# Mental Health Law
## in England & Wales

Sara Miller McCune founded SAGE Publishing in 1965 to support the dissemination of usable knowledge and educate a global community. SAGE publishes more than 1000 journals and over 800 new books each year, spanning a wide range of subject areas. Our growing selection of library products includes archives, data, case studies and video. SAGE remains majority owned by our founder and after her lifetime will become owned by a charitable trust that secures the company's continued independence.

Los Angeles | London | New Delhi | Singapore | Washington DC | Melbourne

4th
Edition

# Mental Health Law
## in England & Wales

A Guide for Mental Health Professionals

PAUL BARBER, ROBERT BROWN & DEBBIE MARTIN

Learning Matters
An imprint of SAGE Publications Ltd
1 Oliver's Yard
55 City Road
London EC1Y 1SP

SAGE Publications Inc.
2455 Teller Road
Thousand Oaks, California 91320

SAGE Publications India Pvt Ltd
B 1/I 1 Mohan Cooperative Industrial Area
Mathura Road
New Delhi 110 044

SAGE Publications Asia-Pacific Pte Ltd
3 Church Street
#10-04 Samsung Hub
Singapore 049483

© Paul Barber, Robert Brown and
Debbie Martin, 2020

First edition published in 2009
Second edition published in 2012
Third edition published in 2017
Fourth edition published in 2020

Editors: Kate Keers/Catriona McMullen
Development editor: Sarah Turpie
Senior project editor: Chris Marke
Project management: Swales & Willis Ltd, Exeter,
Devon
Marketing manager: Samantha Glorioso
Cover design: Wendy Scott
Typeset by: C&M Digitals (P) Ltd, Chennai, India

**Library of Congress Control Number: 2019946424**

**British Library Cataloguing in Publication Data**

A catalogue record for this book is available from
the British Library

ISBN 978-1-5264-9499-3
ISBN 978-1-5264-9498-6 (pbk)

# Contents

## 4 Mental disorder and the availability of appropriate medical treatment     23

## 5 Civil admission and compulsion in hospital     31

## 6 Civil compulsion in the community     45

## 7 Mentally disordered offenders     56

# 8 Medical treatment under the Mental Health Act 65

# 9 The Mental Capacity Act 2005 74

# 10 The interface between the Mental Health Act and the Mental Capacity Act 84

# About the authors

**Paul Barber** qualified as a solicitor in 1976. From 1979 until December 2003 he was a partner at Bevan Ashford (now Bevan Brittan), where for many years he led the firm's NHS Litigation Department, increasingly specialising in the field of Mental Health, Mental Capacity and Human Rights law, being involved in a number of leading cases. Still associated with the firm, he is now largely a freelance trainer and lecturer. He has been extensively involved in training on s12, AC and DoLS courses, and also provides training to AMHPs, nurses, managers and others. Amongst other publications he is co-author of *The Mental Capacity Act 2005: A Guide for Practice*, 3rd edition.

**Robert Brown** is a social worker and a Visiting Fellow at Bournemouth University. He was a founding director of Edge Training and Consultancy Ltd. He provides refresher training for AMHPs and helps to train s12 Approved Doctors and Approved Clinicians. He provides consultation and supervision for the AMHPs/BIAs in the Deprivation of Liberty Team in Cornwall. He also provides consultation for Lead AMHPs in Hampshire, West Berkshire, Portsmouth and Lambeth. Rob was a Mental Health Act Commissioner from 1993 to 2010. Prior to that, Rob worked as a Mental Welfare Officer and then an Approved Social Worker with Hampshire County Council. He has been a lecturer at Southampton University, Stirling University and Croydon College.

**Dr Debbie Martin** is Director of the Bournemouth University Approved Mental Health Professionals' course in South West England. She is also involved in the training of s12 Approval and Approved Clinician courses, and provides training to various NHS Trusts, Health Authorities and Local Authorities. She has published in the field of Mental Health and Mental Capacity Law. She is a registered social worker, and has practised as a social worker, a mental health manager and an Approved Mental Health Professional.

# *Preface*

This book has been designed to provide anyone with an interest in mental health law in England or Wales with access to the Mental Health Act 1983 (as amended by the Mental Health Act 2007) together with a simple commentary to make the law easier to understand.

The law as described relates only to England and Wales. Note that the law is significantly different in Scotland, in Northern Ireland, the Isle of Man and in the Channel Islands and readers will need to look elsewhere for information on each of these. Although the Mental Health Act 1983 (as amended) applies to both England and Wales, there are a few minor differences within the Act itself and some significant differences in subsidiary legislation, such as the Regulations. This means, as an example, that the forms which need to be completed in relation to the use of the Act are different in England from those in Wales. These differences are pointed out in the text and we have sought to include key material for both England and Wales where they are available and where space has allowed.

Where references are made to one of the Codes of Practice, "E Para." refers to the English Code and "W Para." refers to the Welsh Code. This only applies to the Codes of Practice for the Mental Health Act as the Mental Capacity Act Codes are the same for both countries. Where it might not immediately be clear as to which Act the Code relates to, "MHA" or "MCA" will appear before the reference to the Code. Appendix 7 contains a full list of the statutory forms and matches the Welsh forms with those used in England.

At the end of each chapter we have included key points in an attempt to aid learning. Some of the most important points are also summarised in Appendices to try and help busy practitioners.

We would like to thank Anne-Marie Abaecheta, Wendy Barber, Claire Fife, Mark Griffiths, Anthony Harbour, Niall Moore, Mark Spraggs and Susan Thompson, who have all read and commented on the book when it was in its draft form. Their views, based on their experience and knowledge of how the law operates in practice, have been very helpful to us. However, we accept responsibility for any inaccuracies which remain within the text. We are also indebted to Kev Ashill for his technological support.

Paul Barber, Solicitor (non-practising)

Robert Brown, Visiting Fellow at Bournemouth University

Dr Debbie Martin, South West England AMHP Programme Director,
Bournemouth University

# List of abbreviations

| | |
|---|---|
| AC | approved clinician |
| AMHP | approved mental health professional |
| ASW | approved social worker |
| AWOL | absent without leave |
| BIA | best interests assessor (under DoLS procedure) |
| CAMHS | Child and Adolescent Mental Health Services |
| CCfW | Care Council for Wales |
| CoP | Court of Protection |
| CPA | Care Programme Approach |
| CQC | Care Quality Commission |
| CTO | community treatment order |
| dol | deprivation of liberty |
| DoLS | Deprivation of Liberty Safeguards |
| ECHR | European Convention on Human Rights |
| ECT | electro-convulsive therapy |
| HCPC | Health and Care Professions Council |
| HRA | Human Rights Act 1998 |
| HSC2008 | Health and Social Care Act 2008 |
| IMCA | independent mental capacity advocate |
| IMHA | independent mental health advocate |
| LA | local authority |
| LHB | local health board |
| LSSA | local social services authority |
| MCA | Mental Capacity Act 2005 |

| | |
|---|---|
| MHAC | Mental Health Act Commission |
| MHA1983 | Mental Health Act 1983 |
| MHA2007 | Mental Health Act 2007 |
| MHRT | Mental Health Review Tribunal for Wales |
| NHS | National Health Service |
| NR | nearest relative |
| PCT | primary care trust |
| RC | responsible clinician |
| RCP | Royal College of Psychiatrists |
| RMO | responsible medical officer |
| SOAD | second opinion appointed doctor |

# Glossary

**Advance decision** A decision made under the Mental Capacity Act to refuse specified treatment. This is made in advance by a person who has capacity to do so.

**Attorney** Someone appointed under the Mental Capacity Act with the legal right to make decisions (e.g. about treatment) within the scope of the authority, on behalf of the person (the donor) who made the lasting power of attorney (LPA).

**Commission** The Care Quality Commission, which is an independent body that monitors the operation of the MH Act.

**Community patient** A patient subject to a community treatment order.

**Conditional discharge** Discharge from detention in hospital of a restricted patient by the Tribunal or the Secretary of State for Justice subject to specified conditions.

**Deputy** A person appointed by the Court of Protection under s16 of the MCA to take specified decisions on behalf of someone who lacks capacity to take those decisions themselves.

**Liable to be detained** A patient who is subject to a detaining section. This includes people on s17 leave, and those where an application has been made for detention but where they have not yet arrived at the hospital, as well as those actually detained in hospital (it is not just someone who meets the criteria for detention, as is sometimes thought).

**Nominated deputy** A doctor or AC who may make a report detaining a patient under the holding powers in s5 in the absence of the doctor or approved clinician who is in charge of the patient's treatment.

**Patient** Someone who is, or appears to be, suffering from a mental disorder.

**Primary care trust** The NHS body responsible, in particular, for commissioning (arranging) NHS services for a particular part of England. PCTs may also provide NHS services themselves.

**Tribunal** The body to whom a patient (or sometimes the NR) can appeal against compulsion. In England this will be referred to as the Tribunal and in Wales as the Mental Health Review Tribunal.

**Welsh Ministers** Ministers in the Welsh Government.

# Chapter 1

# Background to the Mental Health Act 2007

## Recent history of mental health law

### Introduction

The Mental Health Act amendments, as passed in 2007 and largely implemented in 2008, were the result of ten years of debate. Many saw the revisions to the 1983 Mental Health Act as a disappointing conclusion to such a lengthy period of discussion and analysis. In its final version, the Act was not a particularly radical reform and it preserved most of the existing law. The UK Government's initial plans were more radical but they met significant resistance, as we shall see in this chapter. We will also look at the main changes which came into effect in 2008 in summary form. The main changes to the Act in the last ten years came with the reforms of the Policing and Crime Act 2017. In particular, these reduced the periods of detention from 72 hours to 24 hours and made it much less likely that a police station would be used as the place of safety for s135 or s136.

At the time of writing, the review of the Mental Health Act (*Modernising the Mental Health Act*, DHSC, 2018) has been published but there are no signs of any of the recommendations leading to statutory changes in the near future. There are some references to the review in this text as they provide an indication of the direction any future reform may take. In contrast, the reforms of the Mental Capacity Act 2005 are close to obtaining Royal Assent and may be in force by 2020.

## The structure of this book

This book is essentially concerned with the Mental Health Act 1983 as revised up to May 2019 and as it operates in England and Wales. There are some differences between the two countries in terms of the Act but more significantly with the various rules, regulations and Codes of Practice. We try to highlight the differences where they are significant. The text of the Act itself is included within this book, but occasionally readers may need to access the internet or seek other source materials for particular references (such as the Reference Guide).

The book contains some material on the Mental Capacity Act because of its relevance to mental health law. The aim is to simplify the law as far as possible to make it accessible to professionals and to those affected by the law. The main chapters give details on who operates the Act, who is affected by it, how people may be subject to compulsion, how the law governs issues of capacity and consent to treatment, how to appeal against compulsion, and the role of the nearest relative. There are chapters on advocacy, children and the importance of human rights issues. Where possible, we provide quick summaries of key points as well as grids and diagrams to help explain how the law works in practice.

The Appendices provide access to the Act itself, as well as various rules and regulations and a summary of key cases that have been decided by the courts. Appendix 8 gives guidance to transfers of patients within the British Isles.

In places we refer readers to more detailed texts on some specific areas of the law.

# Why have separate mental health law?

Some authors with a civil libertarian approach (e.g. Thomas Szasz) argue that there should be no need for mental health law. Following this approach, one could argue that there might be a need for law relating to mental incapacity (e.g. for people with brain injury, dementia, learning disability), but no need for a law which allows for the detention and compulsory treatment of people just because a doctor considers them to be suffering from mental illnesses (such as schizophrenia or depression). They should be treated in the same way as anyone with a physical illness, such as diabetes.

The Mental Health Act 1959 took a more welfarist approach, accepting that it may be necessary to intervene against someone's will where they are considered to suffer from a mental disorder, either in order to protect others, or in the interests of the patient's own health or safety.

Even though the Government has recently been expressing a preference for using mental capacity law rather than the Mental Health Act, it resisted early attempts to include an assessment of the patient's capacity as a key element in determining whether or not to intervene without the patient's consent. So, with the significant exception of electro-convulsive therapy (ECT), the Mental Health Act 1983 as amended still allows for the compulsory treatment of a patient with capacity.

The Act also keeps learning disability as well as mental illness and personality disorders within its remit. This has not always been the case, as we can see from the brief historical summary which follows.

# Previous law

A summary of earlier law is set out below, including references to those covered by these Acts. The common law distinguished "idiots" from "lunatics" before the first of the Acts, which are listed here. These terms correspond with the distinction between people with a learning disability and those who are mentally ill. Historically, the groups have sometimes been dealt with in separate legislation and sometimes together, as in the Mental Health Act 1983. Chapter 4 will look at what now amounts to "mental disorder" in more depth.

| | |
|---|---|
| 1713–44 | Vagrancy Acts allowed detention of "Lunaticks or mad persons". |
| 1774 | Act for regulating private madhouses. |
| 1845 | Lunatics Act included "Person of unsound mind". |
| 1886 | Idiots Act provided separately for idiots and imbeciles. |
| 1890 | Lunacy (Consolidation) Act ignored the distinction. |
| 1913 | Mental Deficiency Act – favoured segregation of "mental defectives". In ascending order of vulnerability: |
| | idiots were unable to guard themselves against common physical dangers such as fire, water or traffic; |
| | imbeciles could guard against physical dangers but were incapable of managing themselves or their affairs; |
| | feeble-minded individuals needed care or control for protection of self or others; while |
| | moral defectives had vicious or criminal propensities (use of this category later included many poor women with unsupported babies). |

1927      Mental Deficiency Act emphasised the need for care outside institutions.

               Mental deficiency was defined as "a condition of arrested or incomplete development of mind existing before the age of 18 years whether arising from inherent causes or induced by disease or injury". Chapter 4 will show how close this is to the current definition of learning disability.

1930      Mental Treatment Act allowed for voluntary admissions. This was the first time that it was considered that anyone might actually want to be admitted to a psychiatric hospital without coercion. It enabled patients to enter the county mental hospitals as voluntary patients, as long as they could express volition on admission, it being only necessary for them to sign a form stating they were willing to enter the hospital and would abide by the rules. They could discharge themselves by giving 72 hours' notice in writing (the opposite approach to s5 of the MHA1983). The concept of the "voluntary patient" has gained renewed significance as a result of recent case law.

1946      NHS Act – ended the distinction between paying and non-paying patients.

1948      National Assistance Act – made provisions in the community or in residential settings for those in need (which came to include mentally disordered people).

1959      Mental Health Act – mental disorder meant: "mental illness; arrested or incomplete development of mind, psychopathic disorder, and any other disorder or disability of mind". Further classifications for long-term compulsion were: "mental illness, severe subnormality; subnormality; psychopathic disorder" with a kind of treatability test for the last two. "Voluntary" patients replaced by "informal patients".

1983      Mental Health Act. The broad definition was exactly the same as in the 1959 Act. However the classifications changed to: *mental illness* (undefined); *severe mental impairment; mental impairment; or psychopathic disorder*. These are discussed in more detail in Chapter 4.

1984      Police and Criminal Evidence Act (and its Codes of Practice) uses the term "mental disorder" as per the Mental Health Act and the revised PACE Codes use the concept of the mentally vulnerable adult.

2007      Mental Health Act defines mental disorder as "any disorder or disability of the mind", which would include an even wider group of people than the 1983 Act. The Deprivation of Liberty Safeguards (DoLS) include a mental disorder test using the MHA definition.

A useful summary of the origins of mental health law in England and Wales can be found in Bowen (2007). Larry Gostin's work for MIND (*A Human Condition*, volumes 1 and 2) was very influential in the lead up to the 1982 amendments that form the basis of the 1983 Act. These two short books are still well worth reading, as they provide a critical approach to mental health law (Gostin, 1975, 1977).

# The lead up to the 2007 changes

The main changes brought about by the 2007 Act came into effect almost exactly ten years after the process of change began with the Expert Committee (under Professor Genevra Richardson) in October 1998. There were a number of factors which led to the reform of the 1983 Act. There had been the reduction in the number of hospital beds and a greater emphasis on care in the community, but the MHA1983 seemed primarily concerned with hospital-based treatment.

There were some high-profile cases, such as: the 1992 killing of Jonathan Zito by Christopher Clunis; the incident at the end of 1992 when Ben Silcock climbed into a lion's den and was badly mauled; and the deaths of Megan Russell and Lin Russell at the hands of Michael Stone in 1996. The first two involved mentally ill patients in the community and the third was a man diagnosed with a severe personality disorder. There was concern that the law was not providing adequate protection to those suffering from mental disorders or to those affected by their actions.

In 1997 the "Bournewood" case started its journey through the courts. This involved HL, a man with autism and severe learning disabilities. He was admitted to hospital and kept there against the wishes of his carers. This continued for three months until a decision in the Court of Appeal led to his detention under the MHA1983. During this period he was effectively detained in hospital, but without any of the procedures or protections of the MHA1983. This case is dealt with in more detail in Chapter 11 as the issues it raised have been highly influential in reforming the law, especially those parts of the MHA2007 which reform the MCA.

In 1998 the Human Rights Act was passed and eventually came into effect in 2000. The Government was concerned that mental health legislation should be reformed to be consistent with the requirements of this new Act, which enshrined most of the European Convention on Human Rights (ECHR) within English law. One example involved the relationship between the patient and the nearest relative. In *JT v United Kingdom* (2000) the Government agreed that the Mental Health Act needed reform so that the patient could have some say in who should act as the nearest relative.

The Richardson report was published in 1999 at the same time as the Government published a Green Paper on Reform of the Mental Health Act. One of the main differences between the two approaches was the Expert Committee's recommendations that assessments of mental capacity should play an important part in mental health law. The Green Paper did not take this approach, nor did it support the Richardson proposal of reciprocity where any use of compulsion should be linked to a duty to provide appropriate services. These two reports were followed by a White Paper, which was published in 2000. After a period of consultation we saw the first draft Bill in 2002.

The draft Mental Health Bill was met with fierce criticism from a number of quarters. Issues raised at this stage have continued to be contentious. The definition of mental disorder was seen by many as being too wide and there was concern that this would lower the threshold of compulsion. There also seemed to be a lack of emphasis on therapeutic purpose, with the disappearance of the treatability test and a greater focus on public safety. The proposal that the Mental Health Review Tribunal should have a much greater involvement (including being the body that, in effect, would need to approve long-term compulsion) was seen as cumbersome and impractical.

The Mental Health Alliance was formed to coordinate the views of many of the protesting parties. There was a protest march in London in September 2002, which highlighted concerns about the proposed changes, in particular the community treatment order with the prospect of forcible medical treatment in the community. The Government, however, was determined to introduce some kind of new compulsory treatment provision in the community.

Running alongside the reform of the Mental Health Act was the Government's concern with dangerous people with severe personality disorders (DSPD). This was linked with concerns about cases such as Michael Stone. The Government believed that the definition of mental disorder was too tight and, combined with the treatability test, was preventing some dangerous individuals from being detained in hospital. At one point, separate legislation was considered but eventually the aims of this Home Office-driven approach were subsumed within the amendments to the MHA1983. Some changes in the Act are hard to understand without an awareness of this DSPD agenda.

A second draft Mental Health Bill was produced in 2004. This was examined by a Joint Parliamentary Committee, which reported in 2005. The report recognised the need for reform but considered the Bill to be too long, too complex and too concerned with public safety at the expense of patients' rights. In 2004 the European Court of Human Rights determined that

HL (the Bournewood patient) had been detained under common law and that the lack of any formal procedure or recourse to review had breached Article 5 of the ECHR. This important decision needed to be reflected in the revisions to the MHA1983 and a consultation paper on this aspect of the law was produced in 2005.

While this rather convoluted process continued, the amending of mental health law was over-taken by the Mental Capacity Act, which was passed in 2005. This has had an increasingly significant impact on the use of the Mental Health Act, as we shall see later in the book. The Mental Capacity Act is summarised in Chapter 9 and considered in more detail in a companion volume (Brown et al., 2009).

Then in 2006 the Government announced the demise of the second draft Bill. A further Bill was produced which would amend the 1983 Act rather than replace it. This received Royal Assent in July 2007 as the Mental Health Act 2007. In the final stages (known as "ping-ponging" between the House of Commons and the House of Lords), the Lords wrung a number of concessions from the Government which are of some significance. Ten years of work had culminated in what amounts to a comparatively minor amendment Act, most of which came into effect in November 2008. History may regard this as a wasted opportunity.

# The main changes

As stated above the MHA2007 was an amendment Act rather than a radical overhaul of mental health law. The main changes are summarised below. Key issues arising from the changes are highlighted. Each of them is dealt with in more detail later in the book.

*The definition of "mental disorder"* was broadened with limited exclusions. The definition is: "any disorder or disability of the mind". The specific classifications of mental illness, severe mental impairment, mental impairment and psychopathic disorder all disappeared. Promiscuity, other immoral conduct and sexual deviancy were no longer to be exclusions. Previously, by themselves, they were not to be seen as mental disorders. The only remaining exclusion was to be dependence on alcohol or drugs. Limitations on the use of long-term compulsion remain for people with learning disability unless they are abnormally aggressive or seriously irresponsible.

*The "treatability test"* for s3 and s37 was replaced by an *"appropriate medical treatment"* test. Instead of having to state that treatment is likely to alleviate or prevent a deterioration in the patient's condition, the requirement now is that appropriate medical treatment is available and it is intended to "alleviate, or prevent a worsening of, the disorder or one or more of its symp-toms or manifestations". It is a therapeutic purpose that is required rather than the probability (i.e. more likely than not) of success.

*The approved social worker (ASW)* was replaced by the *approved mental health professional (AMHP)*. The role is essentially that which was fulfilled by the ASW but the change allows for nurses, psychologists and occupational therapists, as well as social workers, to take on the AMHP function. They are still approved by the local authority but can be employed by an NHS Trust or other health organisation. In practice, eight years on, something like 95 per cent of AMHPs are social workers. They retain personal accountability for making a decision whether or not to apply for detention. Notably the other participants in civil detention remain the same, i.e. two doctors provide recommendations (one must be approved under s12 and one must have previous acquaintance with the patient where practicable), and someone acting on behalf of the hospital managers is needed to admit the patient and receive the papers.

*The nearest relative* functions were virtually unchanged. Their identity is arrived at by the same process as before, following the requirements of s26, but with the addition that civil partner-ships are treated exactly the same as marriages. The patient is added to the list of those who can make an application to the county court under s29 and there is a new ground for dis-placement of the nearest relative if they are "unsuitable". At one stage the Government was considering giving the patient the power to nominate someone from the outset, but this proposal was discarded. The 2018 Review suggested that the nearest relative should be replaced by a person nominated by the patient but there are no signs of such a reform at the time of writing.

*The responsible medical officer (RMO)* was replaced by the *responsible clinician (RC)*. In some ways this was more radical than opening up the ASW/AMHP role to other professionals because the role of the RC can be performed by nurses, psychologists, occupational therapists or social workers, as well as doctors. However, again in practice, the impact has been minimal. The vast majority of approved clinicians are doctors. Such staff need to demonstrate certain competences and undertake training to become approved clinicians in order to be eligible to be responsible clinicians for particular patients. Although the initial detention is based on medical recommendations from doctors, decisions on the continuation of compulsion can be taken by the RC. This is based on an assessment that the mental disorder remains of a nature or degree to justify this. It would require medical expertise and challenges might have been expected as to whether all those appointed as RCs possess this. One potential safeguard is that the RC must now obtain the written agreement of someone professionally concerned with the patient's treatment but who is from a different professional group than the RC. However, this need not be a doctor. In practice, there have been no reported challenges to the "medical expertise" of approved clinicians who are not registered medical practitioners.

*Hospital managers* featured in two areas of reform. The managers' power was extended to include the power to discharge a patient from a community treatment order (CTO) as well as retaining the old power to discharge detained patients. Second, the hospital managers are responsible for giving information to patients and their nearest relatives, and the amendments imposed some additional requirements.

*Mental Health Review Tribunals* underwent major structural change, but this had little effect on most people. In England the MHA is covered by the First-tier Tribunals, which also cover matters other than mental health. There is still a Mental Health Review Tribunal for Wales (MHRT). Tribunals did not form the basis of a radically new Act, as was proposed at one stage. In terms of appeals, there were some comparatively minor changes. For example, automatic reference dates were amended, which had the effect in some cases of bringing the review date forward. To be consistent with other changes, discharge criteria were amended to require the Tribunal to consider the availability of appropriate medical treatment. The power to reclassify was abolished, as there are no more classifications. In practice, the changes to the Rules and the Practice Direction have had more impact (see Appendix 2A).

*Consent to treatment rules* were amended to provide new safeguards for electro-convulsive therapy (ECT). A patient is able to make an advance decision to refuse ECT and this is very hard to override, even if the patient is detained. There were additional safeguards for children and a new Part 4A to cover community patients.

*The Mental Health Act Commission* was unchanged by the MHA2007, but the Health and Social Care Act 2008 changes mean that its functions are now performed by the Care Quality Commission (CQC) in England as from April 2009. This body took over the functions of the MHA Commission, the Health Care Commission and the Commission for Social Care Inspection, forming one regulatory body. The visiting and complaints functions remain. In Wales the functions have been taken on by the Healthcare Inspectorate Wales (HIW).

*Independent mental health advocates* were introduced. There are advocacy services for patients subject to community treatment orders, guardianship or detention (except those on s4, 5, 135 or 136) and the services have been extended to other patients in Wales. There is a duty on service providers to provide qualifying patients with information that advocacy services are available. Advocates have an unfettered right to meet with patients in private, and to meet with professionals. They have access to patient records where a capable patient gives consent. For incapable patients, there are rules to govern access.

*The community treatment order (CTO)* was the flagship of the Government's reform, and the determination to have this new provision was apparent in the final stages of the parliamentary process. Attempts to obtain a treatment order for patients not already subject to detention were unsuccessful so, as with its predecessor *supervised aftercare* which is repealed, the CTO requires that the patient is detained on s3 or the equivalent before the order can be made. It contains a recall power and limited powers to treat a patient without their consent.

*Section 17 leave* was only changed in that the RC must consider a CTO before placing a patient on leave for more than seven consecutive days. With the courts having effectively extended the potential for use of longer-term s17 leave in recent years, it was a surprise to most people that the CTO proved so popular that there were over 5,000 people subject to CTOs in March 2015.

*Guardianship under section 7 or s37.* The power to convey patients was extended to include taking them to accommodation in the first instance. The power to convey previously only covered returning a patient who had absented themselves from where they were required to live, and this had created some problems in practice.

*Places of safety under s135 or s136.* Patients may be moved between places of safety as long as this is authorised by an AMHP or police officer and as long as the total period of detention does not exceed 72 hours. This was a pragmatic change which was largely uncontroversial.

*Offender patients (Part 3).* There are no more time-limited restriction orders. Again, this was uncontroversial and the practice of courts placing time limits on restriction orders had already become rare. The 2007 Act amended the Domestic Violence, Crime and Victims Act 2004 with regard to giving notification of Tribunals to victims of all hospital order patients.

*Principles.* These are not set out in detail on the face of the Act (unlike the position with the Mental Capacity Act 2005) but are in the Code of Practice. There are separate Codes for England and Wales and there are differences between the two. The principles need to be used lawfully and in a way that is compliant with the Human Rights Act 1998.

*Admission of children.* There were new restrictions on the informal admission of 16- to 17-year-olds. Section 131 was amended so that if a patient aged 16 or 17 who has capacity does not consent to admission to hospital, the admission cannot be "carried out or determined on the basis of the consent of a person who has parental responsibility for the patient". At the time of writing the Supreme Court decision on one particular case is not known but is likely to be crucial for this area of law.

*Suitable environments for children.* Providers need to ensure that the environment is suitable, having regard to age (subject to needs), and are advised to consult a CAMHS specialist about the fulfilment of this duty.

*Deprivation of Liberty Safeguards.* These are in the MH2007 and amend the Mental Capacity Act 2005 from April 2009. They were designed to fill the "Bournewood Gap" for mentally disordered patients who lack capacity to make a decision about admission to a hospital or care home and are effectively deprived of their liberty. They are likely to survive until at least 2020 but will then probably be replaced by Liberty Protection Safeguards.

# Summary

The mental health law reforms of 2007 became amendments to the 1983 Act rather than a comprehensive new Act. There is no consolidating Act in the way that the 1983 Act consolidated the 1982 amendments with the 1959 Act. We hope that the consolidated version of the MHA1983 as amended, which we have provided at Appendix 1, will be of assistance. It includes the changes to s135 and s136 which took effect in December 2017. In reviewing the amendments it is notable that the risk criteria for detention were left virtually unchanged. This is significant because the Government had wanted provisions whereby certain patients who posed a risk to others would have to be detained, even if they were willing to enter hospital informally. Time will tell if the other changes, and crucially the resources to support them, are seen to achieve an appropriate balance between the autonomy of patients and the need to protect their health and safety, and that of others.

# Chapter 2

# Who operates the Act?

## Introduction

The Mental Health Act 1983 provides for both informal and compulsory care, and treatment of people who have a mental disorder. The legislation prescribes roles, duties and powers that allow, or require, people to take action in relation to the care and treatment of those with mental disorder. This chapter identifies the professionals and others responsible for operating the Act, and describes their functions. These functions are described under the following categories: assessors, professional roles, and safeguarding roles. "Assessors" are professionals who have a responsibility to assess those thought to have a mental disorder, and to make any necessary arrangements for their care and treatment. The section on "professional roles" describes the roles of the "approved mental health professional" (AMHP), the "approved clinician" (AC) and the "responsible clinician" (RC). These roles were introduced by the MHA2007. Finally the chapter will consider "safeguarding roles", which describe the various bodies or individuals who provide safeguards for those receiving compulsory care and treatment under the Act.

## Assessors

The responsibility to assess patients to establish if they have a mental disorder, and if they meet legal criteria set out in the Act, falls to different people depending upon the provision being considered. For example, for civil admissions, doctors and AMHPs fulfil the assessment role, whereas when dealing with mentally disordered offenders the courts, supported by health and social care professionals, fulfil the role.

*Doctors* are needed to provide medical recommendations for detention in hospital or for reception into guardianship. They are required to conduct a personal medical examination of the patient and satisfy themselves that the person has a mental disorder and that they meet legal criteria for use of the compulsory powers. Assuming the patient meets the criteria, doctors are able to complete medical recommendations, which taken together with an application, enable the patient to be detained in hospital, placed on a community treatment order (CTO) or received into guardianship. It is important to note that doctors are not compelled to complete a medical recommendation; they may exercise their discretion and choose not to provide medical recommendations even where the criteria are met. Of the two doctors required to complete medical recommendations for longer-term detention under Part 2 of the Act and reception into guardianship under s7, one must be approved as having special experience in the diagnosis or treatment of mental disorder. In practice this means that they must meet specific requirements and undertake training before they are eligible for approval. Such doctors are referred to as s12 approved doctors. In addition, it is preferable for one of the two doctors to have previous acquaintance with the patient. Previous acquaintance is not defined in the Act, however the case of *Reed (Trainer) v Bronglais Hospital* (2001) offers some clarity of its meaning (see Appendix 6).

The role of the *AMHP* is to coordinate the process of assessment, to interview patients, and to consider medical views, to establish if there is evidence of mental disorder, and whether the legal criteria for compulsion are met. AMHPs have a wider role than that of the doctors in that they are required to satisfy themselves that an application ought to be made, having regard to any wishes expressed by relatives and any other circumstances, and to decide whether it is necessary or proper to make an application. AMHPs cannot be instructed to make a specific decision by their employer or by the local social services authority (LSSA) for whom they are acting. They are individually accountable for their decision-making, and retain discretion over whether to make an application.

If they are satisfied that the criteria are met and that there is no more appropriate alternative, they are able to complete an application. An application can only be completed if the AMHP has the required medical recommendation(s). A completed application, along with the required medical recommendations, provides the legal authority to detain a patient, or to receive them into guardianship. The AMHP has a number of duties, which are discussed in more detail below. The role of applicant is usually taken by an AMHP. However, a patient's nearest relative also has the legal right to make an application for detention or guardianship. In the event of an AMHP not making an application, the Code of Practice (E Para. 14.101) states that the AMHP should "advise the nearest relative of their right to do so instead".

# Professional roles

## The approved mental health professional (AMHP)

The AMHP replaced the role of the approved social worker (ASW). The role and functions of the AMHP remain unchanged from those of the ASW, other than their additional roles in relation to CTOs. Since 1984, ASWs have been social workers who have undertaken additional training to equip them to perform specific functions under the Act. The AMHP role has been broadened to encompass other professional groups. In addition to social workers (registered with the Health and Care Professions Council (HCPC) or Care Council for Wales (CCfW)) the following professional groups are able to train to become AMHPs: nurses (first level mental health and learning disability nurses), registered occupational therapists and chartered psychologists (holding a relevant practising certificate issued by the British Psychological Society). AMHPs do not have to be employed by LSSAs. They do, however, need to be approved by an LSSA. This is because they act on behalf of, and are accountable to, a specific LSSA when performing the functions of an AMHP. The LSSA cannot direct the decisions of an AMHP, who must reach their own independent judgement.

Eligible professionals are required to undertake training before they can be approved. Training courses are delivered by universities which need to be accredited by the HCPC or the CCfW. Staff who successfully complete courses may then be approved by a local authority for a period of up to five years before they are required to go through a re-approval process.

Social workers already undertaking the ASW role automatically became AMHPs at the time of legislative change (November 2008). Most of them completed short courses to acquire knowledge of the changes brought about by the MHA2007.

The *AMHP's Guide to Mental Health Law* (Brown, 2019) lists the following AMHP functions:

- *deciding whether to make an application for compulsory admission to hospital for assessment or for treatment under Part 2 of the Act (s13);*
- *deciding whether to make an application for guardianship under s7 of the Act (s13);*
- *informing or consulting with the nearest relative (NR) about an application (s11);*
- *conveying a patient to hospital (or a place of residence) on the basis of an application as above (s6);*

- *responding to a referral from an NR for an MHA assessment, and, if an application is not made, giving the reasons for this in writing to the NR (s13(4));*

- *providing a social circumstance report for the hospital for any patient detained on the basis of an application made by the NR (s14);*

- *confirming that a CTO should be made and agreeing to any conditions (s17A);*

- *agreeing to the extension of a CTO (s20A);*

- *agreeing to the revocation of a CTO (s17F);*

- *applying to the county court for the displacement of an existing nearest relative and/or the appointment of an acting nearest relative (s29);*

- *having the right to enter and inspect premises where a mentally disordered patient is living (s115);*

- *applying for a warrant to enter premises under section 135 to search for and remove a patient to a place of safety (s135);*

- *having the power to take a patient into custody and take them to the place they ought to be when they have gone absent without leave (AWOL) (s138);*

- *interviewing a patient arrested by the police on s136 (s136(2));*

- *making a decision on whether a patient subject to s136 should be moved from one place of safety to another (s136(3)).*

## The approved clinician (AC)

An AC has a number of functions under the Act but their main purpose is that they are able to act as the responsible clinician (RC) for a detained patient and for a patient subject to guardianship or a CTO. Strategic health authorities and local health boards are responsible for making arrangements for the approval process of ACs in England and Wales respectively. The Welsh Ministers and the Secretary of State have separately issued directions stating that doctors, chartered psychologists, first level nurses (mental health and learning disability), registered occupational therapists and registered social workers may be approved as ACs. Prior to approval, these professionals will have to demonstrate specific competence and complete training. However there were transitional arrangements whereby, for example in England, doctors who were s12 approved and had been in overall charge of the medical treatment for mental disorder of a patient in the 12 months leading up to November 2008 automatically become approved clinicians.

Some of the functions of ACs are:

- using s5(2) powers to detain a patient for a period not exceeding 72 hours;

- writing reports in relation to Part 3 patients;

- visiting and examining a patient on behalf of an NR for the purpose of advising with regard to the possible discharge by the NR of a detained patient or a patient subject to guardianship.

## The responsible clinician (RC)

The responsible clinician replaced the role of the RMO. The RC is the approved clinician who has overall responsibility for the patient's case. This in effect means that a range of professionals will be able to assume the overall responsibility for detained patients and those subject to guardianship or CTOs. They are able to perform functions that have historically been the sole remit of doctors.

Some of the functions that RCs will perform are:

- granting s17 leave;

- making a CTO;

- varying or suspending discretionary conditions attached to a CTO;

- renewing detention or extending a CTO;

- recalling a patient from s17 leave or CTO;

- revoking a CTO;

- discharging a patient from detention, guardianship or a CTO.

It is important to note that RCs will not be able to perform all of these tasks without the involvement of others. For example, a CTO cannot be made or revoked without the agreement of an AMHP (see Chapter 6 for more information). RCs cannot perform tasks that fall outside their professional competence, for example prescribing and administering medication. It is uncertain whether a professional who is not a doctor will be able to demonstrate, if challenged in court, the objective medical expertise which European Convention case law has held to be necessary when renewing detention or extending a CTO. It is expected that the RC will liaise with other ACs and draw upon their particular expertise. Hospital managers are required to have protocols in place to ensure that the most appropriate clinician is appointed to meet a patient's particular needs. It is envisaged that the role of RC will transfer from one professional to another to ensure that a patient is allocated the most appropriate clinician at any given time. The Code of Practice (E Para. 36.5) gives an example of this, stating:

> *where psychological therapies are central to the patient's treatment, it may be appropriate for a professional with particular expertise in this area to act as the responsible clinician.*

Then at E Para. 36.8:

> *As the needs of the patient may change over time, it is important that the appropriateness of the responsible clinician is kept under review throughout the care planning process. It may be appropriate for the patient's responsible clinician to change during a period of care and treatment, if such a change enables the needs of the patient to be met more effectively.*

# Safeguarding roles

The Mental Health Act contains a significant number of safeguarding provisions for patients. These safeguards operate to prevent misuse of the Act, to enable people to challenge the use of the Act and to monitor the use of the Act.

## The assessing team

Those who assess for the potential use of compulsory powers (doctors and AMHPs) have discretion whether or not to use the provisions of the Act, even where the statutory criteria are met.

They are only able to initiate compulsory care and treatment if agreement is reached between the whole assessing team. This requirement of agreement prevents arbitrary decision-making by one professional. They are all trained in the importance of meeting the patient's rights under the ECHR and only using compulsion where justified, and where it is a proportionate response to the risks involved.

## The nearest relative

Section 11 of the Act places a duty upon AMHPs to inform or consult the NR where "practicable", or "reasonably practicable", when considering use of s2 (application for assessment), s3 (application for treatment) or s7 (application for guardianship). The interpretation of "practicable" is discussed within Appendix 6 (see *R (E) v Bristol* 2005). Where an application for either s3 or 7 is being considered, an AMHP is prevented from proceeding with the application if the patient's nearest relative objects. In these circumstances the AMHP may decide to apply to the county court for displacement of the NR (see Chapter 14). In addition, the NR is able to order the discharge of a patient subject to sections 2 (Admission for assessment), 3 (Admission for treatment), 7 (Application for guardianship) and 17A (Community treatment orders). The RC may however prevent discharge of those detained under sections 2, 3 and 17A if they certify that the patient, if discharged, would be likely to act in a manner dangerous to himself or others.

## Tribunals (Mental Health Review Tribunals in Wales)

Section 66 of the Act sets out which patients can apply to a Tribunal and when. The Tribunal provides certain detained patients with a legal right to challenge their detention, which Article 5(4) of the ECHR enshrines. Tribunals have the power to uphold detention and to discharge patients from detention immediately or at a future specified date. They also have the power to make the following recommendations for patients on treatment orders: the granting of s17 leave; transfer to another hospital; transfer into guardianship; or the making of a CTO. Tribunals consist of three members: a legal chair, a medical member and a lay member. They must consider the evidence before them and comply with the requirements of law when determining the outcome of the Tribunal. Patients are entitled to non-means-tested public funding, and can have a solicitor or other person represent them at the Tribunal (see Chapter 12). Nearest relatives also have the right to apply to the Tribunal in certain circumstances (see Chapter 12).

## Hospital managers

*Managers' hearings*. Section 23 gives hospital managers the power to discharge detained patients (apart from those on restriction orders and those still awaiting court decisions) as well as those subject to CTOs. Patients are entitled to apply for a managers' hearing in addition to a Tribunal, but the managers may decide not to proceed with a hearing if a Tribunal hearing is imminent. Managers should also consider holding a hearing if an RC bars a nearest relative's discharge. They must hold a hearing if an RC renews detention or extends a CTO. Whilst the Act does not specify criteria to be considered regarding the decision-making process, the Code of Practice sets out guidance. In essence, managers should consider whether the initial criteria for detention or a CTO continue to be met. Where the legal criteria are not met, the patient must be discharged.

*Information*. Hospital managers have duties to provide information to patients and to nearest relatives about rights of appeal and the existence of the other safeguarding processes (see Chapter 13).

## Independent mental health advocates (IMHAs)

The Mental Health Act 2007 introduced IMHAs, who are available to qualifying patients. Qualifying patients are those subject to detention, those who are liable to be detained (e.g. those who are on leave of absence) and patients subject to conditional discharge, guardianship and CTOs. Some informal patients will also be entitled to an IMHA if, for example, they are being considered for treatment under s57 of the Act, or if ECT is being considered as a means of treatment for a young person or child under the age of 18. In England, patients subject to short-term detention (i.e. s4, 5(2), 5(4), 135 and 136) are not entitled to an IMHA, but in Wales the measure provides that many patients on short-term sections, and voluntary and informal patients, have a statutory entitlement to an IMHA.

Advocates should be independent of the professionals concerned with the care and treatment of the patient. The role of the IMHA is to ensure that patients understand their rights, the rights of others under the Act (for example nearest relatives and RCs), any conditions placed upon the patient and what treatments can be given to them. In order to enable IMHAs to perform these functions, they are able to visit and interview patients and in some circumstances have access to relevant medical and social care records. They are also able to visit and interview any professionals concerned with the patient's treatment. There are a number of people who are able to request the involvement of an IMHA; these include the patient, the patient's nearest relative, an AMHP and the patient's RC. IMHAs must comply with such a request but the patient is not required to accept the support of an IMHA (see Chapter 16).

## The Care Quality Commission (CQC)

The Care Quality Commission and the Healthcare Inspectorate for Wales has responsibility for keeping under review the exercise of the powers and duties conferred by the Act in relation to the detention of patients, including those liable to be detained and patients subject to CTOs. The role of the CQC is to interview patients, investigate complaints, appoint second opinion appointed doctors (SOADs), review decisions regarding the withholding of patients' post and produce reports. They do not have the ability to discharge patients from detention, but the CQC does have powers to impose sanctions where services do not conform to national standards, and they have a role in monitoring the DoLS procedures. (Chapter 15 provides more information on the CQC.)

## Second opinion appointed doctors (SOADs)

SOADs are doctors appointed by the CQC to provide independent medical views. Their role is to assess patients' capacity to consent to treatment, and to give a view regarding the continuation of medical treatment for mental disorder. To assist them in this role, they are entitled to visit and interview patients and relevant professionals concerned with their treatment. They are also able to have access to any relevant records. (Further information regarding SOADs is contained within Chapters 8 and 15.)

## Lasting power of attorney under the Mental Capacity Act (LPA)

Patients, to some degree, can determine who is able to make decisions on their behalf in the event of their lacking capacity to make their own decisions. The Mental Capacity Act 2005 introduced a statutory right to appoint a person or number of people to make decisions on someone's behalf, for a time when they may lose capacity to make those decisions themselves. LPAs can be made by capacitated adults (i.e. those aged 18 and over). They must include specified information and meet a number of formal requirements. There are two types of LPA: a personal welfare (healthcare and social matters) LPA and a property and affairs LPA. The persons appointed are referred to as attorneys. Where a patient has made a personal welfare LPA, the attorney may be entitled to make decisions regarding treatment (including psychiatric treatment). This may include accepting or refusing treatment for mental disorder. However, a refusal of treatment for mental disorder could be overridden if the person were to be detained under a section of the MHA to which Part 4 of that Act applied. Attorneys are also prevented from making decisions about where a person should live if the person is subject to the requirement of residence under s7 (guardianship) of the MHA1983.

Those providing care and treatment should make reasonable efforts to establish whether a patient has appointed an attorney, or whether the courts have appointed a deputy, as decision-making may well be within their remit, rather than that of the professionals (see Chapter 9).

# Key points

1. Initial assessors for detention or guardianship are still two doctors and one applicant, usually an AMHP.

2. ASW replaced by the AMHP, broadening the role out to other professions.

3. AMHPs may be employed by trusts, but are accountable to, and act on behalf of, LSSAs.

4. The RC replaced the RMO.

5. A professional must train and become an AC before they can be appointed as an RC.

6. Doctors, nurses, psychologists, OTs and social workers can train to become ACs.

7. CTO patients are able to apply to Tribunals.

8. Hospital managers must give information to CTO patients.

9. IMHA provisions are available in England and Wales, but entitlement differs in the two countries.

10. The CQC has additional responsibilities in relation to CTO patients.

# Chapter 3
## The Codes of Practice and the Reference Guide

## Introduction

There are separate Codes of Practice for England and for Wales. Following comprehensive revision, the current Code for England was issued in April 2015, and the Code for Wales in October 2016. The Codes are more closely aligned, and in particular adopt the same chapter numbering, making comparisons easier between the two. In places the guidance differs, however, and where appropriate this will be indicated. There is in addition a separate Code (issued with effect from June 2012) in relation to the Mental Health (Wales) Measure 2010.

In this chapter the principles will be outlined, and the purpose and legal effect of the Code and the nature of its obligations will be discussed.

There is also a "Reference Guide" to the amended Mental Health Act. It relates to the Act as it applies in England. There is no separate Guide for Wales. The purpose of the Reference Guide is to explain the legal provisions of the Act rather than offer guidance to professionals and others on how it should be implemented in practice.

England's Code contains boxed case examples of a number of practice points. The Reference Guide explains many of the Act's provisions by means of illustrative tables. There is a measure of overlap between the two documents.

## The duty of the Secretary of State and the Welsh Ministers

Section 118(1) provides that the:

*Secretary of State shall prepare, and from time to time revise, a code of practice –*

(a) *for the guidance of registered medical practitioners, approved clinicians, managers and staff of hospitals, independent hospitals and care homes and approved mental health professionals in relation to the admission of patients to hospitals and registered establishments under this Act and to guardianship and community patients under this Act; and*

(b) *for the guidance of registered medical practitioners and members of other professions in relation to the medical treatment of patients suffering from mental disorder.*

Section 118 (1A) provides that the Code for Wales shall include guidance for independent mental health advocates (IMHAs).

# To whom does the Code apply?

In addition to the above individuals for whom the guidance is specifically intended, the Code itself adds (Introduction, E Para. vi; W Para. xii) that it should prove beneficial to the police and ambulance services and others in health and social services, including the independent and voluntary sectors involved in providing services to people who are or may become subject to compulsory measures under the Act. It is also intended to be helpful to patients, their representatives, carers, families and friends, and others who support them. However, it is only those specifically identified in (a), (b) and (1A) above who are under an obligation under s118(2D) to "have regard" to the Code.

# In what circumstances does the Code apply?

While s118(1)(a) states that the Code is guidance in relation to the admission of patients to hospitals and registered establishments, and to guardianship and community patients *under this Act*, there is no such qualification under s118(1)(b): "guidance in relation to the medical treatment of patients suffering from mental disorder". As a result its impact is wide reaching. In *R (C) v A LA et al.* (see Appendix 6) the Code was held to apply inter alia to the seclusion of a learning disabled child at a school. The court even suggested that it would be unacceptable for the Code not to apply where the learning disability fell outside the definition of mental disorder (because it lacked an association with abnormally aggressive or seriously irresponsible conduct).

# The nature of the obligation to have regard to the Code

As can be seen above, the requirement to "have regard to" the Code appears in the Act itself. This mirrors the position in the Mental Capacity Act 2005. What exactly does "have regard to" mean in practice? The status of the then Code of Practice and the guidance it contained was examined in *R (Munjaz) v Mersey Care NHS Trust* (see Appendix 6). The House of Lords held that although not having statutory force, the Code comprised much more than "mere advice which an addressee is free to follow or not". It was guidance "which any hospital should consider with great care and from which it should depart only if it has cogent reasons for doing so". It was also stated that the Code was "more than something to which those to whom it is addressed must have regard to". In the light of this judgement, it is perhaps surprising that the nature of the obligation is stated in s118 to be merely to "have regard to" the Code.

In the introduction to the Code (para. v) the position is put thus:

> The people listed above to whom the Code is addressed must have regard to the Code. It is important that these persons have training on the Code and ensure that they are familiar with its requirements. As departures from the Code could give rise to legal challenge, reasons for any departure should be recorded clearly. Courts will scrutinise such reasons to ensure that there is sufficiently convincing justification in the circumstances.

Despite the wording in the Act it would be advisable to view the status of and the guidance in the Code in the light of the House of Lords' ruling requiring any departures to be for cogent reasons. This is in fact spelt out in the Code for Wales (but not England) (Introduction W Para. xii). On the other hand, as the *Munjaz* case confirmed, the European Convention on Human Rights has a higher status than the Code: the question is less whether a patient is being managed in accordance with the Code, and more whether his treatment or management breaches his rights under the Convention.

There are gradations of advice within the Code. Where "must" is used, it reflects legal obligations in legislation (including other legislation such as the Human Rights Act 1998) or case law, and must be followed. Where the Code uses the term "should", then departures should be documented and recorded. Where the Code gives guidance using the terms "may", "can" or "could", then the guidance in the Code is to be followed wherever possible (Introduction E Para. ix). The Code for Wales has equivalent provision at Introduction W Para. xiv. Unfortunately the Codes do not always use these distinctions correctly. For example at 27.11 (W Para. 27.8), it is stated that the responsible clinician (RC) "should" consider a community treatment order (CTO) when deciding whether to grant leave of absence for more than seven consecutive days. In fact this is a legal requirement, a "must".

# What must the Code cover?

Section 118(2) provides that the Code must specify any additional forms of treatment to be included within the provisions of s57. However neither Code has done so, and s57 therefore continues to apply only to any surgical operation for destroying brain tissue or the functioning of brain tissue, and to the surgical implantation of hormones for the purposes of reducing male sex drive.

The question whether the principles underpinning the Act should be contained in the Act or in the Code proved controversial during the passage of the Mental Health Act 2007 through Parliament.[1] The end result is a rather curious compromise, whereby s118(2A) states:

> *The code shall include a statement of the principles which the Secretary of State thinks should inform decisions under this Act.*

And then s118(2B) goes on to list those "matters" which must be addressed by the principles:

(a) *respect for patients' past and present wishes and feelings;*

(b) *respect for diversity generally including, in particular, diversity of religion, culture and sexual orientation (within the meaning of section 35 of the Equality Act 2006);*

(c) *minimising restrictions on liberty;*

(d) *involvement of patients in planning, developing and delivering care and treatment appropriate to them;*

(e) *avoidance of unlawful discrimination;*

(f) *effectiveness of treatment;*

(g) *views of carers and other interested parties;*

(h) *patient well-being and safety; and*

(i) *public safety.*

In addition, by s118(2C):

---

[1] The Review of the Mental Health Act, chaired by Sir Simon Wessely and published in December 2018, recommends that the principles should, as they are in the Mental Capacity Act, be located in the Act not the Code.

*The Secretary of State shall also have regard to the desirability of ensuring:*

(a) *the efficient use of resources; and*

(b) *the equitable distribution of services.*

The use of the word "inform" in s118(2A) should be noted. As the English Code makes plain at Para. 1.23, the principles inform decisions; they do not determine them:

*All five sets of principles are of equal importance, and should inform any decision made under the Act. The weight given to each principle in reaching a particular decision will need to be balanced in different ways according to the circumstances and nature of each particular decision.*

There is a similar provision at Para. 1.30 in the Welsh Code.

# The guiding principles

Chapter 1 of each of the Codes for England and Wales, covering the guiding principles, has been expanded in the most recent editions. In addition, the principles themselves have been much more closely aligned in the Codes, though they remain subtly different. Both cover the "matters" referred to in s118. The Code for England contains five "overarching" principles (E Para. 1.1):

1. Least restrictive option and maximising independence

2. Empowerment and involvement

3. Respect and dignity

4. Purpose and effectiveness

5. Efficiency and equity.

The Code for Wales contains six "guiding" principles (W Para. 1.1):

1. Dignity and respect

2. Least restrictive option and maximising independence

3. Fairness, equality and equity

4. Empowerment and involvement

5. Keeping people safe

6. Effectiveness and efficiency.

All are expanded upon at length and it is fair to say that considerable efforts have been made to refer to and embed these principles at appropriate points throughout the guidance contained in the Codes, in particular the "least restriction and maximising independence" principle.

# Some issues raised by the Codes of Practice

The guidance contained in the respective Codes for England and Wales will be referred to at appropriate points in this book. However, a number of the more striking or controversial points are worth underlining here:

1.   The Codes reflect the introduction of the Care Act 2014, in particular the amendments to s117, and the Social Services and Well-being (Wales) Act 2014, as well as the public sector equality duty based on s149 Equality Act 2010 and refer to current safeguarding and whistleblowing provisions.

2.   In England the Code will be the starting point for the CQC's rating system and will help to identify a "good" rating in the care and treatment of people subject to the Act (Intro E Para. xxv). The Health Inspectorate Wales (HIW) will specifically check that the Code is being followed (W Para. Intro xviii).

3.   There are occasions when in particular the Code for England gives guidance which arguably does not accurately reflect the law. For example the guidance at Para. 27.11 that s17 leave "should normally be of short duration" and at Para. 31.5 should be "for a fixed purpose or a fixed period and not normally more than one month" goes well beyond the legal requirement to "consider" a CTO if leave is to be for more than seven consecutive days. It is also inconsistent with long-standing case law, restated recently in *SL v Ludlow Street Healthcare* (2015) confirming the legitimacy of long-term use of s17 leave. Interestingly there are no such statements in the Code for Wales, which adopts a more even-handed (and perhaps more legally correct) approach to the choice between regimes.

4.   Both the Mental Capacity Act and DoLS Codes are now showing their age and the most up-to-date guidance on assessing capacity, deprivation of liberty (in the light of the Supreme Court decision in *Cheshire West* (2014) UKSC 14), and choosing between MHA or DoLS regimes is currently to be found in the MHA Codes for England and Wales. Noteworthy provisions which largely reflect case law developments include:

     (a)   the prescriptive requirements for recording assessments of capacity (E Para. 13.22; W Para. 13.8);

     (b)   the virtual impossibility of now admitting informally incapacitated patients to hospital for treatment of mental disorder where they are likely to be deprived of their liberty, whether content to be admitted or not (E Para. 13.53; W Para. 13.39);

     (c)   the requirement to adopt a level playing field approach to the choice between DoLS and MHA, where both are potentially available (E Para. 13.60);

     (d)   (controversially) the statement that "both regimes (i.e. MHA and DoLS) provide appropriate procedural safeguards to ensure the rights of the person concerned are protected during their detention" (E Para. 13.59). This is not repeated in the Code for Wales, which states that this is a matter for the professional judgement of the decision-maker (W Paras 13.42, 13.43).

5.   Before their current editions, the Codes contained scant reference to the Human Rights Act 1998. The Codes both now contain a chapter on human rights and equality, which are placed at the heart of service delivery, and an effort has been made consistently throughout the Codes to relate specific guidance to the European Convention on Human Rights, in particular Article 8.

6.   There may be a degree of frustration at the number of occasions within the Code when guidance is not in fact given, but rather reference made to the numerous policies and procedures which have to be drawn up (usually by managers) to cover a practice issue. Annex B to the Code for England contains a list of 56 such policies, many of which cover a multiplicity of issues. The Code for Wales has a similar list at Annex 2.

7.   There is an enhanced focus on blanket restrictions, i.e. "rules or policies that restrict a patient's liberty and other rights, which are routinely applied to all patients, or to classes of patients, or within a service, without individual risk assessments to justify their application". These are generally deprecated and should only be applied "as a

proportionate and measured response to an individually identified risk" (E Paras 8.5–8.6; W Para. 8.11).

8.  There is throughout the Codes a noticeably increased frequency of guidance requiring consideration of the views and needs of carers, including child carers, and a greater emphasis on the need to involve at appropriate times an independent mental health advocate (IMHA).

9.  Although the Code for England reaffirms that it is normally the responsibility of the doctor (not the AMHP) to locate a bed to which a patient may be admitted (E Para. 14.77), there is for the first time mention of the role of the bed manager: "Providers should identify a bed manager or other single point of contact who will be responsible for finding a suitable bed as soon as possible and telling the applicant the name of the site at which it is situated" (E Para. 14.89). There is no similar guidance in the Code for Wales.

10. A recurrent practice issue is the determination of whether a patient is objecting to the treatment or care proposed. It is noticeable that both Codes, again reflecting in part recent case law, repeatedly emphasise that decision-makers should err on the side of caution and, where in doubt, take the position that a patient is objecting (see, e.g., E Paras 13.51, 14.20, 24.21; W Paras 13.38, 14.17, 24.21). This has considerable implications for future management, as will be explored in later chapters.

11. In respect of children and young people, the Code for England has dropped use of the rather ungainly phrase "the zone of parental control" in favour of the more logical "scope of parental responsibility" ("PR"). The Code for Wales refers to the consent of someone with parental responsibility. This still leaves open the question what precisely falls within such scope. The Code for England suggests at Para. 19.48 that practitioners keep an eye on case law developments, which are dealt with in Chapters 11 and 18. The Supreme Court has decided (*D (A Child)* (2019) UKSC 42) (see Appendix 6) that confining or authorising the confinement of a young person of 16 or 17 lacking capacity in circumstances which meet the "acid test" of deprivation of liberty does not fall within the scope of PR. In the meantime it is noteworthy that whereas the Code for Wales continues to assert that the best interests of the child must always be the primary consideration (W Para. 19.5) and their welfare and protection of paramount importance (W Para. 19.4), the Code for England refers to the best interests of a child being merely "a significant consideration" (E Para. 19.5). It is also at least arguable that the Code guidance as to when one should not rely on parental consent goes beyond what the law currently requires, as the Supreme Court in *D (A Child)* confined its judgement to the case of deprivation of liberty of an incapacitated young person.

# The Reference Guide to the Mental Health Act (for England)

The Reference Guide was revised in 2015 to coincide with the Code of Practice for England. It consists of 397 pages, is available in electronic form and can be downloaded from **www.gov. uk/government/uploads/system/uploads/attachment_data/file/417412/Reference_Guide. pdf**. It is intended as a source of reference for people who want to understand the provisions of the Mental Health Act 1983 as it applies in England, whereas the Code guides the implementation of the Act in practice. There is no equivalent Reference Guide for Wales.

The Guide is an extremely useful point of reference. Some of the 2007 Act amendments to the 1983 Act are extraordinarily complex and difficult to understand. This applies in particular to the provisions of Part 4A dealing with the treatment of CTO patients while in the community. Chapter 24 of the Guide would be a sensible place for anyone to start who wished to grasp their meaning.

The opportunity presented by the Reference Guide being published shortly after the Code was taken to correct some quite major errors within the Code for England. In particular the Code suggests at Para. 29.46 that the grounds for recalling a CTO patient under s17E(1) are alternatives, whereas in fact both elements at (a) and (b) have to be met. Likewise revocation of a CTO requires agreement of both the responsible clinician (RC) *and* an approved mental health professional (AMHP), whereas the Code wrongly suggests (E Para. 29.64) that either will suffice. The problem is that more people refer to the Code than to the Reference Guide, so these errors are likely to continue to mislead. The errors are not repeated in the Code for Wales, as it was published a year later than its counterpart in England.

Throughout the Guide, extensive use is made of tables to illustrate the Act's provisions. Examples include: the summary at Figure 74 of exemptions from Part 4 certificate requirements for CTO and former CTO patients (which are formidably difficult to understand in the text of the Act itself); the summary of the requirements of s56, s58 and s58A at Para. 23.69; and the tables relating to occasions on which applications may be made to First-tier Tribunals at Figures 13–29.

The Guide also makes use of case studies, for example at Para. 25.27, illustrating the consequences of different categories of patients going absent without leave.

There is a degree of overlap with the Code of Practice. Both contain glossaries of similarly, but not identically, defined terms. The manner in which the exclusion relating to drug or alcohol dependency is covered is virtually identical (Code Paras 3.8–3.12; Guide Paras 1.8–1.11), as are the conditions to be attached to a CTO (Code Paras 25.29–25.35; Guide Paras 15.16–15.19). One wonders whether the two documents might not have been combined to create a single volume both describing and giving guidance on the provisions of the amended Act.

# Key points

1. There are separate Codes of Practice for England and Wales.

2. People need to consider whether they are obliged to "have regard to" the Codes.

3. The Codes are guidance and do not have statutory force.

4. The Codes should not be departed from except for cogent reasons.

5. The European Convention on Human Rights is a higher authority than the Codes.

6. The Codes, not the Act, contain the principles underpinning the operation of the Act.

7. The Codes do not just apply to patients formally detained under the Act.

8. The MHA Codes rather than the MCA Code contain the most up-to-date guidance on assessments of capacity and identification of deprivation of liberty.

9. The Codes contain guidance as to when to use the Mental Capacity Act rather than the Mental Health Act.

10. The Reference Guide contains an explanation of the main legal provisions of the Act and the Regulations.

# Chapter 4

## Mental disorder and the availability of appropriate medical treatment

## Introduction

Before the compulsory powers contained in the Mental Health Act may be used, a series of criteria must be met. Even if the criteria *are* all met, this will not necessarily result in the powers being invoked because health and social care professionals retain the discretion to take a different approach. AMHPs, for example, have an obligation under s13(2) (and restated in Forms A2 and A6 in England; HO2 and HO6 in Wales) in respect of applications for admission of a patient to hospital to satisfy themselves *"that detention in hospital is in all the circumstances of the case the most appropriate way of providing the care or medical treatment of which the patient stands in need"*. Doctors completing recommendations for s3 must state in Form A8 (HO8 in Wales) that the necessary treatment cannot be provided unless the patient is detained under s3. Even for admissions under s2, doctors must (in Forms A4 and HO4 respectively) explain why informal admission is not appropriate.

The first criterion to be met is that the patient is suffering from mental disorder. This is important because it is a legal requirement of the Mental Health Act and the powers can only be exercised precisely within a legal framework. However, it also touches upon one of the essential requirements of Article 5 of the European Convention on Human Rights (see Chapter 17 and Appendix 5) which in certain circumstances permits the detention of *"persons of unsound mind"*. We will therefore, in this chapter, consider the meaning of mental disorder and look at some of the key issues associated with this. We will also look at the "availability of appropriate medical treatment" test introduced by the Mental Health Act 2007.

## The meaning of mental disorder

Mental disorder is succinctly defined in s1(2) as follows: *"mental disorder" means any disorder or disability of the mind.*

It is nowhere further defined in the Act, but, as will be seen, it is qualified in relation to learning disability. A distinction is clearly intended to be made between "a disorder or disability of the **mind**" and a "disorder or disability of the **brain**". The words "or brain" were included within the draft 2002 Bill definition, but then dropped. At Para. 17, the Explanatory Notes state that *"disorders or disabilities of the brain are not mental disorders unless (and only to the extent that) they give rise to a disability or disorder of the mind as well."* The intention is no doubt to create a demarcation line between the Mental Health Act and the Mental Capacity Act (which includes the words "or brain" in its definition of incapacity in s2), but the distinction may not always be clear-cut.

A non-exhaustive list of possible examples of mental disorder is set out in the Code of Practice for England at Para. 2.5:

- *affective disorders, such as depression and bipolar disorder;*

- *schizophrenia and delusional disorders;*

- *neurotic, stress-related and somatoform disorders, such as anxiety, phobic disorders, obsessive compulsive disorders, post-traumatic stress disorder and hypochondriacal disorders;*

- *organic mental disorders such as dementia and delirium (however caused);*

- *personality and behavioural changes caused by brain injury or damage (however acquired);*

- *personality disorders;*

- *mental and behavioural disorders caused by psychoactive substance use …;*

- *eating disorders, non-organic sleep disorders and non-organic sexual disorders;*

- *learning disabilities;*

- *autistic spectrum disorders (including Asperger's syndrome) …;*

- *behavioural and emotional disorders of children and young people.*

The 2016 Code for Wales no longer includes such a list at all, and there is some logic for this approach. The mere presence of such conditions in the Code or in manuals such as ICD-10 or DSM-V does not establish them as mental disorders for the purposes of the Act. Nor does the non-appearance of a condition in the manuals mean that it cannot legally be considered a mental disorder. As was noted by the court in *DL-H v Devon Partnership NHS Trust v Secretary of State* (see Appendix 6), "the specific criteria in ICD 10 are labelled as diagnostic criteria for *research*" and the introduction to DSM-IV confirms that the "clinical diagnosis of a DSM-IV mental disorder is not sufficient to establish the existence for legal purposes of a 'mental disorder'."

## The removal of the classifications

The broad definition of mental disorder is accompanied by the removal of the previous classifications. These classifications (mental illness, mental impairment, severe mental impairment and psychopathic disorder) acted to restrict the application of some sections of the Act to certain categories of mental disorder. Although in relation to the treatment to be given to a patient, case law had decided that the classification of the disorder was not decisive, the distinction was important in determining which parts of the Act applied to which disorder for a variety of purposes. For s3, the longer-term admission for treatment required a patient to be placed within one of the four classifications, whereas s2 did not. Now, whether s2 or s3 is under consideration, the first criterion for either is simply whether the patient is suffering from mental disorder.

Because for the purposes of the Act psychopathic disorder no longer exists, the particular qualifications attaching to the condition disappear likewise. So for s3, there is no requirement that treatment is likely to alleviate or prevent a deterioration of the condition. Further, for all purposes it is unnecessary to establish that the disorder is "persistent" or "resulting in abnormally aggressive or seriously irresponsible conduct" on the part of the patient. All that is required is "mental disorder". This can only mean that more people (particularly the personality disordered) are eligible to be considered for use of the compulsory powers than before the amendments introduced by the Mental Health Act 2007.

# The exclusions

There was a good deal of debate around the proposed removal of the exclusions from mental disorder as the 2007 Bill was passing through Parliament. Section 1 of the unamended Act precluded promiscuity or other immoral conduct, sexual deviancy, or dependence on alcohol or drugs from being considered as mental disorders for the purpose of using the compulsory powers. The House of Lords pressed for the addition of further exclusions, whereas the Government wanted the removal of all of them. In the end only the exclusion relating to dependence on alcohol or drugs was retained. While this means that it is not possible to use the Act's compulsory powers on the basis of drug or alcohol dependence alone, as the Code of Practice points out at E Para. 2.11:

> *Alcohol or drug dependence may be accompanied by, or associated with, a mental disorder which does fall within the Act's definition. If the relevant criteria are met, it is therefore possible (for example) to detain people who are suffering from mental disorder, even though they are also dependent on alcohol or drugs. This is true even if the mental disorder in question results from the person's alcohol or drug dependence.*

(The Code for Wales at 2.6 gives similar guidance.) So a related or consequential mental disorder would not rule out use of the compulsory powers.

The removal of the exclusions relating to promiscuity, other immoral conduct and sexual deviancy is controversial. The Explanatory Notes state at E Para. 24:

> *Clinically, neither promiscuity nor "other immoral conduct" by itself is regarded as a mental disorder, so the deletion of that exclusion makes no practical difference. Similarly, sexual orientation (homo-, hetero- and bi-sexuality) alone is not regarded as a mental disorder. However, there are disorders of sexual preference which are recognised clinically as mental disorders. Some of these disorders might be considered "sexual deviance" in the terms of the current exclusion (for example paraphilias like fetishism or paedophilia). On that basis, the amendment would bring such disorders within the scope of the 1983 Act.*

Clearly the intention is that paedophilia, for example (so long as the other criteria are met), should be capable of being regarded as a mental disorder for the purposes of using the compulsory powers of the Act. If paedophilia could be considered a symptom of a personality disorder, it would not have been excluded from consideration in any event under the unamended Act. The question is whether without being such a symptom, the removal of sexual deviancy as an exclusion makes it easier to argue that such conditions constitute mental disorders eligible for consideration for use of the compulsory powers. Of course all other criteria would have to be met (e.g. as to risk), but an argument can be anticipated that rather than being true mental disorders they are behaviours "deviating from society's norms" and therefore fall foul of the *Winterwerp* criteria for what constitutes lawful detention on the basis of unsoundness of mind (see Appendix 6).

# Learning disability

Although the definition of mental disorder has been simplified and broadened (so as to include some conditions not previously considered eligible for use of the Act's powers), there is one area in which the complexity of the unamended Act has been retained, namely learning disability. This is defined in s1(4) as: *"a state of arrested or incomplete development of the mind which includes significant impairment of intelligence and social functioning".*

As such it would clearly fall within the s1(2) definition of mental disorder. However, as a result of an amendment introduced during the Bill's passage, words familiar from the unamended Act were reintroduced (drawn from the old definition of mental impairment). The effect of s1(2A) is that for all but the short-term sections (2, 4, 5, 135, 136), learning disability will not constitute a mental disorder unless "associated with abnormally aggressive or seriously irresponsible conduct" on the part of the patient. It follows that, for example, neither s3 nor s7 can be invoked without this qualification being met. Given the generally restrictive but not entirely consistent interpretation often placed in particular on the phrase "seriously irresponsible conduct" by the courts (see *Re F (Mental Health: Guardianship* in Appendix 6), there will be some cases where guardianship will not be a possible avenue for a patient because of this requirement. The intention is probably that such patients should be managed for preference under the Mental Capacity Act. The Deprivation of Liberty Safeguards (DoLS) procedure does not require learning disability to be qualified in this way in order to constitute a mental disorder. Whether it is to the advantage of a learning disabled person to be managed under DoLS rather than the Mental Health Act is a moot point among health and social care professionals.

Particular care will need to be taken by AMHPs and doctors in this area as, for some inexplicable reason, the forms for applications and medical recommendations under s3 do not make this behavioural requirement explicit.

The Code of Practice (E Para. 2.17; W Para. 2.13) differentiates autistic spectrum disorders from learning disability, so that the condition for use of the longer-term compulsory powers could be met (albeit rarely) without any other coexisting form of mental disorder and without the association with abnormally aggressive or seriously irresponsible behaviour.

# The availability of appropriate medical treatment

The UK Government was adamant that the "treatability" test contained in the unamended Act was to be removed. It was seen as one of the reasons relied on not to admit certain patients whom the Government did not wish to see excluded. This was one of the principal battlegrounds during the Bill's passage and although the Government had its way, a last-minute amendment was introduced upon which opinion is divided. Does the definition of "appropriate medical treatment" effectively introduce a new more widely applicable treatability test, or is the definition so imprecise that virtually all patients will meet it should the health and social care professionals wish to use the compulsory powers in any given case?

The requirement that appropriate medical treatment is available for the patient applies to all patients suffering from mental disorder, whether at the time of initially considering s3 or of its renewal. In addition it is a requirement for placing a patient on a community treatment order under s17A (and extending it), and for Tribunals considering whether to discharge a patient. It even extends to the exercise by SOADs of their certification responsibilities, where the "alleviation" test is replaced with an "appropriateness" test.

An application for admission for treatment is now possible if three grounds are met for the patient:

(a) *he is suffering from mental disorder of a nature or degree which makes it appropriate for him to receive medical treatment in a hospital; and*

(b) ...

(c) *it is necessary for the health or safety of the patient or for the protection of other persons that he should receive such treatment and it cannot be provided unless he is detained under this section; and*

(d) *appropriate medical treatment is available for him.*

# The meaning of the availability of appropriate medical treatment

Section 3(4) states as follows:

> *In this Act, references to appropriate medical treatment, in relation to a person suffering from mental disorder, are references to medical treatment which is appropriate in his case, taking into account the nature and degree of the mental disorder and all other circumstances of his case.*

"Appropriate medical treatment" is not further defined in the Act, and at first sight the s3(4) definition is not particularly helpful to health and social care professionals in deciding whether this fundamental criterion for admission for treatment is met. The first part of the definition simply repeats itself and the concluding phrase confines itself to directing the professionals to consider anything which may be relevant, the broad ambit of which is stated in the Code of Practice (E Para. 23.12; W Para. 23.13). On one view, the lack of elaboration in the definition will merely serve to underline the professionals' discretion whether to proceed with admission. On the other hand, the broad nature of the phrase might be seen to encompass so much that not to admit would amount to a bold decision. In *MD v Nottinghamshire Healthcare NHS Trust* (see Appendix 6) the judge stated that "appropriateness is an important additional criterion for detention; it is not surplus verbiage." However he did not elaborate further and the Code merely refers back to the statutory definitions (E Para. 23.9; W (in different terms) Para. 23.11).

If "appropriate medical treatment" is not particularly helpfully defined, and the word "appropriate" simply confirms the existence of professional discretion whether to use the compulsory powers, what about "medical treatment"? Section 145(4) states:

> *Any reference in this Act to medical treatment in relation to mental disorder shall be construed as a reference to medical treatment the purpose of which is to alleviate, or prevent a worsening of, the disorder or one or more of its symptoms or manifestations.*

In addition s145(1) states:

> *"Medical treatment" includes nursing, psychological intervention and specialist mental health habilitation, rehabilitation and care.*

The following points should be noted in relation to these definitions:

1.  The courts have tended to adopt a broad view of what medical treatment comprises. In *Reid v Secretary of State for Scotland* (see Appendix 6) it was stated that it was broad enough to include treatment the purpose of which ranged from "cure to containment". The inclusion of "psychological intervention" is spelled out in s145(1) but would have fallen within this broad view in any event.

2.  The s145(4) definition does not require medical treatment to alleviate or prevent a deterioration of the disorder, but merely one or more of its symptoms or manifestations. In *Reid*, however, the same judge stated that "medical treatment" included treatment "designed to alleviate or prevent a deterioration of the mental disorder or the symptoms of the mental disorder"; so as Bowen (2007, 3.55) has pointed out s145(4) simply makes this requirement specific. The inclusion of "manifestations", however, does broaden the scope of the definition still further.

3.  The s145(4) definition does not require that (as in the unamended Act) the medical treatment is "likely" to produce an effect, merely that that is its "purpose": "Purpose is not the same as likelihood" (Codes E Para. 23.4; W Para. 23.3). This would seem to imply

a lowering of the threshold (but see *Reid* above). The Government was anxious that patients should not be denied admission under the compulsory powers merely because, for example, they were unlikely to cooperate with treatment offered, thus rendering it ineffective. As the Code for England states at Para. 23.19 and the Code for Wales at Para. 23.14: "An indication of unwillingness to co-operate with treatment generally, or with a specific aspect of treatment, does not make such treatment inappropriate." See also W Para. 4.17.

Although the decisions of the court all predate the amendments introduced by the 2007 Act, there is no reason to suppose that the amended definitions would be construed differently in any future challenge. So the bar of what is required to meet the "appropriate medical treatment" test is set low. The Code for England states at Para. 23.8 that:

*The appropriate medical treatment test must be applied to ensure that no one is detained (or remains detained) for treatment, or is on a CTO, unless medical treatment for their mental disorder is both appropriate and available.*

And the Code for Wales at Para. 23.8 that:

*The purpose of the "appropriate medical treatment test" is to ensure that no one is detained (or remains detained) for treatment, unless they are actually to be offered medical treatment for their mental disorder.*

And both Codes (E Para. 23.4; W Para. 23.3) make the point that:

*Purpose is not the same as likelihood. Medical treatment must be for the purpose of alleviating or preventing a worsening of mental disorder even if it cannot be shown, in advance, that a particular effect is likely to be achieved.*

So given the broad interpretation of "medical treatment", even though:

*Simply detaining someone – even in a hospital – does not constitute medical treatment* [E Para. 23.18].

very little more than this is required either in terms of specific treatment or its therapeutic "purpose". So we have a situation where:

*There may be patients whose particular circumstances mean that treatment may be appropriate even though it consists only of nursing and specialist day to day care under the clinical supervision of an approved clinician* [W Para. 23.9] *in a safe and secure therapeutic environment with a structured regime* [E Para. 23.17].

That the threshold is low was confirmed by subsequent court decisions. In *MD v Nottinghamshire Healthcare NHS Trust* (see Appendix 6) the court found that in respect of a personality disordered patient:

1.  Detention without reduction of risk did not constitute mere containment.

2.  Merely benefitting from the ward "milieu" meant that appropriate medical treatment was available.

3.  The argument that a theoretical capacity to engage with psychological therapy did not equate to a practical ability to benefit from treatment was "untenable".

In *DL-H v Devon Partnership NHS Trust et al.* (see above) the Court confirmed that the s145(4) definition of medical treatment was broad enough to include attempts by nursing staff to encourage the patient to engage. Recognising that this ran the risk of patients being contained for public safety rather than detained for treatment, the Court suggested that Tribunals avert the danger by investigating behind assertions, generalisations and standard phrases and asking: What treatment could be provided? What benefit might it have for the patient? Is the benefit related to the patient's mental disorder? Is the patient truly resistant to engagement? When this case returned to the Upper Tribunal in 2013, the Court denied that these questions reintroduced a treatability test.

# What is "availability"?

Appropriate medical treatment, whatever it comprises, is not by itself sufficient. Such treatment must also be "available". There is no indication in the Act as to how this word is to be construed in this context. Is treatment for a patient living in Bath but only available in, say, Oxford or Wrexham "available"? Is treatment for a patient available locally but only in the private sector at a price the health authority is not prepared to fund "available"? Is treatment, such as cognitive behavioural therapy (CBT), which because of demands on the service can only be commenced three months after compulsory admission, "available"?

The Code of Practice for England states at Para. 23.14:

> *Medical treatment must actually be available to the patient. It is not sufficient that appropriate treatment could theoretically be provided* [but note the comment in the MD case above].

The Code at E Para. 23.12 (W Para. 3.13) refers to the location of treatment as being part of "all the other circumstances of the patient's case". At Para. 23.10 the Code for England states:

> *The appropriate medical treatment test requires a judgement about whether an appropriate treatment or package of treatment for mental disorder is available for the individual in question. It is not consistent with the least "restrictive option and maximising independence" and "purpose and effectiveness guiding principles" to detain someone for treatment that is not actually available **or may not become available until some future point in time*** [emphasis added].

And at E Paras 23.13, 23.21:

> *Medical treatment must always be an appropriate response to the patient's condition and situation and indeed wherever possible should be the most appropriate treatment available. It may be that a single medical treatment does not address every aspect of a patient's mental disorder … (but) … those making the judgement must satisfy themselves that appropriate medical treatment is available for the time being, given the patient's condition and circumstances as they are currently understood.*

The Code for Wales at Para 23.16 gives guidance in similar vein. Faced with this guidance, health and social care professionals can be forgiven for concluding that "appropriate" means what they say it means. To put it another way, they have a very broad discretion to decide whether any particular form of medical treatment (itself a very broad concept) is "available" in any given case.

# Conclusion

It is reasonable to suggest that the broad definition of mental disorder, the removal of most of the exclusions, the abolition of the classifications of mental disorder, and the replacement of the treatability requirement with a therapeutic purpose test constitute a collective lowering of the threshold for use of compulsory powers; and that this makes those powers more widely available for use, even though the risk and other criteria must be met and health and social care professionals retain their discretion not to use the Act. One might expect this to be reflected in the statistics published since the Mental Health Act 2007 changes came into effect; and indeed these show a rise every year in the use of the compulsory powers. Between 2005–06 and 2015–16 (the last year for which reliable statistics are available) use of the compulsory powers increased by 40%. There are other factors in play – not least the lack of available beds for patients not detained under the Act, a reduction in the availability of community resources and the combined effect of the decision of the Supreme Court in *Cheshire West*, which lowered the threshold for what constitutes deprivation of liberty so requiring an authorisation, and the decision in *A PCT v LDV et al.* (2013) EWHC 272 (Fam) (see Appendix 6) which raised the level of understanding required for a patient to be capable of being admitted informally. However, the ease with which the availability of the appropriate medical treatment test can be met is likely to have contributed to this increase.

One might query whether it is necessary to continue to consider some 12 years on the changes introduced by the 2007 Act rather than simply explaining the Act as it currently stands. The truth is that the Government set up the recent Mental Health Act Review because of concerns inter alia at the increasing use of the compulsory powers since the 2007 Act amendments were introduced, at whether safeguards available to patients were sufficient and at the possibility that detention might be being used to detain rather than treat: all problems anticipated and argued over in the period leading up to the 2007 Act. The review, which reported in December 2018, makes 154 recommendations and has a particular focus on the need to strengthen detention criteria concerning treatment and risk: treatment should be available which would benefit the patient and not just serve public protection, and the risk thresholds raised to that of a substantial likelihood of significant harm to the health or welfare of the person or the safety of any other person – recommendations at least in part prompted by the introduction of the availability of the appropriate treatment test. At the date of writing, the Government's full response to these recommendations is still awaited.

# Key points

1. Mental disorder means any disorder or disability of the mind.

2. Disorders or disabilities of the brain are excluded unless leading to a disorder or disability of the mind.

3. Health and social care professionals retain the discretion not to use the compulsory powers even when the criteria are met.

4. When considering longer-term compulsion, consider whether the learning disability is associated with abnormally aggressive or seriously irresponsible conduct.

5. Drug or alcohol dependence alone is insufficient for use of the compulsory powers.

6. Whether paedophilia is a true mental disorder is uncertain.

7. For s3 detention and for CTOs appropriate medical treatment must be available.

8. Case law confirms that medical treatment is to be very broadly defined and construed.

9. The "treatability" test is replaced with a "therapeutic purpose" test.

10. It is sufficient for the "therapeutic purpose" test merely to relate to a symptom or manifestation of the mental disorder.

# Chapter 5

## Civil admission and compulsion in hospital

## Introduction

This chapter outlines the civil provisions within the Mental Health Act for detaining patients. There are a number of provisions, usually referred to by their section number, that allow people to be detained in hospital settings and places of safety. Each section has distinct criteria that must be met before a person can be compulsorily detained. The different sections allow varying levels of compulsory requirements to be placed upon patients and offer them varying levels of safeguards. Patient safeguards are detailed within a table at the end of this chapter.

## Admission for assessment – s2

Section 2 of the MHA allows a patient to be detained in hospital for up to 28 days. Section 2 may apply to someone who is already an in-patient, either under an existing section (i.e. s5(2), s5(4) or s4) or an informal patient, or to a person living in the community. The purpose of s2 is to enable a person's mental state to be assessed, and, if necessary, for them to be treated following a period of assessment, for their mental disorder. The Code of Practice (E Para. 14.27) suggests the use of s2 in the following circumstances:

- *the full extent of the nature and degree of a patient's condition is unclear;*

- *there is a need to carry out an initial in-patient assessment in order to formulate a treatment plan, or to reach a judgement about whether the patient will accept treatment on a voluntary basis following admission; or*

- *there is a need to carry out a new in-patient assessment in order to re-formulate a treatment plan, or to reach a judgement about whether the patient will accept treatment on a voluntary basis.*

The Welsh Code of Practice (W Para. 14.20) has a broader range of considerations:

- *An assessment as an inpatient is required in order to produce a treatment plan.*

- *A judgement is required on whether the patient will accept treatment on a voluntary/ informal basis after admission.*

- *A judgement has to be made on whether a proposed treatment, which can only be administered to the patient under Part 4 of the Act, is likely to be effective.*

- *The condition of a patient who has already been assessed, and who has been previously admitted compulsorily under the Act, is judged to have changed since the previous admission and further assessment is required.*

- *The diagnosis and/or prognosis of a patient's condition are unclear.*

- *It has not been possible to undertake any other assessment in order to formulate a treatment plan.*

## Section 2 assessment

For a person to be detained under this section he must be assessed as meeting the legal criteria set out at s2(2) of the Act by two doctors and an applicant, either an AMHP or the nearest relative. Of the two doctors, one must be approved under s12 as "having special experience in the diagnosis or treatment of mental disorder", and, unless that doctor also has previous acquaintance with the patient, the other doctor, if practicable, should have previous acquaintance with the patient. See Appendix 6 *(Reed (Trainer) v Bronglais Hospital et al.* (2001)) for the interpretation of "previous acquaintance". Both doctors must personally examine the patient together or separately. Where they have carried out separate examinations, there must be no more than five days between medical examinations. For example, where the first examination takes place on the 1st of the month, the second examination can be no later than the 7th of the month. The applicant has 14 days beginning with the date of the last medical examination to complete their application and convey the patient to hospital. For the purpose of conveyance the AMHP has all the powers of a police constable, but in practice the task of conveyance is usually delegated to the ambulance or police services.

The legal grounds that must be met before a person can be detained under s2 are that the patient:

- is suffering from a mental disorder of a nature or degree which warrants the detention of the patient in a hospital for assessment (or for assessment followed by medical treatment); and

- he ought to be detained in the interests of his own health or safety or with a view to the protection of others.

Mental disorder is defined as "any disorder or disability of the mind", which is a broad definition, leaving the interpretation of what constitutes a mental disorder to the doctors. Dependence on alcohol or drugs by itself is excluded from the definition of mental disorder. However, if a patient is dependent upon alcohol or drugs and displays symptoms of mental disorder, he would fall within the definition of mental disorder. The mental disorder must be of a nature or degree that makes it appropriate for the patient to receive medical treatment in a hospital. The meaning of nature or degree was considered by Popplewell, J. in *R v Mental Health Review Tribunal for the South Thames Region ex parte Smith* (1999), who stated that "nature" refers to the particular mental disorder from which the patient suffers, its chronicity, its prognosis, and the patient's previous response to receiving treatment for the disorder, and the "degree" refers to the current manifestation of the patient's mental disorder.

In addition, there are three risk criteria: health (including both physical and mental health); safety of the patient; and the protection of others. However, it is only necessary for one of these risk criteria to be met, and there is no requirement for the doctors to reach agreement about which risk criteria are met. If both doctors are satisfied that the above criteria are met and that informal admission of the patient is not appropriate, they may complete medical recommendations for the detention of a patient under s2 of the Act.

Once the recommendations are completed, the AMHP, having interviewed the patient, must decide whether to complete an application for detention. The applicant must also satisfy himself that the legal criteria are met and that the application ought to be made having regard to any wishes expressed by relatives and any other relevant circumstances. The applicant has the discretion whether or not to make an application for detention, and may only apply if he is satisfied that it is necessary or proper to do so. The completed application gives the applicant the authority to convey the patient to hospital, and the hospital then has the authority to admit and detain the patient. Where an application is not made by the AMHP they should inform the nearest relative of their right to do so, and where the nearest relative chooses to make an application, the AMHP must interview the patient and provide a social circumstances report in line with s14 of the Act.

Section 2 cannot be renewed and should not immediately be followed by another s2 application. If a patient needs continued treatment beyond 28 days, the responsible clinician should consider whether informal admission or s3 would be appropriate. If s3 is considered appropriate and the patient's nearest relative objects, the process of applying to the county court for the displacement of the nearest relative has the effect of extending the s2 beyond 28 days until the court proceedings have finished.

## Effect of detention

The completed medical recommendations and application provide the authority for the patient to be admitted and detained in hospital for up to 28 days. A patient detained under s2 can be treated, following a period of assessment, without his consent if necessary, for his mental disorder and he can be prevented from leaving the hospital. The only means of lawful absence from hospital during the period of detention is by way of s17 leave (see Chapter 6).

# Admission for treatment – s3

Section 3 allows a patient to be detained in hospital for an initial period of up to six months. The patient could be admitted either from the community or following use of s2, 4 or 5 or even when an informal in-patient. The Code of Practice (E Para. 14.28) suggests the use of s3 where the following criteria are met:

- *the patient is already detained under section 2 (detention under section 2 cannot be renewed by a new section 2 application); or*

- *the nature and current degree of the patient's mental disorder, the essential elements of the treatment plan to be followed and the likelihood of the patient accepting treatment on a voluntary basis are already established to make it unnecessary to undertake a new assessment under section 2.*

The Welsh Code of Practice (W Para. 14.20) has a broader range of considerations:

- *The patient is considered to need compulsory admission for the treatment of a mental disorder, which is already known to his or her clinical team, and has recently been assessed by that team.*

- *The patient is detained under section 2 and assessment indicates a need for compulsory treatment under the Act beyond the existing period of detention. In such circumstances an application for detention under section 3 should be made at the earliest opportunity and should not be delayed until the end of the existing period of detention.*

## Section 3 assessment

As for s2 a patient must be examined by two doctors (one must be s12 approved and one where practicable should have previous acquaintance with the patient). He must also be interviewed by an applicant (an AMHP or nearest relative). The assessing team must establish whether the patient meets the following grounds for detention:

• he must be suffering from a mental disorder[1] of a nature or degree which makes it appropriate for him to receive medical treatment in a hospital; and

• it is necessary for the health or safety of the patient or for the protection of others;

• treatment cannot be provided unless he is detained under this section; and

• appropriate medical treatment is available.

See Appendix 6 (*Re (F) (Mental Health Act: Guardianship) (2000)*) for the interpretation of "seriously irresponsible".

The doctors may complete medical recommendations for detention if they are satisfied that the above criteria are met. Where medical recommendations are completed the applicant may complete an application for detention, if he too is satisfied that the legal criteria are met and that there is no other way of providing the care and medical treatment the patient needs. An AMHP must consult the patient's nearest relative prior to making the application if it is reasonably practicable to do so and would not cause an unreasonable delay. If the nearest relative objects to an application being made, or has notified that professional or the LSSA that he objects to an application being made, the AMHP cannot proceed with an application. In such a case the AMHP should consider whether there are grounds for displacing the nearest relative on the grounds that the nearest relative's objection is unreasonable (see Chapter 14). If, however, the AMHP decides not to make an application for s3, like section 2 (above) the AMHP should inform the nearest relative of their right to do so, and where the nearest relative chooses to make an application, the AMHP must interview the patient and provide a social circumstances report in line with s14 of the Act.

## Renewal of detention

Detention under s3 lasts for up to six months in the first instance and can be renewed under s20 by the patient's responsible clinician for a further six months, and then annually. Renewal of detention can occur if the RC consults one other person professionally concerned with the patient's treatment, and gains the agreement of a professional concerned with the patient's treatment who is of a different profession from the RC. Before agreeing to the renewal of detention, this professional must be satisfied that the grounds for detention under s3 (detailed above) continue to be met. Both of these functions could be performed by the same professional, provided that he is concerned with the patient's treatment and is of a different profession to that of the RC. If the patient's RC is not a doctor, they may be well advised to gain the agreement to continued detention from someone who is a doctor to avoid a challenge under Article 5 of the ECHR regarding the absence of objective medical expertise at the point of renewal (see Chapter 17).

---

[1]For patients with learning disability alone (meaning a "state of arrested or incomplete development of the mind which includes significant impairment of intelligence and social functioning") this must be "associated with abnormally aggressive or seriously irresponsible conduct". This additional criterion of associated abnormally aggressive or seriously irresponsible conduct does not however apply to those with autistic spectrum disorders or those with a learning disability and coexisting mental disorders requiring treatment. These patients are simply to be treated as mentally disordered.

## Effect of detention

Patients detained under s3 are compelled to remain in hospital unless they are granted s17 leave of absence, which provides a lawful means of being absent from hospital. Whilst detained under this section, patients are covered by Part 4 consent to treatment provisions (see Chapter 8), and therefore they can be treated for their mental disorder with or without their consent, and in the face of a valid and applicable advance decision, other than with ECT.

# Admission for assessment in cases of emergency – s4

An emergency application should only be made in cases of urgency where securing the attendance of a second doctor would cause unreasonable delay.

## Section 4 assessment

An emergency application for detention in hospital may be made by an AMHP (provided that he has seen the patient within the previous 24 hours) or the patient's nearest relative, if founded on one medical recommendation by a doctor (who need not be s12 approved). The grounds for detention are the same as for s2 above. The Code of Practice (E Paras 15.7 and 15.8) emphasises that s4 should not be used for administrative convenience and goes on to give examples of what might be considered an emergency:

*An emergency may arise where the patient's mental state or behaviour presents problems which those involved cannot reasonably be expected to manage while waiting for a second doctor. To be satisfied that an emergency has arisen, the person making the application and the doctor making the supporting recommendation should have evidence of:*

- *an immediate and significant risk of mental or physical harm to the patient or to others;*
- *danger of serious harm to property; or*
- *a need for use of restrictive interventions on a patient.*

The Welsh Code of Practice has similar considerations to that of the English Code. See W Para. 15.6.

## Effect of detention

A patient detained under s4 can be kept in hospital for up to 72 hours, during which time a second medical recommendation could be sought and, assuming the medical recommendations comply with the requirements of s12, the s4 will be converted into an s2. In this case the patient can be detained for a period of 28 days, including the time they were detained under the initial s4. There is no procedure for converting an s4 into an s3, and therefore this would require another assessment.

# Applications in respect of patients already in hospital – s5

Section 5 allows in-patients to be detained for short periods of time, either up to six or 72 hours. The purpose of the detention is to lawfully keep patients in hospital to enable a full assessment of their mental state to be carried out to establish if they require continued treatment in hospital under compulsory powers. An in-patient in this context is defined in the Code of Practice (E Paras 18.7 and 18.8) as:

> *any person who is receiving in-patient treatment in a hospital. It does not apply to a patient who is already liable to be detained under section 2, 3 or 4 of the Act, subject to a community treatment order, or a person who is being kept in a hospital as a place of safety under section 135 or 136. It includes patients who are in hospital by virtue of a deprivation of liberty authorisation under the Mental Capacity Act 2005 ... The power cannot be used for an out-patient attending a hospital's accident and emergency department, or any other out-patient. Patients should not be admitted informally with the sole intention of then using the holding power.*

Similar guidance can be found in the Welsh Code of Practice (see W Paras 18.9 and 18.10).

## Section 5(2) assessment

The doctor or approved clinician (AC) who is in charge of the patient's treatment (or one doctor or AC nominated by this person to act in their absence) can detain an informal in-patient in a hospital for a period of up to 72 hours, where they consider that an application under Part 2 of the Act should be made. In other words, they believe that the person meets the grounds for detention on s2 or s3. This section does not apply to patients already detained under Part 2 of the Act or community patients. However it does apply to patients in general hospitals who could just be receiving treatment for physical conditions.

## Section 5(4) assessment

A nurse of a prescribed class (essentially, level one in mental disorder or learning disability) is able to detain an in-patient already receiving treatment for mental disorder for a period of six hours. Before furnishing a report under this section, the nurse must believe:

> (a) *that the patient is suffering from mental disorder to such a degree that it is necessary for his health or safety or for the protection of others for him to be immediately restrained from leaving the hospital; and*

> (b) *that it is not practicable to secure the immediate attendance of a practitioner or clinician for the purpose of furnishing a report under subsection (2) above.*

Section 5(4) cannot be renewed and should only be used as a means of detaining a patient for a short period of time until a doctor or approved clinician can attend to use s5(2) or until a Mental Health Act assessment can be convened. If an s5(2) follows the use of s5(4), the total number of hours of detention must not exceed 72.

## Effect of detention

A patient detained under sections 5(2) or 5(4) can be prevented from leaving hospital (with proportionate restraint where necessary), but in the event of their leaving hospital they can be returned during the time that the holding powers last. Patients detained under sections 5(2) or 5(4) may not, however, be treated under the provisions of Part 4 of the Act. Where treatment is considered necessary a lawful authority must be sought – for example, the capacitous consent of the patient or under the provisions of the Mental Capacity Act provided the requirements of that Act are met (see Chapter 9).

# Warrant to search for and remove patients – s135

A warrant can be issued by a magistrate (justice of the peace, JP) in two sets of circumstances: either to gain access to a person for the purpose of assessing their mental state or to take or retake a person who is already liable to be detained. This last situation might include a patient who has failed to return to hospital after a period of leave of absence. If access is denied by the patient (and any co-occupier), gaining access to, or remaining in, a property that one has been asked to leave is a trespass. A warrant under s135 provides legal authority to gain access to a property for the purpose set out in s135(1) and s135(2) – see below.

## Section 135(1) warrant

An AMHP having given information on oath or affirmation may be granted a warrant in relation to a person believed to be suffering from mental disorder, if the following criteria set out at s135(1) are met. The person:

(a) *has been, or is being, ill-treated, neglected or kept otherwise than under proper control, in any place within the jurisdiction of the justice; or*

(b) *being unable to care for himself, is living alone in any such place.*

## Effect of the warrant

The warrant authorises any constable to enter any premises (if need be by force) specified in the warrant, where the person is thought to be. The constable must be accompanied by an AMHP and a doctor when the warrant is executed. The person who is thought to be mentally disordered may be removed to a place of safety, if thought fit, or be kept at those premises if the premises specified in the warrant are a place of safety. The person may be detained for up to 24 hours (unless extended) to be assessed for a potential application under Part 2 of the Act or for other treatment or care arrangements to be made. The 24-hour period will start either upon arrival at the place of safety where the person is removed to a place of safety, or from the time the constable first entered the premises to execute the warrant where the person is being kept at those premises. They can, however, be moved from one place of safety to one or more other places of safety during the 24-hour period. This may be authorised by a constable, an AMHP or a person authorised by either of them. An exception arises in cases of emergency where such agreement is not required, for example, where a patient requires treatment in an A&E department, in which case the 24-hour period will start upon arrival at A&E. What constitutes a place of safety and the grounds for extending the 24-hour period are set out below.

## Section 135(2) warrant

A constable or other authorised person (any officer on the staff of the hospital, any person authorised by the hospital, any AMHP, or in the case of guardianship, any officer on the staff of the LSSA or any person authorised by the guardian or the LSSA) having given information on oath or affirmation may be granted a warrant in respect of a patient liable to be detained under this Act, authorising him to be taken or retaken if the following criteria at s135(2) are met:

(a) *that there is reasonable cause to believe that the patient is to be found on premises within the jurisdiction of the justice; and*

(b) *that admission to the premises has been refused or that a refusal of such admission is apprehended.*

## Effect of the warrant

The warrant authorises any constable to enter the premises (if need be by force) and remove the patient. A person removed to a place of safety cannot be held there for longer than 24 hours. They can however be moved from one place of safety to one or more other places of safety during the 24-hour period.

## Place of safety

Changes to the Act as a result of the Policing and Crime Act 2017 have broadened what may be regarded as places of safety, and in some environments have introduced differing levels of agreement to their use as a place of safety.

For the purpose of s135 and s136, a place of safety is defined in s135(6) as:

*Residential accommodation provided by a local social services authority under Part 1 of the Care Act 2014 or Part 4 of the Social Services and Well-being (Wales) Act 2014, a hospital as defined by this Act, a police station, an independent hospital or care home for mentally disordered persons or any other suitable place.*

The definition of a hospital is drawn from section 275 of the National Health Service Act 2006, which states:

*"hospital" means –*

(a) *any institution for the reception and treatment of persons suffering from illness,*

(b) *any maternity home, and*

(c) *any institution for the reception and treatment of persons during convalescence or persons requiring medical rehabilitation, and includes clinics, dispensaries and out-patient departments maintained in connection with any such home or institution, and "hospital accommodation" must be construed accordingly.*

In addition, a house, flat or room where a person is living may be regarded as a place of safety provided the required agreement to its use as a place of safety is obtained. The required agreement is most clearly summarised in Para. 3.9 of the guidance document (DoH & HO, 2017):

| Scenario | Agreement required |
| --- | --- |
| If the person believed to be suffering from a mental disorder is the sole occupier of the place. | That person agrees to the use of the place as a place of safety. |
| If the person believed to be suffering from a mental disorder is an occupier of the place but not the sole occupier. | Both that person and one of the other occupiers agree to the use of the place as a place of safety. |
| If the person believed to be suffering from a mental disorder is not an occupier of the place. | Both that person and the occupier (or, if more than one, one of the occupiers) agree to the use of the place as a place of safety. |

While this guidance reflects the wording of the Act in respect of gaining agreement, the guidance then goes on to explain that the person's ability to understand the information relevant to the decision, retain that information, use or weigh that information as part of the process of making the decision, and communicate the decision, is relevant – suggesting that an inability to do the above means that the necessary agreement cannot be obtained. This guidance arguably sets a higher bar of a capacitous consent before a private dwelling may be used as a place of safety, as opposed to a statute which refers to agreement, which may be regarded as a lesser threshold of an absence of dissent. Even where agreement is gained, consideration should be given to the appropriateness of a private dwelling being used as a place of safety.

A place other than a house, flat or room – for example, a voluntary sector provision – may not be used as a place of safety unless a person who appears to the constable to be responsible for the management of the place agrees to its use as a place of safety. While amendments to the Act have broadened the scope of environments that may be regarded as places of safety, limits have been placed on the use of police stations as places of safety. A child (below the age of 18) may not be taken to a police station as a place of safety. Adults may be taken to a police station as a place of safety, but only where an officer of the rank of inspector or above is satisfied that the following grounds are met:

(i) *the behaviour of [adult] poses an imminent risk of serious injury or death to [adult], or to another person,*

(ii) *because of that risk, no place of safety other than a police station in the relevant police area can reasonably be expected to detain [adult].*

Where a police station is used as a place of safety, regulations require that a custody officer at the police station ensures that:

(a) *the welfare of the detained adult is checked by a healthcare professional at least once every thirty minutes, and any appropriate action is taken for the treatment and care of [detained adult], and*

(b) *so far as is reasonably practicable, a healthcare professional is present and available to [detained adult], throughout the period in which [detained adult] is detained at the police station.*

Where these requirements are not met the custody officer must arrange for the detained adult to be taken to another place of safety, unless arrangements for an assessment have been made which would commence sooner at the police station than at another place of safety, and to postpone the assessment would be likely to cause distress to the detained adult. In addition to the above healthcare checks a custody officer at the police station must review the behaviour of the detained adult at least once an hour and determine whether the circumstances for their detention in a police station continue to be met, and where this is no longer the case, they must arrange for the detained adult to be taken to a place of safety other than a police station. The requirement to review the behaviour of the detained adult at least once an hour may be relaxed to no less than once every three hours where the detained adult is sleeping, provided the last healthcare check did not identify any risk that would require the detained adult to be woken more frequently.

# Removal of mentally disordered persons without a warrant – s136

Like section 135 (above), section 136 was altered as a result of the Policing and Crime Act 2017. The main changes include the introduction of a requirement that the police officer consult a healthcare professional, where practicable, to assist in determining whether use of s136 is appropriate, and the broadening of the environments in which s136 may be used.

## Consultation with a healthcare professional prior to use of s136

Section 136 of the MHA allows a constable to remove a person to a place of safety, or if the person is already at a place of safety keep the person at that place or remove to another place of safety for the purpose of examination by a doctor and interview by an AMHP, and to enable any necessary arrangements for the person's treatment or care to be made. However, prior to exercising this power, the police offer is required to consult a healthcare professional, where it is practicable to do so, to gain information and advice to decide on the best course of action. The police officer may consult a registered medical practitioner, a registered nurse, an AMHP, an occupational therapist or a paramedic. Guidance (Para. 2.11, DoH & HO, 2017) sets out the purpose of consultation, and advises on the information and advice that may be sought:

- *an opinion on whether this appears to be a mental health issue based on professional observation and, if possible, questioning of the person;*

- *whether other physical health issues may be of concern or contributing to behaviour (e.g. substance misuse, signs of physical injury or illness);*

- *whether the person is known to local health service providers;*

- *if so, whether it is possible to access medical records or any care plan to determine medical history and suggested strategies for appropriately managing a mental health crisis;*

- *whether in the circumstances, the proposed use of s136 powers is appropriate;*

- *where it is determined that use of s136 powers is appropriate, then identification of a suitable health-based place of safety, and facilitation of access to it;*

- *where it is determined that use of s136 powers is not appropriate, then identification and implementation of alternative arrangements (such as escorting the person home, to their own doctor, to hospital, or to a community place of calm/ respite).*

The police retain responsibility for deciding whether or not to use s136, and for recording the content of their consultation.

## Section 136 assessment

A police constable may exercise this power, if need be by force, in any place other than:

(a) any house, flat or room where that person, or any other person, is living, or

(b) any yard, garden, garage or outhouse that is used in connection with the house, flat or room, other than one that is also used in connection with one or more other houses, flats or rooms.

The constable can remove a person if satisfied that the person meets the following criteria:

- they appear to be suffering from a mental disorder;

- they are in immediate need of care or control; and

- it is in the interests of the person or to protect others to remove them to a place of safety.

Section 136 will end in the event of a doctor concluding that the person does not have a mental disorder, at the expiry of the 24 hours (unless extended, see below), where the person is made subject to detention under s2, 3 or 4, or where arrangements have been made for the person's treatment or care.

## Effect of the detention

Once the person arrives at a place of safety they can be kept there for up to 24 hours, in which time they should be examined by a doctor and interviewed by an AMHP as soon as possible. During the 24 hours (or up to 36 hours if extended) a person can be transferred from one place of safety to one or more other places of safety by a constable, an AMHP or someone authorised by either of them.

The English Code states that the assessing doctor and AMHP should attend the place of safety within three hours where there are no clinical grounds for delay; in contrast the Welsh Code states that in most cases assessors should attend within four hours, and s136 should not exceed 12 hours where a police station is used as a place of safety. Prolonged detention of a vulnerable mentally disordered person in a police station without appropriate psychiatric treatment may constitute a breach of Article 3 ECHR "Prohibition of Torture", as in the case of *MS v UK* (2012) ECHR 804 (see Appendix 6).

# Extensions of detention

The detention period of 24 hours under sections 135 and 136 may be extended for up to 12 hours by the registered medical practitioner who is responsible for examination of the detained patient. The extension must however be authorised within the initial 24-hour period, and may only be authorised for the following reasons set out in s136B of the Act:

> *the extension is necessary because the condition of the person detained is such that it would not be practicable for the assessment of the person for the purpose of section 135 or (as the case may be) section 136 to be carried out before the end of the 24 hours (or, if the assessment began within that period, for it to be completed before the end).*

Where the patient is detained in a police station, an officer of the rank of superintendent or above must approve the extension before the 24-hour period may lawfully be extended.

Guidance (Para. 4.6) gives an example of grounds for extending the 24-hour period, stating: "*if the person is too mentally distressed, or is particularly intoxicated with alcohol or drugs and cannot co-operate with the assessment process. A delay in attendance by an Approved Mental Health Professional or medical practitioner is not a valid reason for extending detention.*" This makes clear that any extension should be as a result of the needs of the patient as opposed to the needs of professionals or deficits in service provision.

# Protective searches

A police officer may search a person subject to sections 135 and 136 MHA if they have reasonable grounds for believing that the person:

(a) *may present a danger to himself or herself or to others, and*

(b) *is concealing on his or her person an item that could be used to cause physical injury to himself or herself or to others.*

The time frames during which the search may be exercised are set out below:

| Section | Time frame |
|---------|-----------|
| S135(1) | From the time when a constable enters the premises specified in the warrant until the ending of detention under that section. |
| S135(2) | Any time while the person is being removed under the authority of the warrant. |
| S136 | At any time while the person is detained under that section. |

The search is however limited to the removal of an outer coat, jacket or gloves and does not authorise a search of the person's mouth. Any item found that might be used to cause physical injury may be seized. Where a more thorough search is considered necessary the police may rely on powers under sections 32 and 54 of the Police and Criminal Evidence Act 1984.

# Safeguards for detained patients

Table 5.1 sets out the various safeguards available to patients when they have been detained. For each section there is information in the table about the nearest relative's powers, whether the patient can be treated without consent under the MHA, and whether they can appeal to a Tribunal or to the hospital managers.

## Aftercare

Section 117 of the MHA1983 places a duty on primary care trusts, local health boards and LSSAs, in cooperation with voluntary agencies, to provide aftercare to patients detained under s3, 37, 45A, 47 or 48, once they leave hospital. This will include patients on s17 leave of absence from hospital and those subject to s17A (the community treatment order – CTO). Aftercare services are defined in s75 of the Care Act 2014 as services for the purposes of *"meeting a need arising from or related to the person's mental disorder; and reducing the risk of a deterioration of the person's mental condition (and, accordingly, reducing the risk of the person requiring admission to a hospital again for treatment for mental disorder)"*. Such services must be provided and paid for by the responsible aftercare bodies until the responsible aftercare bodies are satisfied that the patient is no longer in need of the aftercare services.

## Rectification of errors

Section 15, rectification of applications and recommendations, sets out the basis for rectifying statutory forms where a patient has been admitted to a hospital following an application for admission for assessment or treatment. As a general rule, incorrect or defective forms can, with the agreement of the hospital managers, be amended by the signatory of the form within 14 days of the date of admission. If amended, the forms will have effect as if they were correct at the time of admission. Where one or both of the medical recommendations are found to be insufficient the hospital managers may, within the time frame mentioned above, give written notice to the applicant who can arrange for a fresh recommendation, and if that recommendation complies with the relevant provision of the Act, the application will be deemed to have been sufficient from the date of admission. There are, however,

*Table 5.1    Safeguards for detained patients*

| Section | Nearest relative | Can patient be treated under Part 4 of the MHA? | Can patient apply to a Tribunal? | Can patient apply for managers' hearing? |
|---|---|---|---|---|
| 2 – for assessment | NR should be informed of admission.<br><br>NR is able to order discharge of the patient. | Yes | Yes, within the first 14 days of detention. | Yes |
| 3 – for treatment | NR should be consulted regarding application and can object to it.<br><br>NR is able to order the discharge of the patient. | Yes, but see rules regarding medication after three months. | Yes, once within each period of detention. | Yes |
| 4 – in emergency | NR should be informed of admission.<br><br>No effective power of discharge of the patient unless on s2. | No, but MCA or common law may be used if conditions are met. | Yes, but the Tribunal will only take place if converted to an s2. | Not in effect unless converted to s2. |
| 5(2) – holding power | No function. | No, but MCA or common law may be used if conditions are met. | No | No |
| 135 – warrant for entry | No function. | No, but MCA or common law may be used if conditions are met. | No | No |
| 136 – police powers | No function. | No, but MCA or common law may be used if conditions are met. | No | No |

errors which fall outside the scope of s15, for example failure to comply with the time frame between examinations for medical recommendations set out at s12(1), and failure to sign the form. The Reference Guide at Chapter 2 sets out what might constitute incorrect, defective or insufficient forms.

It is worth noting that s15 has not been amended to allow for the rectification of errors of CTO statutory forms. Therefore it is unclear how any identified error will be dealt with.

# Key points

1.  Sections 2 and 3 require two doctors and an applicant (usually an AMHP).

2.  Detention under s2 lasts for up to 28 days and is not renewable.

3. Detention under s3 lasts for up to six months and can be renewed for six months and then annually.

4. In an emergency, a patient can be detained under s4 with just one doctor and an applicant.

5. An informal patient will have either a doctor or AC in charge of their treatment and in some circumstances this person can stop him from leaving.

6. An s135(1) warrant may be needed if the AMHP cannot gain access to premises, or where it is necessary to remove the patient to a place of safety for the purpose of assessment.

7. An s135(2) warrant may be needed for a patient who is absent without leave, who has failed to return to hospital following a period of s17 leave of absence, has failed to return to hospital following recall from s17 leave of absence or a CTO, or who absents themselves from their place of residence stipulated under s8.

8. Safeguards include NR powers, appeals to Tribunals and hospital managers, IMHAs and consent to treatment provisions.

# Chapter 6

## Civil compulsion in the community

## Introduction

The Mental Health Act 1983 (as amended by the 2007 Act) sets out a number of routes for providing care or treatment to people with mental disorder within the community, as opposed to within hospital settings. This chapter will detail the three civil routes (i.e. not involving the criminal courts) for providing compulsory care or treatment to people within the community. These routes are via guardianship, leave of absence and the community treatment order (CTO). All three have distinct criteria which must be met before the provisions can be used; they enable differing levels of compulsion to be imposed; and they carry varying levels of control should a person fail to comply with the compulsory measures. There are additional community provisions available for offender patients under the Mental Health Act and these are detailed within Chapter 7. It is also possible to use a degree of compulsion with mentally disordered adults where they lack capacity to make particular decisions. This involves the Mental Capacity Act, which is discussed in Chapters 9, 10 and 11.

## Guardianship – s7

Section 7 of the Act enables applications to be made to local authorities for guardianship in respect of non-offender patients. This provision can be used whether or not the person is, or has been, detained under the Act. Guardianship is intended to enable people to receive care within the community when it cannot be provided without the use of compulsion. The Code of Practice (E Para. 30.4) states that guardianship:

> provides an authoritative framework for working with a patient, with a minimum of constraint, to achieve as independent a life as possible within the community. Where it is used, it should be part of the patient's overall care plan.

### Who can be subject to guardianship?

A person aged 16 or over can be received into guardianship if they:

- are suffering from a mental disorder of a nature or degree which warrants reception into guardianship; and

- it is necessary in the interests of their welfare, or for the protection of others.

A person can only be received into guardianship where two doctors complete medical recommendations having satisfied themselves that the grounds listed above are met, and where an application is made either by an AMHP or by the person's nearest relative. Where the AMHP is the applicant (nearest relative applications are so rare that the Government has stopped collecting the statistics), they must satisfy themselves that the grounds are met, that the application ought to be made and that, given the views of relatives and any other relevant circumstances, it is necessary or proper for them to make the application. The application is made to the local social services authority (LSSA). If accepted, it enables the person to be received into guardianship for up to six months. Guardianship is renewable after the initial six months for an additional six months and then yearly. During each period of guardianship the patient is able to appeal against the guardianship by applying to the Tribunal (see Chapter 12).

## The effect of guardianship

A person made subject to guardianship will have a named guardian, either the LSSA, or a private individual approved by the LSSA. The guardian has the authority to require the person to:

- reside at a specified place;
- attend places at specified times for the purpose of medical treatment, occupation, education or training;
- allow access, where they are residing, to any doctor, AMHP, or other specified person.

The imposition of these requirements might be sufficient, by themselves, to encourage cooperation with a care and treatment plan. But if the person fails to cooperate with the requirements, there are limitations on the guardian's power to enforce them.

### Residence
The requirement of residence enables the guardian to specify where the person shall live. The patient can be taken there in the first instance (a power introduced by the 2007 reforms) and they can be returned if they leave with the intention of not returning. Guardianship cannot, however, be used to restrict a person's freedom to come and go in terms of shopping, visiting friends, etc. The Code of Practice (E Para. 30.31) states:

> The power to require patients to reside in a particular place may not be used to require them to live in a situation in which they are deprived of liberty.

In the event of guardianship amounting to deprivation of liberty for a person lacking capacity to decide where to live, this may be authorised separately by the Deprivation of Liberty Safeguards (for those aged 18 and over in hospital or care home settings) or by the Court of Protection (for those aged 16 and over in other community settings, such as domestic or supported living arrangements). Deprivation of liberty is considered in Chapter 11.

### Attendance
A person can be required to attend places for medical treatment, occupation, education or training. However, there is no power to convey the person against their will. Nor is there power to compel a person to receive medical treatment. Treatment can only be given if the person either consents to the treatment, or if they lack capacity to consent, and they meet the requirements of s5 of the MCA2005. Chapter 9 sets out the test for incapacity and gives further information.

### Access
The power of access does not give authority to force an entry if access is denied. If this occurs, consideration should be given to the use of s135(1) of the Act. However, there would be no need to seek a warrant if a co-occupier granted entry. Section 135 is detailed within Chapter 5.

Guardianship is viewed by the Code of Practice (E Para. 30.22) as a means of realising a care plan which would provide:

- *suitable accommodation to help meet the patient's needs;*

- *access to day care, education and training facilities, as appropriate;*

- *effective cooperation and communication between all persons concerned in implementing the plan;*

- *(if there is to be a private guardian) support from the local authority for the guardian.*

However, as already established, a guardian has limited powers of enforcement, and the provision is only likely to achieve its aims if the person responds well to the imposition of a legislative framework.

# Leave of absence from hospital – s17

Section 17 of the Act enables an RC to grant leave of absence to a patient who is liable to be detained in hospital, thereby providing the only lawful means for a detained patient to be absent from hospital. Leave of absence can be granted for specified or indefinite periods of time, and can have conditions attached if thought necessary in the interests of the patient or for the protection of others. The Code of Practice (E Para. 27.18) states:

*Longer-term leave should be planned properly and, where possible, well in advance. Patients should be fully involved in the decision and responsible clinicians should be satisfied that patients are likely to be able to manage outside the hospital.*

Leave of absence is often granted incrementally, facilitating a gradual discharge of patients from hospital, ensuring they are able to manage outside a hospital environment.

## Who can s17 leave apply to?

Section 17 leave of absence can be granted by an RC to patients of all ages who are liable to be detained under Part 2 of this Act, namely s2, 3 and 4. However, a patient's RC must consider use of a CTO if granting leave for more than seven consecutive days or extending a period of leave which will then exceed seven consecutive days. CTOs under s17A are detailed below. Section 17 leave can be granted in certain circumstances to restricted patients. See Chapter 7 for more information.

## Effect of leave of absence

Whilst on leave the patient remains liable to be detained, subject to Part 4 consent to treatment provisions, and can have conditions attached to their leave. This in effect means that a patient can:

- have leave revoked and be recalled to hospital;

- be compelled to receive treatment for mental disorder;

- be compelled to comply with conditions imposed.

The above powers carry considerably more weight than the requirements available under guardianship. They are, however, limited to those already detained under the Act. Ultimately, failure to comply with the conditions can result in recall to hospital, where a patient would continue to be detained until either the section lapses, or it is discharged by the RC, a Tribunal, the hospital managers or the patient's nearest relative.

Section 117 aftercare provisions apply when an s3 patient is granted leave (see Chapter 5).

## Revocation of leave and recall

RCs have the power under s17(4) to revoke leave of absence and recall patients to hospital. This can be done at any time during which a patient remains liable to be detained, provided that the RC thinks it necessary in the interests of the patient's health or safety, or for the protection of others. The revocation of leave must be given to the patient, or the person who is in charge of the patient (assuming this is a condition), in writing. Once leave of absence is revoked the patient must return to hospital. If they fail to do so they can be returned under the authority of s18 of the Act. The revocation of leave does not, however, give authority to force an entry if denied, and a warrant under s135(2) of the Act would be necessary to access the patient for the purpose of returning them to hospital.

## Treatment for mental disorder whilst on leave

A patient who is granted leave of absence remains subject to the consent to treatment provisions contained within Part 4 of this Act (see Chapter 8). This means that the patient can be compelled to receive treatment for mental disorder under the direction of the RC or the approved clinician in charge of the treatment. Treatment can be administered either in the community or in hospital. Reasonable force can be used to administer treatment to a resisting patient, whether or not they have the capacity to refuse the proposed treatment. In practice, nurses are not happy to use force in community settings and if the patient is physically resistant they are more likely to be recalled to hospital. Treatment for anything other than mental disorder cannot be administered under Part 4 of the Act. It can however be administered under s5 of the MCA if the patient meets the requirements of that Act (see Chapter 9).

## Compliance with leave conditions

An RC may attach conditions to a patient's leave of absence if this is considered necessary in the interests of the patient or for the protection of others. The conditions might include matters such as the patient remaining in the custody of a person, or residing at a specified place. Where leave of absence is granted in the custody of a person other than any office on the staff of the hospital, the leave must be authorised in writing by the managers of the hospital, in addition to the RC.

Leave of absence might be granted for short periods of time, and on a few occasions before a patient is discharged from compulsion. It is, however, also used as a means of exercising control over patients for long periods of time within the community. This is most commonly done where patients fail to comply with treatment and as a result have repeated admissions to hospital (sometimes referred to as revolving door patients).

There have been several cases before the courts where patients have challenged the lawfulness of their continued detention where their care and treatment was largely managed outside of a hospital environment (see Appendix 6). The outcomes of the cases to date have established that detention can continue to be renewed, and that leave of absence can continue to be granted long term provided that there is a significant component of the patient's care and treatment plan taking place at a hospital. There is no requirement for the patient to be re-admitted or to be treated as an in-patient.

There is, however, with the introduction of community treatment orders, a requirement that RCs consider the use of a CTO where leave of absence will exceed seven consecutive days. The Code of Practice (E Para. 27.12) states:

> The option of using a CTO does not mean that the responsible clinician cannot use longer-term leave if that is the more suitable option, but the responsible clinician will need to be able to show that both options have been duly considered. Decisions should be explained to the patient and fully documented, including why the patient is not considered suitable for a CTO, and also guardianship or discharge.

Leave of absence has been used successfully for many years, and has, more recently, with the development of case law, as noted above, been used as a means of long-term compulsion within the community. Despite this the Government introduced community treatment orders. Whilst CTOs arguably offer more safeguards to patients (for example, the involvement of AMHPs and limitations on the ability to recall patients), the use of leave of absence enables the management of a patient's care within the community with minimal complexity. For example, there are no requirements to get the agreement of an AMHP, the procedure is less lengthy, the consent to treatment provisions less cumbersome, and revocation and recall is easier. RCs faced with this choice must consider the guidance and balance the complexities of CTOs and additional patient safeguards with the familiar, and less complex arrangements of leave of absence in the knowledge that they both offer a way of structuring compulsion within the community.

# Community treatment orders – s17A

Community treatment orders were introduced on 3 November 2008, coinciding with the repeal of aftercare under supervision (s25A). Like aftercare under supervision, a CTO cannot be made unless a patient is liable to be detained in a hospital for treatment. This will in turn mean that those placed on CTOs will be entitled to s117 aftercare. Whilst there is no obligation to consult the funding authorities before making a patient subject to CTO, there may be practical considerations for those initiating a CTO if any discretionary conditions attached have financial implications. Patients subject to CTOs can be, with certain limitations, compulsorily treated for their mental disorder. This ability might make it a more attractive provision than its predecessor, s25A, which did not allow for compulsory treatment. Indeed, the numbers of CTOs have far exceeded Government projected figures, despite research findings about the effectiveness of the order (Churchill et al. 2007 and the Oxford Community Treatment Order Evaluation Trial (OCTET) 2008, 2013).

## Who can be placed on a CTO?

Patients of all ages who are liable to be detained under s3, and unrestricted Part 3 patients, can be made subject to a CTO by their RC, with the agreement of an AMHP, if the following criteria are met as set out in s17A(5):

(a) the patient is suffering from mental disorder of a nature or degree which makes it appropriate for him to receive medical treatment;

(b) it is necessary for his health or safety or for the protection of other persons that he should receive such treatment;

(c) subject to his being liable to be recalled as mentioned in paragraph (d) below, such treatment can be provided without his continuing to be detained in a hospital;

(d) it is necessary that the responsible clinician should be able to exercise the power under section 17E(1) below to recall the patient to hospital;

(e) appropriate medical treatment is available for him.

The RC and AMHP must both state that the above criteria are met. In addition, the AMHP must state that it is appropriate to make the CTO, and, where discretionary conditions are set, agree that they are necessary or appropriate. A CTO cannot take effect unless an AMHP has agreed to it. This is in contrast to the ability of an RC to grant leave of absence without the agreement of anyone else.

## Conditions attached to community treatment orders

Conditions are split into two categories:

1. mandatory, which will form part of all CTOs; and

2. discretionary, which may form part of CTOs, if certain requirements are met.

### Mandatory conditions

All patients made subject to a CTO will have these two conditions attached to the order which require them to make themselves available for:

1. examination by the RC for the purpose of extending the CTO; and

2. examination by the second opinion appointed doctor (SOAD) for the purpose of consent to treatment provisions.

Examination by the SOAD is however only necessary where the patient either lacks capacity to consent to, or refuse treatment, or who retains capacity and refuses treatment.

### Discretionary conditions

The RC may, with the agreement of the AMHP, specify discretionary conditions. Any discretionary conditions must be considered necessary or appropriate to:

* ensure the patient receives medical treatment; or

* prevent risk of harm to the patient's health or safety; or

* protect others.

These conditions can be varied or suspended by the RC at any time without the agreement of an AMHP. However failure by the patient to comply with a discretionary condition is not a ground by itself to recall the patient to hospital.

The Code of Practice at E Para. 29.32 gives some guidance about the sorts of conditions that might be attached to a patient's CTO. These include where and when the patient is to receive treatment, where the patient should live, and avoidance of known risk factors or high-risk situations relevant to the patient's mental disorder. The guidance suggests that patients should agree to the conditions, which is in line with the principle of patient empowerment and involvement. However, the fact that failure to comply with discretionary conditions does not provide grounds for recall might well lead RCs and AMHPs to consider s17 leave as an alternative.

On the other hand, the RC and AMHP may consider that the fact that they form part of a legislative framework and are part of an "order" will encourage compliance.

### Conditions and the potential for deprivation of liberty

Although this is not made explicit in the Act, case law (*Welsh Ministers (Respondent) v PJ (Appellant)* (2018) UKSC 66) has confirmed that CTOs may not lawfully authorise a deprivation of liberty (see Appendix 6). The Code of Practice (E Para. 31.9) advises that an incapacitated patient whose care and treatment amounts to a deprivation of liberty may be subject to DoLS or a Court of Protection Order alongside a CTO. This would provide a community order and a lawful deprivation of liberty, complying with the requirements of Article 5. However, the Code does not explore how a patient subject to a CTO, whose care and treatment amounts to a deprivation of liberty, can be managed if they do not meet the requirements of DoLS or fall outsider the scope of the Court of Protection (for example, a patient below the age of 18 or a capacitated young person or adult). The answer may lie in the High Court's inherent jurisdiction to authorise a deprivation of liberty of a patient with capacity, as was the case in *Hereford County Council v AB* (2018) EWHC 3103 (Fam) which was concerned with conditional discharge.

## Extension of CTOs

Section 20A of the Act sets out the provisions and criteria for extension of CTOs. A CTO will last for an initial period of six months, and can be extended for a further six months and then yearly.

The RC, with the agreement of an AMHP, can extend a CTO if satisfied that the initial criteria (listed above) are met, and the AMHP thinks it necessary to extend the order. The Code of Practice (E Para. 23.13) stresses the importance of considering whether there has been a need to exercise the power of recall to hospital when questioning whether that criterion is met.

## Recall and revocation

Patients subject to CTOs may be recalled to hospital by their RC. Recall must be in writing and can only take place if either the patient has failed to comply with a mandatory condition or they require medical treatment in hospital for their mental disorder, and there would be a risk of harm to the health or safety of the patient or to others if they were not recalled to hospital for treatment of their mental disorder. In deciding whether to recall a patient, the RC may take into account any failure by the patient to comply with a non-mandatory condition. It is important to note that the RC has discretion when deciding whether to exercise their power of recall. There is no statutory obligation to recall if the criteria are met, merely the power to do so if the RC considers it a proportionate response to the risks posed. The Code of Practice (E Para. 29.49) offers the following guidance regarding recall:

> *The responsible clinician should consider in each case whether recalling the patient to hospital is justified in all the circumstances. For example, it might be sufficient to monitor a patient who has failed to comply with a condition to attend for treatment, before deciding whether the lack of treatment means that recall is necessary.*

> *A patient might agree to admission to hospital on a voluntary basis. Failure to comply with a condition (apart from those relating to availability for medical examination ...) does not in itself trigger recall. Only if the breach of a condition results in an increased risk of harm to the patient or to anyone else will recall be justified.*

The Mental Health Regulations specify that recall may be served in one of three ways, and dependent on the method of serving the recall notice, the patient may be returned to hospital in the following prescribed time frames. The Reference Guide to the Mental Health Act 1983 sets out the following guidance at Para. 15.2:

| Method of serving the recall notice | Notice deemed to have been served |
|---|---|
| Delivering the notice by hand to the patient | As soon as it is given to the patient. |
| Delivering the notice by hand to the patient's usual or last known address | At the start of the day which follows the day on which it is delivered to that address. For example, if it is delivered at noon, it is deemed to have been served immediately after midnight that night, even if it is a weekend or bank holiday. |
| Sending it by pre-paid first class post (or its equivalent) to the patient at the patient's usual or last known address | At the start of the second business day after it is posted. For example, if it is posted on a Monday, it is deemed to have been delivered on Wednesday. But if it is posted on Friday, it is deemed to have been delivered on Tuesday. Weekends and public holidays do not count as business days. |

Recalled patients must return to hospital. If, however, they fail to do so, they can be returned under the authority of s18 of the Act. As with s17, leave of absence, there is no authority to force an entry should a patient deny access, and a warrant under s135(2) of the Act should be considered.

Recalled patients can be detained in hospital for up to 72 hours, during which time the RC may:

- provide necessary treatment and allow the patient to leave hospital within 72 hours from the time of recall; or

- revoke the CTO, with the agreement of an AMHP, assuming the grounds are met; or

- discharge the CTO completely.

### Recall, treat and allow the patient to leave hospital
On recall the RC will consider whether, within the 72-hour period, the problems leading to recall can be resolved and the patient returned to the community. During the period of recall a patient reverts to Part 4 of the Act and this may allow compulsory treatment, with, for example, medication. Assuming the patient does not require care or treatment for a period beyond 72 hours, they can then leave hospital and continue as a CTO patient. Once 72 hours have elapsed (from the time of arrival at hospital after recall) the patient is free to leave (though subject to the CTO) unless the CTO has been revoked by the RC and AMHP.

### Revoking a CTO
If a patient needs care and treatment as an in-patient for a period exceeding 72 hours, the RC should consider revoking the CTO. The RC (with an AMHP) may revoke a CTO if the criteria for detention under s3 are met, i.e.:

- the patient is suffering from a mental disorder of a nature or degree which makes it appropriate for him to receive medical treatment in a hospital; and

- it is necessary for the health or safety of the patient or for the protection of other persons that he should receive such treatment and it cannot be provided unless he is detained under this section; and

- appropriate medical treatment is available for him.

Before an RC can revoke a CTO, an AMHP must agree in writing that the above criteria are met and that it is appropriate to revoke the order. The effect of revocation is that the patient remains in hospital under their original detention section (3, 37 or equivalent). The patient will start a new detention period of six months from the time of revocation. However, for consent to treatment purposes, the time frame continues from their original detention. A patient whose CTO has been revoked can be compelled to receive treatment for mental disorder under Part 4 of the Act. Rights of appeal to Tribunals and hospital managers' hearings are detailed in Chapters 12 and 13.

## Discharge from a CTO

A patient may be discharged from a CTO by their RC, NR (subject to restrictions set out in s25 of the Act whereby the RC can bar the discharge if they believe the patient is dangerous), a Tribunal or the hospital managers. Discharge from a CTO has the effect of discharging the initial liability for detention, resulting in the patient being free from all forms of compulsion. Failure of an RC and AMHP to extend a CTO at the appropriate intervals also results in the patient's freedom from compulsion.

Table 6.1 details the functions, relevant section numbers, statutory forms and responsible professionals for operating the provisions of CTOs. The section references are given to enable individual professionals to refer to Appendix 1 (the Act) to establish their precise responsibilities.

*Table 6.1 Community treatment orders: relevant functions and forms*

| Function | Section numbers | Form in England | Form in Wales | Professionals involved |
|---|---|---|---|---|
| Making a CTO | s17A | CTO 1 | CP1 | RC and AMHP |
| Varying conditions | s17B | CTO 2 | CP2 | RC |
| Recalling to hospital | s17E | CTO 3 | CP5 | RC |
| Record of recall managers | s17E | CTO 4 | CP6 | Hospital |
| Revocation | s17F(4) | CTO 5 | CP7 | RC and AMHP |
| Transfer to a hospital under different management and assignment of responsibility for CTO patient | s17F(2) and s19A | CTO 6 CTO10 | TC6 TC5 | Hospital managers |
| Extension of CTO | s20A | CTO 7 | CP3 | RC and AMHP |

*(Continued)*

*Table 6.1   (Continued)*

| Function | Section numbers | Form in England | Form in Wales | Professionals involved |
|---|---|---|---|---|
| Extension after AWOL beyond 28 days | s21B | CTO 8 | CP4 | RC and AMHP + consultees |
| CTO patients transfer | Part 6 | CTO 9 | TC8 | RC and AMHP |
| Consent to treatment – Part 4A certificate | s64C(4) | CTO 11 | CO7 | SOAD + consultees |

See Appendix 7 for the full list of forms.

The Code of Practice (E Para. 31.7) offers the following guidance regarding the use of the most appropriate community provision:

# CTO or longer-term leave of absence: relevant factors to consider

| Factors suggesting longer-term leave | Factors suggesting a CTO |
|---|---|
| Discharge from hospital is for a specific purpose or a fixed period. | There is confidence that the patient is ready for discharge from hospital on an indefinite basis. |
| The patient's discharge from hospital is deliberately on a "trial" basis. | There are good reasons to expect that the patient will not need to be detained for the treatment they need to be given. |
| The patient is likely to need further in-patient treatment without their consent or compliance. | The patient appears prepared to consent or comply with the treatment they need – but risks as below mean that recall may be necessary. |
| There is a serious risk of arrangements in the community breaking down or being unsatisfactory – more so than for a CTO. | The risk of arrangements in the community breaking down, or of the patient needing to be recalled to hospital for treatment, is sufficiently serious to justify a CTO, but not to the extent that it is very likely to happen. |

# CTO or guardianship: relevant factors to consider

| Factors suggesting guardianship | Factors suggesting a CTO |
|---|---|
| The focus is on the patient's general welfare, rather than specifically on medical treatment. | The main focus is on ensuring that the patient continues to receive necessary medical treatment for mental disorder, without having to be detained again. |
| There is little risk of the patient needing to be admitted compulsorily and quickly to hospital. | Compulsory recall may well be necessary, and speed is likely to be important. |
| There is a need for enforceable power to require the patient to reside at a particular place. | |

(Table from Para. 31.7 of the Code of Practice)

# Key points

1. There are three civil means of compulsion within the community (guardianship, s17 leave and the CTO).

2. The CTO is only available to those who have been detained for treatment.

3. Part 4 applies to most detained patients and to recalled CTO patients.

4. CTO patients are covered by Part 4A for consent to treatment purposes.

5. Guardianship patients are not covered by Part 4 or 4A.

6. There is a power to convey guardianship patients to accommodation.

7. There are significant roles for AMHPs for the CTO.

# Chapter 7
## Mentally disordered offenders

## Introduction

Part 3 of the Mental Health Act 1983 covers patients who are concerned in criminal proceedings or are under sentence. As well as allowing the courts to order patients' admission to hospital, it covers situations where the Secretary of State wants prisoners to be transferred into hospital. There were some changes stemming from the MHA2007 but far more significant changes were implemented in 1984 as part of the consolidated MHA1983.

These changes will be outlined in this chapter, together with a consideration of the impact of the change in the definition of mental disorder which took place in 2008. There are also other pieces of legislation, apart from the Mental Health Act, which affect mentally disordered offenders. These are included here in a summary of law as it may be relevant at different points within the system.

A recent Supreme Court case decision (*Secretary of State for Justice v MM* (2018)) has led to some problems in potentially conditionally discharging patients who have capacity to agree to restrictions in a proposed setting that would amount to a deprivation of liberty. This case, and its implications, is considered in detail after the discussion on s37/41 later in this chapter.

### Changes introduced in 1984

The Mental Health (Amendment) Act 1982 amended the 1959 Act and gave effect to recommendations which were made in the Butler Report of 1975 (Cmnd 6244). That report concluded that too many mentally disordered offenders were being inappropriately placed in prison. Sections 35, 36 and 38 of the 1983 Act were all introduced and were designed to deal with this problem. They did not come into effect until 1984, when it was considered that resources were in place to provide for these new patients. However the number of patients covered by these new sections of the Act (and s45A which was implemented in 2008) remains low. Of 37,709 formal admissions to hospital in England in 2014–15, about 5 per cent (1,930) were under Part 3 of the Act. Only 75 were on s35, 15 on s36 and nine patients were admitted under s45A during that year. More recent statistics show even lower numbers but these statistics from NHS Digital are unreliable and not reported here.

## Key stages where mental disorder may be relevant

There is a more detailed account of the law relevant to mentally disordered offenders in Fennell (2011). This chapter will adopt the approach taken by Brenda Hale in *Mental Health Law* (2017) in outlining the law at key stages:

- at the time of police involvement;

- before the trial;

- at the trial (where mental disorder may be used as a defence);

- at sentencing;

- after sentencing.

# Police involvement

Under s136:

> *If a person appears to a constable to be suffering from mental disorder and to be in immediate need of care or control, the constable may, if he thinks it necessary to do so in the interests of that person or for the protection of other persons (a) remove the person to a place of safety within the meaning of section 135.*

What has then replaced the old requirement that the person had been found in a place to which the public had access is:

> (1A) *The power of a constable under subsection (1) may be exercised where the mentally disordered person is at any place, other than –*
>
> (a) *any house, flat or room where that person, or any other person, is living, or*
>
> (b) *any yard, garden, garage or outhouse that is used in connection with the house, flat or room, other than one that is also used in connection with one or more other houses, flats or rooms.*
>
> (1B) *For the purpose of exercising the power under subsection (1), a constable may enter any place where the power may be exercised, if need be by force.*

This power is considered in more detail in Chapter 5.

Apart from s136 the police have a number of other options when they are dealing with a possible offender whom they think might be mentally disordered. They could:

- check if the person is an absconding detained patient and then return them to the hospital under s18 or s138;

- encourage the person to wait while they set up a Mental Health Act assessment;

- use their powers of arrest for any offence or to prevent a breach of the peace.

The Police and Criminal Evidence Act 1984 (PACE) has its own Codes of Practice which cover the detention, treatment and questioning of persons by police officers. These apply where an officer suspects, or is told in good faith, that a person may be mentally disordered or be unable to understand the significance of questions or their own answers. If the person is detained, an "appropriate adult" must be informed and asked to come to the police station. A person who is trained or experienced in dealing with mentally disordered people may be seen as more appropriate than an unqualified relative. The appropriate adult should be present when the individual is told of their rights or can have them read again. They can also require the presence of a lawyer. Unless delay would involve serious risk to person or property, a mentally disordered person should not be interviewed or asked to sign a statement until the appropriate adult is present. The appropriate adult is not just an observer. They have a role in advising the person being interviewed, observing the fairness of the interview and of facilitating communication with the interviewee.

If a decision is taken to prosecute, the case is then passed to the Crown Prosecution Service, which will decide whether the person should be charged with a criminal offence, and, if so, what that defence should be. The CPS will consider a number of factors, such as: whether there is a realistic prospect of conviction; the public interest; and the likely effect of prosecution on a defendant who was mentally disordered at the time of the offence. In the case of mental disorder, the Crown Prosecutor will require independent evidence of the disorder and the likely adverse effects of prosecution.

Under s17 of PACE a constable may enter and search any premises to: execute a warrant; arrest a person for an arrestable offence; recapture someone unlawfully at large whom he is pursuing; save life or limb; or prevent serious damage to property. There are limited circumstances in which a common law power of arrest may be made. In *Bibby v Chief Constable of Essex Police* (Court of Appeal 2000) these circumstances were summarised: a sufficiently real and present threat to the peace; the threat coming from the person to be arrested; conduct clearly interfering with the rights of others with its natural consequence being "not wholly unreasonable violence" from a third party; and unreasonable conduct from the person to be arrested.

# Before the trial (or awaiting court appearance)

Where possible the courts will remand a person on bail rather than in custody. This could include a condition of residence at a hospital while reports are prepared. In these circumstances the patient would be informal rather than subject to detention. Where a person might otherwise be remanded to prison, the Mental Health Act 1983 introduced two new powers of remand:

### Section 35. Remand to hospital for report on accused's mental condition
Subsection (3) allows an order to be made by the Crown Court or magistrates' court if:

(a) *the court is satisfied, on the written or oral evidence of a registered medical practitioner, that there is reason to suspect that the accused person is suffering from mental disorder; and*

(b) *the court is of the opinion that it would be impracticable for a report on his mental condition to be made if he were remanded on bail.*

There must also be evidence (from the approved clinician who would be responsible for producing the report) that a hospital bed would be available within seven days, beginning with the date of the remand. While waiting for a bed, the accused must be kept in a place of safety, which could be "any police station, prison, or remand centre, or any hospital, the managers of which are willing temporarily to receive him" (s55(1)). The remand is initially for a maximum of 28 days. The court may then renew this for further periods of 28 days to a maximum of 12 weeks. Part 4 provisions on consent to treatment do not apply, so the person should not be treated without their consent under the provisions of the MHA. Some psychiatrists have sought a Part 2 detention to run alongside the s35. Section 5 of the MHA deals with detention of patients who are already in hospital, and does not specifically rule this out. The Code of Practice (E Para. 33.20) states that it might be considered if there is a delay in getting to court. The use of s36 might be more appropriate in most such cases.

## Section 36. Remand of accused person to hospital for treatment

Only the Crown Court can make an s36 order. Again, it is restricted to those cases where it would be an alternative to a remand in custody. Section 36 applies to people waiting for trial or sentence and its use requires the written or oral evidence of two doctors that:

(a) *he is suffering from mental disorder of a nature or degree which makes it appropriate for him to be detained in a hospital for medical treatment; and*

(b) *appropriate medical treatment is available for him.*

"Appropriate medical treatment" is discussed in Chapter 4.

Note that this section used to be applicable only to patients with mental illness or severe mental impairment, so a wider group of patients are now eligible because the broad s1 definition of "any disorder or disability of the mind" applies.

The s36 remand is for a maximum of 28 days although the court may renew this for further periods of 28 days to a maximum of 12 weeks. Part 4 provisions on consent to treatment apply. Again there must be evidence that a hospital bed would be available within seven days, beginning with the date of the remand. While waiting for a bed, the accused must be kept in a "place of safety", as defined earlier. If someone has to wait for more than three months to appear in the Crown Court the general powers of the Secretary of State to transfer prisoners may apply.

## Section 48. Removal to hospital of other prisoners

This section allows the Secretary of State to direct the transfer to hospital of a person who is waiting for trial or sentence, and who has been remanded in custody. The section applies to people who are: detained under the Immigration Act 1971; civil prisoners; remanded in custody by a magistrates' court; or, otherwise detained in a prison or remand centre but not serving a custodial sentence. The Secretary of State needs at least two medical reports on the patient stating:

(a) *that the said person is suffering from mental disorder; and*

(b) *that the mental disorder from which that person is suffering is of a nature or degree which makes it appropriate for him to be detained in a hospital for medical treatment; and*

(c) *that appropriate medical treatment is available for him.*

"Appropriate medical treatment" is discussed in Chapter 4.

There are 14 days for the person to be admitted to the specified hospital. Periods of detention in hospital may vary but a civil or Immigration Act prisoner can never be detained longer than they would have been in prison. Part 4 provisions on consent to treatment apply.

In 2014–15, 440 patients were transferred under s48 in England and all but three of these were subject to the restrictions of s49. It can be seen that this measure is used far more frequently than the court's remands under s35 (only 75 in the same year) and s36 (only 15).

## Unfit to plead

The present procedure for determining whether an accused person is unfit to plead is governed by sections 4 and 4A of the Criminal Procedure (Insanity) Act 1964 ("the 1964 Act"), as amended by the Criminal Procedure (Insanity and Unfitness to Plead) Act 1991 ("the 1991 Act") and the Domestic Violence, Crime and Victims Act 2004. Where an accused person is unfit to be tried, there is provision for a "trial of the facts" to determine whether the judge is satisfied beyond reasonable doubt that the accused did the act or made the omission charged against him. Home Office Circular No. 24/2005 sets out guidance on the trial of the facts and summarises the disposal options which are: a hospital admission order (with or without restrictions), a supervision order, or absolute discharge. Where a hospital order is made the requirements are the same as for s37 listed below. The procedure is currently under review by the Law Commission and changes are expected in the near future.

Supervision orders are sometimes made under the current legislation and recently some AMHPs have been asked to take on the supervisor role. Guidance can be found in an appendix to the sister volume (Brown, 2016).

# At the trial: mental disorder as a defence

### *The insanity defence where sentences are fixed by law (i.e. murder)*
This defence can apply where "the accused was labouring under such defect of reason from disease of the mind that he did not know the nature and quality of the act, so as not to know that what he was doing was wrong" (the McNaghten Rules, 1843–60). If the defence is successful the judge will make the equivalent of a hospital order with restrictions on discharge. Its use is rare. This is still a requirement following the changes of the Criminal Procedure (Insanity and Unfitness to Plead) Act 1991.

### *Diminished responsibility. Section 2 of the Homicide Act 1957*
This applies where the accused was suffering from such abnormality of mind as to substantially impair mental responsibility for the killing. If the defence is successful, the judge has discretion in sentencing. Conviction will be for manslaughter rather than murder and so there is no mandatory life sentence.

### *Infanticide Act 1938*
This may apply to a woman who kills a child under the age of one if her mind "is disturbed by reason of not having fully recovered from the effect of giving birth to the child or by reason of the effect of lactation consequent on the birth". The court may impose any appropriate sentence.

# At sentencing

The Bradley Report (2009) should have led to improvements in the way mentally disordered people are dealt with in prison, although the evidence for this is scant. This may put a new angle on the arguments for diversion from the criminal justice system into hospital. As Hale (2017, p206) states:

> It is of course possible that some offenders would prefer a determinate time in prison to an indeterminate time in hospital where they can be treated against their will and some of the rules may be less congenial than those in prison. An offender may be prepared to accept the loss of a right to a proportionate sentence, in the hope that a therapeutic disposal will do him some good, or at least be more pleasant than the alternative. But if he has the capacity to make the choice, perhaps he should be allowed to decide whether or not to do so.

Bartlett and Sandland (2014) argue that diversion from prison to hospital is more appropriate, but that the system is failing in that the numbers of those who are diverted are very low.

There are five orders which can be made at the point of sentencing which involve a psychiatric element.

### Section 37 of the MHA1983. Hospital or guardianship order

This may be made by the Crown Court in cases where an offender is convicted. A magistrates' court may make an order, even without a conviction, as long as they are satisfied that the offender committed the act or made the omission in question. Requirements set out in s37(2) are that:

(a) *the court is satisfied, on the written or oral evidence of two registered medical practitioners, that the offender is suffering from mental disorder and that either –*

   (i) *the mental disorder from which the offender is suffering is of a nature or degree which makes it appropriate for him to be detained in a hospital for medical treatment and, appropriate medical treatment is available to him; or*

   (ii) *in the case of an offender who has attained the age of 16 years, the mental disorder is of a nature or degree which warrants his reception into guardianship under this Act; and*

(b) *the court is of the opinion, having regard to all the circumstances including the nature of the offence and the character and antecedents of the offender, and to the other available methods of dealing with him, that the most suitable method of disposing of the case is by means of an order under this section.*

What amounts to "appropriate medical treatment" is considered in Chapter 4.

The order is for up to six months in the first instance. This may be renewed for a further six months and then for a year at a time. Apart from a delay until after six months for an appeal to the Tribunal (there is a route for an appeal through the court system within this period), the effect for a hospital order is as if the patient were subject to s3. Part 4 applies. There must also be evidence that a hospital bed would be available within 28 days, beginning with the date of the order. While waiting for a bed a patient may be kept in a "place of safety" as defined above. In 2014–15, there were 486 unrestricted s37 orders and a further 307 restricted orders.

Guardianship orders are rare. Only 14 were made in England in 2014–15. One can only be made if the proposed guardian (usually a local authority) agrees to it. If the patient absconds from the place they are required to live, they may be recaptured and returned there. Part 4 does not apply, so guardianship cannot be used to enforce medication. The Butler Report considered that collaboration between relevant agencies might lead to a welcome increase in the use of guardianship, but there is no evidence that this has occurred.

### Section 38 of the MHA1983. Interim hospital order

If a court is not sure that a full hospital order is appropriate, they can test this out by making an interim hospital order. The order can be made for up to 12 weeks at first instance and can then be renewed by the court for periods of up to 28 days at a time, to a maximum of one year. Two doctors must give written or oral evidence. In effect, by making this order the court is reserving final judgement to itself once it has received reports on how treatment is progressing. Part 4 of the MHA1983 applies, so treatment may be given as per section 37.

### Sections 37/41 MHA1983. Restricted hospital order

The court must have the same evidence needed to make a hospital order and one of the doctors must attend to give evidence in person. Section 41(1) states:

*Where a hospital order is made in respect of an offender by the Crown Court, and it appears to the court, having regard to the nature of the offence, the antecedents of the offender and the risk of his committing further offences if set at large, that it is necessary for the protection of the public from serious harm so to do, the court may, subject to the provisions of this section, further order that the offender shall be subject to the special restrictions set out in this section and an order under this section shall be known as a "restriction order".*

The main restrictions are that the patient can only be discharged, given leave of absence, or transferred to another hospital with the approval of the Secretary of State. As the orders can now only be made without limit of time there is no renewal process and the only review of the order would be via the Tribunal process, which could result in discharge (see Chapter 12). The Secretary of State may discharge the patient absolutely or conditionally. For the latter, the patient is subject to compulsory aftercare, which will involve supervision. Social services departments are now asked to organise a social supervisor and quite often they are AMHPs, even though the role is a very different one.

A recent Supreme Court case decision has led to some problems when seeking to conditionally discharge a patient who has capacity to agree to restrictions in a proposed setting that would amount to a deprivation of liberty. In the *Secretary of State for Justice v MM* (2018), the Supreme Court upheld the ruling of the Court of Appeal that neither the SoS nor the Mental Health Tribunal has the power to impose conditions on the discharge of a restricted patient which would amount objectively to a deprivation of the patient's liberty. MM wanted to leave hospital and was willing to consent to a very restrictive regime in the community to allow this to happen. The court held that this was not legally permissible. It was agreed that MM had capacity to consent to restrictions which would have satisfied the "acid test" set down in Cheshire West. As it stands this decision will prevent some restricted patients from being discharged from hospital and require the recall of any capacitous patients who are out of hospital on conditions amounting to a deprivation of liberty.

Until there is any change in the statute the Mental Health Casework Section of HM Prison and Probation Service has issued guidance proposing that there should be greater use of long-term s17(3) leave. Those already conditionally discharged into confinement are being technically recalled to hospital (without actually having to go there) and are given escorted s17(3) leave for anything up to a year at a time. How this will sit with the case law that has required a significant hospital element in the s17 is not clear from the guidance.

### Section 45A of the MHA1983. Hospital and limitation directions
This is referred to as the "Hybrid Order" as it is a prison sentence together with a requirement for hospital treatment with limitation directions. The provision was brought in by s46 of the Crime (Sentences) Act 1997 on 1 October 1997. It used to be limited to patients with psychopathic disorder until that classification was abolished by the 2007 Act. Although it is now open to all mental disorders, there is no sign of its use increasing. There were only nine orders made in 2014–15. The order is only available to the Crown Court. The grounds set out in subsection (2) are:

(a) that the offender is suffering from mental disorder; and

(b) that the mental disorder from which the offender is suffering is of a nature or degree which makes it appropriate for him to be detained in a hospital for medical treatment; and

(c) that appropriate medical treatment is available for him.

"Appropriate medical treatment" is discussed in Chapter 4. Written or oral evidence from two doctors is required.

### Community orders (formerly psychiatric probation orders)

Community orders may be made in any court and may result from any offence other than one where there is a fixed penalty. They require a conviction before they can be made. They can be made with a mental health treatment requirement (MHTR). The MHTR is intended for offenders who have been convicted of an offence which is below the threshold for a custodial sentence, and where they have a mental health problem that does not require secure in-patient treatment.

An MHTR may be applied to a community order or suspended sentence order in cases where a court is satisfied that a defendant suffers mental health issues which are treatable in the community, and where suitable treatment and support is available to enable the MHTR to be delivered in the community.

Before making an MHTR, the court must be satisfied that:

1. The mental condition of the offender requires treatment and may be helped by treatment, but does not warrant making a hospital or guardianship order (within the meaning of the Mental Health Act 1983).

2. Arrangements have been or can be made for the offender to receive treatment as specified in the order.

3. The offender agrees to undergo treatment for their mental health condition.

# After sentencing

### Section 47 of the MHA 1983. Transfers of persons serving sentences of imprisonment

A prisoner may be transferred to a psychiatric hospital even after sentencing. The Secretary of State can order their transfer under s47 if they are satisfied by reports from at least two doctors:

(a) *that the said person is suffering from mental disorder; and*

(b) *that the mental disorder from which that person is suffering is of a nature or degree which makes it appropriate for him to be detained in a hospital for medical treatment; and*

(c) *that appropriate medical treatment is available for him.*

"Appropriate medical treatment" is discussed in Chapter 4.

The transfer direction has the same effect as an s37 hospital order made without restrictions and the patient is subject to consent to treatment provisions. In most cases a restriction direction is also made under s49. This has the same effect as a restriction order under s41 described above. If the offender was sentenced to a fixed term of imprisonment, the restriction lifts on the expiry of the sentence (allowing for remission). There were 429 restricted transfers made in 2014–15 and only 60 unrestricted transfers.

# Key points

1. Part 3 is based on a philosophy of transferring mentally disordered offenders from the criminal justice system to mental health services where possible.

2.  Courts may place patients in hospital for assessment or treatment before returning to court for a final disposal.

3.  The broader definition of mental disorder means that more people are now eligible for the Part 3 sections and the removal of most of the exclusions also potentially brought more people into the Part 3 system.

4.  However, after a brief increase in the use of Part 3 numbers have now fallen to about the same as they were before the 2007 changes.

5.  It is possible to transfer people from prison to hospital.

6.  Some higher-risk patients may be made subject to certain restrictions.

7.  There is no nearest relative role for restricted patients.

8.  Tribunals have the power to discharge any Part 3 patients.

# Chapter 8

# Medical treatment under the Mental Health Act

## Introduction

This chapter is mainly concerned with medical treatment given under Part 4 to detained patients, or under Part 4A to patients on community treatment orders. After defining medical treatment, the chapter will explore both of these parts of the Act in some detail. Patients not covered by Part 4 or 4A are entitled to refuse or to consent to treatment in the same way as any patient receiving treatment for a physical condition. Where a patient lacks capacity in relation to the treatment the Mental Capacity Act may apply (see Chapter 9). For readers who wish to explore psychiatry and the use of medication, there is a companion volume (Brown et al., 2009).

### Historical background

Until the 1982 amendments there were no special rules for treating detained patients. Under the Mental Health Act 1959 a convention had developed whereby if a patient needed to be detained they would be placed on an s25 (for observation, with or without other medical treatment, lasting up to 28 days), but if a patient was then refusing treatment such as medication or ECT, they would be referred for an s26 which was for treatment for up to a year in the first instance.

The approach adopted in 1982 (and consolidated in the 1983 Act) was based on the idea that some patients who are liable to be detained may need treatment without their consent. Certain procedures should be followed to offer safeguards. What may be seen as particularly controversial by many patients is that s63 allows for a vast array of treatments (including medication for the first three months of detention) to be given without the valid consent of the patient. This can even apply where the patient has capacity with regard to the treatment and where they are no risk to anyone else. Recent case law, however, may have introduced some limitations in this area. (For example see *Nottinghamshire Healthcare NHS Trust and RC* (2014) EWCOP 1317, where the judge ruled that it would be an abuse of power even to think about imposing a blood transfusion on a patient having regard to the judge's findings that he had capacity to refuse blood products and that it was lawful for those responsible for the medical care of him to withhold all and any treatment notwithstanding the existence of powers under s63 MHA.)

### The 2007 reforms

The safeguards for detained patients were altered by the 2007 amendments, but still essentially involve a second medical opinion from outside the hospital for more serious forms of treatment in those cases where valid consent cannot be obtained from the patient. This absence of consent could either be the result of the patient objecting to the treatment, or of their being unable to give valid consent (e.g. because of mental incapacity). New safeguards were introduced for ECT by the 2007 amendments and these will be outlined below.

For the most serious treatments (such as psychosurgery), a second opinion and the valid consent of the patient are required. Because of the invasive nature of these treatments, the safeguards are also extended to informal patients.

With the introduction of the community treatment order (CTO) in 2008 a new set of rules applies to this group of patients and these are set out in Part 4A.

Another complication introduced by the 2007 reforms is that certain treatments can only be given under the direction of an approved clinician. Previously, medical treatment was given under the direction of a doctor but as this is no longer a requirement, there are new safeguards covering who can be in charge of certain treatments.

The Care Quality Commission (CQC) has a general duty to oversee the operation of these two related parts of the Act. The value of the procedures and safeguards may be debated, but the first step is to understand what they cover and how the rules work.

# Definition and categories of medical treatment

As we saw in Chapter 4, s145 of the amended MHA gives a definition of medical treatment which includes "nursing, psychological intervention and specialist mental health habilitation, rehabilitation and care … the purpose of which is to alleviate, or prevent a worsening of, the disorder or one or more of its symptoms or manifestations".

Sections 57, 58 and 58A set out categories of medical treatment which attract special rules and procedures. Some of these treatments require the approval of a second opinion appointed doctor (SOAD) who has been appointed by Secretary of State or the Welsh Ministers for this purpose.

The categories of treatment which are specified in the Act or Regulations are:

*Section 57*:

- any surgical operation for destroying brain tissue or for destroying the functioning of brain tissue (generally known as neurosurgery);
- surgical implantation of hormones to reduce male sex drive.

*Section 58*:

- medicine after three months of treatment while detained.

*Section 58A*:

- electro-convulsive therapy (ECT) and related medicine;
- other forms of treatment could be added to this list by regulations.

## Who is covered by Part 4 and 4A

It is important to understand not just what the legal procedures are, but which patients are covered by them, as not all detained patients are included. Generally, those patients liable to detention for periods of more than 72 hours are covered by Part 4, with the exception of people remanded for reports by the courts under s35. Patients on community treatment orders are subject to Part 4A unless they are recalled to hospital, in which case they are covered by Part 4 during the period of recall.

## The role of approved clinicians

There are a number of situations when the person in charge of the treatment must be registered as an approved clinician.

For a detained patient this will be:

- where treatment is given without the patient's consent;
- where the patient has consented under s58 or 58A and the certificate has been completed by an AC rather than an SOAD;
  - where a CTO patient has been recalled or the CTO revoked, and
  - where the s58 requirements have not yet been met, **but**
  - there is consent and the treatment is necessary to prevent serious suffering to the patient.

For a CTO patient in the community, there needs to be an AC in charge of the treatment being given to a patient who lacks capacity to consent to it unless there is the consent of an attorney (from an LPA), a deputy or the Court of Protection.

(But see s64G for emergencies.)

The Code notes at E Para. 25.6 (W Para. 25.5 is similar) that:

> Hospital managers should keep a record of approved clinicians who are available to treat patients for whom they are responsible and should ensure that approved clinicians are in charge of treatment where the Act requires it.

# Part 4 – Consent to treatment

*Section 56* sets out which patients are covered by Part 4 and this will be considered when we look at each form of treatment.

*Section 57* covers any surgical operation for destroying brain tissue or for destroying the functioning of brain tissue (generally known as neurosurgery), and the surgical implantation of hormones to reduce male sex drive. This section covers informal as well as detained patients.

There are rigorous safeguards under s57. An SOAD and two other persons appointed by the Care Quality Commission (or the Welsh Ministers) need to certify in writing that the patient is capable of understanding the nature, purpose and likely effects of the treatment in question and has consented to it. Second, the SOAD has to certify in writing that it is appropriate for the treatment to be given, having consulted two other persons who have been professionally concerned with the patient's medical treatment. One of these consultees needs to be a nurse and the other should be someone other than a nurse or a doctor.

Neurosurgery under s57 is now very rare. There are usually only three or four cases per year in the whole of England and Wales.

There have been no referrals concerning the surgical implantation of hormones to reduce male sex drive for nearly 30 years. This is probably because the most common treatments are now given orally.

*Section 58* formerly included ECT, but ECT is now regulated by s58A. Therefore s58 only deals with medication for mental disorder after three months of treatment under detention. In effect, then, this will relate to patients who are subject to s3, s37 or the equivalent. It does not cover medication administered as part of ECT treatment, as this is covered by s58A.

The safeguards under s58 are that medication cannot be given unless:

- the patient has consented to that treatment and either the approved clinician in charge of it or an SOAD has certified in writing (on Form T2/CO2) that the patient is capable of understanding its nature, purpose and likely effects and has consented to it; **or**

- an SOAD has certified in writing (on Form T3/CO3) that the patient is not capable of understanding the nature, purpose and likely effects of that treatment, or is capable but has not consented to it, and that it is appropriate for the treatment to be given. The SOAD must have consulted two other persons who have been professionally concerned with the patient's medical treatment. One of these must be a nurse and the other shall be neither a nurse nor a registered medical practitioner; and neither can be the responsible clinician or the person in charge of the treatment in question.

If treatment is based on a Form T2/CO2 the Code recommends that there should be a record in the patient's notes of the relevant discussion where capacity was confirmed and full details of the specific treatment covered. As the Code confirms at E Para. 25.18:

*Certificates under this section must clearly set out the specific forms of treatment to which they apply. All the relevant drugs should be listed, including medication to be given "as required" (prn), either by name or by the classes described in the British National Formulary (BNF). If drugs are specified by class, the certificate should state clearly the number of drugs authorised in each class, and whether any drugs within the class are excluded. The maximum dosage and route of administration should be clearly indicated for each drug or category of drugs proposed. This can exceed the dosages listed in the BNF, but particular care is required in these cases.*

*Section 58A* covers ECT and any medication administered as part of the ECT process. The rules apply to adult detained patients (on s2, s3 etc.) and to all patients under the age of 18, including those who are not detained. The Act contains significant new safeguards and this is the first occasion where the MHA1983 does not automatically take preference over the MCA. A competent refusal or a valid and applicable advance decision will prevent treatment from being given under s58A. No patient under 18 may be given ECT without the approval of an SOAD.

ECT may not be given to an adult unless:

- the patient has consented to that treatment and either the approved clinician in charge of it or an SOAD has certified in writing (on Form T4/CO4) that the patient is capable of understanding its nature, purpose and likely effects and has consented to it; **or**

- an SOAD has certified in writing (on Form T6/CO6) that the patient is not capable of understanding the nature, purpose and likely effects of the treatment, and that it is appropriate for the treatment to be given, and that this will not conflict with a valid and applicable advance decision or a decision made by a donee or a deputy or the Court of Protection. The SOAD must have consulted two other persons who have been professionally concerned with the patient's medical treatment. One of these must be a nurse and the other shall be neither a nurse nor a registered medical practitioner; and neither can be the responsible clinician or the person in charge of the treatment in question.

For someone under 18, a certificate from an SOAD is needed both for patients who have capacity and have consented (FormT5/CO5) or for those who lack capacity (Form T6/CO6). The certificate by itself is not sufficient. The clinician must also have the patient's own consent or some other legal authority at the time of giving the treatment (see Chapter 18 for further discussion about children).

## Section 62 deals with urgent treatment

This provision covers sections 57 and 58, but in practice it is only ever used in relation to s58. It provides for emergencies (e.g. triggered by a patient withdrawing consent in the middle of a course of treatment) and even then it only allows treatment:

1. (a) *which is immediately necessary to save the patient's life; or*

   (b) *which (not being irreversible) is immediately necessary to prevent a serious deterioration of his condition; or*

   (c) *which (not being irreversible or hazardous) is immediately necessary to alleviate serious suffering by the patient; or*

   (d) *which (not being irreversible or hazardous) is immediately necessary and represents the minimum interference necessary to prevent the patient from behaving violently or being a danger to himself or to others.*

In the case of ECT (s58A) only (a) and (b) apply so the risk level needs to be very high before the normal requirements can be dispensed with. It is worth stressing that (c) and (d) are no longer acceptable and this is a significant change for practitioners.

Treatment is irreversible if it has "unfavourable irreversible physical or psychological conse-quences" and hazardous if it entails "significant physical hazard".

There is no certificate for s62 prescribed by the Regulations but the Code of Practice states at E Para. 25.42:

> *Hospital managers should monitor the use of these exceptions to the certificate requirements to ensure that they are not used inappropriately or excessively. They are advised to provide a form (or other method) by which the clinician in charge of the treatment in question can record details of:*
>
> - *the proposed treatment;*
> - *why it is immediately necessary to give the treatment; and*
> - *the length of time for which the treatment was given.*

## Section 63 covers treatment not requiring consent

> *The consent of a patient shall not be required for any medical treatment given to him for the mental disorder from which he is suffering, not being a form of treatment to which section 57, 58 or 58A above applies, if the treatment is given by or under the direction of the approved clinician in charge of the treatment.*

This short section is the source of much concern to many patients. In practice (given the rarity of s57 treatments) it means that, apart from ECT, any treatment can be given to a patient in the first three months of their detention without their valid consent. After three months the safeguard of the SOAD's involvement applies, but only in relation to medication. As a result of the broad definition of medical treatment, many other treatments can continue to be given without the SOAD safeguard.

In *X v Finland* (2012), the European Court of Human Rights held there was a breach of Article 8 because Finnish law permitted the forced administration of medication by doctors despite a refusal by the patient, without immediate judicial scrutiny of its lawfulness and proportionality, and without the court being able to order its discontinuance. It could be argued that s63 creates a similar power. However the combined effect of the procedural requirements of the MHA, the power of Tribunals to discharge, and in particular cases such as *Wilkinson v UK* (2006) and *Nottinghamshire Healthcare NHS Trust v RC* (2014), may mean that sufficient safeguards have been built into the scheme for compulsory treatment for UK law to be compliant with Article 8.

Possibly because of concerns over this issue the Code makes a number of points, such as encouraging staff to seek the patient's consent wherever practicable and to record this (or their refusal) in the notes. Clinicians are reminded (in the Code of Practice at E Para. 24.43) of the relevance of the Human Rights Act and the ECHR.

> *23.40 In particular, the following should be noted:*
>
> - *compulsory administration of treatment which would otherwise require consent is invariably an infringement of Article 8 of the ECHR (respect for family and private life). However, it may be justified where it is in accordance with law (in this case the procedures in the Act) and where it is proportionate to a legitimate aim (in this case, the reduction of the risk posed by a person's mental disorder and the improvement of their health);*
>
> - *compulsory treatment is capable of being inhuman treatment (or in extreme cases even torture) contrary to Article 3 of the ECHR, if its effect on the person concerned reaches a sufficient level of severity. But the European Court of Human Rights has said that a measure which is convincingly shown to be of medical necessity from the point of view of established principles of medicine cannot in principle be regarded as inhuman and degrading.*
>
> *23.41 Scrupulous adherence to the requirements of the legislation and good clinical practice should ensure that there is no such incompatibility. But if clinicians have concerns about a potential breach of a person's human rights they should seek senior clinical and, if necessary, legal advice.*

This may have been drafted in anticipation of future potential challenges to forcible administration of treatment on competent adults who do not pose a risk to others. The *Nottinghamshire Healthcare NHS Trust and RC* (2014) EWCOP 1317 case discussed above means clinicians are more likely to seek legal advice in similar cases.

# Part 4A – Treatment of community patients not recalled to hospital

This part of the Act sets out the law regarding treatment for patients who have been made subject to the new community treatment orders. The House of Lords was particularly concerned about this area of law and the Government made a number of concessions. This leaves the law in a rather complicated state. A patient on s17 leave in the community is covered by Part 4 of the Act, whereas a community patient (i.e. subject to a CTO) is covered by the different rules contained in Part 4A. To be made subject to Part 4, a community patient needs to be recalled to hospital.

While a patient is on a CTO and has not been recalled they cannot be given treatment for mental disorder unless the requirements of Part 4A are met:

- the person giving the treatment must have the authority to do so; and

- in some cases there will be a certification requirement.

A certificate is not needed if the patient has capacity and gives valid consent to the treatment. Given that a major use of the CTO is to require a previously non-compliant patient to take their medication, this is a contentious area in terms of the genuine validity of the consent, which could be seen as being given under duress. Certification is needed for patients who lack capacity. Form CTO11/CO7 is needed for treatments which would require a certificate under s58 or 58A if the patient were detained. This means medication after the initial three-month period and ECT and any related medication.

However, a certificate is not required during the first month following a patient's discharge from detention on to a CTO. This is the case even if the three-month period for s58 has already expired or expires during this first month.

## The role of the SOAD

The Code of Practice (at E Para. 25.32) explains the rather complex situation for the SOAD when using Form CTO10/TC5, which covers Part 4A patients:

> When giving Part 4A certificates, SOADs do not have to certify whether a patient has, or lacks, capacity to consent to the treatments in question, nor whether a patient with capacity is consenting or refusing. They may make it a condition of their approval that particular treatments are given only in certain circumstances. For example, they might specify that a particular treatment is to be given only with the patient's consent. Similarly, they might specify that a medication may be given up to a certain dosage if the patient lacks capacity to consent, but that a higher dosage may be given with the patient's consent.

SOADs also have to consider the possibility that the patient may be recalled to hospital with a view to giving them treatment and/or assessing whether the CTO should be revoked.

They can decide which treatments to approve should the patient be recalled to hospital and whether to impose any conditions on that approval.

Unless it states otherwise, the certificate will then authorise the treatment under Part 4 even if the patient has capacity to refuse it (apart from ECT).

The Code (at E Para. 25.35) identifies that the advantage of authorising treatments to be given on recall to hospital is that it will enable them to be given quickly without the need to obtain a new certificate. However it advises that SOADs should do so only where they believe they have sufficient information on which properly to make such a judgement.

The SOAD must consult two other people who have been professionally concerned with the patient's medical treatment. Only one of these may be a doctor and neither of them can be the patient's responsible clinician or the approved clinician in charge of any of the treatments that are to be specified on the certificate. The Reference Guide (Para. 24.26) notes:

> As a result, the certificate would not authorise any treatment if, at the time it is proposed to give the treatment, the person who is now the patient's responsible clinician or the approved clinician in charge of the treatment in question happens to be one of the two people who were originally consulted by the SOAD before giving the certificate.

## Authority to treat (for patients who are 16 or older)

Where a patient has capacity (as defined by the MCA) to consent to treatment then this provides the authority to treat. Alternatively there may be a donee of an LPA, or a deputy appointed by the Court of Protection, who is able to consent on the patient's behalf (see s64B).

# Adult community patients lacking capacity

Where the CTO patient lacks capacity to consent to the treatment in question, the person wishing to have authority to treat must:

- take reasonable steps to establish that the patient lacks capacity to consent to the treatment. Then, when giving the treatment, he must reasonably believe that the patient lacks capacity to consent to it;

- have no reason to believe that the patient objects to being given the treatment; or, if he does have reason to believe that the patient objects, it is not necessary to use force against the patient in order to give the treatment;

- be the person in charge of the treatment and an approved clinician; or the treatment must be given under the direction of that clinician;

- ensure that giving the treatment will not conflict with an advance decision which he is satisfied is valid and applicable, or with a decision made by a donee or deputy or the Court of Protection.

In an emergency, if treatment is to be given without a certificate, the treatment must fall into one of the following categories set out in s64G(5):

(a) *it is immediately necessary to save the patient's life; or*

(b) *it is immediately necessary to prevent a serious deterioration of the patient's condition and is not irreversible; or*

(c) *it is immediately necessary to alleviate serious suffering by the patient and is not irreversible or hazardous; or*

(d) *it is immediately necessary, represents the minimum interference necessary to prevent the patient from behaving violently or being a danger to himself or others and is not irreversible or hazardous.*

If it is necessary to use force against the patient in order to give the treatment this can only be to prevent harm to the patient; and the use of such force must be a proportionate response to the likelihood of the patient's suffering harm, and to the seriousness of that harm.

## Community patients who are recalled to hospital

The Code of Practice (at E Para. 25.33) sets out the position for this group of patients.

*In general, CTO patients recalled to hospital are subject to sections 58 and 58A in the same way as other detained patients. But there are exceptions, as follows:*

- *a certificate under section 58 is not needed for medication if less than one month has passed since the patient was discharged from hospital and became an CTO patient;*

- *a certificate is not needed under either section 58 or 58A if a Part 4A certificate or Part 4A consent certificate has been issued;*

- *a certificate is not needed under either section 58 or 58A if the treatment in question is already explicitly authorised for administration on recall on the patient's SOAD issued Part 4A certificate; and*

- *treatment that was already being given on the basis of a Part 4A certificate may be continued, even though it is not authorised for administration on recall, if the approved clinician in charge of the treatment considers that discontinuing it would cause the patient serious suffering. It may only be continued pending compliance with section 58 or 58A (as applicable) – in other words while steps are taken to obtain a new certificate.*

## Children as community patients

It is not anticipated that many children under the age of 16 will be placed on community treatment orders. If they are, the law covering their treatment is covered in s64E–F, which can be found in Appendix 1. The rules are similar to those covering adults except that the MCA does not apply. We are therefore concerned with "competence" for the under 16-year-old rather than "capacity" as defined by the MCA.

Where a child has the competence to consent to a particular treatment, their consent will provide the authority required to treat.

Chapter 18 examines the position of children under the Mental Health Act in more detail.

# Key points

1. Part 4 of the Act governs the treatment of most patients who are detained, including those CTO patients who have been recalled to hospital.

2. Part 4A covers those patients on CTOs who have not been recalled.

3. It is more difficult to treat a patient without their consent under Part 4A than under Part 4.

4. In Part 4 the main treatments with specific rules are medication after three months of treatment while detained (s58) and ECT (s58A).

5. Section 62 sets out rules for treating in emergencies without consent or a certificate.

6. Section 63 covers treatments where consent is not required. This includes medication for the first three months and most other treatments.

7. ECT has new safeguards so that a patient with capacity can nearly always refuse.

8. There are special safeguards for children.

9. Consider whether the treatment in question is one that requires an AC to be in charge of it.

# Chapter 9

## The Mental Capacity Act 2005

## Introduction

The Mental Capacity Act 2005 provides a statutory framework for decision-making on behalf of people who lack the capacity to consent to their care or treatment. It also allows capacitated adults to make preparations for a time when they may lack capacity in the future. Prior to the implementation of the Act, incapacitated individuals were most commonly dealt with under the common law doctrine of necessity, which provided for the care or treatment of incapacitated adults in their "best interests". People who have a mental disorder, as well as lacking capacity, could have decisions made for them under the provisions of the MHA1983 as well as the MCA. The interface between the two Acts is addressed within Chapter 10.

Guidance in Chapter 13 of the MCA Code of Practice urges the use of the MCA rather than the MHA wherever possible. This chapter will offer an overview of the main provisions of the Mental Capacity Act and how they operate in practice. The Act provides a framework for acting and making decisions on behalf of people who lack capacity at that point.

For more detailed information in relation to the Mental Capacity Act, please refer to *The Mental Capacity Act 2005: A Guide for Practice* by Brown et al. (2015). This provides a guide which is relevant for many groups and not just social workers.

## Who is the Mental Capacity Act aimed at?

The title of the Act is a little misleading. The inclusion of the word "mental" often leads people to think that the Act only applies to those with mental health problems, but this is not the case. The Act is aimed at people who lack the capacity to make decisions, as well as those who wish to make arrangements for others to be able to make decisions on their behalf, should they lose capacity to make their own decisions in the future.

The Act should be considered by anyone who is providing care or treatment to a person aged 16 and over, living in England or Wales, who lacks the capacity to make particular decisions. For example, the Act may be relied on by informal carers, health and social care professionals, and the police and ambulance services. The term "decision-maker" is used for those who make decisions on behalf of incapacitated people.

This chapter will describe s5 acts and other key aspects of the MCA2005.

### Section 5 acts

If a person (D) performs an act in relation to another person (P) whom they believe to lack capacity in relation to the decision involved, this may be an s5 act. D needs to believe that P lacks capacity for the matter at the point of intervention. D must also believe it is in P's best interests for it to be included as an s5 act. This would then provide legal protection as if P had made the decision himself.

The kind of decisions and actions covered by s5 of the Act are outlined within the Code of Practice (E Para. 6.5), and include:

*Personal care*

- *helping with washing, dressing or personal hygiene;*
- *helping with eating and drinking ...;*
- *doing the shopping or buying necessary goods with the person's money ...;*
- *undertaking actions related to community care services (for example, day care, residential accommodation, nursing care) ...;*
- *helping someone to move home (including moving property and clearing the former home).*

*Healthcare and treatment*

- *carrying out diagnostic examinations and tests (to identify an illness, condition or other problem);*
- *providing professional medical, dental and similar treatment;*
- *giving medication;*
- *taking someone to hospital for assessment or treatment;*
- *providing nursing care (whether in hospital or in the community) ....*

It is important to note that the Act can only be relied on for such interventions if the decision-maker has complied with the requirements of the Act. The checklist in Table 9.1 is designed as a prompt for decision-makers to assist them in ensuring that they have carried out all necessary steps, before intervening on behalf of an incapacitated person. More detailed descriptions of the processes are given after the checklist.

# The five principles

Section 1 of the Act sets out five principles that are to be applied by anyone operating the Act. The principles are intended to protect people who lack capacity, and to help them participate in decision-making as fully as possible.

Section 1 of the Act, "The Principles", states:

(1) *A person must be assumed to have capacity unless it is established that he lacks capacity.*

(2) *A person is not to be treated as unable to make a decision unless all practicable steps to help him to do so have been taken without success.*

(3) *A person is not to be treated as unable to make a decision merely because he makes an unwise decision.*

(4) *An act done, or decision made, under this Act for or on behalf of a person who lacks capacity must be done, or made, in his best interests.*

(5) *Before the act is done, or the decision is made, regard must be had to whether the purpose of which it is needed can be as effectively achieved in a way that is less restrictive of the person's rights and freedom of action.*

*Table 9.1   Mental Capacity Act checklist*

Has the decision-maker:

- Established that the person is 16 or over?
- Established that there is a specific decision to be made?
- Applied the five principles?
- Established that the person is unable to make their own decision because of a negative reply to one or more of the following questions:
  - Do they understand the relevant information?
  - Can they retain it?
  - Can they use or weigh the information up to make a decision?
  - Can they communicate a decision?
- Established that the person's inability to make the decision is because of an impairment of, or a disturbance in the functioning of, the mind or brain?
- Ensured that the person lacks capacity in relation to the particular matter at the particular time?
- Ensured that the decision is not based on assumptions about the person's age, appearance, behaviour etc.?
- Ensured that this is genuine lack of capacity and not merely an unwise decision?
- Applied the best interests checklist?
- Ensured that the care or treatment is a mere restriction of movement rather than a deprivation of liberty?

# Testing capacity

The first of the five principles requires the decision-maker to assume capacity unless the opposite is established. This places a duty upon the decision-maker to assess the person's capacity in relation to the decision(s) to be made. The test for incapacity is set out in s2 and s3 of the Act.

Section 2 of the Act, "inability to make decisions", states:

> for the purpose of this Act, a person lacks capacity in relation to a matter if at the material time he is unable to make a decision for himself in relation to the matter because of an impairment of, or a disturbance in the functioning of, the mind or brain.

This requires the decision-maker to establish two facts.

1. Is there a specific decision to be made now?
2. Is the person unable to make that decision because of an impairment of, or a disturbance in the functioning of the mind or brain, whether temporary or permanent?

If the decision-maker answers "no" to one or both of these questions, the Act will not apply to the person. However, if the answer is "yes" to both of these questions they must go on to establish whether the person is able to make their own decision. This must be done before the decision-maker is able to make decisions on behalf of the person.

Section 3 of the Act sets out a statutory test for determining whether the person is incapable of making their own decisions. It is important to remember that people with an impairment of, or a disturbance in the functioning of, their mind or brain do not necessarily lack the capacity to make all their own decisions. The Act includes an anti-discriminatory statement at s2(3), which states that unjustified assumptions about capacity cannot be made merely on the basis of a person's age, appearance, condition or behaviour.

Section 3 of the Act, "inability to make decisions", states:

> A person is unable to make decisions for himself if he is unable –
>
> (a) to understand the information relevant to the decision;
>
> (b) to retain the information;
>
> (c) to use or weigh that information as part of the process of making the decision; or
>
> (d) to communicate his decision (whether by talking, using sign language or any other means).

The decision-maker must decide what information is relevant, and give that information in a way that the person can understand. While there is no statutory standard for the information to be given, the case of *Montgomery v Lanarkshire Health Board* (2015) UKSC 11 determined that risks were to be discussed with the patient based upon what the reasonable person in the patient's position would be likely to attach significance to, as opposed to the Bolam test, concerned with conduct supported by a responsible body of medical opinion (see Appendix 6). The person needs to demonstrate that they are able to use that information to weigh up the benefits and/or risks of the proposed action, and understand the consequences of inaction. Finally, they need to retain the information for long enough to weigh up the information, and communicate a decision to the decision-maker.

If the decision-maker is satisfied that the person meets all four of the above requirements (a–d) they must regard the person as having the capacity to make the decision in question, and therefore they have no authority to make that decision on the person's behalf. If, however, the decision-maker, on the balance of probabilities, believes that the person is unable to demonstrate one or more of the four requirements, because of an impairment of, or a disturbance in the functioning of, their mind or brain, the person is deemed to lack the capacity to make the specific decision(s). The necessity to establish a causal link between the inability to make the decision, and an impairment or disturbance in the functioning of the mind or brain, was highlighted in the case of *PC v City of York* (2013). It is therefore suggested that decision-makers first establish whether the person can make their own decision (replying on the test at s3), and where an inability to make the decision is established, they must then determine whether the inability to make the decision is as a result of an impairment or disturbance in the functioning of the mind or brain. Where this is the case, the decision-maker is then able to make those decisions on the person's behalf acting in the person's "best interests". Where a person's inability to make a decision is not as a result of an impairment or disturbance in the functioning of the mind or brain, but for example as a result of emotional immaturity or undue influence, the MCA cannot be relied upon, and consideration should be given to making an application to the High Court.

# Determining best interests

Section 4 of the Act does not define "best interests", but sets out a checklist of factors that decision-makers must consider. The aim of the checklist is to ensure that any decisions made, or actions taken, are in the best interests of the incapacitated person. The factors to consider are broad, enabling them to be applied to all decisions and actions. However, there is no statutory guidance about the weight and importance to be given to each aspect of the best interests checklist. That said, the case of *Wye Valley NHS Trust v B and Mr B* (2015) highlighted the importance of the person's wishes and feelings, values and beliefs (see Appendix 6). The following guidance found at Para. 35 in the case of M; *ITW v Z* (2009) might aid those balancing potentially competing factors:

- (a) *the degree of P's incapacity, for the nearer to the borderline the more weight must in principle be attached to P's wishes and feelings: Re MM; Local Authority X v MM (by the Official Solicitor) and KM [2007] EWHC 2003 (Fam), [2009] 1 FLR 443, at para [124];*

- (b) *the strength and consistency of the views being expressed by P;*

- (c) *the possible impact on P of knowledge that her wishes and feelings are not being given effect to: see again Re MM; Local Authority X v MM (by the Official Solicitor) and KM [2007] EWHC 2003 (Fam), [2009] 1 FLR 443, at para [124];*

- (d) *the extent to which P's wishes and feelings are, or are not, rational, sensible, responsible and pragmatically capable of sensible implementation in the particular circumstances; and*

- (e) *crucially, the extent to which P's wishes and feelings, if given effect to, can properly be accommodated within the court's overall assessment of what is in her best interests.*

Based on the checklist from the statute, a quick summary at the beginning of Chapter 5 of the Code of Practice offers the following guidance to decision-makers when determining what is in a person's best interests:

*Encourage participation*

- *Do whatever is possible to permit and encourage the person to take part, or to improve their ability to take part, in making the decision.*

*Identify all relevant circumstances*

- *Try to identify all the things that the person who lacks capacity would take into account if they were making the decision or acting for themselves.*

*Find out the person's views*

- *Try to find out the views of the person who lacks capacity, including:*
    - *the person's past and present wishes and feelings – these may have been expressed verbally, in writing or through behaviour or habits;*
    - *any beliefs and values (e.g. religious, cultural, moral or political) that would be likely to influence the decision in question;*
    - *any other factors the person themselves would be likely to consider if they were making the decision or acting for themselves.*

*Avoid discrimination*

- *Not make assumptions about someone's best interests simply on the basis of the person's age, appearance, condition or behaviour.*

*Assess whether the person might regain capacity*

- *Consider whether the person is likely to regain capacity (e.g. after receiving medical treatment). If so, can the decision wait until then?*

*If the decision concerns life-sustaining treatment*

- *Not be motivated in any way by a desire to bring about the person's death. They should not make assumptions about the person's quality of life.*

*Consult others*

- *If it is practical and appropriate to do so, consult other people for their views about the person's best interests and to see if they have any information about the person's wishes and feelings, beliefs and values. In particular, try to consult:*
  - *anyone previously named by the person as someone to be consulted on either the decision in question or on similar issues;*
  - *anyone engaged in caring for the person;*
  - *close relatives, friends or others who take an interest in the person's welfare;*
  - *any attorney appointed under a lasting power of attorney or enduring power of attorney made by the person;*
  - *any deputy appointed by the Court of Protection to make decisions for the person.*
- *For decisions about major medical treatment or where the person should live and where there is no one who fits into any of the above categories, an independent mental capacity advocate (IMCA) must be consulted.*
- *When consulting, remember that the person who lacks capacity to make the decision or act for themselves still has a right to keep their affairs private – so it would not be right to share every piece of information with everyone.*

*Avoid restricting the person's rights*

- *See if there are other options that may be less restrictive of the person's rights. Take all of this into account.*
- *Weigh up all of these factors in order to work out what is in the person's best interests.*

There are no statutory forms for the best interests checklist, or for the capacity test. However decision-makers are well advised to record their decision-making process, as this will provide authority for their actions and help protect them from liability.

# Acts in connection with care or treatment and protection from liability

Section 5 of the Act allows decision-makers to carry out acts in connection with care or treatment provided that they have followed the requirements of the Act. However, there are limitations, which in effect means that certain actions are not permitted as s5 acts. Exceeding these limitations would amount to unlawful practice.

Section 5 of the Act permits decision-makers to make decisions and carry out actions for or on behalf of an incapacitated person provided that:

- before doing the act the decision-maker takes reasonable steps to establish whether the person lacks capacity in relation to the matter;
- when doing the act they believe the person lacks capacity in relation to the matter; and
- the act will be in the person's best interests (determined in accordance with s4).

If these criteria are met the decision-maker should be protected from liability, assuming that they do not exceed the limitations detailed below, and do not act negligently.

# Limitations of s5 acts

Section 6 of the Act sets out a number of conditions which must be met to ensure that s5 acts are lawful. If decision-makers have followed the procedures explained above and do not exceed the limitations detailed below, their acts of care or treatment will fall within the scope of section 5 of this Act.

Restraint can be used, provided that the following criteria are met:

- the decision-maker believes that the restraint is necessary to do the act in order to prevent harm to the person; and
- the act is a proportionate response to:
    - the likelihood of the person suffering harm; and
    - the seriousness of that harm.

It is important to note that restraint cannot be used to prevent the person causing harm to others. If restraint is needed to prevent harm to others, decision-makers will need to establish if the Mental Health Act or the common law would provide more appropriate means of meeting the person's needs or safeguarding others.

Restraint is defined as the use, or threat of, force to secure the doing of an act which the person resists, or the restriction of the person's liberty of movement, whether or not the person is resisting the act.

Whilst restraint is permitted in certain circumstances, it will only be permitted where it amounts to a restriction of the person's movements, rather than a deprivation of their liberty. This leaves decision-makers with the complex question: what amounts to a deprivation of liberty? This question is explored within Chapter 11.

Decision-makers are also prevented from carrying out s5 acts if they conflict with:

- a person's advance refusal of treatment; or
- the authority of an attorney appointed by the person; or
- the authority of a deputy appointed by the Court of Protection.

See below, under the heading "Planning for loss of capacity" for more information.

# Routes of lawful deprivation of liberty

It has been established that s5 of the Mental Capacity Act cannot be used as a means of depriving a person of their liberty. If a decision-maker concludes that the care or treatment proposed amounts to a deprivation of liberty, the following provisions are available, assuming the criteria are met:

- a personal welfare order of the Court of Protection, under s16 of the MCA2005;
- detention under the MHA1983;

- Deprivation of Liberty Safeguards (introduced in April 2009);

- life-sustaining treatment, or treatment to prevent a deterioration, whilst awaiting a decision by the Court of Protection.

Each of these will now be described in brief.

### Personal welfare order

The Court of Protection has power to make a personal welfare order in respect of a person who lacks capacity. The order can include: decisions about where the person lives; decisions about contact with others; prohibition of contact with others; the giving or refusing of consent to treatment; determining who is responsible for a person's healthcare. The court is also able to make orders in relation to property and affairs.

### Detention under the Mental Health Act

The Mental Health Act provides a number of routes for lawfully depriving a person of their liberty. These apply to people of all ages, who have a mental disorder and who meet specific detention criteria (see Chapters 4, 5 and 6 for more information).

### Deprivation of Liberty Safeguards – "DoLS"

The DoLS are an amendment to the Mental Capacity Act introduced in April 2009. The provisions are intended to provide a procedure for the lawful deprivation of liberty of individuals living in care homes or in hospital settings. They will apply to people aged 18 or over, who lack capacity and who have a mental disorder. As with detention under the MHA, specific criteria need to be met before a deprivation of liberty authorisation is granted (see Chapter 11).

### Life-sustaining treatment

The MCA2005 allows life-sustaining treatment or treatment to prevent a deterioration in someone's condition if an application is being made to the Court of Protection for determination of lack of capacity and best interests.

# Planning for loss of capacity

The Act empowers capacitated people to make arrangements for a time when they might lose capacity to make their own decisions. A person, whilst capacitated can make:

1. An advance decision to refuse treatment.

2. A lasting power of attorney (LPA).

### Advance decisions

These can be made by capacitated adults (aged 18 and over). They need not be in writing unless they concern life-sustaining treatment, in which case they must be in writing, verified and witnessed. Advance decisions need to state what treatment cannot be given, and under what circumstances. They will only be effective if they are valid and applicable, i.e. if the specific treatment is proposed and the person at that point lacks capacity in relation to the treatment decision. Advance decisions only concern the refusal of treatment, not, for example, decisions about social care. They are also limited to refusals, and therefore cannot require a specific treatment to be given. It is important to note that an advance refusal of treatment for mental disorder can be overridden if a person is detained under a section of the Mental Health Act 1983 to which Part 4 applies. However, the MHA2007 has introduced additional safeguards for people who make advance refusals of ECT, to ensure that their refusal is respected, unless certain criteria are met. These changes are detailed within Chapter 8. For more general information in relation to the impact of advance refusals, see Chapter 10.

### Lasting power of attorney (LPA)

LPAs can be made by capacitated adults (aged 18 and over). They must contain prescribed information and be witnessed and registered. There are two types of LPA: one concerning personal welfare matters and the other concerning property and affairs. LPAs allow the appointment of a person or persons to make decisions on behalf of someone once they lose the capacity to make their own decision(s). Anyone appointed is referred to as an attorney or donee.

There are some limitations to an attorney's remit. These include the refusal of treatment for mental disorder, which can be overridden if the person is detained under a section of the MHA to which Part 4 of that Act applies. They are also prevented from making decisions about where a person should live, if the person is subject to the requirement of residence under guardianship under s7 of the MHA.

# Court of Protection

In the event of a person losing capacity to make either personal welfare or property and affairs decisions, the following provisions are also available:

1. Decisions by the Court of Protection.

2. Appointment of a deputy by the Court of Protection.

### Decisions by the Court of Protection

The court is able to make personal welfare and/or property and affairs decisions on behalf of an incapacitated person. It is also able to make decisions about a person's capacity, if this is unclear, and on the lawfulness of any decisions or proposed decisions.

### Deputies appointed by the Court of Protection

Where there are ongoing decisions to be made in relation to personal welfare matters and/or property and affairs, the court can appoint a person to make these decisions, referred to as a deputy. Deputies also have a role if a deprivation of liberty is being considered using the "Deprivation of Liberty Safeguards". More information about these safeguards is contained within Chapter 11.

**Relevant information:** There are a number of cases that assist decision-makers in determining how to interpret the meaning of relevant information. For example, the cases of *CC v KK* (2012) EWHC (COP): salient information; *LBX v K, L, M* (2013) EWHC 3230: capacity in respect of accommodation, care and contact; *A PCT v LDV, CC and B Healthcare Group* (2013) EWHC 272: capacity to consent to admission to hospital; and *Montgomery v Lanarkshire Health Board* (2015) UKSC 11 (outlined above), *Re A (Capacity: Social Media and Internet Use: Best Interests* (2019) EWCOP 2 and *Re B (Capacity: Social Media: Care and Contact)* (2019) EWCOP 3 (see Appendix 6).

# Key points

1. All those acting and making decisions on behalf of incapacitated people must comply with the legal framework of the MCA.

2.  The MCA applies to incapacitated people aged 16 and over living in England and Wales.

3.  Section 5 allows care and treatment (including treatment for mental disorder) to be provided in a person's best interests.

4.  Section 1 of the MCA sets out the five principles to be applied by anyone operating the MCA.

5.  The test for incapacity is set in the Act and must be used by decision-makers in determining the person's ability to make specific decisions at a specific time.

6.  Decisions must be made in the person's best interests.

7.  There are limitations to the use of s5 (e.g. using restraint to protect others from harm or providing care and treatment that amounts to a deprivation of liberty).

8.  The Act allows people to plan ahead and make arrangements for a time when they may lose the capacity to make their own decisions.

9.  The MCA has in the main replaced the common law doctrine of necessity.

# Chapter 10

## The interface between the Mental Health Act and the Mental Capacity Act

## Introduction

The Mental Health Act 2007 (which amended both the Mental Health Act 1983 and the Mental Capacity Act 2005) had a significant impact on the ways individuals can be cared for or treated. Each Act has its own distinct criteria, benefits and limitations. When deciding which legal framework to rely on, the decision-maker will have to consider a range of issues: does the person have capacity, or do they lack capacity in relation to the decision in question? What is the person's age? Do they have a mental disorder? Are there any risks? Does the person need to receive treatment? What restrictions will be placed upon the person? Is the person objecting to treatment? These and other questions will need to be answered before decision-makers can determine which of the available routes can lawfully meet the individual's needs. In addition, decision-makers will need to consider the rights and available safeguards under each of the provisions.

This chapter is intended to help decision-makers understand the main routes of providing care and treatment. It will outline the legislative frameworks, examine the guidance and explore some of the benefits and drawbacks of the various provisions. It is, however, important to remember that the two Acts are not mutually exclusive. It is entirely possible that a patient detained under the MHA receiving treatment for a mental disorder might also receive treatment under the provisions of the MCA. This could happen, for example, when treating physical health problems unrelated to mental disorder. Therefore, decision-makers will need to examine the circumstances of each individual's case and establish which provisions are necessary and appropriate to meet the person's needs.

## Which Act is appropriate?

The following tables aim to:

- give an overview of the legal criteria to be met;

- establish who is responsible for assessment and decision-making;

- explain what care or treatment is authorised under the provision;

- highlight the limitations of the provision;

- consider the protections for the person and for the decision-maker; and

- highlight any other considerations to be borne in mind by the decision-maker.

This is a complex area of law, which may leave decision-makers with a degree of uncertainty regarding how to operate these provisions in practice. For this reason the tables are specific to each of the main routes of providing care or treatment. This is to make the provisions as intelligible as possible. The first two tables deal with the main routes provided by the MCA, s5 acts and Deprivation of Liberty Safeguards (DoLS). The final tables deal with informal admission to hospital and detention in hospital, both under the MHA. It is important to note that these are not the only routes of providing care or treatment to people. The tables are intended as a guide and should not be relied upon in isolation from the more detailed information outlined within this text.

# The Mental Capacity Act 2005 (MCA)

The MCA is aimed at people who lack the capacity to make decisions, as well as those who cur-rently have capacity but wish to choose who should make decisions on their behalf, if they lose capacity in the future. There are a number of provisions within the Act that enable care and treatment to be given to an incapacitated person, in their best interests. This chapter will give an overview of the two main provisions: s5 acts, which came into effect in October 2007 and DoLS, which came into effect in April 2009.

The Code of Practice to the MCA suggests the use of that Act wherever possible, rather than the MHA. Those who have experience in the operation of the MHA will need to familiarise them-selves with the provisions of the MCA and consider its use whenever relevant (see Chapter 9). As a general rule for those aged 16 years and older, whose care and treatment amounts to a mere restriction of movement, s5 of the MCA will apply. However, where a person's care or treatment would amount to a deprivation of liberty, a personal welfare order (by the Court of Protection), DoLS or the use of detention under the MHA should be considered. The use of guardianship (s7 of the Mental Health Act) as a potential means of depriving a person of their liberty is discussed in Chapter 11. In addition, the Children Act may be relied on in some cir-cumstances for children and young persons under 18 (see Chapter 18).

The MCA is mainly concerned with those aged 16 and over. The care and treatment of people under 16 will have to be provided for by an alternative legislative framework:

- the Children Act 1989;
- the Mental Health Act 1983 (amended by the 2007 Act); or
- the common law.

See Chapters 5, 6 and 18 for more information.

That said, the DoLS are only available to those aged 18 or over. Where care or treatment in a hospital or care home is likely to amount to a deprivation of liberty, DoLS should be consid-ered. Where a patient requires treatment for mental disorder in a hospital, in circumstances that amount to a deprivation of liberty, decision-makers must determine which Act should be used. To do so the decision-maker must establish whether the patient is ineligible for DoLS. The case of *GJ v The Foundation Trust et al.* (2009) helped clarify the questions to be addressed in establishing this fact:

- Does the patient require treatment for mental disorder in a hospital?
- Could the patient be detained under the MHA? (i.e. are the legal criteria for sections 2 or 3 met?)
- Is the patient objecting to some or all of the treatment for mental disorder?

Where the three questions are met in the positive, the patient will be ineligible for MCA DoLS. Therefore detention under the MHA must be used.

The first of the three questions requires the decision-maker to establish whether the illness giving rise to the need for treatment in hospital is indeed mental disorder (this may include a physical health problem that is intrinsically linked with the mental disorder, therefore bringing it within the scope of treatment for mental disorder, for example, naso-gastric feeding of a patient with anorexia nervosa (*Re KB* 1994)). In the case of GJ, it was concluded that his physical ill health (poorly controlled diabetes) and his mental disorder (vascular dementia and Korsakoff's syndrome) were unrelated, and "but for" his physical ill health his mental health did not warrant treatment in hospital; therefore he was not ineligible for DoLS, so its use was not unlawful. Put simply, you must ask what the primary need for treatment is. If it is for mental disorder the first of the questions is met in the positive; if it is for physical ill health, unrelated to mental disorder, the MHA cannot be used. When considering the second question the decision-maker must simply ask whether the person could be detained under the MHA. This does not require an MHA assessment, but a judgement to be made as to whether the criteria for s2 or s3 are met. If this is the case, it is to be assumed that the medical recommendations would be made. When addressing the third question, the bar for objection appears to have been set low. A distinction between past or present objection, incapacitated or capacitous objection, and objection to treatment or simply being in hospital has not been made. This is due to the likelihood that the patient will, by reason of incapacity, be unable to make an informed, balanced decision; therefore what matters is simply whether the patient objects.

There will, however, be situations where all three questions are not answered in the positive, in which case the person will not be ineligible for DoLS, and a choice between Acts emerges. This situation arose in the case of *AM v SLAM & Secretary of State for Health* (2013). The case concerned a person subject to Mental Health Act detention in a hospital. She required treatment in hospital for mental disorder, and met the statutory criteria for detention under the Mental Health Act; however she was not objecting to treatment. She was, therefore, not ineligible for DoLS, and so a choice between Acts arose. Mr Justice Charles asserted that the choice should be made on the basis of whether the person's detention under the MHA is or is not warranted, or necessary, and which Act is less restrictive. Decision-makers therefore must exercise this choice when faced with a passive, incompetent patient, requiring treatment in a hospital for mental disorder, who meets the statutory criteria for s2 or s3 of the MHA, and who is in effect deprived of their liberty.

*Table 10.1   Mental Capacity Act – s5 Acts*

| | |
|---|---|
| Criteria as set out in statute | • Aged 16 and over |
| | • Specific decision to be made at a specific time |
| | • Lacks capacity to make specific decision(s), because of an impairment of, or a disturbance in, the functioning of the mind or brain |
| | • The decision is in their best interests (see the MCA checklist in Chapter 9 for more information) |
| Assessor(s)/decision-makers | • The person most closely connected with the decision to be made. This could be a relative, carer or someone acting in a professional capacity. They should speak with others (as part of the best interests checklist). See Chapter 9 |
| Allows | • Acts in relation to the care or treatment of a person with either mental or physical ill health, without time limit |

| | |
|---|---|
| Limitations | • Does not allow restraint to prevent harm to others |
| | • Where restraint is used it must be proportionate |
| | • Cannot be used to deprive a person of their liberty |
| | • No entitlement to free aftercare services |
| | • No automatic legal hearings to challenge the decision |
| | • No consent to treatment safeguards |
| | • No nearest relative protections |
| Protections for the person | • Legal criteria must be met for an act to take place |
| | • Consultation with others (as part of the best interests checklist) |
| | • Challenges to the Court of Protection |
| Protections for the decision-maker | • Protection from liability if the requirements of the Act have been followed (i.e. assessment of incapacity and best interests checklist) and there is no negligence |
| Other considerations | • Use of s5 to admit someone to psychiatric hospital may overlap with s131 of the MHA (see Table 10.3) |
| | • Has the person made a valid and applicable refusal of the treatment proposed? If so s5 cannot be used to override this |
| | • An attorney or deputy can give or withhold consent for care or treatment. If consent is withheld for treatment of mental disorder their authority can be overridden by use of the MHA if Part 4 of the MHA applies |
| | • Is the person subject to a personal welfare order by the Court of Protection? If so, this might give authority for withholding or consenting to care or treatment |
| | • If the person is already detained under the MHA, and covered by Part 4 of that Act, treatment for mental disorder cannot be given under the MCA |

The DoLS procedure, unlike s5 acts, cannot be carried out by anyone closely connected with the person. The responsibility for carrying out the assessments to establish if the person meets the criteria rests with health and social care professionals. The DoLS are discussed in more detail within Chapter 11.

# The Mental Health Act 1983

The MHA enables people of all ages to be treated for mental disorder on an informal basis, or where necessary, under compulsory powers. The main provisions for informal and compulsory treatment are detailed below (see also Chapters 5, 6 and 7).

# The process of assessment

Historically, people with mental health problems have had their needs met by either the provisions of the MHA or by relying on the common law doctrine of necessity. Those responsible for the assessment of people's needs will be familiar with the formal requirements of the MHA and the less formal requirements for the use of the common law. Common law has now largely been replaced by the MCA, so assessors will need to broaden their approach to encompass the criteria for both the MHA and MCA to enable them to establish which criteria are met, and therefore which Act could or should be used.

When considering the use of the MHA assessors have to establish the following:

- mental disorder, i.e. "any disorder or disability of the mind";

- nature or degree of the disorder, warranting detention;

- risks to the health or safety of the person or risks posed to others;

- whether treatment in hospital is necessary, or in some cases whether appropriate medical treatment is available, and;

- whether there are any alternatives to admission.

Table 10.2   Mental Capacity Act – Deprivation of Liberty Safeguards (DoLS)

| | |
|---|---|
| Assessments (all six must be met for an authorisation to be given) | • Aged 18 and over<br>• Mental disorder<br>• Mental incapacity<br>• Best interests<br>• Eligibility<br>• No refusals |
| Assessor(s)/decision-makers | • There will be two or more assessors, each of which will be acting in a professional capacity (for example, a doctor and a social worker) |
| Allows | • Deprivation of liberty within hospital and care home settings, for up to one year in the first instance |
| Limitations | • Does not authorise anything other than a lawful deprivation of liberty (e.g. does not authorise medical treatment)<br>• No entitlement to free aftercare services, unless there is an existing entitlement under s117 of the MHA<br>• No automatic legal hearings to challenge the decision(s) |
| Protections for the person | • Compliance with Article 5 of the ECHR<br>• Reviews<br>• Legal challenge to the Court of Protection<br>• IMCAs where there is no one to consult other than those acting in a professional capacity, and when the decision concerns serious medical treatment or long-term care<br>• An appointed representative for the person<br>• Overview by the Care Quality Commission |
| Protections for the decision-maker | • Assessors (other than age assessor) must be covered by indemnity for any liabilities that might arise in connection with carrying out an assessment |

| Other considerations | • These provisions do not apply to people detained under the MHA, or under a personal welfare order by the Court of Protection (s16 of the MCA) |
|---|---|
| | • An authorisation cannot be granted in the face of a refusal by way of an advance decision (specifying the proposed treatment) or the authority of an attorney or deputy (assuming it is within their authority of decision-making) |
| | • Provision could not be used if the authorisation would be inconsistent with obligations placed upon the person under the following provisions of the MHA: requirement of residence under s7 or s17, CTO or conditional discharge |
| | • A person would not be eligible for the proposed authorisation (for deprivation of liberty in a hospital for treatment of mental disorder) if they are subject to: s17 leave, a CTO or conditional discharge (as the power of recall can be used), or if the person objects to some or all of the proposed treatment for mental disorder, and they meet the criteria for detention under the MHA |

With the introduction of the MCA assessors also need to assess:

• whether there is an "impairment of, or a disturbance in the functioning of, the mind or brain";

• the person's age;

• whether or not they have the capacity to make their own decisions, and;

• whether the care or treatment is likely to be a mere restriction of liberty or a deprivation of liberty.

*Table 10.3   Mental Health Act – informal admission (s131)*

| Criteria | • No lower age restriction |
|---|---|
| | • Mental disorder, i.e. "any disorder or disability of the mind" |
| | • Not objecting to informal admission |
| Assessor(s)/decision-makers | • Likely to be a mental health professional but several people could be involved in the process including family, GP, hospital staff |
| Allows | • Admission to hospital, without time limit |
| Limitations | • Does not authorise treatment to be given unless the person consents to it |
| | • No entitlement to free aftercare services, unless there is an existing entitlement under s117 of the MHA |
| Protections for the person | • They are free to leave the hospital |
| | • They can refuse treatment |
| Other considerations | • Once a person has become an in-patient, staff may prevent the person from leaving (subject to certain criteria being met, see Chapter 5) |
| | • Where a person lacks capacity to consent and their treatment will amount to a deprivation of liberty, use of detention under the MHA or DoLS should be considered |

Depending upon the outcome of the assessment, decision-makers will have to decide which of the Acts, if any, apply. However, there will be circumstances where a person meets the criteria for both Acts. In this case decision-makers will need to establish which of the Acts is more appropriate or if, indeed, both need to be operated to meet the person's needs.

# Government guidance

The Code of Practice to the MCA offers some guidance about the relationship between the MCA and the MHA. It aims to help those making a choice between the legal frameworks, albeit with strong encouragement to use the less restrictive framework of the MCA. Chapter 13 of the Code of Practice to the MCA states at page 225:

*Professionals may need to think about using the MHA to detain and treat somebody who lacks capacity to consent to treatment (rather than use the MCA), if:*

- *it is not possible to give the person the care or treatment they need without doing something that might deprive them of their liberty;*

- *the person needs treatment that cannot be given under the MCA (for example, because the person had made a valid and applicable advance decision to refuse an essential part of treatment);*

- *the person may need to be restrained in a way that is not allowed under the MCA;*

- *it is not possible to assess or treat the person safely or effectively without treatment being compulsory (perhaps because the person is expected to regain capacity to consent, but might then refuse to give consent);*

- *the person lacks capacity to decide on some elements of the treatment but has capacity to refuse a vital part of it – and they have done so; or*

- *there is some other reason why the person might not get treatment, and they or somebody else might suffer harm as a result.*

*Before making an application under the MHA, decision-makers should consider whether they could achieve their aims safely and effectively by using the MCA instead.*

*Compulsory treatment under the MHA is not an option if:*

- *the patient's mental disorder does not justify detention in hospital; or*

- *the patient needs treatment only for a physical illness or disability.*

*The MCA applies to people subject to the MHA in the same way as it applies to anyone else, with four exceptions:*

- *if someone is detained under the MHA, decision-makers cannot normally rely on the MCA to give treatment for mental disorder or make decisions about that treatment on that person's behalf;*

- *if somebody can be treated for their mental disorder without their consent because they are detained under the MHA, healthcare staff can treat them even if it goes against an advance decision to refuse that treatment;*

- *if a person is subject to guardianship, the guardian has the exclusive right to take certain decisions, including where the person is to live; and*

- *independent mental capacity advocates do not have to be involved in decisions about serious medical treatment or accommodation, if those decisions are made under the MHA.*

*Table 10.4    Mental Health Act – detention under Part 2 (civil) or Part 3 (criminal)*

| | |
|---|---|
| Criteria | • No lower age restriction |
| | • Mental disorder, i.e. "any disorder or disability of the mind", of a nature or degree warranting detention |
| | • Risks to health or safety of patient or protection of others |
| | • Informal admission is not appropriate |
| | • It is the most appropriate way of providing care and medical treatment |
| | • Appropriate medical treatment is available (for longer-term detention) |
| Assessor(s)/ decision-makers | • In most cases (for civil admissions) two doctors and an AMHP, see Chapter 5 |
| | • For criminal cases a court advised by mental health professionals, see Chapter 7 |
| Allows | • Detention in hospital |
| | • Treatment to be given for mental disorder (if need be by force, and in some circumstances, against a capacitated refusal – but note limitations in connection with ECT, Chapter 8) |
| | • Time limits vary (see Chapter 5) |
| Limitations | • Does not authorise treatment for physical health problems (unless they are intrinsically linked with mental disorder) |
| Protections for the person | • Detention criteria must be met |
| | • Assessment by three individuals, who must reach agreement |
| | • Nearest relative rights at the point of admission and power of discharge |
| | • Can appeal to hospital managers and Tribunals |
| | • SOAD, CQC |
| Protections for the decision-maker | • Section 139 (action against individual not possible unless they have acted in bad faith or without reasonable care) |
| Other considerations | • An advance decision refusing treatment for mental disorder can be overridden where Part 4 of the Act applies (but note exclusions for ECT) |
| | • Detention can override a refusal of treatment for mental disorder by an attorney and deputy (if however the attorney or deputy is the patient's nearest relative they retain the powers and rights of the NR and may object to s3) |

Further guidance can be found in Chapter 13 of the Mental Health Act 1983: Code of Practice.

Chapter 4 of the Code of Practice to the MHA encourages use of less restrictive measures wherever possible, stating at E Para. 14.11:

> *In deciding whether it is necessary to detain patients, doctors and AMHPs must always consider the alternative ways of providing the treatment or care they need. Decision-makers should always consider whether there are less restrictive alternatives to detention under the Act, which may include:*

> • *informal admission to hospital of a patient based on that person's consent;*

> • *treatment under the Mental Capacity Act (MCA) if the person lacks capacity to consent to admission and treatment. If a deprivation of liberty occurs, or is likely to occur, either the Act, a DoLS authorisation or a deprivation of liberty order by the Court of Protection must be in place;*

- *management in the community – e.g. by a crisis and support team, in a crisis house or with a host family or*

- *guardianship.*

Table 10.5 aims to clarify the ways of providing care or treatment to people by setting out the main provisions, indicating which can be used depending upon the person's age, and whether the care and treatment amounts to a deprivation of the person's liberty. It also prompts decision-makers to consider some key issues.

This is not an exhaustive guide, but an attempt to provide some visual assistance with this complex area.

# Key points

1. Both the MCA and MHA offer frameworks for providing care or treatment to those with a mental disorder.

2. Age is a relevant consideration.

3. Capacity needs to be considered when identifying the legal route to take.

4. There are limitations on where certain types of treatment or care can be provided.

5. Assessors need to understand both Acts and whether they have a right to make a decision.

6. Each Act has a different approach to guiding principles.

7. Codes of Practice exist for both Acts.

8. Decision-makers must uphold the human rights of those they seek to assist.

*Table 10.5   AMHPs carrying out Mental Health Act assessments*

**Possible routes to providing care and treatment assessing: capacity, mental disorder, restriction of movement cf. deprivation of liberty**

| Age | Mental Capacity Act 2005 | Mental Health Act 1983 | Common law | Notes |
|---|---|---|---|---|
| Under 16 years | Does not apply to those under 16 | No age limits<br><br>Mental disorder<br><br>Criteria for provision/ detention met<br><br>May have or lack capacity<br><br>Detention under MHA authorises deprivation of liberty<br><br>Treatment for mental disorder authorised under Part 4 of the Act<br><br>Statutory forms | Gillick competence<br><br>Consider: parental authority, and the ability of a person with PA to authorise a deprivation of liberty (see case of *Trust A v X and A Local Authority* (2015) EWHC 922) | Consider Children Act<br><br>MCA and DoLS cannot be used for this age group |

| | | | | |
|---|---|---|---|---|
| 16+ | If person lacks capacity<br><br>Restriction of liberty only<br><br>Best interests checklist, etc.<br><br>Does not authorise treatment, but care and treatment can be provided subject to the limitations of s6<br><br>No statutory forms, check if you have local policy and/or forms<br><br>Court of Protection (s16) could authorise a deprivation of liberty | As above<br><br>Guardianship (s7) is not seen as a way of depriving a person of their liberty, but it does allow for restriction of movement and is a procedure prescribed by law<br><br>Where patient lacks capacity, establish if needs can be met under the MCA<br><br>Consider Court of Protection where deprivation of liberty is required and cannot be provided for under MHA<br><br>If patient detained under MHA needs treatment not covered by Part 4, consider use of MCA for other care and treatment | Probably just for emergency use only (e.g. to protect others where no risk to person's own health)<br><br>Note: Parental authority cannot be used to authorise a deprivation of liberty (see *D (A Child)* (2019) UKSC 42) | Capacitated acceptance/refusal of admission to hospital for treatment of mental disorder cannot be overridden by someone with parental responsibility<br><br>As well as MHA consider:<br><br>MCA<br><br>Children Act<br><br>Court of Protection Cannot use DoLS until 18 |
| 18+ | DoLS: If person lacks capacity and has mental disorder<br><br>Authorises deprivation of liberty (subject to six assessments)<br><br>Does not authorise treatment but it can be provided subject to limitations of s6<br><br>There will be forms | As 16+ if patient detained under MHA needs treatment not covered by Part 4, consider use of MCA for other care and treatment | As above in respect of emergency treatment<br><br>PR falls away at 18 | |

# Chapter 11

## The Deprivation of Liberty Safeguards

## Introduction

The Deprivation of Liberty Safeguards (DoLS) set out in Schedule A1 are an amendment to the Mental Capacity Act 2005 introduced by the Mental Health Act 2007. The DoLS framework is supported by a supplement to the MCA Code of Practice. DoLS were introduced to ensure that any deprivation of liberty of an incapacitated adult complies with the requirements of the European Convention on Human Rights (ECHR). The need for procedural safeguards, ensuring compliance with the ECHR, was highlighted in the case of *HL v UK* (2004), formerly known as Bournewood. The details of the case are set out below. As a result of the European judgement the Government introduced a procedure that, if followed, will ensure that any deprivation of liberty complies with Article 5 of the ECHR (see Chapter 17 and Appendix 5). This chapter will:

- explore the distinction between restriction of movement and deprivation of liberty;

- set out the process for depriving a person of their liberty under the DoLS regime; and

- outline the alternative routes of providing care and treatment dependent upon whether the care and treatment amounts to a restriction of movement or a deprivation of liberty.

## What is deprivation of liberty?

For a deprivation of liberty to be occurring, the following three criteria must be met:

- the objective component of the confinement in a particular restricted place for a not negligible length of time (deprivation of liberty);

- the subjective component of lack of valid consent; and

- the attribution of responsibility to the state (*Storck v Germany* (2005), paras 74 and 89).

## The objective component of the confinement in a particular restricted place for a not negligible length of time (deprivation of liberty)

Deprivation of liberty was defined in the case of *Cheshire West* (2014) as continuous/complete supervision *and* control, *and* not free to leave. This test is referred to as the "acid test". The decision-maker must therefore ask, first, whether the person is subject to continuous/complete supervision and control and, second, is not free to leave the environment in which they are being kept. Where both questions are answered in the positive, the decision-maker must establish whether the deprivation is for a "not negligible length of time".

There is no prescribed time frame in statute for a not negligible length of time, and so case law and guidance provide the only sources of information to assist decision-makers to answer this element of the question. In the case of *HL v UK* (2004), the court concluded that detention in a psychiatric hospital for a period of three months without legal authority was too long. Later in 2011, the court in the case of *Sessay v South London & Maudsley NHS Foundation Trust & The Commissioner of Police* (2011) concluded that detention in a psychiatric place of safety for 12 hours amounted to an unlawful detention, and more recently the physical restraint of a man with a learning disability by police for 40 minutes constituted an unlawful deprivation of liberty (*ZH v Commissioner of the Police for the Metropolis* (2013)). It is therefore difficult to quantify the time before an unlawful deprivation of liberty may occur. Decision-makers must therefore look at the type of restrictions imposed, and the degree and intensity of them when determining whether an authority is needed. The Law Society strongly suggests that it is not safe to rely on the rule of thumb that deprivation of liberty is unlikely to arise where a person's confinement is less than seven days. They have suggested that a deprivation of liberty is likely to occur where the acid test is met, and the person is confined for more than two or three days.

## The subjective component of lack of valid consent

The second of the three criteria that must be met when determining whether a person is deprived of their liberty concerns the person's inability to consent to the arrangements for their care and/or treatment. A person must be assumed to have the capacity to make decisions. However, where there is doubt about this, the onus is on the decision-maker to rebut the presumption of capacity. This is done by applying the diagnostic and functional tests set out in s2 and s3 of the MCA (see Chapter 9 for information about the application of the test). Where the decision-maker establishes that the person is unable to make a decision because of an impairment of, or a disturbance in the functioning of, the mind or brain, they must finally establish whether the deprivation is imputable to the state (see below).

## The attribution of responsibility to the state

The decision-maker must establish whether the care and/or treatment being provided is attributable to the state (for example, local authority (LA) or NHS). Where, for example, a person is in a placement, part or whole funded by the LA or NHS, the state is clearly responsible in some way for the deprivation of liberty. It is less clear, however, where a person is self-funding a package of care in a domestic setting. The Law Society has suggested that this criterion may be met where, for example, care is provided (albeit self-funded) by an organisation inspected by the Care Quality Commission. Where it is unclear whether the state is responsible, decision-makers would be well advised to seek a legal view.

It is important to understand that providing care and treatment that amounts to a restriction of a person's movement does not engage Article 5, whereas depriving a person of their liberty is unlawful unless the requirements of Article 5 are met. The distinction between the two will have to be made by those providing care and treatment to people, and, in particular, by any best interests assessor (BIA) considering whether deprivation of liberty should be authorised under the DoLS procedure. Assessors will need to establish what restrictions will be, or are being, placed upon the person, and decide if they amount to a deprivation of liberty. If a person is considered to be deprived of their liberty, or at risk of it, the deprivation must be compliant with Article 5 of the ECHR for it to be lawful.

There have been a number of cases before the courts, where the distinction between restriction of movement and deprivation of liberty has been an issue. These cases set precedents, offering assessors some guidance on how to make this distinction in practice. That said, each person has a distinct set of circumstances, and therefore the following judgements and guidance only offer a guide when considering individual cases. The cases appear in date order, concluding with the most recent cases. Of particular importance to decision-makers are the cases of *Cheshire West* (2014), in which the "acid test" was established; *Trust A v X and A Local Authority* (2015); and *Birmingham CC v D* (2016) EWCOP 8. The latter two cases concerned the detention of a 15-year-old male in a psychiatric hospital, and his continued detention in a residential establishment, having attained the age of 16.

# *HL v The United Kingdom* (2004)

This case concerned a man with autism, who was informally admitted to hospital. The European Court of Human Rights had to decide if his management constituted a lawful restriction of movement or an unlawful deprivation of liberty.

HL was without speech, had limited understanding and lacked the capacity to consent to, or refuse, care or treatment. He was often agitated and had a history of self-harming behaviour. During a routine visit to a day centre, his behaviour became unmanageable; he began hitting himself on the head and banging his head against a wall. In the absence of his carers, Mr and Mrs E, those responsible for him in the day centre took steps to manage the situation. This involved a doctor administering sedative medication at the day centre, conveyance to an accident and emergency department for assessment and then informal admission to an intensive behavioural unit. He did not resist admission or attempt to leave the hospital.

HL, like any other person requiring intervention, had a number of needs. It was the responses to these needs that were restrictions leading to possible deprivation of liberty. It is helpful to list the restrictions, as this will assist assessors in determining whether they amount to a deprivation of liberty.

Restrictions placed on HL included:

- administration of sedative medication, prior to admission and during admission;
- conveyance by ambulance to an accident and emergency department;
- conveyance (by two staff) to an in-patient unit;
- admission to an in-patient unit;
- no contact with his carers (contact was discouraged by his doctor);
- Mr and Mrs E's request for HL's discharge was denied;
- HL was not free to leave the hospital;
- HL was under continuous supervision (by nursing staff);
- HL was given treatment without his consent;
- HL remained in hospital for approximately three months under the common law doctrine of necessity.

The European Court of Human Rights decided that HL had been deprived of his liberty. The court placed considerable emphasis on the fact that the healthcare professionals exercised "complete and effective control" over his care and movements from the moment he presented acute behavioural problems until his detention under the MHA, some three months later. It is perhaps not surprising that the court concluded that the "degree and intensity" of the restrictions amounted to a deprivation of liberty.

The Deprivation of Liberty Safeguards (Code to supplement the main Mental Capacity Act 2005 Code of Practice) referred to hereafter as the Code, states at 2.5:

> *The ECHR and UK courts have determined a number of cases about deprivation of liberty. Their judgements indicate that the following factors can be relevant to identifying whether steps taken involve more than restraint and amount to a deprivation of liberty. It is important to remember that this list is not exclusive; other factors may arise in future in particular cases.*
>
> - *Restraint is used, including sedation, to admit a person to an institution where that person is resisting admission.*
>
> - *Staff exercise complete and effective control over the care and movement of a person for a significant period.*
>
> - *Staff exercise control over assessments, treatment, contacts and residence.*
>
> - *A decision has been taken by the institution that the person will not be released into the care of others, or permitted to live elsewhere, unless the staff in the institution consider it appropriate.*
>
> - *A request by carers for a person to be discharged to their care is refused.*
>
> - *The person is unable to maintain social contacts because of restrictions placed on their access to other people.*
>
> - *The person loses autonomy because they are under continuous supervision and control.*

Whilst this offers some guidance it does not suggest how many restrictions result in a deprivation of liberty, or whether more weight should be given to some restrictions than to others. The following case highlights the significance given to the person not being free to leave and live where he chose, which has since become integral to the acid test of deprivation of liberty.

# JE v DE and Surrey County Council (2006)

DE, a man who lacked the capacity to decide where to live, was placed within a local authority residential care home after his wife put him out on the street as a protest against lack of support to care for him. DE repeatedly requested to go home to live with his wife and his wife wanted him to return home, having made her point. The local authority considered it was in DE's best interests to remain in the care home. Again the court had to determine whether his movements were restricted or if he was deprived of his liberty. The High Court concluded that DE was deprived of his liberty.

The judge, Mr Justice Munby, stated:

> *It seems to me that DE quite plainly was not "free to leave" the X home and has not been "free to leave" the Y home, with the consequence, in my judgement, that he has been and continues to be "deprived of his liberty".*

Whilst there were other restrictions considered during the court proceedings, it appears that the sole factor of not being free to leave and live where he chose was sufficient for the judge to determine that DE was deprived of his liberty. This is in contrast to the following case, in which weight was given to the degree and intensity of the restrictions imposed, in addition to E's confinement in a residential establishment.

# G v E v A Local Authority v F (2010)

In the case of *G v E v A Local Authority v F* (2010), the court was asked amongst other things to determine whether E, aged 19, was being deprived of his liberty in a residential establishment, having been removed from the care of his long-term carer by the local authority. E has physical health problems, a learning disability and the language skills equivalent to an 18–24-month-old child. E displays some behavioural difficulties, and these appear to worsen when outside the care of F, his long-term carer.

Mr Justice Baker concluded that the local authority care arrangements deprived E of his liberty. This conclusion was drawn having considered the complete control over his care and movements (assessments, treatment, contacts and residence). Some of the factors that led to this conclusion included:

- confinement to a residential establishment, other than escorted visits and activities;
- no private space or possessions;
- an inability to maintain social contacts;
- administration of a neuroleptic medication to manage behaviour, over which E had no control.

The degree and intensity of conditions, along with an infringement of Article 8 ECHR – a failure to respect family life – contributed to the conclusion of unlawful deprivation of liberty in the case of *Hillingdon v Neary* (2011).

# Hillingdon v Neary (2011)

Steven Neary, aged 21, has childhood autism and a severe learning disability. He requires supervision and support at all times. He was brought up by both his parents until they separated in 2009, after which he resided with his father, who received high levels of support with Steven's care from Hillingdon social services. In December 2009, Mr Neary agreed that Steven could be accommodated in respite care for a couple of weeks whilst he recovered his health. Hillingdon kept Steven in its care between January and December 2010 (during which time the DoLS were used) in the face of his father's request for his son's return home.

Mr Justice Jackson was to determine whether the local authority had acted unlawfully by depriving him of his liberty by failing to respect his right to family life. It was concluded that the "degree and intensity" of the restrictions imposed amounted to a deprivation of his liberty. The following features led to that conclusion: Steven's objection to being at the support unit, the objection of his father, and "the total and effective control of Steven's every waking moment in an environment that was not his home".

A number of general principles flow from the judgement:

- In cases of disagreement, local authority powers are limited to investigating, providing support services and, where appropriate, referring the matter to the Court of Protection. The DoLS should not be used as a means by which the local authority can get its own way on the question of best interests.
- Use of the DoLS will not make lawful what is unlawful, for example, failure to properly carry out the best interests assessment (in this case failure to consider the less restrictive option of Steven returning home).

- The role of the supervisory body and case planning should be independent of one another.

- The supervisory body should provide independent scrutiny of the required assessments, not simply authorise a deprivation of liberty upon receipt of assessments that on the face of it meet the criteria.

- The primary concern of where a person should live (i.e. what is in their best interests) (Article 8) and whether they are deprived of their liberty (Article 5) should not be conflated. This is in keeping with previous judgements (*Re Mig and Meg* at the Court of Appeal).

- A breach of Article 5(4) may be found, and was in this case on the basis of three factors coming together: no IMCA, no effective review and no timely issue of proceeding. The case of *Cheshire and Chester v P* (2011) also highlighted the need for court reviews where deprivation of liberty is occurring to meet the requirements of Article 5(4) ECHR. Given the lack of automatic legal review under the DoLS, consideration should be given to the necessity to refer cases to the Court of Protection to ensure compliance with Article 5(4) ECHR.

More recent cases assist decision-makers in determining whether a deprivation of liberty is occurring on the basis of the "acid test", and the role of parental consent to what would otherwise amount to deprivation of liberty. The cases of Mig and Meg (aka P and Q) and P were heard in the Supreme Court together, concluding that all three were deprived of their liberty. Mig has a mental age of two-and-a-half, and Meg has a mental age of four to five; both lack capacity in relation to their care and treatment. Mig and Meg lived with their mother until 2007, when they were accommodated by the local authority as a result of a dysfunctional and abusive family home. Mig resides in a foster home and Meg in a small residential home. Mig is "under continuous supervision and control", and if she attempted to leave she would be prevented from doing so. Meg has 1:1 and sometimes 2:1 support, and behavioural management techniques and occasional restraint are used to manage her challenging behaviour. She is under continuous supervision and control and receives medication to stabilise her mood and calm her down. P, an adult male, who was born with cerebral palsy and Down's syndrome, resided in a small residential establishment (housing four residents) that was not designed for compulsory detention. He had regular contact with his family; he attended a day service and enjoyed a good social life. He was under 1:1 or 2:1 supervision at all times and occasional restraint was used to manage his challenging behaviour.

In the case of Mig and Meg, both the Court of Protection and the Court of Appeal concluded that their care did not amount to a deprivation of liberty, in spite of extensive restrictions. P, in contrast, was found by the Court of Protection to be deprived of his liberty, as his "life [was] completely under the control of members of staff" and occasional restraint was used. However, in contrast, Munby, LJ in the Court of Appeal concluded that P was not deprived of his liberty. The Court of Appeal found that the Court of Protection had not questioned whether the "limitations and restrictions on P's life ... are anything more than the inevitable corollary of his various disabilities" (E Para. 110). In addition, the restrictions placed upon P were seen as necessary regardless of environment, and not capable of tipping the balance from restriction of movement to deprivation of liberty. Both judgements were overruled by the Supreme Court in the case of *Cheshire West*. The tests of "relevant comparator" and "relative normality" – introduced by Munby, LJ in the Court Of Appeal – were viewed as discriminatory, affording differing levels of liberty dependent upon the differing characteristics of individuals. A new "acid test" of deprivation of liberty was established, and was to be applied to all regardless of mental or physical disability (see above, "What is deprivation of liberty?"). However, differing approaches appear to be emerging when determining deprivation of liberty for children and young people.

# Deprivation of liberty – children (below the age of 16)

The case of *Trust A v X and A Local Authority* (2015) concerned the detention of a 15-year-old male (referred to as D) in a psychiatric hospital. D is diagnosed with mental disorder, and is awaiting a suitable residential placement. The court were asked to determine whether his placement in hospital satisfied the "acid test", whether his parents could consent to his deprivation of liberty, and (if the parents' consent could not be relied upon) whether the court should exercise its powers under the inherent jurisdiction to consider declaring that D's deprivation of liberty at the hospital is lawful and in his best interests. (Given D's age he falls outside the scope of the MCA DoLS regime and the Court of Protection (CoP).)

Restrictions placed on D included:

- D is residing in a six-bedded unit. He has his own room, but shares bathroom and living facilities;

- D receives full-time education on site;

- D's unit is staffed 24 hours a day, and has a locked front door. D does not leave the ward unaccompanied;

- D is subject to half-hourly observation, but he seeks out contact with staff more regularly;

- D leaves the unit on a daily basis, but is accompanied by staff. He has stated that he would be anxious to go out on his own;

- D is considered anxious about his impending discharge from hospital.

First, the court concluded that these restrictions met the acid test. Second, the question of consent arose. D was unable to consent; however the court concluded "the consent of D's parents to his placement at Hospital B, with all of the restrictions placed upon his life there, falls within the 'zone of parental responsibility'" (para. 66). D's parents were therefore able to, and did consent to, what would otherwise have amounted to deprivation of liberty. The court steered away from giving guidance to hospitals and local authorities faced with similar circumstances, stressing that "cases are invariably fact specific and require a close examination of the 'concrete' situation" (para. 68). That said, the appropriate exercise of parental responsibility was discussed in light of age and disability:

> *An appropriate exercise of parental responsibility in respect of a 5 year old child will differ very considerably from what is or is not an appropriate exercise of parental responsibility in respect of a 15 year old young person ... The decisions which might be said to come within the zone of parental responsibility for a 15 year old who did not suffer from the conditions with which D has been diagnosed will be of a wholly different order from those decisions which have to be taken by parents whose 15 year old son suffers with D's disabilities. Thus a decision to keep such a 15 year old boy under constant supervision and control would undoubtedly be considered an inappropriate exercise of parental responsibility and would probably amount to ill treatment. The decision to keep an autistic 15 year old boy who has erratic, challenging and potentially harmful behaviours under constant supervision and control is a quite different matter; to do otherwise would be neglectful. In such a case I consider the decision to keep this young person under constant supervision and control is the proper exercise of parental responsibility.*

This statement appears to reintroduce the comparator established by Munby, LJ, which was viewed in the case of *Cheshire West* (2014) as inherently discriminatory.

# Deprivation of liberty – young people (those aged 16 and 17)

The case of D (above) came before the Court of Protection once he had attained the age of 16 and had moved to a residential establishment funded by the LA, and with his parent's consent under s20 of the Children Act 1989. The court was to determine whether parental consent could still be replied upon, now that D had attained the age of 16, and whether the arrangements were imputable to the state. All parties were satisfied that the circumstances in which he resided met the acid test. Whist parental responsibility lasts up until a person's eighteenth birthday, it was concluded that a greater degree of autonomy should be afforded to those aged 16 and 17. Therefore a parent of a 16- or 17-year-old may not consent to their child's confinement, negating a deprivation of liberty. However, this decision was overturned in the case of *D (A Child)* (2017) EWCA Civ 1695, concluding that parents (with parental responsibility) may in some circumstances consent to what would otherwise be a deprivation of liberty for an incapable 16/17-year-old. This case was however appealed to the Supreme Court, and with a majority decision concluded that those with parental responsibility for an incapable 16- or 17-year-old may not consent to their deprivation of liberty. Consenting to deprivation of liberty was viewed as going beyond the scope of parental decision making, and therefore the protections of A5 ECHR must be afforded. The fact that restrictions may be necessary to prevent harm and that arrangements are close to normal life is irrelevant to whether a deprivation of liberty is occurring. Professionals must therefore establish whether the degree of supervision and control goes beyond what is normal for a child of 16 or 17 years of age, and where this is the case an appropriate authority, complying with A5 ECHR must be sought.

If, after careful consideration of the potential restrictions to be placed upon a person, the assessor concludes that the person will merely be restricted of their movement, this will be lawful under s5 of the MCA (assuming all other criteria are met). If, however, the assessor concludes that the restriction(s) amount to a deprivation of liberty, this will not be permitted under s5 of the Act. Where deprivation of liberty is considered likely, consideration will have to be given to other means of lawfully depriving a person of their liberty, for example the DoLS procedure, detention under the MHA or a personal welfare order made by the Court of Protection (s16 MCA), or parental consent for those aged under 16 years.

# The Deprivation of Liberty Safeguards (DoLS): standard authorisation

Where an incapacitated adult is deprived of their liberty, or at risk of being deprived of their liberty within a care home or hospital, setting the DoLS procedure should be instigated. The managing authority has the responsibility for applying for an authorisation of deprivation of liberty. The Code at E Para. 3.1 gives the following guidance regarding identification of the managing authority:

- *In the case of an NHS hospital, the managing authority is the NHS body responsible for the running of the hospital in which the relevant person is, or is to be, a resident.*

- *In the case of a care home or a private hospital, the managing authority will be the person registered, or required to be registered, under part 2 of the Care Standards Act 2000 in respect of the hospital or care home.*

Once the "managing authority" has applied for an authorisation of deprivation of liberty, the "supervisory body" becomes responsible for considering the request. It will commission the six assessments (see below) and, if all six assessment criteria are met, will authorise a deprivation of liberty. Amendments to Schedule A1 of the MCA by Schedule 5 of the Health and Social Care Act 2012 transferred hospital supervisory body responsibilities to local authorities in England. This means that local authorities are the only supervisory bodies in England authorising deprivation of liberty (in hospital and care home settings). Supervisory responsibility arrangements in Wales were unchanged. Supervisory body responsibilities are as follows:

## Hospitals situated in England

- *Where the Deprivation of Liberty Safeguards are applied to a person in a hospital situated in England, the supervisory body will be the local authority for the area in which the person is ordinarily resident.*

- *Where the Deprivation of Liberty Safeguards are applied to a person not ordinarily resident in England and the National Assembly for Wales or the local health board commission the relevant care or treatment, the National Assembly are the supervisory body.*

- *In any other case, the supervisory body is the local authority for the area in which the relevant hospital is situated.*

## Hospitals situated in Wales

- *Where the Deprivation of Liberty Safeguards are applied to a person in a hospital situated in Wales, the supervisory body will be the National Assembly for Wales.*

- *Where the Deprivation of Liberty Safeguards are applied to a person ordinarily resident in the area of a local authority in England, the supervisory body is that local authority.*

## Care homes

- *Where the Deprivation of Liberty Safeguards are applied to a person in a care home, whether situated in England or Wales, the supervisory body will be the local authority for the area in which the person is ordinarily resident. However, if the person is not ordinarily resident in the area of any local authority (for example a person of no fixed abode), the supervisory body will be the local authority for the area in which the care home is situated (MoJ 2008, Para 3.3)*

An application for a standard authorisation must be made by the managing authority to the supervisory body. Applications must be in writing and must be on a prescribed form. The form content varies depending upon whether the request is within England or Wales. Once an application has been made, there is an expectation that certain people are informed of the request.

The Code offers further information relating to this requirement (E MCA Para. 3.15). Assuming that the supervisory body considers the request appropriate, and has all the relevant information, it should commission assessors to perform the following six assessments: age, no refusals, mental capacity, mental health, eligibility and best interests. The assessors have 21 days in which to complete the assessments for a standard authorisation of deprivation of liberty. The 21 days start from the date that the supervisory body receives the request in England, and from the date that the supervisory body instructs the assessors in Wales. Assuming that the equivalents of these assessments have not been carried out within the last 12 months, new assessments will be required.

*Table 11.1   The assessors for the six DoLS assessments*

| Assessments | Persons eligible to assess |
|---|---|
| Mental health | A doctor approved under s12 of the MHA, or a doctor with a minimum of three years post-registration experience in the diagnosis or treatment of mental disorder. Both need to complete a DoLS course provided by RCP |
| Best interests | AMHP, social worker, nurse, OT or psychologist. All need to be two years post-qualification and have completed approved BIA training |
| Age | Anyone eligible to carry out a best interests assessment |
| No refusals | Anyone eligible to carry out a best interests assessment |
| Mental capacity | A doctor approved as a mental health assessor or a BIA |
| Eligibility | A doctor approved as a mental health assessor or a BIA who is also an AMHP |

Notes:  • The mental health assessor and BIA must be different people. Therefore, there will always be two or more assessors.

• England and Wales have different regulations for the DoLS procedure.

# The six assessments

## Age

The person must be, or believed to be, 18 years of age or older.

## No refusals

This assessment requires the assessor to establish if a deprivation of liberty would conflict with any advance or substituted decision-making. This could be an advance decision made by the person refusing all or part of the proposed care and treatment, or a refusal by either a donee (under an LPA) or a deputy appointed by the Court of Protection.

## Mental capacity

The relevant person's capacity must be assessed in relation to the decision about residence in a residential care home or a hospital for the purpose of providing care and treatment. The test for incapacity must be in accordance with sections 1–3 of the MCA; Chapter 9 offers a more detailed description of the test for incapacity. If the person has capacity the DoLS procedure cannot be used.

## Mental health

A doctor must establish if the relevant person has a mental disorder, i.e. "any disorder or disability of the mind" as defined by the Mental Health Act 1983 as amended by the 2007 Act. This will exclude those solely with dependence upon alcohol or drugs, but will include those with a learning disability. The requirement of a learning disabled person to be "abnormally aggressive or seriously irresponsible" does not apply when considering the DoLS procedure. Therefore the MCA may well be used for people with a learning disability who would not be eligible for guardianship (s7) or detention for treatment (s3) of the MHA (see Chapter 4 for more information).

## Eligibility

This requires the assessor to establish if there are requirements placed upon the relevant person that would mean that they are not eligible for DoLS. A patient subject to most forms of detention in hospital under the MHA is not eligible for DoLS. Nor could a deprivation of liberty be granted if it were inconsistent with an obligation placed upon a patient subject to s17 leave of absence, a patient subject to s7 guardianship, s17A community treatment order or conditional discharge. Where a patient requires treatment for mental disorder in a hospital in circumstances that amount to a deprivation of liberty, the decision-maker must determine whether the patient is ineligible for DoLS. To do this, three questions must be addressed: (1) Does the patient require treatment for mental disorder in a hospital? (2) Could the patient be detained under the MHA? (3) Is the patient objecting? If all of these questions are answered in the positive, the patient is ineligible for DoLS and the MHA must be used (see Chapter 10 for more detailed information).

## Best interests

Best interests assessors (BIAs) must satisfy themselves that:

- the person is, or is going to be a detained resident in a care home or hospital. This requires the BIA to establish if the person's care and treatment is, or will amount to, a deprivation of liberty;

- it would be in the person's best interests to be a detained resident;

- it is necessary for the person to be a detained resident to prevent harm to himself; and

- deprivation of liberty is a proportionate response to the likelihood of the person suffering harm, and the seriousness of that harm.

In addition, the BIA will identify a representative for the person, consider any conditions to be attached to the deprivation of liberty, and suggest the length of time for which a deprivation of liberty should be granted. In order to carry out this assessment, the BIA must comply with s4 of the MCA (see Chapter 9 for more information).

As part of the assessment, the BIAs must establish if there is an independent person to be consulted with as part of the process of determining best interests. If they conclude that there is no such person an IMCA must be appointed (see Chapter 16). In addition to the best interest checklist set out at s4 of the MCA, BIAs must also consider the additional factors outlined at E Para. 4.61 of the Code:

- *whether any harm to the person could arise if the deprivation of liberty does not take place;*

- *what that harm would be;*

- *how likely that harm is to arise (i.e. is the level of risk sufficient to justify a step as serious as depriving a person of liberty?);*

- *what other care options there are which could avoid deprivation of liberty; and*

- *if deprivation of liberty is currently unavoidable, what action could be taken to avoid it in the future.*

## Decision

If any of the six assessments is negative, a standard authorisation cannot be given. In this case (assuming it is not seen as practicable to reduce the limitations on the person so that they fall short of deprivation of liberty), consideration should be given to alternative means of lawfully depriving a person of their liberty, e.g. detention under the MHA or a personal welfare order from the Court of Protection. If, however, on written evidence and after proper scrutiny (*LBH v Neary* (2011), see Appendix 6) they are satisfied that all of the assessments are met, the supervisory body must give a standard authorisation, on the prescribed form.

# Urgent authorisation

Where there is not time to gain a standard authorisation, an urgent authorisation may be given by the managing authority itself where a simultaneous request for a standard authorisation is made. This urgent self-authorisation will make lawful the deprivation of liberty whilst the six assessments take place to determine if a standard authorisation can be given. An urgent authorisation may be made in cases of urgency; for example, a deterioration in someone's health requiring immediate care in a care home or hospital in circumstances which amount to a deprivation of liberty, or the need to move someone urgently from one establishment to another, who is already subject to DoLS, but where there has not been time to complete the required assessments before the move takes place. An urgent authorisation should not be used as a general means to authorise a short-term deprivation of liberty. An urgent authorisation may be granted for up to seven days and be renewed for a further seven days. Assessments for a standard authorisation must be completed by the expiry date of the urgent authorisation.

## Effect of an authorisation for a deprivation of liberty

A standard authorisation for a deprivation of liberty cannot exceed 12 months. The BIA should recommend the length of the deprivation of liberty, which should be for the shortest period possible, given the person's particular needs. A further period of deprivation of liberty can be authorised, provided that the six assessments have been met, either afresh or where equivalent assessments have taken place within the previous 12 months. A standard or urgent deprivation of liberty merely authorises deprivation of liberty; it does not give authority to impose other forms of treatment, such as treatment for physical or mental health problems. If such treatment is needed in addition to the deprivation of liberty, usual procedures must take place: assessment of capacity and, dependent upon the outcome of that assessment, establishing if consent can be relied upon or if the authority of s5 of the MCA or detention under the MHA is necessary.

A deprivation of liberty in one establishment is not transferable to another establishment if the person needs to be moved. New assessments would be necessary, or, in cases of urgency, an urgent authorisation may be granted, giving time for the six assessments to be completed.

A person subject to a standard authorisation for DoLS will have a representative appointed for them by the supervisory body. In practice the representative will be selected by the relevant person (the subject of the procedure), where they have capacity to do so, or by the BIA during the assessment process. The representative should maintain contact with the person whom they are representing, they should offer support to that person, they may ask for a review, instigate complaints procedures and make an application to the Court of Protection. Reviews may be at the request of the relevant person, the representative, or as a result of criteria being met for a statutory review, e.g. where one of the six requirements is no longer met. Reviews will generally follow the assessment process, and will involve one or more new assessments being carried out, assuming that a recent equivalent assessment has not taken place. The review may conclude in continued deprivation of liberty, short-term suspension of the deprivation of liberty, or ending of the deprivation of liberty. In addition to a review, the relevant person and their representative have a right to apply to the Court of Protection.

The Code (E Paras 10.2 and 10.3) sets out what questions the court is able to address:

- *whether the relevant person meets one or more of the qualifying requirements for deprivation of liberty;*
- *the period for which the standard authorisation is to be in force;*
- *the purpose for which the standard authorisation is given; or*
- *the conditions subject to which the standard authorisation is given.*

In the case of an urgent authorisation the relevant person, their donee or deputy has the right to apply to the Court of Protection, which is able to address:

- *whether the urgent authorisation should have been given;*
- *the period for which the urgent authorisation is to be in force; or*
- *the purpose for which the urgent authorisation has been given.*

The Court of Protection can make decisions in relation to people subject to a standard or urgent authorisation. They may vary or terminate the deprivation of liberty, or direct the supervisory body or managing authority to vary or terminate the deprivation of liberty. Monitoring the use of the DoLS falls to the Care Quality Commission (see Chapter 15).

*Table 11.2   Restriction of movement compared with deprivation of liberty*

| Restriction of movement | Deprivation of liberty |
|---|---|
| Mental Health Act: | Mental Health Act: |
| s7 guardianship | detention (for example, under sections 2, 3, 4 or via the courts s37) |
| s17A community treatment order (see Chapter 6) | |
| Mental Capacity Act: | Mental Capacity Act: |
| s5 act, complying with the limitations set out at s6 | s16, personal welfare order by the Court of Protection |
| | s4A and Schedule A1 (DoLS provisions) |
| | s4B life-sustaining treatment in certain situations |
| Common law in cases of urgency where the above provisions cannot be instigated because of time limitations, or limitations of the provisions | Common law in cases of urgency where the above provisions cannot be instigated because of time limitations |

# Summary of routes of providing care and treatment with compulsion

Table 11.2 sets out the possible routes to providing care and treatment to people, determined by whether their care and treatment amounts to a restriction of movement or a deprivation of liberty. It is important to remember that one person may require the provisions of both the MHA and MCA to fully and lawfully meet their needs. Chapter 10 addresses the interface between these two Acts.

Guardianship is generally not viewed as a means of depriving a person of liberty, but is a legislative provision to manage patients within the community with a minimum of restraint. However, the requirement of residence under s8 of the MHA would equate to the notion that the person is not free to leave and live where they choose, and so the second element of the acid test is met. If this is the case, decision-makers should question whether the care plan amounts to complete and effective control. If this is the case, and the person lacks capacity to consent to the arrangements, a lawful means of dol should be sought.

# Key points

1. It is important to distinguish between restriction of movement and deprivation of liberty.

2. The DoLS procedure was introduced by the Government in April 2009 to provide a lawful means of deprivation of liberty, complying with Article 5 ECHR.

3. The DoLS procedure covers residential settings as well as hospitals.

4. The DoLS procedure is under the MCA2005 rather than the MHA1983.

5. Any appeal will be to the Court of Protection (not Tribunals).

6. There are six assessments to be carried out by two or more assessors.

7. Assessors for DoLS will require specific training.

8. In an urgent situation a managing authority can self-authorise for a short period.

9. There are plans to replace DoLS with Liberty Protection Safeguards (LPS), extending it to those aged 16 and over, living in supported accommodation, shared lives accommodation and domestic settings. Implementation is intended from 1 October 2020.

# Chapter 12
# Tribunals

## Introduction: the structural reforms

The Tribunal system in England has undergone major structural reform. Under the Tribunals, Courts and Enforcement Act 2007 a new Tribunal framework was established which created two new Tribunals, a First-tier Tribunal and an Upper Tribunal. The Upper Tribunal largely deals with reviews of and hears appeals from the First-tier Tribunal. It also hears appeals from the Mental Health Review Tribunal for Wales (but not reviews). Within the two Tribunals, "chambers" have been created. From 3 November 2008, when most of the amendments to the Mental Health Act 1983 took effect, Mental Health Review Tribunals were abolished as a free-standing legal entity for England, and now sit within a new Health Education and Social Care (HESC) chamber. At the same time the First-tier Tribunal (Health Education and Social Care Chamber) Rules 2008 (see Appendix 2A) replaced the previous Mental Health Review Tribunal Rules. They have been supplemented by Practice Directions (see Appendix 2B), most recently with effect from October 2013, which cover the contents of reports that must be provided to the Tribunal.

In Wales, the Mental Health Review Tribunal remains (known as the Mental Health Review Tribunal for Wales). As noted above, a new appeal right (s78A in MHA1983) has been created to the Upper Tribunal. There are Rules governing its procedure, known as the *Mental Health Review Tribunal for Wales Rules* 2008 (see Appendix 2C). No Practice Direction has been issued for the Mental Health Review Tribunal for Wales. However in *WH v Partnerships in Care* (2015) the court said that it would be desirable for Wales to adopt the English Practice Direction as "the Welsh Rules provided little useful guidance and full reports would have assisted in this difficult case." At Para. 12.15 the Code of Practice for Wales states:

> *Whilst the Practice Direction First-tier Tribunal Health Education and Social Care Chamber: Statements and Reports in Mental Health Cases relates to England only, it may be helpful to use this as the basis for reports produced for the MHRT for Wales.*

## The composition of the Tribunal

The Tribunal taking on the role of the former Mental Health Review Tribunal in England sits within the Health and Social Care Chamber. The members of the Tribunal are appointed by the Lord Chancellor, and fall into three categories: legal members referred to as Judges, medical members who are registered medical practitioners and other members. The third category consists of people who have substantial experience of health or social care matters. Each Tribunal sitting must include at least one person from each category of member. Subject to this requirement, a Tribunal could in theory consist of more than three members. Decisions of the Tribunal are by majority. The Judge is the Tribunal chairman. In the case of a hearing involving a patient subject to a restriction order, the Judge is drawn from a special panel primarily consisting of Circuit Judges. The medical member has a dual role; in addition to being a decision-maker with the other members, he examines the patient before the hearing when this is required. It has been argued that examining the patient in advance means that having reached a provisional conclusion as to the patient's mental state, the medical member runs the risk of approaching the hearing and the evidence to be given at it with a preconceived idea of the outcome, thus breaching the patient's right under Article 5(4) (see Chapter 17). In *R (S) v MHRT* (2002) it was held that so long as the medical member does not form a concluded view as to the patient's mental condition, there will be no prejudice. The substance of the medical member's views should, however, be made known to the patient and his representative at the outset of the hearing to ensure fairness (*R (RD) v MHRT* (2007)).

# The role of the Tribunal

The Tribunal's role is to decide whether at the time of the hearing a patient should remain subject to the relevant compulsory powers of the Mental Health Act, and, if appropriate, to make statutory recommendations. It is not therefore its purpose to decide whether the initial detention was lawful or justified. In fulfilling this role, the Tribunal is ensuring that the patient's right under Article 5(4) to a speedy and effective challenge to his detention is respected (see Chapter 17). It must therefore have the right to discharge patients, including restricted patients, from detention. The remit of Tribunals has been extended to cover community treatment orders under s17A so that such patients, too, can seek their discharge.

The burden of proof before the Tribunal rests on those arguing for the continued use of the compulsory powers in relation to the patient. Until 2001 the reverse was true, and under s72 and s73 the patient had to establish that he was no longer suffering from the mental disorder justifying his continued detention. The court held in *R (H) v MHRT for NE London* (2001) that this was incompatible with the patient's rights under Article 5 and the Government consequently cured the incompatibility by means of a remedial order.

The standard of proof is the balance of probabilities (*R (AN) v MHRT (Northern Region)* (2005) – see Appendix 6). The Court of Appeal stated in this case that "the standard of proof will have a much more important part to play in the determination of disputed issues of fact than it will generally have in matters of judgement as to appropriateness and necessity."

# Applications to a Tribunal

Patients and nearest relatives have certain defined *rights* to apply to a Tribunal. The Secretary of State and the Welsh Ministers have the *discretion* to refer cases to the Tribunal. The hospital managers have an *obligation* to refer certain patients to a Tribunal. These will be looked at in turn. The Reference Guide contains a very helpful set of summaries in grid form of the occasions when patients and nearest relatives may apply and the hospital managers must refer to the Tribunal. They are to be found in the Guide at Figures 13–31.

## The rights of the patient

These are defined in s66. In brief, a patient detained under s2 may apply, but only within the first 14 days of his detention. A patient detained under s3 or subject to guardianship may apply once in the initial six-month period and then once in each subsequent renewal period. A patient subject to a CTO may apply once within six months of the making of the order, once during each period of extension, and also within six months of the revocation of the order. A patient subject to a hospital order under Part 3 is not entitled to apply within the first six-month period, but can do so once in each of the subsequent periods of renewal.

## The rights of the nearest relative

If the responsible clinician issues a barring report under s25 in response to an NR ordering the discharge of a patient detained under s3 (but not s2) or of a CTO patient, the NR has a period of 28 days from the date he or she is so informed within which to apply to a Tribunal. In relation to a patient subject to an unrestricted hospital order under Part 3, the NR may apply during each period of renewal. If the NR is displaced under s29 on the ground either that he has unreasonably objected to an application being made under s3 or s7 or that he has exercised the power to discharge (including from a CTO) without due regard to the welfare of the patient or the interests of the public, he may apply to the Tribunal within twelve months of the county court order. He may apply again once during each further 12-month period the order remains in force.

## The discretion of the Secretary of State and the Welsh Ministers

Under s67, the Secretary of State or the Welsh Ministers may, if they think fit, at any time refer to a Tribunal the case of a patient who is liable to be detained or subject to guardianship under Part 2, or any CTO patient. Anyone may request such a reference and according to the Code of Practice (E Para. 37.46; W Para. 37.41) managers in particular should seek a reference where:

- *a patient's detention under section 2 has been extended under section 29 of the Act pending the outcome of an application to the county court for the displacement of their nearest relative;*
- *the patient lacks the capacity to request a reference, or;*
- *either the patient's case has never been considered by the Tribunal, or a significant period has passed since it was last considered.*

Although expressed as a discretion and not an obligation, this is nevertheless an important safeguard for the patient. Article 5(4) of the ECHR requires there to be the right to a speedy and effective challenge to a detention. The relevance to this right of the role of the discretion of the Secretary of State, of the hospital managers and of the independent mental health advocate (IMHA), and the special safeguards that may be needed to make such a challenge effective for those lacking capacity, was raised in *MH v UK* App'n No 11577/06 (2014) (see Appendix 6 and the discussion in Chapter 17).

## The obligation of the managers

Under s68 the hospital managers are under an obligation to refer patients automatically to a Tribunal in certain circumstances. A reference must be made if six months has passed since the patient was first detained, whether under s3 or s2. In other words, the six months runs from the date of admission under s2 if this preceded an s3, or under s3 if there was no preceding s2. This means that if a patient's s2 is extended by virtue of an application to the court under s29 for displacement of his NR, he will have a referral to a Tribunal six months from his date of admission in any event. The six-month period also runs in respect of s3 patients, whether or not previously detained under s2, who are subsequently made subject to a CTO.

However, this obligation to refer patients automatically does not arise if the patient has himself applied (except while under s2); nor if the NR has applied having been displaced by the court under s29 when his discharge order was barred by the RC; nor if the managers have already made a referral under s68(7) following revocation of a patient's CTO; nor if the Secretary of State (or Welsh Ministers) has exercised his discretion to refer under s67 above.

The managers must also under s68(6) refer unrestricted and CTO patients to a Tribunal if more than three years (one year if under 18) has passed since the Tribunal last considered their cases.

Finally, the managers are obliged to refer a patient to a Tribunal "as soon as possible" after his CTO is revoked (s68(7)). If, before the application is heard, the patient is placed on a CTO again this reference will lapse (Tribunal Guidance Note, August 2010).

These are the principal occasions when applications can or must be made to Tribunals. There are other categories of patient to whom separate provisions apply. See the Figures in the Reference Guide noted above. The Code of Practice at Para. 37.39 (E Para. 37.33) has a similarly useful table relating to the managers' obligations to refer patients at Figure 20.

# Documentation for Tribunals

The statements to be provided by the responsible authority (normally the managers) for the Tribunal under Rule 32(6), and the contents of the various reports required (clinician's, social circumstances, nursing, etc.), including for patients on CTOs, are covered by the Practice Direction (see Appendix 2B). This Practice Direction, which came into force in England on 28 October 2013, is very much more comprehensive and prescriptive than its predecessors. The Responsible Clinician's Report must now include inter alia: a chronology of the patient's involvement with mental health services; factors affecting the patient's understanding or ability to cope with the hearing; details of appropriate available medical treatment prescribed, provided, offered or planned; a summary of the patient's current progress, behaviour, capacity and insight; and, for eligible compliant incapacitated patients, whether the Deprivation of Liberty Safeguards (DoLS) would be appropriate and less restrictive (see Chapter 10). As mentioned above, although there is no equivalent Practice Direction in Wales, the Code of Practice for Wales suggests the Practice Direction in England may be helpful in the preparation of reports. In addition to up-to-date clinical reports, copies of all background papers relating to the patient's detention (including s17 leave forms, consent to treatment papers, managers' hearings decisions and all section papers) must be supplied.

# Proceedings before the Tribunal

The Tribunal has wide powers to regulate its own procedure. It can:

- Require documents to be provided.
- Hold preliminary hearings and adjourn hearings.
- Appoint legal representatives.
- Regulate the use of expert evidence.
- Decide which evidence can be given orally and which in writing.
- Admit hearsay evidence.
- Summon witnesses.
- Regulate the examination of witnesses.
- Decide whether the hearing or part of it should be held in public.
- Proceed with the hearing in the absence of a party.

The following points are worth noting in relation to the Tribunal Rules for England:

- Rule 11 covers Representation. The Tribunal may appoint a legal representative for a patient where

    (a) the patient has stated that they do not wish to conduct their own case or that they wish to be represented; or

    (b) the patient lacks the capacity to appoint a representative but the Tribunal believes that it is in the patient's best interests for the patient to be represented.

    (Note the state's positive obligation to secure Convention rights, including the right to a fair trial under Article 6, to everyone within its jurisdiction.) The issue will continue to arise whether the RC will attend merely as a witness, or as representative of the responsible authority. If the latter, he will have the right to ask questions but there may be implications for his relationship with the patient and indeed with the responsible authority if their views and interests do not coincide.

- Medical examination of the patient before the hearing is covered by Rule 34. This Rule was substantially amended with effect from 6 April 2014. For a patient detained under s2 there must be an examination by the medical member unless the Tribunal is satisfied that the patient does not want it. In other cases there will be no such examination unless:

    (a) the Tribunal is notified by or on behalf of the patient not less than 14 days before the hearing that this is wanted, in which case it will be granted automatically. Otherwise a Tribunal decision will be required; or

    (b) the Tribunal has directed that there must be an examination to enable it to deal with the case fairly and justly; or

    (c) the patient completely fails to attend the hearing, in which case the panel should direct an examination unless this is impractical or unnecessary.

- Rule 14 deals with the withholding of documents. The Tribunal may prohibit the disclosure of documents or information to a person if it is satisfied this would be likely to cause that person or some other person serious harm *and* that it is proportionate to do so, having regard to the interests of justice. In *RM v St Andrew's Healthcare* (2010) (see Appendix 6), even though it was considered that disclosure (that the patient was being covertly medicated) might well cause serious harm to his health, this was ordered in the interests of justice because without it he could not have had a fair hearing. Documents withheld from the patient for this reason can be disclosed to his representative. The Tribunal will rule on the issue of disclosure as a preliminary issue, but in *Dorset Healthcare NHS Foundation Trust v MHRT* (2009) (see Appendix 6) the Upper Tribunal urged the parties to reach agreement without involving the Tribunal and stated that the starting point is that full disclosure of all relevant material should generally be given.

- Rule 38 provides that all hearings must be held in private unless the Tribunal considers that it is in the interests of justice for the hearing to be held in public. In *AH v W London MHT* (2011) (see Appendix 6), bearing in mind the right to a public hearing protected by Article 6 ECHR, this was directed despite the practical problems and expense involved: "Open justice is a right, which does not require justification on a case by case basis. On the contrary it is the exceptions which need to be justified."

- Tribunals cannot usually dispose of proceedings without a hearing. However, under a recent amendment to Rule 35 a patient aged 18 or over subject to a community treatment order (CTO) whose case is referred to a Tribunal by the hospital managers under s68 may state in writing that they do not wish to attend or be represented, in which case the Tribunal can dispense with a hearing and a preliminary medical examination, though it will still call for full reports so it can decide the case on the papers. The responsible clinician must include in the Report to the Tribunal an assessment of the patient's capacity to make such a decision.

# The powers of the Tribunal

Tribunals do not have power to discharge patients detained under s5 (holding powers), s135 or s136 (place of safety); nor may they discharge Part 3 patients remanded under s35 or s36, or subject to an interim hospital order under s38.

The Tribunal has *discretion* under s72 to discharge patients, including CTO and guardianship patients (but not restricted patients), even if the criteria for continued detention are met. However the Tribunal *must* discharge such patients if the relevant criteria for detention under s2, s3, hospital order, CTO or guardianship respectively are not met. Except for a guardianship patient, the Tribunal may defer discharge to a future date. Discharge will take place on or before that date irrespective of whether the proposed community arrangements for the patient have been put into effect. If not discharging the patient from detention, the Tribunal can make a recommendation that the patient be considered for:

- a community treatment order under s17A;

- s17 leave;

- transfer to another hospital;

- transfer into guardianship.

However, the Tribunal has no power to make or insist on a CTO, nor to revoke or vary any of the conditions attaching to an existing CTO. Conditions may not amount to a deprivation of the patient's liberty but any challenge based on alleged consequential unlawful deprivation of liberty must be by judicial review or habeas corpus (see *Welsh Ministers v PJ* (2018) in Appendix 6). Faced with a refusal by the RC to accept and act on a recommendation for a CTO, it is open to the Tribunal to reconvene and discharge the patient (*KL v Somerset Partnership NHS Foundation Trust* (2011)).

The issue whether a patient recently discharged by a Tribunal may lawfully be "re-detained" under the compulsory powers arose in the case of *R (von Brandenburg) v East London and City Mental Health NHS Trust* (2003). This involves consideration of the patient's rights under Article 5(4) of the ECHR (see Chapter 17 and Appendix 6). It is important that the Tribunal gives early and fully reasoned decisions.

**In relation to restricted patients** the Tribunal's powers are set out in s73. It does not have the same overriding s72 discretion to discharge such patients, but can discharge absolutely or conditionally and, if conditionally, it can defer the discharge. In summary:

- if the criteria for continued detention are met, discharge will not be ordered;

- if the Tribunal is not satisfied both that the criteria for continued detention are met and that it is appropriate for the patient to remain liable to be recalled to hospital for further treatment, the discharge must be absolute;

- if the Tribunal is not satisfied that the criteria are met but is satisfied that the patient needs to be subject to recall, the discharge must be conditional. Conditional discharge may be deferred;

- if the Tribunal is minded to make a deferred conditional discharge, it should not make such a decision immediately but should adjourn and monitor attempts to implement the proposed arrangements in the community. There is no absolute obligation on the health authority or any individual psychiatrist to comply with such conditions, but rather an obligation to use their "best endeavours" to implement them. If bona fide attempts to implement the proposed arrangements failed, the Tribunal should then reconvene and either alter or withdraw its original proposed conditions, defer for a further period or decide that the patient remain in hospital. This was explained in *R (IH) v Secretary of State for the Home Department* (2003) (see Appendix 6).

# The appeal process

The appeal process in England may be summarised as follows:

- The Tribunal can *set aside and remake* a decision if in interests of justice and there has been a procedural irregularity such as documents not being sent or received or a party or representative not being present (Rule 45).

- A party can apply for *leave to appeal* a Tribunal decision identifying the alleged errors of law and stating the result sought (Rule 46).

- The Tribunal will then consider under Rule 47 whether to *review* the decision itself under Rule 49 on the basis that there was an error of law.

- If the Tribunal decides not to review or reviews and makes no change, it must then decide whether to grant leave to appeal to the Upper Tribunal.

- If the Tribunal refuses leave to appeal, it must notify the party of the right to apply direct to the Upper Tribunal for leave to appeal (Rule 47).

- The Tribunal can suspend the effect of a decision in the meantime (Rule 5(3)(l)).

- Appeal from the Upper Tribunal is to the Court of Appeal.

Although appeals are on a point of law, this is a less narrow ground than might be imagined. In particular this could include:

- Basing a decision on an incorrect proposition of law.

- Making a decision which was unsupported by evidence.

- Making a decision which no reasonable person acting judicially could have reached.

- Breaching a requirement of natural justice or of a duty to act fairly.

- Taking into account irrelevant matters or not taking into account relevant matters.

- Giving inadequate reasons.

As mentioned above, appeal from the Mental Health Review Tribunal for Wales is to the Upper Tribunal in England.

# Key points

1. There are separate Tribunal systems for England and Wales.

2. Each Tribunal must have a legal, medical and lay member.

3. The medical member will examine the patient before the hearing only in specified circumstances.

4. The Tribunal has to address whether the patient should continue to be detained, based on the situation at the time of the hearing.

5. The burden of proof is on those arguing for the continued detention of the patient.

6. The managers must decide whether to ask the Secretary of State to consider referring a patient to a Tribunal.

7. The managers must refer a patient automatically to a Tribunal if six months have passed since he was detained, including under s2.

8. The RC should consider whether he is appearing as a witness or as a representative.

9. The Tribunal can discharge an unrestricted patient even if the criteria for continued detention are met.

10. The Tribunal can recommend that a patient be placed on a CTO, but cannot order it.

# Chapter 13
## Hospital managers

## Introduction

Hospital managers constitute one of the major safeguards for patients detained under the Act. They have the power to discharge unrestricted detained patients and have the primary responsibility for ensuring that relevant information about the admission and its consequences is given both to patients and nearest relatives amongst others. Their responsibilities, however, go much further than this and have increased over the years, now including CTO patients and ranging from referring patients to Tribunals to ensuring age-appropriate accommodation, etc. for children; from allocating the responsible clinician (RC) for patients to ensuring that the detention is managed in accordance with the requirements of the Act.

Annex B to the Code of Practice for England contains a list of 56 policies, procedures and guidance to be put in place. It is the responsibility of the hospital managers to draw up most of these. The Reference Guide at E Para. 31.5 contains a list (which is "not definitive") of 16 such policies. The Code of Practice for Wales adopts a similar approach at Annex 2.

This chapter will set out who the managers are and who can exercise specific functions for them; it will look in more detail at their functions and how they are carried out.

## Who are the managers?

The effect of the definition of hospital managers in s145(1) is that they are the NHS Trust or foundation trust, or in Wales the local health board (LHB), in which the respective hospital is vested. For an independent hospital they are whoever is registered in respect of the hospital under the Health and Social Care Act 2008.

The legal status of the managers is that of the formal detaining authority of a patient admitted pursuant to an application, which s11(2) states must be addressed to them.

Section 6(2) provides:

> Where a patient is admitted ... to the hospital specified in such an application ... the application shall be sufficient authority for the managers to detain the patient in the hospital in accordance with the provisions of this Act.

This does not mean that the managers are obliged to accept all such applications and there have been occasions where they have refused to admit particular patients, e.g. where there were no beds available or because of the risk the patient would pose to themselves or others on a particular unit. In such situations, the professionals involved have to liaise with the relevant health body on how to resolve the problem. In some cases funding might be found for a private hospital bed.

It follows from their legal status that it is the managers who must ensure that the legal requirements of the Act are observed. As the Code of Practice for England states at E Para. 37.2 (W Para. 37.4):

*In particular, they must ensure that patients are detained only as the Act allows, that their treatment and care accord fully with its provisions, and that they are fully informed of, and are supported in exercising, their statutory rights.*

The managers of the "responsible hospital" (see Chapter 6) have equivalent responsibilities for CTO patients. As a result, the managers have the responsibility for ensuring, through proper admission and scrutiny procedures (see Chapter 5), that the documents on which the admission is based are valid. If they are not valid, the managers must arrange for them to be amended where this is permitted under s15.

# Who can exercise the managers' functions?

The hospital managers' functions can, for the most part, be delegated to officers. However, it is important to note that this does not include the s23 power to discharge, which cannot be exercised by officers or employees – see further details below under "Managers' hearings". However, the NHS Trust or organisation in charge of the hospital retains responsibility for the performance of the managers' functions so delegated, and therefore for the competence of those performing them. The Code of Practice suggests (E Para. 37.11; W Para. 37.10) that a Mental Health Act steering or scrutiny group be established to monitor and review the manner in which the functions are exercised.

# The powers of the hospital managers

## Transfers of patients and CTO patients under s19 and s19A respectively

The Mental Health (Hospital, Guardianship and Treatment) Regulations 2008 ("the Regulations") require all such transfers to be given and recorded in the appropriate prescribed forms (H4 and CTO6 respectively). This is not a matter of simple routine. There is the potential to breach the Article 8 rights of the patient (the right to respect for private and family life – see Chapter 17). So the Code for England emphasises that the needs and interests of the patient (who should be involved in the process) must be considered and the reasons for transfer explained. Every effort should be made to meet the patient's wishes where he or she suggests a transfer. The factors that the Code suggests be considered are set out at E Para. 37.21 (W Para. 37.20):

- *whether the transfer would give the patient greater access to carers, or have the opposite effect;*

- *what effect a transfer is likely to have on the course of the patient's disorder or their recovery;*

- *the availability of appropriate beds at the potential receiving hospital (this does not appear in W37.20); and*

- *whether a transfer would be appropriate to enable the patient to be in a more culturally suitable or compatible environment, or whether it would have the opposite effect.*

The managers of a hospital to which a CTO patient has been recalled may authorise the patient's transfer to another hospital during the maximum 72-hour period of recall (s17F(2)).

## Requests to the Secretary of State to refer patient to MHRT

In *R (MH) v Sec of State for Health* (2005) (see Appendix 6) the House of Lords relied on the existence of the power of the Secretary of State under s67 to refer a patient to an MHRT for its finding that there was no breach under Article 5(4) of the rights of a patient who was unable to make her own Tribunal application when her s2 was extended as the result of an application to displace her NR. It is for the managers to ensure that in such cases the Secretary of State (or in Wales, the Welsh Ministers) is notified of the situation and asked to consider making a reference. In addition the Code (E Para. 37.46; W Para. 37.41) suggests that managers should make a similar request of the Secretary of State where the patient lacks capacity to make the request himself or significant time has passed since the Tribunal last considered the patient's case. This requirement is underlined by the decision of the ECHR when it considered the *MH* case and concluded that because of the need for special safeguards for detained patients lacking capacity, the failure to ensure that a patient detained under s2 was provided with a means of challenging that detention constituted a breach of Article 5(4).

## Post

Section 134 gives persons appointed by the managers for the purpose limited powers in respect of the outgoing post of all detained patients, and in respect of the incoming post of patients detained in high security hospitals. For the latter, they can open and inspect post to decide whether and what to withhold. For incoming post it must be necessary to do so in the interests of the safety of the patient or for the protection of others. For outgoing post it must be likely to cause distress or danger. However, for patients other than those in high security hospitals, outgoing post should not be opened, but merely checked to ensure that it is not addressed to someone who has made a request that it should be withheld. Post to and from certain persons, such as Members of Parliament or Welsh Assembly Members, is exempt from these provisions in respect of all patients. The Care Quality Commission or the Welsh Ministers have powers to review decisions as to withholding of post in high security hospitals and patients must be informed of their right to request a review. Part 7 of the Regulations sets out the procedure for inspection and opening of post.

## Discharge of patients under s23

This is dealt with separately below.

# The duties of the hospital managers

## Information for patients and nearest relatives

Under s132, s132A and s133 the managers are under an obligation to provide certain information to patients and nearest relatives. In respect of detained patients the obligation is expressed as follows in s132, to take:

*such steps as are practicable to ensure that the patient understands*

(a) *under which of the provisions of this Act he is for the time being detained and the effect of that provision; and*

(b) *what rights of applying to a Mental Health Review Tribunal are available to him in respect of his detention under that provision;*

*and those steps shall be taken as soon as practicable after the commencement of the patient's detention under the provision in question.*

This information has to be given both orally and in writing. It may need to be given on more than one occasion. Equivalent information has to be given to CTO patients. Unless the patient requests to the contrary, a copy of the written information should be given to the patient's nearest relative.

The Code of Practice for England in Chapter 4 elaborates on the statutory obligation, suggesting that the information should cover:

1. the rights of the nearest relative to discharge and apply to an MHRT;

2. the reasons for detention or CTO;

3. the CTO conditions and when the patient could be recalled;

4. the length of the detention or CTO and how and when it might be ended, renewed or extended;

5. the legal and factual basis of the detention or CTO;

6. when the patient can be treated without consent, and the role of the SOAD;

7. the rules relating to ECT (where relevant);

8. the managers' power of discharge;

9. the role of the Care Quality Commission;

10. how to obtain assistance in applying to a Tribunal or for a managers' hearing;

11. information about and assistance in making complaints.

Section 133 provides that the managers must, giving at least seven days notice if practicable, inform the NR if a patient is discharged (including where being discharged from hospital on a CTO) unless either has requested otherwise. Part 4 of the Regulations largely covers other occasions when the managers are obliged (unless the patient requests otherwise) to give information to the NR where practicable, in particular on renewal of the patient's detention or his transfer to another hospital, and how that information is to be given. The principles arising from the case of *R (E) v Bristol City Council* (2005) (see Appendix 6) will apply in considering "practicability" in this context. This is made clear in the Code of Practice for England at Para. 4.36 (W Para. 4.40).

In relation to the independent mental health advocacy (IMHA) provisions, there is a requirement under s130D to ensure both orally and in writing that "qualifying patients" (see Chapter 16) understand that help is available from an IMHA and how to obtain it. For a detained patient the responsibility falls on the managers; for other patients, the identity of the person responsible is set out in a grid in the Code of Practice for England at Para. 6.15 (W Para. 6.16) reflecting s130D(2). Written information given to the patient must be copied to the nearest relative unless the patient otherwise requests.

In relation to the various obligations to give information to patients and nearest relatives, the Code of Practice E Para. 4.48 (and in much less detail at W Para. 4.50) advises that the managers should draw up policies to ensure that:

- *the correct information is given to patients and their nearest relatives;*

- *information is given in accordance with the requirements of the legislation, at a suitable time and in an accessible format, where appropriate with the aid of assistive technologies and interpretative and advocacy services;*

- *people who give the information have received sufficient training and guidance and if relevant have specialist skills in relation to people with learning disabilities, autism and/ or children and young people;*

- *a record is kept of the information given, including how, when, where and by whom it was given, and an assessment made of how well the information was understood by the recipient;*

- *a regular check is made that information has been properly given to each patient and understood by them; and*

- *information must be provided in a format and/or language that the individual understands (e.g. Braille, easy read or Moon).*

# Information for victims

The Mental Health Act 2007 amends the Domestic Violence, Crime and Victims Act 2004 by extending the circumstances in which the victim of a violent or sexual offence is entitled to information and to make representations about the discharge and discharge conditions relating to Part 3 patients. Previously, the provisions applied to restricted patients, but the new provisions apply to unrestricted patients as well. In relation to unrestricted offenders the Code of Practice (E Para. 40.19; W Para. 40.18) summarises the statutory minimum information to be communicated to victims as follows:

- whether the patient is to be discharged;

- whether a community treatment order (CTO) is to be made, including allowing the victim to make representations about the conditions attached to the CTO;

- what conditions of the CTO relate to the victim;

- when the CTO ceases;

- when authority to detain the patient expires;

- when the Part 3 patient is discharged, including allowing the victim to make representations about discharge conditions; and

- what conditions of discharge relate to the victim, and when these cease.

In relation to restricted patients, the provision of information to victims is managed by the probation service, not by the hospital managers, and delivered through a victim liaison officer (VLO). The key information to be shared is summarised in the Code of Practice at E Para. 40.13 (W Para. 40.11).

## Allocation of responsible clinician

The managers have the responsibility for ensuring that a detained patient has an RC allocated promptly and that this remains the most appropriate AC to take on this function as the patient's particular needs evolve. At Para. 36.3 the Code of Practice for England (W Para. 36.3) advises that the managers draw up local protocols which should:

- *ensure that the patient's responsible clinician is the available approved clinician with the most appropriate expertise to meet the patient's main assessment and treatment needs;*

- *ensure that it can be easily determined who a particular patient's responsible clinician is;*

- *ensure that cover arrangements are in place when the responsible clinician is not available (e.g. during nonworking hours, annual leave etc.);*

- *include a system for keeping the appropriateness of the responsible clinician under review.*

In relation to a child or young person, the Code of Practice (E Para. 36.6; W Para. 36.6) advises that the responsible clinician should, whenever possible, be a CAMHS specialist.

## References to Tribunals

The managers have an obligation on a number of occasions set out in s68 to refer patients automatically to a Mental Health (Review) Tribunal. These are identified and discussed in Chapter 12.

## Suitable environment for children

Since April 2010, managers have been under a duty to ensure that the environment of all children and young people admitted for treatment of mental disorder is suitable having regard to their age and subject to their needs. This is covered in Chapter 18.

## Other responsibilities

The many other issues in respect of which the Code of Practice for England states that managers should draw up policies include:

1. identifying the second professional who has to agree in writing that the criteria for renewal of a patient's detention under s20 are met (E Para. 32.5; W Para. 32.6);

2. ensuring that the 72-hour period during which a CTO patient is recalled to hospital is not exceeded (E Para. 29.69; W Para. 29.73);

3. ensuring that where a Tribunal or managers' hearing is arranged in relation to a patient who might be entitled to s117 aftercare, the relevant CCG and local authority are informed (E Para. 33.12);

4. ensuring that they are alerted when automatic MHRT referrals are due (E Paras 39.41, 19.110; W Para. 37.35);

5. the action to be taken when a patient or CTO patient goes missing (E Para. 28.11; W Para. 28.11);

6. observation, seclusion and restrictive interventions (E Paras 26.5–26.7, 26.33; W Paras 26.13, 26.29);

7. "blanket" use of locked doors and the impact on each patient (E Para. 8.12; W Para. 8.16);

8. monitoring the use of s4 emergency applications (E Para. 15.11; W Para. 15.15) and s5 holding powers (E Para. 18.39; W Para. 18.33);

9. use of s135 and s136 in conjunction with local authorities and police (E Para. 16.31; W Para. 16.38);

10. ensuring reviews take place before the period of detention or CTO expires (E Para. 38.50; W Para. 38.45).

## Managers' hearings and the power of discharge

As mentioned above, the managers have retained their power to discharge unrestricted patients, including CTO patients and to hold hearings in relation to restricted Part 3 patients, though without the power to discharge them without the agreement of the Ministry of Justice. The importance of this power, and of the independence of their decision-making (from e.g. Tribunals) was recently emphasised by the Court in *South Stafford and Shropshire Healthcare NHSFT v St George's Hospital* (2016). One of the recommendations of the Mental Health Act Review, which reported in December 2018, is that managers should lose this power.

The managers *may* review a patient's detention at any time but *must* review it if the patient's detention is renewed under s20, or if his CTO is extended under s20A. They should *consider* reviewing it if the RC has issued a barring order under s25, and indeed at any time at the patient's request or at their discretion. The Code of Practice states (E Para. 38.13; W Para. 38.10) that in deciding whether to conduct a review where they have a discretion, they are entitled to *"take into account whether the Tribunal has recently considered the patient's case or is due to do so in the near future"*.

In exercising the power to discharge, the managers must consider whether the grounds for continued detention or continued CTO under the relevant section are satisfied. In addition (if the review follows the RC's use of the barring order under s25 to prevent discharge by the NR), they should consider whether the patient, if discharged, would be likely to act in a manner dangerous to other people or to themselves. Dangerousness, which is a more stringent test than the basic risk criteria which refer to health, safety or protection of others, might include psychological as well as physical harm.

Unlike for most of the managers' powers and responsibilities, the function of discharging patients may not be delegated to employees or officers of the Trust. Those appointed are often referred to as "associate managers". The managers' panel must consist of at least three qualifying and authorised people. The Reference Guide has a useful table at Figure 77 setting out in relation to NHS Trusts and other bodies who may exercise the function of deciding whether to discharge.

In reaching a decision, a majority decision to discharge is insufficient, unless the panel comprises more than three people, and at least three decide in favour of discharge.

The managers should be provided with CPA documentation and written reports from the RC and other appropriate professionals, and the patient should normally be given copies.

There is no prescribed procedure for the conduct of managers' hearings. At E Para. 38.34 (W Para. 38.30) the Code of Practice suggests the need to balance informality with rigour and emphasises the following key points:

- *the patient should be given a full opportunity, and any necessary help, to explain why they should be no longer be detained or on a CTO;*

- *the patient should be allowed to be accompanied by a representative of their own choosing to help in putting their point of view to the panel. If the patient lacks capacity to put their point of view their deputy, attorney or other representative of their choosing should be allowed to represent them;*

- *the patient should also be allowed to have a relative, friend, carer, deputy, attorney, or advocate attend to support them; and*

- *the responsible clinician and other professionals should be asked to give their views on whether the patient's continued detention or CTO is justified and to explain the grounds on which those views are based.*

If the renewal or extension of the patient's detention or CTO is uncontested, the managers may decide to consider the case on the papers without a hearing, but the patient should be offered the opportunity to be interviewed by at least one member of the managers' panel.

## Key points

1. The managers are the formal detaining authority for the patient.

2. It is the managers' responsibility to ensure that the procedures and formalities in relation to the patient's admission have been correctly followed.

3. The managers have the power to discharge an unrestricted patient.

4. The managers have to give prescribed information to the patient, including CTO patients, and to nearest relatives.

5. The managers must ensure that a detained patient has the most appropriate responsible clinician at all times.

6. The managers must ensure that the environment is suitable for a patient under the age of 18.

7. Managers must consider whether the Domestic Violence, Crime and Victims Act 2004 applies to this patient.

8. Managers holding hearings may not be employees or officers of the NHS Trust.

9. There is no prescribed procedure for managers' hearings.

10. Consider whether this is an occasion where a managers' hearing must be held.

# Chapter 14

# The nearest relative

## Introduction

The nearest relative is an intriguing figure within the Mental Health Act. They have a number of important functions and yet at times their actions can be blocked, or they may find themselves being denied information about the patient's situation. The situation is probably best summed up by Hale, LJ in *R (S) v Plymouth City Council* (2002), where a patient's mother was seeking information about her son who had been made subject to guardianship under the MHA:

> *Although the identity of the nearest relative is prescribed by statute, the object of the statute is to identify the person with the closest family relationship to the patient. The powers are given to the nearest relative partly for the protection of the patient and partly for the protection of the family which may otherwise face intolerable burdens in looking after him.*

This chapter will explain how to identify the nearest relative, will explain their powers and responsibilities, and will explore some of the issues that arise for the various parties involved. The main impact of the MHA2007 was the introduction of the patient's right to make an application to the county court and the new ground to displace, i.e. where a nearest relative is seen as unsuitable.

## Identifying relatives and the nearest relative

The nearest relative will not necessarily be the person identified by the patient as their next of kin and, indeed, the patient has little control over who will be seen in law as the nearest relative in the first instance. The legal rules governing the process of identifying the nearest relative were designed to meet the aim referred to by Hale above, i.e. that the nearest relative should be the person with the closest family relationship to the patient. However, they do not always achieve this result. It is a complex area of law where many mistakes are made, and legal challenges are not infrequent.

Section 26 includes a list of people who are considered to be relatives under the Act. Having the status of "relative" is of itself important: AMHPs should have regard to any wishes they express (see s13(1A)); it may enable them to apply to the county court for a ruling on a nearest relative issue (see later in the chapter); and being such a relative is a pre-requisite to being the nearest relative (apart from where the court intervenes or where powers are transferred under Regulation 24 in England and Regulation 33 in Wales).

What follows is the list of those relationships which qualify people as relatives for the purpose of this Act. Note that some potentially quite significant relationships (such as cousins) are not listed and are therefore not relatives for the purposes of the MHA.

- Husband or wife or civil partner (this may be someone who has lived as husband or wife or civil partner for at least six months)

- Son or Daughter

- Father or Mother

- Brother or Sister

- Grandparent

- Grandchild

- Uncle or Aunt (if related by blood)

- Nephew or Niece (if related by blood)

- Any other person with whom the patient has ordinarily resided for five years or more.

This last category of people is added by s26(7) as a group to be treated as if they are relatives. It is not uncommon to find that someone in this category becomes the nearest relative because of the preference that is given to anyone ordinarily residing with or caring for the patient at the point when they enter hospital.

For the purpose of making the list, half-blood relationships should be included, illegitimate children should be regarded as the legitimate children of their mothers, and in-law relationships are not to be included. "Illegitimate" is an archaic word and it is somewhat surprising to find it in modern legislation. Given the number of parents who are not married, it immediately poses a problem in identifying relatives. AMHPs are often the first people who have to identify the nearest relative and it is doubtful if many have pursued this issue vigorously in the past. Recent challenges to AMHPs on nearest relative issues (e.g. *TW v Enfield Borough Council* (2014) and *BB v Cygnet Healthcare and Another* (2008)) may encourage AMHPs to be rigorous in their approach to identifying and dealing with nearest relatives. On the question of patients, where the father has never had parental responsibility so that only the mother is considered as a relative, the issue probably continues into adulthood (Hale, 2017), which may cause some problems.

Another odd question which emerges from the list of relatives is: "When aren't aunts aunts?" It would seem that only blood relationships would count here, so that your mother's brother is your uncle, but this uncle's wife is not your aunt for the purposes of the MHA1983. This is a recipe for confusion and mistakes.

If this were not difficult enough, it is then necessary to follow a definite sequence if you are to identify the correct nearest relative.

We will start with the situation where the patient is ordinarily resident in England, Wales, Scotland, Northern Ireland, the Channel Islands or the Isle of Man. If anyone on the list above is not so resident, cross them out, as the Act, in rather dramatic language at s26(5), states that "the nearest relative of the patient shall be ascertained as if that person were dead." If the patient themselves ordinarily resides abroad and is just visiting, then this rule does not apply and the nearest relative could be anywhere in the world. You would just follow the next stages.

## Steps to identify the nearest relative

1. **Cross out** anyone on the list who is under the age of 18 unless they are the patient's spouse, civil partner or parent.

2. **Cross out** the husband, wife or civil partner of the patient if they:

   – *are permanently separated from the patient either by agreement or under an order of a court, or*

    –   *have deserted the patient or been deserted by them for a period which has not come to an end.*

3.   **Circle** anyone on the list who ordinarily resides with **or** cares for the patient (or did so before the patient was admitted to hospital). "Caring for" is a matter of judgement and could include shopping, cooking or providing other care. In *Re D (Mental patient: Habeas corpus* (2000)) the judge stated "the words *'cared for'* were not defined in the Act but they were clear everyday words set in the context where a social worker had to act in a common sense manner." The judge also noted that the word "ordinarily" in subsection 4 applied to "residing with" and not to "caring", so a person may only recently have started providing the care.

4.   If only one person is circled then they are the nearest relative. If more than one person (or no one) is circled then go to:

5.   **Ranking** in order of priority. If more than one person was circled above under (3) then rank only those who were circled. If no one was circled the ranking applies to everyone on the list. The person highest in the list is the nearest relative. If there is more than one person in the same category, then whole blood relatives are preferred to half-blood and then elder is preferred to younger.

Those who have read the passage above and now have some sympathy with AMHPs trying to identify the nearest relative, often in a crisis, may appreciate a further statement from the judge in the *Re D* case (2000):

> *the question the court had to consider in deciding whether the application for detention had been validly made was not whether the social worker consulted with the legally correct nearest relative, but whether the patient's daughter appeared to him to be the correct relative.*

As long as the AMHP takes reasonable steps and also does so in good faith any application will not be invalidated if later information (which had not been known to them) reveals that someone else should have been identified as the nearest relative.

It should be noted that there have been some problems where the applicant or the hospital managers have decided after an admission that the wrong person has been identified as the nearest relative. There are different views as to the correct way to respond to this situation and in such a case the hospital would be well advised to seek a view from their legal advisers.

# Further points on identifying the nearest relative

Some further issues are discussed in this section which may appear odd. Readers should not despair. If the issues result in perverse outcomes, there are usually (but not always) ways of dealing with the situation and a description of these methods follows later.

## Patients on restriction orders

In a judicial review *R v MHRT for West Midlands and North West ex parte H* (2000) it was held that restricted patients do not have a nearest relative. This is because there is no legal function for a nearest relative for such a patient. When compiling reports for Tribunals it is important, therefore, not to refer to anyone as the nearest relative. The person who would otherwise have been the nearest relative may be of significance but they should just be referred to in terms of their relationship with the patient and there should be no heading in the report for the nearest relative's views.

## Children and young people

It is comparatively unusual for children and young persons under 18 to be detained under the Mental Health Act, but it does happen and the numbers have been increasing in recent years. There is a lower age limit of 16 for guardianship but there is no lower age limit for detention. Where admission is considered, the nearest relative will usually be the older parent. However, where a guardian has been appointed under the Children Act 1989 (or is a person named in a child arrangements order as a person with whom the child is to live) then that person will be the nearest relative (see s28). If there are two such people, they share the role. If a local authority is responsible for the child under a care order, then the local authority will be the nearest relative as a result of s27 MHA. In those rare cases where the child is a ward of court, no application for detention may be made without the leave of the court.

## The five year rule

The 1983 Act introduced a new category of persons to be treated as if they were relatives. These are defined in s26(7) as persons with whom the patient has been "ordinarily residing for a period of not less than five years". Together with the preference in s26(4) for making the nearest relative the person whom "the patient ordinarily resides with or is cared for by", this has created some odd situations in practice and some conflict of opinion. A group of young friends who have shared a flat for five years and eat together and share common facilities should probably be included within the meaning of "the patient ordinarily resides with" if one of them is assessed under the MHA. The patient may regard one of their parents as their next of kin and the person they would expect to be their nearest relative, but it would probably be the oldest of their flat mates (unless a blood relative was providing significant care).

Possibly even more controversially, consider someone who has been in an older persons' home with the same group of people for more than five years. Depending on the living arrangements, one or more people may be seen as someone "the patient ordinarily resides with". Assuming none of the other residents is a blood relative, the eldest of this group could be seen as the nearest relative. Again, this will apply even if the patient has blood relatives elsewhere, unless one is "caring for" the patient.

## The patient objects to the nearest relative

In certain situations the Act requires an AMHP to inform, or consult with, the nearest relative where practicable, but this poses a problem where the patient objects to contact (e.g. where there has been abuse) on the grounds that it violates their human rights. Article 8 of the European Convention on Human Rights states that everyone has a right to respect for their private and family life, their home and correspondence.

In the case of *JT v United Kingdom* (2000) (see Appendix 6), JT was detained under s3. She was moved to a secure unit in November 1984 and to a special hospital in 1987. Her detention was subject to periodic review by MHRTs and she was discharged in January 1996. JT complained to the European Commission (the executive branch of the European Union) that she had been unable to change her nearest relative in violation of Article 8. Her nearest relative was her mother, with whom she had had a difficult relationship. JT had wanted to nominate another person so personal information, mainly in relation to MHRTs, was not released to her mother, or to her stepfather (against whom the applicant had made allegations of sexual abuse). The UK Government agreed to amend the law to allow a detainee to apply to the county court to have a nearest relative replaced if the patient reasonably objected to that person acting in that capacity. With the delays in amending the Mental Health Act it took eight years to address the problem and the patient's right to apply to the county court where they consider the nearest relative to be unsuitable is outlined below.

In the meantime in the case of *R v Bristol City Council* (2005) the court had determined that the words "reasonably practicable" allowed the approved social worker (ASW) discretion to decide not to consult the nearest relative in some circumstances where the human rights of the patient were affected. In the particular case (which is set out in Appendix 6) the judge stated that the ASW had discretion to decide not to consult the nearest relative of a competent patient who objected, and whose psychiatrist said that such consultation would be detrimental to the patient's health.

In 2014 this position was amended by the decision in the case of *TW v Enfield Borough Council* (2014). This case focused on the role of the nearest relative in protecting a patient's Article 5 rights. AMHPs will now need to show an awareness of this protective role and where they are not consulting the nearest relative, they would usually be expected to apply to the county court for someone else to take on this function.

The Code of Practice reflects this new position at E Para. 14.61:

> *There may also be cases where, although physically possible, it would not be reasonably practicable to inform or consult the nearest relative because the detrimental impact of this on the patient would interfere with the patient's right to respect for their privacy and family life under Article 8 of the European Convention on Human Rights to an extent that would not be justified and proportionate in the particular circumstances of the case. Detrimental impact may include cases where patients are likely to suffer emotional distress, deterioration in their mental health, physical harm, or financial or other exploitation as a result of the consultation. Consultation with the nearest relative that interferes with the patient's Article 8 rights may be justified to protect the patient's Article 5 right to liberty.*

What follows is an examination of two ways of responding to difficulties.

# Changing or displacing the person acting as nearest relative

## Regulation 24 (England) and Regulation 33 (Wales)

If mentally capable, a nearest relative may authorise someone else to perform their functions under Regulation 24 of the Mental Health (Hospital, Guardianship and Treatment) Regulations 1983. In Wales this would be under Regulation 33 of the Mental Health (Hospital, Guardianship, Community Treatment and Consent to Treatment) (Wales) Regulations 2008. This other person need not be a relative as defined by the Act, but they must not be in one of the categories (such as persons under the age of 18) excluded under s26(5). The authorisation needs to be in writing and copies lodged with the person authorised and with the hospital managers (for detained patients) or the local authority (for guardianship). The procedure may be useful in the circumstances outlined above (where under the five year rule the eldest resident was identified as the nearest relative but did not consider themselves to be the most suitable person to act as such), or in any other cases where both parties are agreeable. This might be any situation where those involved do not feel that the legal nearest relative is the right person to carry out that function. Strictly speaking, the patient does not have a say in this process, which seems unfortunate and one might hope that they would be consulted. If the patient considered the outcome was unacceptable, they could consider applying to the county court in a process we shall now consider.

An application to the county court would also be the correct response where the nearest relative was too ill to authorise someone else under the Regulations.

## The county court (appointing someone to carry out NR functions)

Section 29(2) sets out the county court's powers regarding nearest relatives:

> (2)  An order under this section may be made on the application of –
>> (za) the patient;
>> (a)  any relative of the patient;
>> (b)  any other person with whom the patient is residing (or, if the patient is then an in-patient in a hospital, was last residing before he was admitted); or
>> (c)  an approved mental health professional.
>
> (3)  An application for an order under this section may be made upon any of the following grounds, that is to say –
>> (a)  that the patient has no nearest relative within the meaning of this Act, or that it is not reasonably practicable to ascertain whether he has such a relative, or who that relative is;
>> (b)  that the nearest relative of the patient is incapable of acting as such by reason of mental disorder or other illness;
>> (c)  that the nearest relative of the patient unreasonably objects to the making of an application for admission for treatment or a guardianship application in respect of the patient;
>> (d)  that the nearest relative of the patient has exercised without due regard to the welfare of the patient or the interests of the public his power to discharge the patient from hospital or guardianship under this Part of this Act, or is likely to do so; or
>> (e)  that the nearest relative of the patient is otherwise not a suitable person to act as such.

The last of the grounds (e) was added by the MHA2007 and, combined with the patient's new right to apply to the court, is the Government's response to *JT v United Kingdom* (2000). There had been hopes that the patient might be able to nominate the nearest relative more directly.

Readers who wish to explore what might have been and read an in-depth account of the nearest relative issues may wish to consult *The Nearest Relative Handbook* by David Hewitt (2007).

Where (a), (b) or (e) are the grounds, the court can specify a time limit for the order. If (c) or (d) are the grounds, or where no time limit is set under (a) or (b), the order lasts until the patient is no longer liable to detention or subject to guardianship.

Where (c) or (d) apply, and the patient is already detained under s2, the detention will last until the court reaches a decision. If the decision is to make an order giving someone else the functions of the nearest relative, there is a further seven-day period, which would allow an s3 application form to be completed.

In the case of (e), the applicant can nominate someone that they wish to take on the role if the nearest relative is indeed seen as unsuitable.

## Unsuitability test

Where either the patient or the AMHP decides to apply to displace on the new ground that "the nearest relative of the patient is otherwise not a suitable person to act as such", the question naturally arises as to what would amount to unsuitability. Essentially, it is for the court to decide. Even if the AMHP is not the applicant it may be that the court will ask their opinion.

E Para. 5.14 of the Code (Para. 5.21 in the Welsh Code) gives some guidance on factors that might lead an AMHP to consider that a nearest relative is unsuitable to act as such:

> *any reason to think that the patient has suffered, or is suspected to have suffered, abuse at the hands of the nearest relative (or someone with whom the nearest relative is in a relationship), or is at risk of suffering such abuse;*

> *whether the patient is afraid of the nearest relative or seriously distressed by the possibility of the nearest relative being involved in their life or their care; and*

> *whether the patient and nearest relative are unknown to each other, there is only a distant relationship, or their relationship has broken down irretrievably.*

# Rights and functions of the nearest relative

There are a number of areas where the MHA gives the nearest relative powers or rights and these are summarised in this next section.

## Applying for detention or guardianship

The nearest relative, as well as the AMHP, is able to apply for the patient's detention in hospital under sections 2, 3 and 4 and they can apply for reception into guardianship under s7. However, the Code of Practice suggests at E Para. 14.30:

> *An AMHP is usually a more appropriate applicant than a patient's nearest relative, given their professional training and knowledge of the legislation and local resources. This also removes the risk that an application by the nearest relative might have an adverse effect on their relationship with the patient.*

Then at E Para. 14.32:

> *Doctors who are approached directly by a nearest relative about the possibility of an application being made should advise the nearest relative of their right to require a local authority to arrange for an AMHP to consider the patient's case.*

The number of nearest relative applications each year fell so low that the Department of Health stopped collecting the statistics. The Government had planned to remove this power and rely on the nearest relative's rights under s13(4) as detailed below. A concern that, for whatever reason, an area might find itself with insufficient AMHPs is apparently one of the reasons that changed their minds.

Where the nearest relative is the applicant, s14 requires an AMHP to provide a social circumstances report to the hospital. If the AMHP had earlier refused to make an application, the report is likely to include an account of the reasons for this. The Code of Practice recommends that AMHPs provide assistance but in much more guarded tones than the Code in operation before 2008. E Para. 17.11 states:

*If the nearest relative is the applicant, any AMHP and other professionals involved in the assessment of the patient should give advice and assistance. However, they should not assist in a patient's detention unless they believe it is justified and lawful.*

## Discharging the patient from detention or guardianship

Section 11(3) requires the AMHP to "take such steps as are practicable" to explain to the nearest relative "before or within a reasonable time after an application for the admission of a patient for assessment" that an application is being, or has been, made and of their rights to discharge a patient under s23. In exercising this power, the nearest relative must give the hospital managers 72 hours' written notice of their intention. It would be advisable for the AMHP to explain that the RC may bar this discharge if able to produce within the 72 hours "a report certifying that in the opinion of that clinician, the patient, if discharged, would be likely to act in a manner dangerous to other persons or to himself."

## The right to object to s3 admission or guardianship

The AMHP must not make an application for the detention of a patient under s3 or for reception into guardianship under s7 if the nearest relative objects. Under the provisions of s11(4), the AMHP must consult with the nearest relative before making such an application unless "it appears to the professional that in the circumstances such consultation is not reasonably practicable or would involve unreasonable delay." (See discussion re: Article 8 of the ECHR and *R (E) v Bristol City Council* (2005) above and *TW v Enfield Borough Council* (2014).) Recent cases illustrate the importance of this area of law. See the case summaries in Appendix 6 (*TTM v Hackney BC et al.* (2011) and *BB v Cygnet Healthcare and Another* (2008)).

## The right to an assessment

Under s13(4) it is:

> the duty of a local social services authority, if so required by the nearest relative of a patient residing in their area, to make arrangements under subsection (1) above for an approved mental health professional to consider the patient's case with a view to making an application for his admission to hospital; and if in any such case that professional decides not to make an application he shall inform the nearest relative of his reasons in writing.

Although the section does not explicitly say that an AMHP must carry out a Mental Health Act assessment, it is hard to see how the AMHP could realistically take the case into consideration *"with a view to making an application for his admission to hospital"* without doing so. From a nearest relative perspective, Yeates (2005) has argued that she is very much in favour of the s13(4) right and would use it in preference to seeking to be the applicant. Yeates also argued for the retention of the nearest relative function rather than the proposed "nominated person", as she was concerned about close blood relatives being excluded from Mental Health Act matters. The late change in the Government's plans met her preference while giving the patient the right to seek to displace an NR if they can show that they are "unsuitable".

## Rights to information

Section 132 requires hospital managers to give information about a patient's detention and the legal implications of this to the nearest relative unless the patient objects. Section 132A extends this same principle to the community treatment order. Both sets of Regulations place further requirements on hospital managers to give information.

Section 133 requires hospitals to give the nearest relative seven days' notice of the intended discharge of a detained patient unless the patient or nearest relative has asked for this information not to be given. It would be difficult to see why this would not usually be practicable when considering the use of s17A. This is an area where some hospitals may need to improve their practice in meeting the requirements of s133.

## Key points

1. The NR will usually be identified by the AMHP during an MHA assessment.

2. The rules determining the identity of the NR are complex.

3. The NR is not necessarily the same person as the next of kin.

4. The NR could apply for detention, but such instances are very rare.

5. The AMHP will usually inform or consult the NR.

6. The NR can block an s3 or s7 application but the AMHP may then apply to court.

7. There are circumstances where the NR has power to discharge the patient, but this may be blocked by the RC if the patient is "dangerous".

8. The patient has a right to apply to the county court to replace their NR.

9. There is a ground to displace the NR if they are "unsuitable" to act as such.

10. The NR is entitled to information about the patient in many circumstances.

# Chapter 15

# The Care Quality Commission (England) and the Healthcare Inspectorate Wales

## Introduction

The Mental Health Act Commission was established by the 1983 Mental Health Act. Its over-all function was to keep under review the exercise of powers relating to detained patients. There is a long history of having an independent body to seek to protect the rights of detained patients. Since the development of statutory mental health law in England and Wales, there have been a number of bodies performing similar protective functions. For example, there was a Parliamentary Inquiry into Madhouses in 1815–16, which was followed by the Lunacy Commission and then the Board of Control, both reporting to Parliament.

In April 2009 the Mental Health Act Commission was subsumed within the Care Quality Commission for England, and for Wales the functions of monitoring of the Act were returned to the Welsh Ministers. The Healthcare Inspectorate for Wales performs these functions in practice. Whilst some argue that the new bodies were given greater powers of enforce-ment, others are concerned that there was a loss of focus on the specific situation of detained patients.

This chapter will outline the main functions of the Care Quality Commission and describe how it operates in practice. It will consider some of the issues highlighted in the Commission's most recent Annual Report on monitoring the MHA in 2017–18. Finally, there is a brief summary of its main functions at the end of the chapter together with information on how people can access the Commission. Information on the Healthcare Inspectorate Wales can be found at **www.hiw.org.uk**.

## Statutory basis of the Care Quality Commission

The Health and Social Care Act 2008 received Royal Assent in July 2008 and repealed section 121 of the Mental Health Act 1983. This had established the Mental Health Act Commission. The 2008 Act establishes the Care Quality Commission, which combines the functions of the old Healthcare Commission, the Commission for Social Care Inspection and the Mental Health Act Commission.

# Overall functions of the Care Quality Commission

The CQC has a broad remit in health and social care, including:

- Registering providers of health and social care to ensure that they are meeting the essential standards of quality and safety.

- Monitoring how providers comply with the standards. The CQC gathers information and visits providers if it thinks this is needed.

- Using enforcement powers. This might include fines or public warnings if services drop below essential standards. The CQC has the power to close a service down if necessary.

- Acting to protect patients whose rights are restricted under the Mental Health Act.

- Promoting improvement in services by conducting regular reviews of how well those who arrange and provide services locally are performing.

- Carrying out special reviews of particular types of services and pathways of care, or undertaking investigations on areas where there are concerns about quality.

- Seeking the views of people who use services by involving them in the work of the CQC and publishing a statement on how this is done.

- Telling people about the quality of their local care services to help providers and commissioners of services to learn from each other about what works best and where improvement is needed, and to help to shape national policy.

Some specific mental health functions have been inherited from the Mental Health Act Commission, as below.

# CQC and HIW mental health functions

Section 120 requires:

(1) The regulatory authority must keep under review and, where appropriate, investigate the exercise of the powers and the discharge of the duties conferred or imposed by this Act so far as relating to the detention of patients or their reception into guardianship or to relevant patients.

(2) Relevant patients are –

    (a) patients liable to be detained under this Act,

    (b) community patients, and

    (c) patients subject to guardianship.

(3) The regulatory authority must make arrangements for persons authorised by it to visit and interview relevant patients in private –

    (a) in the case of relevant patients detained under this Act, in the place where they are detained, and

    (b) in the case of other relevant patients, in hospitals and regulated establishments and, if access is granted, other places.

(4) The regulatory authority must also make arrangements for persons authorised by it to investigate any complaint as to the exercise of the powers or the discharge of the duties conferred or imposed by this Act in respect of a patient who is or has been detained under this Act or who is or has been a relevant patient.

(5) The arrangements made under subsection (4) –

    (a) may exclude matters from investigation in specified circumstances, and

    (b) do not require any person exercising functions under the arrangements to undertake or continue with any investigation where the person does not consider it appropriate to do so.

In England, the Mental Health Act Commissioners who used to visit patients have been replaced by Mental Health Act Reviewers. There are less of them and many are full time. In Wales, this function is now performed by Reviewers appointed by the Healthcare Inspectorate.

# Membership of the Care Quality Commission and MHA role

The Chair is appointed by the Secretary of State. There are 15 members of the Board with a Chair, a Chief Executive, chief inspectors and the executive and non-executive directors. People undertaking visiting functions in relation to psychiatric compulsion are no longer called Mental Health Act Commissioners, but Mental Health Act Reviewers.

The CQC role in protecting people who are detained under the MHA is now just one part of their overall role in monitoring, inspecting and regulating mental health services. Since April 2014, the CQC has included a Mental Health Act Reviewer as part of the inspection team for every inspection of NHS services where there are detained patients.

The CQC website states:

> *reviewers make sure that the powers of the Mental Health Act are used properly. Mental Health Act reviewers come from a variety of professional backgrounds, from doctors to lawyers, and are independent of the service providing care. They can visit patients detained in hospital and meet with them in private to find out about their experiences. Where requested, they can also meet patients who are on a community treatment order.*

| *Reviewers can …* | *Reviewers can't …* |
|---|---|
| *Listen to your issues* | *Discharge patients* |
| *Raise problems with ward managers* | *Arrange patient transfers* |
| *Help patients write letters or complain* | *Offer medical advice* |
| *Check paperwork* | *Give legal advice* |
| *Publish reports on wards* | *Arrange leave for patients* |

In 2017–18, Mental Health Act Reviewers met with 3,993 patients (down from 5,937 in 2014–15 and overall there were less visits). The regulatory bodies' annual reports contain their overall findings. The major concerns that have emerged from these visits in recent years are: treatment and medication; choice and access, including food options and ward activities; s17 leave of absence; patient information and rights; how information is provided to patients and other relevant people, privacy, dignity and safety, and patient involvement in care planning.

# Investigating complaints

The CQC and the HIW have duties to investigate complaints concerning detained patients, community patients and those subject to guardianship. These have included: issues with medication, including allegations of inappropriately prescribed medication and or/poor side effects of drugs; concerns with the care and services provided by doctors and nurses (e.g. regarding the detention process, medical professionals not explaining rights, or not providing documents to make an appeal); challenges with taking leave from hospital, including leave not being granted on clinical grounds, or escorted leave being agreed but the patient not being able to take it because there were not enough staff. Safeguarding concerns have included issues or allegations of offences against the person, and allegations of physical or verbal abuse by staff or other patients.

# Second opinion appointed doctors (SOADs)

The CQC and the HIW appoint second opinion appointed doctors (SOADs) to provide second opinions when required by s57, s58 or s58A of the MHA. SOADs are required to give their own independent judgement on whether treatment proposed by the AC should go ahead. In *R (on the application of Wooder) v Fegetter and the Mental Health Act Commission* (2002) it was decided that the SOAD owes a duty to give reasons for his opinion in writing to the AC together with any opinion he may have on the desirability of withholding them from the patient on "serious harm" grounds. Unless the AC agrees that these grounds exist, he will give the information to the patient.

The English Code of Practice at para. 25.60 describes the role of the SOAD as follows:

> *The SOAD's role is to provide an additional safeguard to protect the patient's rights, primarily by deciding whether certain treatments are appropriate and issuing certificates accordingly. Although appointed by the Commission, SOADs act as independent professionals and must reach their own judgement about whether the proposed treatment is appropriate.*

E Para. 25.61:

> *When deciding whether it is appropriate for treatment to be given to a patient, SOADs are required to consider both the clinical appropriateness of the treatment to the patient's mental disorder and its appropriateness in the light of all the other circumstances of the patient's case.*

E Para. 25.62: SOADs should, in particular:

- *seek to understand the patient's views on the proposed treatment, and the reasons for them. This includes involving an advocate, carers or making any reasonable adjustments, as appropriate;*
- *give due weight to the patient's views, including any objection to the proposed treatment and any preference for an alternative;*
- *consider the appropriateness of alternative forms of treatment, not just that proposed;*
- *balance the potential therapeutic efficacy of the proposed treatment against the side effects and any other potential disadvantages to the patient;*

- *take into account any previous experience of comparable treatment for a similar episode of disorder; and*

- *give due weight to the opinions, knowledge, experience and skills of those consulted.*

# Annual Report on Care Quality Commission mental health functions

The Mental Health Act Commission used to produce a Biennial Report for Parliament and this provided an invaluable critique of mental health services. Section 120D now requires the regulatory authorities to produce an Annual Report on their activities and the exercise of their functions under the Mental Health Act. The CQC's first such report was published in October 2010.

## Contact details

CQC (Mental Health Act)

Citygate

Gallowgate

Newcastle

NE1 4PA

Tel: 03000 616161

Healthcare Inspectorate Wales

Bevan House

Rhydycar Business Park

Merthyr Tydfil

CF48 1UZ

Tel: 0300 062 8163

# Key points

The regulatory bodies are the Care Quality Commission for England and the Healthcare Inspectorate Wales.

In briefest summary, the Care Quality Commission's functions are to:

1. review the working of the MHA1983 for detained patients and those subject to CTOs or guardianship;

2. visit and interview, in private, detained patients and those subject to CTOs or guardianship;

3. investigate complaints;

4. appoint SOADs;

5. review decisions to withhold mail of patients detained in high security hospitals;

6. produce an Annual Report for Parliament;

7. monitor the Code of Practice and propose amendments to Ministers;

8. offer advice to Ministers on matters falling within the Commission's remit.

Note: The Care Quality Commission also has a role in monitoring DoLS.

# Chapter 16

## Independent mental health advocates

## Introduction

The Mental Health Act 2007 introduced a new role, that of the independent mental health advocate (IMHA). An advocate is available for most detained patients, patients subject to CTOs or guardianship, and patients for whom treatment under s57 and s58A are under discussion. The scheme in Wales extends beyond the English equivalent. This chapter will examine the background to this service and will then consider the legal basis for it and how it operates in practice. The scheme was implemented in Wales in November 2008, which is earlier than in England where it was not implemented until April 2009. The chapter will conclude with an outline of the independent mental capacity advocate (IMCA) scheme and how this links with the Mental Health Act and IMHAs.

## Background to the IMHA scheme

The provision of mental health advocacy in England and Wales had been developing in the years before 2007 but it was still variable. A Welsh Assembly report considered that there was adequate provision in in-patient settings, but less than adequate provision within the community. It stated that:

> the nature of mental health advocacy services was also very variable. It could be provided by volunteers, paid staff or peer advocates and it was often funded to meet the needs of specific groups of service users, such as:
>
> • people with mental health problems in the community
>
> • patients in specific psychiatric in-patient units
>
> • patients in forensic settings.

(Welsh Assembly, 2008, p4)

The White Paper *Reforming the Mental Health Act* (Department of Health, 2000) recognised that specialist advocacy services should be provided for detained patients. This was followed by a project linked with Durham University, which was subject to a national consultation exercise in both England and Wales. Despite some problems in the intervening years, these proposals eventually formed the basis of the proposed IMHA provision. An example of the need for advocacy could be found in the Kerr/Haslam Inquiry, which reported in 2005.

### The Kerr/Haslam Inquiry

In 2000 and then 2003 two consultant psychiatrists, who worked in the same psychiatric hospital in York during the 1970s and 1980s, were convicted on several counts of indecent assault.

The victims were all vulnerable female psychiatric patients who had gone to their consultants for treatment, seeking help. The patients of Kerr and Haslam made complaints but then went on to withdraw them or declined to pursue matters. The Inquiry concluded that had someone been readily available to step in at the beginning (referred to in the report as "patient champions") to offer support and mentoring, to refer the patients for appropriate assistance, and to ensure that any investigation was appropriate to their vulnerabilities, the Inquiry might have been unnecessary.

The Inquiry concluded that:

> in relation to disclosures of alleged abuse, voluntary advocacy and advice services (independent of the NHS) should be supported by central public funding to offer advice and assistance to patients and former patients (particularly those who are mentally unwell, or who are otherwise vulnerable).
>
> (Department of Health, 2005, p26)

# The legal basis for the IMHA scheme

Section 130A requires local authorities in England to make such arrangements as they consider reasonable to enable independent mental health advocates to be available to help qualifying patients. Section 130A includes the principle that any help available to a patient under the arrangements should, so far as practicable, be provided by a person who is independent of any person who is professionally concerned with the patient's medical treatment.

A patient in England is a qualifying patient if he is liable to be detained on any section that lasts longer than 72 hours or is subject to guardianship or is a community patient (someone subject to a CTO). An informal patient will also qualify for an advocate if he discusses with a doctor or approved clinician the possibility of being given a form of treatment to which s57 applies, or, not having attained the age of 18 years, he discusses with a registered medical practitioner or approved clinician the possibility of being given a form of treatment to which s58A applies (ECT). The IMHA scheme has a wider application in Wales, where it was expanded by Part 4 of the Mental Health (Wales) Measure 2010 (the Measure). This brings patients who are not detained but who are patients receiving assessment or treatment for mental disorder in hospitals in Wales within the scope of the IMHA service.

Section 130B states that advocacy should include help in obtaining information about and understanding:

- the relevant sections of the Act and any conditions or restrictions on the patient;
- details of any medical treatment and why it is being given, proposed or discussed;
- the authority under which it is, or would be, given and any further requirements.

Then, in order to act on this, the patient should be offered help with information on any rights which may be exercised and help, by way of representation or otherwise, in exercising those rights.

If the patient consents to this, then under s130B(3):

> For the purpose of providing help to a patient in accordance with the arrangements, an independent mental health advocate may –
>
> (a) visit and interview the patient in private;
>
> (b) visit and interview any person who is professionally concerned with his medical treatment;

(c) require the production of and inspect any records relating to his detention or treatment in any hospital or registered establishment or to any aftercare services provided for him under section 117 above;

(d) require the production of and inspect any records of, or held by, a local social services authority which relate to him.

(4) But an independent mental health advocate is not entitled to the production of, or to inspect, records in reliance on subsection (3)(c) or (d) above unless –

(a) in a case where the patient has capacity or is competent to consent, he does consent; or

(b) in any other case, the production or inspection would not conflict with a decision made by a donee or deputy or the Court of Protection and the person holding the records, having regard to such matters as may be prescribed in regulations under section 130A above, considers that –

(i) the records may be relevant to the help to be provided by the advocate; and

(ii) the production or inspection is appropriate.

# Code of Practice Guidance (Wales)

The revised Welsh Code of Practice was implemented in 2016. Not only is the scheme more extensive in Wales than in England, but there is more guidance in the Code. For example at W Para. 6.6, there is an extensive list of situations in which IMHAs might support patients to ensure that they can participate in decisions about care and treatment:

- *attending meetings with the patient to discuss their care and treatment;*
- *attending meetings at the patient's request and on their behalf (subject to the consent of the mental health professional who is convening the meeting);*
- *supporting the patient in exploring alternatives to the proposed treatment;*
- *supporting the patient in understanding their rights of appeal;*
- *supporting the patient in applying to and obtaining legal representation for the Mental Health Review Tribunal for Wales (MHRT for Wales) or hospital managers' hearings, and in attending these if requested;*
- *supporting the patient in understanding and following up the decisions or directions made by the MHRT for Wales or hospital managers;*
- *supporting the patient in understanding their rights regarding their nearest relative;*
- *supporting the patient in understanding, applying to and obtaining legal representation for county court hearings;*
- *supporting the patient in raising concerns or in accessing the relevant complaints process about any aspect of their hospital or community treatment order experience;*
- *supporting the patient in accessing relevant records;*
- *supporting the patient over the provision of appropriate aftercare;*
- *signposting other services to the patient and vice versa.*

The detailed guidance in the Code covers providing support to qualifying patients who cannot instruct the advocate, visits and interviews, providing information about the service, etc. There is a grid at W Para. 6.26 which sets out who would be responsible for informing qualifying patients in various circumstances.

# Code of Practice Guidance (England)

The 2015 edition of the Code states at E Para. 6.6:

> To ensure that IMHA services reflect the diversity of the local population and that they are as independent as possible, they are commissioned by local authorities, as follows:
>
> • for detained patients, by the local authority for the area in which the hospital in which they are detained is located;
>
> • for community treatment order (CTO) patients, by the local authority for the area in which their responsible hospital is located;
>
> • for people subject to guardianship, by the local authority which is acting as the guardian or, if the patient has a private guardian, by the local authority for the area in which the private guardian lives.

It continues to state that patients are eligible for support from an IMHA, irrespective of their age, if they are: detained under the Act; liable to be detained under the Act, even if not actually detained, including those who are currently on leave of absence from hospital or absent without leave, or those for whom an application or court order for admission has been completed; conditionally discharged restricted patients; subject to guardianship; or patients subject to community treatment orders (CTOs).

There was more emphasis in the 2015 Code on the importance of the IMHA. This may, to some extent have been influenced by the undoubted impact IMCAs had had on the Mental Capacity Act in the preceding years. The CQC then decided to focus on the role in 2015.

# The IMHA scheme in practice

For several years leading up to 2015, CQC reports had highlighted concerns with provision and access for patients, as well as the understanding of staff working with detained patients on how and when to refer to the IMHA service. The English Code of Practice implemented in April 2015 advises hospitals to make sure patients have an opportunity to meet an IMHA so they can explain to the patient what the service can offer. In the first three months of 2015, the CQC carried out a survey to see how ready services were to implement the new Code of Practice especially with regard to the IMHA service. They asked ward managers how they monitored IMHA provision. Of 200 wards, fewer than one in five monitored referrals and IMHA contacts. Fifty-eight per cent of all ward managers said that they automatically referred patients who lacked capacity to an IMHA service. Of the remaining 42 per cent, managers told us the decision to refer a patient would be made in multidisciplinary reviews of care plans, or was subject to whether it was in the patient's best interests.

In almost 40 per cent of wards visited, staff had not received training on the IMHA service or how to refer a patient to that service. In some of these cases the CQC was told that, because the hospital's MHA administrator had been given the responsibility for managing IMHA referrals, it was not considered necessary to train other staff on IMHA. The CQC's view is that all staff involved in the clinical care of eligible patients should receive training on IMHA, to make sure that they understand their role and that they recognise when patients need to be referred. They expect training on IMHA to be a part of routine training on the Act for staff, particularly in relation to their duties to provide patients and relatives with information.

The CQC stated that it would issue requirement notices or take enforcement action where providers have failed to put in place systems that enable staff to support the important IMHA role. The scheme itself received a significant boost from the 2015 Code of Practice.

# Independent mental capacity advocates (IMCAs) under the Mental Capacity Act

There is a risk that this similarly named scheme might be confused with the IMHA system. There are some areas where this Mental Capacity Act service may be relevant to patients who are also covered by the Mental Health Act, but in most situations where a patient has an IMHA they will not be eligible for an IMCA. For example, IMCAs do not become involved in Part 4 or 4A treatment issues, although they may be involved in serious treatment issues for informal patients. Similarly, they would only be involved in accommodation issues for a patient who was not subject to compulsion under the Mental Health Act. Conversely, they may well be involved in the deprivation of liberty procedures under the Mental Capacity Act (see Chapter 11).

The IMCA service has been available in England and Wales since 2007 so staff should know how to contact the service. The service is limited to specific situations and the amount of time allocated for an IMCA to make a decision is also limited. Most people who lack capacity to make an important decision (for example, about treatment or where to live) will have family or friends who will be consulted by any decision-maker because of the requirements of the Mental Capacity Act. The IMCA service is for people who lack such people to help represent them.

Money is allocated to local authorities (in England) and local health boards (in Wales) so that they can commission IMCA services. Advocates are trained to provide what is, in effect, non-instructional or "best interests" advocacy. This is where an advocate represents what they consider a person's wishes would be, if they were able to express them. This is a new area for many advocates, who are more used to working with people who can clearly express what they want.

The role of the IMCA is summarised by the MCA Code of Practice at Chapter 10, as to:

> help particularly vulnerable people who lack the capacity to make important decisions about serious medical treatment and changes of accommodation, and who have no family or friends that it would be appropriate to consult about those decisions. IMCAs will work with and support people who lack capacity, and represent their views to those who are working out their best interests.

The role of the IMCA is to support and represent the person concerned, to ascertain their wishes and feelings and to check that the Act's principles and best interests checklist are followed. The IMCA cannot veto certain decisions, but the relevant authority must take into account any information or submissions provided by the IMCA. If the IMCA is very concerned that the person's best interests are not being followed, the IMCA could challenge a decision by going to the Court of Protection.

# Key points

1. The IMHA scheme came into effect in Wales in November 2008 and in England in April 2009.

2. People should not confuse IMHAs (MHA1983) with IMCAs (MCA2005).

3. Some patients may require both an IMHA and an IMCA.

4. IMHAs provide any patients subject to compulsion under the Mental Health Act (under a section that lasts more than 72 hours) with an explanation of:

    (i) the relevant sections of the Act and any conditions or restrictions on the patient;

    (ii) details of any medical treatment and why it is being given, proposed or discussed;

    (iii) the authority under which this treatment is, or would be, given as well as any further requirements.

5. An IMHA would help the patient to exercise any rights in relation to these issues.

6. Readers in Wales can check for details on the Welsh Government website, which can be found at: **www.wales.gov.uk**.

7. The revised Codes of Practice for both England and Wales place new emphasis on the importance of the IMHA service.

# Chapter 17
## Human Rights Act implications

## Introduction

References are made throughout this book to the Human Rights Act 1998 ("HRA") implications of various provisions in the Mental Health Act. In this chapter a brief overview of the HRA will be given, followed by an outline of the main Articles of the European Convention on Human Rights ("the Convention") and some leading court cases. We will then identify and discuss some of the current uncertainties and challenges. As mentioned in Chapter 3, the new Codes of Practice have a considerably enhanced and consistent focus on human rights which is entrenched in the guidance. The relevance of Article 8 in particular to the care and treatment of those detained under the Act is ever present. This is unsurprising, given that hardly a case comes before the courts involving an issue of practice within the mental health field in which neither the main nor at least a subsidiary issue is whether there has been a breach of an individual's rights under the Convention. The issues, decisions and implications of a number of the most significant cases are summarised in Appendix 6. The Convention rights as they apply in England and Wales are set out at Appendix 5.

## Overview of the Human Rights Act 1998

The HRA took effect in England and Wales in October 2000. However, it is important to understand that the Act did not create any new, substantive "human rights". The UK has been a signatory to the Convention since the early 1950s and the Act is largely procedural, allowing (by incorporating the Convention into United Kingdom law) alleged infringements of the Convention to be brought directly before the United Kingdom courts. The Government referred appropriately to the effect being to "bring rights home".

The HRA provides that it is unlawful for a public authority to act in a way which is incompatible with a Convention right. Although "public authority" is not defined, it includes anyone "certain of whose functions are functions of a public nature". Thus health and social care professionals carrying out their obligations under the Mental Health Act are almost certainly individually "public authorities" and caught by the provisions of the HRA.

Courts are required to construe legislation, if possible, in a way which is compatible with Convention rights. In practice this means that where there are different possible interpretations of a provision in, for example the Mental Health Act, the court will, if it can, adopt one which does not infringe Convention rights. The case of *R (E) v Bristol City Council* (2005) (see Appendix 6) is one such example. To interpret the words "reasonably practicable" in relation to the obligation of the ASW (now AMHP) under s11(4) of the Act to consult with the nearest relative as meaning "appropriate" rather than that the nearest relative was "available", would avoid a potential infringement of the patient's rights under Article 8 where the patient had a strong wish that the nearest relative should not be consulted. This was the construction adopted by the court. In *TW v Enfield BC* (2014), the court emphasised the need to balance the patient's Article 8 rights with his rights under Article 5 not to be deprived of his liberty arbitrarily or otherwise than in accordance with a procedure prescribed by law, which might justify a breach of Article 8 (see Code of Practice E Para. 14.61; W Para. 14.53).

If it is not possible for the court to interpret a statute compatibly with a person's Convention rights, it cannot disapply the provision in question because Parliament and not the court is sovereign. However, it can do so in respect of subordinate legislation such as a statutory instrument (e.g. the Mental Health (Hospital, Guardianship and Treatment) (England) Regulations 2008).

Faced with a statutory provision which is incompatible with a person's Convention rights, the court can make a "declaration of incompatibility". Then one of two things can happen. The Government can make use of the "fast track" procedure of the HRA to introduce a "remedial order" and thereby amend the legislation in question. Alternatively the Government might take no action, in which case the legislation remains unaltered.

An example of a case in which a declaration of incompatibility was made which was followed by a remedial order is *R (H) v MHRT for NE London* (2001). Here the court stated that to place on the patient the burden of establishing before an MHRT that the criteria for continued detention were no longer met was incompatible with his Convention rights. A remedial order followed quickly, reversing the burden of proof. On the other hand, the declaration of incompatibility made in the case of *R (M) v Sec of State for Health* (2003), which followed the European Court of Human Rights' ruling in *JT v UK* (2000) that the inability of a patient to apply to court for the displacement of his nearest relative was in breach of his Convention rights resulted in no such remedial order. The incompatibility was not addressed until the Mental Health Act 2007 introduced the limited right of the patient to apply to the court under s29 (see below and Chapter 14).

It is the obligation of States to "secure to everyone within their jurisdiction" the Convention rights. These rights are not for people to opt into. This is a positive obligation of Government. For example, it would be no answer to an allegation of breach of the Article 2 right to life of a patient committing suicide for the NHS Trust or the health and social care professionals to argue that they were not themselves directly responsible for the death and therefore for the breach, if they had not taken reasonable steps to minimise the possibility of the patient harming himself. The scope of this positive obligation includes patients formally detained under the Mental Health Act (see *Savage v South Essex Partnership NHS Foundation Trust* (2008) (Appendix 6)) and even informal patients, depending upon the presence of relevant factors such as the vulnerability of the patient, the nature of the risk (e.g. of self-harm) and the assumption of responsibility by the NHS Trust concerned (see *Rabone v Pennine Care NHS Trust* (2012)). In *LBH v Neary* (2011) (see Appendix 6), a DoLS case, the court emphasised that it was not enough that a person could apply to the Court of Protection if so minded: the supervisory body must enable and *ensure* that this took place.

The Convention rights, although traditionally divided into qualified and non-qualified rights, are in practice rarely absolute. If a Convention right under Article 8 has been breached, the issue will usually be whether this was justified on the basis that it was lawful, intended to pursue a legitimate aim, necessary in a democratic society, non-discriminatory and proportionate.

Almost always the court is required to undertake a balancing act, as different Convention rights may exist in a situation facing a single individual. Similarly, individuals in conflict with one another may both have Convention rights "engaged" by a set of circumstances. A terminally ill patient's right to life under Article 2 and to treatment to prolong it may be in conflict with his right under Article 3 not to be subjected to futile measures constituting inhuman and degrading treatment. In the case of conjoined twins, each will have the same Article 2 right to life potentially at risk from an operation to separate them. A parent has a right under Article 8 to make decisions as to the treatment his child should receive; but the child has a right to life which might be put at risk by a parent's decision, for example, to refuse a blood transfusion.

A policy of force-feeding a prisoner may under the Convention legitimately be regarded as upholding the positive obligation to preserve life or as subjecting him to inhuman and degrading treatment under Article 3.

The Convention is a "living instrument". This means that although courts are required to have regard to the case law of the European Court of Human Rights, caution is required as it is possible to reinterpret the Convention in the light of changing social conditions, opening the way to a different decision being reached on the same or similar facts in the future.

# The main Convention articles

**Article 5** of the ECHR provides that

> *Everyone has the right to liberty and security of person. No one should be deprived of his liberty save in the following cases and in accordance with a procedure prescribed by law …*
>
> *the lawful detention of … persons of unsound mind.* (Art 5(1)(e))
>
> *Everyone who is deprived of his liberty by arrest or detention shall be entitled to take proceedings by which the lawfulness of his detention shall be decided speedily by a court and his release ordered if the detention is not lawful.* (Art 5(4))

This raises a large number of significant issues:

1. What is the meaning of "deprivation of liberty"? This vexed issue is discussed in detail in Chapter 11. Only deprivation of liberty is covered by Article 5 – mere restrictions of movement are not. The Mental Capacity Act prior to the introduction of the DoLS did not allow deprivation of liberty without an order of the Court of Protection under s16. The meaning and application in various contexts of the "acid test" of deprivation of liberty expounded in the Supreme Court's decision in *Cheshire West* (2014) – that a person is (for a non-negligible period of time) under continuous supervision and control and not free to leave – is in the process of being worked out in subsequent and not yet always consistent case law. This "objective" element is just one of the three elements required for Article 5 to be engaged. The other two, the "subjective" element (i.e. whether the person has with capacity validly consented to restrictions which would otherwise amount to a deprivation of liberty), and the "imputable (directly or indirectly) to the state" element are equally subject to case law developments which are not at the time of writing always easy to reconcile.

2. What in this context is a "lawful" detention? The case of *Winterwerp v Netherlands* (1979) established that as a minimum:

   - A person must be reliably shown to be suffering from a true mental disorder, based on objective medical expertise, save in emergencies.

   - The mental disorder must be of a kind or degree justifying compulsory confinement.

   - Continued confinement must be justified on the basis of the persistence of the disorder.

3. What is "unsoundness of mind"? Although this is undefined in the Convention, it is to be distinguished from "behaviour deviating from society's norms" – in other words there must be a true mental disorder, established on the basis of objective medical expertise.

4. Is the deprivation of liberty authorised by a "procedure prescribed by law"? This was one of the issues in *HL v UK* (2004) where the patient was detained on the basis of the common law doctrine of necessity, which the European Court held was arbitrary and unlawful because no procedure was either prescribed or followed (unlike a detention under the

provisions of the Mental Health Act). The "Deprivation of Liberty Safeguards" procedure (DoLS) under the Mental Capacity Act needs to be seen in this light – a response to the decision in *HL v UK* characterised by a new procedure which, if followed, would render the detention lawful. It is concerned with establishing a new lawful procedure rather than introducing substantive new patient safeguards, although the patient may incidentally benefit from increased attention from health and social care professionals during the process. The paucity and potential weakness of DoLS safeguards was recognised by the court in *Neary* (see Appendix 6) which inter alia established that a supervisory body had to scrutinise DoLS assessments and not automatically grant authorisations when it received six positive assessments. This development of the DoLS safeguards was subsequently taken further in *AJ v A LA* (2015) and *Re RD et al.* (2016) (see Appendix 6).

5.  A patient lawfully detained must under Article 5(4) above have the right to a means of speedy and effective challenge. Again this was missing in the case of the common law detention in *HL v UK*, which did not provide, for example, for applications to Mental Health Review Tribunals, nor for discharge by the nearest relative.

6.  Any challenge to a patient's detention must be speedy. A delay in a Mental Health Review Tribunal hearing could give rise to a breach of Article 5(4), even if the Tribunal eventually decided against discharge; the infringement is not of any right to be discharged but of the right speedily to challenge the detention.

7.  Any challenge to a patient's detention under Article 5(4) must be effective, i.e. "his release ordered if the detention is not lawful". In what circumstances then may a patient recently discharged by a Tribunal be lawfully re-detained under the Mental Health Act? This was one of the issues in *R (von Brandenburg) v East London and City Mental Health NHS Trust* (2003) (see Appendix 6). The health and social care professionals argued that they had a continuing obligation to consider the use of the compulsory powers under the Mental Health Act, which did not end with discharge ordered by the Tribunal. The patient argued that if he were to be re-detained immediately after discharge that would be to undermine fatally his right under Article 5(4) to an effective challenge to his detention. The House of Lords held that there would be no necessary infringement of Article 5(4) if the ASW (now AMHP) bona fide believed that they had information not known to the Tribunal which placed a significantly different complexion on the matter, and gave a number of examples, such as a decision being made by the Tribunal in ignorance of an earlier serious suicide attempt.

8.  Article 5 refers to detention, not treatment. There is no right to specific treatment conferred by the Convention, but where detained the patient is entitled to be placed in a "therapeutic environment" which in *Aerts v Belgium* (2000) (see Appendix 6), for example, the prison hospital wing was held not to constitute.

**Article 3** provides that:

> *No one shall be subjected to torture or to inhuman or degrading treatment or punishment.*

Attempts have been made to argue that various psychiatric practices constitute inhuman and degrading treatment. Most have failed because although the courts have conceded that there might in theory be circumstances where the argument would succeed they have set the threshold high. It was argued unsuccessfully in the House of Lords in relation to seclusion in *R (Munjaz) v Mersey Care NHS Trust* (2005). However when this case reached the ECHR under the title *Munjaz v UK*, the Court did not rule out the possibility that seclusion might amount to a breach of a patient's residual right to liberty under Article 5, as had indeed been held by the minority in the House of Lords. In relation to forcing treatment on a capable but refusing patient suffering from mental disorder, while the medical necessity for the treatment to be given must be convincingly established, a measure which is a "thera-peutic necessity" will not generally be regarded as inhuman or degrading (*Herczegfalvy v Austria* (1992)).

One significant case in which the threshold was reached was that of *Keenan v UK* (2001), in which it was held that the lack of effective monitoring of a prisoner known to be suffering from serious long-standing mental disorder and the failure to provide him with informed psy-chiatric input might amount to inhuman and degrading treatment. Treatment falling short of being inhuman and degrading might nevertheless constitute a breach of Article 8 and might need to be justified under Article 8(2) (see below).

Another was *MS v UK* (2012) (see Appendix 6) in which an extremely mentally ill person was detained under s136 and kept in a police cell for a period in excess of the then maximum 72 hours without receiving treatment. This itself constituted inhuman and degrading treatment. The Policing and Crime Act 2017 reduced this maximum period to 24 hours (extendable in some circumstances by up to a further 24 hours) (see Chapter 5).

**Article 8** provides that:

> *Everyone has the right to respect for his private and family life, his home and his correspondence.* (Art 8(1))

> *There shall be no interference by a public authority with the exercise of this right except such as is in accordance with law and is necessary in a democratic society in the interests of national security, public safety or the economic well-being of the country, for the prevention of disorder or crime, for the protection of health or morals or for the protection of the rights and freedoms of others.* (Art 8(2))

The rights set out at Art 8(1) are extremely broad and would inter alia be engaged by the following issues:

1. A patient's right to confidentiality.
2. A patient's right to autonomy in respect of medical treatment decisions; e.g. not to have treatment forced upon him if refusing with capacity.
3. A patient's right to apply to the court under s29 for his nearest relative to be displaced or in some circumstances to prevent his nearest relative from being consulted under s11(4) (see *JT v UK* and *R (E) v Bristol City Council* above).
4. The imposition of seclusion.
5. Being managed on a mixed sex ward.
6. A parent's right to consent to or refuse treatment of his child.
7. A person being kept on a waiting list for treatment to the point where his condition deteriorated.
8. A patient suffering serious side effects from medication imposed upon him.
9. The searching of patients.
10. Visiting rights by or to children and young persons.
11. Children being managed on an adult ward.
12. Whether to go to a care home or stay at home with a package of care.
13. Deciding best interests for a person lacking capacity.

While Article 8 is very broad-ranging in terms of what it covers within the field of mental health law and practice, it is by no means an unqualified right and its effect is limited by Article 8(2), which provides a large number of potential justifications for breaches. Although any breach must be proportionate, going no further than necessary to achieve a legitimate objective, and the exceptions narrowly interpreted, there is still considerable scope in particular on grounds of the protection of the health of the patient or of the rights or freedoms of others for justifying breaches of this Convention right. It might be used to justify breaching confidentiality where a third party was at risk; or for secluding a patient; or for imposing treatment on a competently refusing patient; although in the latter case the courts may be moving in the direction of limiting the scope for doing so (see *X v Finland* in Appendix 6).

# Current challenges and uncertainties

Challenges based on alleged breaches of the Convention are a common occurrence and show no signs of abating. The fallout from the *Cheshire West* decision is but one example. There is no shortage of current issues arising from the use of the Mental Health Act being tested in the courts on this basis. What follows therefore is merely a selection of current uncertainties confronting health and social care professionals.

- Under s20 a patient's detention can be renewed by his RC, who may not be a doctor. The RC has to consult with one or more other persons professionally concerned with the patient's medical treatment, none of whom has to be a doctor. Additionally, under s20(5A) someone professionally concerned with the patient's treatment must state in writing that the renewal conditions are met, and this person (although from a different profession from the RC) does not have to be a doctor either. Although local policies may provide that where the RC is not a doctor the second professional should be, this would not be a legal requirement, and the Codes of Practice do not suggest it, so it is possible that no doctor will be involved in the procedure at all. The issue is whether this conflicts with the Article 5 requirement expounded in *Winterwerp* above that detention or continued detention be based on objective medical expertise. The Government believes that the training, professional background and competencies required of approved clinicians means that they will have that expertise even if they are not doctors. It will have to be seen whether the courts agree. If a non-doctor RC can renew a patient's detention, why should it still be necessary for two doctors to provide medical reports upon which the initial detention must be founded?

- A similar issue arises in relation to placing a patient on a CTO, or to extending it, which also does not require the involvement of a doctor. Again, in relation to revoking a CTO, the effect of which is to start a new six-month period of detention under s3, there is no requirement for a doctor to be involved.

- The reduction in the threshold for what constitutes a deprivation of liberty within the meaning of Article 5 is creating many problems for health and social care professionals in operating the Mental Health Act. A Mental Health Tribunal may not impose conditions on the discharge of a restricted patient, which amount to a deprivation of liberty even if they consent to them with capacity (see *SoS for Justice v MM* (2018) in Appendix 6). Likewise, a responsible clinician may not impose such conditions on a CTO patient (see *Welsh Ministers v PJ* (2018) in Appendix 6). Guardianship may not be used to deprive someone of their liberty (see MCA Code 13.16 and *NL v Hampshire CC* (2015)). Parents (probably) may not deprive their children of their liberty (see *RK v BCC* (2011) under *D (A Child) Deprivation of Liberty* (2015) and *D (A Child)* (2019) UKSC 42 in Appendix 6) (which itself gives rise to the question whether consent of someone with parental responsibility to the child's confinement can negate any such deprivation of liberty). Before the decision of the Supreme Court in *Cheshire West*, this was rarely a practical problem as the restrictions so imposed would generally be regarded as falling below the deprivation of liberty threshold. Now the threshold has been effectively lowered, such restrictive conditions risk engaging Article 5, and so require formal authorisation which the Mental Health Act or parental responsibility may not always be able to provide. This may lead to more patients remaining in hospital, more applications to court for formal authorisations and more detentions under the Mental Health Act or DoLS (and from October 2020 its successor scheme the Liberty Protection Safeguards which will operate from age 16) where the patient lacks capacity to consent to the arrangements or where his consent cannot legitimise them. The situation has been exacerbated by the relatively high level of understanding of the implications of admission to hospital for treatment of mental disorder required before the patient can consent to informal admission (see *A PCT v LDV* (2013) in Appendix 6). "Rescuing" the concept of the informal patient is one of the aims of the Mental Health Act Review recommendations, but this will be difficult given the current state of case law.

- The removal of the exclusions relating to promiscuity, other immoral conduct and sexual deviancy (see Chapter 4) raises the issue whether detention on grounds of, for example, paedophilia (which the Government clearly intends should be within the definition of mental disorder) will breach Article 5, which distinguishes behaviour "deviating from society's norms" from true mental disorder.

- The inability of a parent to prevent a child receiving ECT under s58A to which the child consents, or to refuse ECT for a child who lacks capacity or competence is a potential breach of Article 8.

- Under s58 an SOAD becomes involved where medicine is administered to a patient by any means as medical treatment for mental disorder after three months have elapsed since it was first given during their detention where they either do not consent or lack capacity to consent to it. The SOAD must then certify that it is appropriate for the treatment (to continue) to be given. However it is arguable that the delay in operation of this safeguard for three months constitutes an unjustified breach of Article 8.

- The provisions enabling a patient to apply to the court under s29 to displace his NR may not go far enough to ensure compliance with Article 8 in two respects. First, the right will usually arise in practice at a time when the patient may be at his most vulnerable and least able to exercise the right, or indeed may lack capacity to exercise it. It is not clear how far in advance of an application for detention under the Act the court would entertain a prospective attempt to displace the NR. Second, it is not sufficient for the patient to have someone in mind who might be more suitable to act as his NR; he has to show that the existing nearest relative is "unsuitable". Other than in extreme cases, this might be difficult.

- The managers are required to make an automatic reference to a Mental Health Review Tribunal in respect of a patient six months after he has been detained under the Act, including time detained under s2. This means that there is a long stop provision ensuring that a patient whose s2 is extended where an application has been made under s29 to displace an NR will not have to wait indefinitely for a Tribunal reference. There is, however, a concern that the occasions for applying to or being referred to Tribunals are too infrequent and widely spaced to be compliant with the Convention. The Government has recognised this in principle by creating a power to reduce the periods between applications at some time in the future (s68A). It is uncertain if or when these powers will be exercised. Increased opportunities for challenging detention at a Tribunal are one of the recommendations of the Wessely Mental Health Act Review.

- In *MH v UK* (2012) (see Chapter 13 and Appendix 6) the ECHR found a breach of Article 5(4) in the failure of the MHA to provide safeguards to ensure that patients lacking capacity would have their initial detention under s2 challenged. The court also suggested that the reference to the Secretary of State in respect of the extension of the s2 (as the result of an application to court to remove the nearest relative) only happened because the patient's nearest relative was in fact willing and able to instruct solicitors in the matter; so protecting the patient's rights became a matter of chance rather than inevitability. It is uncertain whether the guidance to managers in the Code of Practice at E Para. 37.46 (W Para. 37.41) as to when they "should normally" make a reference to the Secretary of State (including on such occasions as this) is sufficiently robust. The increased potential involvement of an IMHA, in particular where a patient lacks the capacity to decide whether to seek such help (see Code for England Paras 4.23 and 6.23; W Para. 6.32), again may be insufficient to ensure that such patients have their right to a speedy and effective challenge under Article 5(4) protected.

- Under s63 the consent of a patient is not required for medical treatment for mental disorder if given by or under the direction of the AC in charge. This provision authorising the treatment of a refusing capacitated patient detained under a section to which Part 4 of the Act applies constitutes on the face of it a potential breach of Article 3 and clear breach of Article 8(1) requiring justification under Article 8(2). The ECHR case of *X v Finland* (2012) (see Appendix 6) suggests this may not be straightforward, and cases in the English courts appear to require in effect a best interests test to be applied, namely whether the therapeutic necessity of proceeding to treat in such circumstances can be "convincingly demonstrated". This would require consideration of delaying treatment, possible alternatives or even not treating. It is arguable that the courts are moving in the direction of supporting the wishes of patients even when detained under the Act and when the power to override a capacitated refusal exists in law. Section 63 is a power to treat, not an obligation to do so and must not be exercised arbitrarily. In *Nottinghamshire Healthcare NHS Trust v RC* (2014) (see Appendix 6) the court stated that it would be lawful not to treat with blood products a detained patient who was refusing this with capacity (and had made an advance decision to the same effect), even though to do so would constitute medical treatment for mental disorder and so fall within s63 and might be potentially life-saving. The judge stated that it would be "an abuse of power even to think of imposing a blood transfusion" in the circumstances. (The judge stated that where not to exercise a power to treat placed the patient's life at risk, the NHS Trust would be well advised to apply to the court.) The Code of Practice for England guidance at Paras 24.6 and 24.41 also emphasises respect for the wishes of a detained patient to refuse treatment (including where expressed in an advance decision). The Code for Wales at Para. 24.43 emphasises the importance of Article 8 in this respect and in particular, at Paras 9.8 and 9.12, the need to try to comply with the patient's wishes, whether they have capacity at the time or are covered by an advance decision or statement of wishes. The Wessely Review of the Mental Health Act recommends introducing a right for an objecting detained patient to challenge at a Tribunal the decision compulsorily to treat.

- The obligation under s131A to ensure an age-appropriate environment in hospital for children and young persons, being somewhat elastic (see Chapter 18), may not satisfy the requirements of Article 8. It could lead to children being admitted to adult wards by adult professionals and to an argument that this did not constitute a therapeutic environment (*Aerts v Belgium* (2000), see Appendix 6) for the child.

- The extension of victims' rights under the Domestic Violence, Crime and Victims Act 2004 (see Chapter 13) potentially infringes the right of the patient to confidentiality under Article 8.

# Key points

1. It is unlawful for a public authority to act in a way incompatible with a person's Convention rights.

2.  The court can make a declaration of incompatibility with a Convention right.

3.  Is the person being deprived of his liberty?

4.  Establish whether the patient was detained in accordance with a procedure prescribed by law.

5.  Exercising caution before re-detaining a patient shortly after discharge by a Tribunal.

6.  Medical treatment for mental disorder must convincingly be shown to be a therapeutic necessity before imposition on an objecting patient.

7.  Article 8(2) provides potential grounds for justifying a breach of the right to respect for private and family life.

8.  Those lawfully detained have the right to a speedy and effective challenge to a court.

9.  Failure to provide appropriate psychiatric care of a detained person might amount to a breach of Article 3.

10. Admission of a child by an adult team to an adult ward may breach the Convention rights of the child.

# Chapter 18

## Children and young persons

## Introduction

This chapter will outline the main provisions of the Mental Health Act 1983 as amended which make specific, or different, provisions for children (aged under 16) and young persons (aged 16 and 17). Relevant provisions in other legislation will be referred to. The question of admission to hospital for treatment of mental disorder, the treatment itself, and who can or should make those decisions (the child or young person, the parent, the local authority, the health and social care professionals or the court) will be considered.

## Age-specific provisions in the Mental Health Act 1983 as amended

There is generally no lower age limit for use of the compulsory powers under the Act, including s17A community treatment orders. However:

**Guardianship** under s7 and s37 is only available for a patient or offender who has attained the age of 16 years.

**Relying on parental responsibility**. Since January 2008 under s131(2)–(5), a patient aged 16 or 17 who requires treatment for mental disorder and who has capacity (within the meaning of the MCA) can be admitted to hospital informally with his consent, and no one with parental responsibility (as defined in the Children Act 1989) can override that decision. Perhaps of greater importance, where such a young person has capacity and is refusing admission for that purpose it is no longer possible to rely on the consent of someone with parental responsibility to override his refusal. These statutory amendments are of limited effect. In particular it should be noted that they do not apply to:

1.  children under 16, whether "Gillick competent" or not;

2.  admission to hospital for treatment of a physical disorder;

3.  the issue of the treatment for mental disorder once admitted;

4.  young persons aged 16 or 17 who lack capacity.

In these cases the common law, the MHA, the MCA or the Children Act would be expected to apply as before the 2007 Act amendments in line with developing case law. The difficulty is that the Codes of Practice arguably seek by guidance to alter the existing legal balance between relying on parental responsibility, using the compulsory powers or applying to the court for authority. In particular the Code seeks to go beyond the statutory amendments to s131 and to limit the reliance on parental responsibility as authority for decisions to admit and treat. This will be dealt with in further detail below.

**Age-appropriate facilities**. From April 2010 the hospital managers have had an obligation in respect of any child or young person admitted to hospital, whether under the compulsory powers or not. Under s131A(2):

> The managers of the hospital shall ensure that the patient's environment in the hospital is suitable having regard to his age (subject to his needs).

Under s131A(3):

> For the purpose of deciding how to fulfil the duty under subsection (2) above, the managers shall consult a person who appears to them to have knowledge or experience of cases involving patients who have not attained the age of 18 years which makes him suitable to be consulted.

These provisions fall short of requiring that all children and young persons be admitted to dedicated CAMHS facilities, or that the person consulted need have any professional qualification. The Code of Practice advises (E Para. 19.91) that the effect of these provisions is that, after consultation with someone "experienced in CAMHS cases", children and young persons should have:

- *appropriate physical facilities;*
- *staff with the right training, skills and knowledge to understand and address their specific needs;*
- *a hospital routine that will allow their personal, social and educational development to continue as normally as possible; and*
- *equal access to educational opportunities as their peers, in so far as that is consistent with their ability to make use of them, considering their mental state.*

There is similarly no legal requirement for any of the professionals involved in the assessment for admission of a child or young person to be a CAMHS specialist. The Code of Practice for England states at Para. 19.73:

> At least one of the people involved in assessing whether a child or young person should be admitted to hospital, and if so whether they should be detained under the Act (i.e. one of the two medical practitioners or the approved mental health professional (AMHP)), should be a child and adolescent mental health services (CAMHS) professional. Where this is not possible, and admission to hospital is considered necessary, the AMHP should have access to an AMHP with experience of working in CAMHS, and the medical practitioners should consult a CAMHS clinician as soon as possible and involve them as closely as the circumstances of the case allow.

This would include involvement of a CAMHS consultant with relevant experience of learning disability or autism where relevant (E Para. 20.49).

The Code for Wales has similar guidance at W Paras 19.54 and 20.18.

All these provisions fall short of being absolute legal requirements. It continues to be possible (though undesirable) for a child or young person to be admitted to an adult ward on the basis of an application and medical recommendations from professionals whose expertise is entirely in relation to adult patients.

Under s140, primary care trusts and local health boards must notify their local social services authority of hospitals within their area which provide accommodation or facilities designed so as to be specially suitable for children and young persons. Note that this does not create an obligation to provide such accommodation or facilities.

**Nearest relative** and related issues. No one under the age of 18 may be the NR of a patient (nor may he have the NR functions delegated to him under Regulation 24) unless he is that patient's parent, spouse or civil partner or treated as such (s26(5),(6)). Under s27, if a child or young person is subject to a care order under the Children Act 1989 the local authority will be deemed to be the patient's NR in preference to anyone except the patient's spouse or civil partner (if any).

Section 116 provides that in relation to a patient who is a child or young person subject to a care order, the guardianship of a local social services authority or in respect of whom the authority has had transferred to it the NR functions, the authority must arrange for the patient to be visited and take such other steps as would expect to be taken by the parents.

If a child or young person is a ward of court, an application for admission to hospital under the Mental Health Act requires leave of the court; the AMHP does not need to consult with the NR in respect of an s3 application, nor can the NR block such an application (s33). The power of the NR to discharge the patient or apply to the Mental Health Review Tribunal can only be exercised with leave of the court.

**Part 3**. Under s39 a court considering making a hospital order or interim hospital order (including remands under s35 and s36 and committals under s44) in relation to a person under 18 may request information about accommodation and facilities designed to be specially suitable for such patients.

**Part 4 – ECT**. There are special provisions relating to the giving of ECT to children and young persons. The impact of s58A is described generally in Chapter 8. In relation to patients who are children or young persons, whether informal or admitted under the compulsory powers, the position is governed by s58A(4), the effect of which is that ECT may not be given unless:

1. the patient has consented to ECT; *and*

2. a second opinion appointed doctor (SOAD) (not the approved clinician in charge of the treatment) certifies in writing that:

    (a) the patient is capable of understanding the nature, purpose and likely effects of the treatment;

    (b) the patient has consented to it;

    (c) it is appropriate for the treatment to be given.

These provisions apply to all s58A treatments, but so far only ECT has been designated as such. If the child is not "Gillick competent", or the young person lacks capacity, ECT may not be given unless a SOAD (not the RC or AC) certifies in writing that:

    (a) the patient is *not* capable of understanding the nature, purpose and likely effects of the treatment;

    (b) it is appropriate for the treatment to be given;

    (c) (in the case of a young person) giving the treatment would not conflict with a decision made by a deputy or by the Court of Protection.

The additional requirement for incapacitated adults that giving the treatment would not conflict with a valid and applicable advance decision or with a decision made by a donee (attorney) does not apply because neither a child nor a young person can make an advance decision or a lasting power of attorney.

If the child or young person is an informal patient then additional authority is required before ECT can be given which will derive from the Mental Capacity Act for a young person and from parental authority or the court for a child (s56(7)). This is subject to the authorisation of ECT being seen as within the scope of parental responsibility in respect of which the Code of Practice urges caution (E Para. 19.41).

The s62 "urgent treatment" provisions allow the processes described above to be dispensed with in the case of patients of any age where ECT is immediately necessary to save the patient's life or prevent a serious deterioration in his condition, i.e. falling only within s62(1)(a) or (b).

**Part 4A**. Treatment of a CTO patient while in the community is dealt with in Chapter 8. In relation to CTO patients under the age of 18 it should be noted that, somewhat confusingly, the distinction is made between "adult community patients" – i.e. those over the age of 16 and "child community patients" – those under 16. Therefore it needs to be remembered that:

1.   The MCA broadly applies to those over the age of 16, but the provisions relating to advance decisions and lasting powers of attorney only apply to persons over the age of 18. So they are not relevant to authorising or refusing treatment in the community for young persons subject to CTOs in the way that they are relevant for those over 18.

2.   A distinction will need to be made in relation to competence for those CTO patients under 16 and capacity as defined in the Mental Capacity Act for those over 16. Whether the relevant tests are significantly different is a moot point, but the presumption of capacity to make decisions only applies in relation to those over the age of 16.

**Tribunals**. The managers' responsibility to refer automatically a patient's case to a Mental Health Review Tribunal arises in the case of a child or young person if more than one year has elapsed since the Tribunal last considered his case, whether on his own application or otherwise (s68(6)).

# Age-specific provisions in other relevant legislation

**The Mental Capacity Act 2005** generally applies to those over the age of 16.

However:

*   No one under the age of 18 can make an advance decision.

*   No one under the age of 18 can make or be appointed under a lasting power of attorney.

*   No one under the age of 18 can be appointed a deputy.

*   The "Deprivation of Liberty Safeguards" procedure (DoLS) only applies to those over the age of 18. Note that from October 2020 the Liberty Protection Safeguards ("LPS"), which replace DoLS, will apply from age 16.

**Under the Children Act 1989:**

*   A specific issues order under s8 will only in exceptional circumstances last beyond the child's sixteenth birthday.

*   A secure accommodation order under s25 cannot be made in respect of a child under the age of 13 without approval of the Secretary of State.

*   An application for a care order may only be made up to a child's seventeenth birthday, even though it can last until the child is 18.

## Parental responsibility

Parental responsibility ("PR") is defined in s3 of the Children Act 1989 as meaning all the rights, duties, powers, responsibilities and authority which by law a parent has in relation to a child and his property. Who can acquire PR and by what means is outside the scope of this book, but certainly can include people who are not the child's parents, and can be obtained by agreement or court order which might oust the birth parents. Accordingly, as the Code of Practice for England states at Para. 19.8 (and the Code for Wales to similar effect at Para. 19.6):

> *Those taking decisions under the Act must be clear about who has parental responsibility. When seeking to identify who has parental responsibility for the child or young person, practitioners should always check whether the child or young person's medical and/or social service files include any relevant court orders, and request copies of any such orders. These orders may include care orders, child arrangements orders (which replace residence orders and contact orders), special guardianship orders, evidence of appointment as the child or young person's guardian, parental responsibility agreements or orders under section 4 of the Children Act 1989 and any order under wardship. Practitioners should always check with those caring for the child or young person whether any child arrangements orders, parental responsibility agreements or orders, or special guardianship orders have been obtained.*

# The scope of parental responsibility

It is not always obvious what the "rights, duties, powers, responsibilities and authority which by law a parent has in relation to a child" comprise, as they are not codified. The Code of Practice seeks to make a distinction between decisions falling within and those falling outside the scope of PR. Only in respect of those areas of decision-making falling within that scope is it appropriate to rely on parental consent. Where do decisions to admit a child or young person to hospital for treatment of mental disorder, or in relation to the treatment once in hospital or outside fall? The scope of PR is merely another way of describing, but not defining, those "rights, duties etc." The Code of Practice for England states at Para. 19.41 (W Paras 19.28–19.30) that two questions need to be considered:

*First, is this a decision that a parent should reasonably be expected to make?* In this connection relevant considerations might include:

- the type and invasiveness of the proposed intervention – the more extreme the intervention (e.g. ECT) the greater the justification required;
- the age, maturity and understanding of the child or young person;
- the extent to which the decision accords with the wishes of the child or young person, and whether the child or young person is resisting the decision;
- whether the child or young person had expressed any views about the proposed intervention when they had the competence or capacity to make such decisions.

*Second, are there any factors that might undermine the validity of parental consent?* Such factors might include:

- where the parent lacks capacity to make the decision;
- where the parent is unable to focus on what course of action is in the best interests of the child;
- where the child's poor mental health has led to conflict between the parents;
- where one parent agrees with the decision and the other is opposed to it.

# Parental responsibility and deprivation of liberty

Three issues arise here. First, may a parent as a matter of law consent to or authorise the detention of their child or young person in circumstances which meet the "objective" element of a deprivation of liberty (the acid test) (with the result that Article 5 is not breached because of that consent)? Second, if so, in what circumstances would to do so fall within the scope of PR? Third, if not, how should the deprivation of liberty be authorised? The uncertainty around these questions is reflected in the Code of Practice for England which states at Para. 19.48:

> *Prior to the Supreme Court's judgment in Cheshire West case law had established that persons with parental responsibility cannot authorise a deprivation of liberty. Cheshire West clarified the elements establishing a deprivation of liberty, but did not expressly decide whether a person with parental responsibility could, and if so in what circumstances, consent to restrictions that would, without their consent, amount to a deprivation of liberty. In determining whether a person with parental responsibility can consent to the arrangements which would, without their consent, amount to a deprivation of liberty, practitioners will need to consider and apply developments in case law following Cheshire West.*

There have been a number of such developments.

Dealing with these questions in turn, it is true that in *RK v BCC et al.* (2011) the court had said that a parent could not consent to the deprivation of liberty of their child. However, most incidents of parental control fall far short of the threshold for a deprivation of liberty so in practice this did not create a problem. Since the decision in *Cheshire West* lowered the threshold the situation is less clear cut, which explains the cautious Code guidance. In *D (A Child) Deprivation of Liberty* (2015) (see Appendix 6) the court held that *RK* was an obiter decision, incorrect and not binding. Thus parents (in this case of a 15-year-old child) could authorise the deprivation of liberty of their child as a matter of law.

The judge went on to consider the second question and decided that what fell within the scope of PR for a 15-year-old child would depend inter alia upon the level of that child's disabilities, and that for a child with (as in this case) multiple disabilities, what fell within the scope was greater than for a child without disabilities (which appears inconsistent with the approach in *Cheshire West*). In *A LA v D* (2015), the court held that, depending on the circumstances, the same might apply where a child had been voluntarily accommodated by the local authority, but not where the child was subject to a care order.

In *D (A Child)* (2019) UKSC 42 (see Appendix 6) the Supreme Court held that consenting to the deprivation of liberty of a 16- or 17-year-old lacking capacity was outside the scope of PR and thus formal authorisation would be required following a procedure prescribed by law in accordance with Article 5.

So as to the third question, the implication of these recent decisions is that the authorisation for the deprivation of liberty of a child or young person will be required as appropriate from either:

1. The Mental Health Act 1983 **OR**

2. S25 Children Act 1989 (Secure Accommodation Order) **OR**

3. The court **OR**

4. Parental responsibility (for some under 16-year-olds) **OR**

5. From October 2020 under the Liberty Protection Safeguards for those over 16 lacking capacity (see above).

The approach of the Code of Practice for Wales to the issue of deprivation of liberty and parental responsibility is to emphasise the need to balance the child's right to liberty under Article 5 and to autonomy under Article 8 against the parent's right to respect for the right to family life under Article 8, which includes the exercise of parental responsibilities (W Para. 19.34).

# Decisions to admit and treat children and young persons

Quite apart from the issue of parental responsibility and deprivation of liberty discussed above, the question of how to authorise the admission to hospital and the treatment of mental disorder of a child or young person is fraught with difficulty and uncertainty, whether in statute law, case law or the guidance contained in the Code of Practice. It is convenient to consider these issues (with paragraph references) under the same headings as does the English Code. The Code for Wales adopts a similar approach at Paras 19.40–19.47. Guidance on the assessment of capacity of young people and of competence of children is to be found in the Code at E Paras 19.24–19.37. The Code for Wales at Paras 19.15–19.24 gives guidance to the same effect.

## Admission of a capacitated young person

Here, at least, as mentioned above, the amended provisions of s131 make the position clear. A young person with capacity (determined in accordance with the Mental Capacity Act) can consent to his own admission for treatment of mental disorder. A parent cannot overrule him; neither, if the young person refuses admission, can the parent authorise his admission. The compulsory powers must be used if the criteria are met and admission is necessary (E Para. 19.55). If they are not, only the court could authorise his admission. It is important to remember that a person only lacks capacity within the meaning of the Mental Capacity Act if the inability to make the decision is "because of an impairment of or disturbance in the functioning of the mind or brain". If a young person is unable to make a decision whether to be admitted to hospital but this is because, for example, they are overwhelmed by the implications or simply find the decision too difficult, this falls outside the Mental Capacity Act and, it being impossible to rely in that situation upon parental consent, court authorisation might be necessary (E Para. 19.54).

## Admission of an incapacitated young person

Section 131 does not apply, as the young person lacks capacity (again within the meaning of the MCA). Being over 16 the MCA applies, so if the admission falls short of being a deprivation of liberty, this route to admission could be used. If it does constitute a deprivation of liberty, the DoLS procedure will not be available as the patient is under 18. But as noted above the LPS will be available from October 2020 from age 16 for those lacking capacity. It will not be possible to rely on parental authority (see above). Alternatively the MHA could be used if the criteria are met; if not, court authorisation may be necessary (Para. 19.57).

## Treatment of a capacitated young person*

Clearly the Mental Capacity Act will not apply. By s8 Family Law Reform Act 1969 a young person is presumed capable of consenting to his own medical treatment. The refusal of consent by a young person can be overruled by the court. Case law suggests that a parent may likewise overrule such a refusal. In *Re W (a minor)* (1992) (medical treatment) (see Appendix 6 under *Gillick*) the Court of Appeal stated that: *"no minor of whatever age has power by refusing consent to treatment to override a consent to treatment by someone who has parental responsibility."*

However, the Code of Practice advises that it is inadvisable to rely on parental consent any longer but that instead the Mental Health Act should be used where the criteria are met or the authority of the court sought where not (E Paras 19.39, 19.59). This view is supported by the recommendations of the Wessely Review of the Mental Health Act.

## Treatment of an incapacitated young person*

In this case the Mental Capacity Act applies and treatment falling short of a deprivation of liberty can be given in accordance with its provisions. It may also be possible to rely on the consent of a parent (whether or not the young person lacks capacity within the meaning of the Mental Capacity Act), so long as the decision falls within the scope of PR (see above). If the circumstances surrounding the treatment constitute a deprivation of liberty, then as discussed this might, following recent case law, fall outside such scope. If neither the Mental Capacity Act nor parental consent can in the circumstances be relied on, the Mental Health Act could be considered if appropriate and the criteria are met; failing this, an application to court for authorisation should be considered (E Paras 19.61–19.64).

## Admission and treatment of a Gillick competent child*

Gillick competence is the term used to describe a child who has a full understanding of the nature of the proposed treatment, including the consequences of failure to treat, and sufficient maturity to be able to make up his or her own mind. In practice it is hard to discern any significant difference between the test of Gillick competence and the s3 MCA test for those over 16. However, whereas for the over 16-year-old there is a presumption of capacity, for the under 16-year-old there is no presumption of competence. If the child is Gillick competent, he or she can be admitted and treatment given without parental authority (E Para. 19.65). If the child is refusing, despite the decision in *Re W* above, the Code of Practice, anticipating potentially successful future challenges under the Human Rights Act, states that it "may be inadvisable" to rely on parental consent (E Paras 19.66, 19.39). Instead it advises using the MHA if the criteria are met and otherwise seeking legal advice on the need to obtain authorisation from the court (E Para. 19.66).

## Admission and treatment of non-Gillick competent child*

If the child is not Gillick competent and the decision falls within the scope of PR (see above) consent to admit and treat from someone with PR can be relied on. If the decision as to admission and/or treatment falls outside the scope of PR (see above) parental consent may not be relied upon, and again the Code guidance is that if necessary and the criteria are met the Mental Health Act should be considered, or otherwise legal advice sought on the need for court authorisation (E Para. 19.70).

At the end of Chapter 19 of the Code, there are some useful flowcharts (at Figures 7–9) and case examples, summarising the issues that practitioners will need to consider when determining the legal authority to admit and/or treat a child or young person.

---

* In relation to the treatment of a capacitous or incapacitous young person or to the admission and treatment of a Gillick competent or non-Gillick competent child under 16, the position is not directly affected by the Supreme Court decision in *D (A Child)* (2019) (see above and Appendix 6) which dealt only with the scope of PR in relation to confinement and deprivation of liberty.

## Comments

The advice contained in the Code of Practice presents certain difficulties for health and social care professionals. It places emphasis on the limits to the scope of PR. It acknowledges past court decisions confirming a parent's ability to overrule a child's refusal but advises against relying on these (E Para. 19.39). As a result, the overall impact of the guidance (coupled with the effect of the Supreme Court decision in *D (A Child)* (2019)) may be to:

1. reduce the occasions on which parental consent can be relied on even for non-Gillick competent children, and correspondingly;

2. increase the number of admissions of children and young people under the compulsory powers of the Mental Health Act;

3. increase the number of applications to court in respect of children and young persons; and

4. increase the number of LPS procedures for young persons from October 2020.

While this may increase the formal safeguards available it is debatable whether this is always in the overall interests of the child or young person. Whether it is the intended effect of the legislation is also hard to square with the strictly limited effect of the changes to s131 noted above, pace the Supreme Court decision in *D (A Child)* (2019).

Although the Code for Wales is particularly strong in its emphasis on the interests of the child being the primary consideration (see W Para. 19.5), the Code for England is less firm, suggesting merely that the best interests of the child or young person must always be "a significant consideration" (E Para. 19.5).

# Emergency treatment

The guidance in the Code of Practice for England confirms the exceptions to the usual requirement for authorisation to treat a child or young person as follows:

> *19.71 A life-threatening emergency may arise when treatment needs to be given but it is not possible to rely on the consent of the child, young person or person with parental responsibility and there is no time to seek authorisation from the court or (where applicable) to detain and treat under the Act. If the failure to treat the child or young person would be likely to lead to their death or to severe permanent injury, treatment may be given without their consent, even if this means overriding their refusal when they have the competence (children) or the capacity (young people and those with parental responsibility), to make this treatment decision. In such cases, the courts have stated that doubt should be resolved in favour of the preservation of life, and it will be acceptable to undertake treatment to preserve life or prevent irreversible serious deterioration of the child or young person's condition.*

> *19.72 The treatment given must be no more than necessary and in the best interests of the child or young person. Once the child or young person's condition is stabilised, legal authority for on-going treatment must be established; this might be on an informal basis or in accordance with either a court order or, if the child or young person is detained, under part 4 of the Act.*

The Code of Practice for Wales gives similar advice at Paras 19.36–19.39.

# Secure accommodation orders

There is one further route to lawful detention of children and young persons which requires consideration, and that is the use of a secure accommodation order under s25 of the Children

Act 1989, which the courts have held amounts to a deprivation of liberty within the meaning of Article 5. A detailed consideration of s25 is outside the scope of this book, but in short the grounds are that the child or young person:

- **either** has a history of absconding, is likely to abscond from any other kind of accommodation and in so doing is likely to suffer significant harm;

- **or** is likely to injure himself or other persons if kept in any other kind of accommodation.

As can be seen, the emphasis of this provision is on safe containment of the child rather than treatment, and indeed the section confers no additional powers to treat. Accordingly, in deciding which route to take, the traditional distinction made between the Children Act and Mental Health Act has been whether the primary purpose is to provide medical treatment for mental disorder or rather to control disturbed behaviour. Unlike the Code for England, the Code for Wales elaborates on this at Paras 19.48–19.52.

Orders under s25 are initially for a period of three months. Without a court order, a local authority can place a child or young person in secure accommodation for up to 72 hours in any 28-day period. If the child is under the age of 13, the prior agreement of the Secretary of State is needed before an order can be obtained. If for any reason it is not possible for the local authority to obtain an order under s25 (e.g. because the accommodation does not satisfy the definition of secure accommodation), in limited circumstances the High Court may make an order under s100 using its inherent jurisdiction. However, this will not lightly be granted and the court is likely in any event to require the strict criteria of s25 to be met before deciding to use its inherent jurisdiction. In *D (A Child)* (2019) (see above and Appendix 6) the Supreme Court considered (obiter) the meaning of "secure accommodation" within s25 and tentatively suggested that this turned on the nature of the accommodation itself rather than on the regime operating within it. So, many children would not be covered by the automatic need for court authorisation and the scope of PR becomes therefore relevant.

# Key points

1. Parental responsibility cannot be relied on to admit a capacitous 16/17-year-old to hospital informally for treatment of mental disorder.

2. Managers are obliged to ensure suitable environments for children.

3. ECT may never be given to a child or young person, even if informal, without the involvement of an SOAD, save in limited s62 circumstances.

4. No one under the age of 18 may make an advance decision to refuse medical treatment.

5. There is no lower age limit for a CTO.

6. Establish who has parental responsibility for a child or young person.

7. The scope of parental responsibility may sometimes include deprivation of liberty of a child under 16 but not of a 16- or 17-year-old.

8. Consider whether the MCA rather than the MHA could be used for the young person's treatment.

9. If the MHA criteria are not met, consider whether to rely on parental responsibility or to obtain authority from the court.

10. Consider whether a secure accommodation order under the Children Act may be more appropriate than the Mental Health Act.

# Appendix 1

## Mental Health Act 1983

## ARRANGEMENT OF SECTIONS

## PART 5: MENTAL HEALTH REVIEW TRIBUNALS

*Constitution etc.*

*Applications and references concerning Part 2 patients*

*Applications and references concerning Part 3 patients*

*Discharge of patients*

*General*

## PART 6: REMOVAL AND RETURN OF PATIENTS
## WITHIN THE UNITED KINGDOM

*Removal to and from Scotland*

## PART 9: OFFENCES

## PART 10: MISCELLANEOUS AND SUPPLEMENTARY

*Miscellaneous provisions*

## SCHEDULE 2. MENTAL HEALTH REVIEW TRIBUNALS FOR WALES

(Other schedules omitted here)

### PART 1: APPLICATION OF ACT

### 1. Application of Act: "mental disorder"

(1)    The provisions of this Act shall have effect with respect to the reception, care and treatment of mentally disordered patients, the management of their property and other related matters.

(2)    In this Act –

"mental disorder" means any disorder or disability of the mind; and "mentally disordered" shall be construed accordingly;

and other expressions shall have the meanings assigned to them in section 145 below.

(2A) But a person with learning disability shall not be considered by reason of that disability to be –

(a) suffering from mental disorder for the purposes of the provisions mentioned in sub-section (2B) below; or

(b) requiring treatment in hospital for mental disorder for the purposes of sections 17E and 50 to 53 below,

unless that disability is associated with abnormally aggressive or seriously irresponsible conduct on his part.

(2B) The provisions are –

(a) sections 3, 7, 17A, 20 and 20A below;

(b) sections 35 to 38, 45A, 47, 48 and 51 below; and

(c) section 72(1)(b) and (c) and (4) below.

(3) Dependence on alcohol or drugs is not considered to be a disorder or disability of the mind for the purposes of subsection (2) above.

(4) In subsection (2A) above, "learning disability" means a state of arrested or incomplete development of the mind which includes significant impairment of intelligence and social functioning.

## PART 2: COMPULSORY ADMISSION TO HOSPITAL AND GUARDIANSHIP

*Procedure for hospital admission*

### 2. Admission for assessment

(1) A patient may be admitted to a hospital and detained there for the period allowed by subsection (4) below in pursuance of an application (in this Act referred to as "an application for admission for assessment") made in accordance with subsections (2) and (3) below.

(2) An application for admission for assessment may be made in respect of a patient on the grounds that –

(a) he is suffering from mental disorder of a nature or degree which warrants the detention of the patient in a hospital for assessment (or for assessment followed by medical treatment) for at least a limited period; and

(b) he ought to be so detained in the interests of his own health or safety, or with a view to the protection of other persons.

(3) An application for admission for assessment shall be founded on the written recommendations in the prescribed form of two registered medical practitioners, including in each case a statement that in the opinion of the practitioner the conditions set out in subsection (2) above are complied with.

(4) Subject to the provisions of section 29(4) below, a patient admitted to hospital in pursuance of an application for admission for assessment may be detained for a period not exceeding 28 days beginning with the day on which he is admitted, but shall not be detained after the expiration of that period unless before it has expired he has become liable to be detained by virtue of a subsequent application, order or direction under the following provisions of this Act.

### 3. Admission for treatment

(1)    A patient may be admitted to a hospital and detained there for the period allowed by the following provisions of this Act in pursuance of an application (in this Act referred to as "an application for admission for treatment") made in accordance with this section.

(2)    An application for admission for treatment may be made in respect of a patient on the grounds that –

(a)   he is suffering from mental disorder of a nature or degree which makes it appropriate for him to receive medical treatment in a hospital; and

(b)   (repealed);

(c)   it is necessary for the health or safety of the patient or for the protection of other persons that he should receive such treatment and it cannot be provided unless he is detained under this section; and

(d)   appropriate medical treatment is available for him.

(3)    An application for admission for treatment shall be founded on the written recommendations in the prescribed form of two registered medical practitioners, including in each case a statement that in the opinion of the practitioner the conditions set out in subsection (2) above are complied with;

and each such recommendation shall include –

(a)   such particulars as may be prescribed of the grounds for that opinion so far as it relates to the conditions set out in paragraphs (a) and (d) of that subsection; and

(b)   a statement of the reasons for that opinion so far as it relates to the conditions set out in paragraph (c) of that subsection, specifying whether other methods of dealing with the patient are available and, if so, why they are not appropriate.

(4)    In this Act, references to appropriate medical treatment, in relation to a person suffering from mental disorder, are references to medical treatment which is appropriate in his case, taking into account the nature and degree of the mental disorder and all other circumstances of his case.

### 4. Admission for assessment in cases of emergency

(1)    In any case of urgent necessity, an application for admission for assessment may be made in respect of a patient in accordance with the following provisions of this section, and any application so made is in this Act referred to as "an emergency application".

(2)    An emergency application may be made either by an approved mental health professional or by the nearest relative of the patient; and every such application shall include a statement that it is of urgent necessity for the patient to be admitted and detained under section 2 above, and that compliance with the provisions of this Part of this Act relating to applications under that section would involve undesirable delay.

(3)    An emergency application shall be sufficient in the first instance if founded on one of the medical recommendations required by section 2 above, given, if practicable, by a practitioner who has previous acquaintance with the patient and otherwise complying with the requirements of section 12 below so far as applicable to a single recommendation, and verifying the statement referred to in subsection (2) above.

(4)   An emergency application shall cease to have effect on the expiration of a period of 72 hours from the time when the patient is admitted to the hospital unless –

   (a)   the second medical recommendation required by section 2 above is given and received by the managers within that period; and

   (b)   that recommendation and the recommendation referred to in subsection (3) above together comply with all the requirements of section 12 below (other than the requirement as to the time of signature of the second recommendation).

(5)   In relation to an emergency application, section 11 below shall have effect as if in subsection (5) of that section for the words "the period of 14 days ending with the date of the application" there were substituted the words "the previous 24 hours".

## 5. Application in respect of patient already in hospital

(1)   An application for the admission of a patient to a hospital may be made under this Part of this Act notwithstanding that the patient is already an in-patient in that hospital or, in the case of an application for admission for treatment, that the patient is for the time being liable to be detained in the hospital in pursuance of an application for admission for assessment; and where an application is so made the patient shall be treated for the purposes of this Part of this Act as if he had been admitted to the hospital at the time when that application was received by the managers.

(2)   If, in the case of a patient who is an in-patient in a hospital, it appears to the registered medical practitioner or approved clinician in charge of the treatment of the patient that an application ought to be made under this Part of this Act for the admission of the patient to hospital, he may furnish to the managers a report in writing to that effect; and in any such case the patient may be detained in the hospital for a period of 72 hours from the time when the report is so furnished.

(3)   The registered medical practitioner or approved clinician in charge of the treatment of a patient in a hospital may nominate one (but not more than one) person to act for him under subsection (2) above in his absence.

(3A)  For the purposes of subsection (3) above –

   (a)   the registered medical practitioner may nominate another registered medical practitioner, or an approved clinician, on the staff of the hospital; and

   (b)   the approved clinician may nominate another approved clinician, or a registered medical practitioner, on the staff of the hospital.

(4)   If, in the case of a patient who is receiving treatment for mental disorder as an in-patient in a hospital, it appears to a nurse of the prescribed class –

   (a)   that the patient is suffering from mental disorder to such a degree that it is necessary for his health or safety or for the protection of others for him to be immediately restrained from leaving the hospital; and

   (b)   that it is not practicable to secure the immediate attendance of a practitioner or clinician for the purpose of furnishing a report under subsection (2) above,

   the nurse may record that fact in writing; and in that event the patient may be detained in the hospital for a period of six hours from the time when that fact is so recorded or until the earlier arrival at the place where the patient is detained of a practitioner or clinician having power to furnish a report under that subsection.

(5)   A record made under subsection (4) above shall be delivered by the nurse (or by a person authorised by the nurse in that behalf) to the managers of the hospital as soon as possible after it is made; and where a record is made under that subsection the period mentioned in subsection (2) above shall begin at the time when it is made.

(6)   The reference in subsection (1) above to an in-patient does not include an in-patient who is liable to be detained in pursuance of an application under this Part of this Act or a community patient and the references in subsections (2) and (4) above do not include an in-patient who is liable to be detained in a hospital under this Part of this Act or a community patient.

(7)   In subsection (4) above "prescribed" means prescribed by an order made by the Secretary of State.

## 6. Effect of application for admission

(1)   An application for the admission of a patient to a hospital under this Part of this Act, duly completed in accordance with the provisions of this Part of this Act, shall be sufficient authority for the applicant, or any person authorised by the applicant, to take the patient and convey him to the hospital at any time within the following period, that is to say –

    (a)   in the case of an application other than an emergency application, the period of 14 days beginning with the date on which the patient was last examined by a registered medical practitioner before giving a medical recommendation for the purposes of the application;

    (b)   in the case of an emergency application, the period of 24 hours beginning at the time when the patient was examined by the practitioner giving the medical recommendation which is referred to in section 4(3) above, or at the time when the application is made, whichever is the earlier.

(2)   Where a patient is admitted within the said period to the hospital specified in such an application as is mentioned in subsection (1) above, or, being within that hospital, is treated by virtue of section 5 above as if he had been so admitted, the application shall be sufficient authority for the managers to detain the patient in the hospital in accordance with the provisions of this Act.

(3)   Any application for the admission of a patient under this Part of this Act which appears to be duly made and to be founded on the necessary medical recommendations may be acted upon without further proof of the signature or qualification of the person by whom the application or any such medical recommendation is made or given or of any matter of fact or opinion stated in it.

(4)   Where a patient is admitted to a hospital in pursuance of an application for admission for treatment, any previous application under this Part of this Act by virtue of which he was liable to be detained in a hospital or subject to guardianship shall cease to have effect.

*Guardianship*

## 7. Application for guardianship

(1)   A patient who has attained the age of 16 years may be received into guardianship, for the period allowed by the following provisions of this Act, in pursuance of an application (in this Act referred to as "a guardianship application") made in accordance with this section.

(2) A guardianship application may be made in respect of a patient on the grounds that –

    (a) he is suffering from mental disorder of a nature or degree which warrants his reception into guardianship under this section;

    (b) it is necessary in the interests of the welfare of the patient or for the protection of other persons that the patient should be so received.

(3) A guardianship application shall be founded on the written recommendations in the prescribed form of two registered medical practitioners, including in each case a statement that in the opinion of the practitioner the conditions set out in subsection (2) above are complied with; and each such recommendation shall include –

    (a) such particulars as may be prescribed of the grounds for that opinion so far as it relates to the conditions set out in paragraph (a) of that subsection; and

    (b) a statement of the reasons for that opinion so far as it relates to the conditions set out in paragraph (b) of that subsection.

(4) A guardianship application shall state the age of the patient or, if his exact age is not known to the applicant, shall state (if it be the fact) that the patient is believed to have attained the age of 16 years.

(5) The person named as guardian in a guardianship application may be either a local social services authority or any other person (including the applicant himself); but a guardianship application in which a person other than a local social services authority is named as guardian shall be of no effect unless it is accepted on behalf of that person by the local social services authority for the area in which he resides, and shall be accompanied by a statement in writing by that person that he is willing to act as guardian.

## 8. Effect of guardianship application, etc.

(1) Where a guardianship application, duly made under the provisions of this Part of this Act and forwarded to the local social services authority within the period allowed by subsection (2) below is accepted by that authority, the application shall, subject to regulations made by the Secretary of State, confer on the authority or person named in the application as guardian, to the exclusion of any other person –

    (a) the power to require the patient to reside at a place specified by the authority or person named as guardian;

    (b) the power to require the patient to attend at places and times so specified for the purpose of medical treatment, occupation, education or training;

    (c) the power to require access to the patient to be given, at any place where the patient is residing, to any registered medical practitioner, approved mental health professional or other person so specified.

(2) The period within which a guardianship application is required for the purposes of this section to be forwarded to the local social services authority is the period of 14 days beginning with the date on which the patient was last examined by a registered medical practitioner before giving a medical recommendation for the purposes of the application.

(3) A guardianship application which appears to be duly made and to be founded on the necessary medical recommendations may be acted upon without further proof of the signature or qualification of the person by whom the application or any such medical recommendation is made or given, or of any matter of fact or opinion stated in the application.

(4)    If within the period of 14 days beginning with the day on which a guardianship application has been accepted by the local social services authority the application, or any medical recommendation given for the purposes of the application, is found to be in any respect incorrect or defective, the application or recommendation may, within that period and with the consent of that authority, be amended by the person by whom it was signed; and upon such amendment being made the application or recommendation shall have effect and shall be deemed to have had effect as if it had been originally made as so amended.

(5)    Where a patient is received into guardianship in pursuance of a guardianship application, any previous application under this Part of this Act by virtue of which he was subject to guardianship or liable to be detained in a hospital shall cease to have effect.

## 9. Regulations as to guardianship

(1)    Subject to the provisions of this Part of this Act, the Secretary of State may make regulations –

(a)    for regulating the exercise by the guardians of patients received into guardianship under this Part of this Act of their powers as such; and

(b)    for imposing on such guardians, and upon local social services authorities in the case of patients under the guardianship of persons other than local social services authorities, such duties as he considers necessary or expedient in the interests of the patients.

(2)    Regulations under this section may in particular make provision for requiring the patients to be visited, on such occasions or at such intervals as may be prescribed by the regulations, on behalf of such local social services authorities as may be so prescribed, and shall provide for the appointment, in the case of every patient subject to the guardianship of a person other than a local social services authority, of a registered medical practitioner to act as the nominated medical attendant of the patient.

## 10. Transfer of guardianship in case of death, incapacity, etc. of guardian

(1)    If any person (other than a local social services authority) who is the guardian of a patient received into guardianship under this Part of this Act –

(a)    dies; or

(b)    gives notice in writing to the local social services authority that he desires to relinquish the functions of guardian, the guardianship of the patient shall thereupon vest in the local social services authority, but without prejudice to any power to transfer the patient into the guardianship of another person in pursuance of regulations under section 19 below.

(2)    If any such person, not having given notice under subsection (1)(b) above, is incapacitated by illness or any other cause from performing the functions of guardian of the patient, those functions may, during his incapacity, be performed on his behalf by the local social services authority or by any other person approved for the purposes by that authority.

(3)    If it appears to the county court, upon application made by an approved mental health professional acting on behalf of the local social services authority, that any person other than a local social services authority having the guardianship of a patient received into guardianship under this Part of this Act has performed his functions negligently or in a manner contrary to the interests of the welfare of the patient, the court may order that

the guardianship of the patient be transferred to the local social services authority or to any other person approved for the purpose by that authority.

(4) Where the guardianship of a patient is transferred to a local social services authority or other person by or under this section, subsection (2)(c) of section 19 below shall apply as if the patient had been transferred into the guardianship of that authority or person in pursuance of regulations under that section.

(5) In this section "the local social services authority", in relation to a person (other than a local social services authority) who is the guardian of a patient, means the local social services authority for the area in which that person resides (or resided immediately before his death).

*General provisions as to applications and recommendations*

## 11. General provisions as to applications

(1) Subject to the provisions of this section, an application for admission for assessment, an application for admission for treatment and a guardianship application may be made either by the nearest relative of the patient or by an approved mental health professional; and every such application shall specify the qualification of the applicant to make the application.

(1A) No application mentioned in subsection (1) above shall be made by an approved mental health professional if the circumstances are such that there would be a potential conflict of interest for the purposes of regulations under section 12A below.

(2) Every application for admission shall be addressed to the managers of the hospital to which admission is sought and every guardianship application shall be forwarded to the local social services authority named in the application as guardian, or, as the case may be, to the local social services authority for the area in which the person so named resides.

(3) Before or within a reasonable time after an application for the admission of a patient for assessment is made by an approved mental health professional, that professional shall take such steps as are practicable to inform the person (if any) appearing to be the nearest relative of the patient that the application is to be or has been made and of the power of the nearest relative under section 23(2)(a) below.

(4) An approved mental health professional may not make an application for admission for treatment or a guardianship application in respect of a patient in either of the following cases –

    (a) the nearest relative of the patient has notified that professional, or the local social services authority on whose behalf the professional is acting, that he objects to the application being made; or

    (b) that professional has not consulted the person (if any) appearing to be the nearest relative of the patient, but the requirement to consult that person does not apply if it appears to the professional that in the circumstances such consultation is not reasonably practicable or would involve unreasonable delay.

(5) None of the applications mentioned in subsection (1) above shall be made by any person in respect of a patient unless that person has personally seen the patient within the period of 14 days ending with the date of the application.

(6) (repealed).

(7)     Each of the applications mentioned in subsection (1) above shall be sufficient if the recommendations on which it is founded are given either as separate recommendations, each signed by a registered medical practitioner, or as a joint recommendation signed by two such practitioners.

## 12. General provisions as to medical recommendations

(1)     The recommendations required for the purposes of an application for the admission of a patient under this Part of this Act or a guardianship application (in this Act referred to as "medical recommendations") shall be signed on or before the date of the application, and shall be given by practitioners who have personally examined the patient either together or separately, but where they have examined the patient separately not more than five days must have elapsed between the days on which the separate examinations took place.

(2)     Of the medical recommendations given for the purposes of any such application, one shall be given by a practitioner approved for the purposes of this section by the Secretary of State as having special experience in the diagnosis or treatment of mental disorder; and unless that practitioner has previous acquaintance with the patient, the other such recommendation shall, if practicable, be given by a registered medical practitioner who has such previous acquaintance.

(2A)   A registered medical practitioner who is an approved clinician shall be treated as also approved for the purposes of this section under subsection (2) above as having special experience as mentioned there.

(3)     No medical recommendation shall be given for the purposes of an application mentioned in subsection (1) above if the circumstances are such that there would be a potential conflict of interest for the purposes of regulations under section 12A below.

## 12ZA. Agreement for exercise of approval function: England

(1)     The Secretary of State may enter into an agreement with another person for an approval function of the Secretary of State to be exercisable by the Secretary of State concurrently –

   (a)  with that other person; and

   (b)  if a requirement under section 12ZB has effect, with the other person by whom the function is exercisable under that requirement.

(2)     In this section and sections 12ZB and 12ZC, "approval function" means –

   (a)  the function under section 12(2); or

   (b)  the function of approving persons as approved clinicians.

(3)     An agreement under this section may, in particular, provide for an approval function to be exercisable by the other party –

   (a)  in all circumstances or only in specified circumstances;

   (b)  in all areas or only in specified areas.

(4)     An agreement under this section may provide for an approval function to be exercisable by the other party –

   (a)  for a period specified in the agreement; or

   (b)  for a period determined in accordance with the agreement.

(5)   The other party to an agreement under this section must comply with such instructions as the Secretary of State may give with respect to the exercise of the approval function.

(6)   An instruction under subsection (5) may require the other party to cease to exercise the function to such extent as the instruction specifies.

(7)   The agreement may provide for the Secretary of State to pay compensation to the other party in the event of an instruction such as is mentioned in subsection (6) being given.

(8)   An instruction under subsection (5) may be given in such form as the Secretary of State may determine.

(9)   The Secretary of State must publish instructions under subsection (5) in such form as the Secretary of State may determine; but that does not apply to an instruction such as is mentioned in subsection (6).

(10)   An agreement under this section may provide for the Secretary of State to make payments to the other party; and the Secretary of State may make payments to other persons in connection with the exercise of an approval function by virtue of this section.

## 12ZB. Requirement to exercise approval functions: England

(1)   The Secretary of State may impose a requirement on the National Health Service Commissioning Board ("the Board") or a Special Health Authority for an approval function of the Secretary of State to be exercisable by the Secretary of State concurrently –

(a)   with the Board or (as the case may be) Special Health Authority; and

(b)   if an agreement under section 12ZA has effect, with the other person by whom the function is exercisable under that agreement.

(2)   The Secretary of State may, in particular, require the body concerned to exercise an approval function –

(a)   in all circumstances or only in specified circumstances;

(b)   in all areas or only in specified areas.

(3)   The Secretary of State may require the body concerned to exercise an approval function –

(a)   for a period specified in the requirement, or

(b)   for a period determined in accordance with the requirement.

(4)   Where a requirement under subsection (1) is imposed, the Board or (as the case may be) Special Health Authority must comply with such instructions as the Secretary of State may give with respect to the exercise of the approval function.

(5)   An instruction under subsection (4) may be given in such form as the Secretary of State may determine.

(6)   The Secretary of State must publish instructions under subsection (4) in such form as the Secretary of State may determine.

(7)   Where the Board or a Special Health Authority has an approval function by virtue of this section, the function is to be treated for the purposes of the National Health Service Act 2006 as a function that it has under that Act.

(8)  The Secretary of State may make payments in connection with the exercise of an approval function by virtue of this section.

### 12ZC. Provision of information for the purposes of section 12ZA or 12ZB

(1)  A relevant person may provide another person with such information as the relevant person considers necessary or appropriate for or in connection with –

  (a)  the exercise of an approval function; or

  (b)  the exercise by the Secretary of State of the power –

    (i)   to enter into an agreement under section 12ZA;

    (ii)  to impose a requirement under section 12ZB; or

    (iii) to give an instruction under section 12ZA(5) or 12ZB(4).

(2)  The relevant persons are –

  (a)  the Secretary of State;

  (b)  a person who is a party to an agreement under section 12ZA; or

  (c)  if the Secretary of State imposes a requirement under section 12ZB on the National Health Service Commissioning Board or a Special Health Authority, the Board or (as the case may be) Special Health Authority.

(3)  This section, in so far as it authorises the provision of information by one relevant person to another relevant person, has effect notwithstanding any rule of common law which would otherwise prohibit or restrict the provision.

(4)  In this section, "information" includes documents and records.

### 12A. Conflicts of interest

(1)  The appropriate national authority may make regulations as to the circumstances in which there would be a potential conflict of interest such that –

  (a)  an approved mental health professional shall not make an application mentioned in section 11(1) above;

  (b)  a registered medical practitioner shall not give a recommendation for the purposes of an application mentioned in section 12(1) above.

(2)  Regulations under subsection (1) above may make –

  (a)  provision for the prohibitions in paragraphs (a) and (b) of that subsection to be subject to specified exceptions;

  (b)  different provision for different cases; and

  (c)  transitional, consequential, incidental or supplemental provision.

(3)  In subsection (1) above, "the appropriate national authority" means –

  (a)  in relation to applications in which admission is sought to a hospital in England or to guardianship applications in respect of which the area of the relevant local social services authority is in England, the Secretary of State;

  (b)  in relation to applications in which admission is sought to a hospital in Wales or to guardianship applications in respect of which the area of the relevant local social services authority is in Wales, the Welsh Ministers.

(4)     References in this section to the relevant local social services authority, in relation to a guardianship application, are references to the local social services authority named in the application as guardian or (as the case may be) the local social services authority for the area in which the person so named resides.

## 13. Duty of approved mental health professionals to make applications for admission or guardianship

(1)     If a local social services authority has reason to think that an application for admission to hospital or a guardianship application may need to be made in respect of a patient within their area, they shall make arrangements for an approved mental health professional to consider the patient's case on their behalf.

(1A)    If that professional is –

(a)   satisfied that such an application ought to be made in respect of the patient; and

(b)   of the opinion, having regard to any wishes expressed by relatives of the patient or any other relevant circumstances, that it is necessary or proper for the application to be made by him, he shall make the application.

(1B)    Subsection (1C) below applies where –

(a)   a local social services authority makes arrangements under subsection (1) above in respect of a patient;

(b)   an application for admission for assessment is made under subsection (1A) above in respect of the patient;

(c)   while the patient is liable to be detained in pursuance of that application, the authority has reason to think that an application for admission for treatment may need to be made in respect of the patient; and

(d)   the patient is not within the area of the authority.

(1C)    Where this subsection applies, subsection (1) above shall be construed as requiring the authority to make arrangements under that subsection in place of the authority mentioned there.

(2)     Before making an application for the admission of a patient to hospital an approved mental health professional shall interview the patient in a suitable manner and satisfy himself that detention in a hospital is in all the circumstances of the case the most appropriate way of providing the care and medical treatment of which the patient stands in need.

(3)     An application under subsection (1A) above may be made outside the area of the local social services authority on whose behalf the approved mental health professional is considering the patient's case.

(4)     It shall be the duty of a local social services authority, if so required by the nearest relative of a patient residing in their area, to make arrangements under subsection (1) above for an approved mental health professional to consider the patient's case with a view to making an application for his admission to hospital; and if in any such case that professional decides not to make an application he shall inform the nearest relative of his reasons in writing.

(5)     Nothing in this section shall be construed as authorising or requiring an application to be made by an approved mental health professional in contravention of the provisions of section 11(4) above or of regulations under section 12A above, or as restricting

the power of a local social services authority to make arrangements with an approved mental health professional to consider a patient's case or of an approved mental health professional to make any application under this Act.

## 14. Social reports

Where a patient is admitted to a hospital in pursuance of an application (other than an emergency application) made under this Part of this Act by his nearest relative, the managers of the hospital shall as soon as practicable give notice of that fact to the local social services authority for the area in which the patient resided immediately before his admission; and that authority shall as soon as practicable arrange for an approved mental health professional to interview the patient and provide the managers with a report on his social circumstances.

## 15. Rectification of applications and recommendations

(1)   If within the period of 14 days beginning with the day on which a patient has been admitted to a hospital in pursuance of an application for admission for assessment or for treatment the application, or any medical recommendation given for the purposes of the application, is found to be in any respect incorrect or defective, the application or recommendation may, within that period and with the consent of the managers of the hospital, be amended by the person by whom it was signed; and upon such amendment being made the application or recommendation shall have effect and shall be deemed to have had effect as if it had been originally made as so amended.

(2)   Without prejudice to subsection (1) above, if within the period mentioned in that subsection it appears to the managers of the hospital that one of the two medical recommendations on which an application for the admission of a patient is founded is insufficient to warrant the detention of the patient in pursuance of the application, they may, within that period, give notice in writing to that effect to the applicant; and where any such notice is given in respect of a medical recommendation, that recommendation shall be disregarded, but the application shall be, and shall be deemed always to have been, sufficient if –

   (a)  a fresh medical recommendation complying with the relevant provisions of this Part of this Act (other than the provisions relating to the time of signature and the interval between examinations) is furnished to the managers within that period; and

   (b)  that recommendation, and the other recommendation on which the application is founded, together comply with those provisions.

(3)   Where the medical recommendations upon which an application for admission is founded are, taken together, insufficient to warrant the detention of the patient in pursuance of the application, a notice under subsection (2) above may be given in respect of either of those recommendations.

(4)   Nothing in this section shall be construed as authorising the giving of notice in respect of an application made as an emergency application, or the detention of a patient admitted in pursuance of such an application, after the period of 72 hours referred to in section 4(4) above, unless the conditions set out in paragraphs (a) and (b) of that section are complied with or would be complied with apart from any error or defect to which this section applies.

## 16. (repealed)

## 17. Leave of absence from hospital

(1)   The responsible clinician may grant to any patient who is for the time being liable to be detained in a hospital under this Part of this Act leave to be absent from the hospital

subject to such conditions (if any) as that clinician considers necessary in the interests of the patient or for the protection of other persons.

(2) Leave of absence may be granted to a patient under this section either indefinitely or on specified occasions or for any specified period; and where leave is so granted for a specified period, that period may be extended by further leave granted in the absence of the patient.

(2A) But longer-term leave may not be granted to a patient unless the responsible clinician first considers whether the patient should be dealt with under section 17A instead.

(2B) For these purposes, longer-term leave is granted to a patient if –

(a) leave of absence is granted to him under this section either indefinitely or for a specified period of more than seven consecutive days; or

(b) a specified period is extended under this section such that the total period for which leave of absence will have been granted to him under this section exceeds seven consecutive days.

(3) Where it appears to the responsible clinician that it is necessary so to do in the interests of the patient or for the protection of other persons, he may, upon granting leave of absence under this section, direct that the patient remain in custody during his absence; and where leave of absence is so granted the patient may be kept in the custody of any officer on the staff of the hospital, or of any other person authorised in writing by the managers of the hospital or, if the patient is required in accordance with conditions imposed on the grant of leave of absence to reside in another hospital, of any officer on the staff of that other hospital.

(4) In any case where a patient is absent from a hospital in pursuance of leave of absence granted under this section, and it appears to the responsible clinician that it is necessary so to do in the interests of the patient's health or safety or for the protection of other persons, that clinician may, subject to subsection (5) below, by notice in writing given to the patient or to the person for the time being in charge of the patient, revoke the leave of absence and recall the patient to the hospital.

(5) A patient to whom leave of absence is granted under this section shall not be recalled under subsection (4) above after he has ceased to be liable to be detained under this Part of this Act.

(6) Subsection (7) below applies to a person who is granted leave by or by virtue of a provision –

(a) in force in Scotland, Northern Ireland, any of the Channel Islands or the Isle of Man; and

(b) corresponding to subsection (1) above.

(7) For the purpose of giving effect to a direction or condition imposed by virtue of a provision corresponding to subsection (3) above, the person may be conveyed to a place in, or kept in custody or detained at a place of safety in, England and Wales by a person authorised in that behalf by the direction or condition.

## 17A. Community treatment orders

(1) The responsible clinician may by order in writing discharge a detained patient from hospital subject to his being liable to recall in accordance with section 17E below.

(2) A detained patient is a patient who is liable to be detained in a hospital in pursuance of an application for admission for treatment.

(3)    An order under subsection (1) above is referred to in this Act as a "community treatment order".

(4)    The responsible clinician may not make a community treatment order unless –

  (a)   in his opinion, the relevant criteria are met; and

  (b)   an approved mental health professional states in writing –

    (i)   that he agrees with that opinion; and

    (ii)   that it is appropriate to make the order.

(5)    The relevant criteria are –

  (a)   the patient is suffering from mental disorder of a nature or degree which makes it appropriate for him to receive medical treatment;

  (b)   it is necessary for his health or safety or for the protection of other persons that he should receive such treatment;

  (c)   subject to his being liable to be recalled as mentioned in paragraph (d) below, such treatment can be provided without his continuing to be detained in a hospital;

  (d)   it is necessary that the responsible clinician should be able to exercise the power under section 17E(1) below to recall the patient to hospital;

  (e)   appropriate medical treatment is available for him.

(6)    In determining whether the criterion in subsection (5)(d) above is met, the responsible clinician shall, in particular, consider, having regard to the patient's history of mental disorder and any other relevant factors, what risk there would be of a deterioration of the patient's condition if he were not detained in a hospital (as a result, for example, of his refusing or neglecting to receive the medical treatment he requires for his mental disorder).

(7)    In this Act –

"community patient" means a patient in respect of whom a community treatment order is in force;

"the community treatment order", in relation to such a patient, means the community treatment order in force in respect of him; and

"the responsible hospital", in relation to such a patient, means the hospital in which he was liable to be detained immediately before the community treatment order was made, subject to section 19A below.

## 17B. Conditions

(1)    A community treatment order shall specify conditions to which the patient is to be subject while the order remains in force.

(2)    But, subject to subsection (3) below, the order may specify conditions only if the responsible clinician, with the agreement of the approved mental health professional mentioned in section 17A(4)(b) above, thinks them necessary or appropriate for one or more of the following purposes –

  (a)   ensuring that the patient receives medical treatment;

  (b)   preventing risk of harm to the patient's health or safety;

  (c)   protecting other persons.

(3)    The order shall specify –

    (a)    a condition that the patient make himself available for examination under section 20A below; and

    (b)    a condition that, if it is proposed to give a certificate under Part 4A of this Act in his case, he make himself available for examination so as to enable the certificate to be given.

(4)    The responsible clinician may from time to time by order in writing vary the conditions specified in a community treatment order.

(5)    He may also suspend any conditions specified in a community treatment order.

(6)    If a community patient fails to comply with a condition specified in the community treatment order by virtue of subsection (2) above, that fact may be taken into account for the purposes of exercising the power of recall under section 17E (1) below.

(7)    But nothing in this section restricts the exercise of that power to cases where there is such a failure.

## 17C. Duration of community treatment order

A community treatment order shall remain in force until –

(a)    the period mentioned in section 20A(1) below (as extended under any provision of this Act) expires, but this is subject to sections 21 and 22 below;

(b)    the patient is discharged in pursuance of an order under section 23 below or a direction under section 72 below;

(c)    the application for admission for treatment in respect of the patient otherwise ceases to have effect; or

(d)    the order is revoked under section 17F below, whichever occurs first.

## 17D. Effect of community treatment order

(1)    The application for admission for treatment in respect of a patient shall not cease to have effect by virtue of his becoming a community patient.

(2)    But while he remains a community patient –

    (a)    the authority of the managers to detain him under section 6(2) above in pursuance of that application shall be suspended; and

    (b)    reference (however expressed) in this or any other Act, or in any subordinate legislation (within the meaning of the Interpretation Act 1978), to patients liable to be detained, or detained, under this Act shall not include him.

(3)    And section 20 below shall not apply to him while he remains a community patient.

(4)    Accordingly, authority for his detention shall not expire during any period in which that authority is suspended by virtue of subsection (2)(a) above.

## 17E. Power to recall to hospital

(1)    The responsible clinician may recall a community patient to hospital if in his opinion –

    (a)    the patient requires medical treatment in hospital for his mental disorder; and

(b) there would be a risk of harm to the health or safety of the patient or to other persons if the patient were not recalled to hospital for that purpose.

(2) The responsible clinician may also recall a community patient to hospital if the patient fails to comply with a condition specified under section 17B(3) above.

(3) The hospital to which a patient is recalled need not be the responsible hospital.

(4) Nothing in this section prevents a patient from being recalled to a hospital even though he is already in the hospital at the time when the power of recall is exercised; references to recalling him shall be construed accordingly.

(5) The power of recall under subsections (1) and (2) above shall be exercisable by notice in writing to the patient.

(6) A notice under this section recalling a patient to hospital shall be sufficient authority for the managers of that hospital to detain the patient there in accordance with the provisions of this Act.

## 17F. Powers in respect of recalled patients

(1) This section applies to a community patient who is detained in a hospital by virtue of a notice recalling him there under section 17E above.

(2) The patient may be transferred to another hospital in such circumstances and subject to such conditions as may be prescribed in regulations made by the Secretary of State (if the hospital in which the patient is detained is in England) or the Welsh Ministers (if that hospital is in Wales).

(3) If he is so transferred to another hospital, he shall be treated for the purposes of this section (and section 17E above) as if the notice under that section were a notice recalling him to that other hospital and as if he had been detained there from the time when his detention in hospital by virtue of the notice first began.

(4) The responsible clinician may by order in writing revoke the community treatment order if –

(a) in his opinion the conditions mentioned in section 3(2) above are satisfied in respect of the patient; and

(b) an approved mental health professional states in writing –

(i) that he agrees with that opinion; and

(ii) that it is appropriate to revoke the order.

(5) The responsible clinician may at any time release the patient, but not after the community treatment order has been revoked.

(6) If the patient has not been released, nor the community treatment order revoked, by the end of the period of 72 hours, he shall then be released.

(7) But a patient who is released under this section remains subject to the community treatment order.

(8) In this section –

(a) "the period of 72 hours" means the period of 72 hours beginning with the time when the patient's detention in hospital by virtue of the notice under section 17E above begins; and

(b)  references to being released shall be construed as references to being released from that detention (and accordingly from being recalled to hospital).

## 17G. Effect of revoking community treatment order

(1)  This section applies if a community treatment order is revoked under section 17F above in respect of a patient.

(2)  Section 6(2) above shall have effect as if the patient had never been discharged from hospital by virtue of the community treatment order.

(3)  The provisions of this or any other Act relating to patients liable to be detained (or detained) in pursuance of an application for admission for treatment shall apply to the patient as they did before the community treatment order was made, unless otherwise provided.

(4)  If, when the order is revoked, the patient is being detained in a hospital other than the responsible hospital, the provisions of this Part of this Act shall have effect as if –

(a)  the application for admission for treatment in respect of him were an application for admission to that other hospital; and

(b)  he had been admitted to that other hospital at the time when he was originally admitted in pursuance of the application.

(5)  But, in any case, section 20 below shall have effect as if the patient had been admitted to hospital in pursuance of the application for admission for treatment on the day on which the order is revoked.

## 18. Return and readmission of patients absent without leave

(1)  Where a patient who is for the time being liable to be detained under this Part of this Act in a hospital –

(a)  absents himself from the hospital without leave granted under section 17 above; or

(b)  fails to return to the hospital on any occasion on which, or at the expiration of any period for which, leave of absence was granted to him under that section, or upon being recalled under that section; or

(c)  absents himself without permission from any place where he is required to reside in accordance with conditions imposed on the grant of leave of absence under that section,

he may, subject to the provisions of this section, be taken into custody and returned to the hospital or place by any approved mental health professional, by any officer on the staff of the hospital, by any constable, or by any person authorised in writing by the managers of the hospital.

(2)  Where the place referred to in paragraph (c) of subsection (1) above is a hospital other than the one in which the patient is for the time being liable to be detained, the references in that subsection to an officer on the staff of the hospital and the managers of the hospital shall respectively include references to an officer on the staff of the first-mentioned hospital and the managers of that hospital.

(2A)  Where a community patient is at any time absent from a hospital to which he is recalled under section 17E above, he may, subject to the provisions of this section, be taken into custody and returned to the hospital by any approved mental health professional, by any officer on the staff of the hospital, by any constable, or by any person authorised in writing by the responsible clinician or the managers of the hospital.

(3) Where a patient who is for the time being subject to guardianship under this Part of this Act absents himself without the leave of the guardian from the place at which he is required by the guardian to reside, he may, subject to the provisions of this section, be taken into custody and returned to that place by any officer on the staff of a local social services authority, by any constable, or by any person authorised in writing by the guardian or a local social services authority.

(4) A patient shall not be taken into custody under this section after the later of –

    (a) the end of the period of six months beginning with the first day of his absence without leave; and

    (b) the end of the period for which (apart from section 21 below) he is liable to be detained or subject to guardianship or, in the case of a community patient, the community treatment order is in force.

(4A) In determining for the purposes of subsection (4)(b) above or any other provision of this Act whether a person who is or has been absent without leave is at any time liable to be detained or subject to guardianship, a report furnished under section 20 or 21B below before the first day of his absence without leave shall not be taken to have renewed the authority for his detention or guardianship unless the period of renewal began before that day.

(4B) Similarly, in determining for those purposes whether a community treatment order is at any time in force in respect of a person who is or has been absent without leave, a report furnished under section 20A or 21B below before the first day of his absence without leave shall not be taken to have extended the community treatment period unless the extension began before that day.

(5) A patient shall not be taken into custody under this section if the period for which he is liable to be detained is that specified in section 2(4), 4(4) or 5(2) or (4) above and that period has expired.

(6) In this Act "absent without leave" means absent from any hospital or other place and liable to be taken into custody and returned under this section, and related expressions shall be construed accordingly.

(7) In relation to a patient who has yet to comply with a requirement imposed by virtue of this Act to be in a hospital or place, references in this Act to his liability to be returned to the hospital or place shall include his liability to be taken to that hospital or place; and related expressions shall be construed accordingly.

### 19. Regulations as to transfer of patients

(1) In such circumstances and subject to such conditions as may be prescribed by regulations made by the Secretary of State –

    (a) a patient who is for the time being liable to be detained in a hospital by virtue of an application under this Part of this Act may be transferred to another hospital or into the guardianship of a local social services authority or of any person approved by such an authority;

    (b) a patient who is for the time being subject to the guardianship of a local social services authority or other person by virtue of an application under this Part of this Act may be transferred into the guardianship of another local social services authority or person, or be transferred to a hospital.

(2)  Where a patient is transferred in pursuance of regulations under this section, the provisions of this Part of this Act (including this subsection) shall apply to him as follows, that is to say –

(a)  in the case of a patient who is liable to be detained in a hospital by virtue of an application for admission for assessment or for treatment and is transferred to another hospital, as if the application were an application for admission to that other hospital and as if the patient had been admitted to that other hospital at the time when he was originally admitted in pursuance of the application;

(b)  in the case of a patient who is liable to be detained in a hospital by virtue of such an application and is transferred into guardianship, as if the application were a guardianship application duly accepted at the said time;

(c)  in the case of a patient who is subject to guardianship by virtue of a guardianship application and is transferred into the guardianship of another authority or person, as if the application were for his reception into the guardianship of that authority or person and had been accepted at the time when it was originally accepted;

(d)  in the case of a patient who is subject to guardianship by virtue of a guardianship application and is transferred to a hospital, as if the guardianship application were an application for admission to that hospital for treatment and as if the patient had been admitted to the hospital at the time when the application was originally accepted.

(3)  Without prejudice to subsections (1) and (2) above, any patient who is for the time being liable to be detained under this Part of this Act in a hospital vested in the Secretary of State for the purposes of his functions under the National Health Service Act 2006, in a hospital vested in the Welsh Ministers for the purposes of their functions under the National Health Service (Wales) Act 2006, in any accommodation used under either of those Acts, by the managers of such a hospital or in a hospital vested in a National Health Service trust, NHS foundation trust, Local Health Board or Primary Care Trust, may at any time be removed to any other such hospital or accommodation which is managed by the managers of, or is vested in the National Health Service trust, NHS foundation trust, Local Health Board or Primary Care Trust for, the first mentioned hospital; and paragraph (a) of subsection (2) above shall apply in relation to a patient so removed as it applies in relation to a patient transferred in pursuance of regulations made under this section.

(4)  Regulations made under this section may make provision for regulating the conveyance to their destination of patients authorised to be transferred or removed in pursuance of the regulations or under subsection (3) above.

## 19A. Regulations as to assignment of responsibility for community patients

(1)  Responsibility for a community patient may be assigned to another hospital in such circumstances and subject to such conditions as may be prescribed by regulations made by the Secretary of State (if the responsible hospital is in England) or the Welsh Ministers (if that hospital is in Wales).

(2)  If responsibility for a community patient is assigned to another hospital –

(a)  the application for admission for treatment in respect of the patient shall have effect (subject to section 17D above) as if it had always specified that other hospital;

(b)  the patient shall be treated as if he had been admitted to that other hospital at the time when he was originally admitted in pursuance of the application (and as if he had subsequently been discharged under section 17A above from there); and

(c) that other hospital shall become "the responsible hospital" in relation to the patient for the purposes of this Act.

*Duration of authority and discharge*

## 20. Duration of authority

(1) Subject to the following provisions of this Part of this Act, a patient admitted to hospital in pursuance of an application for admission for treatment, and a patient placed under guardianship in pursuance of a guardianship application, may be detained in a hospital or kept under guardianship for a period not exceeding six months beginning with the day on which he was so admitted, or the day on which the guardianship application was accepted, as the case may be, but shall not be so detained or kept for any longer period unless the authority for his detention or guardianship is renewed under this section.

(2) Authority for the detention or guardianship of a patient may, unless the patient has previously been discharged under section 23 below, be renewed –

(a) from the expiration of the period referred to in subsection (1) above, for a further period of six months;

(b) from the expiration of any period of renewal under paragraph (a) above, for a further period of one year,

and so on for periods of one year at a time.

(3) Within the period of two months ending on the day on which a patient who is liable to be detained in pursuance of an application for admission for treatment would cease under this section to be so liable in default of the renewal of the authority for his detention, it shall be the duty of the responsible clinician –

(a) to examine the patient; and

(b) if it appears to him that the conditions set out in subsection (4) are satisfied, to furnish to the managers of the hospital where the patient is detained a report to that effect in the prescribed form;

and where such a report is furnished in respect of a patient the managers shall, unless they discharge the patient under section 23 below, cause him to be informed.

(4) The conditions referred to in subsection (3) above are that –

(a) the patient is suffering from mental disorder of a nature or degree which makes it appropriate for him to receive medical treatment in a hospital; and

(b) (repealed);

(c) it is necessary for the health or safety of the patient or for the protection of other persons that he should receive such treatment and that it cannot be provided unless he continues to be detained; and

(d) appropriate medical treatment is available for him.

(5) Before furnishing a report under subsection (3) above the responsible clinician shall consult one or more other persons who have been professionally concerned with the patient's medical treatment.

(5A) But the responsible clinician may not furnish a report under subsection (3) above unless a person –

(a)   who has been professionally concerned with the patient's medical treatment; but

(b)   who belongs to a profession other than that to which the responsible clinician belongs, states in writing that he agrees that the conditions set out in subsection (4) above are satisfied.

(6)   Within the period of two months ending with the day on which a patient who is subject to guardianship under this Part of this Act would cease under this section to be so liable in default of the renewal of the authority for his guardianship, it shall be the duty of the appropriate practitioner –

(a)   to examine the patient; and

(b)   if it appears to him that the conditions set out in subsection (7) below are satisfied, to furnish to the guardian and, where the guardian is a person other than a local social services authority, to the responsible local social services authority a report to that effect in the prescribed form;

and where such a report is furnished in respect of a patient, the local social services authority shall, unless they discharge the patient under section 23 below, cause him to be informed.

(7)   The conditions referred to in subsection (6) above are that –

(a)   the patient is suffering from mental disorder of a nature or degree which warrants his reception into guardianship; and

(b)   it is necessary in the interests of the welfare of the patient or for the protection of other persons that the patient should remain under guardianship.

(8)   Where a report is duly furnished under subsection (3) or (6) above, the authority for the detention or guardianship of the patient shall be thereby renewed for the period pre-scribed in that case by subsection (2) above.

## 20A. Community treatment period

(1)   Subject to the provisions of this Part, a community treatment order shall cease to be in force on expiry of the period of six months beginning with the day on which it was made.

(2)   That period is referred to in this Act as "the community treatment period".

(3)   The community treatment period may, unless the order has previously ceased to be in force, be extended –

(a)   from its expiration for a period of six months;

(b)   from the expiration of any period of extension under paragraph (a) above for a fur-ther period of one year, and so on for periods of one year at a time.

(4)   Within the period of two months ending on the day on which the order would cease to be in force in default of an extension under this section, it shall be the duty of the responsible clinician –

(a)   to examine the patient; and

(b)   if it appears to him that the conditions set out in subsection (6) below are satisfied and if a statement under subsection (8) is made, to furnish to the managers of the responsible hospital a report to that effect in the prescribed form.

(5) Where such a report is furnished in respect of the patient, the managers shall, unless they discharge him under section 23 below, cause him to be informed.

(6) The conditions referred to in subsection (4) above are that –

(a) the patient is suffering from mental disorder of a nature or degree which makes it appropriate for him to receive medical treatment;

(b) it is necessary for his health or safety or for the protection of other persons that he should receive such treatment;

(c) subject to his continuing to be liable to be recalled as mentioned in paragraph (d) below, such treatment can be provided without his being detained in a hospital;

(d) it is necessary that the responsible clinician should continue to be able to exercise the power under section 17E(1) above to recall the patient to hospital; and

(e) appropriate medical treatment is available for him.

(7) In determining whether the criterion in subsection (6)(d) above is met, the responsible clinician shall, in particular, consider, having regard to the patient's history of mental disorder and any other relevant factors, what risk there would be of a deterioration of the patient's condition if he were to continue not to be detained in a hospital (as a result, for example, of his refusing or neglecting to receive the medical treatment he requires for his mental disorder).

(8) The statement referred to in subsection (4) above is a statement in writing by an approved mental health professional –

(a) that it appears to him that the conditions set out in subsection (6) above are satisfied; and

(b) that it is appropriate to extend the community treatment period.

(9) Before furnishing a report under subsection (4) above the responsible clinician shall consult one or more other persons who have been professionally concerned with the patient's medical treatment.

(10) Where a report is duly furnished under subsection (4) above, the community treatment period shall be thereby extended for the period prescribed in that case by subsection (3) above.

### 20B. Effect of expiry of community treatment order

(1) A community patient shall be deemed to be discharged absolutely from liability to recall under this Part of this Act, and the application for admission for treatment cease to have effect, on expiry of the community treatment order, if the order has not previously ceased to be in force.

(2) For the purposes of subsection (1) above, a community treatment order expires on expiry of the community treatment period as extended under this Part of this Act, but this is subject to sections 21 and 22 below.

### 21. Special provisions as to patients absent without leave

(1) Where a patient is absent without leave –

(a) on the day on which (apart from this section) he would cease to be liable to be detained or subject to guardianship under this Part of this Act or, in the case of a community patient, the community treatment order would cease to be in force; or

(b)  within the period of one week ending with that day,

he shall not cease to be so liable or subject, or the order shall not cease to be in force, until the relevant time.

(2)  For the purposes of subsection (1) above the relevant time –

(a)  where the patient is taken into custody under section 18 above, is the end of the period of one week beginning with the day on which he is returned to the hospital or place where he ought to be;

(b)  where the patient returns himself to the hospital or place where he ought to be within the period during which he can be taken into custody under section 18 above, is the end of the period of one week beginning with the day on which he so returns himself; and

(c)  otherwise, is the end of the period during which he can be taken into custody under section 18 above.

(3)  Where a patient is absent without leave on the day on which (apart from this section) the managers would be required under section 68 below to refer the patient's case to a Mental Health Review Tribunal, that requirement shall not apply unless and until –

(a)  the patient is taken into custody under section 18 above and returned to the hospital where he ought to be; or

(b)  the patient returns himself to the hospital where he ought to be within the period during which he can be taken into custody under section 18 above.

(4)  Where a community patient is absent without leave on the day on which (apart from this section) the 72-hour period mentioned in section 17F above would expire, that period shall not expire until the end of the period of 72 hours beginning with the time when –

(a)  the patient is taken into custody under section 18 above and returned to the hospital where he ought to be; or

(b)  the patient returns himself to the hospital where he ought to be within the period during which he can be taken into custody under section 18 above.

(5)  Any reference in this section, or in sections 21A to 22 below, to the time when a community treatment order would cease, or would have ceased, to be in force shall be construed as a reference to the time when it would cease, or would have ceased, to be in force by reason only of the passage of time.

## 21A. Patients who are taken into custody or return within 28 days

(1)  This section applies where a patient who is absent without leave is taken into custody under section 18 above, or returns himself to the hospital or place where he ought to be, not later than the end of the period of 28 days beginning with the first day of his absence without leave.

(2)  Where the period for which the patient is liable to be detained or subject to guardianship is extended by section 21 above, any examination and report to be made and furnished in respect of the patient under section 20(3) or (6) above may be made and furnished within the period as so extended.

(3)  Where the authority for the detention or guardianship of the patient is renewed by virtue of subsection (2) above after the day on which (apart from section 21 above) that authority would have expired, the renewal shall take effect as from that day.

(4)   In the case of a community patient, where the period for which the community treatment order is in force is extended by section 21 above, any examination and report to be made and furnished in respect of the patient under section 20A(4) above may be made and furnished within the period as so extended.

(5)   Where the community treatment period is extended by virtue of subsection (4) above after the day on which (apart from section 21 above) the order would have ceased to be in force, the extension shall take effect as from that day.

### 21B. Patients who are taken into custody or return after more than 28 days

(1)   This section applies where a patient who is absent without leave is taken into custody under section 18 above, or returns himself to the hospital or place where he ought to be, later than the end of the period of 28 days beginning with the first day of his absence without leave.

(2)   It shall be the duty of the appropriate practitioner, within the period of one week beginning with the day on which the patient is returned or returns himself to the hospital or place where he ought to be (his "return day") –

    (a)   to examine the patient; and

    (b)   if it appears to him that the relevant conditions are satisfied, to furnish to the appropriate body a report to that effect in the prescribed form;

and where such a report is furnished in respect of the patient the appropriate body shall cause him to be informed.

(3)   Where the patient is liable to be detained or is a community patient (as opposed to subject to guardianship) the appropriate practitioner shall, before furnishing a report under subsection (2) above, consult –

    (a)   one or more other persons who have been professionally concerned with the patient's medical treatment; and

    (b)   an approved mental health professional.

(4)   Where –

    (a)   the patient would (apart from any renewal of the authority for his detention or guardianship on or after his return day) be liable to be detained or subject to guardianship after the end of the period of one week beginning with that day; or

    (b)   in the case of a community patient, the community treatment order would (apart from any extension of the community treatment period on or after that day) be in force after the end of that period,

he shall cease to be so liable or subject, or the community treatment period shall be deemed to expire, at the end of that period unless a report is duly furnished in respect of him under subsection (2) above.

(4A)  If, in the case of a community patient, the community treatment order is revoked under section 17F above during the period of one week beginning with his return day –

    (a)   subsections (2) and (4) above shall not apply; and

    (b)   any report already furnished in respect of him under subsection (2) above shall be of no effect.

(5)   Where the patient would (apart from section 21 above) have ceased to be liable to be detained or subject to guardianship on or before the day on which a report is duly fur-

nished in respect of him under subsection (2) above, the report shall renew the authority for his detention or guardianship for the period prescribed in that case by section 20(2) above.

(6) Where the authority for the detention or guardianship of the patient is renewed by virtue of subsection (5) above –

(a) the renewal shall take effect as from the day on which (apart from section 21 above and that subsection) the authority would have expired; and

(b) if (apart from this paragraph) the renewed authority would expire on or before the day on which the report is furnished, the report shall further renew the authority, as from the day on which it would expire, for the period prescribed in that case by section 20(2) above.

(6A) In the case of a community patient, where the community treatment order would (apart from section 21 above) have ceased to be in force on or before the day on which a report is duly furnished in respect of him under subsection (2) above, the report shall extend the community treatment period for the period prescribed in that case by section 20A(3) above.

(6B) Where the community treatment period is extended by virtue of subsection (6A) above –

(a) the extension shall take effect as from the day on which (apart from section 21 above and that subsection) the order would have ceased to be in force; and

(b) if (apart from this paragraph) the period as so extended would expire on or before the day on which the report is furnished, the report shall further extend that period, as from the day on which it would expire, for the period prescribed in that case by section 20A(3) above.

(7) Where the authority for the detention or guardianship of the patient would expire within the period of two months beginning with the day on which a report is duly furnished in respect of him under subsection (2) above, the report shall, if it so provides, have effect also as a report duly furnished under section 20(3) or (6) above; and the reference in this subsection to authority includes any authority renewed under subsection (5) above by the report.

(7A) In the case of a community patient, where the community treatment order would (taking account of any extension under subsection (6A) above) cease to be in force within the period of two months beginning with the day on which a report is duly furnished in respect of him under subsection (2) above, the report shall, if it so provides, have effect also as a report duly furnished under section 20A(4) above.

(8) (repealed)

(9) (repealed)

(10) In this section –

"the appropriate body" means –

(a) in relation to a patient who is liable to be detained in a hospital, the managers of the hospital;

(b) in relation to a patient who is subject to guardianship, the responsible local social services authority;

(c) in relation to a community patient, the managers of the responsible hospital; and

"the relevant conditions" means –

(a) in relation to a patient who is liable to be detained in a hospital, the conditions set out in subsection (4) of section 20 above;

(b) in relation to a patient who is subject to guardianship, the conditions set out in subsection (7) of that section;

(c) in relation to a community patient, the conditions set out in section 20A(6) above.

## 22. Special provisions as to patients sentenced to imprisonment, etc.

(1) If –

(a) a qualifying patient is detained in custody in pursuance of any sentence or order passed or made by a court in the United Kingdom (including an order committing or remanding him in custody); and

(b) he is so detained for a period exceeding, or for successive periods exceeding in the aggregate, six months,

the relevant application shall cease to have effect on expiry of that period.

(2) A patient is a qualifying patient for the purposes of this section if –

(a) he is liable to be detained by virtue of an application for admission for treatment;

(b) he is subject to guardianship by virtue of a guardianship application; or

(c) he is a community patient.

(3) "The relevant application", in relation to a qualifying patient, means –

(a) in the case of a patient who is subject to guardianship, the guardianship application in respect of him;

(b) in any other case, the application for admission for treatment in respect of him.

(4) The remaining subsections of this section shall apply if a qualifying patient is detained in custody as mentioned in subsection (1)(a) above but for a period not exceeding, or for successive periods not exceeding in the aggregate, six months.

(5) If apart from this subsection –

(a) the patient would have ceased to be liable to be detained or subject to guardianship by virtue of the relevant application on or before the day on which he is discharged from custody; or

(b) in the case of a community patient, the community treatment order would have ceased to be in force on or before that day, he shall not cease and shall be deemed not to have ceased to be so liable or subject, or the order shall not cease and shall be deemed not to have ceased to be in force, until the end of that day.

(6) In any case (except as provided in subsection (8) below), sections 18, 21 and 21A above shall apply in relation to the patient as if he had absented himself without leave on that day.

(7) In its application by virtue of subsection (6) above section 18 shall have effect as if –

(a) in subsection (4) for the words from "later of" to the end there were substituted "end of the period of 28 days beginning with the first day of his absence without leave"; and

(b) subsections (4A) and (4B) were omitted.

(8)  In relation to a community patient who was not recalled to hospital under section 17E above at the time when his detention in custody began –

(a)  section 18 above shall not apply; but

(b)  sections 21 and 21A above shall apply as if he had absented himself without leave on the day on which he is discharged from custody and had returned himself as provided in those sections on the last day of the period of 28 days beginning with that day.

## 23. Discharge of patients

(1)  Subject to the provisions of this section and section 25 below, a patient who is for the time being liable to be detained or subject to guardianship under this Part of this Act shall cease to be so liable or subject if an order in writing discharging him absolutely from detention or guardianship is made in accordance with this section.

(1A)  Subject to the provisions of this section and section 25 below, a community patient shall cease to be liable to recall under this Part of this Act, and the application for admission for treatment cease to have effect, if an order in writing discharging him from such liability is made in accordance with this section.

(1B)  An order under subsection (1) or (1A) above shall be referred to in this Act as "an order for discharge".

(2)  An order for discharge may be made in respect of a patient –

(a)  where the patient is liable to be detained in a hospital in pursuance of an application for admission for assessment or for treatment by the responsible clinician, by the managers or by the nearest relative of the patient;

(b)  where the patient is subject to guardianship, by the responsible clinician, by the responsible local social services authority or by the nearest relative of the patient

(c)  where the patient is a community patient, by the responsible clinician, by the managers of the responsible hospital or by the nearest relative of the patient.

(3)  (repealed)

(4)  The powers conferred by this section on any authority, trust, board (other than an NHS foundation trust) or body of persons may be exercised subject to subsection (3) below by any three or more members of that authority, trust, board or body authorised by them in that behalf or by three or more members of a committee or sub-committee of that authority, trust, board or body which has been authorised by them in that behalf.

(5)  The reference in subsection (4) above to the members of an authority, trust, board or body or the members of a committee or sub-committee of an authority, trust, board or body –

(a)  in the case of a Local Health Board, Special Health Authority or Primary Care Trust or a committee or sub-committee of a Local Health Board, Special Health Authority or Primary Care Trust, is a reference only to the chairman of the authority, trust or board and such members (of the authority, trust, board, committee or sub-committee, as the case may be) as are not also officers of the authority, trust or board, within the meaning of the National Health Service Act 2006 or the National Health Service (Wales) Act 2006; and

(b)  in the case of a National Health Service trust or a committee or sub-committee of such a trust, is a reference only to the chairman of the trust and such directors or (in the case of a committee or sub-committee) members as are not also employees of the trust.

(6) The powers conferred by this section on any NHS foundation trust may be exercised by any three or more persons authorised by the board of the trust in that behalf each of whom is neither an executive director of the board nor an employee of the trust.

## 24. Visiting and examination of patients

(1) For the purpose of advising as to the exercise by the nearest relative of a patient who is liable to be detained or subject to guardianship under this Part of this Act, or who is a community patient, of any power to order his discharge, any registered medical practitioner or approved clinician authorised by or on behalf of the nearest relative of the patient may, at any reasonable time, visit the patient and examine him in private.

(2) Any registered medical practitioner or approved clinician authorised for the purposes of subsection (1) above to visit and examine a patient may require the production of and inspect any records relating to the detention or treatment of the patient in any hospital or to any aftercare services provided for the patient under section 117 below.

## 25. Restrictions on discharge by nearest relative

(1) An order for the discharge of a patient who is liable to be detained in a hospital shall not be made under section 23 above by his nearest relative except after giving not less than 72 hours' notice in writing to the managers of the hospital; and if, within 72 hours after such notice has been given, the responsible clinician furnishes to the managers a report certifying that in the opinion of that clinician the patient, if discharged, would be likely to act in a manner dangerous to other persons or to himself –

  (a) any order for the discharge of the patient made by that relative in pursuance of the notice shall be of no effect; and

  (b) no further order for the discharge of the patient shall be made by that relative during the period of six months beginning with the date of the report.

(1A) Subsection (1) above shall apply to an order for the discharge of a community patient as it applies to an order for the discharge of a patient who is liable to be detained in a hospital, but with the reference to the managers of the hospital being read as a reference to the managers of the responsible hospital.

(2) In any case where a report under subsection (1) above is furnished in respect of a patient who is liable to be detained in pursuance of an application for admission for treatment, or in respect of a community patient, the managers shall cause the nearest relative of the patient to be informed.

*Functions of relatives of patients*

## 26. Definition of "relative" and "nearest relative"

(1) In this Part of this Act "relative" means any of the following persons –

  (a) husband or wife or civil partner;

  (b) son or daughter;

  (c) father or mother;

  (d) brother or sister;

  (e) grandparent;

(f)   grandchild;

(g)   uncle or aunt;

(h)   nephew or niece.

(2)   In deducing relationships for the purposes of this section, any relationship of the half-blood shall be treated as a relationship of the whole blood, and an illegitimate person shall be treated as the legitimate child of

(a)   his mother, and

(b)   if his father has parental responsibility for him within the meaning of section 3 of the Children Act 1989, his father.

(3)   In this Part of this Act, subject to the provisions of this section and to the following provisions of this Part of this Act, the "nearest relative" means the person first described in subsection (1) above who is for the time being surviving, relatives of the whole blood being preferred to relatives of the same description of the half-blood and the elder or eldest of two or more relatives described in any paragraph of that subsection being preferred to the other or others of those relatives, regardless of sex.

(4)   Subject to the provisions of this section and to the following provisions of this Part of this Act, where the patient ordinarily resides with or is cared for by one or more of his relatives (or, if he is for the time being an in-patient in a hospital, he last ordinarily resided with or was cared for by one or more of his relatives) his nearest relative shall be determined –

(a)   by giving preference to that relative or those relatives over the other or others; and

(b)   as between two or more such relatives, in accordance with subsection (3) above.

(5)   Where the person who, under subsection (3) or (4) above, would be the nearest relative of a patient –

(a)   in the case of a patient ordinarily resident in the United Kingdom, the Channel Islands or the Isle of Man, is not so resident; or

(b)   is the husband or wife or civil partner of the patient, but is permanently separated from the patient, either by agreement or under an order of a court, or has deserted or has been deserted by the patient for a period which has not come to an end; or

(c)   is a person other than the husband, wife, civil partner, father or mother of the patient, and is for the time being under 18 years of age;

(d)   (repealed);

the nearest relative of the patient shall be ascertained as if that person were dead.

(6)   In this section "husband", "wife" and "civil partner" include a person who is living with the patient as the patient's husband or wife or as if they were civil partners, as the case may be (or, if the patient is for the time being an in-patient in a hospital, was so living until the patient was admitted), and has been or had been so living for a period of not less than six months; but a person shall not be treated by virtue of this subsection as the nearest relative of a married patient or a patient in a civil partnership unless the husband, wife or civil partner of the patient is disregarded by virtue of paragraph (b) of subsection (5) above.

(7)   A person, other than a relative, with whom the patient ordinarily resides (or, if the patient is for the time being an in-patient in a hospital, last ordinarily resided before he was admitted), and with whom he has or had been ordinarily residing for a period of not

less than five years, shall be treated for the purposes of this Part of this Act as if he were a relative but –

(a) shall be treated for the purposes of subsection (3) above as if mentioned last in sub-section (1) above; and

(b) shall not be treated by virtue of this subsection as the nearest relative of a married patient or a patient in a civil partnership unless the husband, wife or civil partner of the patient is disregarded by virtue of paragraph (b) of subsection (5) above.

### 27. Children and young persons in care

Where –

(a) a patient who is a child or young person is in the care of a local authority by virtue of a care order within the meaning of the Children Act 1989; or

(b) the rights and powers of a parent of a patient who is a child or young person are vested in a local authority by virtue of section 16 of the Social Work (Scotland) Act 1968,

the authority shall be deemed to be the nearest relative of the patient in preference to any person except the patient's husband or wife or civil partner (if any).

### 28. Nearest relative of minor under guardianship, etc.

(1) Where –

(a) a guardian has been appointed for a person who has not attained the age of 18 years; or

(b) a residence order (as defined by section 8 of the Children Act 1989) is in force with respect to such a person, the guardian (or guardians, where there is more than one) or the person named in the residence order shall, to the exclusion of any other person, be deemed to be his nearest relative.

(2) Subsection (5) of section 26 above shall apply in relation to a person who is, or who is one of the persons, deemed to be the nearest relative of a patient by virtue of this section as it applies in relation to a person who would be the nearest relative under sub-section (3) of that section.

(3) In this section "guardian" includes a special guardian (within the meaning of the Children Act 1989), but does not include a guardian under this Part of this Act.

(4) In this section "court" includes a court in Scotland or Northern Ireland, and "enactment" includes an enactment of the Parliament of Northern Ireland, a Measure of the Northern Ireland Assembly and an Order in Council under Schedule 1 of the Northern Ireland Act 1974.

### 29. Appointment by court of acting nearest relative

(1) The county court may, upon application made in accordance with the provisions of this section in respect of a patient, by order direct that the functions of the nearest relative of the patient under this Part of this Act and sections 66 and 69 below shall, during the continuance in force of the order, be exercisable by the person specified in the order.

(1A) If the court decides to make an order on an application under subsection (1) above, the following rules have effect for the purposes of specifying a person in the order –

(a) if a person is nominated in the application to act as the patient's nearest relative and that person is, in the opinion of the court, a suitable person to act as such and is willing to do so, the court shall specify that person (or, if there are two or more such persons, such one of them as the court thinks fit);

    (b)  otherwise, the court shall specify such person as is, in its opinion, a suitable person to act as the patient's nearest relative and is willing to do so.

(2)    An order under this section may be made on the application of –

    (za) the patient;

    (a)  any relative of the patient;

    (b)  any other person with whom the patient is residing (or, if the patient is then an in-patient in a hospital, was last residing before he was admitted); or

    (c)  approved mental health professional.

(3)    An application for an order under this section may be made upon any of the following grounds, that is to say –

    (a)  that the patient has no nearest relative within the meaning of this Act, or that it is not reasonably practicable to ascertain whether he has such a relative, or who that relative is;

    (b)  that the nearest relative of the patient is incapable of acting as such by reason of mental disorder or other illness;

    (c)  that the nearest relative of the patient unreasonably objects to the making of an application for admission for treatment or a guardianship application in respect of the patient;

    (d)  that the nearest relative of the patient has exercised without due regard to the welfare of the patient or the interests of the public his power to discharge the patient from hospital or guardianship under this Part of this Act, or is likely to do so; or

    (e)  that the nearest relative of the patient is otherwise not a suitable person to act as such.

(4)    If, immediately before the expiration of the period for which a patient is liable to be detained by virtue of an application for admission for assessment, an application under this section, which is an application made on the ground specified in subsection (3)(c) or (d) above, is pending in respect of the patient, that period shall be extended –

    (a)  in any case, until the application under this section has been finally disposed of; and

    (b)  if an order is made in pursuance of the application under this section, for a further period of seven days;

    and for the purposes of this subsection an application under this section shall be deemed to have been finally disposed of at the expiration of the time allowed for appealing from the decision of the court or, if notice of appeal has been given within that time, when the appeal has been heard or withdrawn, and "pending" shall be construed accordingly.

(5)    An order made on the ground specified in subsection (3)(a), (b) or (e) above may specify a period for which it is to continue in force unless previously discharged under section 30 below,

(6)    While an order made under this section is in force, the provisions of this Part of this Act (other than this section and section 30 below) and sections 66, 69, 132(4) and 133 below shall apply in relation to the patient as if for any reference to the nearest relative of the patient there were substituted a reference to the person having the functions of that relative and (without prejudice to section 30 below) shall so apply notwithstanding

that the person who was the patient's nearest relative when the order was made is no longer his nearest relative; but this subsection shall not apply to section 66 below in the case mentioned in paragraph (h) of subsection (1) of that section.

### 30. Discharge and variation of orders under section 29

(1) An order made under section 29 above in respect of a patient may be discharged by the county court upon application made –

   (a) in any case, by the patient or the person having the functions of the nearest relative of the patient by virtue of the order;

   (b) where the order was made on the ground specified in paragraph (a), (b) or (e) of section 29(3) above, or where the person who was the nearest relative of the patient when the order was made has ceased to be his nearest relative, on the application of the nearest relative of the patient.

(1A) But, in the case of an order made on the ground specified in paragraph (e) of section 29(3) above, an application may not be made under subsection (1)(b) above by the person who was the nearest relative of the patient when the order was made except with leave of the county court.

(2) An order made under section 29 above in respect of a patient may be varied by the county court, on the application of the person having the functions of the nearest relative by virtue of the order or on the application of the patient or of an approved mental health professional, by substituting another person for the person having those functions.

(2A) If the court decides to vary an order on an application under subsection (2) above, the following rules have effect for the purposes of substituting another person –

   (a) if a person is nominated in the application to act as the patient's nearest relative and that person is, in the opinion of the court, a suitable person to act as such and is willing to do so, the court shall specify that person (or, if there are two or more such persons, such one of them as the court thinks fit);

   (b) otherwise, the court shall specify such person as is, in its opinion, a suitable person to act as the patient's nearest relative and is willing to do so.

(3) If the person having the functions of the nearest relative of a patient by virtue of an order under section 29 above dies –

   (a) subsections (1) and (2) above shall apply as if for any reference to that person there were substituted a reference to any relative of the patient, and

   (b) until the order is discharged or varied under those provisions the functions of the nearest relative under this Part of this Act and sections 66 and 69 below shall not be exercisable by any person.

(4) An order made on the ground specified in paragraph (c) or (d) of section 29(3) above shall, unless previously discharged under subsection (1) above, cease to have effect as follows –

   (a) if –

      (i) on the date of the order the patient was liable to be detained or subject to guardianship by virtue of a relevant application, order or direction; or

      (ii) he becomes so liable or subject within the period of three months beginning with that date; or

      (iii) he was a community patient on the date of the order,

it shall cease to have effect when he is discharged under section 23 above or 72 below or the relevant application, order or direction otherwise ceases to have effect (except as a result of his being transferred in pursuance of regulations under section 19 above);

(b)  otherwise, it shall cease to have effect at the end of the period of three months beginning with the date of the order.

(4A)  In subsection (4) above, reference to a relevant application, order or direction is to any of the following –

(a)  an application for admission for treatment;

(b)  a guardianship application;

(c)  an order or direction under Part 3 of this Act (other than under section 35, 36 or 38).

(4B)  An order made on the ground specified in paragraph (a), (b) or (e) of section 29(3) above shall –

(a)  if a period was specified under section 29(5) above, cease to have effect on expiry of that period, unless previously discharged under subsection (1) above;

(b)  if no such period was specified, remain in force until it is discharged under subsection (1) above.

(5)  The discharge or variation under this section of an order made under section 29 above shall not affect the validity of anything previously done in pursuance of the order.

*Supplemental*

## 31. Procedure on applications to county court

Rules of court which relate to applications authorised by this Part of this Act to be made to the county court may make provision –

(a)  for the hearing and determination of such applications otherwise than in open court;

(b)  for the admission on the hearing of such applications of evidence of such descriptions as may be specified in the rules notwithstanding anything to the contrary in any enactment or rule of law relating to the admissibility of evidence;

(c)  for the visiting and interviewing of patients in private by or under the directions of the court.

## 32. Regulations for purposes of Part 2

(1)  The Secretary of State may make regulations for prescribing anything which, under this Part of this Act, is required or authorised to be prescribed, and otherwise for carrying this Part of this Act into full effect.

(2)  Regulations under this section may in particular make provision –

(a)  for prescribing the form of any application, recommendation, report, order, notice or other document to be made or given under this Part of this Act;

(b)  for prescribing the manner in which any such application, recommendation, report, order, notice or other document may be proved, and for regulating the service of any such application, report, order or notice;

(c)   for requiring such bodies as may be prescribed by the regulations to keep such registers or other records as may be so prescribed in respect of patients liable to be detained or subject to guardianship under this Part of this Act or community patients, and to furnish or make available to those patients, and their relatives, such written statements of their rights and powers under this Act as may be so prescribed;

(d)   for the determination in accordance with the regulations of the age of any person whose exact age cannot be ascertained by reference to the registers kept under the Births and Deaths Registration Act 1953; and

(e)   for enabling the functions under this Part of this Act of the nearest relative of a patient to be performed, in such circumstances and subject to such conditions (if any) as may be prescribed by the regulations, by any person authorised in that behalf by that relative;

and for the purposes of this Part of this Act any application, report or notice the service of which is regulated under paragraph (b) above shall be deemed to have been received by or furnished to the authority or person to whom it is authorised or required to be furnished, addressed or given if it is duly served in accordance with the regulations.

(3)   Without prejudice to subsections (1) and (2) above, but subject to section 23(4) and (6) above, regulations under this section may determine the manner in which functions under this Part of this Act of the managers of hospitals, local social services authorities, Local Health Board, Special Health Authorities, Primary Care Trusts, National Health Service trusts or NHS foundation trusts are to be exercised, and such regulations may in particular specify the circumstances in which, and the conditions subject to which, any such functions may be performed by officers of or other persons acting on behalf of those managers, boards, authorities and trusts.

### 33. Special provisions as to wards of court

(1)   An application for the admission to hospital of a minor who is a ward of court may be made under this Part of this Act with the leave of the court; and section 11(4) above shall not apply in relation to an application so made.

(2)   Where a minor who is a ward of court is liable to be detained in a hospital by virtue of an application for admission under this Part of this Act or is a community patient, any power exercisable under this Part of this Act or under section 66 below in relation to the patient by his nearest relative shall be exercisable by or with the leave of the court.

(3)   Nothing in this Part of this Act shall be construed as authorising the making of a guardianship application in respect of a minor who is a ward of court, or the transfer into guardianship of any such minor.

(4)   Where a community treatment order has been made in respect of a minor who is a ward of court, the provisions of this Part of this Act relating to community treatment orders and community patients have effect in relation to the minor subject to any order which the court makes in the exercise of its wardship jurisdiction; but this does not apply as regards any period when the minor is recalled to hospital under section 17E above.

### 34. Interpretation of Part 2

(1)   In this Part of this Act –

"the appropriate practitioner" means –

(a) in the case of a patient who is subject to the guardianship of a person other than a local social services authority, the nominated medical attendant of the patient; and

(b) in any other case, the responsible clinician;

"the nominated medical attendant", in relation to a patient who is subject to the guardianship of a person other than a local social services authority, means the person appointed in pursuance of regulations made under section 9(2) above to act as the medical attendant of the patient;

"registered establishment" means an establishment –

(a) which would not, apart from subsection (2) below, be a hospital for the purposes of this Part; and

(b) in respect of which a person is registered under Part 2 of the Care Standards Act 2000 as an independent hospital in which treatment or nursing (or both) are provided for persons liable to be detained under this Act;

"the responsible clinician" means –

(a) in relation to a patient liable to be detained by virtue of an application for admission for assessment or an application for admission for treatment, or a community patient, the approved clinician with overall responsibility for the patient's case;

(b) in relation to a patient subject to guardianship, the approved clinician authorised by the responsible local social services authority to act (either generally or in any particular case or for any particular purpose) as the responsible clinician;

(2) Except where otherwise expressly provided, this Part of this Act applies in relation to a registered establishment, as it applies in relation to a hospital, and references in this Part of this Act to a hospital, and any reference in this Act to a hospital to which this Part of this Act applies, shall be construed accordingly.

(3) In relation to a patient who is subject to guardianship in pursuance of a guardianship application, any reference in this Part of this Act to the responsible local social services authority is a reference –

(a) where the patient is subject to the guardianship of a local social services authority, to that authority;

(b) where the patient is subject to the guardianship of a person other than a local social services authority, to the local social services authority for the area in which that person resides.

## PART 3: PATIENTS CONCERNED IN CRIMINAL PROCEEDINGS OR UNDER SENTENCE

*Remands to hospital*

### 35. Remand to hospital for report on accused's mental condition

(1) Subject to the provisions of this section, the Crown Court or a magistrates' court may remand an accused person to a hospital specified by the court for a report on his mental condition.

(2) For the purposes of this section an accused person is –

(a) in relation to the Crown Court, any person who is awaiting trial before the court for an offence punishable with imprisonment or who has been arraigned before the court for such an offence and has not yet been sentenced or otherwise dealt with for the offence on which he has been arraigned;

(b) in relation to a magistrates' court, any person who has been convicted by the court of an offence punishable on summary conviction with imprisonment and any person charged with such an offence if the court is satisfied that he did the act or made the omission charged or he has consented to the exercise by the court of the powers conferred by this section.

(3) Subject to subsection (4) below, the powers conferred by this section may be exercised if –

(a) the court is satisfied, on the written or oral evidence of a registered medical practitioner, that there is reason to suspect that the accused person is suffering from mental disorder; and

(b) the court is of the opinion that it would be impracticable for a report on his mental condition to be made if he were remanded on bail;

but those powers shall not be exercised by the Crown Court in respect of a person who has been convicted before the court if the sentence for the offence of which he has been convicted is fixed by law.

(4) The court shall not remand an accused person to a hospital under this section unless satisfied, on the written or oral evidence of the approved clinician who would be responsible for making the report or of some other person representing the managers of the hospital, that arrangements have been made for his admission to that hospital and for his admission to it within the period of seven days beginning with the date of the remand; and if the court is so satisfied it may, pending his admission, give directions for his conveyance to and detention in a place of safety.

(5) Where a court has remanded an accused person under this section it may further remand him if it appears to the court, on the written or oral evidence of the approved clinician responsible for making the report, that a further remand is necessary for completing the assessment of the accused person's mental condition.

(6) The power of further remanding an accused person under this section may be exercised by the court without his being brought before the court if he is represented by counsel or a solicitor and his counsel or solicitor is given an opportunity of being heard.

(7) An accused person shall not be remanded or further remanded under this section for more than 28 days at a time or for more than 12 weeks in all; and the court may at any time terminate the remand if it appears to the court that it is appropriate to do so.

(8) An accused person remanded to hospital under this section shall be entitled to obtain at his own expense an independent report on his mental condition from a registered medical practitioner or approved clinician chosen by him and to apply to the court on the basis of it for his remand to be terminated under subsection (7) above.

(9) Where an accused person is remanded under this section –

(a) a constable or any other person directed to do so by the court shall convey the accused person to the hospital specified by the court within the period mentioned in subsection (4) above; and

(b) the managers of the hospital shall admit him within that period and thereafter detain him in accordance with the provisions of this section.

(10) If an accused person absconds from a hospital to which he has been remanded under this section, or while being conveyed to or from that hospital, he may be arrested

without warrant by any constable and shall, after being arrested, be brought as soon as practicable before the court that remanded him; and the court may thereupon terminate the remand and deal with him in any way in which it could have dealt with him if he had not been remanded under this section.

## 36. Remand of accused person to hospital for treatment

(1) Subject to the provisions of this section, the Crown Court may, instead of remanding an accused person in custody, remand him to a hospital specified by the court if satisfied, on the written or oral evidence of two registered medical practitioners, that

(a) he is suffering from mental disorder of a nature or degree which makes it appropriate for him to be detained in a hospital for medical treatment; and

(b) appropriate medical treatment is available for him.

(2) For the purposes of this section an accused person is any person who is in custody awaiting trial before the Crown Court for an offence punishable with imprisonment (other than an offence the sentence for which is fixed by law) or who at any time before sentence is in custody in the course of a trial before that court for such an offence.

(3) The court shall not remand an accused person under this section to a hospital unless it is satisfied, on the written or oral evidence of the approved clinician who would have overall responsibility for his case or of some other person representing the managers of the hospital, that arrangements have been made for his admission to that hospital and for his admission to it within the period of seven days beginning with the date of the remand; and if the court is so satisfied it may, pending his admission, give directions for his conveyance to and detention in a place of safety.

(4) Where a court has remanded an accused person under this section it may further remand him if it appears to the court, on the written or oral evidence of the responsible clinician, that a further remand is warranted.

(5) The power of further remanding an accused person under this section may be exercised by the court without his being brought before the court if he is represented by counsel or a solicitor and his counsel or solicitor is given an opportunity of being heard.

(6) An accused person shall not be remanded or further remanded under this section for more than 28 days at a time or for more than 12 weeks in all; and the court may at any time terminate the remand if it appears to the court that it is appropriate to do so.

(7) An accused person remanded to hospital under this section shall be entitled to obtain at his own expense an independent report on his mental condition from a registered medical practitioner or approved clinician chosen by him and to apply to the court on the basis of it for his remand to be terminated under subsection (6) above.

(8) Subsections (9) and (10) of section 35 above shall have effect in relation to a remand under this section as they have effect in relation to a remand under that section.

*Hospital and guardianship orders*

## 37. Powers of courts to order hospital admission or guardianship

(1) Where a person is convicted before the Crown Court of an offence punishable with imprisonment other than an offence the sentence for which is fixed by law, or is convicted by a magistrates' court of an offence punishable on summary conviction with imprisonment, and the conditions mentioned in subsection (2) below are satisfied, the court may by order authorise his admission to and detention in such hospital as may be specified in the order or, as the case may be, place him under the guardianship of a

local social services authority or of such other person approved by a local social services authority as may be so specified.

(1A)  In the case of an offence the sentence for which would otherwise fall to be imposed –

(za)  under section 1A(5) of the Prevention of Crime Act 1953,

(a)  under section 51A(2) of the Firearms Act 1968,

(aa)  under section 139AA(7 |) of the Criminal Justice Act 1988,

(b)  under section 110(2) or 111(2) of the Powers of Criminal Courts (Sentencing) Act 2000

(ba)  under section 224A of the Criminal Justice Act 2003,

(c)  under any of sections 225 to 228 of the Criminal Justice Act 2003, or

(d)  under section 29(4) or (6) of the Violent Crime Reduction Act 2006 (minimum sentences in certain cases of using someone to mind a weapon),

nothing in those provisions shall prevent a court from making an order under subsection (1) above for the admission of the offender to a hospital.

(1B)  References in subsection (1A) above to a sentence falling to be imposed under any of the provisions mentioned in that subsection are to be read in accordance with section 305(4) of the Criminal Justice Act 2003.

(2)  The conditions referred to in subsection (1) above are that –

(a)  the court is satisfied, on the written or oral evidence of two registered medical practitioners, that the offender is suffering from mental disorder and that either –

(i)  the mental disorder from which the offender is suffering is of a nature or degree which makes it appropriate for him to be detained in a hospital for medical treatment and, appropriate medical treatment is available for him; or

(ii)  in the case of an offender who has attained the age of 16 years, the mental disorder is of a nature or degree which warrants his reception into guardianship under this Act; and

(b)  the court is of the opinion, having regard to all the circumstances including the nature of the offence and the character and antecedents of the offender, and to the other available methods of dealing with him, that the most suitable method of disposing of the case is by means of an order under this section.

(3)  Where a person is charged before a magistrates' court with any act or omission as an offence and the court would have power, on convicting him of that offence, to make an order under subsection (1) above in his case, then, if the court is satisfied that the accused did the act or made the omission charged, the court may, if it thinks fit, make such an order without convicting him.

(4)  An order for the admission of an offender to a hospital (in this Act referred to as "a hospital order") shall not be made under this section unless the court is satisfied on the written or oral evidence of the approved clinician who would have overall responsibility for his case or of some other person representing the managers of the hospital that arrangements have been made for his admission to that hospital, and for his admission to it within the period of 28 days beginning with the date of the making of such an order; and the court may, pending his admission within that period, give such directions as it thinks fit for his conveyance to and detention in a place of safety.

(5)     If within the said period of 28 days it appears to the Secretary of State that by reason of an emergency or other special circumstances it is not practicable for the patient to be received into the hospital specified in the order, he may give directions for the admission of the patient to such other hospital as appears to be appropriate instead of the hospital so specified; and where such directions are given –

(a)   the Secretary of State shall cause the person having the custody of the patient to be informed, and

(b)   the hospital order shall have effect as if the hospital specified in the directions were substituted for the hospital specified in the order.

(6)     An order placing an offender under the guardianship of a local social services author-ity or of any other person (in this Act referred to as "a guardianship order") shall not be made under this section unless the court is satisfied that that authority or person is will-ing to receive the offender into guardianship.

(7)     (repealed)

(8)     Where an order is made under this section, the court shall not –

(a)   pass sentence of imprisonment or impose a fine or make a community order (within the meaning of Part 12 of the Criminal Justice Act 2003) in respect of the offence,

(b)   if the order under this section is a hospital order, make a referral order (within the meaning of the Powers of Criminal Courts (Sentencing) Act 2000) in respect of the offence, or

(c)   make in respect of the offender a supervision order (within the meaning of that Act) or an order under section 150 of that Act (binding over of parent or guardian),

but the court may make any other order which it has power to make apart from this sec-tion; and for the purposes of this subsection "sentence of imprisonment" includes any sentence or order for detention.

## 38. Interim hospital orders

(1)     Where a person is convicted before the Crown Court of an offence punishable with imprisonment (other than an offence the sentence for which is fixed by law) or is con-victed by a magistrates' court of an offence punishable on summary conviction with imprisonment and the court before or by which he is convicted is satisfied, on the written or oral evidence of two registered medical practitioners –

(a)   that the offender is suffering from mental disorder; and

(b)   that there is reason to suppose that the mental disorder from which the offender is suffering is such that it may be appropriate for a hospital order to be made in his case,

the court may, before making a hospital order or dealing with him in some other way, make an order (in this Act referred to as "an interim hospital order") authorising his admission to such hospital as may be specified in the order and his detention there in accordance with this section.

(2)     In the case of an offender who is subject to an interim hospital order the court may make a hospital order without his being brought before the court if he is represented by counsel or a solicitor and his counsel or solicitor is given an opportunity of being heard.

(3)     At least one of the registered medical practitioners whose evidence is taken into account under subsection (1) above shall be employed at the hospital which is to be specified in the order.

(4)     An interim hospital order shall not be made for the admission of an offender to a hospital unless the court is satisfied, on the written or oral evidence of the approved clinician who would have overall responsibility for his case or of some other person representing the managers of the hospital, that arrangements have been made for his admission to that hospital and for his admission to it within the period of 28 days beginning with the date of the order; and if the court is so satisfied the court may, pending his admission, give directions for his conveyance to and detention in a place of safety.

(5)     An interim hospital order –

  (a)   shall be in force for such period, not exceeding 12 weeks, as the court may specify when making the order; but

  (b)   may be renewed for further periods of not more than 28 days at a time if it appears to the court, on the written or oral evidence of the responsible clinician, that the continuation of the order is warranted;

but no such order shall continue in force for more than 12 months in all and the court shall terminate the order if it makes a hospital order in respect of the offender or decides after considering the written or oral evidence of the responsible clinician, to deal with the offender in some other way.

(6)     The power of renewing an interim hospital order may be exercised without the offender being brought before the court if he is represented by counsel or a solicitor and his counsel or solicitor is given an opportunity of being heard.

(7)     If an offender absconds from a hospital in which he is detained in pursuance of an interim hospital order, or while being conveyed to or from such a hospital, he may be arrested without warrant by a constable and shall, after being arrested, be brought as soon as practicable before the court that made the order; and the court may thereupon terminate the order and deal with him in any way in which it could have dealt with him if no such order had been made.

## 39. Information as to hospitals

(1)     Where a court is minded to make a hospital order or interim hospital order in respect of any person it may request –

  (a)   the Primary Care Trust or Local Health Board for the area in which that person resides or last resided; or

  (b)   the National Assembly for Wales or any other Primary Care Trust or Local Health Board that appears to the court to be appropriate,

to furnish the court with such information as that Primary Care Trust or Local Health Board or National Assembly for Wales have or can reasonably obtain with respect to the hospital or hospitals (if any) in their area or elsewhere at which arrangements could be made for the admission of that person in pursuance of the order, and that Primary Care Trust or Local Health Board National Assembly for Wales shall comply with any such request.

(1A)  In relation to a person who has not attained the age of 18 years, subsection (1) above shall have effect as if the reference to the making of a hospital order included a reference to a remand under section 35 or 36 above or the making of an order under section 44 below.

(1B)    Where the person concerned has not attained the age of 18 years, the information which may be requested under subsection (1) above includes, in particular, information about the availability of accommodation or facilities designed so as to be specially suitable for patients who have not attained the age of 18 years.

(2)    (repealed)

## 39A. Information to facilitate guardianship orders

Where a court is minded to make a guardianship order in respect of any offender, it may request the local social services authority for the area in which the offender resides or last resided, or any other local social services authority that appears to the court to be appropriate –

(a)    to inform the court whether it or any other person approved by it is willing to receive the offender into guardianship; and

(b)    if so, to give such information as it reasonably can about how it or the other person could be expected to exercise in relation to the offender the powers conferred by section 40(2) below;

and that authority shall comply with any such request.

## 40. Effect of hospital orders, guardianship orders and interim hospital orders

(1)    A hospital order shall be sufficient authority –

(a)  for a constable, an approved mental health professional or any other person directed to do so by the court to convey the patient to the hospital specified in the order within a period of 28 days; and

(b)  for the managers of the hospital to admit him at any time within that period and thereafter detain him in accordance with the provisions of this Act.

(2)    A guardianship order shall confer on the authority or person named in the order as guardian the same powers as a guardianship application made and accepted under Part 2 of this Act.

(3)    Where an interim hospital order is made in respect of an offender –

(a)  a constable or any other person directed to do so by the court shall convey the offender to the hospital specified in the order within the period mentioned in section 38(4) above; and

(b)  the managers of the hospital shall admit him within that period and thereafter detain him in accordance with the provisions of section 38 above.

(4)    A patient who is admitted to a hospital in pursuance of a hospital order, or placed under guardianship by a guardianship order, shall, subject to the provisions of this subsection, be treated for the purposes of the provisions of this Act mentioned in Part 1 of Schedule 1 to this Act as if he had been so admitted or placed on the date of the order in pursuance of an application for admission for treatment or a guardianship application, as the case may be, duly made under Part 2 of this Act, but subject to any modifications of those provisions specified in that Part of that Schedule.

(5)    Where a patient is admitted to a hospital in pursuance of a hospital order, or placed under guardianship by a guardianship order, any previous application, hospital order or guardianship order by virtue of which he was liable to be detained in a hospital or subject to guardianship shall cease to have effect; but if the first-mentioned order, or the conviction on which it was made, is quashed on appeal, this subsection shall not apply and section 22 above shall have effect as if during any period for which the patient was

liable to be detained or subject to guardianship under the order, he had been detained in custody as mentioned in that section.

(6)   Where –

(a)   a patient admitted to a hospital in pursuance of a hospital order is absent without leave;

(b)   a warrant to arrest him has been issued under section 72 of the Criminal Justice Act 1967; and

(c)   he is held pursuant to the warrant in any country or territory other than the United Kingdom, any of the Channel Islands and the Isle of Man,

he shall be treated as having been taken into custody under section 18 above on first being so held.

*Restriction orders*

### 41. Power of higher courts to restrict discharge from hospital

(1)   Where a hospital order is made in respect of an offender by the Crown Court, and it appears to the court, having regard to the nature of the offence, the antecedents of the offender and the risk of his committing further offences if set at large, that it is necessary for the protection of the public from serious harm so to do, the court may, subject to the provisions of this section, further order that the offender shall be subject to the special restrictions set out in this section and an order under this section shall be known as "a restriction order".

(2)   A restriction order shall not be made in the case of any person unless at least one of the registered medical practitioners whose evidence is taken into account by the court under section 37(2)(a) above has given evidence orally before the court.

(3)   The special restrictions applicable to a patient in respect of whom a restriction order is in force are as follows –

(a)   none of the provisions of Part 2 of this Act relating to the duration, renewal and expiration of authority for the detention of patients shall apply, and the patient shall continue to be liable to be detained by virtue of the relevant hospital order until he is duly discharged under the said Part II or absolutely discharged under section 42, 73, 74 or 75 below;

(aa)   none of the provisions of Part 2 of this Act relating to community treatment orders and community patients shall apply;

(b)   no application shall be made to the appropriate tribunal in respect of a patient under section 66 or 69(1) below;

(c)   the following powers shall be exercisable only with the consent of the Secretary of State, namely –

(i)   power to grant leave of absence to the patient under section 17 above;

(ii)   power to transfer the patient in pursuance of regulations under section 19 above or in pursuance of subsection (3) of that section; and

(iii)   power to order the discharge of the patient under section 23 above;

and if leave of absence is granted under the said section 17 power to recall the patient under that section shall vest in the Secretary of State as well as the responsible clinician; and

(d) the power of the Secretary of State to recall the patient under the said section 17 and power to take the patient into custody and return him under section 18 above may be exercised at any time;

and in relation to any such patient section 40(4) above shall have effect as if it referred to Part 2 of Schedule 1 to this Act instead of Part 1 of that Schedule.

(4) A hospital order shall not cease to have effect under section 40(5) above if a restriction order in respect of the patient is in force at the material time.

(5) Where a restriction order in respect of a patient ceases to have effect while the relevant hospital order continues in force, the provisions of section 40 above and Part 1 of Schedule 1 to this Act shall apply to the patient as if he had been admitted to the hospital in pursuance of a hospital order (without a restriction order) made on the date on which the restriction order ceased to have effect.

(6) While a person is subject to a restriction order the responsible clinician shall at such intervals (not exceeding one year) as the Secretary of State may direct examine and report to the Secretary of State on that person; and every report shall contain such particulars as the Secretary of State may require.

## 42. Powers of Secretary of State in respect of patients subject to restriction orders

(1) If the Secretary of State is satisfied that in the case of any patient a restriction order is no longer required for the protection of the public from serious harm, he may direct that the patient cease to be subject to the special restrictions set out in section 41(3) above; and where the Secretary of State so directs, the restriction order shall cease to have effect, and section 41(5) above shall apply accordingly.

(2) At any time while a restriction order is in force in respect of a patient, the Secretary of State may, if he thinks fit, by warrant discharge the patient from hospital, either absolutely or subject to conditions; and where a person is absolutely discharged under this subsection, he shall thereupon cease to be liable to be detained by virtue of the relevant hospital order, and the restriction order shall cease to have effect accordingly.

(3) The Secretary of State may at any time during the continuance in force of a restriction order in respect of a patient who has been conditionally discharged under subsection (2) above by warrant recall the patient to such hospital as may be specified in the warrant.

(4) Where a patient is recalled as mentioned in subsection (3) above –

(a) if the hospital specified in the warrant is not the hospital from which the patient was conditionally discharged, the hospital order and the restriction order shall have effect as if the hospital specified in the warrant were substituted for the hospital specified in the hospital order;

(b) in any case, the patient shall be treated for the purposes of section 18 above as if he had absented himself without leave from the hospital specified in the warrant.

(5) If a restriction order in respect of a patient ceases to have effect after the patient has been conditionally discharged under this section, the patient shall, unless previously recalled under subsection (3) above, be deemed to be absolutely discharged on the date when the order ceases to have effect, and shall cease to be liable to be detained by virtue of the relevant hospital order accordingly.

(6) The Secretary of State may, if satisfied that the attendance at any place in Great Britain of a patient who is subject to a restriction order is desirable in the interests of justice or for the purposes of any public inquiry, direct him to be taken to that place; and where

a patient is directed under this subsection to be taken to any place he shall, unless the Secretary of State otherwise directs, be kept in custody while being so taken, while at that place and while being taken back to the hospital in which he is liable to be detained.

### 43. Power of magistrates' courts to commit for restriction order

(1) If in the case of a person of or over the age of 14 years who is convicted by a magistrates' court of an offence punishable on summary conviction with imprisonment –

   (a) the conditions which under section 37(1) above are required to be satisfied for the making of a hospital order are satisfied in respect of the offender; but

   (b) it appears to the court, having regard to the nature of the offence, the antecedents of the offender and the risk of his committing further offences if set at large, that if a hospital order is made a restriction order should also be made,

   the court may, instead of making a hospital order or dealing with him in any other manner, commit him in custody to the Crown Court to be dealt with in respect of the offence.

(2) Where an offender is committed to the Crown Court under this section, the Crown Court shall inquire into the circumstances of the case and may –

   (a) if that court would have power so to do under the foregoing provisions of this Part of this Act upon the conviction of the offender before that court of such an offence as is described in section 37(1) above, make a hospital order in his case, with or without a restriction order;

   (b) if the court does not make such an order, deal with the offender in any other manner in which the magistrates' court might have dealt with him.

(3) The Crown Court shall have the same power to make orders under sections 35, 36 and 38 above in the case of a person committed to the court under this section as the Crown Court has under those sections in the case of an accused person within the meaning of section 35 or 36 above or of a person convicted before that court as mentioned in section 38 above.

(4) The powers of a magistrates' court under section 3 or 3B of the Powers of Criminal Courts (Sentencing) Act 2000 (which enable such a court to commit an offender to the Crown Court where the court is of the opinion, or it appears to the court, as mentioned in the section in question) shall also be exercisable by a magistrates' court where it is of that opinion (or it so appears to it) unless a hospital order is made in the offender's case with a restriction order.

(5) The power of the Crown Court to make a hospital order, with or without a restriction order, in the case of a person convicted before that court of an offence may, in the same circumstances and subject to the same conditions, be exercised by such a court in the case of a person committed to the court under section 5 of the Vagrancy Act 1824 (which provides for the committal to the Crown Court of persons who are incorrigible rogues within the meaning of that section).

### 44. Committal to hospital under section 43

(1) Where an offender is committed under section 43(1) above and the magistrates' court by which he is committed is satisfied on written or oral evidence that arrangements have been made for the admission of the offender to a hospital in the event of an order being made under this section, the court may, instead of committing him in custody, by order direct him to be admitted to that hospital, specifying it, and to be detained there until

the case is disposed of by the Crown Court, and may give such directions as it thinks fit for his production from the hospital to attend the Crown Court by which his case is to be dealt with.

(2)   The evidence required by subsection (1) above shall be given by the approved clinician who would have overall responsibility for the offender's case or by some other person representing the managers of the hospital in question.

(3)   The power to give directions under section 37(4) above, section 37(5) above and section 40(1) above shall apply in relation to an order under this section as they apply in relation to a hospital order, but as if references to the period of 28 days mentioned in section 40(1) above were omitted; and subject as aforesaid an order under this section shall, until the offender's case is disposed of by the Crown Court, have the same effect as a hospital order together with a restriction order.

## 45. Appeals from magistrates' courts

(1)   Where on the trial of an information charging a person with an offence a magistrates' court makes a hospital order or guardianship order in respect of him without convicting him, he shall have the same right of appeal against the order as if it had been made on his conviction; and on any such appeal the Crown Court shall have the same powers as if the appeal had been against both conviction and sentence.

(2)   An appeal by a child or young person with respect to whom any such order has been made, whether the appeal is against the order or against the finding upon which the order was made, may be brought by him or by his parent or guardian on his behalf.

*Hospital and limitation directions*

## 45A. Power of higher courts to direct hospital admission

(1)   This section applies where, in the case of a person convicted before the Crown Court of an offence the sentence for which is not fixed by law –

(a)   the conditions mentioned in subsection (2) below are fulfilled; and

(b)   the court considers making a hospital order in respect of him before deciding to impose a sentence of imprisonment ("the relevant sentence") in respect of the offence.

(2)   The conditions referred to in subsection (1) above are that the court is satisfied, on the written or oral evidence of two registered medical practitioners –

(a)   that the offender is suffering from mental disorder;

(b)   that the mental disorder from which the offender is suffering is of a nature or degree which makes it appropriate for him to be detained in a hospital for medical treatment; and

(c)   that appropriate medical treatment is available for him.

(3)   The court may give both of the following directions, namely –

(a)   a direction that, instead of being removed to and detained in a prison, the offender be removed to and detained in such hospital as may be specified in the direction (in this Act referred to as a "hospital direction"); and

(b)   a direction that the offender be subject to the special restrictions set out in section 41 above (in this Act referred to as a "limitation direction").

(4)   A hospital direction and a limitation direction shall not be given in relation to an offender unless at least one of the medical practitioners whose evidence is taken into account by the court under subsection (2) above has given evidence orally before the court.

(5)   A hospital direction and a limitation direction shall not be given in relation to an offender unless the court is satisfied on the written or oral evidence of the approved clinician who would have overall responsibility for his case, or of some other person representing the managers of the hospital that arrangements have been made –

(a)   for his admission to that hospital; and

(b)   for his admission to it within the period of 28 days beginning with the day of the giving of such directions;

and the court may, pending his admission within that period, give such directions as it thinks fit for his conveyance to and detention in a place of safety.

(6)   If within the said period of 28 days it appears to the Secretary of State that by reason of an emergency or other special circumstances it is not practicable for the patient to be received into the hospital specified in the hospital direction, he may give instructions for the admission of the patient to such other hospital as appears to be appropriate instead of the hospital so specified.

(7)   Where such instructions are given –

(a)   the Secretary of State shall cause the person having the custody of the patient to be informed, and

(b)   the hospital direction shall have effect as if the hospital specified in the instructions were substituted for the hospital specified in the hospital direction.

(8)   Section 38(1) and (5) and section 39 above shall have effect as if any reference to the making of a hospital order included a reference to the giving of a hospital direction and a limitation direction.

(9)   A hospital direction and a limitation direction given in relation to an offender shall have effect not only as regards the relevant sentence but also (so far as applicable) as regards any other sentence of imprisonment imposed on the same or a previous occasion.

(10)   (repealed)

(11)   (repealed)

## 45B. Effect of hospital and limitation directions

(1)   A hospital direction and a limitation direction shall be sufficient authority –

(a)   for a constable or any other person directed to do so by the court to convey the patient to the hospital specified in the hospital direction within a period of 28 days; and

(b)   for the managers of the hospital to admit him at any time within that period and thereafter detain him in accordance with the provisions of this Act.

(2)   With respect to any person –

(a)   a hospital direction shall have effect as a transfer direction; and

(b)   a limitation direction shall have effect as a restriction direction.

(3)     While a person is subject to a hospital direction and a limitation direction the responsible clinician shall at such intervals (not exceeding one year) as the Secretary of State may direct examine and report to the Secretary of State on that person; and every report shall contain such particulars as the Secretary of State may require.

## 46. (repealed)

*Transfer to hospital of prisoners etc.*

## 47. Removal to hospital of persons serving sentences of imprisonment, etc.

(1)     If in the case of a person serving a sentence of imprisonment the Secretary of State is satisfied, by reports from at least two registered medical practitioners –

(a)   that the said person is suffering from mental disorder; and

(b)   that the mental disorder from which that person is suffering is of a nature or degree which makes it appropriate for him to be detained in a hospital for medical treatment; and

(c)   that appropriate medical treatment is available for him;

the Secretary of State may, if he is of the opinion having regard to the public interest and all the circumstances that it is expedient so to do, by warrant direct that that person be removed to and detained in such hospital as may be specified in the direction; and a direction under this section shall be known as "a transfer direction".

(2)     A transfer direction shall cease to have effect at the expiration of the period of 14 days beginning with the date on which it is given unless within that period the person with respect to whom it was given has been received into the hospital specified in the direction.

(3)     A transfer direction with respect to any person shall have the same effect as a hospital order made in his case.

(4)     (repealed)

(5)     References in this Part of this Act to a person serving a sentence of imprisonment include references –

(a)   to a person detained in pursuance of any sentence or order for detention made by a court in criminal proceedings or service disciplinary proceedings (other than an order made in consequence of a finding of insanity or unfitness to stand trial or a sentence of service detention within the meaning of the Armed Forces Act 2006);

(b)   to a person committed to custody under section 115(3) of the Magistrates' Courts Act 1980 (which relates to persons who fail to comply with an order to enter into recognisances to keep the peace or be of good behaviour); and

(c)   to a person committed by a court to a prison or other institution to which the Prison Act 1952 applies in default of payment of any sum adjudged to be paid on his conviction.

(6)     In subsection (5)(a) "service disciplinary proceedings" means proceedings in respect of a service offence within the meaning of the Armed Forces Act 2006.

## 48. Removal to hospital of other prisoners

(1)     If in the case of a person to whom this section applies the Secretary of State is satisfied by the same reports as are required for the purposes of section 47 above that –

(a) that person is suffering from mental disorder of a nature or degree which makes it appropriate for him to be detained in hospital for medical treatment; and

(b) he is in urgent need of such treatment; and

(c) appropriate medical treatment is available for him;

the Secretary of State shall have the same power of giving a transfer direction in respect of him under that section as if he were serving a sentence of imprisonment.

(2) This section applies to the following persons, that is to say –

(a) persons detained in a prison, not being person serving a sentence of imprisonment or persons falling within the following paragraphs of this subsection;

(b) persons remanded in custody by a magistrates' court;

(c) civil prisoners, that is to say, persons committed by a court to prison for a limited term, who are not persons falling to be dealt with under section 47 above;

(d) persons detained under the Immigration Act 1971 or under section 62 of the Nationality, Immigration and Asylum Act 2002 (detention by Secretary of State).

(3) Subsections (2) and (3) of section 47 above shall apply for the purposes of this section and of any transfer direction given by virtue of this section as they apply for the purposes of that section and of any transfer direction under that section.

### 49. Restriction on discharge of prisoners removed to hospital

(1) Where a transfer direction is given in respect of any person, the Secretary of State, if he thinks fit, may by warrant further direct that that person shall be subject to the special restrictions set out in section 41 above; and where the Secretary of State gives a transfer direction in respect of any such person as is described in paragraph (a) or (b) of section 48(2) above, he shall also give a direction under this section applying those restrictions to him.

(2) A direction under this section shall have the same effect as a restriction order made under section 41 above and shall be known as "a restriction direction".

(3) While a person is subject to a restriction direction the responsible clinician shall at such intervals (not exceeding one year) as the Secretary of State may direct examine and report to the Secretary of State on that person; and every report shall contain such particulars as the Secretary of State may require.

### 50. Further provisions as to prisoners under sentence

(1) Where a transfer direction and a restriction direction have been given in respect of a person serving a sentence of imprisonment and before his release date the Secretary of State is notified by the responsible clinician, any other approved clinician or the appropriate tribunal that that person no longer requires treatment in hospital for mental disorder or that no effective treatment for his disorder can be given in the hospital to which he has been removed, the Secretary of State may –

(a) by warrant direct that he be remitted to any prison or other institution in which he might have been detained if he had not been removed to hospital, there to be dealt with as if he had not been so removed; or

(b) exercise any power of releasing him on licence or discharging him under supervision which could have been exercisable if he had been remitted to such a prison or institution as aforesaid, and on his arrival in the prison or other institution or, as the case may be, his release or discharge as aforesaid, the transfer direction and the restriction direction shall cease to have effect.

(2)    A restriction direction in the case of a person serving a sentence of imprisonment shall cease to have effect, if it has not previously done so, on his release date.

(3)    In this section, references to a person's release date are to the day (if any) on which he would be entitled to be released (whether unconditionally or on licence) from any prison or other institution in which he might have been detained if the transfer direction had not been given; and in determining that day there shall be disregarded –

   (a)   any powers that would be exercisable by the Parole Board if he were detained in such a prison or other institution, and

   (b)   any practice of the Secretary of State in relation to the early release under discretionary powers of persons detained in such a prison or other institution.

(4)    For the purposes of section 49(2) of the Prison Act 1952 (which provides for discounting from the sentences of certain prisoners periods while they are unlawfully at large) a patient who, having been transferred in pursuance of a transfer direction from any such institution as is referred to in that section, is at large in circumstances in which he is liable to be taken into custody under any provision of this Act, shall be treated as unlawfully at large and absent from that institution.

(5)    The preceding provisions of this section shall have effect as if –

   (a)   the reference in subsection (1) to a transfer direction and a restriction direction having been given in respect of a person serving a sentence of imprisonment included a reference to a hospital direction and a limitation direction having been given in respect of a person sentenced to imprisonment;

   (b)   the reference in subsection (2) to a restriction direction included a reference to a limitation direction; and

   (c)   references in subsections (3) and (4) to a transfer direction included references to a hospital direction.

## 51. Further provisions as to detained persons

(1)    This section has effect where a transfer direction has been given in respect of any such person as is described in paragraph (a) of section 48(2) above and that person is in this section referred to as "the detainee".

(2)    The transfer direction shall cease to have effect when the detainee's case is disposed of by the court having jurisdiction to try or otherwise deal with him, but without prejudice to any power of that court to make a hospital order or other order under this Part of this Act in his case.

(3)    If the Secretary of State is notified by the responsible clinician, any other approved clinician or a Mental Health Review Tribunal at any time before the detainee's case is disposed of by that court –

   (a)   that the detainee no longer requires treatment in hospital for mental disorder; or

   (b)   that no effective treatment for his disorder can be given at the hospital to which he has been removed,

   the Secretary of State may by warrant direct that he be remitted to any place where he might have been detained if he had not been removed to hospital, there to be dealt with as if he had not been so removed, and on his arrival at the place to which he is so remitted the transfer direction shall cease to have effect.

(4) If (no direction having been given under subsection (3) above) the court having jurisdiction to try or otherwise deal with the detainee is satisfied on the written or oral evidence of the responsible clinician –

(a) that the detainee no longer requires treatment in hospital for mental disorder; or

(b) that no effective treatment for his disorder can be given at the hospital to which he has been removed,

the court may order him to be remitted to any such place as is mentioned in subsection (3) above or, subject to section 25 of the Criminal Justice and Public Order Act 1994, released on bail and on his arrival at that place or, as the case may be, his release on bail the transfer direction shall cease to have effect.

(5) If (no direction or order having been given or made under subsection (3) or (4) above) it appears to the court having jurisdiction to try or otherwise deal with the detainee –

(a) that it is impracticable or inappropriate to bring the detainee before the court; and

(b) that the conditions set out in subsection (6) below are satisfied,

the court may make a hospital order (with or without a restriction order) in his case in his absence and, in the case of a person awaiting trial, without convicting him.

(6) A hospital order may be made in respect of a person under subsection (5) above if the court –

(a) is satisfied, on the written or oral evidence of at least two registered medical practitioners, that –

(i) the detainee is suffering from mental disorder of a nature or degree which makes it appropriate for the patient to be detained in a hospital for medical treatment; and

(ii) appropriate medical treatments is available for him; and

(b) is of the opinion, after considering any depositions or other documents required to be sent to the proper officer of the court, that it is proper to make such an order.

(7) Where a person committed to the Crown Court to be dealt with under section 43 above is admitted to a hospital in pursuance of an order under section 44 above, subsections (5) and (6) above shall apply as if he were a person subject to a transfer direction.

### 52. Further provisions as to persons remanded by magistrates' courts

(1) This section has effect where a transfer direction has been given in respect of any such person as is described in paragraph (b) of section 48(2) above; and that person is in this section referred to as "the accused".

(2) Subject to subsection (5) below, the transfer direction shall cease to have effect on the expiration of the period of remand unless the accused is sent in custody to the Crown Court for trial or to be otherwise dealt with.

(3) Subject to subsection (4) below, the power of further remanding the accused under section 128 of the Magistrates' Courts Act 1980 may be exercised by the court without his being brought before the court; and if the court further remands the accused in custody (whether or not he is brought before the court) the period of remand shall, for the purposes of this section, be deemed not to have expired.

(4)     The court shall not under subsection (3) above further remand the accused in his absence unless he has appeared before the court within the previous six months.

(5)     If the magistrates' court is satisfied, on the written or oral evidence of the responsible clinician –

   (a)   that the accused no longer requires treatment in hospital for mental disorder; or

   (b)   that no effective treatment for his disorder can be given in the hospital to which he has been removed,

   the court may direct that the transfer direction shall cease to have effect notwithstanding that the period of remand has not expired or that the accused is sent to the Crown Court as mentioned in subsection (2) above.

(6)     If the accused is sent to the Crown Court as mentioned in subsection (2) above and the transfer direction has not ceased to have effect under subsection (5) above, section 51 above shall apply as if the transfer direction given in his case were a direction given in respect of a person falling within that section.

(7)     The magistrates' court may, in the absence of the accused, send him to the Crown Court for trial under section 51 or 51A of the Crime and Disorder Act 1998 if –

   (a)   the court is satisfied, on the written or oral evidence of the responsible clinician, that the accused is unfit to take part in the proceedings; and

   (b)   the accused is represented by an authorised person.

## 53. Further provisions as to civil prisoners and persons detained under the Immigration Acts

(1)     Subject to subsection (2) below, a transfer direction given in respect of any such person as is described in paragraph (c) or (d) of section 48(2) above shall cease to have effect on the expiration of the period during which he would, but for his removal to hospital, be liable to be detained in the place from which he was removed.

(2)     Where a transfer direction and a restriction direction have been given in respect of any such person as is mentioned in subsection (1) above, then, if the Secretary of State is notified by the responsible clinician, any other approved clinician or the appropriate tribunal at any time before the expiration of the period there mentioned –

   (a)   that that person no longer requires treatment in hospital for mental disorder; or

   (b)   that no effective treatment for his disorder can be given in the hospital to which he has been removed,

   the Secretary of State may by warrant direct that he be remitted to any place where he might have been detained if he had not been removed to hospital, and on his arrival at the place to which he is so remitted the transfer direction and the restriction direction shall cease to have effect

*Supplemental*

## 54. Requirements as to medical evidence

(1)     The registered medical practitioner whose evidence is taken into account under section 35(3)(a) above and at least one of the registered medical practitioners whose evidence is taken into account under sections 36(1), 37(2)(a), 38(1), 45A(2) and 51(6)(a) above and whose reports are taken into account under sections 47(1) and 48(1) above shall be a practitioner approved for the purposes of section 12 above by the Secretary of State, or

by another person by virtue of section 12ZA or 12 ZB above, as having special experience in the diagnosis or treatment of mental disorder.

(2) For the purposes of any provision of this Part of this Act under which a court may act on the written evidence of any person, a report in writing purporting to be signed by that person may, subject to the provisions of this section, be received in evidence without proof of the following –

    (a) the signature of the person; or

    (b) his having the requisite qualifications or approval or authority or being of the requisite description to give the report.

(2A) But the court may require the signatory of any such report to be called to give oral evidence.

(3) Where, in pursuance of a direction of the court, any such report is tendered in evidence otherwise than by or on behalf of the person who is the subject of the report, then –

    (a) if that person is represented by an authorised person, a copy of the report shall be given to that authorised person;

    (b) if that person is not so represented, the substance of the report shall be disclosed to him or, where he is a child or young person, to his parent or guardian if present in court; and

    (c) except where the report relates only to arrangements for his admission to a hospital, that person may require the signatory of the report to be called to give oral evidence, and evidence to rebut the evidence contained in the report may be called by or on behalf of that person.

## 54A. Reduction of period for making hospital orders

(1) The Secretary of State may by order reduce the length of the periods mentioned in sections 37(4) and (5) and 38(4) above.

(2) An order under subsection (1) above may make such consequential amendments of sections 40(1) and 44(3) above as appear to the Secretary of State to be necessary or expedient.

## 55. Interpretation of Part 3

(1) In this Part of this Act –

"authorised person" means a person who, for the purposes of the Legal Services Act 2007, is an authorised person in relation to an activity which constitutes the exercise of a right of audience (within the meaning of that Act);

"child" and "young person" have the same meaning as in the Children and Young Persons Act 1933;

"civil prisoner" has the meaning given to it by section 48(2)(c) above;

"guardian", in relation to a child or young person, has the same meaning as in the Children and Young Persons Act 1933;

"place of safety", in relation to a person who is not a child or young person, means any police station, prison or remand centre, or any hospital the managers of which are willing temporarily to receive him, and in relation to a child or young person has the same meaning as in the Children and Young Persons Act 1933;

"responsible clinician", in relation to a person liable to be detained in a hospital within the meaning of Part 2 of this Act, means the approved clinician with overall responsibility for the patient's case.

(2)    Any reference in this Part of this Act to an offence punishable on summary conviction with imprisonment shall be construed without regard to any prohibition or restriction imposed by or under any enactment relating to the imprisonment of young offenders.

(3)    (repealed)

(4)    Any reference to a hospital order, a guardianship order or a restriction order in section 40(2), (4) or (5), section 41(3) to (5), or section 42 above or section 69(1) below shall be construed as including a reference to any order or direction under this Part of this Act having the same effect as the first mentioned order; and the exceptions and modifications set out in Schedule 1 to this Act in respect of the provisions of this Act described in that Schedule accordingly include those which are consequential on the provisions of this subsection.

(5)    Section 34(2) above shall apply for the purposes of this Part of this Act as it applies for the purposes of Part 2 of this Act.

(6)    References in this Part of this Act to persons serving a sentence of imprisonment shall be construed in accordance with section 47(5) above.

(7)    Section 99 of the Children and Young Persons Act 1933 (which relates to the presumption and determination of age) shall apply for the purposes of this Part of this Act as it applies for the purposes of that Act.

## PART 4: CONSENT TO TREATMENT

### 56. Patients to whom Part 4 applies

(1)    Section 57 and, so far as relevant to that section, sections 59 to 62 below apply to any patient.

(2)    Subject to that and to subsection (5) below, this Part of this Act applies to a patient only if he falls within subsection (3) or (4) below.

(3)    A patient falls within this subsection if he is liable to be detained under this Act but not if –

   (a)   he is so liable by virtue of an emergency application and the second medical recommendation referred to in section 4(4)(a) above has not been given and received;

   (b)   he is so liable by virtue of section 5(2) or (4) or 35 above or section 135 or 136 below or by virtue of a direction for his detention in a place of safety under section 37(4) or 45A(5) above; or

   (c)   he has been conditionally discharged under section 42(2) above or section 73 or 74 below and he is not recalled to hospital.

(4)    A patient falls within this subsection if

   (a)   he is a community patient; and

   (b)   he is recalled to hospital under section 17E above.

(5)    Section 58A and, so far as relevant to that section, sections 59 to 62 below also apply to any patient who –

   (a)   does not fall within subsection (3) above;

(b)  is not a community patient; and

(c)  has not attained the age of 18 years.

## 57. Treatment requiring consent and a second opinion

(1)  This section applies to the following forms of medical treatment for mental disorder –

(a)  any surgical operation for destroying brain tissue or for destroying the functioning of brain tissue; and

(b)  such other forms of treatment as may be specified for the purposes of this section by regulations made by the Secretary of State.

(2)  Subject to section 62 below, a patient shall not be given any form of treatment to which this section applies unless he has consented to it and –

(a)  a registered medical practitioner appointed for the purposes of this Part of this Act by the regulatory authority (not being the responsible clinician (if there is one) or the person in charge of the treatment in question) and two other persons appointed for the purposes of this paragraph by the regulatory authority (not being registered medical practitioners) have certified in writing that the patient is capable of understanding the nature, purpose and likely effects of the treatment in question and has consented to it; and

(b)  the registered medical practitioner referred to in paragraph (a) above has certified in writing that, it is appropriate for the treatment to be given.

(3)  Before giving a certificate under subsection (2)(b) above the registered medical practitioner concerned shall consult two other persons who have been professionally concerned with the patient's medical treatment but of those persons –

(a)  one shall be a nurse and the other shall be neither a nurse nor a registered medical practitioner; and

(b)  neither shall be the responsible clinician (if there is one) or the person in charge of the treatment in question.

(4)  Before making any regulations for the purpose of this section the Secretary of State shall consult such bodies as appear to him to be concerned.

## 58. Treatment requiring consent or a second opinion

(1)  This section applies to the following forms of medical treatment for mental disorder –

(a)  such forms of treatment as may be specified for the purposes of this section by regulations made by the Secretary of State;

(b)  the administration of medicine to a patient by any means (not being a form of treatment specified under paragraph (a) above or section 57 above or section 58A(1)(b) below) at any time during a period for which he is liable to be detained as a patient to whom this Part of this Act applies if three months or more have elapsed since the first occasion in that period when medicine was administered to him by any means for his mental disorder.

(2)  The Secretary of State may by order vary the length of the period mentioned in subsection (1)(b) above.

(3)  Subject to section 62 below, a patient shall not be given any form of treatment to which this section applies unless –

(a)  he has consented to that treatment and either the approved clinician in charge of it or a registered medical practitioner appointed for the purposes of this Part of this Act by the regulatory authority has certified in writing that the patient is capable of understanding its nature, purpose and likely effects and has consented to it;

(b)  a registered medical practitioner appointed as aforesaid (not being the responsible clinician or the approved clinician in charge of the treatment in question) has certified in writing that the patient is not capable of understanding the nature, purpose and likely effects of that treatment or being so capable has not consented to it but that it is appropriate for the treatment to be given.

(4)  Before giving a certificate under subsection (3)(b) above the registered medical practitioner concerned shall consult two other persons who have been professionally concerned with the patient's medical treatment, but of those persons –

(a)  one shall be a nurse and the other shall be neither a nurse nor a registered medical practitioner; and

(b)  neither shall be the responsible clinician or the person in charge of the treatment in question.

(5)  Before making any regulations for the purposes of this section the Secretary of State shall consult such bodies as appear to him to be concerned.

## 58A. Electro-convulsive therapy, etc.

(1)  This section applies to the following forms of medical treatment for mental disorder –

(a)  electro-convulsive therapy; and

(b)  such other forms of treatment as may be specified for the purposes of this section by regulations made by the appropriate national authority.

(2)  Subject to section 62 below, a patient shall be not be given any form of treatment to which this section applies unless he falls within subsection (3), (4) or (5) below.

(3)  A patient falls within this subsection if –

(a)  he has attained the age of 18 years;

(b)  he has consented to the treatment in question; and

(c)  either the approved clinician in charge of it or a registered medical practitioner appointed as mentioned in section 58(3) above has certified in writing that the patient is capable of understanding the nature, purpose and likely effects of the treatment and has consented to it.

(4)  A patient falls within this subsection if –

(a)  he has not attained the age of 18 years; but

(b)  he has consented to the treatment in question; and

(c)  a registered medical practitioner appointed as aforesaid (not being the approved clinician in charge of the treatment) has certified in writing –

(i)  that the patient is capable of understanding the nature, purpose and likely effects of the treatment and has consented to it; and

(ii)  that it is appropriate for the treatment to be given.

(5) A patient falls within this subsection if a registered medical practitioner appointed as aforesaid (not being the responsible clinician (if there is one) or the approved clinician in charge of the treatment in question) has certified in writing –

    (a) that the patient is not capable of understanding the nature, purpose and likely effects of the treatment; but

    (b) that it is appropriate for the treatment to be given; and

    (c) that giving him the treatment would not conflict with –

        (i) an advance decision which the registered medical practitioner concerned is satisfied is valid and applicable;

        (ii) a decision made by a donee or deputy or by the Court of Protection.

(6) Before giving a certificate under subsection (5) above the registered medical practitioner concerned shall consult two other persons who have been professionally concerned with the patient's medical treatment, but of those persons –

    (a) one shall be a nurse and the other shall be neither a nurse nor a registered medical practitioner; and

    (b) neither shall be the responsible clinician (if there is one) or the approved clinician in charge of the treatment in question.

(7) This section shall not by itself confer sufficient authority for a patient who falls within section 56(5) above to be given a form of treatment to which this section applies if he is not capable of understanding the nature, purpose and likely effects of the treatment (and cannot therefore consent to it).

(8) Before making any regulations for the purposes of this section, the appropriate national authority shall consult such bodies as appear to it to be concerned.

(9) In this section –

    (a) a reference to an advance decision is to an advance decision (within the meaning of the Mental Capacity Act 2005) made by the patient;

    (b) "valid and applicable", in relation to such a decision, means valid and applicable to the treatment in question in accordance with section 25 of that Act;

    (c) a reference to a donee is to a donee of a lasting power of attorney (within the meaning of section 9 of that Act) created by the patient, where the donee is acting within the scope of his authority and in accordance with that Act; and

    (d) a reference to a deputy is to a deputy appointed for the patient by the Court of Protection under section 16 of that Act, where the deputy is acting within the scope of his authority and in accordance with that Act.

(10) In this section, "the appropriate national authority" means –

    (a) in a case where the treatment in question would, if given, be given in England, the Secretary of State;

    (b) in a case where the treatment in question would, if given, be given in Wales, the Welsh Ministers.

### 59. Plans of treatment

Any consent or certificate under section 57, 58 or 58A above may relate to a plan of treatment under which the patient is to be given (whether within a specified period or otherwise) one or more of the forms of treatment to which that section applies.

## 60. Withdrawal of consent

(1)     Where the consent of a patient to any treatment has been given for the purposes of section 57, 58 or 58A above, the patient may, subject to section 62 below, at any time before the completion of the treatment withdraw his consent, and those sections shall then apply as if the remainder of the treatment were a separate form of treatment.

(1A)   Subsection (1B) below applies where –

(a)   the consent of a patient to any treatment has been given for the purposes of section 57, 58 or 58A above; but

(b)   before the completion of the treatment, the patient ceases to be capable of understanding its nature, purpose and likely effects.

(1B)   The patient shall, subject to section 62 below, be treated as having withdrawn his consent, and those sections shall then apply as if the remainder of the treatment were a separate form of treatment.

(1C)   Subsection (1D) below applies where –

(a)   a certificate has been given under section 58 or 58A above that a patient is not capable of understanding the nature, purpose and likely effects of the treatment to which the certificate applies; but

(b)   before the completion of the treatment, the patient becomes capable of understanding its nature, purpose and likely effects.

(1D)   The certificate shall, subject to section 62 below, cease to apply to the treatment and those sections shall then apply as if the remainder of the treatment were a separate form of treatment.

(2)     Without prejudice to the application of subsections (1) to (1D) above to any treatment given under the plan of treatment to which a patient has consented, a patient who has consented to such a plan may, subject to section 62 below, at any time withdraw his consent to further treatment, or to further treatment of any description, under the plan.

## 61. Review of treatment

(1)     Where a patient is given treatment in accordance with section 57(2) or 58(3)(b), 58(3)(b) or 58A(4) or (5) above, or by virtue of section 62A below in accordance with a Part 4A certificate (within the meaning of that section), a report on the treatment and the patient's condition shall be given by the approved clinician in charge of the treatment to the regulatory authority –

(a)   on the next occasion on which the responsible clinician furnishes a report under section 20(3), 20A(4) or 21B(2) above in respect of the patient; and

(b)   at any other time if so required by the regulatory authority.

(2)     In relation to a patient who is subject to a restriction order, limitation direction or restriction direction subsection (1) above shall have effect as if paragraph (a) required the report to be made –

(a)   in the case of treatment in the period of six months beginning with the date of the order or direction, at the end of that period;

(b)   in the case of treatment at any subsequent time, on the next occasion on which the responsible clinician makes a report in respect of the patient under section 41(6), 45B(3) or 49(3) above.

(3)  The regulatory authority may at any time give notice directing that, subject to section 62 below, a certificate given in respect of a patient under section 57(2), 58(3(b) or 58A(4) or (5) above shall not apply to treatment given to him whether in England or Wales after a date specified in the notice and sections 57, 58 and 58A above shall then apply to any such treatment as if that certificate had not been given.

(3A)  The notice under subsection (3) above shall be given to the approved clinician in charge of the treatment.

## 62. Urgent treatment

(1)  Sections 57 and 58 above shall not apply to any treatment –

   (a)  which is immediately necessary to save the patient's life; or

   (b)  which (not being irreversible) is immediately necessary to prevent a serious deterioration of his condition; or

   (c)  which (not being irreversible or hazardous) is immediately necessary to alleviate serious suffering by the patient; or

   (d)  which (not being irreversible or hazardous) is immediately necessary and represents the minimum interference necessary to prevent the patient from behaving violently or being a danger to himself or to others.

(1A)  Section 58A above, in so far as it relates to electro-convulsive therapy by virtue of subsection (1)(a) of that section, shall not apply to any treatment which falls within paragraph (a) or (b) of subsection (1) above.

(1B)  Section 58A above, in so far as it relates to a form of treatment specified by virtue of subsection (1)(b) of that section, shall not apply to any treatment which falls within such of paragraphs (a) to (d) of subsection (1) above as may be specified in regulations under that section.

(1C)  For the purposes of subsection (1B) above, the regulations –

   (a)  may make different provision for different cases (and may, in particular, make different provision for different forms of treatment);

   (b)  may make provision which applies subject to specified exceptions; and

   (c)  may include transitional, consequential, incidental or supplemental provision.

(2)  Sections 60 and 61(3) above shall not preclude the continuation of any treatment or of treatment under any plan pending compliance with section 57, 58 or 58A above if the approved clinician in charge of the treatment considers that the discontinuance of the treatment or of treatment under the plan would cause serious suffering to the patient.

(3)  For the purposes of this section treatment is irreversible if it has unfavourable irreversible physical or psychological consequences and hazardous if it entails significant physical hazard.

## 62A. Treatment on recall of community patient or revocation of order

(1)  This section applies where –

   (a)  a community patient is recalled to hospital under section 17E above; or

   (b)  a patient is liable to be detained under this Act following the revocation of a community treatment order under section 17F above in respect of him.

(2)    For the purposes of section 58(1)(b) above, the patient is to be treated as if he had remained liable to be detained since the making of the community treatment order.

(3)    But section 58 above does not apply to treatment given to the patient if –

    (a)  the certificate requirement is met for the purposes of section 64C or 64E below; or

    (b)  as a result of section 64B(4) or 64E(4) below, the certificate requirement would not apply (were the patient a community patient not recalled to hospital under section 17E above).

(4)    Section 58A above does not apply to treatment given to the patient if there is authority to give the treatment, and the certificate requirement is met, for the purposes of section 64C or 64E below.

(5)    In a case where this section applies, the certificate requirement is met only in so far as –

    (a)  the Part 4A certificate expressly provides that it is appropriate for one or more specified forms of treatment to be given to the patient in that case (subject to such conditions as may be specified); or

    (b)  a notice having been given under subsection (5) of section 64H below, treatment is authorised by virtue of subsection (8) of that section.

(6)    Subsection (5)(a) above shall not preclude the continuation of any treatment, or of treatment under any plan, pending compliance with section 58 or 58A above if the approved clinician in charge of the treatment considers that the discontinuance of the treatment, or of the treatment under the plan, would cause serious suffering to the patient.

(7)    In a case where subsection (1)(b) above applies, subsection (3) above only applies pending compliance with section 58 above.

(8)    In subsection (5) above –

    "Part 4A certificate" has the meaning given in section 64H below; and "specified", in relation to a Part 4A certificate, means specified in the certificate.

### 63. Treatment not requiring consent

    The consent of a patient shall not be required for any medical treatment given to him for the mental disorder from which he is suffering, not being a form of treatment to which section 57, 58 or 58A above applies, if the treatment is given by or under the direction of the approved clinician in charge of the treatment.

### 64. Supplementary provisions for Part 4

(1)    In this Part of this Act "the responsible clinician" means the approved clinician with overall responsibility for the case of the patient in question and "hospital" includes a registered establishment.

(1A)  References in this Part of this Act to the approved clinician in charge of a patient's treatment shall, where the treatment in question is a form of treatment to which section 57 above applies, be construed as references to the person in charge of the treatment.

(1B)  References in this Part of this Act to the approved clinician in charge of a patient's treatment shall, where the treatment in question is a form of treatment to which section 58A above applies and the patient falls within section 56(5) above, be construed as references to the person in charge of the treatment.

(1C)  Regulations made by virtue of section 32(2)(d) above apply for the purposes of this Part as they apply for the purposes of Part 2 of this Act.

(2)  Any certificate for the purposes of this Part of this Act shall be in such form as may be prescribed by regulations made by the Secretary of State.

(3)  For the purposes of this Part of this Act, it is appropriate for treatment to be given to a patient if the treatment is appropriate in his case, taking into account the nature and degree of the mental disorder from which he is suffering and all other circumstances of his case.

## PART 4A: TREATMENT OF COMMUNITY PATIENTS NOT RECALLED TO HOSPITAL

### 64A. Meaning of "relevant treatment"

In this Part of this Act "relevant treatment", in relation to a patient, means medical treatment which –

(a)  is for the mental disorder from which the patient is suffering; and

(b)  is not a form of treatment to which section 57 above applies.

### 64B. Adult community patients

(1)  This section applies to the giving of relevant treatment to a community patient who –

    (a)  is not recalled to hospital under section 17E above; and

    (b)  has attained the age of 16 years.

(2)  The treatment may not be given to the patient unless –

    (a)  there is authority to give it to him; and

    (b)  if it is section 58 type treatment or section 58A type treatment, the certificate requirement is met.

(3)  But the certificate requirement does not apply if –

    (a)  giving the treatment to the patient is authorised in accordance with section 64G below; or

    (b)  the treatment is immediately necessary and –

        (i)  the patient has capacity to consent to it and does consent to it; or

        (ii)  a donee or deputy or the Court of Protection consents to the treatment on the patient's behalf.

(4)  Nor does the certificate requirement apply in so far as the administration of medicine to the patient at any time during the period of one month beginning with the day on which the community treatment order is made is section 58 type treatment.

(5)  The reference in subsection (4) above to the administration of medicine does not include any form of treatment specified under section 58(1)(a) above.

### 64C. Section 64B: supplemental

(1)  This section has effect for the purposes of section 64B above.

(2)  There is authority to give treatment to a patient if –

(a)  he has capacity to consent to it and does consent to it;

(b)  a donee or deputy or the Court of Protection consents to it on his behalf; or

(c)  giving it to him is authorised in accordance with section 64D or 64G below.

(3)  Relevant treatment is section 58 type treatment or section 58A type treatment if, at the time when it is given to the patient, section 58 or 58A (respectively) would have applied to it, had the patient remained liable to be detained at that time (rather than being a community patient).

(4)  The certificate requirement is met in respect of treatment to be given to a patient if –

(a)  a registered medical practitioner appointed for the purposes of Part 4 of this Act (not being the responsible clinician or the person in charge of the treatment) has certified in writing that it is appropriate for the treatment to be given or for the treatment to be given subject to such conditions as may be specified in the certificate; and

(b)  if conditions are so specified, the conditions are satisfied.

(5)  In a case where the treatment is section 58 type treatment, treatment is immediately necessary if –

(a)  it is immediately necessary to save the patient's life; or

(b)  it is immediately necessary to prevent a serious deterioration of the patient's condition and is not irreversible; or

(c)  it is immediately necessary to alleviate serious suffering by the patient and is not irreversible or hazardous; or

(d)  it is immediately necessary, represents the minimum interference necessary to prevent the patient from behaving violently or being a danger to himself or others and is not irreversible or hazardous.

(6)  In a case where the treatment is section 58A type treatment by virtue of subsection (1)(a) of that section, treatment is immediately necessary if it falls within paragraph (a) or (b) of subsection (5) above.

(7)  In a case where the treatment is section 58A type treatment by virtue of subsection (1)(b) of that section, treatment is immediately necessary if it falls within such of paragraphs (a) to (d) of subsection (5) above as may be specified in regulations under that section.

(8)  For the purposes of subsection (7) above, the regulations –

(a)  may make different provision for different cases (and may, in particular, make different provision for different forms of treatment);

(b)  may make provision which applies subject to specified exceptions; and

(c)  may include transitional, consequential, incidental or supplemental provision.

(9)  Subsection (3) of section 62 above applies for the purposes of this section as it applies for the purposes of that section.

## 64D. Adult community patients lacking capacity

(1)  A person is authorised to give relevant treatment to a patient as mentioned in section 64C(2)(c) above if the conditions in subsections (2) to (6) below are met.

(2)     The first condition is that, before giving the treatment, the person takes reasonable steps to establish whether the patient lacks capacity to consent to the treatment.

(3)     The second condition is that, when giving the treatment, he reasonably believes that the patient lacks capacity to consent to it.

(4)     The third condition is that –

(a)   he has no reason to believe that the patient objects to being given the treatment; or

(b)   he does have reason to believe that the patient so objects, but it is not necessary to use force against the patient in order to give the treatment.

(5)     The fourth condition is that –

(a)   he is the person in charge of the treatment and an approved clinician; or

(b)   the treatment is given under the direction of that clinician.

(6)     The fifth condition is that giving the treatment does not conflict with –

(a)   an advance decision which he is satisfied is valid and applicable; or

(b)   a decision made by a donee or deputy or the Court of Protection.

(7)     In this section –

(a)   reference to an advance decision is to an advance decision (within the meaning of the Mental Capacity Act 2005) made by the patient; and

(b)   "valid and applicable", in relation to such a decision, means valid and applicable to the treatment in question in accordance with section 25 of that Act.

## 64E. Child community patients

(1)     This section applies to the giving of relevant treatment to a community patient who –

(a)   is not recalled to hospital under section 17E above; and

(b)   has not attained the age of 16 years.

(2)     The treatment may not be given to the patient unless –

(a)   there is authority to give it to him; and

(b)   if it is section 58 type treatment or section 58A type treatment, the certificate requirement is met.

(3)     But the certificate requirement does not apply if –

(a)   giving the treatment to the patient is authorised in accordance with section 64G below; or

(b)   in a case where the patient is competent to consent to the treatment and does consent to it, the treatment is immediately necessary.

(4)     Nor does the certificate requirement apply in so far as the administration of medicine to the patient at any time during the period of one month beginning with the day on which the community treatment order is made is section 58 type treatment.

(5)     The reference in subsection (4) above to the administration of medicine does not include any form of treatment specified under section 58(1)(a) above.

(6)    For the purposes of subsection (2)(a) above, there is authority to give treatment to a patient if –

(a)   he is competent to consent to it and he does consent to it; or

(b)   giving it to him is authorised in accordance with section 64F or 64G below.

(7)    Subsections (3) to (9) of section 64C above have effect for the purposes of this section as they have effect for the purposes of section 64B above.

(8)    Regulations made by virtue of section 32(2)(d) above apply for the purposes of this section as they apply for the purposes of Part 2 of this Act.

## 64F. Child community patients lacking competence

(1)    A person is authorised to give relevant treatment to a patient as mentioned in section 64E(6)(b) above if the conditions in subsections (2) to (5) below are met.

(2)    The first condition is that, before giving the treatment, the person takes reasonable steps to establish whether the patient is competent to consent to the treatment.

(3)    The second condition is that, when giving the treatment, he reasonably believes that the patient is not competent to consent to it.

(4)    The third condition is that –

(a)   he has no reason to believe that the patient objects to being given the treatment; or

(b)   he does have reason to believe that the patient so objects, but it is not necessary to use force against the patient in order to give the treatment.

(5)    The fourth condition is that –

(a)   he is the person in charge of the treatment and an approved clinician; or

(b)   the treatment is given under the direction of that clinician.

## 64G. Emergency treatment for patients lacking capacity or competence

(1)    A person is also authorised to give relevant treatment to a patient as mentioned in section 64C(2)(c) or 64E(6)(b) above if the conditions in subsections (2) to (4) below are met.

(2)    The first condition is that, when giving the treatment, the person reasonably believes that the patient lacks capacity to consent to it or, as the case may be, is not competent to consent to it.

(3)    The second condition is that the treatment is immediately necessary.

(4)    The third condition is that if it is necessary to use force against the patient in order to give the treatment –

(a)   the treatment needs to be given in order to prevent harm to the patient; and

(b)   the use of such force is a proportionate response to the likelihood of the patient's suffering harm, and to the seriousness of that harm.

(5)    Subject to subsections (6) to (8) below, treatment is immediately necessary if –

(a)   it is immediately necessary to save the patient's life; or

(b)   it is immediately necessary to prevent a serious deterioration of the patient's condition and is not irreversible; or

(c)  it is immediately necessary to alleviate serious suffering by the patient and is not irreversible or hazardous; or

(d)  it is immediately necessary, represents the minimum interference necessary to prevent the patient from behaving violently or being a danger to himself or others and is not irreversible or hazardous.

(6)  Where the treatment is section 58A type treatment by virtue of subsection (1)(a) of that section, treatment is immediately necessary if it falls within paragraph (a) or (b) of subsection (5) above.

(7)  Where the treatment is section 58A type treatment by virtue of subsection (1)(b) of that section, treatment is immediately necessary if it falls within such of paragraphs (a) to (d) of subsection (5) above as may be specified in regulations under section 58A above.

(8)  For the purposes of subsection (7) above, the regulations –

(a)  may make different provision for different cases (and may, in particular, make different provision for different forms of treatment);

(b)  may make provision which applies subject to specified exceptions; and

(c)  may include transitional, consequential, incidental or supplemental provision.

(9)  Subsection (3) of section 62 above applies for the purposes of this section as it applies for the purposes of that section.

#### 64H. Certificates: supplementary provisions

(1)  A certificate under section 64B(2)(b) or 64E(2)(b) above (a "Part 4A certificate") may relate to a plan of treatment under which the patient is to be given (whether within a specified period or otherwise) one or more forms of section 58 type treatment or section 58A type treatment.

(2)  A Part 4A certificate shall be in such form as may be prescribed by regulations made by the appropriate national authority.

(3)  Before giving a Part 4A certificate, the registered medical practitioner concerned shall consult two other persons who have been professionally concerned with the patient's medical treatment but, of those persons –

(a)  at least one shall be a person who is not a registered medical practitioner; and

(b)  neither shall be the patient's responsible clinician or the person in charge of the treatment in question.

(4)  Where a patient is given treatment in accordance with a Part 4A certificate, a report on the treatment and the patient's condition shall be given by the person in charge of the treatment to the regulatory authority if required by that authority.

(5)  The regulatory authority may at any time give notice directing that a Part 4A certificate shall not apply to treatment given to a patient after a date specified in the notice, and the relevant section shall then apply to any such treatment as if that certificate had not been given.

(6)  The relevant section is –

(a)  if the patient is not recalled to hospital in accordance with section 17E above, section 64B or 64E above;

(b)  if the patient is so recalled or is liable to be detained under this Act following revocation of the community treatment order under section 17F above –

(i) section 58 above, in the case of section 58 type treatment;

(ii) section 58A above, in the case of section 58A type treatment; (subject to section 62A(2) above).

(7) The notice under subsection (5) above shall be given to the person in charge of the treatment in question.

(8) Subsection (5) above shall not preclude the continuation of any treatment or of treatment under any plan pending compliance with the relevant section if the person in charge of the treatment considers that the discontinuance of the treatment or of treatment under the plan would cause serious suffering to the patient.

(9) In this section, "the appropriate national authority" means –

(a) in relation to community patients in respect of whom the responsible hospital is in England, the Secretary of State;

(b) in relation to community patients in respect of whom the responsible hospital is in Wales, the Welsh Ministers.

### 64I. Liability for negligence

Nothing in sections 64D, 64F or 64G above excludes a person's civil liability for loss or damage, or his criminal liability, resulting from his negligence in doing anything authorised to be done by that section.

### 64J. Factors to be considered in determining whether patient objects to treatment

(1) In assessing for the purposes of this Part whether he has reason to believe that a patient objects to treatment, a person shall consider all the circumstances so far as they are reasonably ascertainable, including the patient's behaviour, wishes, feelings, views, beliefs and values.

(2) But circumstances from the past shall be considered only so far as it is still appropriate to consider them.

### 64K. Interpretation of Part 4A

(1) This Part of this Act is to be construed as follows.

(2) References to a patient who lacks capacity are to a patient who lacks capacity within the meaning of the Mental Capacity Act 2005.

(3) References to a patient who has capacity are to be read accordingly.

(4) References to a donee are to a donee of a lasting power of attorney (within the meaning of section 9 of the Mental Capacity Act 2005) created by the patient, where the donee is acting within the scope of his authority and in accordance with that Act.

(5) References to a deputy are to a deputy appointed for the patient by the Court of Protection under section 16 of the Mental Capacity Act 2005, where the deputy is acting within the scope of his authority and in accordance with that Act.

(6) Reference to the responsible clinician shall be construed as a reference to the responsible clinician within the meaning of Part 2 of this Act.

(7)     References to a hospital include a registered establishment.

(8)     Section 64(3) above applies for the purposes of this Part of this Act as it applies for the purposes of Part 4 of this Act.

## PART 5: MENTAL HEALTH REVIEW TRIBUNALS

*Constitution etc.*

### 65. Mental Health Review Tribunals for Wales

(1)     There shall be a Mental Health Review Tribunal for Wales.

(1A)   The purpose of that tribunal is to deal with applications and references by and in respect of patients under the provisions of this Act.

(2)     The provisions of Schedule 2 to this Act shall have effect with respect to the constitution of the Mental Health Review Tribunal for Wales.

(3)     Subject to the provisions of Schedule 2 to this Act, and to rules made by the Lord Chancellor under this Act, the jurisdiction of the Mental Health Review Tribunal for Wales may be exercised by any three or more of its members, and references in this Act to a Mental Health Review Tribunal for Wales shall be construed accordingly.

(4)     The Welsh Ministers may pay to the members of Mental Health Review Tribunal for Wales such remuneration and allowances as they may determine, and defray the expenses of that tribunal to such amount as they may determine, and may provide for that tribunal such officers and servants, and such accommodation, as that tribunal may require.

*Applications and references concerning Part 2 patients*

### 66. Applications to tribunals

(1)     Where –

(a)   a patient is admitted to a hospital in pursuance of an application for admission for assessment; or

(b)   a patient is admitted to a hospital in pursuance of an application for admission for treatment; or

(c)   a patient is received into guardianship in pursuance of a guardianship application; or

(ca)   a community treatment order is made in respect of a patient; or

(cb)   a community treatment order is revoked under section 17F above in respect of a patient; or

(d)   (repealed)

(e)   a patient is transferred from guardianship to a hospital in pursuance of regulations made under section 19 above; or

(f)   a report is furnished under section 20 above in respect of a patient and the patient is not discharged under section 23 above; or

(fza)   a report is furnished under section 20A above in respect of a patient and the patient is not discharged under section 23 above; or

(fa)   a report is furnished under subsection (2) of section 21B above in respect of a patient and subsection (5) of that section applies (or subsections (5) and (6)(b) of that section apply) in the case of the report; or

> > (faa)  a report is furnished under subsection (2) of section 21B above in respect of a community patient and subsection (6A) of that section applies (or subsections (6A) and (6B)(b) of that section apply) in the case of the report; or

> (g)  a report is furnished under section 25 above in respect of a patient who is detained in pursuance of an application for admission for treatment or a community patient; or

> (h)  an order is made under section 29 above on the ground specified in paragraph (c) or (d) of subsection (3) of that section in respect of a patient who is or subsequently becomes liable to be detained or subject to guardianship under Part 2 of this Act or who is a community patient,

an application may be made to the appropriate Tribunal within the relevant period –

> (i)  by the patient (except in the cases mentioned in paragraphs (g) and (h) above)

> (ii)  in the cases mentioned in paragraphs (g) and (h) above, by his nearest relative.

(2)  In subsection (1) above "the relevant period" means –

(a)  in the case mentioned in paragraph (a) of that subsection, 14 days beginning with the day on which the patient is admitted as so mentioned;

(b)  in the case mentioned in paragraph (b) of that subsection, six months beginning with the day on which the patient is admitted as so mentioned;

(c)  in the case mentioned in paragraph (c) of that subsection, six months beginning with the day on which the application is accepted;

> (ca)  in the case mentioned in paragraph (ca) of that subsection, six months beginning with the day on which the community treatment order is made;

> (cb)  in the case mentioned in paragraph (cb) of that subsection, six months beginning with the day on which the community treatment order is revoked;

(d)  in the case mentioned in paragraph (g) and (gb) of that subsection, 28 days beginning with the day on which the applicant is informed that the report has been furnished;

(e)  in the case mentioned in paragraph (e) of that subsection, six months beginning with the day on which the patient is transferred;

(f)  in the case mentioned in paragraph (f) or (fa) of that subsection, the period or periods for which authority for the patient's detention or guardianship is renewed by virtue of the report;

> (fza)  in the cases mentioned in paragraphs (fza) and (faa) of that subsection, the period or periods for which the community treatment period is extended by virtue of the report;

(g)  in the case mentioned in paragraph (h) of that subsection, 12 months beginning with the date of the order, and in any subsequent period of 12 months during which the order continues in force.

(2A)  Nothing in subsection (1)(b) above entitles a community patient to make an application by virtue of that provision even if he is admitted to a hospital on being recalled there under section 17E above.

(3)  Section 32 above shall apply for the purposes of this section as it applies for the purposes of Part 2 of this Act.

(4)    In this Act "the appropriate tribunal" means the First-tier Tribunal or the Mental Health Review Tribunal for Wales.

(5)    For provision determining to which of those tribunals applications by or in respect of a patient under this Act shall be made, see section 77(3) and (4) below.

### 67. References to tribunals by Secretary of State concerning Part 2 patients

(1)    The Secretary of State may, if he thinks fit, at any time refer to the appropriate tribunal the case of any patient who is liable to be detained or subject to guardianship under Part 2 of this Act or of any community patient.

(2)    For the purpose of furnishing information for the purposes of a reference under subsection (1) above any registered medical practitioner or approved clinician authorised by or on behalf of the patient may, at any reasonable time, visit the patient and examine him in private and require the production of and inspect any records relating to the detention or treatment of the patient in any hospital or to any aftercare services provided for the patient under section 117 below.

(3)    Section 32 above shall apply for the purposes of this section as it applies for the purposes of Part 2 of this Act.

### 68. Duty of managers of hospitals to refer cases to tribunal

(1)    This section applies in respect of the following patients –

   (a)  a patient who is admitted to a hospital in pursuance of an application for admission for assessment;

   (b)  a patient who is admitted to a hospital in pursuance of an application for admission for treatment;

   (c)  a community patient;

   (d)  a patient whose community treatment order is revoked under section 17F above;

   (e)  a patient who is transferred from guardianship to a hospital in pursuance of regulations made under section 19 above.

(2)    On expiry of the period of six months beginning with the applicable day, the managers of the hospital shall refer the patient's case to the appropriate tribunal.

(3)    But they shall not do so if during that period –

   (a)  any right has been exercised by or in respect of the patient by virtue of any of paragraphs (b), (ca), (cb) (e), (g) and (h) of section 66(1) above;

   (b)  a reference has been made in respect of the patient under section 67(1) above, not being a reference made while the patient is or was liable to be detained in pursuance of an application for admission for assessment; or

   (c)  a reference has been made in respect of the patient under subsection (7) below.

(4)    A person who applies to a tribunal but subsequently withdraws his application shall be treated for these purposes as not having exercised his right to apply, and if he withdraws his application on a date after expiry of the period mentioned in subsection (2) above, the managers shall refer the patient's case as soon as possible after that date.

(5)    In subsection (2) above, "the applicable day" means –

   (a)  in the case of a patient who is admitted to a hospital in pursuance of an application for admission for assessment, the day on which the patient was so admitted;

(b) in the case of a patient who is admitted to a hospital in pursuance of an application for admission for treatment –

    (i) the day on which the patient was so admitted; or

    (ii) if, when he was so admitted, he was already liable to be detained in pursuance of an application for admission for assessment, the day on which he was originally admitted in pursuance of the application for admission for assessment;

(c) in the case of a community patient or a patient whose community treatment order is revoked under section 17F above, the day mentioned in sub-paragraph (i) or (ii), as the case may be, of paragraph (b) above;

(d) in the case of a patient who is transferred from guardianship to a hospital, the day on which he was so transferred.

(6) The managers of the hospital shall also refer the patient's case to a Mental Health Review Tribunal if a period of more than three years (or, if the patient has not attained the age of 18 years, one year) has elapsed since his case was last considered by such a tribunal, whether on his own application or otherwise.

(7) If, in the case of a community patient, the community treatment order is revoked under section 17F above, the managers of the hospital shall also refer the patient's case to the appropriate tribunal as soon as possible after the order is revoked.

(8) For the purposes of furnishing information for the purposes of a reference under this section, a registered medical practitioner or approved clinician authorised by or on behalf of the patient may at any reasonable time –

(a) visit and examine the patient in private; and

(b) require the production of and inspect any records relating to the detention or treatment of the patient in any hospital or any aftercare services provided for him under section 117 below.

(9) Reference in this section to the managers of the hospital –

(a) in relation to a community patient, is to the managers of the responsible hospital;

(b) in relation to any other patient, is to the managers of the hospital in which he is liable to be detained.

## 68A. Power to reduce periods under section 68

(1) The appropriate national authority may from time to time by order amend subsections (2) or (6) of section 68 above so as to substitute for a period mentioned there such shorter period as is specified in the order.

(2) The order may include such transitional, consequential, incidental or supplemental provision as the appropriate national authority thinks fit.

(3) The order may, in particular, make provision for a case where –

(a) a patient in respect of whom subsection (1) of section 68 above applies is, or is about to be, transferred from England to Wales or from Wales to England; and

(b) the period by reference to which subsection (2) or (6) of that section operates for the purposes of the patient's case is not the same in one territory as it is in the other.

(4) A patient is transferred from one territory to the other if –

(a) he is transferred from a hospital, or from guardianship, in one territory to a hospital in the other in pursuance of regulations made under section 19 above;

(b)  he is removed under subsection (3) of that section from a hospital or accommodation in one territory to a hospital or accommodation in the other;

(c)  he is a community patient responsibility for whom is assigned from a hospital in one territory to a hospital in the other in pursuance of regulations made under section 19A above; or

(d)  on the revocation of a community treatment order in respect of him under section 17F above he is detained in a hospital in the territory other than the one in which the responsible hospital was situated;

(5)  Provision made by virtue of subsection (3) above may require or authorise the managers of a hospital determined in accordance with the order to refer the patient's case to the appropriate tribunal.

(6)  In so far as making provision by virtue of subsection (3) above, the order –

(a)  may make different provision for different cases;

(b)  may make provision which applies subject to specified exceptions.

(7)  Where the appropriate national authority for one territory makes an order under subsection (1) above, the appropriate national authority for the other territory may by order make such provision in consequence of the order as it thinks fit.

(8)  An order made under subsection (7) above may, in particular, make provision for a case within subsection (3) above (and subsections (4) to (6) above shall apply accordingly).

(9)  In this section, "the appropriate national authority" means –

(a)  in relation to the managers of a hospital in England, the Secretary of State;

(b)  in relation to the managers of a hospital in Wales, the Welsh Ministers.

*Applications and references concerning Part 3 patients*

### 69. Applications to tribunals concerning patients subject to hospital and guardianship orders

(1)  Without prejudice to any provision of section 66(1) above as applied by section 40(4) above, an application to the appropriate tribunal may also be made –

(a)  in respect of a patient liable to be detained in pursuance of a hospital order or a community patient who was so liable immediately before he became a community patient, by the nearest relative of the patient in any period in which an application may be made by the patient under any such provision as so applied;

(b)  in respect of a patient placed under guardianship by a guardianship order –

(i)  by the patient, within the period of six months beginning with the date of the order;

(ii)  by the nearest relative of the patient, within the period of 12 months beginning with the date of the order and in any subsequent period of 12 months.

(2)  Where a person detained in a hospital –

(a)  is treated as subject to a hospital order, hospital direction or transfer direction by virtue of section 41(5) above, or section 80B(2), 82(2) or 85(2) below; or

(b)  is subject to a direction having the same effect as a hospital order by virtue of section 47(3) or 48(3) above, then, without prejudice to any provision of Part 2 of this Act as applied by section 40 above, that person may make an application to the appropriate tribunal in the period of six months beginning with the date of the order or direction mentioned in paragraph (a) above or, as the case may be, the date of the direction mentioned in paragraph (b) above.

(3)  The provisions of section 66 above as applied by section 40(4) above are subject to sub-section (4) below.

(4)  If the initial detention period has not elapsed when the relevant application period begins, the right of a hospital order patient to make an application by virtue of par-agraph (ca) or (cb) of section 66(1) above shall be exercisable only during whatever remains of the relevant application period after the initial detention period has elapsed.

(5)  In subsection (4) above –

    (a)  "hospital order patient" means a patient who is subject to a hospital order, exclud-ing a patient of a kind mentioned in paragraph (a) or (b) of subsection (2) above;

    (b)  "the initial detention period", in relation to a hospital order patient, means the period of six months beginning with the date of the hospital order; and

    (c)  "the relevant application period" means the relevant period mentioned in paragraph (ca) or (cb), as the case may be, of section 66(2) above.

## 70. Applications to tribunals concerning restricted patients

A patient who is a restricted patient within the meaning of section 79 below and is detained in a hospital may apply to the appropriate tribunal –

(a)  in the period between the expiration of six months and the expiration of 12 months begin-ning with the date of the relevant hospital order, hospital direction or transfer direction; and

(b)  in any subsequent period of 12 months.

## 71. References by Secretary of State concerning restricted patients

(1)  The Secretary of State may at any time refer the case of a restricted patient to the appro-priate tribunal.

(2)  The Secretary of State shall refer to the appropriate tribunal the case of any restricted patient detained in a hospital whose case has not been considered by such a tribunal, whether on his own application or otherwise, within the last three years.

(3)  The Secretary of State may by order vary the length of the period mentioned in subsec-tion (2) above.

(3A)  An order under subsection (3) above may include such transitional, consequential, inci-dental or supplemental provision as the Secretary of State thinks fit.

(4)  Any reference under subsection (1) above in respect of a patient who has been condi-tionally discharged and not recalled to hospital shall be made to the tribunal for the area in which the patient resides.

(5), (6)  (repealed)

*Discharge of patients*

## 72. Powers of tribunals

(1)  Where application is made to the appropriate tribunal by or in respect of a patient who is liable to be detained under this Act or is a community patient, the tribunal may in any case direct that the patient be discharged, and –

(a)  the tribunal shall direct the discharge of a patient liable to be detained under section 2 above if they are not satisfied –

   (i)   that he is then suffering from mental disorder or from mental disorder of a nature or degree which warrants his detention in a hospital for assessment (or for assessment followed by medical treatment) for at least a limited period; or

   (ii)  that his detention as aforesaid is justified in the interests of his own health or safety or with a view to the protection of other persons;

(b)  the tribunal shall direct the discharge of a patient liable to be detained otherwise than under section 2 above if they are not satisfied –

   (i)   that he is then suffering from mental disorder or from mental disorder of a nature or degree which makes it appropriate for him to be liable to be detained in a hospital for medical treatment; or

   (ii)  that it is necessary for the health of safety of the patient or for the protection of other persons that he should receive such treatment; or

   (iia) that appropriate medical treatment is available for him; or

   (iii) in the case of an application by virtue of paragraph (g) of section 66(1) above, that the patient, if released, would be likely to act in a manner dangerous to other persons or to himself.

(c)  the tribunal shall direct the discharge of a community patient if they are not satisfied –

   (i)   that he is then suffering from mental disorder or mental disorder of a nature or degree which makes it appropriate for him to receive medical treatment; or

   (ii)  that it is necessary for his health or safety or for the protection of other persons that he should receive such treatment; or

   (iii) that it is necessary that the responsible clinician should be able to exercise the power under section 17E(1) to recall the patient to hospital; or

   (iv)  that appropriate medical treatment is available for him; or

   (v)   in the case of an application by virtue of paragraph (g) of section 66(1) above, that the patient, if discharged, would be likely to act in a manner dangerous to other persons or to himself.

(1A)  In determining whether the criterion in subsection (1)(c)(iii) above is met, the tribunal shall, in particular, consider, having regard to the patient's history of mental disorder and any other relevant factors, what risk there would be of a deterioration of the patient's condition if he were to continue not to be detained in a hospital (as a result, for example, of his refusing or neglecting to receive the medical treatment he requires for his mental disorder).

(2)   (repealed)

(3)   A tribunal may under subsection (1) above direct the discharge of a patient on a future date specified in the direction; and where a tribunal do not direct the discharge of a patient under that subsection the tribunal may –

(a)   with a view to facilitating his discharge on a future date, recommend that he be granted leave of absence or transferred to another hospital or into guardianship; and

(b)   further consider his case in the event of any such recommendation not being complied with.

(3A)  Subsection (1) above does not require a tribunal to direct the discharge of a patient just because they think it might be appropriate for the patient to be discharged (subject to the possibility of recall) under a community treatment order; and a tribunal –

    (a)  may recommend that the responsible clinician consider whether to make a community treatment order; and

    (b)  may (but need not) further consider the patient's case if the responsible clinician does not make an order.

(4)  Where application is made to a Mental Health Review Tribunal by or in respect of a patient who is subject to guardianship under this Act, the tribunal may in any case direct that the patient be discharged, and shall so direct if they are satisfied –

    (a)  that he is not then suffering from mental disorder; or

    (b)  that it is not necessary in the interests of the welfare of the patient, or for the protection of other persons, that the patient should remain under such guardianship.

(4A), (5)  (repealed)

(6)  Subsections (1) to (4) above apply in relation to references to a Mental Health Review Tribunal as they apply in relation to applications made to such a tribunal by or in respect of a patient.

(7)  Subsection (1) above shall not apply in the case of a restricted patient except as provided in sections 73 and 74 below.

## 73. Power to discharge restricted patients

(1)  Where an application to the appropriate tribunal is made by a restricted patient who is subject to a restriction order, or where the case of such a patient is referred to such a tribunal, the tribunal shall direct the absolute discharge of the patient if –

    (a)  the tribunal are not satisfied as to the matters mentioned in paragraph (b)(i),(ii) or (iia) of section 72(1) above;

    (b)  the tribunal are satisfied that it is not appropriate for the patient to remain liable to be recalled to hospital for further treatment.

(2)  Where in the case of any such patient as is mentioned in subsection (1) above –

    (a)  paragraph (a) of that subsection applies; but

    (b)  paragraph (b) of that subsection does not apply, the tribunal shall direct the conditional discharge of the patient.

(3)  Where a patient is absolutely discharged under this section he shall thereupon cease to be liable to be detained by virtue of the relevant hospital order, and the restriction order shall cease to have effect accordingly.

(4)  Where a patient is conditionally discharged under this section –

    (a)  he may be recalled by the Secretary of State under subsection (3) of section 42 above as if he had been conditionally discharged under subsection (2) of that section; and

    (b)  the patient shall comply with such conditions (if any) as may be imposed at the time of discharge by the tribunal or at any subsequent time by the Secretary of State.

(5)     The Secretary of State may from time to time vary any condition imposed (whether by the tribunal or by him) under subsection (4) above.

(6)     Where a restriction order in respect of a patient ceases to have effect after he has been conditionally discharged under this section the patient shall, unless previously recalled, be deemed to be absolutely discharged on the date when the order ceases to have effect and shall cease to be liable to be detained by virtue of the relevant hospital order.

(7)     A tribunal may defer a direction for the conditional discharge of a patient until such arrangements as appear to the tribunal to be necessary for that purpose have been made to their satisfaction; and where by virtue of any such deferment no direction has been given on an application or reference before the time when the patient's case comes before the tribunal on a subsequent application or reference, the previous application or reference shall be treated as one on which no direction under this section can be given.

(8)     This section is without prejudice to section 42 above.

## 74. Restricted patients subject to restriction directions

(1)     Where an application to the appropriate tribunal is made by a restricted patient who is subject to a limitation direction or restriction direction, or where the case of such a patient is referred to the appropriate tribunal the tribunal –

   (a)   shall notify the Secretary of State whether, in their opinion, the patient would, if subject to a restriction order, be entitled to be absolutely or conditionally discharged under section 73 above; and

   (b)   if they notify him that the patient would be entitled to be conditionally discharged, may recommend that in the event of his not being discharged under this section he should continue to be detained in hospital.

(2)     If in the case of a patient not falling within subsection (4) below –

   (a)   the tribunal notify the Secretary of State that the patient would be entitled to be absolutely or conditionally discharged; and

   (b)   within the period of 90 days beginning with the date of that notification the Secretary of State gives notice to the tribunal that the patient may be so discharged, the tribunal shall direct the absolute or, as the case may be, the conditional discharge of the patient.

(3)     Where a patient continues to be liable to be detained in a hospital at the end of the period referred to in subsection (2)(b) above because the Secretary of State has not given the notice there mentioned, the managers of the hospital shall, unless the tribunal have made a recommendation under subsection (1)(b) above, transfer the patient to a prison or other institution in which he might have been detained if he had not been removed to hospital, there to be dealt with as if he had not been so removed.

(4)     If, in the case of a patient who is subject to a transfer direction under section 48 above, the tribunal notify the Secretary of State that the patient would be entitled to be absolutely or conditionally discharged, the Secretary of State shall, unless the tribunal have made a recommendation under subsection (1)(b) above, by warrant direct that the patient be remitted to a prison or other institution in which he might have been detained if he had not been removed to hospital, there to be dealt with as if he had not been so removed.

(5)     Where a patient is transferred or remitted under subsection (3) or (4) above the relevant hospital direction and the limitation direction or, as the case may be, the relevant transfer direction and the restriction direction shall cease to have effect on his arrival in the prison or other institution.

(5A) Where the tribunal have made a recommendation under subsection (1)(b) above in the case of a patient who is subject to a restriction direction or a limitation direction –

(a) the fact that the restriction direction or limitation direction remains in force does not prevent the making of any application or reference to the Parole Board by or in respect of him or the exercise by him of any power to require the Secretary of State to refer his case to the Parole Board, and

(b) if the Parole Board make a direction or recommendation by virtue of which the patient would become entitled to be released (whether unconditionally or on licence) from any prison or other institution in which he might have been detained if he had not been removed to hospital, the restriction direction or limitation direction shall cease to have effect at the time when he would become entitled to be so released.

(6) Subsections (3) to (8) of section 73 above shall have effect in relation to this section as they have effect in relation to that section, taking references to the relevant hospital order and the restriction order as references to the hospital direction and the limitation direction or, as the case may be, to the transfer direction and the restriction direction.

(7) This section is without prejudice to sections 50 to 53 above in their application to patients who are not discharged under this section.

## 75. Applications and references concerning conditionally discharged restricted patients

(1) Where a restricted patient has been conditionally discharged under section 42(2), 73 or 74 above and is subsequently recalled to hospital –

(a) the Secretary of State shall, within one month of the day on which the patient returns or is returned to hospital, refer his case to the appropriate tribunal; and

(b) section 70 above shall apply to the patient as if the relevant hospital order, hospital direction or transfer direction had been made on that day.

(2) Where a restricted patient has been conditionally discharged as aforesaid but has not been recalled to hospital he may apply to the appropriate tribunal –

(a) in the period between the expiration of 12 months and the expiration of two years beginning with the date on which he was conditionally discharged; and

(b) in any subsequent period of two years.

(3) Sections 73 and 74 above shall not apply to an application under subsection (2) above but on any such application the tribunal may –

(a) vary any condition to which the patient is subject in connection with his discharge or impose any condition which might have been imposed in connection therewith; or

(b) direct that the restriction order, limitation direction or restriction direction to which he is subject shall cease to have effect;

and if the tribunal give a direction under paragraph (b) above the patient shall cease to be liable to be detained by virtue of the relevant hospital order, hospital direction or transfer direction.

*General*

## 76. Visiting and examination of patients

(1) For the purpose of advising whether an application to the appropriate tribunal should be made by or in respect of a patient who is liable to be detained or subject to guardianship

under Part 2 of this Act or a community patient, or of furnishing information as to the condition of a patient for the purposes of such an application, any registered medical practitioner or approved clinician authorised by or on behalf of the patient or other person who is entitled to make or has made the application –

(a) may at any reasonable time visit the patient and examine him in private, and

(b) may require the production of and inspect any records relating to the detention or treatment of the patient in any hospital or to any aftercare services provided for the patient under section 117 below.

(2) Section 32 above shall apply for the purposes of this section as it applies for the purposes of Part 2 of this Act.

### 77. General provisions concerning tribunal applications

(1) No application shall be made to the appropriate tribunal by or in respect of a patient except in such cases and at such times as are expressly provided by this Act.

(2) Where under this Act any person is authorised to make an application to a Mental Health Review Tribunal within a specified period, not more than one such application shall be made by that person within that period but for that purpose there shall be disregarded any application which is withdrawn in accordance with rules made under section 78 below.

(3) Subject to subsection (4) below an application to a Tribunal authorised to be made by or in respect of a patient under this Act shall be made by notice in writing addressed

(a) in the case of a patient who is liable to be detained in a hospital, to the First-tier tribunal where that hospital is in England and to the Mental Health Review Tribunal for Wales where that hospital is in Wales;

(b) in the case of a community patient, to the First-tier Tribunal where the responsible hospital is in England and to the Mental Health Review Tribunal for Wales where that hospital is in Wales;

(c) in the case of a patient subject to guardianship, to the First-tier Tribunal where the patient resides in England and to the Mental Health Review Tribunal for Wales where the patient resides in Wales.

(4) Any application under section 75(2) above shall be made to the First-tier Tribunal where the patient resides in England and to the Mental Health Review Tribunal for Wales where the patient resides in Wales.

### 78. Procedure of tribunals

(1) The Lord Chancellor may make rules with respect to the making of applications to Mental Health Review Tribunal for Wales and with respect to the proceedings of such tribunals and matters incidental to or consequential on such proceedings.

(2) Rules made under this section may in particular make provision –

(a) for enabling a tribunal, or the chairman of the tribunal, to postpone the consideration of any application by or in respect of a patient, or of any such application of any specified class, until the expiration of such period (not exceeding 12 months) as may be specified in the rules from the date on which an application by or in respect of the same patient was last considered and determined by the tribunal or the First-tier tribunal;

(b) for the transfer of proceedings to or from the Mental Health Review Tribunal for Wales in any case where, after the making of the application, the patient is moved into or out of Wales;

(c) for restricting the persons qualified to serve as members of the tribunal for the consideration of any application, or of an application of any specified class;

(d) for enabling the tribunal to dispose of an application without a formal hearing where such a hearing is not requested by the applicant or it appears to the tribunal that such a hearing would be detrimental to the health of the patient;

(e) for enabling the tribunal to exclude members of the public, or any specified class of members of the public, from any proceedings of the tribunal, or to prohibit the publication of reports of any such proceedings or the names of any persons concerned in such proceedings;

(f) for regulating the circumstances in which, and the persons by whom, applicants and patients in respect of whom applications are made to the tribunal may, if not desiring to conduct their own case, be represented for the purposes of those applications;

(g) for regulating the methods by which information relevant to an application may be obtained by or furnished to the tribunal, and in particular for authorising the members of the tribunal, or any one or more of them, to visit and interview in private any patient by or in respect of whom an application has been made;

(h) for making available to any applicant, and to any patient in respect of whom an application is made to the tribunal, copies of any documents obtained by or furnished to the tribunal in connection with the application, and a statement of the substance of any oral information so obtained or furnished except where the tribunal considers it undesirable in the interests of the patient or for other special reasons;

(i) for requiring the tribunal, if so requested in accordance with the rules, to furnish such statements of the reasons for any decision given by the tribunal as may be prescribed by the rules, subject to any provision made by the rules for withholding such a statement from a patient or any other person in cases where the tribunal considers that furnishing it would be undesirable in the interests of the patient or for other special reasons;

(j) for conferring on the tribunal such ancillary powers as the Lord Chancellor thinks necessary for the purposes of the exercise of its functions under this Act;

(k) for enabling any functions of the tribunal which relate to matters preliminary or incidental to an application to be performed by the chairman of the tribunal.

(3) Subsections (1) and (2) above apply in relation to references to Mental Health Review Tribunal for Wales as they apply in relation to applications to that tribunals by or in respect of patients.

(4) Rules under this section may make provision as to the procedure to be adopted in cases concerning restricted patients and, in particular –

(a) for restricting the persons qualified to serve as chairman of the tribunal for the consideration of an application or reference relating to a restricted patient;

(b) for the transfer of proceedings to or from the tribunal in any case where, after the making of a reference or application in accordance with section 71(4) or 77(4) above, the patient begins or ceases to reside in Wales.

(5)    Rules under this section may be so framed as to apply to all applications or references or to applications or references of any specified class and may make different provision in relation to different cases.

(6)    Any functions conferred on the chairman of the Mental Health Review Tribunal for Wales by rules under this section may be exercised by another member of that tribunal appointed by him for the purpose.

(7)    The Mental Health Review Tribunal for Wales may pay allowances in respect of travelling expenses, subsistence and loss of earnings to any person attending the tribunal as an applicant or witness, to the patient who is the subject of the proceedings if he attends otherwise than as the applicant or a witness and to any person (other than counsel or a solicitor) who attends as the representative of an applicant.

(8)    (repealed)

(9)    Part I of the Arbitration Act 1996 shall not apply to any proceedings before the Mental Health Review Tribunal for Wales except so far as any provisions of that Act may be applied, with or without modifications, by rules made under this section.

### 78A. Appeal from the Mental Health Review Tribunal for Wales to the Upper Tribunal

(1)    A party to any proceedings before the Mental Health Review Tribunal for Wales may appeal to the Upper tribunal on any point of law arising from a decision made by the Mental Health Review Tribunal for Wales in those proceedings.

(2)    An appeal may be brought under subsection (1) above only if, on an application made by the party concerned, the Mental Health Review Tribunal for Wales or the Upper Tribunal has given its permission for the appeal to be brought.

(3)    Section 12 of the Tribunals, Courts and Enforcement Act 2007 (proceedings on appeal to the Upper Tribunal) applies in relation to appeals to the Upper Tribunal under this section as it applies in relation to appeals to it under section 11 of that Act, but as if references to the First-tier Tribunal were references to the Mental Health Review Tribunal for Wales.

### 79. Interpretation of Part 5

(1)    In this Part of this Act "restricted patient" means a patient who is subject to a restriction order, limitation direction or restriction direction and this Part of this Act shall, subject to the provisions of this section, have effect in relation to any person who –

   (a)   is treated by virtue of any enactment as subject to a hospital order and a restriction order; or

   (b)   (repealed)

   (c)   is treated as subject to a hospital order and a restriction order, or to a hospital direction and a limitation direction, or to a transfer direction and a restriction direction, by virtue of any provision of Part 6 of this Act (except section 80D(3), 82A(2) or 85A(2) below),

as it has effect in relation to a restricted patient.

(2)    Subject to the following provisions of this section, in this Part of this Act "the relevant hospital order", "the relevant hospital direction" and "the relevant transfer direction", in relation to a restricted patient, mean the hospital order, the hospital direction or transfer direction by virtue of which he is liable to be detained in a hospital.

(3)    In the case of a person within paragraph (a) of subsection (1) above, references in this Part of this Act to the relevant hospital order or restriction order shall be construed as references to the direction referred to in that paragraph.

(4)     In the case of a person within paragraph (b) of subsection (1) above, references in this Part of this Act to the relevant hospital order or restriction order shall be construed as references to the order under the provisions mentioned in that paragraph.

(5)     In the case of a person within paragraph (c) of subsection (1) above, references in this Part of this Act to the relevant hospital order, the relevant hospital direction, the relevant transfer direction, the restriction order, limitation direction or the restriction direction or to a transfer direction under section 48 above shall be construed as references to the hospital order, hospital direction, transfer direction, restriction order, limitation direction, restriction direction or transfer direction under that section to which that person is treated as subject by virtue of the provisions mentioned in that paragraph.

(5A)    Section 75 above shall, subject to the modifications in subsection (5C) below, have effect in relation to a qualifying patient as it has effect in relation to a restricted patient who is conditionally discharged under section 42(2), 73 or 74 above.

(5B)    A patient is a qualifying patient if he is treated by virtue of section 80D(3), 82A(2) or 85A(2) below as if he had been conditionally discharged and were subject to a hospital order and a restriction order, or to a hospital direction and a limitation direction, or to a transfer direction and a restriction direction.

(5C)    The modifications mentioned in subsection (5A) above are –

(a)    references to the relevant hospital order, hospital direction or transfer direction, or to the restriction order, limitation direction or restriction direction to which the patient is subject, shall be construed as references to the hospital order, hospital direction or transfer direction, or restriction order, limitation direction or restriction direction, to which the patient is treated as subject by virtue of section 80D(3), 82A(2) or 85A(2) below; and

(b)    the reference to the date on which the patient was conditionally discharged shall be construed as a reference to the date on which he was treated as conditionally discharged by virtue of a provision mentioned in paragraph (a) above.

(6)     In this Part of this Act, unless the context otherwise requires, "hospital" means a hospital, and "the responsible clinician" means the responsible clinician, within the meaning of Part 2 II of this Act.

(7)     (repealed)

## PART 6: REMOVAL AND RETURN OF PATIENTS WITHIN UNITED KINGDOM, ETC.

*Removal to and from Scotland*

### 80. Removal of patients to Scotland

(1)     If it appears to the Secretary of State, in the case of a patient who is for the time being liable to be detained under this Act (otherwise than by virtue of section 35, 36 or 38 above), that it is in the interests of the patient to remove him to Scotland, and that arrangements have been made for admitting him to a hospital or, where he is not to be admitted to a hospital, for his detention in hospital to be authorised by virtue of the Mental Health (Care and Treatment) (Scotland) Act 2003 or the Criminal Procedure (Scotland) Act 1995 the Secretary of State may authorise his removal to Scotland and may give any necessary directions for his conveyance to his destination.

(2)–(6)    (repealed)

(7)    In this section "hospital" has the same meaning as in the Mental Health (Care and Treatment) (Scotland) Act 2003.

(8)    Reference in this section to a patient's detention in hospital being authorised by virtue of the Mental Health (Care and Treatment) (Scotland) Act 2003 or the Criminal Procedure (Scotland) Act 1995 shall be read as including references to a patient in respect of whom a certificate under one of the provisions listed in section 290(7)(a) of the Act of 2003 is in operation.

### 80ZA. Transfer of responsibility for community patients to Scotland

(1)    If it appears to the appropriate national authority, in the case of a community patient, that the conditions mentioned in subsection (2) below are met, the authority may authorise the transfer of responsibility for him to Scotland.

(2)    The conditions are –

    (a)  a transfer under this section is in the patient's interests; and

    (b)  arrangements have been made for dealing with him under enactments in force in Scotland corresponding or similar to those relating to community patients in this Act.

(3)    The appropriate national authority may not act under subsection (1) above while the patient is recalled to hospital under section 17E above.

(4)    In this section, "the appropriate national authority" means –

    (a)  in relation to a community patient in respect of whom the responsible hospital is in England, the Secretary of State;

    (b)  in relation to a community patient in respect of whom the responsible hospital is in Wales, the Welsh Ministers.

### 80A. Transfer of responsibility for conditionally discharged patients to Scotland

(1)    If it appears to the Secretary of State, in the case of a patient who –

    (a)  is subject to a restriction order under section 41 above; and

    (b)  has been conditionally discharged under section 42 or 73 above,

    that a transfer under this section would be in the interests of the patient, the Secretary of State may, with the consent of the Minister exercising corresponding functions in Scotland, transfer responsibility for the patient to that Minister.

(2), (3)  (repealed)

### 80B. Removal of detained patients from Scotland

(1)    This section applies to a patient if –

    (a)  he is removed to England and Wales under regulations made under section 290(1)(a) of the Mental Health (Care and Treatment) (Scotland) Act 2003 ("the 2003 Act");

    (b)  immediately before his removal, his detention in hospital was authorised by virtue of that Act or the Criminal Procedure (Scotland) Act 1995; and

    (c)  on his removal, he is admitted to a hospital in England or Wales.

(2)    He shall be treated as if, on the date of his admission to the hospital, he had been so admitted in pursuance of an application made, or an order or direction made or given,

on that date under the enactment in force in England and Wales which most closely corresponds to the enactment by virtue of which his detention in hospital was authorised immediately before his removal.

(3)    If, immediately before his removal, he was subject to a measure under any enactment in force in Scotland restricting his discharge, he shall be treated as if he were subject to an order or direction under the enactment in force in England and Wales which most closely corresponds to that enactment.

(4)    If, immediately before his removal, the patient was liable to be detained under the 2003 Act by virtue of a transfer for treatment direction, given while he was serving a sentence of imprisonment (within the meaning of section 136(9) of that Act) imposed by a court in Scotland, he shall be treated as if the sentence had been imposed by a court in England and Wales.

(5)    If, immediately before his removal, the patient was subject to a hospital direction or transfer for treatment direction, the restriction direction to which he is subject by virtue of subsection (3) above shall expire on the date on which that hospital direction or transfer for treatment direction (as the case may be) would have expired if he had not been so removed.

(6)    If, immediately before his removal, the patient was liable to be detained under the 2003 Act by virtue of a hospital direction, he shall be treated as if any sentence of imprisonment passed at the time when that hospital direction was made had been imposed by a court in England and Wales.

(7)    Any directions given by the Scottish Ministers under regulations made under section 290 of the 2003 Act as to the removal of a patient to which this section applies shall have effect as if they were given under this Act.

(8)    Subsection (8) of section 80 above applies to a reference in this section as it applies to one in that section.

(9)    In this section –

"hospital direction" means a direction made under section 59A of the Criminal Procedure (Scotland) Act 1995; and

"transfer for treatment direction" has the meaning given by section 136 of the 2003 Act.

## 80C. Removal of patients subject to compulsion in the community from Scotland

(1)    This section applies to a patient if –

    (a)  he is subject to an enactment in force in Scotland by virtue of which regulations under section 289(1) of the Mental Health (Care and Treatment) (Scotland) Act 2003 apply to him; and

    (b)  he is removed to England and Wales under those regulations.

(2)    He shall be treated as if on the date of his arrival at the place where he is to reside in England or Wales –

    (a)  he had been admitted to a hospital in England or Wales in pursuance of an application or order made on that date under the corresponding enactment; and

    (b)  a community treatment order had then been made discharging him from the hospital.

(3)    For these purposes –

    (a)    if the enactment to which the patient was subject in Scotland was an enactment contained in the Mental Health (Care and Treatment) (Scotland) Act 2003, the corresponding enactment is section 3 of this Act;

    (b)    if the enactment to which he was subject in Scotland was an enactment contained in the Criminal Procedure (Scotland) Act 1995, the corresponding enactment is section 37 of this Act.

(4)    "The responsible hospital", in the case of a patient in respect of whom a community treatment order is in force by virtue of subsection (2) above, means the hospital to which he is treated as having been admitted by virtue of that subsection, subject to section 19A above.

(5)    As soon as practicable after the patient's arrival at the place where he is to reside in England or Wales, the responsible clinician shall specify the conditions to which he is to be subject for the purposes of section 17B(1) above, and the conditions shall be deemed to be specified in the community treatment order.

(6)    But the responsible clinician may only specify conditions under subsection (5) above which an approved mental health professional agrees should be specified.

## 80D. Transfer of conditionally discharged patients from Scotland

(1)    This section applies to a patient who is subject to –

    (a)    a restriction order under section 59 of the Criminal Procedure (Scotland) Act 1995; and

    (b)    a conditional discharge under section 193(7) of the Mental Health (Care and Treatment) (Scotland) Act 2003 ("the 2003 Act").

(2)    A transfer of the patient to England and Wales under regulations made under section 290 of the 2003 Act shall have effect only if the Secretary of State has consented to the transfer.

(3)    If a transfer under those regulations has effect, the patient shall be treated as if –

    (a)    on the date of the transfer he had been conditionally discharged under section 42 or 73 above; and

    (b)    he were subject to a hospital order under section 37 above and a restriction order under section 41 above.

(4)    If the restriction order to which the patient was subject immediately before the transfer was of limited duration, the restriction order to which he is subject by virtue of subsection (3) above shall expire on the date on which the first mentioned order would have expired if the transfer had not been made.

*Removal to and from Northern Ireland*

## 81. Removal of patients to Northern Ireland

(1)    If it appears to the Secretary of State, in the case of a patient who is for the time being liable to be detained or subject to guardianship under this Act (otherwise than by virtue of section 35, 36 or 38 above), that it is in the interests of the patient to remove him to Northern Ireland, and that arrangements have been made for admitting him to a hospital or, as the case may be, for receiving him into guardianship there, the Secretary of State may authorise his removal to Northern Ireland and may give any necessary directions for his conveyance to his destination.

(2) Subject to the provisions of subsections (4) and (5) below, where a patient liable to be detained under this Act by virtue of an application, order or direction under any enactment in force in England and Wales is removed under this section and admitted to a hospital in Northern Ireland, he shall be treated as if on the date of his admission he had been so admitted in pursuance of an application made, or an order or direction made or given, on that date under the corresponding enactment in force in Northern Ireland, and, where he is subject to a hospital order and a restriction order or a transfer direction and a restriction direction under any enactment in this Act, as if he were subject to a hospital order and a restriction order or a transfer direction and a restriction direction under the corresponding enactment in force in Northern Ireland.

(3) Where a patient subject to guardianship under this Act by virtue of an application, order or direction under any enactment in force in England and Wales is removed under this section and received into guardianship in Northern Ireland, he shall be treated as if on the date on which he arrives at the place where he is to reside he had been so received in pursuance of an application, order or direction under the corresponding enactment in force in Northern Ireland, and as if the application had been accepted or, as the case may be, the order or direction had been made or given on that date.

(4) Where a person removed under this section was immediately before his removal liable to be detained by virtue of an application for admission for assessment under this Act, he shall, on his admission to a hospital in Northern Ireland, be treated as if he had been admitted to the hospital in pursuance of an application for assessment under Article 4 of the Mental Health (Northern Ireland) Order 1986 made on the date of his admission.

(5) Where a person removed under this section was immediately before his removal liable to be detained by virtue of an application for admission for treatment under this Act, he shall, on his admission to a hospital in Northern Ireland, be treated as if he were detained for treatment under Part 2 of the Mental Health (Northern Ireland) Order 1986 by virtue of a report under Article 12(1) of that Order made on the date of his admission.

(6) Where a patient removed under this section was immediately before his removal liable to be detained under this Act by virtue of a transfer direction given while he was serving a sentence of imprisonment (within the meaning of section 47(5) above) imposed by a court in England and Wales, he shall be treated as if the sentence had been imposed by a court in Northern Ireland.

(7) Where a person removed under this section was immediately before his removal subject to a restriction direction of limited duration, the restriction direction to which he is subject by virtue of subsection (2) above shall expire on the date on which the first-mentioned restricted direction would have expired if he had not been so removed.

(8) In this section "hospital" has the same meaning as in the (Northern Ireland) Order 1986.

## 81ZA. Removal of community patients to Northern Ireland

(1) Section 81 above shall apply in the case of a community patient as it applies in the case of a patient who is for the time being liable to be detained under this Act, as if the community patient were so liable.

(2) Any reference in that section to the application, order or direction by virtue of which a patient is liable to be detained under this Act shall be construed, for these purposes, as a reference to the application, order or direction under this Act in respect of the patient.

## 81A. Transfer of responsibility for patients to Northern Ireland

(1)    If it appears to the Secretary of State, in the case of a patient who –

(a)    is subject to a hospital order under section 37 above and a restriction order under section 41 above or to a transfer direction under section 47 above and a restriction direction under section 49 above; and

(b)    has been conditionally discharged under section 42 or 73 above,

that a transfer under this section would be in the interests of the patient, the Secretary of State may, with the consent of the Minister exercising corresponding functions in Northern Ireland, transfer responsibility for the patient to that Minister.

(2)    Where responsibility for such a patient is transferred under this section, the patient shall be treated –

(a)    as if on the date of the transfer he had been conditionally discharged under the corresponding enactment in force in Northern Ireland; and

(b)    as if he were subject to a hospital order and a restriction order, or to a transfer direction and a restriction direction, under the corresponding enactment in force in Northern Ireland.

(3)    Where a patient responsibility for whom is transferred under this section was immediately before the transfer subject to a restriction direction of limited duration, the restriction direction to which he is subject by virtue of subsection (2) above shall expire on the date on which the first- mentioned direction would have expired if the transfer had not been made.

## 82. Removal to England and Wales of patients from Northern Ireland

(1)    If it appears to the responsible authority, in the case of a patient who is for the time being liable to be detained or subject to guardianship under the (Northern Ireland) Order 1986 (otherwise than by virtue of Article 42, 43 or 45 of that Order), that it is in the interests of the patient to remove him to England and Wales, and that arrangements have been made for admitting him to a hospital or, as the case may be, for receiving him into guardianship there, the responsible authority may authorise his removal to England and Wales and may give any necessary directions for his conveyance to his destination.

(2)    Subject to the provisions of subsections (4) and (4A) below, where a patient who is liable to be detained under the Mental Health (Northern Ireland) Order 1986 by virtue of an application, order or direction under any enactment in force in Northern Ireland is removed under this section and admitted to a hospital in England and Wales, he shall be treated as if on the date of his admission he had been so admitted in pursuance of an application made, or an order or direction made or given, on that date under the corresponding enactment in force in England and Wales and, where he is subject to a hospital order and a restriction order or a transfer direction and a restriction direction under any enactment in that Order, as if he were subject to a hospital order and a restriction order or a transfer direction and a restriction direction under the corresponding enactment in force in England and Wales.

(3)    Where a patient subject to guardianship under the Mental Health (Northern Ireland) Order 1986 by virtue of an application, order or direction under any enactment in force in Northern Ireland is removed under this section and received into guardianship in England and Wales, he shall be treated as if on the date on which he arrives at the place where he is to reside he had been so received in pursuance of an application, order or direction under the corresponding enactment in force in England and Wales and as if the

application had been accepted or, as the case may be, the order or direction had been made or given on that date.

(4)    Where a person removed under this section was immediately before his removal liable to be detained for treatment by virtue of a report under Article 12(1) or 13 of the Mental Health (Northern Ireland) Order 1986, he shall be treated, on his admission to a hospital in England and Wales, as if he had been admitted to the hospital in pursuance of an application for admission for treatment made on the date of his admission.

(4A)   Where a person removed under this section was immediately before his removal liable to be detained by virtue of an application for assessment under Article 4 of the Mental Health (Northern Ireland) Order 1986, he shall be treated, on his admission to a hospital in England and Wales, as if he had been admitted to the hospital in pursuance of an application for admission for assessment made on the date of his admission.

(5)    Where a patient removed under this section was immediately before his removal liable to be detained under the Mental Health (Northern Ireland) Order 1986 by virtue of a transfer direction given while he was serving a sentence of imprisonment (within the meaning of Article 53(5) of that Order) imposed by a court in Northern Ireland, he shall be treated as if the sentence had been imposed by a court in England and Wales.

(6)    Where a person removed under this section was immediately before his removal subject to a restriction order or restriction direction of limited duration, the restriction order or restriction direction to which he is subject by virtue of subsection (2) above shall expire on the date on which the first-mentioned restriction order or restriction direction would have expired if he had not been so removed.

(7)    In this section "the responsible authority" means the Department of Health and Social Services for Northern Ireland or, in relation to a patient who is subject to a restriction order or restriction direction, the Department of Justice in Northern Ireland.

## 82A. Transfer of responsibility for conditionally discharged patients to England and Wales from Northern Ireland

(1)    If it appears to the relevant Minister, in the case of a patient who –

(a)    is subject to a restriction order or restriction direction under Article 47(1) or 55(1) of the Mental Health (Northern Ireland) Order 1986; and

(b)    has been conditionally discharged under Article 48(2) or 78(2) of that Order,

that a transfer under this section would be in the interests of the patient, that Minister may, with the consent of the Secretary of State, transfer responsibility for the patient to the Secretary of State.

(2)    Where responsibility for such a patient is transferred under this section, the patient shall be treated –

(a)    as if on the date of the transfer he had been conditionally discharged under section 42 or 73 above; and

(b)    as if he were subject to a hospital order under section 37 above and a restriction order under section 41 above or to a transfer direction under section 47 above and a restriction direction under section 49 above.

(3)    Where a patient responsibility for whom is transferred under this section was immediately before the transfer subject to a restriction order or restriction direction of limited

duration, the restriction order or restriction direction to which he is subject by virtue of subsection (2) above shall expire on the date on which the first-mentioned order or direction would have expired if the transfer had not been made.

(4)    (repealed).

*Removal to and from Channel Islands and Isle of Man*

### 83. Removal of patients to Channel Islands or Isle of Man

If it appears to the Secretary of State, in the case of a patient who is for the time being liable to be detained or subject to guardianship under this Act (otherwise than by virtue of section 35, 36 or 38 above), that it is in the interests of the patient to remove him to any of the Channel Islands or to the Isle of Man, and that arrangements have been made for admitting him to a hospital or, as the case may be, for receiving him into guardianship there, the Secretary of State may authorise his removal to the island in question and may give any necessary directions for his conveyance to his destination.

### 83ZA. Removal or transfer of community patients to Channel Islands or Isle of Man

(1)    Section 83 above shall apply in the case of a community patient as it applies in the case of a patient who is for the time being liable to be detained under this Act, as if the community patient were so liable.

(2)    But if there are in force in any of the Channel Islands or the Isle of Man enactments ("relevant enactments") corresponding or similar to those relating to community patients in this Act –

   (a)   subsection (1) above shall not apply as regards that island; and

   (b)   subsections (3) to (6) below shall apply instead.

(3)    If it appears to the appropriate national authority, in the case of a community patient, that the conditions mentioned in subsection (4) below are met, the authority may authorise the transfer of responsibility for him to the island in question.

(4)    The conditions are –

   (a)   a transfer under subsection (3) above is in the patient's interests; and

   (b)   arrangements have been made for dealing with him under the relevant enactments.

(5)    But the authority may not act under subsection (3) above while the patient is recalled to hospital under section 17E above.

(6)    In this section, "the appropriate national authority" means –

   (a)   in relation to a community patient in respect of whom the responsible hospital is in England, the Secretary of State;

   (b)   in relation to a community patient in respect of whom the responsible hospital is in Wales, the Welsh Ministers.

### 83A. Transfer of responsibility for conditionally discharged patients to Channel Islands or Isle of Man

If it appears to the Secretary of State, in the case of a patient who –

(a)    is subject to a restriction order or restriction direction under section 41 or 49 above; and

(b)     has been conditionally discharged under section 42 or 73 above,

that a transfer under this section would be in the interests of the patient, the Secretary of State may, with the consent of the authority exercising corresponding functions in any of the Channel Islands or in the Isle of Man, transfer responsibility for the patient to that authority.

### 84. Removal to England and Wales of offenders found insane in Channel Islands and Isle of Man

(1)     The Secretary of State may by warrant direct that any offender found by a court in any of the Channel Islands or in the Isle of Man to be insane or to have been insane at the time of the alleged offence, and ordered to be detained during Her Majesty's pleasure, be removed to a hospital in England and Wales.

(2)     A patient removed under subsection (1) above shall, on his reception into the hospital in England and Wales, be treated as if he were subject to a hospital order together with a restriction order.

(3)     The Secretary of State may by warrant direct that any patient removed under this section from any of the Channel Islands or from the Isle of Man be returned to the island from which he was so removed, there to be dealt with according to law in all respects as if he had not been removed under this section.

### 85. Patients removed from Channel Islands or Isle of Man

(1)     This section applies to any patient who is removed to England and Wales from any of the Channel Islands or the Isle of Man under a provision corresponding to section 83 above and who immediately before his removal was liable to be detained or subject to guardianship in the island in question under a provision corresponding to an enactment contained in this Act (other than section 35, 36 or 38 above).

(2)     Where the patient is admitted to a hospital in England and Wales he shall be treated as if on the date of his admission he had been so admitted in pursuance of an application made, or an order or direction made or given, on that date under the corresponding enactment contained in this Act and, where he is subject to an order or direction restricting his discharge, as if he were subject to a hospital order and a restriction order or to a hospital direction and a limitation direction or to a transfer direction and a restriction direction.

(3)     Where the patient is received into guardianship in England and Wales, he shall be treated as if on the date on which he arrives at the place where he is to reside he had been so received in pursuance of an application, order or direction under the corresponding enactment contained in this Act and as if the application had been accepted or, as the case may be, the order or direction had been made or given on that date.

(4)     Where the patient was immediately before his removal liable to be detained by virtue of a transfer direction given while he was serving a sentence of imprisonment imposed by a court in the island in question, he shall be treated as if the sentence had been imposed by a court in England and Wales.

(5)     Where the patient was immediately before his removal subject to an order or direction restricting his discharge, being an order or direction of limited duration, the restriction order or restriction direction to which he is subject by virtue of subsection (2) above shall expire on the date on which the first-mentioned order or direction would have expired if he had not been removed.

(6)    While being conveyed to the hospital referred to in subsection (2) or, as the case may be, the place referred to in subsection (3) above, the patient shall be deemed to be in legal custody, and section 138 below shall apply to him as if he were in legal custody by virtue of section 137 below.

(7)    In the case of a patient removed from the Isle of Man the reference in subsection (4) above to a person serving a sentence of imprisonment includes a reference to a person detained as mentioned in section 60(6)(a) of the Mental Health Act 1974 (an Act of Tynwald).

## 85ZA. Responsibility for community patients transferred from Channel Islands or Isle of Man

(1)    This section shall have effect if there are in force in any of the Channel Islands or the Isle of Man enactments ("relevant enactments") corresponding or similar to those relating to community patients in this Act.

(2)    If responsibility for a patient is transferred to England or Wales under a provision corresponding to section 83ZA(3) above, he shall be treated as if on the date of his arrival at the place where he is to reside in England or Wales –

(a)    he had been admitted to the hospital in pursuance of an application made, or an order or direction made or given, on that date under the enactment in force in England and Wales which most closely corresponds to the relevant enactments; and

(b)    a community treatment order had then been made discharging him from the hospital.

(3)    "The responsible hospital", in his case, means the hospital to which he is treated as having been admitted by virtue of subsection (2), subject to section 19A above.

(4)    As soon as practicable after the patient's arrival at the place where he is to reside in England or Wales, the responsible clinician shall specify the conditions to which he is to be subject for the purposes of section 17B(1) above, and the conditions shall be deemed to be specified in the community treatment order.

(5)    But the responsible clinician may only specify conditions under subsection (4) above which an approved mental health professional agrees should be specified.

## 85A. Responsibility for conditionally discharged patients transferred from Channel Islands or Isle of Man

(1)    This section applies to any patient responsibility for whom is transferred to the Secretary of State by the authority exercising corresponding functions in any of the Channel Islands or the Isle of Man under a provision corresponding to section 83A above.

(2)    The patient shall be treated –

(a)    as if on the date of the transfer he had been conditionally discharged under section 42 or 73 above; and

(b)    as if he were subject to a hospital order under section 37 above and a restriction order under section 41 above, or to a hospital direction and a limitation direction under section 45A above, or to a transfer direction under section 47 above and a restriction direction under section 49 above.

(3)    Where the patient was immediately before the transfer subject to an order or direction restricting his discharge, being an order or direction of limited duration, the restriction

order, limitation direction or restriction direction to which he is subject by virtue of subsection (2) above shall expire on the date on which the first-mentioned order or direction would have expired if the transfer had not been made.

*Removal of aliens*

## 86. Removal of alien patients

(1)   This section applies to any patient who is neither a British citizen nor a Commonwealth citizen having the right of abode in the United Kingdom by virtue of section 2(1)(b) of the Immigration Act 1971, being a patient who is receiving treatment for mental disorder as an in-patient in a hospital in England and Wales or a hospital within the meaning of the Mental Health (Northern Ireland) Order 1986 and is detained pursuant to –

(a)   an application for admission for treatment or a report under Article 12(1) or 13 of that Order;

(b)   a hospital order under section 37 above or Article 44 of that Order; or

(c)   an order or direction under this Act (other than under section 35, 36 or 38 above) or under that Order (other than under Article 42, 43 or 45 of that Order) having the same effect as such a hospital order.

(2)   If it appears to the Secretary of State that proper arrangements have been made for the removal of a patient to whom this section applies to a country or territory outside the United Kingdom, the Isle of Man and the Channel Islands and for his care or treatment there and that it is in the interests of the patient to remove him, the Secretary of State may, subject to subsection (3) below –

(a)   by warrant authorise the removal of the patient from the place where he is receiving treatment as mentioned in subsection (1) above, and

(b)   give such directions as the Secretary of State thinks fit for the conveyance of the patient to his destination in that country or territory and for his detention in any place or on board any ship or aircraft until his arrival at any specified port or place in any such country or territory.

(3)   The Secretary of State shall not exercise his powers under subsection (2) above in the case of any patient except with the approval of the appropriate tribunal or, as the case may be, of the Mental Health Review Tribunal for Northern Ireland.

(4)   In relation to a patient receiving treatment in a hospital within the meaning of the Mental Health (Northern Ireland) Order 1986, the reference in subsection (1) above to mental disorder shall be construed in accordance with that Order.

*Return of patients absent without leave*

## 87. Patients absent from hospitals in Northern Ireland

(1)   Any person who –

(a)   under Article 29 or 132 of the Mental Health (Northern Ireland) Order 1986 (which provide, respectively, for the retaking of patients absent without leave and for the retaking of patients escaping from custody); or

(b)   under the said Article 29 as applied by Article 31 of the said Order (which makes special provision as to persons sentenced to imprisonment);

may be taken into custody in Northern Ireland, may be taken into custody in, and returned to Northern Ireland from, England and Wales by an approved mental health professional, by any constable or by any person authorised by or by virtue of the said Order to take him into custody.

(2)     This section does not apply to any person who is subject to guardianship.

### 88. Patients absent from hospitals in England and Wales

(1)     Subject to the provisions of this section, any person who, under section 18 above or section 138 below or under the said section 18 as applied by section 22 above, may be taken into custody in England and Wales may be taken into custody in, and returned to England and Wales from Northern Ireland.

(2)     For the purposes of the enactments referred to in subsection (1) above in their application by virtue of this section, the expression "constable" includes an officer or constable of the Police Service of Northern Ireland.

(3)     For the purposes of the said enactments in their application by virtue of this section, any reference to an approved mental health professional shall be construed as including a reference to any approved social worker within the meaning of the Mental Health (Northern Ireland) Order 1986.

(4)     This section does not apply to any person who is subject to guardianship.

### 89. Patients absent from hospitals in the Channel Islands or Isle of Man

(1)     Any person who under any provision corresponding to section 18 above or 138 below may be taken into custody in any of the Channel Islands or the Isle of Man may be taken into custody in, and returned to the island in question from, England and Wales by an approved mental health professional or a constable.

(2)     This section does not apply to any person who is subject to guardianship.

*General*

### 90. Regulations for purposes of Part 6

Section 32 above shall have effect as if references in that section to Part 2 of this Act included references to this Part of this Act so far as this Part of this Act applies to patients removed to England and Wales or for whom responsibility is transferred to England and Wales.

### 91. General provisions as to patients removed from England and Wales

(1)     Subject to subsection (2) below, where a patient liable to be detained or subject to guardianship by virtue of an application, order or direction under Part 2 or 3 of this Act (other than section 35, 36 or 38 above) is removed from England and Wales in pursuance of arrangements under this Part of this Act, the application, order or direction shall cease to have effect when he is duly received into a hospital or other institution, or placed under guardianship or, where he is not received into a hospital but his detention in hospital is authorised by virtue of the Mental Health (Care and Treatment) (Scotland) Act 2003 or the Criminal Procedure (Scotland) Act 1995, in pursuance of those arrangements.

(2)     Where the Secretary of State exercises his powers under section 86(2) above in respect of a patient who is detained pursuant to a hospital order under section 37 above and in respect of whom a restriction order is in force, those orders shall continue in force so as to apply to the patient if he returns to England and Wales.

(2A)   Where responsibility for a community patient is transferred to a jurisdiction outside England and Wales (or such a patient is removed outside England and Wales) in pursuance of arrangements under this Part of this Act, the application, order or direction mentioned in subsection (1) above in force in respect of him shall cease to have effect on the date on which responsibility is so transferred (or he is so removed) in pursuance of those arrangements.

(3)   Reference in this section to a patient's detention in hospital being authorised by virtue of the Mental Health (Care and Treatment) (Scotland) Act 2003 or the Criminal Procedure (Scotland) Act 1995 shall be read as including references to a patient in respect of whom a certificate under one of the provisions listed in section 290(7)(a) of the Act of 2003 is in operation.

## 92. Interpretation of Part 6

(1)   References in this Part of this Act to a hospital, being a hospital in England and Wales, shall be construed as references to a hospital within the meaning of Part 2 of this Act.

(1A)  References in this Part of this Act to the responsible clinician shall be construed as references to the responsible clinician within the meaning of Part 2 of this Act.

(2)   Where a patient is treated by virtue of this Part of this Act as if he had been removed to a hospital in England and Wales in pursuance of a direction under Part 3 of this Act, that direction shall be deemed to have been given on the date of his reception into the hospital.

(3)   (repealed)

(4)   Sections 80 to 85A above shall have effect as if –

   (a)  any hospital direction under section 45A above were a transfer direction under section 47 above; and

   (b)  any limitation direction under section 45A above were a restriction direction under section 49 above.

(5)   Sections 80(5), 81(6) and 85(4) above shall have effect as if any reference to a transfer direction given while a patient was serving a sentence of imprisonment imposed by a court included a reference to a hospital direction given by a court after imposing a sentence of imprisonment on a patient.

## PART 7 (sections 93–113) repealed by Mental Capacity Act 2005

## PART 8: MISCELLANEOUS FUNCTIONS OF LOCAL AUTHORITIES AND THE SECRETARY OF STATE

*Approved mental health professionals*

## 114. Approval by local social services authority

(1)   A local social services authority may approve a person to act as an approved mental health professional for the purposes of this Act.

(2)   But a local social services authority may not approve a registered medical practitioner to act as an approved mental health professional.

(3)   Before approving a person under subsection (1) above, a local social service authority shall be satisfied that he has appropriate competence in dealing with persons who are suffering from mental disorder.

(4)   The appropriate national authority may by regulations make provision in connection with the giving of approvals under subsection (1) above.

(5)    The provision which may be made by regulations under subsection (4) above includes, in particular, provision as to –

    (a)    the period for which approvals under subsection (1) above have effect;

    (b)    the courses to be undertaken by persons before such approvals are to be given and during the period for which such approvals have effect;

    (c)    the conditions subject to which such approvals are to be given; and

    (d)    the factors to be taken into account in determining whether persons have appropriate competence as mentioned in subsection (3) above.

(6)    Provision made by virtue of subsection (5)(b) above may relate to courses approved or provided by such person as may be specified in the regulations (as well as to courses approved under section 114ZA or 114A below).

(7)    An approval by virtue of subsection (6) above may be in respect of a course in general or in respect of a course in relation to a particular person.

(8)    The power to make regulations under subsection (4) above includes power to make different provision for different cases or areas.

(9)    In this section "the appropriate national authority" means –

    (a)    in relation to persons who are or wish to become approved to act as approved mental health professionals by a local social services authority whose area is in England, the Secretary of State;

    (b)    in relation to persons who are or wish to become approved to act as approved mental health professionals by a local social services authority whose area is in Wales, the Welsh Ministers.

(10)    In this Act "approved mental health professional" means –

    (a)    in relation to acting on behalf of a local social services authority whose area is in England, a person approved under subsection (1) above by any local social services authority whose area is in England, and

    (b)    in relation to acting on behalf of a local social services authority whose area is in Wales, a person approved under that subsection by any local social services authority whose area is in Wales.

### 114ZA. Approval of courses: England

(1)    The Health and Care Professions Council may approve courses for persons who are, or wish to become, approved to act as approved mental health professionals by a local social services authority whose area is in England.

(2)    The Council must publish a list of –

    (a)    the courses which are approved under this section; and

    (b)    the courses which have been, but are no longer, approved under this section and the periods for which they were so approved.

(3)    The functions of an approved mental health professional are not to be considered to be relevant social work for the purposes of Part 4 of the Care Standards Act 2000.

(4)    Where the function under subsection (1) is, in accordance with the Health and Social Work Professions Order 2001, exercisable by a committee of the Council, the committee may arrange for another person to exercise the function on the Council's behalf.

### 114A. Approval of courses: Wales

(1)    The Care Council for Wales may, in accordance with rules made by it, approve courses for persons who are, or wish to become, approved to act as approved mental health professionals by a local social services authority whose area is in Wales.

(2)    For that purpose –

   (a) subsections (2) to (4)(a) and (7) of section 63 of the Care Standards Act 2000 apply as they apply to approvals given, rules made and courses approved under that section; and

   (b) sections 66 and 71 of that Act apply accordingly.

(3)    (repealed)

(4)    The functions of an approved mental health professional shall not be considered to be relevant social work for the purposes of Part 4 of the Care Standards Act 2000.

(5)    The Care Council for Wales may also carry out, or assist other persons in carrying out, research into matters relevant to training for approved mental health professionals.

### 115. Powers of entry and inspection

(1)    An approved mental health professional may at all reasonable times enter and inspect any premises (other than a hospital) in which a mentally disordered patient is living, if he has reasonable cause to believe that the patient is not under proper care.

(2)    The power under subsection (1) above shall be exercisable only after the professional has produced, if asked to do so, some duly authenticated document showing that he is an approved mental health professional.

*Visiting patients*

### 116. Welfare of certain hospital patients

(1)    Where a patient to whom this section applies is admitted to a hospital, independent hospital or care home in England and Wales (whether for treatment for mental disorder or for any other reason) then, without prejudice to their duties in relation to the patient apart from the provisions of this section, the authority shall arrange for visits to be made to him on behalf of the authority, and shall take such other steps in relation to the patient while in the hospital, independent hospital or care home as would be expected to be taken by his parents.

(2)    This section applies to –

   (a) a child or young person –

      (i)    who is in the care of a local authority by virtue of a care order within the meaning of the Children Act 1989, or

      (ii)   in respect of whom the rights and powers of a parent are vested in a local authority by virtue of section 16 of the Social Work (Scotland) Act 1968;

(b)  a person who is subject to the guardianship of a local social services authority under the provisions of this Act; or

(c)  a person the functions of whose nearest relative under this Act are for the time being transferred to a local social services authority.

*Aftercare*

### 117. Aftercare

(1)  This section applies to persons who are detained under section 3 above, or admitted to a hospital in pursuance of a hospital order made under section 37 above, or transferred to a hospital in pursuance of a hospital direction made under section 45A above or a transfer direction made under section 47 or 48 above, and then cease to be detained and (whether or not immediately after so ceasing) leave hospital.

(2)  It shall be the duty of the clinical commissioning group or Local Health Board and of the local social services authority to provide, or arrange for the provision of, in cooperation with relevant voluntary agencies, aftercare services for any person to whom this section applies until such time as the clinical commissioning group or Local Health Board and the local social services authority are satisfied that the person concerned is no longer in need of such services; but they shall not be so satisfied in the case of a community patient while he remains such a patient.

(2A)  (repealed)

(2B)  Section 32 above shall apply for the purposes of this section as it applies for the purposes of Part 2 of this Act.

(2C)  References in this Act to aftercare services provided for a patient under this section include references to services provided for the patient –

(a)  in respect of which direct payments are made under:

(i)  sections 31 to 33 of the Care Act 2014 (as applied by Schedule 4 to that Act);

(ii)  sections 50, 51 and 53 of the Social Services and Well-being (Wales) Act 2014 (as applied by Schedule A1 to that Act); or

(iii)  regulations under; and

(b)  which would be provided under this section apart from those sections (as so applied) or the regulations.

(2D)  Subsection (2), in its application to the clinical commissioning group, has effect as if the words "provide or" were omitted.

(2E)  The Secretary of State may by regulations provide that the duty imposed on the clinical commissioning group by subsection (2) is, in the circumstances or to the extent prescribed by the regulations, to be imposed instead on another clinical commissioning group or the National Health Service Commissioning Board.

(2F)  Where regulations under subsection (2E) provide that the duty imposed by subsection (2) is to be imposed on the National Health Service Commissioning Board, subsection (2D) has effect as if the reference to the clinical commissioning group were a reference to the National Health Service Commissioning Board.

(2G)  Section 272(7) and (8) of the National Health Service Act 2006 applies to the power to make regulations under subsection (2E) as it applies to a power to make regulations under that Act.

(3)   In this section "the clinical commissioning group or Local Health Board" means the clinical commissioning group or Local Health Board, and "the local social services authority" means the local social services authority –

(a)   if, immediately before being detained, the person concerned was ordinarily resident in England, for the area in England in which he was ordinarily resident;

(b)   if, immediately before being detained, the person concerned was ordinarily resident in Wales, for the area in Wales in which he was ordinarily resident; or

(c)   in any other case, for the area in which the person concerned is resident or to which he is sent on discharge by the hospital in which he was detained.

(4)   Where there is a dispute about where a person was ordinarily resident for the purposes of subsection (3) above –

(a)   if the dispute is between local social services authorities in England, section 40 of the Care Act 2014 applies to the dispute as it applies to a dispute about where a person was ordinarily resident for the purposes of Part 1 of that Act;

(b)   if the dispute is between local social services authorities in Wales, section 195 of the Social Services and Well-being (Wales) Act 2014 applies to a dispute about where a person was ordinarily resident for the purposes of that Act;

(c)   if the dispute is between a local social services authority in England and a local social services authority in Wales, it is to be determined by the Secretary of State or the Welsh Ministers.

(5)   The Secretary of State and the Welsh Ministers shall make and publish arrangements for determining which of them is to determine a dispute under subsection (4) (c); and the arrangements may, in particular, be determined by whichever of them they agree is to do so.

(6)   in this section, "aftercare services", in relation to a person, means services which have both of the following purposes:

(a)   meeting a need arising from or related to the person's mental disorder; and

(b)   reducing the risk of a deterioration of the person's mental condition (and, accordingly, reducing the risk of the person requiring admission to a hospital again for treatment for mental disorder).

## 117A. Aftercare: preference for particular accommodation

(1)   The Secretary of State may by regulations provide that where –

(a)   the local social services authority under section 117 is, in discharging its duty under subsection (2) of that section, providing or arranging for the provision of accommodation for the person concerned;

(b)   the person concerned expresses a preference for particular accommodation; and

(c)   any prescribed conditions are met,

the local social services authority must provide or arrange for the provision of the person's preferred accommodation.

(2)   Regulations under this section may provide for the person concerned, or a person of a prescribed description, to pay for some or all of the additional cost in prescribed cases.

(3)   In subsection (2), "additional cost" means the cost of providing or arranging for the provision of the person's preferred accommodation less the amount that the local social

services authority would expect to be the usual cost of providing or arranging for the provision of accommodation of that kind.

(4)     The power to make regulations under this section –

(a)   is exercisable only in relation to local social services authorities in England;

(b)   includes the power to make different provision for different cases or areas.

## 117B.

(1)     Section 117 does not authorise or require a local social services authority in England, in or in connection with the provision of services under that section, to provide or arrange for the provision of nursing care by a registered nurse.

(2)     In this section "nursing care by a registered nurse" means a services provided by a registered nurse involving –

(a)   the provision of care; or

(b)   the planning, supervision or delegation of the provision of care,

other than a service which, having regard to its nature and the circumstances in which it is provided, does not need to be provided by a registered nurse.

*Functions of the Secretary of State*

## 118. Code of practice

(1)     The Secretary of State shall prepare, and from time to time revise, a code of practice –

(a)   for the guidance of registered medical practitioners, approved clinicians, managers and staff of hospitals, independent hospitals and care homes and approved mental health professionals in relation to the admission of patients to hospitals and registered establishments under this Act and to guardianship and community patients under this Act; and

(b)   for the guidance of registered medical practitioners and members of other professions in relation to the medical treatment of patients suffering from mental disorder.

(1A)   The Code which must be prepared, and from time to time revised, in relation to Wales shall also be for the guidance of independent mental health advocates appointed under arrangements made under section 130E below.

(2)     The code shall, in particular, specify forms of medical treatment in addition to any specified by regulations made for the purposes of section 57 above which in the opinion of the Secretary of State give rise to special concern and which should accordingly not be given by a registered medical practitioner unless the patient has consented to the treatment (or to a plan of treatment including that treatment) and a certificate in writing as to the matters mentioned in subsection (2)(a) and (b) of that section has been given by another registered medical practitioner, being a practitioner appointed for the purposes of this section by the regulatory authority.

(2A)   The code shall include a statement of the principles which the Secretary of State thinks should inform decisions under this Act.

(2B)   In preparing the statement of principles the Secretary of State shall, in particular, ensure that each of the following matters is addressed –

(a)   respect for patients' past and present wishes and feelings,

(b) respect for diversity generally including, in particular, diversity of religion, culture and sexual orientation (within the meaning of section 35 of the Equality Act 2006),

(c) minimising restrictions on liberty,

(d) involvement of patients in planning, developing and delivering care and treatment appropriate to them,

(e) avoidance of unlawful discrimination,

(f) effectiveness of treatment,

(g) views of carers and other interested parties,

(h) patient wellbeing and safety, and

(i) public safety.

(2C) The Secretary of State shall also have regard to the desirability of ensuring –

(a) the efficient use of resources, and

(b) the equitable distribution of services.

(2D) In performing functions under this Act persons mentioned in subsection (1)(a) or (b) and subsection 1A shall have regard to the code.

(3) Before preparing the code or making any alteration in it the Secretary of State shall consult such bodies as appear to him to be concerned.

(4) The Secretary of State shall lay copies of the code and of any alteration in the code before Parliament; and if either House of Parliament passes a resolution requiring the code or any alteration in it to be withdrawn the Secretary of State shall withdraw the code or alteration and, where he withdraws the code, shall prepare a code in substitution for the one which is withdrawn.

(5) No resolution shall be passed by either House of Parliament under subsection (4) above in respect of a code or alteration after the expiration of the period of 40 days beginning with the day on which a copy of the code or alteration was laid before that House; but for the purposes of this subsection no account shall be taken of any time during which Parliament is dissolved or prorogued or during which both Houses are adjourned for more than four days.

(6) The Secretary of State shall publish the code as for the time being in force.

(7) The Care Quality Commission may at any time make proposals to the Secretary of State as to the content of the code of practice which the Secretary of State must prepare, and from time to time revise, under this section in relation to England.

## 119. Practitioners approved for Part 4 and s118

(1) The regulatory authority may make such provision as he it may with the approval of the Treasury determine for the payment of remuneration, allowances, pensions or gratuities to or in respect of registered medical practitioners appointed by the authority for the purposes of Part 4 of this Act and section 118 above and to or in respect of other persons appointed for the purposes of section 57(2)(a) above.

(2) A registered medical practitioner or other person appointed for the purposes of the provisions mentioned in subsection (1) above may, for the purpose of exercising his functions under those provisions or under Part 4A of this Act, at any reasonable time –

(a) visit and interview and, in the case of a registered medical practitioner, examine in private any patient detained in a hospital or registered establishment or any community patient in a hospital or regulated establishment (other than a hospital) or (if access is granted) other place; and

(b) require the production of and inspect any records relating to the treatment of the patient there.

(3) In this section, "regulated establishment" means –

(a) an establishment in respect of which a person is registered under Part 2 of the Care Standards Act 2000; or

(b) premises used for the carrying on of a regulated activity, within the meaning of Part 1 of the Health and Social care Act 2008, in respect of which a person is registered under Chapter 2 of that Part.

### 120. General protection of detained patients

(1) The regulatory authority must keep under review, and where appropriate, investigate the exercise of the powers and the discharge of the duties conferred or imposed by this Act so far as relating to the detention of patients or their reception into guardianship or to relevant patients.

(2) Relevant patients are –

(a) patients liable to be detained under this Act,

(b) community patients, and

(c) patients subject to guardianship.

(3) The regulatory authority must make arrangements for persons authorised by it to visit and interview relevant patients in private –

(a) in the case of relevant patients detained under this Act, in the place where they are detained, and

(b) in the case of other relevant patients, in hospitals and regulated establishments and, if access is granted, other places.

(4) The regulatory authority must also make arrangements for persons authorised by it to investigate any complaint as to the exercise of the powers or the discharge of the duties conferred or imposed by this Act in respect of a patient who is or has been detained under this Act or who is or has been a relevant patient.

(5) The arrangements made under subsection (4) –

(a) may exclude matters from investigation in specified circumstances, and

(b) do not require any person exercising functions under the arrangements to undertake or continue with any investigation where the person does not consider it appropriate to do so.

(6) Where any such complaint as is mentioned in subsection (4) is made by a Member of Parliament or a member of the National Assembly for Wales, the results of the investigation must be reported to the Member of Parliament or member of the Assembly.

(7) For the purposes of a review or investigation under subsection (1) or the exercise of functions under arrangements made under this section, a person authorised by the regulatory authority may at any reasonable time –

(a) visit and interview in private any patient in a hospital or registered establishment,

(b) if the authorised person is a registered medical practitioner or approved clinician, examine the patient in private there, and

(c) require the production of and inspect any records relating to the detention or treatment of any person who is or has been detained under this Act or has been a community patient or a patient subject to guardianship.

(8) The regulatory authority may make provision fore the payment of remuneration, allowances, pensions or gratuities to or in respect of persons exercising functions in relation to any review or investigation for which it is responsible under subsection (1) or functions under arrangements may by it under this section.

(9) In this section "registered establishment" means –

(a) an establishment in respect of which a person is registered under Part 2 of the Care Standards Act 2000; or

(b) premises used for the carrying on of a regulated activity, within the meaning of Part 1 of the Health and Social care Act 2008, in respect of which a person is registered under Chapter 2 of that Part.

## 120A. Investigation reports

(1) The regulatory authority may publish a report of a review or investigation carried out by it under section 120(1).

(2) The Secretary of State may by regulations make provision as to the procedure to be followed in respect of the making of representations to the Care Quality Commission before the publication of a report by the Commission under subsection (1).

(3) The Secretary of State must consult the Care Quality Commission before making any such regulations.

(4) The Welsh Ministers may by regulations make provision as to the procedure to be followed in respect of the making of representations to them before the publication of a report by them under subsection (1).

## 120B. Action statements

(1) The regulatory authority may direct a person mentioned in subsection (2) to publish a statement as to the action the person proposes to take as a result of a review or investigation under section 120(1).

(2) The persons are –

(a) the managers of a hospital within the meaning of Part 2 of this Act;

(b) a local social services authority;

(c) persons of any other description prescribed in regulations.

(3) Regulations may make further provision about the content and publication of statements under this section.

(4) "Regulations" means regulations made –

(a) by the Secretary of State, in relation to England;

(b) by the Welsh Ministers, in relation to Wales.

## 120C. Provision of information

(1)　This section applies to the following persons –

    (a)　the managers of a hospital within the meaning of Part 2 of this Act;

    (b)　a local social services authority;

    (c)　persons of any other description prescribed in regulations.

(2)　A person to whom this section applies must provide the regulatory authority with such information as the authority may reasonably request for or in connection with the exercise of its functions under section 120.

(3)　A person to whom this section applies must provide a person authorised under section 120 with such information as the person so authorised may reasonably request for or in connection with the exercise of its functions under arrangements made under that section.

(4)　This section is in addition to the requirements of section 120(7)(c).

(5)　"Information" includes documents and records.

(6)　"Regulations" means regulations made –

    (a)　by the Secretary of State, in relation to England;

    (b)　by the Welsh Ministers, in relation to Wales.

## 120D. Annual reports

(1)　The regulatory authority must publish an annual report on its activities in the exercise of its functions under this Act.

(2)　The report must be published as soon as possible after the end of each financial year.

(3)　The Care Quality Commission must send a copy of its annual report to the Secretary of State who must lay the copy before Parliament.

(4)　The Welsh Ministers must lay a copy of their annual report before the National Assembly for Wales.

(5)　In this section "financial year" means –

    (a)　the period beginning with the date on which section 52 of the Health and Social care Act 2008 comes into force and ending with the next 31 March following that date, and

    (b)　each successive period of 12 months ending with 31 March.

## 121. (repealed)

## 122. Provision of pocket money for in-patients in hospital

(1)　Welsh Ministers may (in relation to Wales) pay to persons who are receiving treatment as in-patients (whether liable to be detained or not) in hospitals wholly or mainly used for the treatment of persons suffering from mental disorder, such amounts as the Welsh Ministers think fit in respect of those persons occasional personal expenses where it appears to the Welsh Ministers that those persons would otherwise be without resources to meet those expenses.

(2)　For the purposes of the National Health Service (Wales) Act 2006, the making of payments under this section to persons for whom hospital services are provided under that Act shall be treated as included among those services.

123. (repealed)

124. (repealed)

125. (repealed)

## PART 9: OFFENCES

### 126. Forgery, false statements, etc.

(1)  Any person who without lawful authority or excuse has in his custody or under his control any document to which this subsection applies, which is, and which he knows or believes to be, false within the meaning of Part I of the Forgery and Counterfeiting Act 1981, shall be guilty of an offence.

(2)  Any person who without lawful authority or excuse makes, or has in his custody or under his control, any document so closely resembling a document to which subsection (1) above applies as to be calculated to deceive shall be guilty of an offence.

(3)  The documents to which subsection (1) above applies are any documents purporting to be –

(a)  an application under Part 2 of this Act;

(b)  a medical or other recommendation or report under this Act; and

(c)  any other document required or authorised to be made for any of the purposes of this Act.

(4)  Any person who –

(a)  wilfully makes a false entry or statement in any application, recommendation, report, record or other document required or authorised to be made for any of the purposes of this Act; or

(b)  with intent to deceive, makes use of any such entry or statement which he knows to be false, shall be guilty of an offence.

(5)  Any person guilty of an offence under this section shall be liable –

(a)  on summary conviction, to imprisonment for a term not exceeding six months or to a fine not exceeding the statutory maximum, or to both;

(b)  on conviction on indictment, to imprisonment for a term not exceeding two years or to a fine of any amount, or to both.

### 127. Ill-treatment of patients

(1)  It shall be an offence for any person who is an officer on the staff of or otherwise employed in, or who is one of the managers of, a hospital, independent hospital or care home –

(a)  to ill-treat or wilfully to neglect a patient for the time being receiving treatment for mental disorder as an in-patient in that hospital or home; or

(b)  to ill-treat or wilfully to neglect, on the premises of which the hospital or home forms part, a patient for the time being receiving such treatment there as an out-patient.

(2)  It shall be an offence for any individual to ill-treat or wilfully to neglect a mentally disordered patient who is for the time being subject to his guardianship under this Act or

otherwise in his custody or care (whether by virtue of any legal or moral obligation or otherwise).

(3)   Any person guilty of an offence under this section shall be liable –

(a)   on summary conviction, to imprisonment for a term not exceeding six months or to a fine not exceeding the statutory maximum, or to both;

(b)   on conviction on indictment, to imprisonment for a term not exceeding five years or to a fine of any amount, or to both.

(4)   No proceedings shall be instituted for an offence under this section except by or with the consent of the Director of Public Prosecutions.

### 128. Assisting patients to absent themselves without leave, etc.

(1)   Where any person induces or knowingly assists another person who is liable to be detained in a hospital within the meaning of Part 2 of this Act or is subject to guardian-ship under this Act or is a community patient to absent himself without leave he shall be guilty of an offence.

(2)   Where any person induces or knowingly assists another person who is in legal custody by virtue of section 137 below to escape from such custody he shall be guilty of an offence.

(3)   Where any person knowingly harbours a patient who is absent without leave or is oth-erwise at large and liable to be retaken under this Act or gives him any assistance with intent to prevent, hinder or interfere with his being taken into custody or returned to the hospital or other place where he ought to be he shall be guilty of an offence.

(4)   Any person guilty of an offence under this section shall be liable –

(a)   on summary conviction, to imprisonment for a term not exceeding six months or to a fine not exceeding the statutory maximum, or to both;

(b)   on conviction on indictment, to imprisonment for a term not exceeding two years or to a fine of any amount, or to both.

### 129. Obstruction

(1)   Any person who without reasonable cause –

(a)   refuses to allow the inspection of any premises; or

(b)   refuses to allow the visiting, interviewing or examination of any person by a person authorised in that behalf by or under this Act or to give access to any person to a person so authorised; or

(c)   refuses to produce for the inspection of any person so authorised any document or record the production of which is duly required by him; or

(ca)  fails to comply with a request under section 120C; or

(d)   otherwise obstructs any such person in the exercise of his functions, shall be guilty of an offence.

(2)   Without prejudice to the generality of subsection (1) above, any person who insists on being present when required to withdraw by a person authorised by or under this Act to interview or examine a person in private shall be guilty of an offence.

(3)   Any person guilty of an offence under this section shall be liable on summary conviction5 to a fine not exceeding level 4 on the standard scale or to both.

## 130. Prosecutions by local authorities

A local social services authority may institute proceedings for any offence under this Part of this Act, but without prejudice to any provision of this Part of this Act requiring the consent of the Director of Public Prosecutions for the institution of such proceedings.

## PART 10: MISCELLANEOUS AND SUPPLEMENTARY

*Miscellaneous provisions*

## 130A. Independent mental health advocates

(1) A local social services authority whose area is in England shall make such arrangements as it considers reasonable to enable persons' ("independent mental health advocates") to be available to help qualifying patients for whom the authority is responsible for the purposes of this section.

(2) The appropriate national authority may by regulations make provision as to the appointment of persons as independent mental health advocates.

(3) The regulations may, in particular, provide –

    (a) that a person may act as an independent mental health advocate only in such circumstances, or only subject to such conditions, as may be specified in the regulations;

    (b) for the appointment of a person as an independent mental health advocate to be subject to approval in accordance with the regulations.

(4) In making arrangements under this section, a local social services authority shall have regard to the principle that any help available to a patient under the arrangements should, so far as practicable, be provided by a person who is independent of any person who is professionally concerned with the patient's medical treatment.

(5) For the purposes of subsection (4) above, a person is not to be regarded as professionally concerned with a patient's medical treatment merely because he is representing him in accordance with arrangements –

    (a) under section 35 of the Mental Capacity Act 2005; or

    (b) of a description specified in regulations under this section.

(6) Arrangements under this section may include provision for payments to be made to, or in relation to, persons carrying out functions in accordance with the arrangements.

(7) Regulations under this section –

    (a) may make different provision for different cases;

    (b) may make provision which applies subject to specified exceptions;

    (c) may include transitional, consequential, incidental or supplemental provision.

## 130B. Arrangements under section 130A

(1) The help available to a qualifying patient under arrangements under section 130A above shall include help in obtaining information about and understanding –

    (a) the provisions of this Act by virtue of which he is a qualifying patient;

    (b) any conditions or restrictions to which he is subject by virtue of this Act;

(c) what (if any) medical treatment is given to him or is proposed or discussed in his case;

(d) why it is given, proposed or discussed;

(e) the authority under which it is, or would be, given; and

(f) the requirements of this Act which apply, or would apply, in connection with the giving of the treatment to him.

(2) The help available under the arrangements to a qualifying patient shall also include –

(a) help in obtaining information about and understanding any rights which may be exercised under this Act by or in relation to him; and

(b) help (by way of representation or otherwise) in exercising those rights.

(3) For the purpose of providing help to a patient in accordance with the arrangements, an independent mental health advocate may –

(a) visit and interview the patient in private;

(b) visit and interview any person who is professionally concerned with his medical treatment;

(c) require the production of and inspect any records relating to his detention or treatment in any hospital or registered establishment or to any aftercare services provided for him under section 117 above;

(d) require the production of and inspect any records of, or held by, a local social services authority which relate to him.

(4) But an independent mental health advocate is not entitled to the production of, or to inspect, records in reliance on subsection (3)(c) or (d) above unless –

(a) in a case where the patient has capacity or is competent to consent, he does consent; or

(b) in any other case, the production or inspection would not conflict with a decision made by a donee or deputy or the Court of Protection and the person holding the records, having regard to such matters as may be prescribed in regulations under section 130A above, considers that –

(i) the records may be relevant to the help to be provided by the advocate; and

(ii) the production or inspection is appropriate.

(5) For the purpose of providing help to a patient in accordance with the arrangements, an independent mental health advocate shall comply with any reasonable request made to him by any of the following for him to visit and interview the patient –

(a) the person (if any) appearing to the advocate to be the patient's nearest relative;

(b) the responsible clinician for the purposes of this Act;

(c) an approved mental health professional.

(6) But nothing in this Act prevents the patient from declining to be provided with help under the arrangements.

(7) In subsection (4) above –

(a) the reference to a patient who has capacity is to be read in accordance with the Mental Capacity Act 2005;

(b)  the reference to a donee is to a donee of a lasting power of attorney (within the meaning of section 9 of that Act) created by the patient, where the donee is acting within the scope of his authority and in accordance with that Act;

(c)  the reference to a deputy is to a deputy appointed for the patient by the Court of Protection under section 16 of that Act, where the deputy is acting within the scope of his authority and in accordance with that Act.

## 130C. Section 130A: supplemental

(1)  This section applies for the purposes of section 130A above.

(2)  A patient is a qualifying patient if he is –

(a)  liable to be detained under this Act (otherwise than by virtue of section 4 or 5(2) or (4) above or section 135 or 136 below);

(b)  subject to guardianship under this Act; or

(c)  a community patient.

(3)  A patient is also a qualifying patient if –

(a)  not being a qualifying patient falling within subsection (2) above, he discusses with a registered medical practitioner or approved clinician the possibility of being given a form of treatment to which section 57 above applies; or

(b)  not having attained the age of 18 years and not being a qualifying patient falling within subsection (2) above, he discusses with a registered medical practitioner or approved clinician the possibility of being given a form of treatment to which section 58A above applies.

(4)  Where a patient who is a qualifying patient falling within subsection (3) above is informed that the treatment concerned is proposed in his case, he remains a qualifying patient falling within that subsection until –

(a)  the proposal is withdrawn; or

(b)  the treatment is completed or discontinued.

(4A)  A local social services authority is responsible for a qualifying patient if –

(a)  in the case of a qualifying patient falling within subsection (2)(a) above, the hospital or registered establishment in which he is liable to be detained is situated in that authority's area;

(b)  in the case of a qualifying patient falling within subsection (2)(b) above, that authority is the responsible local social services authority within the meaning of section 34(3) above;

(c)  in the case of a qualifying patient falling within subsection (2)(c), the responsible hospital is situated in that authority's area;

(d)  in the case of a qualifying patient falling within subsection (3) –

(i)  in a case where the patient has capacity or is competent to do so, he nominates that authority as responsible for him for the purposes of section 130A above, or

(ii)  in any other case, a donee or deputy or the Court of Protection, or a person engaged in caring for the patient or interested in his welfare, nominates that authority on his behalf as responsible for him for the purposes of that section.

(4B)  In subsection (4A)(d) above –

    (a)  the reference to a patient who has capacity is to be read in accordance with the Mental Capacity Act 2005;

    (b)  the reference to a donee is to a donee of a lasting power of attorney (within the meaning of section 9 of that Act) created by the patient, where the donee is acting within the scope of his authority and in accordance with that Act;

    (c)  the reference to a deputy is to a deputy appointed for the patient by the Court of Protection under section 16 of that Act, where the deputy is acting within the scope of his authority and in accordance with that Act.

(5)  References to the appropriate national authority are –

    (a)  in relation to a qualifying patient in England, to the Secretary of State;

    (b)  in relation to a qualifying patient in Wales, to the Welsh Ministers.

(6)  For the purposes of subsection (5) above –

    (a)  a qualifying patient falling within subsection (2)(a) above is to be regarded as being in the territory in which the hospital or registered establishment in which he is liable to be detained is situated;

    (b)  a qualifying patient falling within subsection (2)(b) above is to be regarded as being in the territory in which the area of the responsible local social services authority within the meaning of section 34(3) above is situated;

    (c)  a qualifying patient falling within subsection (2)(c) above is to be regarded as being in the territory in which the responsible hospital is situated;

    (d)  a qualifying patient falling within subsection (3) above is to be regarded as being in the territory determined in accordance with arrangements made for the purposes of this paragraph, and published, by the Secretary of State and the Welsh Ministers.

**130D. Duty to give information about independent mental health advocates**

(1)  The responsible person in relation to a qualifying patient (within the meaning given by section 130C above) shall take such steps as are practicable to ensure that the patient understands –

    (a)  that help is available to him from an independent mental health advocate; and

    (b)  how he can obtain that help.

(2)  In subsection (1) above, "the responsible person" means –

    (a)  in relation to a qualifying patient falling within section 130C(2)(a) above (other than one also falling within paragraph (b) below), the managers of the hospital or registered establishment in which he is liable to be detained;

    (b)  in relation to a qualifying patient falling within section 130C(2)(a) above and conditionally discharged by virtue of section 42(2), 73 or 74 above, the responsible clinician;

    (c)  in relation to a qualifying patient falling within section 130C(2)(b) above, the responsible local social services authority within the meaning of section 34(3) above;

    (d)  in relation to a qualifying patient falling within section 130C(2)(c) above, the managers of the responsible hospital;

(e)  in relation to a qualifying patient falling within section 130C(3) above, the registered medical practitioner or approved clinician with whom the patient first discusses the possibility of being given the treatment concerned.

(3)  The steps to be taken under subsection (1) above shall be taken –

(a)  where the responsible person falls within subsection (2)(a) above, as soon as practicable after the patient becomes liable to be detained;

(b)  where the responsible person falls within subsection (2)(b) above, as soon as practicable after the conditional discharge;

(c)  where the responsible person falls within subsection (2)(c) above, as soon as practicable after the patient becomes subject to guardianship;

(d)  where the responsible person falls within subsection (2)(d) above, as soon as practicable after the patient becomes a community patient;

(e)  where the responsible person falls within subsection (2)(e) above, while the discussion with the patient is taking place or as soon as practicable thereafter.

(4)  The steps to be taken under subsection (1) above shall include giving the requisite information both orally and in writing.

(5)  The responsible person in relation to a qualifying patient falling within section 130C(2) above (other than a patient liable to be detained by virtue of Part 3 of this Act) shall, except where the patient otherwise requests, take such steps as are practicable to furnish the person (if any) appearing to the responsible person to be the patient's nearest relative with a copy of any information given to the patient in writing under subsection (1) above.

(6)  The steps to be taken under subsection (5) above shall be taken when the information concerned is given to the patient or within a reasonable time thereafter.

## 130E. Independent mental health advocates: Wales

(1)  The Welsh Ministers shall make such arrangements as they consider reasonable to enable persons ("independent mental health advocates") to be available to help –

(a)  Welsh qualifying compulsory patients; and

(b)  Welsh qualifying informal patients.

(2)  The Welsh Ministers may by regulations make provision as to the appointment of persons as independent mental health advocates.

(3)  The regulations may, in particular, provide –

(a)  that a person may act as an independent mental health advocate only in such circumstances, or only subject to such conditions, as may be specified in the regulations;

(b)  for the appointment of a person as an independent mental health advocate to be subject to approval in accordance with the regulations.

(4)  In making arrangements under this section, the Welsh Ministers shall have regard to the principle that any help available to a patient under the arrangements should, so far as practicable, be provided by a person who is independent of any person who –

(a)  is professionally concerned with the patient's medical treatment; or

(b)  falls within a description specified in regulations made by the Welsh Ministers.

(5) For the purposes of subsection (4) above, a person is not to be regarded as professionally concerned with a patient's medical treatment merely because he is representing him in accordance with arrangements –

    (a) under section 35 of the Mental Capacity Act 2005; or

    (b) of a description specified in regulations under this section.

(6) Arrangements under this section may include provision for payments to be made to, or in relation to, persons carrying out functions in accordance with the arrangements.

(7) Regulations under this section and sections 130F to 130H –

    (a) may make different provision for different cases;

    (b) may make provision which applies subject to specified exceptions;

    (c) may include transitional, consequential, incidental or supplemental provision.

**130F. Arrangements under section 130E for Welsh qualifying compulsory patients**

(1) The help available to a Welsh qualifying compulsory patient under arrangements under section 130E shall include help in obtaining information about and understanding –

    (a) the provisions of this Act by virtue of which he is a qualifying compulsory patient;

    (b) any conditions or restrictions to which he is subject by virtue of this Act;

    (c) what (if any) medical treatment is given to him or is proposed or discussed in his case;

    (d) why it is given, proposed or discussed;

    (e) the authority under which it is, or would be, given; and

    (f) the requirements of this Act which apply, or would apply, in connection with the giving of the treatment to him.

(2) The help available under the arrangements to a Welsh qualifying compulsory patient shall also include –

    (a) help in obtaining information about and understanding any rights which may be exercised under this Act by or in relation to him;

    (b) help (by way of representation or otherwise) –

        (i) in exercising the rights referred to in paragraph (a);

        (ii) for patients who wish to become involved, or more involved, in decisions made about their care or treatment, or care or treatment generally;

        (iii) for patients who wish to complain about their care or treatment;

    (a) the provision of information about other services which are or may be available to the patient;

    (b) other help specified in regulations made by the Welsh Ministers.

**130G. Arrangements under section 130E for Welsh qualifying informal patients**

(1) The help available to a Welsh qualifying informal patient under arrangements under section 130E shall include help in obtaining information about and understanding –

(a)  what (if any) medical treatment is given to him or is proposed or discussed in his case;

(b)  why it is given, proposed or discussed;

(c)  the authority under which it is, or would be, given.

(2)  The help available under the arrangements to a Welsh qualifying informal patient shall also include –

(a)  help (by way of representation or otherwise) –

(i)  for patients who wish to become involved, or more involved, in decisions made about their care or treatment, or care or treatment generally;

(ii)  for patients who wish to complain about their care or treatment;

(b)  the provision of information about other services which are or may be available to the patient;

(c)  other help specified in regulations made by the Welsh Ministers.

## 130H. Independent mental health advocates for Wales: supplementary powers and duties

(1)  For the purpose of providing help to a patient in accordance with arrangements made under section 130E, an independent mental health advocate may –

(a)  visit and interview the patient in private;

(b)  visit and interview –

(i)  any person who is professionally concerned with his medical treatment;

(ii)  any other person who falls within a description specified in regulations made by the Welsh Ministers;

(c)  require the production of and inspect any records relating to his detention, treatment or assessment in any hospital or registered establishment or to any aftercare services provided for him under section 117 above;

(d)  require the production of and inspect any records of, or held by, a local social services authority which relate to him.

(2)  But an independent mental health advocate is not entitled to the production of, or to inspect, records in reliance on subsection (1)(c) or (d) above unless –

(a)  in a case where the patient has capacity or is competent to consent, he does consent; or

(b)  in any other case, the production or inspection would not conflict with a decision made by a donee or deputy or the Court of Protection and the person holding the records, having regard to such matters as may be prescribed in regulations under section 130E above, considers that –

(i)  the records may be relevant to the help to be provided by the advocate;

(ii)  the production or inspection is appropriate.

(3)  For the purpose of providing help to a Welsh qualifying compulsory patient in accordance with the arrangements, an independent mental health advocate shall comply with any reasonable request made to him by any of the following for him to visit and interview the patient –

(a)  the patient;

(b)  the person (if any) appearing to the advocate to be the patient's nearest relative;

(c)  the responsible clinician for the purposes of this Act;

(d)  an approved mental health professional;

(e)  a registered social worker who is professionally concerned with the patient's care, treatment or assessment;

(f)  where the patient is liable to be detained in a hospital or registered establishment, the managers of the hospital or establishment;

(g)  the patient's donee or deputy.

(4)  For the purpose of providing help to a Welsh qualifying informal patient in accordance with the arrangements, an independent mental health advocate shall comply with any reasonable request made to him by any of the following for him to visit and interview the patient –

(a)  the patient;

(b)  the managers of the hospital or establishment in which the patient is an in-patient or a person duly authorised on their behalf;

(c)  any person appearing to the advocate to whom the request is made to be the patient's carer;

(d)  the patient's donee or deputy;

(e)  a registered social worker who is professionally concerned with the patient's care, treatment or assessment.

(5)  But nothing in this Act prevents the patient from declining to be provided with help under the arrangements.

(6)  In subsection (2) above the reference to a patient who has capacity is to be read in accordance with the Mental Capacity Act 2005.

(7)  In subsection (4) above –

(a)  "carer", in relation to a Welsh qualifying informal patient, means an individual who provides or intends to provide a substantial amount of care on a regular basis for the patient, but does not include any individual who provides, or intends to provide care by virtue of a contract of employment or other contract with any person or as a volunteer for a body (whether or not incorporated);

(b)  "registered social worker" means a person included in the principal part or the visiting European part of a register maintained under section 56(1) of the Care Standards Act 2000.

(8)  In subsections (2) to (4) above –

(a)  the reference to a donee is to a donee of a lasting power of attorney (within the meaning of section 9 of the Mental Capacity Act 2005) created by the patient, where the donee, in making the decision referred to in subsection (2) or the request referred to in subsection (3) or (4), is acting within the scope of his authority and in accordance with that Act;

(b)  the reference to a deputy is to a deputy appointed for the patient by the Court of Protection under section 16 of that Act, where the deputy, in making the decision referred to in subsection (2) or the request referred to in subsection (3) or (4), is acting within the scope of his authority and in accordance with that Act.

## 130I. Welsh qualifying compulsory patients

(1)   This section applies for the purposes of section 130E above.

(2)   A patient is a Welsh qualifying compulsory patient if he is –

(a)   liable to be detained under this Act (other than under section 135 or 136 below) and the hospital or registered establishment in which he is liable to be detained is situated in Wales;

(b)   detained under section 135 or 136 below in a place of safety situated in Wales;

(c)   subject to guardianship under this Act and the area of the responsible local social services authority within the meaning of section 34(3) above is situated in Wales; or

(d)   a community patient and the responsible hospital is situated in Wales.

(3)   A patient is also a Welsh qualifying compulsory patient if the patient is to be regarded as being in Wales for the purposes of this subsection and –

(a)   not being a qualifying patient falling within subsection (2) above, he discusses with a registered medical practitioner or approved clinician the possibility of being given a form of treatment to which section 57 above applies; or

(b)   not having attained the age of 18 years and not being a qualifying patient falling within subsection (2) above, he discusses with a registered medical practitioner or approved clinician the possibility of being given a form of treatment to which section 58A above applies.

(4)   For the purposes of subsection (3), a patient is to be regarded as being in Wales if that has been determined in accordance with arrangements made for the purposes of that subsection and section 130C(3), and published, by the Secretary of State and the Welsh Ministers.

(5)   Where a patient who is a Welsh qualifying compulsory patient falling within subsection (3) above is informed that the treatment concerned is proposed in his case, he remains a qualifying patient falling within that subsection until –

(a)   the proposal is withdrawn; or

(b)   the treatment is completed or discontinued.

## 130J. Welsh qualifying informal patients

(1)   This section applies for the purposes of section 130E above.

(2)   A patient is a Welsh qualifying informal patient if he is admitted as an in-patient for treatment for, or assessment in relation to, mental disorder to a hospital or registered establishment situated in Wales (whether or not the patient is also admitted for any other purpose) without any application, order, direction or report rendering him liable to be detained under this Act.

## 130K. Duty to give information about independent mental health advocates to Welsh qualifying compulsory patients

(1)   The responsible person in relation to a Welsh qualifying compulsory patient (within the meaning given by section 130I above) shall take such steps as are practicable to ensure that the patient understands –

(a) that help is available to him from an independent mental health advocate; and

(b) how he can obtain that help.

(2) In subsection (1) above, the "responsible person" means –

(a) in relation to a Welsh qualifying compulsory patient falling within section 130I(2)(a) above (other than one also falling within paragraph (b) below), the managers of the hospital or registered establishment in which he is liable to be detained; or

(b) in relation to a Welsh qualifying compulsory patient falling within section 130I(2)(a) above and conditionally discharged by virtue of section 42(2), 73 or 74 above, the responsible clinician;

(c) in relation to a Welsh qualifying compulsory patient falling within section 130I(2)(b) above, the responsible local social services authority within the meaning of section 34(3) above;

(d) in relation to a Welsh qualifying compulsory patient falling within section 130I(2)(c) above, the managers of the responsible hospital;

(e) in relation to a Welsh qualifying compulsory patient falling within section 130I(3) above, the registered medical practitioner or approved clinician with whom the patient first discusses the possibility of being given the treatment concerned.

(3) The steps to be taken under subsection (1) above shall be taken –

(a) where the responsible person falls within subsection (2)(a) above, as soon as practicable after the patient becomes liable to be detained;

(b) where the responsible person falls within subsection (2)(b) above, as soon as practicable after the conditional discharge;

(c) where the responsible person falls within subsection (2)(c) above, as soon as practicable after the patient becomes subject to guardianship;

(d) where the responsible person falls within subsection (2)(d) above, as soon as practicable after the patient becomes a community patient;

(e) where the responsible person falls within subsection (2)(e) above, while the discussion with the patient is taking place or as soon as practicable thereafter.

(4) The steps to be taken under subsection (1) above shall include giving the requisite information both orally and in writing.

(5) The responsible person in relation to a Welsh qualifying compulsory patient falling within section 130I(2) above (other than a patient liable to be detained by virtue of Part 3 of this Act) shall, except where the patient otherwise requests, take such steps as are practicable to furnish any person falling within subsection (6) with a copy of any information given to the patient in writing under subsection (1) above.

(6) A person falls within this subsection if –

(a) the person appears to the responsible person to be the patient's nearest relative;

(b) the person is a donee of a lasting power of attorney (within the meaning of the section 9 of the Mental Capacity Act 2005) created by the patient and the scope of the donee's authority includes matters related to the care and treatment of the patient;

(c)   the person is a deputy appointed for the patient by the Court of Protection under section 16 of that Act and the scope of the deputy's includes matters related to the care and treatment of the patient.

(7)   The steps to be taken under subsection (5) above shall be taken when the information concerned is given to the patient or within a reasonable time thereafter.

### 130L. Duty to give information about independent mental health advocates to Welsh qualifying informal patients

(1)   The responsible person in relation to a Welsh qualifying informal patient (within the meaning given by section 130J above) shall take such steps as are practicable to ensure that the patient understands –

(a)   that help is available to him from an independent mental health advocate; and

(b)   how he can obtain that help.

(2)   In subsection (1) above, the "responsible person" means the managers of the hospital or registered establishment to which the patient is admitted as an in-patient.

(3)   The steps to be taken under subsection (1) above shall be taken as soon as practicable after the patient becomes an in-patient.

(4)   The steps to be taken under subsection (1) above shall include giving the requisite information both orally and in writing.

(5)   The responsible person in relation to a Welsh qualifying informal patient shall, except where the patient otherwise requests, take such steps as are practicable to furnish any person falling within subsection (6) with a copy of any information given to the patient in writing under subsection (1) above.

(6)   A person falls within this subsection if –

(a)   the person appears to the responsible person to be a carer of the patient;

(b)   the person is a donee of a lasting power of attorney (within the meaning of section 9 of the Mental Capacity Act 2005) created by the patient and the scope of the donee's authority includes matters related to the care and treatment of the patient;

(c)   the person is a deputy appointed for the patient by the Court of Protection under section 16 of that Act and the scope of the deputy's authority includes matters related to the care and treatment of the patient.

(7)   In subsection (6), "carer", in relation to a Welsh qualifying informal patient, means an individual who provides or intends to provide a substantial amount of care on a regular basis for the patient, but does not include any individual who provides, or intends to provide care by virtue of a contract of employment or other contract with any person or as a volunteer for a body (whether or not incorporated).

(8)   The steps to be taken under subsection (5) above shall be taken when the information concerned is given to the patient or within a reasonable time thereafter.

### 131. Informal admission of patients

(1)   Nothing in this Act shall be construed as preventing a patient who requires treatment for mental disorder from being admitted to any hospital or registered establishment in pursuance of arrangements made in that behalf and without any application, order or direction rendering him liable to be detained under this Act, or from remaining in any hospital or registered establishment in pursuance of such arrangements after he has ceased to be so liable to be detained.

(2)    Subsections (3) and (4) below apply in the case of a patient aged 16 or 17 years who has capacity to consent to the making of such arrangements as are mentioned in subsection (1) above.

(3)    If the patient consents to the making of the arrangements, they may be made, carried out and determined on the basis of that consent even though there are one or more persons who have parental responsibility for him.

(4)    If the patient does not consent to the making of the arrangements, they may not be made, carried out or determined on the basis of the consent of a person who has parental responsibility for him.

(5)    In this section –

    (a)  the reference to a patient who has capacity is to be read in accordance with the Mental Capacity Act 2005; and

    (b)  "parental responsibility" has the same meaning as in the Children Act 1989.

### 131A. Accommodation, etc. for children

(1)    This section applies in respect of any patient who has not attained the age of 18 years and who –

    (a)  is liable to be detained in a hospital under this Act; or

    (b)  is admitted to, or remains in, a hospital in pursuance of such arrangements as are mentioned in section 131(1) above.

(2)    The managers of the hospital shall ensure that the patient's environment in the hospital is suitable having regard to his age (subject to his needs).

(3)    For the purpose of deciding how to fulfil the duty under subsection (2) above, the managers shall consult a person who appears to them to have knowledge or experience of cases involving patients who have not attained the age of 18 years which makes him suitable to be consulted.

(4)    In this section, "hospital" includes a registered establishment.

### 132. Duty of managers of hospitals to give information to detained patients

(1)    The managers of a hospital or registered establishment in which a patient is detained under this Act shall take such steps as are practicable to ensure that the patient understands –

    (a)  under which of the provisions of this Act he is for the time being detained and the effect of that provision; and

    (b)  what rights of applying to a Tribunal are available to him in respect of his detention under that provision; and those steps shall be taken as soon as practicable after the commencement of the patient's detention under the provision in question.

(2)    The managers of a hospital or registered establishment in which a patient is detained as aforesaid shall also take such steps as are practicable to ensure that the patient understands the effect, so far as relevant in his case, of sections 23, 25, 56 to 64, 66(1)(g), 118 and 120 above and section 134 below; and those steps shall be taken as soon as practicable after the commencement of the patient's detention in the hospital or establishment.

(3)    The steps to be taken under subsections (1) and (2) above shall include giving the requisite information both orally and in writing.

(4)    The managers of a hospital or registered establishment in which a patient is detained as aforesaid shall, except where the patient otherwise requests, take such steps as are practicable to furnish the person (if any) appearing to them to be his nearest relative with a copy of any information given to him in writing under subsections (1) and (2) above; and those steps shall be taken when the information is given to the patient or within a reasonable time thereafter.

## 132A. Duty of managers of hospitals to give information to community patients

(1)    The managers of the responsible hospital shall take such steps as are practicable to ensure that a community patient understands –

   (a)   the effect of the provisions of this Act applying to community patients; and

   (b)   what rights of applying to a Tribunal are available to him in that capacity;

   and those steps shall be taken as soon as practicable after the patient becomes a community patient.

(2)    The steps to be taken under subsection (1) above shall include giving the requisite information both orally and in writing.

(3)    The managers of the responsible hospital shall, except where the community patient otherwise requests, take such steps as are practicable to furnish the person (if any) appearing to them to be his nearest relative with a copy of any information given to him in writing under subsection (1) above; and those steps shall be taken when the information is given to the patient or within a reasonable time thereafter.

## 133. Duty of managers of hospitals to inform nearest relatives of discharge

(1)    Where a patient liable to be detained under this Act in a hospital or registered establishment is to be discharged otherwise than by virtue of an order for discharge made by his nearest relative, the managers of the hospital or registered establishment shall, subject to subsection (2) below, take such steps as are practicable to inform the person (if any) appearing to them to be the nearest relative of the patient; and that information shall, if practicable, be given at least seven days before the date of discharge.

(1A)  The reference in subsection (1) above to a patient who is to be discharged includes a patient who is to be discharged from hospital under section 17A above.

(1B)  Subsection (1) above shall also apply in a case where a community patient is discharged under section 23 or 72 above (otherwise than by virtue of an order for discharge made by his nearest relative), but with the reference in that subsection to the managers of the hospital or registered establishment being read as a reference to the managers of the responsible hospital.

(2)    Subsection (1) above shall not apply if the patient or his nearest relative has requested that information about the patient's discharge should not be given under this section.

## 134. Correspondence of patients

(1)    A postal packet addressed to any person by a patient detained in a hospital under this Act and delivered by the patient for dispatch may be withheld from the postal operator concerned –

   (a)   if that person has requested that communications addressed to him by the patient should be withheld; or

   (b)   subject to subsection (3) below, if the hospital is one at which high security psychiatric services are provided and the managers of the hospital consider that the postal packet is likely –

> (i) to cause distress to the person to whom it is addressed or to any other person (not being a person on the staff of the hospital); or
>
> (ii) to cause danger to any person;
>
> and any request for the purposes of paragraph (a) above shall be made by a notice in writing given to the managers of the hospital, or the approved clinician with overall responsibility for the patient's case.

(2) Subject to subsection (3) below, a postal packet addressed to a patient detained under this Act in a hospital at which high security psychiatric services are provided may be withheld from the patient if, in the opinion of the managers of the hospital, it is necessary to do so in the interests of the safety of the patient or for the protection of other persons.

(3) Subsections (1)(b) and (2) above do not apply to any postal packet addressed by a patient to, or sent to a patient by or on behalf of –

> (a) any Minister of the Crown or the Scottish Ministers or Member of either House of Parliament or member of the Scottish Parliament or of the Northern Ireland Assembly;
>
> (aa) any of the Welsh Ministers, the Counsel general of the Welsh Assembly Government or a member of the National Assembly for Wales;
>
> (b) any judge or officer of the Court of Protection, any of the Court of Protection Visitors or any person asked by that Court for a report under section 49 of the Mental Capacity Act 2005 concerning the patient;
>
> (c) the Parliamentary Commissioner for Administration, the Scottish Public Services Ombudsman, the Public Services Ombudsman for Wales, the Health Service Commissioner for England or a Local Commissioner within the meaning of Part 3 of the Local Government Act 1974;
>
> (ca) the Care Quality Commission;
>
> (d) the First-tier Tribunal or the Mental Health Review Tribunal for Wales;
>
> (e) a Strategic Health Authority, Local Health Board, Special Health Authority or Primary Care Trust, a local social services authority, a Community Health Council, or a local probation board established under section 4 of the Criminal Justice and Court Services Act 2000 or a provider of probation services;
>
> (ea) a provider of a patient advocacy and liaison service for the assistance of patients at the hospital and their families and carers;
>
> (eb) a provider of independent advocacy services for the patient;
>
> (f) the managers of the hospital in which the patient is detained;
>
> (g) any legally qualified person instructed by the patient to act as his legal adviser; or
>
> (h) the European Commission of Human Rights or the European Court of Human Rights;
>
> and for the purposes of paragraph (d) above the reference to the First-tier Tribunal is a reference to that tribunal so far as it is acting for the purposes of any proceedings under this Act or paragraph 5(2) of the Schedule to the Repatriation of Prisoners Act 1984.

(3A) In subsection (3) above –

> (a) "patient advocacy and liaison service" means a service of a description prescribed by regulations made by the Secretary of State, and

(b) "independent advocacy services" means services provided under –

    (i) arrangements under section 130A above;

    (ii) arrangements under section 248 of the National Health Service Act 2006 or section 187 of the National Health Service (Wales) Act 2006; or

    (iii) arrangements of a description prescribed as mentioned in paragraph (a) above.

(4) The managers of a hospital may inspect and open any postal packet for the purposes of determining –

    (a) whether it is one to which subsection (1) or (2) applies, and

    (b) in the case of a postal packet to which subsection (1) or (2) above applies, whether or not it should be withheld under that subsection;

and the power to withhold a postal packet under either of those subsections includes power to withhold anything contained in it.

(5) Where a postal packet or anything contained in it is withheld under subsection (1) or (2) above the managers of the hospital shall record that fact in writing.

(6) Where a postal packet or anything contained in it is withheld under subsection (1)(b) or (2) above the managers of the hospital shall within seven days give notice of that fact to the patient and, in the case of a packet withheld under subsection (2) above, to the person (if known) by whom the postal packet was sent; and any such notice shall be given in writing and shall contain a statement of the effect of section 134A(1) to (4).

(7) The functions of the managers of a hospital under this section shall be discharged on their behalf by a person on the staff of the hospital appointed by them for that purpose and different persons may be appointed to discharge different functions.

(8) The Secretary of State may make regulations with respect to the exercise of the powers conferred by this section.

(9) In this section and section 134A "hospital" has the same meaning as in Part 2 of this Act and "postal operator" and "postal packet" have the same meaning as in the Postal Services Act 2000.

## 134A. Review of decisions to withhold correspondence

(1) The regulatory authority must review any decision to withhold a postal packet (or anything contained in it) under subsection (1)(b) or (2) of section 134 if an application for a review of the decision is made –

    (a) in a case under subsection (1)(b) of that section, by the patient; or

    (b) in a case under subsection (2) of that section, either by the patient or by the person by whom the postal packet was sent.

(2) An application under subsection (1) must be made within 6 months of receipt by the applicant of the notice referred to in section 134(6).

(3) On an application under subsection (1), the regulatory authority may direct that the postal packet (or anything contained in it) is not to be withheld.

(4) The managers of the hospital concerned must comply with any such direction.

(5) The Secretary of State may by regulations make provision in connection with the making to them of applications under subsection (1), including provision for the production to them of any postal packet which is the subject of such an application.

(6)     The Welsh Ministers may by regulations make provision in connection with the making to them of applications under subsection (1), including the provision for the production to them of any postal packet which is the subject of such an application.

### 135. Warrant to search for and remove patients

(1)     If it appears to a justice of the peace, on information on oath laid by an approved mental health professional, that there is reasonable cause to suspect that a person believed to be suffering from mental disorder –

(a)   has been, or is being, ill-treated, neglected or kept otherwise than under proper control, in any place within the jurisdiction of the justice, or

(b)   being unable to care for himself, is living alone in any such place,

the justice may issue a warrant authorising any constable to enter, if need be by force, any premises specified in the warrant in which that person is believed to be, and, if thought fit, to remove him to a place of safety with a view to the making of an application in respect of him under Part 2 of this Act, or of other arrangements for his treatment or care.

(1A)   If the premises specified in the warrant are a place of safety, the constable executing the warrant may, instead of removing the person to another place of safety, keep the person at those premises for the purpose mentioned in subsection (1).

(2)     If it appears to a justice of the peace, on information on oath laid by any constable or other person who is authorised by or under this Act or under article 8 of the Mental Health (Care and Treatment) (Scotland) Act 2003 (Consequential Provisions) Order 2005 to take a patient to any place, or to take into custody or retake a patient who is liable under this Act or under the said article 8 to be so taken or retaken –

(a)   that there is reasonable cause to believe that the patient is to be found on premises within the jurisdiction of the justice; and

(b)   that admission to the premises has been refused or that a refusal of such admission is apprehended,

the justice may issue a warrant authorising any constable to enter the premises, if need be by force, and remove the patient.

(3)     A patient who is removed to a place of safety in the execution of a warrant issued under subsection (1), or kept at the premises specified in the warrant under subsection (1A), may be detained there for a period not exceeding the permitted period of detention.

(3ZA)  In subsection (3), "the permitted period of detention" means –

(a)   the period of 24 hours beginning with –

(i)   in a case where the person is removed to a place of safety, the time when the person arrives at that place;

(ii)  in a case where the person is kept at the premises specified in the warrant, the time when the constable first entered the premises to execute the warrant; or

(b)   where an authorisation is given in relation to the person under section 136B, that period of 24 hours and such further period as is specified in the authorisation.

(3A)   A constable, an approved mental health professional or a person authorised by either of them for the purposes of this subsection may, before the end of the permitted period of detention mentioned in subsection (3) above, take a person detained in a place of safety under that subsection to one or more other places of safety.

(3B) A person taken to a place of safety under subsection (3A) above may be detained there for a period ending no later than the end of the permitted period of detention mentioned in subsection (3) above.

(4) In the execution of a warrant issued under subsection (1) above, a constable shall be accompanied by an approved mental health professional and by a registered medical practitioner, and in the execution of a warrant issued under subsection (2) above a constable may be accompanied –

(a) by a registered medical practitioner;

(b) by any person authorised by or under this Act or under article 8 of the Mental Health (Care and Treatment) (Scotland) Act 2003 (Consequential Provisions) Order 2005 to take or retake the patient.

(5) It shall not be necessary in any information or warrant under subsection (1) above to name the patient concerned.

(6) In this section "place of safety" means residential accommodation provided by a local social services authority under Part 1 of the Care Act 2014 or Part 4 of the Social Services and Well-being (Wales) Act 2014, a hospital as defined by this Act, a police station, an independent hospital or care home for mentally disordered persons or any other suitable place.

(7) For the purpose of subsection (6) –

(a) a house, flat or room where a person is living may not be regarded as a suitable place unless –

(i) if the person believed to be suffering from a mental disorder is the sole occupier of the place, that person agrees to the use of the place as a place of safety;

(ii) if the person believed to be suffering from a mental disorder is an occupier of the place but not the sole occupier, both that person and one of the other occupiers agree to the use of the place as a place of safety;

(iii) if the person believed to be suffering from a mental disorder is not an occupier of the place, both that person and the occupier (or, if more than one, one of the occupiers) agree to the use of the place as a place of safety;

(b) a place other than one mentioned in paragraph (a) may not be regarded as a suitable place unless a person who appears to the constable exercising powers under this section to be responsible for the management of the place agrees to its use as a place of safety.

(8) This section is subject to section 136A which makes provision about the removal and taking of persons to a police station under this section.

### 136. Removal etc. of mentally disordered persons without a warrant

(1) If a person appears to a constable to be suffering from mental disorder and to be in immediate need of care or control, the constable may, if he thinks it necessary to do so in the interests of that person or for the protection of other persons –

(a) remove the person to a place of safety within the meaning of section 135, or

(b) if the person is already at a place of safety within the meaning of that section, keep the person at that place or remove the person to another place of safety.

(1A) The power of a constable under subsection (1) may be exercised where the mentally disordered person is at any place, other than –

(a)  any house, flat or room where that person, or any other person, is living, or

(b)  any yard, garden, garage or outhouse that is used in connection with the house, flat or room, other than one that is also used in connection with one or more other houses, flats or rooms.

(1B)  For the purpose of exercising the power under subsection (1), a constable may enter any place where the power may be exercised, if need be by force.

(1C)  Before deciding to remove a person to, or to keep a person at, a place of safety under subsection (1), the constable must, if it is practicable to do so, consult –

(a)  a registered medical practitioner,

(b)  a registered nurse,

(c)  an approved mental health professional, or

(d)  a person of a description specified in regulations made by the Secretary of State.

(2)  A person removed to, or kept at a place of safety under this section may be detained there for a period not exceeding the permitted period of detention for the purpose of enabling him to be examined by a registered medical practitioner and to be interviewed by an approved mental health professional and of making any necessary arrangements for his treatment or care.

(2A)  In subsection (2), "the permitted period of detention" means –

(a)  the period of 24 hours beginning with –

(i)  in a case where the person is removed to a place of safety, the time when the person arrives at that place;

(ii)  in a case where the person is kept at a place of safety, the time when the constable decides to keep the person at that place; or

(b)  where an authorisation is given in relation to the person under section 136B, that period of 24 hours and such further period as is specified in the authorisation.

(3)  A constable, an approved mental health professional or a person authorised by either of them for the purposes of this subsection may, before the end of the permitted period of detention mentioned in subsection (2) above, take a person detained in a place of safety under that subsection to one or more other places of safety.

(4)  A person taken to a place of a safety under subsection (3) above may be detained there for a purpose mentioned in subsection (2) above for a period ending no later than the end of the permitted period of detention mentioned in that subsection.

(5)  This section is subject to section 136A which makes provision about the removal and taking of persons to a police station, and the keeping of persons at a police station, under this section.

## 136A. Use of police stations as places of safety

(1)  A child may not, in the exercise of a power to which this section applies, be removed to, kept at or taken to a place of safety that is a police station.

(2)  The Secretary of State may by regulations –

(a)  provide that an adult may be removed to, kept at or taken to a place of safety that is a police station, in the exercise of a power to which this section applies, only in circumstances specified in the regulations;

(b)  make provision about how adults removed to, kept at or taken to a police station, in the exercise of a power to which this section applies, are to be treated while at the police station, including provision for review of their detention.

(3)  Regulations under this section –

(a)  may make different provision for different cases;

(b)  may make provision that applies subject to specified exceptions;

(c)  may include incidental, supplementary or consequential provision or transitional, transitory or saving provision.

(4)  The powers to which this section applies are –

(a)  the power to remove a person to a place of safety under a warrant issued under section 135(1);

(b)  the power to take a person to a place of safety under section 135(3A);

(c)  the power to remove a person to, or to keep a person at, a place of safety under section 136(1);

(d)  the power to take a person to a place of safety under section 136(3).

(5)  In this section –

(a)  "child" means a person aged under 18;

(b)  "adult" means a person aged 18 or over.

## 136B. Extension of detention

(1)  The registered medical practitioner who is responsible for the examination of a person detained under section 135 or 136 may, at any time before the expiry of the period of 24 hours mentioned in section 135(3ZA) or (as the case may be) 136(2A), authorise the detention of the person for a further period not exceeding 12 hours (beginning immediately at the end of the period of 24 hours).

(2)  An authorisation under subsection (1) may be given only if the registered medical practitioner considers that the extension is necessary because the condition of the person detained is such that it would not be practicable for the assessment of the person for the purpose of section 135 or (as the case may be) section 136 to be carried out before the end of the period of 24 hours (or, if the assessment began within that period, for it to be completed before the end).

(3)  If the person is detained at a police station, and the assessment would be carried out or completed at the station, the registered medical practitioner may give an authorisation under subsection (1) only if an officer of the rank of superintendent or above approves it.

## 136C. Protective searches

(1)  Where a warrant is issued under section 135(1) or (2), a constable may search the person to whom the warrant relates if the constable has reasonable grounds for believing that the person –

(a)  may present a danger to himself or herself or to others, and

(b)  is concealing on his or her person an item that could be used to cause physical injury to himself or herself or to others.

(2)     The power to search conferred by subsection (1) may be exercised –

    (a)   in a case where a warrant is issued under section 135(1), at any time during the period beginning with the time when a constable enters the premises specified in the warrant and ending when the person ceases to be detained under section 135;

    (b)   in a case where a warrant is issued under section 135(2), at any time while the person is being removed under the authority of the warrant.

(3)     Where a person is detained under section 136(2) or (4), a constable may search the person, at any time while the person is so detained, if the constable has reasonable grounds for believing that the person –

    (a)   may present a danger to himself or herself or to others, and

    (b)   is concealing on his or her person an item that could be used to cause physical injury to himself or herself or to others.

(4)     The power to search conferred by subsection (1) or (3) is only a power to search to the extent that is reasonably required for the purpose of discovering the item that the constable believes the person to be concealing.

(5)     The power to search conferred by subsection (1) or (3) –

    (a)   does not authorise a constable to require a person to remove any of his or her clothing other than an outer coat, jacket or gloves, but

    (b)   does authorise a search of a person's mouth.

(6)     A constable searching a person in the exercise of the power to search conferred by subsection (1) or (3) may seize and retain anything found, if he or she has reasonable grounds for believing that the person searched might use it to cause physical injury to himself or herself or to others.

(7)     The power to search a person conferred by subsection (1) or (3) does not affect any other power to search the person.

### 137. Provisions as to custody, conveyance and detention

(1)     Any person required or authorised by or by virtue of this Act to be conveyed to any place or to be kept in custody or detained in a place of safety or at any place to which he is taken under section 42(6) above shall, while being so conveyed, detained or kept, as the case may be, be deemed to be in legal custody.

(2)     A constable or any other person required or authorised by or by virtue of this Act to take any person into custody, or to convey or detain any person shall, for the purposes of taking him into custody or conveying or detaining him, have all the powers, authorities, protection and privileges which a constable has within the area for which he acts as constable.

(3)     In this section "convey" includes any other expression denoting removal from one place to another.

### 138. Retaking of patients escaping from custody

(1)     If any person who is in legal custody by virtue of section 137 above escapes, he may, subject to the provisions of this section, be retaken –

    (a)   in any case, by the person who had his custody immediately before the escape, or by any constable or approved mental health professional;

(b) if at the time of the escape he was liable to be detained in a hospital within the meaning of Part 2 of this Act, or subject to guardianship under this Act, or a community patient who was recalled to hospital under section 17E above, by any other person who could take him into custody under section 18 above if he had absented himself without leave.

(2) A person to whom paragraph (b) of subsection (1) above applies shall not be retaken under this section after the expiration of the period within which he could be retaken under section 18 above if he had absented himself without leave on the day of the escape unless he is subject to a restriction order under Part 3 of this Act or an order or direction having the same effect as such an order; and subsection (4) of the said section 18 shall apply with the necessary modifications accordingly.

(3) A person who escapes while being taken to or detained in a place of safety under section 135 or 136 above shall not be retaken under this section after the expiration of the period of 72 hours beginning with the time when he escapes or the period during which he is liable to be so detained, whichever expires first.

(4) This section, so far as it relates to the escape of a person liable to be detained in a hospital within the meaning of Part 2 of this Act, shall apply in relation to a person who escapes –

(a) while being taken to or from such a hospital in pursuance of regulations under section 19 above, or of any order, direction or authorisation under Part 3 or 6 of this Act (other than under section 35, 36, 38, 53, 83 or 85); or

(b) while being taken to or detained in a place of safety in pursuance of an order under Part 3 of this Act (other than under section 35, 36 or 38 above) pending his admission to such a hospital, as if he were liable to be detained in that hospital and, if he had not previously been received in that hospital, as if he had been so received.

(5) In computing for the purposes of the power to give directions under section 37(4) above and for the purposes of sections 37(5) and 40(1) above the period of 28 days mentioned in those sections, no account shall be taken of any time during which the patient is at large and liable to be retaken by virtue of this section.

(6) Section 21 above shall, with any necessary modifications, apply in relation to a patient who is at large and liable to be retaken by virtue of this section as it applies in relation to a patient who is absent without leave and references in that section to section 18 above shall be construed accordingly.

### 139. Protection for acts done in pursuance of this Act

(1) No person shall be liable, whether on the ground of want of jurisdiction or on any other ground, to any civil or criminal proceedings to which he would have been liable apart from this section in respect of any act purporting to be done in pursuance of this Act or any regulations or rules made under this Act, unless the act was done in bad faith or without reasonable care.

(2) No civil proceedings shall be brought against any person in any court in respect of any such act without the leave of the High Court; and no criminal proceedings shall be brought against any person in any court in respect of any such act except by or with the consent of the Director of Public Prosecutions.

(3) This section does not apply to proceedings for an offence under this Act, being proceedings which, under any other provision of this Act, can be instituted only by or with the consent of the Director of Public Prosecutions.

(4) This section does not apply to proceedings against the Secretary of State or against the National Health Service Commissioning Board, a clinical commissioning group, Local

Health Board or Special Health Authority or against a National Health Service trust established under the National Health Service Act 2006 or the National Health Service (Wales) Act 2006 or NHS foundation trust or against the Department of Justice in Northern Ireland or against a person who has functions under this Act by virtue of section 12ZA in so far as the proceedings relate to the exercise of those functions.

(5)     In relation to Northern Ireland the reference in this section to the Director of Public Prosecutions shall be construed as a reference to the Director of Public Prosecutions for Northern Ireland.

### 140. Notification of hospitals having arrangements for reception of urgent cases

It shall be the duty of every clinical commissioning group and of every Local Health Board to give notice to every local social services authority for an area wholly or partly comprised within the area of the clinical commissioning group or Local Health Board specifying the hospital or hospitals administered by or otherwise available to the clinical commissioning group or Local Health Board in which arrangements are from time to time in force –

(a)     for the reception of patients in cases of special urgency;

(b)     or the provision of accommodation or facilities designed so as to be specially suitable for patients who have not attained the age of 18 years.

### 141. (repealed)

### 142....

### 142A. Regulations as to approvals in relation to England and Wales

The Secretary of State jointly with the Welsh Ministers may by regulations make provision as to the circumstances in which –

(a)     a practitioner approved for the purposes of section 12 above, or

(b)     a person approved to act as an approved clinician for the purposes of this Act,

approved in relation to England is to be treated, by virtue of his approval, as approved in relation to Wales too, and vice versa.

### 142B. Delegation of powers of managers of NHS foundation trusts

(1)     The constitution of an NHS foundation trust may not provide for a function under this Act to be delegated otherwise than in accordance with provision made by or under this Act.

(2)     Paragraph 15(3) of Schedule 7 to the National Health Service Act 2006 (which provides that the powers of a public benefit corporation may be delegated to a committee of directors or to an executive director) shall have effect subject to this section.

*Supplemental*

### 143. General provisions as to regulations, orders and rules

(1)     Any power of the Secretary of State or the Lord Chancellor to make regulations, orders or rules under this Act shall be exercisable by statutory instrument.

(2)     Any Order in Council under this Act or any order made by the Secretary of State under section 54A or 68A(7) above and any statutory instrument containing regulations made by the Secretary of State, or rules made, under this Act shall be subject to annulment in pursuance of a resolution of either House of Parliament.

(3) No order shall be made by the Secretary of State under section 45A(10), 68A(1) or 71(3) above unless a draft of it has been approved by a resolution of each House of Parliament.

(3A) Subsections (3B) to (3DB) apply where power to make regulations or an order under this Act is conferred on the Welsh Ministers (other than by or by virtue of the Government of Wales Act 2006).

(3B) Any power of the Welsh Ministers to make regulations or an order shall be exercisable by statutory instrument.

(3C) Any statutory instrument containing regulations made by the Welsh Ministers, or an order under section 68A(7) above, made by the Welsh Ministers shall be subject to annulment in pursuance of a resolution of the National Assembly for Wales.

(3D) No order shall be made under section 68A(1) above by the Welsh Ministers unless a draft of it has been approved by a resolution of the National Assembly for Wales.

(3DA) Subsection (3C) does not apply to regulations to which subsection (3DB) applies.

(3DB) A statutory instrument which contains (alone or with other provisions) the first regulations to be made under any of the following provisions –

(a) section 130E(2),

(b) section 130E(4)(b),

(c) section 130E(5)(b),

(d) section 130F(2)(d),

(e) section 130G(2)(c), or

(f) section 130H(1)(b)(ii),

must not be made unless a draft of the instrument containing the regulations has been laid before, and approved by resolution of, the National Assembly for Wales.

(3E) In this section –

(a) references to the Secretary of State include the Secretary of State and the Welsh Ministers acting jointly; and

(b) references to the Welsh Ministers include the Welsh Ministers and the Secretary of State acting jointly.

(4) This section does not apply to rules which are, by virtue of section 108 of this Act, to be made in accordance with Part 1 of Schedule 1 to the Constitutional Reform Act 2005.

## 144. Power to amend local Acts

Her Majesty may by Order in Council repeal or amend any local enactment so far as appears to Her Majesty to be necessary in consequence of this Act.

## 145. Interpretation

(1) In this Act, unless the context otherwise requires –

"absent without leave" has the meaning given to it by section 18 above and related expressions (including expressions relating to a patient's liability to be returned to a hospital or other place) shall be construed accordingly;

"application for admission for assessment" has the meaning given in section 2 above;

"application for admission for treatment" has the meaning given in section 3 above;

"the appropriate tribunal" has the meaning given by section 66(4) above;

"approved clinician" means a person approved by the Secretary of State or by another person by virtue of section 12ZA or 12ZB above (in relation to England) or by the Welsh Ministers (in relation to Wales) to act as an approved clinician for the purposes of this Act;

"approved mental health professional" has the meaning given in section 114 above;

"care home" –

(a)  has the same meaning as in the Care Standards Act 2000 in respect of a care home in England; and

(b)  means a place in Wales at which a care home service within the meaning of Part 1 of the Regulation and Inspection of Social Care (Wales) Act 2016 is provided wholly or mainly to persons aged 18 or over;

"community patient" has the meaning given in section 17A above;

"community treatment order" and "the community treatment order" have the meanings given in section 17A above;

"the community treatment period" has the meaning given in section 20A above;

"high security psychiatric services" has the same meaning as in section 4 of the National Health Service Act 2006 or section 4 of the National Health Service (Wales) Act 2006;

"hospital" means –

(a)  any health service hospital within the meaning of the National Health Service Act 2006 or the National Health Service (Wales) Act 2006; and

(b)  any accommodation provided by a local authority and used as a hospital by or on behalf of the Secretary of State under the National Health Service Act 2006, or of the Welsh Ministers under the National Health Service (Wales) Act 2006; and

(c)  any hospital as defined by section 206 of the National Health Service (Wales) Act 2006 which is vested in a Local Health Board;

and "hospital within the meaning of Part 2 of this Act" has the meaning given in section 34 above;

"hospital direction" has the meaning given in section 45A(3)(a) above;

"hospital order" and "guardianship order" have the meanings respectively given in section 37 above;

"independent hospital" –

(a)  in relation to England, means a hospital as defined by section 275 of the National Health Service Act 2006 that is not a health service hospital as defined by that section, and

(b)  in relation to Wales has the same meaning as in the Care Standards Act 2000;

"interim hospital order" has the meaning given in section 38 above;

"limitation direction" has the meaning given in section 45A(3)(b) above;

"Local Health Board" means a Local Health Board established under section 11 of the

National Health Services (Wales) Act 2006.

"local social services authority" means

(a) an authority in England which is local authority for the purposes of Part I of the Care Act 2014; or

(b) an authority in Wales which is local authority for the purposes of the Social Services and Well-being (Wales) Act 2014.

"the managers" means –

(a) in relation to a hospital vested in the Secretary of State for the purposes of his functions under the National Health Service Act 2006, or in the Welsh Ministers for the purposes of their functions under the National Health Service (Wales) Act 2006, and in relation to any accommodation provided by a local authority and used as a hospital by or on behalf of the Secretary of State under the National Health Service Act 2006, or of the Welsh Ministers under the National Health Service (Wales) Act 2006, the Secretary of State where the Secretary is responsible for the administration of the hospital or the Local Health Board or Special Health Authority responsible for the administration of the hospital;

(bb) in relation to a hospital vested in a Primary Care Trust or a National Health Service trust, the trust;

(bc) in relation to a hospital vested in an NHS foundation trust, the trust;

(bd) in relation to a hospital vested in a Local Health Board, the Board;

(c) in relation to a registered establishment –

(i) if the establishment is in England, the person or persons registered as a service provider under Chapter 2 of Part 1 of the Health and Social Care Act 2008 in respect of the regulated activity (within the meaning of that Part) relating to the assessment or medical treatment of mental disorder that is carried out in the establishment, and

(ii) if the establishment is in Wales, the person or persons registered in respect of the establishment under Part 2 of the Care Standards Act 2000;

and in this definition "hospital" means a hospital within the meaning of Part 2 of this Act;

"medical treatment" includes nursing, psychological intervention and specialist mental health habilitation, rehabilitation and care (but see also subsection (4) below);

"mental disorder" has the meaning given in section 1 above (subject to sections 86(4) and 141(6B));

"nearest relative", in relation to a patient, has the meaning given in Part 2 of this Act;

"patient" means a person suffering or appearing to be suffering from mental disorder;

"Primary Care Trust" means a Primary Care Trust established under section 18 of the National Health Service Act 2006;

"registered establishment" has the meaning given in section 34 above;

the regulatory authority" means –

(a) in relation to England, the Care Quality Commission;

(b) in relation to Wales, the Welsh Ministers.

"the responsible hospital" has the meaning given in section 17A above;

"restriction direction" has the meaning given to it by section 49 above;

"restriction order" has the meaning given to it by section 41 above;

"Special Health Authority" means a Special Health Authority established under section 28 of the National Health Service Act 2006, or section 22 of the National Health Service (Wales) Act 2006;

"transfer direction" has the meaning given to it by section 47 above.

(1AA) Where high security psychiatric services and other services are provided at a hospital, the part of the hospital at which high security psychiatric services are provided and the other part shall be treated as separate hospitals for the purposes of this Act.

(1AB) References in this Act to appropriate medical treatment shall be construed in accordance with section 3(4) above.

(1AC) References in this Act to an approved mental health professional shall be construed as references to an approved mental health professional acting on behalf of a local social services authority, unless the context otherwise requires.

(3) In relation to a person who is liable to be detained or subject to guardianship or a community patient by virtue of an order or direction under Part 3 of this Act (other than under section 35, 36 or 38), any reference in this Act to any enactment contained in Part 2 of this Act or in section 66 or 67 above shall be construed as a reference to that enactment as it applies to that person by virtue of Part 3 of this Act.

(4) Any reference in this Act to medical treatment, in relation to mental disorder, shall be construed as a reference to medical treatment the purpose of which is to alleviate, or prevent a worsening of, the disorder or one or more of its symptoms or manifestations.

## 146. Application to Scotland

Sections 42(6), 80, 116, 137, 139(1), 141, 142, 143 (so far as applicable to any Order in Council extending to Scotland) and 144 above shall extend to Scotland together with any amendment or repeal by this Act of or any provision of Schedule 5 to this Act relating to any enactment which so extends; but, except as aforesaid and except so far as it relates to the interpretation or commencement of the said provisions, this Act shall not extend to Scotland.

## 147. Application to Northern Ireland

Sections 81, 82, 86, 87, 88 (and so far as applied by that section sections 18, 22 and 138), section 128 (except so far as it relates to patients subject to guardianship), 137, 139, 141, 142, 143 (so far as applicable to any Order in Council extending to Northern Ireland) and 144 above shall extend to Northern Ireland together with any amendment or repeal by this Act of or any provision of Schedule 5 to this Act relating to any enactment which so extends; but except as aforesaid and except so far as it relates to the interpretation or commencement of the said provisions, this Act shall not extend to Northern Ireland.

## 148. Consequential and transitional provisions and repeals

(1) Schedule 4 (consequential amendments) and Schedule 5 (transitional and saving provisions) to this Act shall have effect but without prejudice to the operation of sections 15 to 17 of the Interpretation Act 1978 (which relate to the effect of repeals).

(2)   Where any amendment in Schedule 4 to this Act affects an enactment amended by the Mental Health (Amendment) Act 1982 the amendment in Schedule 4 shall come into force immediately after the provision of the Act of 1982 amending that enactment.

(3)   The enactments specified in Schedule 6 to this Act are hereby repealed to the extent mentioned in the third column of that Schedule.

### 149. Short title, commencement and application to Scilly Isles

(1)   This Act may be cited as the Mental Health Act 1983.

(2)   Subject to subsection (3) below and Schedule 5 to this Act, this Act shall come into force on 30th September 1983.

(3)   (repealed)

(4)   Section 130(4) of the National Health Service Act 1977 (which provides for the extension of that Act to the Isles of Scilly) shall have effect as if the references to that Act included references to this Act.

### SCHEDULE 2 MENTAL HEALTH REVIEW TRIBUNAL FOR WALES

### Section 65(2)

(1)   The Mental Health Review Tribunals for Wales shall consist of –

(a)   a number of persons (referred to in this Schedule as "the legal members") appointed by the Lord Chancellor and having such legal experience as the Lord Chancellor considers suitable;

(b)   a number of persons (referred to in this Schedule as "the medical members") being registered medical practitioners appointed by the Lord Chancellor; and

(c)   a number of persons appointed by the Lord Chancellor having such experience in administration, such knowledge of social services or such other qualifications or experience as the Lord Chancellor considers suitable.

(1A)   As part of the selection process for an appointment under paragraph 1(b) or (c) the Judicial Appointments Commission shall consult the Secretary of State.

(2)   Subject to paragraph 2A below the members of the Mental Health Review Tribunals for Wales shall hold and vacate office under the terms of the instrument under which they are appointed, but may resign office by notice in writing to the Lord Chancellor; and any such member who ceases to hold office shall be eligible for re-appointment.

(2A)   A member of the Mental Health Review Tribunal for Wales shall vacate office on the day on which he attains the age of 70 years; but this paragraph is subject to section 26(4) to (6) of the Judicial Pensions and Retirement Act 1993 (power to authorise continuance in office up to the age of 75 years).

(3)   (1)   (repealed)

(2)   The Lord Chancellor shall appoint one of the legal members of the Mental Health Review Tribunal for Wales to be the President of that tribunal.

(4)   Subject to rules made by the Lord Chancellor under section 78(2)(c) above, the members who are to constitute the Mental Health Review Tribunal for Wales for the purposes of any proceedings or class or group of proceedings under this Act shall be appointed by the President of the tribunal or by another member of the tribunal appointed for the purpose by the President; and of the members so appointed –

(a)  one or more shall be appointed from the legal members;

(b)  one or more shall be appointed from the medical members; and

(c)  one or more shall be appointed from the members who are neither legal nor medical members.

(5)  (1)  A member of the First-tier Tribunal who is eligible to decide any matter in a case under this Act may, at the request of the President of the Mental Health Review Tribunal for Wales and with the approval of the Senior President of Tribunals, act as a member of the Mental Health Review Tribunal for Wales.

(2)  Every person while acting under this paragraph may perform any of the functions of a member of the Mental Health Review Tribunal for Wales.

(3)  Until section 38(7) of the Mental Health Act 2007 comes into force, the reference in sub- paragraph (1) to the President of the Mental Health Review Tribunal for Wales is to be read as a reference to the chairman of the tribunal.

(6)  Subject to any rules made by the Lord Chancellor under section 78(4)(a) above, where the President of the tribunal is included among the persons appointed under paragraph 4 above, he shall be chairman of the tribunal; and in any other case the chairman of the tribunal shall be such one of the members so appointed (being one of the legal members) as the President may nominate.

# The Tribunal Procedure (First-tier Tribunal) (Health, Education and Social Care Chamber) Rules 2008 (SI 2008/2699)

## CONTENTS

**PART 4**

*Proceedings before the Tribunal in mental health cases*

**CHAPTER 1**

**CHAPTER 2**

**CHAPTER 3**

**PART 5**

**PART 1**

*Introduction*

Citation, commencement, application and interpretation

1. (1)   These Rules may be cited as the Tribunal Procedure (First-tier Tribunal) (Health, Education and Social Care Chamber) Rules 2008 and come into force on 3 November 2008.

(2)   These Rules apply to proceedings before the Health, Education and Social Care Chamber the First-tier Tribunal.

(3)   In these Rules –

"the 2007 Act" means the Tribunals, Courts and Enforcement Act 2007;

"applicant" means a person who –

(a)   starts Tribunal proceedings, whether by making an application, an appeal, a claim or a reference;

(b)   makes an application to the Tribunal for leave to start such proceedings; or

(c)   is substituted as an applicant under rule 9(1) (substitution and addition of parties);

"childcare provider" means a person who is a childminder or provides day care as defined in section 19 of the Children and Families (Wales) Measure 2010, or a person who provides childcare as defined in section 18 of the Childcare Act 2006;

"disability discrimination in schools case" means proceedings concerning disability discrimination in the education of a child or young person or related matters;

"dispose of proceedings" includes, unless indicated otherwise, disposing of a part of the proceedings;

"document" means anything in which information is recorded in any form, and an obligation under these Rules or any practice direction or direction to provide or allow access to a document or a copy of a document for any purpose means, unless the Tribunal directs otherwise, an obligation to provide or allow access to such document or copy in a legible form or in a form which can be readily made into a legible form;

"health service case" means a case under the National Health Service Act 2006, the National Health Service (Wales) Act 2006, regulations made under either of those Acts, or regulations having effect as if made under either of those Acts by reason of section 4 of and Schedule 2 by reason of the National Health Service (Consequential Provisions) Act 2006;

"hearing" means an oral hearing and includes a hearing conducted in whole or in part by video link, telephone or other means of instantaneous two-way electronic communication;

"legal representative" means a person who, for the purposes of the Legal Services Act 2007, is an authorised person in relation to an activity which constitutes the exercise of a right of audience or the conduct of litigation within the meaning of that Act;

"mental health case" means proceedings brought under the Mental Health Act 1983 or paragraph 5(2) of the Schedule to the Repatriation of Prisoners Act 1984;

"nearest relative" has the meaning set out in section 26 of the Mental Health Act 1983;

"party" means –

(a)   in a mental health case, the patient, the responsible authority, the Secretary of State (if the patient is a restricted patient or in a reference under rule 32(8) (seeking approval under section 86 of the Mental Health Act 1983)), and any other person who starts a mental health case by making an application;

(b)   in any other case, a person who is an applicant or respondent in proceedings before the Tribunal or, if the proceedings have been concluded, a person who was an applicant or respondent when the Tribunal finally disposed of all issues in the proceedings;

"patient" means the person who is the subject of a mental health case;

"practice direction" means a direction given under section 23 of the 2007 Act;

"respondent" means –

(a)   in an appeal against an order made by a justice of the peace, the person who applied to the justice of the peace for the order;

(b)  in an appeal against any other decision, the person who made the decision;

(c)  in proceedings on a claim under section 28I of the Disability Discrimination Act 1995, the body responsible for the school as determined in accordance with paragraph 1 of Schedule 4A to that Act or, if the claim concerns the residual duties of a local education authority under section 28F of that Act, that local education authority;

(d)  in proceedings on an application under section 4(2) of the Protection of Children Act 1999 or section 86(2) of the Care Standards Act 2000, the Secretary of State;

(da)  in an application for, or for a review of, a stop order under the National Health Service (Optical Charges and Payments) Regulations 1997 –

  (i)  the supplier, where the Secretary of State is the applicant;

  (ii)  the Secretary of State, where the supplier is the applicant;

(db)  in any other health service case –

  (i)  the practitioner, performer or person against whom the application is made, where the National Health Service Commissioning Board or a Local Health Board is, or is deemed to be, the applicant;

  (ii)  the National Health Service Commissioning Board or Local Health Board that served the notice, obtained the order or confirmation of the order, where any other person is the applicant; or

(e)  a person substituted or added as a respondent under rule 9 (substitution and addition of parties);

"responsible authority" means –

(a)  in relation to a patient detained under the Mental Health Act 1983 in a hospital within the meaning of Part 2 of that Act, the managers (as defined in section 145 of that Act);

(b)  in relation to a patient subject to guardianship, the responsible local social services authority (as defined in section 34(3) of the Mental Health Act 1983);

(c)  in relation to a community patient, the managers of the responsible hospital (as defined in section 145 of the Mental Health Act 1983);

"restricted patient" has the meaning set out in section 79(1) of the Mental Health Act 1983;

"special educational needs case" means proceedings concerning –

(a)  an EHC needs assessment within the meaning of section 36(2) of the Children and Families Act 2014(a),

(aa)  a detained person's EHC needs assessment within the meaning of section 70(5) of the Children and Families Act 2014, or

(b)  an EHC plan within the meaning of section 37(2) of that Act,

of a child or young person who has or may have special educational needs;

"Suspension Regulations" means regulations which provide for a right of appeal against a decision to suspend, or not to lift the suspension of, a person's registration as a childcare provider;

"Tribunal" means the First-tier Tribunal;

"working day" means any day except a Saturday or Sunday, Christmas Day, Good Friday or a bank holiday under section 1 of the Banking and Financial Dealings Act 1971;

"young person" means, in relation to a special educational needs case or a disability discrimination in schools case, a person over compulsory school age but under 25.

*Overriding objective and parties' obligation to co-operate with the Tribunal*

2.  (1) The overriding objective of these Rules is to enable the Tribunal to deal with cases fairly and justly.

    (2) Dealing with a case fairly and justly includes –

        (a) dealing with the case in ways which are proportionate to the importance of the case, the complexity of the issues, the anticipated costs and the resources of the parties;

        (b) avoiding unnecessary formality and seeking flexibility in the proceedings;

        (c) ensuring, so far as practicable, that the parties are able to participate fully in the proceedings;

        (d) using any special expertise of the Tribunal effectively; and

        (e) avoiding delay, so far as compatible with proper consideration of the issues.

3.  The Tribunal must seek to give effect to the overriding objective when it –

    (a) exercises any power under these Rules; or

    (b) interprets any rule or practice direction.

4.  Parties must –

    (a) help the Tribunal to further the overriding objective; and

    (b) cooperate with the Tribunal generally.

*Alternative dispute resolution and arbitration*

3.  (1) The Tribunal should seek, where appropriate –

        (a) to bring to the attention of the parties the availability of any appropriate alternative procedure for the resolution of the dispute; and

        (b) if the parties wish and provided that it is compatible with the overriding objective, to facilitate the use of the procedure.

    (2) Part 1 of the Arbitration Act 1996(b) does not apply to proceedings before the Tribunal.

## PART 2

*General powers and provisions*

### Delegation to staff

4.  (1) Staff appointed under section 40(1) of the 2007 Act (tribunal staff and services) may, with the approval of the Senior President of Tribunals, carry out functions of a judicial nature permitted or required to be done by the Tribunal.

    (2) The approval referred to at paragraph (1) may apply generally to the carrying out of specified functions by members of staff of a specified description in specified circumstances.

(3) Within 14 days after the date on which the Tribunal sends notice of a decision made by a member of staff under paragraph (1) to a party, that party may apply in writing to the Tribunal for that decision to be considered afresh by a judge.

## Case management powers

5. (1) Subject to the provisions of the 2007 Act and any other enactment, the Tribunal may regulate its own procedure.

   (2) The Tribunal may give a direction in relation to the conduct or disposal of proceedings at any time, including a direction amending, suspending or setting aside an earlier direction.

   (3) In particular, and without restricting the general powers in paragraphs (1) and (2), the Tribunal may –

   (a) extend or shorten the time for complying with any rule, practice direction or direction, unless such extension or shortening would conflict with a provision of another enactment containing a time limit;

   (b) consolidate or hear together two or more sets of proceedings or parts of proceedings raising common issues, or treat a case as a lead case;

   (c) permit or require a party to amend a document;

   (d) permit or require a party or another person to provide documents, information or submissions to the Tribunal or a party;

   (e) deal with an issue in the proceedings as a preliminary issue;

   (f) hold a hearing to consider any matter, including a case management issue;

   (g) decide the form of any hearing;

   (h) adjourn or postpone a hearing;

   (i) require a party to produce a bundle for a hearing;

   (j) stay proceedings;

   (k) transfer proceedings to another court or tribunal if that other court or tribunal has jurisdiction in relation to the proceedings and –

   (i) because of a change of circumstances since the proceedings were started, the Tribunal no longer has jurisdiction in relation to the proceedings; or

   (ii) the Tribunal considers that the other court or tribunal is a more appropriate forum for the determination of the case; or

   (l) suspend the effect of its own decision pending the determination by the Tribunal or the Upper Tribunal of an application for permission to appeal against, and any appeal or review of, that decision.

## Procedure for applying for and giving directions

6. (1) The Tribunal may give a direction on the application of one or more of the parties or on its own initiative.

   (2) An application for a direction may be made –

(a)   by sending or delivering a written application to the Tribunal; or

(b)   orally during the course of a hearing.

(3)   An application for a direction must include the reason for making that application.

(4)   Unless the Tribunal considers that there is good reason not to do so, the Tribunal must send written notice of any direction to every party and to any other person affected by the direction.

(5)   If a party, or any other person given notice of the direction under paragraph (4), wishes to challenge a direction which the Tribunal has given, they may do so by applying for another direction which amends, suspends or sets aside the first direction.

### Failure to comply with rules etc.

7.   (1)   An irregularity resulting from a failure to comply with any requirement in these Rules, a practice direction or a direction, does not of itself render void the proceedings or any step taken in the proceedings.

(2)   If a party has failed to comply with a requirement in these Rules, a practice direction or a direction, the Tribunal may take such action as it considers just, which may include –

(a)   waiving the requirement;

(b)   requiring the failure to be remedied;

(c)   exercising its power under rule 8 (striking out a party's case);

(d)   exercising its power under paragraph (3); or

(e)   except in mental health cases, restricting a party's participation in the proceedings.

(3)   The Tribunal may refer to the Upper Tribunal, and ask the Upper Tribunal to exercise its power under section 25 of the 2007 Act in relation to, any failure by a person to comply with a requirement imposed by the Tribunal –

(a)   to attend at any place for the purpose of giving evidence;

(b)   otherwise to make themselves available to give evidence;

(c)   to swear an oath in connection with the giving of evidence;

(d)   to give evidence as a witness;

(e)   to produce a document; or

(f)   to facilitate the inspection of a document or any other thing (including any premises).

### Striking out a party's case

8.   (1)   With the exception of paragraph (3), this rule does not apply to mental health cases.

(2)   The proceedings, or the appropriate part of them, will automatically be struck out if the applicant has failed to comply with a direction that stated that failure by the applicant to comply with the direction would lead to the striking out of the proceedings or that part of them.

(3)   The Tribunal must strike out the whole or a part of the proceedings if the Tribunal –

(a) does not have jurisdiction in relation to the proceedings or that part of them; and

(b) does not exercise its power under rule 5(3)(k)(i) (transfer to another court or tribunal) in relation to the proceedings or that part of them.

## Substitution and addition of parties

9. (1) The Tribunal may give a direction substituting a party if –

(a) the wrong person has been named as a party; or

(b) the substitution has become necessary because of a change in circumstances since the start of proceedings.

(2) The Tribunal may give a direction adding a person to the proceedings as a respondent.

(3) If the Tribunal gives a direction under paragraph (1) or (2) it may give such consequential directions as it considers appropriate.

## Orders for costs

10. (1) Subject to paragraph (2), the Tribunal may make an order in respect of costs only –

(a) under section 29(4) of the 2007 Act (wasted costs); or

(b) if the Tribunal considers that a party or its representative has acted unreasonably in bringing, defending or conducting the proceedings.

(2) The Tribunal may not make an order under paragraph (1)(b) in mental health cases.

(3) The Tribunal may make an order in respect of costs on an application or on its own initiative.

(4) A person making an application for an order under this rule must –

(a) send or deliver a written application to the Tribunal and to the person against whom it is proposed that the order be made; and

(b) send or deliver a schedule of the costs claimed with the application.

(5) An application for an order under paragraph (1) may be made at any time during the proceedings but may not be made later than 14 days after the date on which the Tribunal sends –

(a) a decision notice recording the decision which finally disposes of all issues in the proceedings; or

(b) notice under rule 17(6) that a withdrawal which ends the proceedings has taken effect.

(6) The Tribunal may not make an order under paragraph (1) against a person (the "paying person") without first –

(a) giving that person an opportunity to make representations; and

(b) if the paying person is an individual, considering that person's financial means.

(7) The amount of costs to be paid under an order under paragraph (1) may be ascertained by –

(a) summary assessment by the Tribunal;

(b) agreement of a specified sum by the paying person and the person entitled to receive the costs ("the receiving person"); or

(c) assessment of the whole or a specified part of the costs including the costs of the assessment incurred by the receiving person, if not agreed.

(8) Following an order for assessment under paragraph (7)(c), the paying person or the receiving person may apply to a county court for a detailed assessment of costs in accordance with the Civil Procedure Rules 1998 on the standard basis or, if specified in the order, on the indemnity basis.

(9) Upon making an order under paragraph (5) or (7)(c), the Tribunal may order an amount to be paid on account before the costs or expenses are assessed.

## Representatives

11. (1) A party may appoint a representative (whether a legal representative or not) to represent that party in the proceedings.

(1A) Where a child or young person is a party to proceedings, that child or young person may appoint a representative under paragraph (1).

(2) If a party appoints a representative, that party (or the representative if the representative is a legal representative) must send or deliver to the Tribunal and to each other party written notice of the representative's name and address.

(3) Anything permitted or required to be done by a party under these Rules, a practice direction or a direction may be done by the representative of that party, except –

(a) signing a witness statement; or

(b) signing an application notice under rule 20 (the application notice) if the representative is not a legal representative.

(4) A person who receives due notice of the appointment of a representative –

(a) must provide to the representative any document which is required to be provided to the represented party, and need not provide that document to the represented party; and

(b) may assume that the representative is and remains authorised as such until they receive written notification that this is not so from the representative or the represented party.

(5) At a hearing a party may be accompanied by another person whose name and address has not been notified under paragraph (2) but who, subject to paragraph (8) and with the permission of the Tribunal, may act as a representative or otherwise assist in presenting the party's case at the hearing.

(6) Paragraphs (2) to (4) do not apply to a person who accompanies a party under paragraph (5).

(7) In a mental health case, if the patient has not appointed a representative, the Tribunal may appoint a legal representative for the patient where –

(a) the patient has stated that they do not wish to conduct their own case or that they wish to be represented; or

(b) the patient lacks the capacity to appoint a representative but the Tribunal believes that it is in the patient's best interests for the patient to be represented.

(8) In a mental health case a party may not appoint as a representative, or be represented or assisted at a hearing by –

(a)  a person liable to be detained or subject to guardianship, or who is a community patient, under the Mental Health Act 1983; or

(b)  a person receiving treatment for mental disorder at the same hospital as the patient.

## Calculating time

12. (1)  An act required by these Rules, a practice direction or a direction to be done on or by a particular day must be done by 5pm on that day.

(2)  If the time specified by these Rules, a practice direction or a direction for doing any act ends on a day other than a working day, the act is done in time if it is done on the next working day.

(3)  In a special educational needs case or a disability discrimination in schools case –

(a)  if the time for starting proceedings by providing the application notice to the Tribunal under rule 20 (the application notice) ends on a day from 25 December to 1 January inclusive, or on any day in August, the application notice is provided in time if it is provided to the Tribunal on the first working day after 1 January or 31 August, as appropriate; and

(b)  the days from 25 December to 1 January inclusive and any day in August must not be counted when calculating the time by which any other act must be done.

(4)  Paragraph (3)(b) does not apply where the Tribunal directs that an act must be done by or on a specified date.

## Sending and delivery of documents

13. (1)  Any document to be provided to the Tribunal under these Rules, a practice direction or a direction must be –

(a)  sent by pre-paid post or delivered by hand to the address specified for the proceedings;

(b)  sent by fax to the number specified for the proceedings; or

(c)  sent or delivered by such other method as the Tribunal may permit or direct.

(1A)  If the Tribunal permits or directs documents to be provided to it by email, the requirement for a signature on applications or references under rules 20(2), 22(4)(a) or 32(1)(b) may be satisfied by a typed instead of a handwritten signature.

(2)  Subject to paragraph (3), if a party provides a fax number, email address or other details for the electronic transmission of documents to them, that party must accept delivery of documents by that method.

(3)  If a party informs the Tribunal and all other parties that a particular form of communication, other than pre-paid post or delivery by hand, should not be used to provide documents to that party, that form of communication must not be so used.

(4)  If the Tribunal or a party sends a document to a party or the Tribunal by email or any other electronic means of communication, the recipient may request that the sender provide a hard copy of the document to the recipient. The recipient must make such a request as soon as reasonably practicable after receiving the document electronically.

(5)  The Tribunal and each party may assume that the address provided by a party or its representative is and remains the address to which documents should be sent or delivered until receiving written notification to the contrary.

## Use of documents and information

14. (1) The Tribunal may make an order prohibiting the disclosure or publication of –

    (a) specified documents or information relating to the proceedings; or

    (b) any matter likely to lead members of the public to identify any person whom the Tribunal considers should not be identified.

    (2) The Tribunal may give a direction prohibiting the disclosure of a document or information to a person if –

    (a) the Tribunal is satisfied that such disclosure would be likely to cause that person or some other person serious harm; and

    (b) the Tribunal is satisfied, having regard to the interests of justice, that it is proportionate to give such a direction.

    (3) If a party ("the first party") considers that the Tribunal should give a direction under paragraph (2) prohibiting the disclosure of a document or information to another party ("the second party"), the first party must –

    (a) exclude the relevant document or information from any documents that will be provided to the second party; and

    (b) provide to the Tribunal the excluded document or information, and the reason for its exclusion, so that the Tribunal may decide whether the document or information should be disclosed to the second party or should be the subject of a direction under paragraph (2).

    (4) The Tribunal must conduct proceedings as appropriate in order to give effect to a direction given under paragraph (2).

    (5) If the Tribunal gives a direction under paragraph (2) which prevents disclosure to a party who has appointed a representative, the Tribunal may give a direction that the documents or information be disclosed to that representative if the Tribunal is satisfied that –

    (a) disclosure to the representative would be in the interests of the party; and

    (b) the representative will act in accordance with paragraph (6).

    (6) Documents or information disclosed to a representative in accordance with a direction under paragraph (5) must not be disclosed either directly or indirectly to any other person without the Tribunal's consent.

    (7) Unless the Tribunal gives a direction to the contrary, information about mental health cases and the names of any persons concerned in such cases must not be made public.

## Evidence and submissions

15. (1) Without restriction on the general powers in rule 5(1) and (2) (case management powers), the Tribunal may give directions as to –

    (a) issues on which it requires evidence or submissions;

    (b) the nature of the evidence or submissions it requires;

    (c) whether the parties are permitted or required to provide expert evidence, and if so whether the parties must jointly appoint a single expert to provide such evidence;

(d)  any limit on the number of witnesses whose evidence a party may put forward, whether in relation to a particular issue or generally;

(e)  the manner in which any evidence or submissions are to be provided, which may include a direction for them to be given –

(i)  orally at a hearing; or

(ii)  by written submissions or witness statement; and

(f)  the time at which any evidence or submissions are to be provided.

(2)  The Tribunal may –

(a)  admit evidence whether or not –

(i)  the evidence would be admissible in a civil trial in England and Wales; or

(ii)  the evidence was available to a previous decision-maker; or

(b)  exclude evidence that would otherwise be admissible where –

(i)  the evidence was not provided within the time allowed by a direction or a practice direction;

(ii)  the evidence was otherwise provided in a manner that did not comply with a direction or a practice direction; or

(iii)  it would otherwise be unfair to admit the evidence.

(3)  The Tribunal may consent to a witness giving, or require any witness to give, evidence on oath, and may administer an oath for that purpose.

(4)  In a special educational needs case the Tribunal may require –

(a)  the parents of the child, or any other person with care of the child or parental responsibility for the child (as defined in section 3 of the Children Act 1989), to make the child available for examination or assessment by a suitably qualified professional person; or

(b)  the person responsible for a school or educational setting to allow a suitably quali-fied professional person to have access to the school or educational setting for the purpose of assessing the child or the provision made, or to be made, for the child.

(5)  The Tribunal may consider a failure by a party to comply with a requirement made under paragraph (4), in the absence of any good reason for such failure, as a failure to cooperate with the Tribunal, which could lead to a result which is adverse to that party's case.

### Summoning of witnesses and orders to answer questions or produce documents

16.  (1)  On the application of a party or on its own initiative, the Tribunal may –

(a)  by summons require any person to attend as a witness at a hearing at the time and place specified in the summons; or

(b)  order any person to answer any questions or produce any documents in that person's possession or control which relate to any issue in the proceedings.

(2) A summons under paragraph (1)(a) must –

    (a) give the person required to attend 14 days' notice of the hearing, or such shorter period as the Tribunal may direct; and

    (b) where the person is not a party, make provision for the person's necessary expenses of attendance to be paid, and state who is to pay them.

(3) No person may be compelled to give any evidence or produce any document that the person could not be compelled to give or produce on a trial of an action in a court of law.

(4) A summons or order under this rule must –

    (a) state that the person on whom the requirement is imposed may apply to the Tribunal to vary or set aside the summons or order, if they have not had an opportunity to object to it; and

    (b) state the consequences of failure to comply with the summons or order.

## Withdrawal

17. (1) Subject to paragraphs (2) and (3), a party may give notice of the withdrawal of its case, or any part of it –

    (a) by sending or delivering to the Tribunal a written notice of withdrawal; or

    (b) orally at a hearing, or

    (c) where a local authority notifies the Tribunal before the expiry of the time limit for submitting a response that it will not oppose the appeal in a special educational needs case.

  (2) Notice of withdrawal will not take effect unless the Tribunal consents to the withdrawal except –

    (a) in proceedings concerning the suitability of a person to work with children or vulnerable adults; or

    (b) in proceedings started by a reference under section 67 or 71(1) of the Mental Health Act 1983.

  (3) A party which started a mental health case by making a reference to the Tribunal under section 68, 71(2) or 75(1) of the Mental Health Act 1983 may not withdraw its case.

  (4) A party which has withdrawn its case may apply to the Tribunal for the case to be reinstated.

  (5) An application under paragraph (4) must be made in writing and be received by the Tribunal within 28 days after –

    (a) the date on which the Tribunal received the notice under paragraph (1)(a); or

    (b) the date of the hearing at which the case was withdrawn orally under paragraph (1)(b).

  (6) The Tribunal must notify each party in writing of a withdrawal under this rule.

## PART 3

### Proceedings before the Tribunal other than in mental health cases (not reproduced here)

## PART 4

### Proceedings before the Tribunal in mental health cases

### CHAPTER 1

### Before the hearing Application of Part 4

31. This Part applies only to mental health cases.

### Procedure in mental health cases

32. (1) An application or reference must be –

    (a) made in writing;

    (b) signed (in the case of an application, by the applicant or any person authorised by the applicant to do so); and

    (c) sent or delivered to the Tribunal so that it is received within the time specified in the Mental Health Act 1983 or the Repatriation of Prisoners Act 1984.

  (2) An application must, if possible, include –

    (a) the name, address and date of birth of the patient;

    (b) if the application is made by the patient's nearest relative, the name, address and relationship to the patient of the patient's nearest relative;

    (c) the provision under which the patient is detained, liable to be detained, subject to guardianship, a community patient or subject to aftercare under supervision;

    (d) whether the person making the application has appointed a representative or intends to do so, and the name and address of any representative appointed;

    (e) the name and address of the responsible authority in relation to the patient.

  (2A) A reference must, if possible, include –

    (a) the name and address of the person or body making the reference;

    (b) the name, address and date of birth of the patient;

    (c) the name and address of any representative of the patient;

    (d) the provision under which the patient is detained, liable to be detained, subject to guardianship or a community patient (as the case may be);

    (e) whether the person or body making the reference has appointed a representative or intends to do so, and the name and address of any representative appointed;

    (f) if the reference is made by the Secretary of State, the name and address of the responsible authority in relation to the patient, or, in the case of a conditionally discharged patient, the name and address of the responsible clinician and any social supervisor in relation to the patient.

(3) Subject to rule 14(2) (withholding evidence likely to cause harm), when the Tribunal receives a document from any party it must send a copy of that document to each other party.

(4) If the patient is a conditionally discharged patient (as defined in the Mental Health Act 1983) the Secretary of State must send or deliver a statement containing the information and documents required by the relevant practice direction to the Tribunal so that it is received by the Tribunal as soon as practicable and in any event within 6 weeks after the Secretary of State received a copy of the application or a request from the Tribunal.

(5) In proceedings under section 66(1)(a) of the Mental Health Act 1983 (application for admission for assessment), on the earlier of receipt of the copy of the application or a request from the Tribunal, the responsible authority must send or deliver to the Tribunal –

   (a) the application for admission;

   (b) the medical recommendations on which the application is founded;

   (c) such of the information specified in the relevant practice direction as is within the knowledge of the responsible authority and can reasonably be provided in the time available; and

   (d) such of the documents specified in the relevant practice direction as can reasonably be provided in the time available.

(6) If paragraph (4) or (5) does not apply, the responsible authority must send or deliver a statement containing the information and documents required by the relevant practice direction to the Tribunal so that it is received by the Tribunal as soon as practicable and in any event within three weeks after the responsible authority received a copy of the application or reference.

(7) If the patient is a restricted patient, a person or body providing a document to the Tribunal in accordance with paragraph (4)(b) or (6) must also send or deliver a copy of the document to the Secretary of State.

(7A) The Secretary of State must send the information specified in paragraph (7B) and any observations the Secretary of State wishes to make to the Tribunal as soon as practicable and in any event –

   (a) in proceedings under section 75(1) of the Mental Health Act 1983 (reference concerning a conditionally discharged restricted patient who has been recalled to hospital), within two weeks after the Secretary of State received the documents sent or delivered in accordance with paragraph (7);

   (b) otherwise, within three weeks after the Secretary of State received the documents sent or delivered in accordance with paragraph (7).

(7B) The information specified in this paragraph is –

   (a) a summary of the offence or alleged offence that resulted in the patient being detained in hospital subject to a restriction order or, in the case of a patient subject to a restriction or limitation direction, that resulted in the patient being remanded in custody, kept in custody or sentenced to imprisonment;

   (b) a record of any other criminal convictions or findings recorded against the patient;

(c) full details of the history of the patient's liability to detention under the Mental Health Act 1983 since the restrictions were imposed;

(d) any further information in the Secretary of State's possession that the Secretary of State considers relevant to the proceedings.

(8) If the Secretary of State wishes to seek the approval of the Tribunal under section 86(3) of the Mental Health Act 1983, (removal of alien patients), the Secretary of State must refer the patient's case to the Tribunal and the provisions of these Rules applicable to references under that Act apply to the proceedings.

(9) The responsible authority must make records relating to the detention or treatment of the patient and any aftercare services available to the Tribunal on request and the Tribunal or an appropriate member of the Tribunal may, before or at the hearing, examine and take notes and copies of such records for use in connection with the proceedings.

## Notice of proceedings to interested persons

33. When the Tribunal receives the information required by rule 32(4), (5) or (6) (procedure in mental health cases) the Tribunal must give notice of the proceedings –

(a) where the patient is subject to the guardianship of a private guardian, to the guardian;

(b) where there is an extant order of the Court of Protection, to that court;

(c) subject to a patient with capacity to do so requesting otherwise, where any person other than the applicant is named by the authority as exercising the functions of the nearest relative, to that person;

(d) where a health authority, Primary Care Trust, National Health Service trust or NHS foundation trust has a right to discharge the patient under the provisions of section 23(3) of the Mental Health Act 1983, to that authority or trust; and

(e) to any other person who, in the opinion of the Tribunal, should have an opportunity of being heard.

## Medical examination of the patient

34. (1) Where paragraph (2) applies, an appropriate member of the Tribunal must, so far as practicable, examine the patient in order to form an opinion of the patient's mental condition, and may do so in private.

(2) This paragraph applies –

(a) in proceedings under section 66(1)(a) of the Mental Health Act 1983(b) (application in respect of an admission for assessment), unless the Tribunal is satisfied that the patient does not want such an examination;

(b) in any other case, if the patient or the patient's representative has informed the Tribunal in writing, not less than 14 days before the hearing, that –

(i) the patient; or

(ii) if the patient lacks the capacity to make such a decision, the patient's representative, wishes there to be such an examination; or

(c) if the Tribunal has directed that there be such an examination.

## CHAPTER 2

### Hearings

35. (1) Subject to the following paragraphs, the Tribunal must hold a hearing before making a decision which disposes of proceedings.

    (2) This rule does not apply to a decision under Part 5.

    (3) The Tribunal may make a decision on a reference under section 68 of the Mental Health Act 1983 (duty of managers of hospitals to refer cases to tribunal) without a hearing if the patient is a community patient aged 18 or over and either –

    (a) the patient has stated in writing that the patient does not wish to attend or be represented at a hearing of the reference and the Tribunal is satisfied that the patient has the capacity to decide whether or not to make that decision; or

    (b) the patient's representative has stated in writing that the patient does not wish to attend or be represented at the hearing of the reference.

    (4) The Tribunal may dispose of proceedings without a hearing under rule 8(3) (striking out a party's case).

### Entitlement to attend a hearing

36. (1) Subject to rule 38(4) (exclusion of a person from a hearing), each party to proceedings is entitled to attend a hearing.

    (2) Any person notified of the proceedings under rule 33 (notice of proceedings to interested persons) may –

    (a) attend and take part in a hearing to such extent as the Tribunal considers proper; or

    (b) provide written submissions to the Tribunal.

### Time and place of hearings

37. (1) In proceedings under section 66(1)(a) of the Mental Health Act 1983 the hearing of the case must start within seven days after the date on which the Tribunal received the application notice.

    (2) In proceedings under section 75(1) of that Act, the hearing of the case must start at least 5 weeks but no more than 8 weeks after the date on which the Tribunal received the reference.

    (3) The Tribunal must give reasonable notice of the time and place of the hearing (including any adjourned or postponed hearing), and any changes to the time and place of the hearing, to –

    (a) each party entitled to attend a hearing; and

    (b) any person who has been notified of the proceedings under rule 33 (notice of proceedings to interested persons).

    (4) The period of notice under paragraph (3) must be at least 21 days, except that –

    (a) in proceedings under section 66(1)(a) of the Mental Health Act 1983 the period must be at least three working days; and

    (b) the Tribunal may give shorter notice –

  (i)   with the parties' consent; or

  (ii)  in urgent or exceptional circumstances.

## Public and private hearings

38. (1)   All hearings must be held in private unless the Tribunal considers that it is in the interests of justice for the hearing to be held in public.

  (2)   If a hearing is held in public, the Tribunal may give a direction that part of the hearing is to be held in private.

  (3)   Where a hearing, or part of it, is to be held in private, the Tribunal may determine who is permitted to attend the hearing or part of it.

  (4)   The Tribunal may give a direction excluding from any hearing, or part of it –

   (a)   any person whose conduct the Tribunal considers is disrupting or is likely to disrupt the hearing;

   (b)   any person whose presence the Tribunal considers is likely to prevent another person from giving evidence or making submissions freely;

   (c)   any person who the Tribunal considers should be excluded in order to give effect to a direction under rule 14(2) (withholding information likely to cause harm); or

   (d)   any person where the purpose of the hearing would be defeated by the attendance of that person.

  (5)   The Tribunal may give a direction excluding a witness from a hearing until that witness gives evidence.

## Hearings in a party's absence

39. (1)   Subject to paragraph (2), if a party fails to attend a hearing the Tribunal may proceed with the hearing if the Tribunal –

   (a)   is satisfied that the party has been notified of the hearing or that reasonable steps have been taken to notify the party of the hearing; and

   (b)   considers that it is in the interests of justice to proceed with the hearing.

  (2)   The Tribunal may not proceed with a hearing that the patient has failed to attend unless the Tribunal is satisfied that –

   (a)   the patient –

    (i)   has decided not to attend the hearing; or

    (ii)  is unable to attend the hearing for reasons of ill health; and

   (b)   an examination under rule 34 (medical examination of the patient)

    (i)   has been carried out; or

    (ii)  is impractical or unnecessary.

## Power to pay allowances

40. The Tribunal may pay allowances in respect of travelling expenses, subsistence and loss of earnings to –

(a) any person who attends a hearing as an applicant or a witness;

(b) a patient who attends a hearing otherwise than as the applicant or a witness; and

(c) any person (other than a legal representative) who attends as the representative of an applicant.

## CHAPTER 3

### Decisions

### Decisions

41. (1) The Tribunal may give a decision orally at a hearing.

    (2) Subject to rule 14(2) (withholding information likely to cause harm), the Tribunal must provide to each party as soon as reasonably practicable after making a decision (except a decision under Part 5) which finally disposes of all issues in the proceedings or a preliminary issue dealt with following a direction under rule 5(3)(e) –

        (a) a decision notice stating the Tribunal's decision;

        (b) written reasons for the decision; and

        (c) notification of any right of appeal against the decision and the time within which, and the manner in which, such right of appeal may be exercised.

    (3) The documents and information referred to in paragraph (2) must –

        (a) in proceedings under section 66(1)(a) of the Mental Health Act 1983, be provided at the hearing or sent within 3 working days after the hearing; and

        (b) in other cases, be provided at the hearing or sent within 7 days after the hearing.

    (4) The Tribunal may provide written reasons for any decision to which paragraph (2) does not apply.

### Provisional decisions

42. For the purposes of this Part and Parts 1, 2 and 5, a decision with recommendations under section 72(3)(a) or (3A)(a) of the Mental Health Act 1983(a) or a deferred direction for conditional discharge under section 73(7) of that Act is a decision which disposes of the proceedings.

## PART 5

### Correcting, setting aside, reviewing and appealing Tribunal decisions

### Interpretation

43. In this Part –

"appeal" means the exercise of a right of appeal on a point of law under section 11 of the 2007 Act; and

"review" means the review of a decision by the Tribunal under section 9 of the 2007 Act.

### Clerical mistakes and accidental slips or omissions

44. The Tribunal may at any time correct any clerical mistake or other accidental slip or omission in a decision, direction or any document produced by it, by –

(a) sending notification of the amended decision or direction, or a copy of the amended document, to all parties; and

(b) making any necessary amendment to any information published in relation to the decision, direction or document.

### Setting aside a decision which disposes of proceedings

45. (1) The Tribunal may set aside a decision which disposes of proceedings, or part of such a decision, and re-make the decision or the relevant part of it, if –

    (a) the Tribunal considers that it is in the interests of justice to do so; and

    (b) one or more of the conditions in paragraph (2) are satisfied.

  (2) The conditions are –

    (a) a document relating to the proceedings was not sent to, or was not received at an appropriate time by, a party or a party's representative;

    (b) a document relating to the proceedings was not sent to the Tribunal at an appropriate time;

    (c) a party, or a party's representative, was not present at a hearing related to the proceedings; or

    (d) there has been some other procedural irregularity in the proceedings.

  (3) A party applying for a decision, or part of a decision, to be set aside under paragraph (1) must make a written application to the Tribunal so that it is received no later than 28 days after the date on which the Tribunal sent notice of the decision to the party.

### Application for permission to appeal

46. (1) A person seeking permission to appeal must make a written application to the Tribunal for permission to appeal.

  (2) An application under paragraph (1) must be sent or delivered to the Tribunal so that it is received no later than 28 days after the latest of the dates that the Tribunal sends to the person making the application –

    (za) the relevant decision notice;

    (a) written reasons for the decision if the decision disposes of –

      (i) all issues in the proceedings; or

      (ii) subject to paragraph (2A), a preliminary issue dealt with following a direction under rule 5(3)(e);

    (b) notification of amended reasons for, or correction of, the decision following a review; or

    (c) notification that an application for the decision to be set aside has been unsuccessful.

  (2) The Tribunal may direct that the 28 days within which a party may send or deliver to the Tribunal an application for permission to appeal against a decision that disposes of a preliminary issue shall run from the date of the decision that disposes of all issues in the proceedings.

(3) The date in paragraph (2)(c) applies only if the application for the decision to be set aside was made within the time stipulated in rule 45 (setting aside a decision which disposes of proceedings) or any extension of that time granted by the Tribunal.

(4) If the person seeking permission to appeal sends or delivers the application to the Tribunal later than the time required by paragraph (2) or by any extension of time under rule 5(3)(a) (power to extend time) –

    (a) the application must include a request for an extension of time and the reason why the application was not provided in time; and

    (b) unless the Tribunal extends time for the application under rule 5(3)(a) (power to extend time) the Tribunal must not admit the application.

(5) An application under paragraph (1) must –

    (a) identify the decision of the Tribunal to which it relates;

    (b) identify the alleged error or errors of law in the decision; and

    (c) state the result the party making the application is seeking.

## Tribunal's consideration of application for permission to appeal

47. (1) On receiving an application for permission to appeal the Tribunal must first consider, taking into account the overriding objective in rule 2, whether to review the decision in accordance with rule 49 (review of a decision).

(2) If the Tribunal decides not to review the decision, or reviews the decision and decides to take no action in relation to the decision, or part of it, the Tribunal must consider whether to give permission to appeal in relation to the decision or that part of it.

(3) The Tribunal must send a record of its decision to the parties as soon as practicable.

(4) If the Tribunal refuses permission to appeal it must send with the record of its decision –

    (a) a statement of its reasons for such refusal; and

    (b) notification of the right to make an application to the Upper Tribunal for permission to appeal and the time within which, and the method by which, such application must be made.

(5) The Tribunal may give permission to appeal on limited grounds, but must comply with paragraph (4) in relation to any grounds on which it has refused permission.

## Application for review in special educational needs cases

48. *omitted here*

## Review of a decision

49. (1) The Tribunal may only undertake a review of a decision –

    (a) pursuant to rule 47(1) (review on an application for permission to appeal) if it is satisfied that there was an error of law in the decision; or

    (b) pursuant to rule 48 (application for review in special educational needs cases).

(2) The Tribunal must notify the parties in writing of the outcome of any review, and of any right of appeal in relation to the outcome.

(3) If the Tribunal takes any action in relation to a decision following a review without first giving every party an opportunity to make representations, the notice under paragraph (2) must state that any party that did not have an opportunity to make representations may apply for such action to be set aside and for the decision to be reviewed again.

**Power to treat an application as a different type of application**

50. The Tribunal may treat an application for a decision to be corrected, set aside or reviewed, or for permission to appeal against a decision, as an application for any other one of those things.

# Appendix 2B

## Practice Direction (First-tier Tribunal) (Health, Education and Social Care Chamber) Statements and Reports in Mental Health Cases

1.  This practice direction is made by the Senior President of Tribunals with the agreement of the Lord Chancellor in the exercise of powers conferred by section 23 of the Tribunals, Courts and Enforcement Act 2007. It applies to a "mental health case" as defined in rule 1(3) the Tribunal Procedure (First-tier Tribunal) (Health, Education and Social Care Chamber) Rules 2008. Rule 32 requires that certain documents are to be sent or delivered to the Tribunal (and, in restricted cases, to the Secretary of State) by the responsible authority, the responsible clinician and any social supervisor (as the case may be). This practice direction specifies the contents of such documents. It replaces the previous Practice Directions on mental health cases dated 30 October 2008 and 6 April 2012, with effect from 28 October 2013.

2.  In this practice direction "the Act" refers to the Mental Health Act 1983 (as amended by the Mental Health Act 2007).

### A. IN-PATIENTS (NON-RESTRICTED AND RESTRICTED)

5.  For the purposes of this Practice Direction, a patient is an in-patient if they are detained in hospital to be assessed or treated for a mental disorder, whether admitted through civil or criminal justice processes, including a restricted patient (i.e. subject to special restrictions under the Act), and including a patient transferred to hospital from custody. A patient is to be regarded as an in-patient detained in a hospital even if they have been permitted leave of absence, or have gone absent without leave.

6.  In the case of a restricted patient detained in hospital, the tribunal may make a provisional decision to order a Conditional Discharge. However, before it finally decides to grant a Conditional Discharge, the tribunal may defer its decision so that satisfactory arrangements can be made. The patient will remain an in-patient unless and until the tribunal finally grants a Conditional Discharge, so this part of the Practice Direction applies.

7.  If the patient is an in-patient, the Responsible Authority must send or deliver to the tribunal the following documents containing the specified information in accordance with the relevant paragraphs below:

    - *Statement of Information about the Patient.*

- *Responsible Clinician's Report, including any relevant forensic history.*

- *Nursing Report, with the patient's current nursing plan attached.*

- *Social Circumstances Report including details of any Care Pathway Approach (CPA) and/or Section 117 aftercare plan in full or in embryo and, where appropriate, the additional information required for patients under the age of 18, and any input from a Multi Agency Public Protection Arrangements (MAPPA) agency or meeting.*

8. In all in-patient cases, except where a patient is detained under Section 2 of the Act, the Responsible Authority must send to the tribunal the required documents containing the specified information, so that they are received by the tribunal as soon as practicable and in any event within three weeks after the Authority made or received the application or reference. If the patient is a restricted patient, the Authority must also, at the same time, send copies of the documents to the Secretary of State (Ministry of Justice).

9. Where a patient is detained under Section 2 of the Act, the Responsible Authority must prepare the required documents as soon as practicable after receipt of a copy of the application or a request from the tribunal. If specified information has to be omitted because it is not available, then this should be mentioned in the statement or report. These documents must be made available to the tribunal panel and the patient's representative at least one hour before the hearing is due to start.

10. The authors of reports should have personally met and be familiar with the patient. If an existing report becomes out-of-date, or if the status or the circumstances of the patient change after the reports have been written but before the tribunal hearing takes place (e.g. if a patient is discharged, or is recalled), the author of the report should then send to the tribunal an addendum addressing the up-to-date situation and, where necessary, the new applicable statutory criteria.

### Statement of Information about the Patient – in-patients

11. The statement provided to the tribunal must be up-to-date, specifically prepared for the tribunal, signed and dated, and must include:

   (a) the patient's full name, date of birth, and usual place of residence;

   (b) the full official name of the Responsible Authority;

   (c) the patient's first language/dialect and, if it is not English, whether an interpreter is required and, if so, in which language/dialect;

   (d) if the patient is deaf, whether the patient will require the services of British Sign Language Interpreters and/or a Relay Interpreter;

   (e) a chronological table listing:

   - the dates of any previous admissions to, discharge from, or recall to hospital, stating whether the admissions were compulsory or voluntary;

   - the date when the current period of detention in hospital originally commenced, stating the nature of the application, order or direction that is the authority for the detention of the patient;

   - the dates of any subsequent renewal of, or change in, the authority for the patient's detention, and any changes in the patient's status under the Act;

   - dates and details of any hospital transfers since the patient's original detention;

- the date of admission or transfer to the hospital where the patient now is;

- the dates and outcomes of any tribunal hearings over the last three years;

(f) the name of the patient's responsible clinician and the date when the patient came under the care of that clinician;

(g) the name and contact details of the patient's care coordinator, community psychiatric nurse, social worker/AMHP or social supervisor;

(h) where the patient is detained in an independent hospital, details of any NHS body that funds, or will fund, the placement;

(i) the name and address of the local social services authority which, were the patient to leave hospital, would have a duty to provide Section 117 aftercare services;

(j) the name and address of the NHS body which, were the patient to leave hospital, would have a duty to provide Section 117 aftercare services;

(k) the name and address of any legal representative acting for the patent;

(l) except in the case of a restricted patient, the name and address of the patient's nearest relative or of the person exercising that function, whether the patient has made any request that their nearest relative should not be consulted or should not be kept informed about the patient's care or treatment and, if so, the details of any such request, whether the responsible authority believes that the patient has capacity to make such a request and the reasons for that belief;

(m) the name and address of any other person who plays a significant part in the care of the patient but who is not professionally involved;

(n) details of any legal proceedings or other arrangements relating to the patient's mental capacity, or their ability to make decisions or handle their own affairs.

## Responsible Clinician's Report – in-patients

12. The report must be up-to-date, specifically prepared for the tribunal and have numbered paragraphs and pages. It should be signed and dated. The report should be written or counter-signed by the patient's responsible clinician. The sources of information for the events and incidents described must be made clear. This report should not be an addendum to (or reproduce extensive details from) previous reports, or recite medical records, but must briefly describe the patient's recent relevant medical history and current mental health presentation, and must include:

(a) whether there are any factors that may affect the patient's understanding or ability to cope with a hearing and whether there are any adjustments that the tribunal may consider in order to deal with the case fairly and justly;

(b) details of any index offence(s) and other relevant forensic history;

(c) a chronology listing the patient's previous involvement with mental health services, including any admissions to, discharge from and recall to hospital;

(d) reasons for any previous admission or recall to hospital;

(e) the circumstances leading up to the patient's current admission to hospital;

(f) whether the patient is now suffering from a mental disorder and, if so, whether a diagnosis has been made, what the diagnosis is, and why;

(g) whether the patient has a learning disability and, if so, whether that disability is associated with abnormally aggressive or seriously irresponsible conduct;

(h) depending upon the statutory criteria, whether any mental disorder present is of a nature or degree to warrant, or make appropriate, liability to be detained in a hospital for assessment and/or medical treatment;

(i) details of any appropriate and available medical treatment prescribed, provided, offered or planned for the patient's mental disorder;

(j) the strengths or positive factors relating to the patient;

(k) a summary of the patient's current progress, behaviour, capacity and insight;

(l) the patient's understanding of, compliance with, and likely future willingness to accept any prescribed medication or comply with any appropriate medical treatment for mental disorder that is or might be made available;

(m) in the case of an eligible compliant patient who lacks capacity to agree or object to their detention or treatment, whether or not deprivation of liberty under the Mental Capacity Act 2005 (as amended) would be appropriate and less restrictive;

(n) details of any incidents where the patient has harmed themselves or others, or threatened harm, or damaged property, or threatened damage;

(o) whether (in Section 2 cases) detention in hospital, or (in all other cases) the provision of medical treatment in hospital, is justified or necessary in the interests of the patient's health or safety, or for the protection of others;

(p) whether the patient, if discharged from hospital, would be likely to act in a manner dangerous to themselves or others;

(q) whether, and if so how, any risks could be managed effectively in the community, including the use of any lawful conditions or recall powers;

(r) any recommendations to the tribunal, with reasons.

### Nursing Report – in-patients

13. The report must be up-to-date, specifically prepared for the tribunal and have numbered paragraphs and pages. It should be signed and dated. The sources of information for the events and incidents described must be made clear. This report should not recite the details of medical records, or be an addendum to (or reproduce extensive details from) previous reports, although the patient's current nursing plan should be attached. In relation to the patient's current in-patient episode, the report must briefly describe the patient's current mental health presentation, and must include:

(a) whether there are any factors that might affect the patient's understanding or ability to cope with a hearing, and whether there are any adjustments that the tribunal may consider in order to deal with the case fairly and justly;

(b) the nature of nursing care and medication currently being made available;

(c) the level of observation to which the patient is currently subject;

(d) whether the patient has contact with relatives, friends or other patients, the nature of the interaction, and what community support the patient has;

(e) strengths or positive factors relating to the patient;

(f) a summary of the patient's current progress, engagement with nursing staff, behaviour, cooperation, activities, self-care and insight;

(g) any occasions on which the patient has been absent without leave whilst liable to be detained, or occasions when the patient has failed to return as and when required, after having been granted leave;

(h) the patient's understanding of, compliance with, and likely future willingness to accept any prescribed medication or treatment for mental disorder that is or might be made available;

(i) details of any incidents in hospital where the patient has harmed themselves or others, or threatened harm, or damaged property, or threatened damage;

(j) any occasions on which the patient has been secluded or restrained, including the reasons why such seclusion or restraint was necessary;

(k) whether (in Section 2 cases) detention in hospital, or (in all other cases) the provision of medical treatment in hospital, is justified or necessary in the interests of the patient's health or safety, or for the protection of others;

(l) whether the patient, if discharged from hospital, would be likely to act in a manner dangerous to themselves or others;

(m) whether, and if so how, any risks could be managed effectively in the community, including the use of any lawful conditions or recall powers;

(n) any recommendations to the tribunal, with reasons.

## Social Circumstances Report – in-patients

14. The report must be up-to-date, specifically prepared for the tribunal and have numbered paragraphs and pages. It should be signed and dated. The sources of information for the events and incidents described must be made clear. This report should not be an addendum to (or reproduce extensive details from) previous reports, but must briefly describe the patient's recent relevant history and current presentation, and must include:

(a) whether there are any factors that might affect the patient's understanding or ability to cope with a hearing, and whether there are any adjustments that the tribunal may consider in order to deal with the case fairly and justly;

(b) details of any index offence(s) and other relevant forensic history;

(c) a chronology listing the patient's previous involvement with mental health services, including any admissions to, discharge from and recall to hospital;

(d) the patient's home and family circumstances;

(e) the housing or accommodation available to the patient if discharged;

(f) the patient's financial position (including benefit entitlements);

(g) any available opportunities for employment;

(h) the patient's previous response to community support or Section 117 aftercare;

(i) so far as is known, details of the care pathway and Section 117 aftercare to be made available to the patient, together with details of the proposed care plan;

(j) the likely adequacy and effectiveness of the proposed care plan;

(k) whether there are any issues as to funding the proposed care plan and, if so, the date by which those issues will be resolved;

(l) the strengths or positive factors relating to the patient;

(m) a summary of the patient's current progress, behaviour, compliance and insight;

(n) details of any incidents where the patient has harmed themselves or others, or threatened harm, or damaged property, or threatened damage;

(o) the patient's views, wishes, beliefs, opinions, hopes and concerns;

(p) except in restricted cases, the views of the patient's nearest relative unless (having consulted the patient) it would inappropriate or impractical to consult the nearest relative, in which case give reasons for this view and describe any attempts to rectify matters;

(q) the views of any other person who takes a lead role in the care and support of the patient but who is not professionally involved;

(r) whether the patient is known to any MAPPA meeting or agency and, if so, in which area, for what reason, and at what level – together with the name of the Chair of any MAPPA meeting concerned with the patient, and the name of the representative of the lead agency;

(s) in the event that a MAPPA meeting or agency wishes to put forward evidence of its views in relation to the level and management of risk, a summary of those views (or an Executive Summary may be attached to the report); and where relevant, a copy of the Police National Computer record of previous convictions should be attached;

(t) in the case of an eligible compliant patient who lacks capacity to agree or object to their detention or treatment, whether or not deprivation of liberty under the Mental Capacity Act 2005 (as amended) would be appropriate and less restrictive;

(u) whether (in Section 2 cases) detention in hospital, or (in all other cases) the provision of medical treatment in hospital, is justified or necessary in the interests of the patient's health or safety, or for the protection of others;

(v) whether the patient, if discharged from hospital, would be likely to act in a manner dangerous to themselves or others;

(w) whether, and if so how, any risks could be managed effectively in the community, including the use of any lawful conditions or recall powers;

(x) any recommendations to the tribunal, with reasons.

## B. COMMUNITY PATIENTS

15. The Responsible Authority must send to the tribunal the following documents, containing the specified information, so that the documents are received by the tribunal as soon as practicable and in any event within 3 weeks after the Authority made or received the application or reference:

- *Statement of Information about the Patient.*

- *Responsible Clinician's Report, including any relevant forensic history.*

- *Social Circumstances Report including details of any Section 117 aftercare plan and, where appropriate, the additional information required for patients under the age of 18, and any input from a Multi Agency Public Protection Arrangements (MAPPA) agency or meeting.*

16. The authors of reports should have personally met and be familiar with the patient. If an existing report becomes out-of-date, or if the status or the circumstances of the patient change after the reports have been written but before the tribunal hearing takes place

(e.g. if a patient is recalled, or again discharged into the community), the author of the report should then send to the tribunal an addendum addressing the up-to-date situation and, where necessary, the new applicable statutory criteria.

## Statement of Information about the Patient – community patients

17. The statement provided to the tribunal should be up-to-date, signed and dated, specifically prepared for the tribunal, and must include:

    (a) the patient's full name, date of birth, and current place of residence;

    (b) the full official name of the responsible authority;

    (c) the patient's first language/dialect and, if it is not English, whether an interpreter is required and, if so, in which language/dialect;

    (d) if the patient is deaf, whether the patient will require the services of British Sign Language Interpreters and/or a Relay Interpreter;

    (e) a chronological table listing:

    - the dates of any previous admissions to, discharge from, or recall to hospital, stating whether the admissions were compulsory or voluntary, and including any previous instances of discharge on to a community treatment order (CTO);

    - the date of the underlying order or direction for detention in hospital prior to the patient's discharge onto the current CTO;

    - the date of the current CTO;

    - the dates of any subsequent renewal of, or change in, the authority for the patient's CTO, and any changes in the patient's status under the Act;

    - the dates and outcomes of any tribunal hearings over the last three years;

    (f) the name of the patient's responsible clinician and the date when the patient came under the care of that clinician;

    (g) the name and contact details of the patient's care coordinator, community psychiatric nurse, and/or social worker/AMHP;

    (h) the name and address of the local social services authority which has the duty to provide Section 117 aftercare services;

    (i) the name and address of the NHS body which has the duty to provide Section 117 aftercare services;

    (j) the name and address of any legal representative acting for the patent;

    (k) the name and address of the patient's nearest relative or of the person exercising that function, whether the patient has made any request that their nearest relative should not be consulted or should not be kept informed about the patient's care or treatment and, if so, the details of any such request, whether the responsible authority believes that the patient has capacity to make such a request and the reasons for that belief;

    (l) the name and address of any other person who plays a significant part in the care of the patient but who is not professionally involved;

    (m) details of any legal proceedings or other arrangements relating to the patient's mental capacity, or their ability to make decisions or handle their own affairs.

## Responsible Clinician's Report – community patients

18. The report must be up-to-date, specifically prepared for the tribunal and have numbered paragraphs and pages. It should be signed and dated. This report should be written or counter-signed by the patient's responsible clinician. The sources of information for the events and incidents described must be made clear. The report should not be an addendum to (or reproduce extensive details from) previous reports, or recite medical records, but must briefly describe the patient's recent relevant medical history and current mental health presentation, and must include:

    (a) where the patient is aged 18 or over and the case is a reference to the tribunal, whether the patient has capacity to decide whether or not to attend or be represented at a tribunal hearing;

    (b) whether, if there is a hearing, there are any factors that may affect the patient's understanding or ability to cope with it, and whether there are any adjustments that the tribunal may consider in order to deal with the case fairly and justly;

    (c) details of any index offence(s) and other relevant forensic history;

    (d) a chronology listing the patient's previous involvement with mental health services, including any admissions to, discharge from and recall to hospital;

    (e) reasons for any previous admission or recall to hospital;

    (f) the circumstances leading up to the patient's most recent admission to hospital;

    (g) the circumstances leading up to the patient's discharge onto a CTO;

    (h) any conditions to which the patient is subject under Section 17B, and details of the patient's compliance;

    (i) whether the patient is now suffering from a mental disorder and, if so, what the diagnosis is and why;

    (j) whether the patient has a learning disability and, if so, whether that disability is associated with abnormally aggressive or seriously irresponsible conduct;

    (k) whether the patient has a mental disorder of a nature or degree such as to make it appropriate for the patient to receive medical treatment;

    (l) details of any appropriate and available medical treatment prescribed, provided, offered or planned for the patient's mental disorder;

    (m) the strengths or positive factors relating to the patient;

    (n) a summary of the patient's current progress, behaviour, capacity and insight;

    (o) the patient's understanding of, compliance with, and likely future willingness to accept any prescribed medication or comply with any appropriate medical treatment for mental disorder that is or might be made available;

    (p) details of any incidents where the patient has harmed themselves or others, or threatened harm, or damaged property, or threatened damage;

    (q) whether it is necessary for the patient's health or safety, or for the protection of others, that the patient should receive medical treatment and, if so, why;

    (r) whether the patient, if discharged from the CTO, would be likely to act in a manner dangerous to themselves or others;

    (s) whether, and if so how, any risks could be managed effectively in the community;

(t)  whether it continues to be necessary that the responsible clinician should be able to exercise the power of recall and, if so, why;

(u)  any recommendations to the tribunal, with reasons.

## Social Circumstances Report – community patients

19. The report must be up-to-date, specifically prepared for the tribunal and have numbered paragraphs and pages. It should be signed and dated. The sources of information for the events and incidents described must be made clear. This report should not be an addendum to (or reproduce extensive details from) previous reports, but must briefly describe the patient's recent relevant history and current presentation, and must include:

(a)  whether there are any factors that might affect the patient's understanding or ability to cope with a hearing, and whether there are any adjustments that the tribunal may consider in order to deal with the case fairly and justly;

(b)  details of any index offence(s), and other relevant forensic history;

(c)  a chronology listing the patient's previous involvement with mental health services, including any admissions to, discharge from and recall to hospital;

(d)  the patient's home and family circumstances;

(e)  the housing or accommodation currently available to the patient;

(f)  the patient's financial position (including benefit entitlements);

(g)  any employment or available opportunities for employment;

(h)  any conditions to which the patient is subject under Section 17B, and details of the patient's compliance;

(i)  the patient's previous response to community support or Section 117 aftercare;

(j)  details of the community support or Section 117 aftercare that is being, or could be made available to the patient, together with details of the current care plan;

(k)  whether there are any issues as to funding the current or future care plan and, if so, the date by which those issues will be resolved;

(l)  the current adequacy and effectiveness of the care plan;

(m)  the strengths or positive factors relating to the patient;

(n)  a summary of the patient's current progress, behaviour, compliance and insight;

(o)  details of any incidents where the patient has harmed themselves or others, or threatened harm, or damaged property, or threatened damage;

(p)  the patient's views, wishes, beliefs, opinions, hopes and concerns;

(q)  the views of the patient's Nearest Relative unless (having consulted the patient) it would inappropriate or impractical to consult the Nearest Relative, in which case give reasons for this view and describe any attempts to rectify matters;

(r)  the views of any other person who takes a lead role in the care and support of the patient but who is not professionally involved;

(s)  whether the patient is known to any Multi Agency Public Protection Arrangements (MAPPA) meeting or agency and, if so, in which area, for what reason, and at what level – together with the name of the Chair of any MAPPA meeting concerned with the patient, and the name of the representative of the lead agency;

(t)  in the event that a MAPPA meeting or agency wishes to put forward evidence of its views in relation to the level and management of risk, a summary of those views (or an Executive Summary may be attached to the report); and where relevant, a copy of the Police National Computer record of previous convictions should be attached;

(u)  whether it is necessary for the patient's health or safety, or for the protection of others, that the patient should receive medical treatment and, if so, why;

(v)  whether the patient, if discharged from the CTO, would be likely to act in a manner dangerous to themselves or others;

(w)  whether, and if so how, any risks could be managed effectively in the community;

(x)  whether it continues to be necessary that the responsible clinician should be able to exercise the power of recall and, if so, why;

(y)  any recommendations to the tribunal, with reasons.

## C. GUARDIANSHIP PATIENTS

20. If the patient has been received into guardianship the Responsible Authority must send to the tribunal the following documents, containing the specified information, so that they are received by the tribunal as soon as practicable and in any event within three weeks after the Authority made or received a copy of the application or reference:

- *Statement of Information about the Patient.*

- *Responsible Clinician's Report, including any relevant forensic history.*

- *Social Circumstances Report including details of any Care Programme Approach (CPA) and, where appropriate, the additional information required for patients under the age of 18, and any input from a Multi Agency Public Protection Arrangements (MAPPA) agency or meeting.*

21. The authors of reports should have personally met and be familiar with the patient. If an existing report becomes out-of-date, or if the status or the circumstances of the patient change after the reports have been written but before the tribunal hearing takes place, the author of the report should then send to the tribunal an addendum addressing the up-to-date situation and, where necessary, the new applicable statutory criteria.

### Statement of Information about the Patient – guardianship patients

22. The statement provided to the tribunal should be up-to-date, signed and dated, specifically prepared for the tribunal, and must include:

(a)  the patient's full name, date of birth, and current place of residence;

(b)  the full official name of the responsible authority;

(c)  the patient's first language/dialect and, if it is not English, whether an interpreter is required and, if so, in which language/dialect;

(d)  if the patient is deaf, whether the patient will require the services of British Sign Language Interpreters and/or a Relay Interpreter;

(e)  a chronological table listing:

- the dates of any previous admissions to, discharge from or recall to hospital, stating whether the admissions were compulsory or voluntary;

- the dates of any previous instances of reception into guardianship;

- the date of reception into current guardianship, stating the nature of the application, order or direction that constitutes the original authority for the guardianship of the patient;

- the dates and outcomes of any tribunal hearings over the last three years;

(f) the name and address of any private guardian;

(g) the name of the patient's responsible clinician and the date when the patient came under the care of that clinician;

(h) the name and contact details of the patient's care coordinator, community psychiatric nurse, and/or social worker/AMHP;

(i) the name and address of any legal representative acting for the patent;

(j) the name and address of the patient's nearest relative or of the person exercising that function, whether the patient has made any request that their nearest relative should not be consulted or should not be kept informed about the patient's care or treatment and, if so, the details of any such request, whether the responsible authority believes that the patient has capacity to make such a request and the reasons for that belief;

(k) the name and address of any other person who plays a significant part in the care of the patient but who is not professionally involved;

(l) details of any legal proceedings or other arrangements relating to the patient's mental capacity, or their ability to make decisions or handle their own affairs.

## Responsible Clinician's Report – guardianship patients

23. The report must be up-to-date, specifically prepared for the tribunal and have numbered paragraphs and pages. It should be signed and dated. The report should be written or counter-signed by the patient's responsible clinician. The sources of information for the events and incidents described must be made clear. This report should not be an addendum to (or reproduce extensive details from) previous reports, or recite medical records, but must briefly describe the patient's recent relevant medical history and current mental health presentation, and must include:

(a) whether there are any factors that may affect the patient's understanding or ability to cope with a hearing, and whether there are any adjustments that the tribunal may consider in order to deal with the case fairly and justly;

(b) details of any index offence(s), and other relevant forensic history;

(c) a chronology listing the patient's previous involvement with mental health services including any admissions to, discharge from and recall to hospital, and any previous instances of reception into guardianship;

(d) the circumstances leading up to the patient's reception into guardianship;

(e) any requirements to which the patient is subject under Section 8(1), and details of the patient's compliance,

(f) whether the patient is now suffering from a mental disorder and, if so, what the diagnosis is and why;

(g) whether the patient has a learning disability and, if so, whether that disability is associated with abnormally aggressive or seriously irresponsible conduct;

(h) details of any appropriate and available medical treatment prescribed, provided offered or planned for the patient's mental disorder;

(i) the strengths or positive factors relating to the patient;

(j) a summary of the patient's current progress, behaviour, capacity and insight;

(k) the patient's understanding of, compliance with, and likely future willingness to accept any prescribed medication or comply with any appropriate medical treatment for mental disorder that is, or might be, made available;

(l) details of any incidents where the patient has harmed themselves or others, or threatened harm, or damaged property, or threatened damage;

(m) whether, and if so how, any risks could be managed effectively in the community;

(n) whether it is necessary for the welfare of the patient, or for the protection of others, that the patient should remain under guardianship and, if so, why;

(o) any recommendations to the tribunal, with reasons.

## Social Circumstances Report – guardianship patients

24. The report must be up-to-date, specifically prepared for the tribunal and have numbered paragraphs and pages. It should be signed and dated. The sources of information for the events and incidents described should be made clear. This report should not be an addendum to (or reproduce extensive details from) previous reports, but must briefly describe the patient's recent relevant history and current presentation, and must include:

(a) whether there are any factors that might affect the patient's understanding or ability to cope with a hearing, and whether there are any adjustments that the tribunal may consider in order to deal with the case fairly and justly;

(b) details of any index offence(s), and other relevant forensic history;

(c) a chronology listing the patient's previous involvement with mental health services including any admissions to, discharge from and recall to hospital, and any previous instances of reception into guardianship;

(d) the patient's home and family circumstances;

(e) the housing or accommodation currently available to the patient;

(f) the patient's financial position (including benefit entitlements);

(g) any employment or available opportunities for employment;

(h) any requirements to which the patient is subject under Section 8(1), and details of the patient's compliance,

(i) the patient's previous response to community support;

(j) details of the community support that is being, or could be, made available to the patient, together with details of the current care plan;

(k) the current adequacy and effectiveness of the care plan;

(l) whether there are any issues as to funding the current or future care plan and, if so, the date by which those issues will be resolved;

(m) the strengths or positive factors relating to the patient;

(n)  a summary of the patient's current progress, behaviour, compliance and insight;

(o)  details of any incidents where the patient has harmed themselves or others, or threatened harm, or damaged property, or threatened damage;

(p)  the patient's views, wishes, beliefs, opinions, hopes and concerns;

(q)  the views of the guardian;

(r)  the views of the patient's nearest relative unless (having consulted the patient) it would inappropriate or impractical to consult the nearest relative, in which case give reasons for this view and describe any attempts to rectify matters;

(s)  the views of any other person who takes a lead role in the care and support of the patient but who is not professionally involved;

(t)  whether the patient is known to any MAPPA meeting or agency and, if so, in which area, for what reason, and at what level – together with the name of the Chair of any MAPPA meeting concerned with the patient, and the name of the representative of the lead agency;

(u)  in the event that a MAPPA meeting or agency wishes to put forward evidence of its views in relation to the level and management of risk, a summary of those views (or an Executive Summary may be attached to the report); and where relevant, a copy of the Police National Computer record of previous convictions should be attached;

(v)  whether, and if so how, any risks could be managed effectively in the community;

(w)  whether it is necessary for the welfare of the patient, or for the protection of others, that the patient should remain under guardianship and, if so, why;

(x)  any recommendations to the tribunal, with reasons.

## D. CONDITIONALLY DISCHARGED PATIENTS

25.  A conditionally discharged patient is a restricted patient who has been discharged from hospital into the community, subject to a condition that the patient will remain liable to be recalled to hospital for further treatment, should it become necessary. Other conditions may, in addition, be imposed by the tribunal, or by the Secretary of State (Ministry of Justice).

26.  This part only applies to restricted patients who have actually been granted a Conditional Discharge and who are living in the community. In the case of a restricted patient detained in hospital, the tribunal may make a provisional decision to order a Conditional Discharge. Before it finally grants a Conditional Discharge, the tribunal may defer its decision so that satisfactory arrangements can be put in place. Unless and until the tribunal finally grants a Conditional Discharge, the patient remains an in-patient, and so the in-patient part of this Practice Direction (and not this part) applies.

27.  Upon being notified by the tribunal of an application or reference, the responsible clinician must send or deliver the Responsible Clinician's Report, and any social supervisor must send or deliver the Social Circumstances Report. If there is no social supervisor, the Responsible Clinician's Report should also provide the required social circumstances information.

28.  The required reports, which must contain the specified information, are:

*   *Responsible Clinician's Report, including any relevant forensic history.*

*   *Social Circumstances Report from the patient's social supervisor, including details of any Section 117 aftercare plan and, where appropriate, the additional information required for patients under the age of 18, and any input from a Multi Agency Public Protection Arrangements (MAPPA) agency or meeting.*

29. The reports must be sent or delivered to the tribunal so that they are received by the tribunal as soon as practicable and in any event within three weeks after the Responsible Clinician or Social Supervisor (as the case may be) received the notification.

30. The responsible clinician and any social supervisor must also, at the same time, send copies of their reports to the Secretary of State (Ministry of Justice).

31. The authors of reports should have personally met and be familiar with the patient. If an existing report is more than six weeks old, or if the status or the circumstances of the patient change after the reports have been written but before the tribunal hearing takes place (e.g. if a patient is recalled), the author of the report should then send to the tribunal an addendum addressing the up-to-date situation and, where necessary, the new applicable statutory criteria.

### Responsible Clinician's Report – conditionally discharged patients

32. The report must be up-to-date, specifically prepared for the tribunal and have numbered paragraphs and pages. It should be signed and dated. The report should be written or counter-signed by the patient's responsible clinician. If there is no social supervisor, the Responsible Clinician's Report should also provide the required social circumstances information. The sources of information for the events and incidents described must be made clear. This report should not be an addendum to (or reproduce extensive details from) previous reports, or recite medical records, but must briefly describe the patient's recent relevant medical history and current mental health presentation, and must include:

    (a) whether there are any factors that might affect the patient's understanding or ability to cope with a hearing, and whether there are any adjustments that the tribunal may consider in order to deal with the case fairly and justly;

    (b) details of the patient's index offence(s), and any other relevant forensic history;

    (c) details and details of the patient's relevant forensic history;

    (d) a chronology listing the patient's involvement with mental health services, including any admissions to, discharge from and recall to hospital;

    (e) reasons for any previous recall following a Conditional Discharge and details of any previous failure to comply with conditions;

    (f) the circumstances leading up to the current Conditional Discharge;

    (g) any conditions currently imposed (whether by the tribunal or the Secretary of State), and the reasons why the conditions were imposed;

    (h) details of the patient's compliance with any current conditions;

    (i) whether the patient is now suffering from a mental disorder and, if so, what the diagnosis is and why;

    (j) whether the patient has a learning disability and, if so, whether that disability is associated with abnormally aggressive or seriously irresponsible conduct;

    (k) details of any legal proceedings or other arrangements relating to the patient's mental capacity, or their ability to make decisions or handle their own affairs;

    (l) details of any appropriate and available medical treatment prescribed, provided, offered or planned for the patient's mental disorder;

(m)  the strengths or positive factors relating to the patient;

(n)  a summary of the patient's current progress, behaviour, capacity and insight;

(o)  the patient's understanding of, compliance with, and likely future willingness to accept any prescribed medication or comply with any appropriate medical treatment for mental disorder;

(p)  details of any incidents where the patient has harmed themselves or others, or threatened harm, or damaged property, or threatened damage;

(q)  an assessment of the patient's prognosis, including the risk and likelihood of a recurrence or exacerbation of any mental disorder;

(r)  the risk and likelihood of the patient re-offending and the degree of harm to which others may be exposed if the patient does re-offend;

(s)  whether it is necessary for the patient's health or safety, or for the protection of others, that the patient should receive medical treatment and, if so, why;

(t)  whether the patient, if absolutely discharged, would be likely to act in a manner harmful to themselves or others, whether any such risks could be managed effectively in the community and, if so, how;

(u)  whether it continues to be appropriate for the patient to remain liable to be recalled for further medical treatment in hospital and, if so, why;

(v)  whether, and if so the extent to which, it is desirable to continue, vary and/or add to any conditions currently imposed;

(w)  any recommendations to the tribunal, with reasons.

## Social Circumstances Report – conditionally discharged patients

33.  The report must be up-to-date, specifically prepared for the tribunal and have numbered paragraphs and pages. It should be signed and dated. The sources of information for the events and incidents described should be made clear. This report should not be an addendum to (or reproduce extensive details from) previous reports, but must briefly describe the patient's recent relevant history and current presentation, and must include:

(a)  the patient's full name, date of birth, and current address;

(b)  the full official name of the responsible authority;

(c)  whether there are any factors that might affect the patient's understanding or ability to cope with a hearing, and whether there are any adjustments that the tribunal may consider in order to deal with the case fairly and justly;

(d)  details of the patient's index offence(s), and any other relevant forensic history;

(e)  a chronology listing the patient's involvement with mental health services including any admissions to, discharge from and recall to hospital;

(f)  any conditions currently imposed (whether by the Tribunal or the Secretary of State), and the reasons why the conditions were imposed;

(g)  details of the patient's compliance with any past or current conditions;

(h)  the patient's home and family circumstances;

(i)  the housing or accommodation currently available to the patient;

(j)   the patient's financial position (including benefit entitlements);

(k)   any employment or available opportunities for employment;

(l)   details of the community support or Section 117 aftercare that is being, or could be made available to the patient, together with details of the current care plan;

(m)   whether there are any issues as to funding the current or future care plan and, if so, the date by which those issues will be resolved;

(n)   the current adequacy and effectiveness of the care plan;

(o)   the strengths or positive factors relating to the patient;

(p)   a summary of the patient's current progress, compliance, behaviour and insight;

(q)   details of any incidents where the patient has harmed themselves or others, or threatened harm, or damaged property, or threatened damage;

(r)   the patient's views, wishes, beliefs, opinions, hopes and concerns;

(s)   the views of any partner, family member or close friend who takes a lead role in the care and support of the patient but who is not professionally involved;

(t)   whether the patient is known to any Multi Agency Public Protection Arrangements (MAPPA) meeting or agency and, if so, in which area, for what reason, and at what level – together with the name of the Chair of any MAPPA meeting concerned with the patient, and the name of the representative of the lead agency;

(u)   in the event that a MAPPA meeting or agency wishes to put forward evidence of its views in relation to the level and management of risk, a summary of those views (or an Executive Summary may be attached to the report); and where relevant, a copy of the Police National Computer record of previous convictions should be attached;

(v)   in the case of an eligible compliant patient who lacks capacity to agree or object to their placement or treatment, whether or not deprivation of liberty under the Mental Capacity Act 2005 (as amended) would be more appropriate;

(w)   whether the patient, if absolutely discharged, would be likely to act in a manner harmful to themselves or others, whether any such risks could be managed effectively in the community and, if so, how;

(x)   whether it continues to be appropriate for the patient to remain liable to be recalled for further medical treatment in hospital and, if so, why;

(y)   whether, and if so the extent to which, it is desirable to continue, vary and/or add to any conditions currently imposed;

(z)   any recommendations to the tribunal, with reasons.

## E. PATIENTS UNDER THE AGE OF 18

34.   All the above requirements in respect of statements and reports apply, as appropriate, depending upon the type of case.

35.   In addition, *for all patients under the age of 18*, the Social Circumstances Report must also state:

(a)   the names and addresses of any people with parental responsibility, and how they acquired parental responsibility;

(b) which public bodies either have worked together or need to liaise in relation to aftercare services that may be provided under Section 117 of the Act;

(c) the outcome of any liaison that has taken place;

(d) if liaison has not taken place, why not – and when liaison will take place;

(e) the details of any multi-agency care plan in place or proposed;

(f) whether there are any issues as to funding the care plan and, if so, the date by which those issues will be resolved;

(g) the name and contact details of the patient's care coordinator, community psychiatric nurse, social worker/AMHP or social supervisor;

(h) whether the patient's needs have been assessed under the Children Act 1989 or the Chronically Sick and Disabled Persons Act 1970 and, if not, the reasons why such an assessment has not been carried out and whether it is proposed to carry out such an assessment;

(i) if there has been such an assessment, what needs or requirements have been identified and how those needs or requirements will be met;

(j) if the patient is subject to or has been the subject of a care order or an interim care order:

- the date and duration of any such order;

- the identity of the relevant local authority;

- the identity of any person(s) with whom the local authority shares parental responsibility;

- whether there are any proceedings which have yet to conclude and, if so, the court in which proceedings are taking place and the date of the next hearing;

- whether the patient comes under the Children (Leaving Care) Act 2000;

- whether there has been any liaison between, on the one hand, social workers responsible for mental health services to children and adolescents and, on the other hand, those responsible for such services to adults;

- the name of the social worker within the relevant local authority who is discharging the function of the nearest relative under Section 27 of the Act;

(k) if the patient is subject to guardianship under Section 7 of the Act, whether any orders have been made under the Children Act 1989 in respect of the patient, and what consultation there has been with the guardian;

(l) if the patient is a ward of court, when the patient was made a ward of court and what steps have been taken to notify the court that made the order of any significant steps taken, or to be taken, in respect of the patient;

(m) whether any other orders under the Children Act 1989 are in existence in respect of the patient and, if so, the details of those orders, together with the date on which such orders were made, and whether they are final or interim orders;

(n) if a patient has been or is a looked after child under section 20 of the Children Act 1989, when the child became looked after, why the child became looked after, what steps have been taken to discharge the obligations of the local authority under paragraph 17(1) of Schedule 2 of the Children Act 1989, and what steps are being taken (if required) to discharge the obligations of the local authority under paragraph 10 (b) of Schedule 2 of the Children Act 1989;

(o) if a patient has been treated by a local authority as a child in need (which includes a child who has a mental disorder) under Section 17(11) of the Children Act 1989, the period or periods for which the child has been so treated, why they were considered to be a child in need, what services were or are being made available to the child by virtue of that status, and details of any assessment of the child;

(p) if a patient has been the subject of a secure accommodation order under Section 25 of the Children Act 1989, the date on which the order was made, the reasons it was made, and the date it expired;

(q) if a patient is a child provided with accommodation under Sections 85 and 86 of the Children Act 1989, what steps have been taken by the accommodating authority or the person carrying on the establishment in question to discharge their notification responsibilities, and what steps have been taken by the local authority to discharge their obligations under Sections 85, 86 and 86A of the Children Act 1989.

# The Mental Health Review Tribunal for Wales Rules 2008

## CONTENTS

## CHAPTER 2

## CHAPTER 3

## PART 4

## PART 5

## PART 1

*Introduction*

### Citation and commencement

1. These Rules may be cited as the Mental Health Review Tribunal for Wales Rules 2008 and come into force on 3 November 2008.

### Interpretation

2. (1) In these Rules –

"the Act" means the Mental Health Act 1983;

"applicant" means a person who –

(a) starts Tribunal proceedings, whether by making an application or a reference, or

(b) is substituted as a party under rule 12 (substitution and addition of parties);

"document" means anything in which information is recorded in any form, and an obligation under these Rules to provide or allow access to a document or a copy of a document for any purpose means, unless the Tribunal directs otherwise, an obligation to provide or allow access to such document or copy in a legible form or in a form which can be readily made into a legible form;

"final determination" means a decision of the Tribunal which disposes of proceedings, including a decision with recommendations or a deferred decision for conditional discharge, but a refusal of an application for permission to appeal under rule 30 (application for permission to appeal) is not a final determination;

"hearing" means an oral hearing and includes a hearing conducted in whole or in part by video link, telephone or other means of instantaneous two-way electronic communication;

"interested party" means a person added as an interested party under rule 12 (substitution and addition of parties);

"legal representative" means an authorised advocate or authorised litigator as defined by section 119(1) of the Courts and Legal Services Act 1990;

"party" means the patient, the responsible authority, the Secretary of State (if the patient is a restricted patient), the Welsh Ministers or Secretary of State in a reference under rule 15(7) (seeking approval under section 86 of the Act) and any other person who starts a case by making an application or referring a matter to the Tribunal under the Act;

"registered person" means the person or persons registered in respect of a registered establishment;

"responsible authority" means –

(a)   in relation to a patient detained under the Act in a hospital within the meaning of Part 2 of that Act, the managers (as defined in section 145 of the Act);

(b)   in relation to a patient subject to guardianship, the responsible local social services authority as defined in section 34(3) of the Act;

(c)   in relation to a community patient, the managers of the responsible hospital (as defined in section 145 of the Act);

(d)   in relation to a patient subject to aftercare under supervision, the local health board or primary care trust which has the duty to provide such aftercare for the patient;

"restricted patient" has the meaning set out in section 79(1) of the Act;

"Tribunal" means the Mental Health Review Tribunal for Wales;

"working day" means any day except a Saturday or Sunday, Christmas Day, Good Friday or a bank holiday under section 1 of the Banking and Financial Dealings Act 1971.

(2)   In these Rules, any reference to a rule or Schedule alone is a reference to a rule or Schedule in these Rules.

## Overriding objective

3.   (1)   The overriding objective of these Rules is to enable the Tribunal to deal with cases fairly, justly, efficiently and expeditiously.

(2)   Dealing with a case in accordance with paragraph (1) includes –

(a)   avoiding unnecessary formality and seeking flexibility in the proceedings;

(b)   ensuring, so far as practicable, that the parties are able to participate fully in the proceedings;

(c)   using any special expertise of the Tribunal effectively; and

(d)   avoiding delay, so far as compatible with proper consideration of the issues.

(3) The Tribunal must seek to give effect to the overriding objective when it –

    (a) exercises any power under these Rules; or

    (b) interprets any rule.

## PART 2

## General powers and provisions

### Preliminary and incidental matters

4. As regards matters preliminary or incidental to an application or reference, the chairman may, at any time up to the hearing of an application or reference by the Tribunal, exercise the powers of the Tribunal under rules 5, 6, 10, 12, 13, 14, 15, 16, 17, 21, 22, 26, 28 and 29.

### Case management powers

5. (1) The Tribunal may give directions at any time in relation to the conduct or disposal of proceedings.

    (2) In particular, and without restriction on the general power to give directions under paragraph (1) and any other provisions within these Rules, the Tribunal may by directions –

        (a) extend or shorten the time for complying with any rule or direction (unless such extension or abridgement would conflict with a provision of an enactment containing a time limit) if –

            (i) the party requiring the extension or abridgement has shown a good reason why it is necessary; and

            (ii) the Tribunal considers the extension or abridgement to be in the interests of justice;

        (b) permit or require a party to amend a document;

        (c) permit or require a party or another person to provide documents, information or submissions to the Tribunal or, subject to rule 17 (withholding documents or information likely to cause harm), a party;

        (d) provide that an issue in the proceedings will be dealt with as a preliminary issue;

        (e) hold a hearing to consider any matter, including a case management issue;

        (f) decide the form of any hearing;

        (g) stay execution of its own decision pending an appeal of such decision;

        (h) stay proceedings.

    (3) Rule 6 (directions) sets out the procedures for applying for and giving directions.

### Directions

6. (1) The Tribunal may give a direction at any time, including a direction amending or suspending an earlier direction.

    (2) The Tribunal may give a direction –

        (a) on the application of one or more of the parties; or

        (b) on its own initiative.

(3)   An application for directions must include the reason for making that application.

(4)   An application for directions may be made either –

(a)   by sending or delivering a written application to the Tribunal; or

(b)   orally during the course of a hearing.

(5)   Unless the Tribunal considers that there is a good reason not to do so, the Tribunal must send written notice of any direction to every party and any other person affected by the direction.

## Failure to comply with rules or directions

7.  (1)   An irregularity resulting from a failure to comply with any provision of these Rules or a direction does not of itself render void the proceedings or any step taken in the proceedings.

(2)   If a party has failed to comply with a requirement in these Rules or a direction, the Tribunal may take such action the Tribunal considers just, which may include –

(a)   waiving the requirement; or

(b)   requiring the failure to be remedied.

## Calculating time

8.  (1)   An act required by these Rules or a direction to be done on or by a particular day must be done before 5pm on that day.

(2)   If the time specified by these Rules or a direction for doing any act ends on a day other than a working day, the act is done in time if it is done on the next working day.

## Sending and delivery of documents

9.  (1)   Any document to be sent or delivered to the Tribunal under these Rules must be –

(a)   sent by pre-paid post or delivered by hand;

(b)   sent by facsimile transmission to the number specified by the Tribunal; or

(c)   sent or delivered by such other method as the Tribunal may permit or direct.

(2)   Subject to paragraph (3), a party may inform the Tribunal and all other parties that a particular form of communication (other than pre-paid post or delivery by hand) should not be used to send documents to that party.

(3)   If a party provides a facsimile transmission number, email address or other details for the electronic transmission of documents to them, that party must accept delivery of documents by that method.

(4)   Subject to paragraph (3), where any document is required or authorised by these Rules to be sent to any person it may be sent by prepaid post or delivered to the last known address of the person to whom the document is directed.

## Prohibitions on disclosure or publication

10. (1)   Unless the Tribunal gives a direction to the contrary, information about proceedings before the Tribunal and the names of any persons concerned in such proceedings must not be made public.

(2) The Tribunal may make an order prohibiting the disclosure or publication of –

    (a) specified documents or information relating to the proceedings; or

    (b) any matter likely to lead members of the public to identify any person who the Tribunal considers should not be identified.

(3) The Tribunal may use the power in paragraph (2) in order to take action under rule 17 (withholding documents or information likely to cause harm) and in such other circumstances as it considers just.

## Appointment of the tribunal

11. (1) A person shall not be qualified to serve as a member of a Tribunal for the purpose of any proceedings where –

    (a) that person is a member, director or registered person (as the case may be) of the responsible authority concerned in the proceedings; or

    (b) that person is a member or director of a local health board or National Health Service trust which has the right to discharge the patient under section 23(3) of the Act; or

    (c) the chairman or, as the case may be, president of the Tribunal considers that that person appears to have a conflict of interest or bias of opinion in respect of the patient, or any other member of that Tribunal or party to the proceedings, or has recently been involved with the medical treatment of the patient in a professional capacity.

(2) The persons qualified to serve as president of the Tribunal for the consideration of an application or reference relating to a restricted patient shall be restricted to those legal members who have been approved for that purpose by the Lord Chief Justice after consulting the Lord Chancellor.

(3) The Lord Chief Justice may nominate a judicial office holder (as defined in section 109(4) of the Constitutional Reform Act 2005) to exercise his functions referred to in paragraph (2).

## Substitution and addition of parties

12. (1) The Tribunal may give a direction substituting a party if –

    (a) the wrong person has been named as a party; or

    (b) the substitution has become necessary because of a change in circumstances since the start of proceedings.

(2) The Tribunal may give a direction adding a person to the proceedings as an interested party.

(3) If the Tribunal gives a direction under paragraph (1) or (2) it may give such consequential directions as it considers appropriate.

## Representatives

13. (1) A party may appoint a representative (whether legally qualified or not) to represent that party in the proceedings, not being a person liable to be detained or subject to guardianship or aftercare under supervision or a community patient under the Act, or a person receiving treatment for mental disorder at the same hospital or registered establishment as the patient.

(2) If a party appoints a representative, that party or representative must send or deliver to the Tribunal written notice of the representative's name and address.

(3)  Anything permitted or required to be done by or provided to a party under these Rules or a direction, other than signing a witness statement, may be done by or provided to the representative of that party.

(4)  In the event of a representative being duly appointed –

    (a)  the Tribunal and other parties may assume that the representative is and remains authorised until receiving written notification to the contrary from the representative or the represented party; and

    (b)  the Tribunal must provide to the representative any document which is required to be sent to the represented party, and need not provide that document to the represented party.

(5)  The Tribunal may appoint a legal representative for the patient if –

    (a)  the patient has not appointed a representative; and

    (b)  (i)  the patient has stated that they do not wish to conduct their own case or that they wish to be represented; or

       (ii)  the patient lacks the capacity to appoint a representative but the Tribunal believes that it is in the patient's best interests for the patient to be represented.

(6)  Unless the Tribunal otherwise directs, a patient or any other party may be accompanied by such other person as the patient or party wishes, in addition to any representative that may have been appointed under this Rule, provided that such person does not act as the representative of the patient or other party.

## PART 3

*Proceedings before the Tribunal*

## CHAPTER 1

*Before the final determination*

### Procedure for applications and references

14.  (1)  An application or reference must be made in writing, be signed (in the case of an application, by the applicant or any person authorised by the applicant to do so) and be provided to the Tribunal so that it is received within the time specified in the Act or the Repatriation of Prisoners Act 1984.

    (2)  An application or reference must, if possible, include –

       (a)  the name and address of the patient;

       (b)  in the event of an application being made by the patient's nearest relative, that person's name, address and relationship to the patient;

       (c)  the provision under which the patient is detained or liable to be detained, subject to guardianship or aftercare under supervision or a community patient;

       (d)  whether the person making the application has appointed a representative or intends to do so, and the name and address of any representative appointed;

       (e)  the name and address of the responsible authority in relation to the patient.

    (3)  On receipt of an application or reference, the Tribunal must send notice of the same to –

(a)   the responsible authority;

(b)   the patient (where the patient is not the applicant); and

(c)   if the patient is a restricted patient, the Secretary of State.

### Statements, reports and documents

15. (1)   Subject to rule 17 (withholding documents or information likely to cause harm), when the Tribunal receives a document from any party it must send a copy of that document to each other party.

(2)   When the Tribunal receives an application or reference it must send to the responsible authority or the Secretary of State, as the case may be, a request for the documents and information required to be provided under paragraph (3), (4) or (5).

(3)   In proceedings under section 66(1)(a) of the Act (application for admission for assessment), on the earlier of receipt of the copy of the application or receipt of a request from the Tribunal, the responsible authority must send or deliver to the Tribunal by the commencement of the hearing –

(a)   the application for admission;

(b)   the written medical recommendation or recommendations, as the case may be, of the registered medical practitioners on which the application is founded;

(c)   such of the information specified in Part A of the Schedule as is within the knowledge of the responsible authority and can reasonably be provided in the time available; and

(d)   such of the reports specified in Part B of the Schedule as can reasonably be provided in the time available.

(4)   If the patient is a conditionally discharged patient the Secretary of State shall send to the Tribunal as soon as practicable, and in any event within six weeks of receipt by the Secretary of State of a copy of the application or request from the Tribunal, a statement which shall contain –

(a)   the information specified in Part C of the Schedule, in so far as it is within the knowledge of the Secretary of State; and

(b)   the reports specified in Part D of the Schedule, in so far as it is reasonably practicable to provide them.

(5)   If neither paragraph (3) nor (4) applies, the responsible authority must send a statement to the Tribunal as soon as practicable, and in any event within three weeks of receipt by the responsible authority of a copy of the application or receipt of a request from the Tribunal, a statement which shall contain –

(a)   the information specified in Part A of the Schedule, in so far as it is within the knowledge of the responsible authority;

(b)   the report specified in paragraph 1 of Part B of that Schedule; and

(c)   the other reports specified in Part B of the Schedule, in so far as it is reasonably practicable to provide them.

(6)   If the patient is a restricted patient the responsible authority must also send the statement under paragraph (5) to the Secretary of State, and the Secretary of State must send a statement of any further relevant information to the Tribunal as soon as practicable and in any event –

(a)  in proceedings under section 75(1) of the Act, within two weeks of receipt by the Secretary of State of the relevant authority's statement; or

(b)  otherwise, within three weeks of receipt by the Secretary of State of the relevant authority's statement.

(7)  If the Welsh Ministers or Secretary of State wish to seek the approval of the Tribunal under section 86(3) of the Act, the Welsh Ministers or Secretary of State, as the case may be, must refer the patient's case to the Tribunal and the provisions of these Rules applicable to references under the Act apply to the proceedings.

## Notice of proceedings

16. (1)  When the Tribunal receives the information required by rule 15(3), (4) or (5), the Tribunal must give notice of the proceedings –

(a)  where the patient is subject to the guardianship of a private guardian, to the guardian;

(b)  where there is an extant order of the superior court of record established by section 45(1) of the Mental Capacity Act 2005, to that court;

(c)  unless the patient requests otherwise, where any person other than the applicant is named in the responsible authority's statement as exercising the functions of the nearest relative, to that person;

(d)  where a local health board, a National Health Service trust, a primary care trust, a NHS Foundation Trust, a Strategic Health Authority, the Welsh Ministers or the Secretary of State has or have a right to discharge the patient under the provisions of section 23(3) of the Act, to such board, trust, authority, person or persons; and

(e)  to any other person the Tribunal may consider should have an opportunity of being heard.

## Withholding documents or information likely to cause harm

17. (1)  The Tribunal must give a direction prohibiting the disclosure of a document or information to a person if it is satisfied that –

(a)  such disclosure would be likely to cause that person or some other person serious harm; and

(b)  having regard to the interests of justice that it is proportionate to give such a direction.

(2)  If a party ("the first party") considers that the Tribunal should give a direction under paragraph (1) prohibiting the disclosure of part or all of a document or of information to another party ("the second party"), the first party must –

(a)  exclude that part of the relevant document or that information from any document that will be provided to the second party; and

(b)  provide to the Tribunal the excluded part of document or information and the reason for its exclusion, in order that the Tribunal may decide whether the document or information should be disclosed to the second party or should be the subject of a direction under paragraph (1).

(3)  The Tribunal must conduct proceedings as appropriate in order to avoid undermining a direction given under paragraph (1).

(4) If the Tribunal gives a direction under paragraph (1) which prevents disclosure to a party who has a representative, the Tribunal may give a direction that the document or information be disclosed to that representative if it is satisfied that –

    (a) disclosure to the representative would be in the interests of the party; and

    (b) the representative would not be likely to act contrary to paragraph (5).

(5) Documents or information disclosed to a representative in accordance with a direction under paragraph (4) must not –

    (a) be disclosed either directly or indirectly to any other person without the Tribunal's consent; or

    (b) be used otherwise than in connection with the proceedings.

## Further evidence and submissions

18. (1) Without restriction on the general powers in rule 5(1) and (2) (case management powers), the Tribunal may give directions as to –

    (a) issues on which it requires evidence or submissions;

    (b) the nature of the evidence or submissions it requires;

    (c) whether the parties are permitted or requested to provide expert evidence;

    (d) any limit on the number of witnesses whose evidence a party may put forward, whether in relation to a particular issue or generally;

    (e) the manner in which any evidence or submissions are to be provided, which may include a direction for them to be given –

        (i) orally at a hearing; or

        (ii) by written submissions or witness statement; and

    (f) the time in which any evidence or submissions are to be provided.

(2) The Tribunal may –

    (a) admit evidence whether or not –

        (i) the evidence would be admissible in a civil trial in the United Kingdom; or

        (ii) the evidence was available to a previous decision maker;

    (b) exclude evidence that would otherwise be admissible where –

        (i) the evidence was not provided within the time allowed by a direction;

        (ii) the evidence was otherwise provided in a manner that did not comply with a direction; or

        (iii) it would otherwise be unfair to admit the evidence.

(3) The Tribunal may require any witness to give evidence on oath or affirmation, and may administer an oath or affirmation for that purpose.

## Summoning of witnesses and orders to answer questions or produce documents

19. (1) On the application of a party or on its own initiative, the Tribunal may –

(a) by summons require any person to attend as a witness at a hearing at the time and place specified in the summons, provided that –

    (i) the person has been given reasonable notice of the hearing; and

    (ii) unless the person is a party to the proceedings, the summons makes provision for the person's necessary expenses of attendance to be paid, and states by whom; and

(b) by order require any person to answer any questions or produce any documents in that person's possession or control which relate to any issue in the proceedings.

(2) A summons under this rule must, if the person to whom it is addressed has not had an opportunity to object to it, state that the person may apply to the Tribunal to vary or set aside the summons.

(3) When a summons is issued, the Tribunal must send a copy of the summons to each party to the proceedings.

(4) No person may be compelled to give any evidence or produce any document that the person could not be compelled to give or produce on a trial of an action in a court of law in England or Wales.

## Medical examination

20. (1) Before the hearing to consider the final determination, a medical member of the Tribunal must, so far as practicable –

    (a) examine the patient; and

    (b) take such other steps as that member considers necessary to form an opinion of the patient's mental condition.

(2) For the purposes of paragraph (1) that member may –

    (a) examine the patient in private;

    (b) examine records relating to the detention or treatment of the patient and any aftercare services;

    (c) take notes and copies of records for use in connection with the proceedings.

(3) At any time before the Tribunal makes the final determination, the Tribunal or any one or more of its members may interview the patient, which interview may take place in the absence of any other person.

## Postponement and adjournment

21. (1) The Tribunal may at any time postpone or adjourn a hearing for the purpose of obtaining further information or for such other purposes as it may think appropriate.

(2) Before postponing or adjourning any hearing, the Tribunal may give such direction as it thinks fit for ensuring the prompt consideration of the application at a postponed or adjourned hearing.

(3) Where a party requests that a hearing postponed or adjourned in accordance with this rule be reconvened, the hearing must be reconvened if the Tribunal is satisfied that reconvening would be in the interests of the patient.

(4) Save in respect of an application under section 66(1)(a) of the Act, before the Tribunal reconvenes any hearing which has been adjourned without a further hearing date being

fixed, it must give to all parties not less than 14 days' notice (or such shorter notice as all parties may consent to) of the date, time and place of the reconvened hearing.

## Withdrawal

22. (1) Subject to paragraphs (2) to (3), an applicant may withdraw an application by sending to the Tribunal a written notice of withdrawal stating reasons.

    (2) Before making a withdrawal under paragraph (1), the consent of the Tribunal must be obtained.

    (3) Where an application is withdrawn, the Tribunal shall so inform the parties and such other persons as the Tribunal considers necessary.

    (4) A reference made by the Welsh Ministers or the Secretary of State in circumstances in which they are not by the terms of the Act obliged to make a reference may be withdrawn by the Welsh Ministers or the Secretary of State, as the case may be, at any time before it is considered by the Tribunal and, where a reference is so withdrawn, the Tribunal shall inform the patient and the other parties that the reference has been withdrawn.

## Transfer of proceedings

23. (1) Where any proceedings in relation to a patient have not been disposed of by the members of the Tribunal appointed for the purpose, and the chairman is of the opinion that it is not practicable or not possible without undue delay for the consideration of those proceedings to be completed by those members, he shall make arrangements for them to be heard by other members of the Tribunal.

    (2) Where a patient in respect of whom proceedings are pending moves to the jurisdiction of the First-tier Tribunal, the proceedings shall, if the chairman of the Tribunal so directs, be transferred to the First-tier Tribunal and notice of the transfer of proceedings shall be given to the parties and such other persons as the Tribunal considers necessary.

## CHAPTER 2

*Hearings*

## Time and place of hearings

24. (1) In proceedings under section 66(1)(a) of the Act the hearing of the case must start within 7 days after the date on which the Tribunal received the application.

    (2) In proceedings under section 75(1) of the Act, the hearing of the case must start at least 5 weeks but no more than eight weeks after the date that the Tribunal received the reference.

    (3) Subject to paragraph (4), the Tribunal must give the parties reasonable notice, and in any event no less than 14 days' notice, of the date, time and place of any hearing (including any adjourned or postponed hearing) and any changes to the time and place of any hearing, except that in proceedings under section 66(1)(a) of the Act the Tribunal must give at least three days' notice.

    (4) The Tribunal may give less notice than that required under paragraph (3) –

(a) with the parties' consent; or

(b) in urgent or exceptional circumstances.

## Privacy of hearings

25. (1) Except where a patient requests a hearing in public and the Tribunal is satisfied that that would be in the interests of the patient, all hearings must be held in private.

    (2) Where the Tribunal refuses a request for a public hearing or directs that a hearing which has begun in public shall continue in private, the Tribunal must record in writing its reasons for holding the hearing in private and shall inform the patient of those reasons.

    (3) Where a hearing is held in private, the Tribunal may –

        (a) exclude particular individuals from the hearing or part of it; or

        (b) permit particular individuals to attend the hearing or part of it on such terms as it considers appropriate.

    (4) The Tribunal may give a direction excluding from the hearing, or part of it –

        (a) any person whose conduct, in the opinion of the Tribunal, is disrupting or is likely to disrupt the hearing;

        (b) any person whose presence the Tribunal considers is likely to prevent another person from giving evidence or making submissions freely; or

        (c) any person who the Tribunal considers should be excluded in order to give effect to a direction under rule 17 (withholding information likely to cause harm).

    (5) The Tribunal may give a direction excluding a witness from a hearing until that witness gives evidence.

## Request to appear at and take part in a hearing

26. The Tribunal may give a direction permitting or requesting any person to –

    (a) attend and take part in a hearing to such extent as the Tribunal considers appropriate; or

    (b) make written submissions in relation to a particular issue.

## Hearings in a party's absence

27. (1) If a party fails to attend a hearing, the Tribunal may proceed with the hearing if –

        (a) the Tribunal –

            (i) is satisfied that the party has been notified of the hearing or that reasonable steps have been taken to notify the party of the hearing; and

            (ii) the Tribunal is not aware of any good reason for the failure to attend; or

        (b) the Tribunal otherwise considers that it is in the interests of the patient to proceed with the hearing.

## CHAPTER 3

*Decisions*

**Decisions**

28. (1) The Tribunal may give a decision orally at a hearing or may reserve its decision.

    (2) The Tribunal must send to each party as soon as reasonably practicable following a final determination –

      (a) a notice stating the Tribunal's decision; and

      (b) written reasons for the decision.

    (3) The documents referred to in paragraph (2) must be sent –

      (a) in proceedings under section 66(1)(a) of the Act, within three working days of the hearing; and

      (b) in other proceedings, within seven days of the hearing.

    (4) Where the Tribunal considers that the full disclosure of the recorded reasons for its decision to the patient would cause the patient or any other person serious harm, the Tribunal may instead communicate its decision to him in such manner as it thinks appropriate and may communicate its decision to the other parties subject to any conditions it may think appropriate as to the disclosure thereof to the patient.

    (5) Where the Tribunal makes a decision with recommendations, the decision may specify any period at the expiration of which the Tribunal will consider the case further in the event of those recommendations not being complied with.

    (6) Subject to rule 10 (prohibitions on disclosure or publication) the Tribunal may, where appropriate, send notice of a decision or the reasons for it to any person.

## PART 4

*Correcting and appealing Tribunal decisions*

**Clerical mistakes, accidental slips or omissions and irregularities**

29. (1) The Tribunal may at any time correct any clerical mistake or other accidental slip or omission in a decision, direction or any document produced by it, by sending notification of the amended decision or direction, or a copy of the amended document, to all parties.

    (2) Any irregularity resulting from failure to comply with these Rules before the Tribunal has determined an application shall not of itself render the proceedings void, but the Tribunal may, and must if it considers that any person may have been prejudiced, take such steps to cure the irregularity as it thinks fit before determining the application, whether by the amendment of any document, the giving of any notice or otherwise.

**Application for permission to appeal**

30. (1) This rule applies to an application for permission to appeal against a decision of the Tribunal on a point of law under section 78A of the Act (appeal from the Tribunal to the Upper Tribunal).

    (2) A party seeking permission to appeal must send or deliver to the Tribunal a written application for permission to appeal so that it is received no later than 28 days after

the date that the Tribunal sent written reasons for the decision to the party making the application.

(3)  If the party sends or delivers the application to the Tribunal later than the time required by paragraph (2) or by any extension of time under rule 5(2)(a) (power to extend time) –

   (a)  the application must include a request for an extension of time and the reason why the application was not provided in time; and

   (b)  unless the Tribunal extends time for the application under rule 5(2)(a), the Tribunal must not admit the application.

(4)  An application under paragraph (2) must –

   (a)  identify the decision of the Tribunal to which it relates;

   (b)  identify the alleged error or errors of law in the decision; and

   (c)  state the result the party making the application seeks.

(5)  Upon considering the application for permission to appeal, the Tribunal must send to the parties as soon as practicable –

   (a)  a record of its decision; and

   (b)  if the Tribunal has refused to grant permission –

      (i)  reasons for such refusal; and

      (ii)  notification of the right to make an application to the Upper Tribunal for permission to appeal and the time within which, and the method by which, such application must be made.

(6)  The Tribunal may grant permission to appeal on limited grounds, but must comply with paragraph (5)(b) in relation to any grounds on which it has refused permission.

## PART 5

*Revocations*

### Revocations

31.  The Mental Health Review Tribunal Rules 1983, the Mental Health Review Tribunal (Amendment) Rules 1996 and the Mental Health Review Tribunal (Amendment) Rules 1998 are revoked.

# SCHEDULE (Rule 15)

## Statements by the Responsible Authority and the Secretary of State

### PART A

### Information about patients (other than conditionally discharged patients)

1.  The patient's full name (and any alternative names used in patient records).

2.  The patient's date of birth and age.

3. The patient's language of choice and, if it is not English or Welsh, whether an interpreter is required.

4. The application, order or direction made under the Act to which the tribunal proceedings relate and the date on which that application, order or direction commenced.

5. Details of the original authority for the detention or guardianship of the patient, including the statutory basis for that authority and details of any subsequent renewal of or change in that authority.

6. In cases where a patient has been transferred to hospital under section 45A, 47 or 48 of the Act, details of the order, direction or authority under which the patient was being held in custody before his transfer to hospital.

7. Except in relation to a patient subject to guardianship or aftercare under supervision, or a community patient, the hospital or hospital unit at which the patient is presently liable to be detained under the Act, and the ward or unit on which he is presently detained.

8. If a condition or requirement has been imposed that requires the patient to reside at a particular place, details of the condition or requirement and the address at which the patient is required to reside;

9. In the case of a community patient, details of any conditions attaching to the patient's community treatment order under section 17B(2) of the Act.

10. The name of the patient's responsible clinician and the length of time the patient has been under their care.

11. Where another approved clinician is or has recently been largely concerned in the treatment of the patient, the name of that clinician and the period that the patient has spent in that clinician's care.

12. The name of any care coordinator appointed for the patient.

13. Where the patient is subject to the guardianship of a private guardian, the name and address of that guardian.

14. Where there is an extant order of the superior court of record established by section 45(1) of the Mental Capacity Act 2005, the details of that order.

15. Unless the patient requests otherwise, the name and address of the person exercising the functions of the nearest relative of the patient.

16. Where a local health board, a National Health Service trust, a primary care trust, a NHS Foundation Trust, a Strategic Health Authority, the Welsh Ministers or the Secretary of State has or have a right to discharge the patient under the provisions of section 23(3) of the Act, the name and address of such board, trust, authority, person or persons.

17. In the case of a patient subject to aftercare under supervision, the name and address of the local social services authority and NHS body that are responsible for providing the patient with aftercare under section 117 of the Act, or will be when he leaves hospital.

18. The name and address of any person who plays a substantial part in the care of the patient but who is not professionally concerned with it.

19. The name and address of any other person who the responsible authority considers should be notified to the Tribunal.

## PART B

### Reports relating to patients (other than conditionally discharged patients)

1. An up-to-date clinical report, prepared for the Tribunal, including the relevant clinical history and a full report on the patient's mental condition.

2. An up-to-date social circumstances report prepared for the tribunal including reports on the following –

   (a) the patient's home and family circumstances, including the views of the patient's nearest relative or the person so acting;

   (b) the opportunities for employment or occupation and the housing facilities which would be available to the patient if discharged;

   (c) the availability of community support and relevant medical facilities;

   (d) the financial circumstances of the patient.

3. The views of the responsible authority on the suitability of the patient for discharge.

4. Where the provisions of section 117 of the Act may apply to the patient, a proposed aftercare plan in respect of the patient.

5. Any other information or observations on the application which the responsible authority wishes to make.

## PART C

### Information about conditionally discharged patients

1. The patient's full name (and any alternative names used in patient records).

2. The patient's date of birth and age.

3. The patient's language of choice and, if it is not English or Welsh, whether an interpreter is required.

4. The history of the patient's present liability to detention including details of the offence or offences, and the dates of the original order or direction and of the conditional discharge.

5. The name and address of any clinician responsible for the care and supervision of the patient in the community, and the period that the patient has spent under the care and supervision of that clinician.

6. The name and address of any social worker or probation officer responsible for the care and supervision of the patient in the community and the period that the patient has spent under the care and supervision of that person.

## PART D

### Reports relating to conditionally discharged patients

1. Where there is a clinician responsible for the care and supervision of the patient in the community, an up-to-date report prepared for the Tribunal including the relevant medical history and a full report on the patient's mental condition.

2. Where there is a social worker, probation officer or community psychiatric nurse responsible for the patient's care and supervision in the community, an up-to-date report prepared for the Tribunal on the patient's progress in the community since discharge from hospital.

3. A report on the patient's home circumstances.

4. The views of the Secretary of State on the suitability of the patient for absolute discharge.

5. Any other observations on the application which the Secretary of State wishes to make.

# Appendix 3

# The Mental Health Regulations

## 3A – MENTAL HEALTH (ENGLAND)

### Statutory Instrument No. 1184 2008

**The Mental Health (Hospital, Guardianship and Treatment) (England) Regulations 2008**

The Secretary of State for Health, in exercise of the powers conferred by sections 9, 17F(2), 19(1) and (4), 19A(1), 32(1), (2) and (3), 57(1)(b), 58A(1)(b), 64(2), 64H(2), 134(3A)(a) and 134(8) of the Mental Health Act 1983, makes the following regulations:

In accordance with sections 57A(4) and 58A(8) of that Act, the Secretary of State has consulted with such bodies as appear to the Secretary of State to be concerned.

### PART 1: GENERAL

#### Citation and commencement

1.  (1)  These Regulations may be cited as the Mental Health (Hospital, Guardianship and Treatment) (England) Regulations 2008 and shall come into force on 3 November 2008.

    (2)  These Regulations apply to England only.

#### Interpretation

2.  (1)  In these Regulations –

    "the Act" means the Mental Health Act 1983;

    "bank holiday" includes New Year's Day, Good Friday, Easter Monday, Christmas Day and Boxing Day;

    "business day" means any day except Saturday, Sunday or a bank holiday;

    "the Commission" means the Mental Health Act Commission referred to in section 121;

    "document" means any application, recommendation, record, report, order, notice or other document;

    "electronic communication" has the same meaning as in section 15(1) of the Electronic Communications Act 2000;

    "guardianship patient" means a person who is subject to guardianship under the Act;

"private guardian", in relation to a patient, means a person, other than a local social services authority, who acts as guardian under the Act;

"responsible registered establishment" is a registered establishment which is a responsible hospital;

"served", in relation to a document, includes addressed, delivered, given, forwarded, furnished or sent.

(2) Unless otherwise stated, any reference in these Regulations to –

    (a) a numbered section is to the section of the Act bearing that number;

    (b) an alphanumeric form is a reference to the form in Schedule 1 bearing that designation.

## Documents

3. (1) Except in a case to which paragraph (2), (3), (4) or (5) applies, or in a case to which regulation 6(3) (recall notices in respect of community patients) applies, any document required or authorised to be served upon any authority, body or person by or under Part 2 of the Act (compulsory admission to hospital, guardianship or community treatment orders) or these Regulations may be served by delivering it to –

    (a) the authority, body or person upon whom it is to be served;

    (b) any person authorised by that authority, body or person to receive it;

    (c) by sending it by pre-paid post addressed to –

        (i) the authority or body at their registered or principal office; or

        (ii) the person upon whom it is to be served at that person's usual or last known residence, or

    (d) by delivering it using an internal mail system operated by the authority, body or person upon whom it is to be served, if that authority, body or person agrees.

(2) Any application for the admission of a patient to a hospital under Part 2 of the Act shall be served by delivering the application to an officer of the managers of the hospital to which it is proposed that the patient shall be admitted, who is authorised by them to receive it.

(3) Where a patient is liable to be detained in a hospital under Part 2 of the Act –

    (a) any order by the nearest relative of the patient under section 23 for the patient's discharge, and

    (b) the notice of such order given under section 25(1), shall be served either by –

        (i) delivery of the order or notice at that hospital to an officer of the managers authorised by the managers to receive it, or

        (ii) sending it by pre-paid post to those managers at that hospital, or

        (iii) delivering it using an internal mail system operated by the managers upon whom it is to be served, if those managers agree.

(4) Where a patient is a community patient –

    (a) any order by the nearest relative of the patient under section 23 for the patient's discharge, and

(b) the notice of such order given under section 25(1A), shall be served by –

    (i) delivery of the order or notice at the patient's responsible hospital to an officer of the managers authorised by the managers to receive it,

    (ii) sending it by pre-paid post to those managers at that hospital, or

    (iii) delivering it using an internal mail system operated by the managers upon whom it is to be served, if those managers agree.

(5) Any report made under subsection (2) of section 5 (detention of patient already in hospital for 72 hours) shall be served by –

(a) delivery of the report to an officer of the managers of the hospital authorised by those managers to receive it, or

(b) delivering it using an internal mail system operated by the managers upon whom it is to be served, if those managers agree

(6) Where a document referred to in this regulation is sent by pre-paid –

(a) first class post, service is deemed to have taken place on the second business day following the day of posting;

(b) second class post, service is deemed to have taken place on the fourth business day following posting, unless the contrary is shown.

(7) Where a document under this regulation is delivered using an internal mail system, service is considered to have taken place immediately it is delivered into the internal mail system.

(8) Subject to sections 6(3) and 8(3) (proof of applications), any document –

(a) required or authorised by or under Part 2 of the Act or these Regulations, and

(b) purporting to be signed by a person required or authorised by or under that Part or these Regulations to do so, shall be received in evidence and be deemed to be such a document without further proof.

(9) Where under Part 2 of the Act or these Regulations the managers of a hospital are required to make any record or report, that function may be performed by an officer authorised by those managers in that behalf.

(10) Where under these Regulations the decision to accept service by a particular method requires the agreement of the managers of a hospital, that agreement may be given by an officer authorised by those managers in that behalf.

## PART 2: PROCEDURES AND RECORDS RELATING TO HOSPITAL ADMISSIONS, GUARDIANSHIP AND COMMUNITY TREATMENT ORDERS

### Procedure for and record of hospital admissions

4. (1) Subject to paragraph (2), for the purposes of admission to hospital under Part 2 of the Act –

(a) any application for admission for assessment under section 2 shall be in the form set out –

    (i) where made by the nearest relative, in Form A1,

    (ii) where made by an approved mental health professional, in Form A2;

    (b)  any medical recommendation for the purposes of section 2 shall be in the form set out –

        (i)   in the case of joint recommendations, in Form A3,

        (ii)  in any other case, in Form A4;

    (c)  any application for admission for treatment under section 3 shall be in the form set out –

        (i)   where made by the nearest relative, in Form A5,

        (ii)  where made by an approved mental health professional, in Form A6;

    (d)  any medical recommendation for the purposes of section 3 shall be in the form set out –

        (i)   in the case of joint recommendations, in Form A7,

        (ii)  in any other case, in Form A8;

    (e)  any emergency application under section 4 shall be in the form set out –

        (i)   where made by the nearest relative, in Form A9,

        (ii)  where made by an approved mental health professional, in Form A10;

    (f)  any medical recommendation for the purposes of section 4 shall be in the form set out in Form A11;

    (g)  any report made under subsection (2) of section 5 (detention of in-patient already in hospital for a maximum 72 hours) by –

        (i)   the registered medical practitioner or approved clinician in charge of the treatment of the patient, or

        (ii)  any person nominated by the registered medical practitioner or approved clinician to act for them, shall be in the form set out in Part 1 of Form H1 and the hospital managers shall record receipt of that report in Part 2 of that Form;

    (h)  any record made under subsection (4) of section 5 (power to detain an in-patient for a maximum of 6 hours) by a nurse of the class for the time being prescribed for the purposes of that subsection shall be in the form set out in Form H2.

(2)  For the purposes of any medical recommendation under sections 2, 3, 4 and 7 (admission for assessment, admission for treatment, admission for assessment in cases of emergency and application for guardianship respectively) in the case of –

    (a)  a single recommendation made in respect of a patient whom a doctor has examined in Wales, the medical recommendation shall be in the form required by Regulations made by the Welsh Ministers to similar effect for Wales;

    (b)  joint recommendations made in respect of a patient whom both doctors have examined in Wales, the medical recommendation shall be in the form required by Regulations made by the Welsh Ministers to similar effect for Wales;

    (c)  joint recommendations made in respect of a patient whom one doctor has examined in Wales and one doctor has examined in England, the medical recommendation shall either be in the form required by these Regulations or in the form required by Regulations made by the Welsh Ministers to similar effect for Wales.

(3)  For the purposes of section 15 (rectification of applications and recommendations), the managers of the hospital to which a patient has been admitted in pursuance of an application for assessment or for treatment may authorise an officer on their behalf –

    (a)  to consent under subsection (1) of that section to the amendment of the application or any medical recommendation given for the purposes of the application;

    (b)  to consider the sufficiency of a medical recommendation and, if the recommendation is considered insufficient, to give written notice as required by subsection (2) of that section.

(4)  Where a patient has been admitted to a hospital pursuant to an application under section 2, 3 or 4 (admission for assessment, admission for treatment and admission for assessment in cases of emergency respectively), a record of admission shall be made by the managers of that hospital in the form set out in Part 1 of Form H3 and shall be attached to the application.

(5)  Where a patient has been admitted to a hospital pursuant to an application under section 4 (admission for assessment in cases of emergency), a record of receipt of a second medical recommendation in support of the application for admission of the patient shall be made by the managers in the form set out in Part 2 of Form H3 and shall be attached to the application.

## Procedure for and acceptance of guardianship applications

5.  (1)  For the purposes of section 7 (application for guardianship) –

    (a)  an application for guardianship shall be in the form set out –

        (i)  where made by the nearest relative, in Part 1 of Form G1,

        (ii)  where made by an approved mental health professional, in Part 1 of Form G2;

    (b)  where a person other than a local social services authority is named as guardian, the statement of willingness of that person to act as guardian shall be in the form set out in Part 2 of Form G1 or, as the case may be, G2;

    (c)  any medical recommendation shall be in the form set out –

        (i)  in the case of joint recommendations, in Form G3,

        (ii)  in any other case, in Form G4.

(2)  Where an application for guardianship is accepted by the responsible local social services authority, it shall record its acceptance of the application in the form set out in Form G5 (which shall be attached to the application).

## Procedure for and records relating to community treatment orders

6.  (1)  For the purposes of section 17A (community treatment orders) –

    (a)  an order made by the responsible clinician shall be in the form set out in Parts 1 and 3 of Form CTO1;

    (b)  the agreement of the approved mental health professional shall be in the form set out in Part 2 of Form CTO1;

    (c)  as soon as reasonably practicable, the responsible clinician shall furnish the managers of the responsible hospital with that order.

(2)  For the purposes of section 17B (conditions in community treatment orders) –

    (a)  the conditions to which the patient is subject whilst the order remains in force shall be in the form set out in Form CTO1;

(b)  a variation of any of those conditions by the responsible clinician shall be in the form set out in Form CTO2;

(c)  as soon as reasonably practicable, the responsible clinician shall furnish the managers of the responsible hospital with Form CTO2.

(3)  For the purposes of section 17E (power to recall a community patient to hospital) –

(a)  a responsible clinician's notice recalling a patient to hospital shall be in the form set out in Form CTO3;

(b)  as soon as reasonably practicable, the responsible clinician shall furnish the managers of the hospital to which the patient is recalled with a copy of the notice recalling the patient to hospital;

(c)  where the patient is recalled to a hospital which is not the responsible hospital, the responsible clinician shall notify the managers of the hospital to which the patient is recalled in writing of the name and address of the responsible hospital;

(d)  the managers of the hospital to which the patient is recalled shall record the time and date of the patient's detention pursuant to that notice in the form set out in Form CTO4.

(4)  Where the patient's responsible hospital is in Wales, the patient's recall shall be effected in accordance with Regulations made by the Welsh Ministers to similar effect for Wales.

(5)  A responsible clinician's notice recalling a patient to hospital for the purposes of section 17E (power to recall a community patient to hospital) in Form CTO3 shall be served by –

(a)  delivering it by hand to the patient,

(b)  delivering it by hand to the patient's usual or last known address, or

(c)  sending it by pre-paid first class post addressed to the patient at the patient's usual or last known address.

(6)  Notice of recall in Form CTO3 is considered served –

(a)  in the case of sub-paragraph 5(a), immediately on delivery of the notice to the patient;

(b)  in the case of sub-paragraph 5(b), on the day (which does not have to be a business day) after it is delivered;

(c)  in the case of sub-paragraph 5(c), on the second business day after it was posted.

(7)  As soon as practicable following the patient's recall, the managers of the responsible hospital shall take such steps as are reasonably practicable to –

(a)  cause the patient to be informed, both orally and in writing, of the provisions of the Act under which the patient is for the time being detained and the effect of those provisions, and

(b)  ensure that the patient understands the effect, so far as is relevant to the patient's case, of sections 56 to 64 (consent to treatment).

(8)  For the purposes of section 17F (powers in respect of recalled patients) –

(a)  an order referred to in subsection (4) (responsible clinician's order revoking a community treatment order) shall be in the form set out in Parts 1 and 3 of Form CTO5;

(b)  a statement of an approved mental health professional referred to in that subsection (signifying agreement with the responsible clinician's opinion and that it is appropriate to revoke the order) shall be in the form set out in Part 2 of Form CTO5;

(c) as soon as practicable, the responsible clinician shall furnish the managers of the hospital to which the patient is recalled with that Form;

(d) where the patient is recalled to a hospital which is not the responsible hospital, the managers of that hospital shall (as soon as reasonably practicable) furnish the managers of the hospital which was the patient's responsible hospital prior to the revocation of the patient's community treatment order, with a copy of Form CTO5.

## Transfer from hospital to hospital or guardianship

7. (1) This regulation shall apply in respect of any patient ("a hospital patient") to whom section 19(1)(a) applies and who is not a patient transferred under –

(a) section 19(3) (transfer between hospitals under the same managers), or

(b) section 123(1) and (2) (transfers between and from special hospitals).

(2) A hospital patient may be transferred to another hospital where –

(a) an authority for transfer is given by the managers of the hospital in which the patient is liable to be detained in the form set out in Part 1 of Form H4, and

(b) those managers are satisfied that arrangements have been made for the admission of the patient to the hospital to which the patient is being transferred within a period of 28 days beginning with the date of the authority for transfer.

(3) Upon completion of the transfer of the patient, the managers of the hospital to which the patient is transferred shall record the patient's admission in the form set out in Part 2 of Form H4.

(4) A hospital patient may be transferred into the guardianship of a local social services authority, or a person approved by a local social services authority, where –

(a) an authority for transfer is given by the managers of the hospital in which the patient is detained in the form set out in Part 1 of Form G6;

(b) the transfer has been agreed by the local social services authority, which will be the responsible local social services authority if the proposed transfer takes effect;

(c) that local social services authority has specified the date on which the transfer shall take place;

(d) the managers of the transferring hospital have recorded the agreement of the local social services authority referred to in paragraph (b) and the date for transfer referred to in paragraph (c), in the form set out in Part 1 of that Form;

(e) in the case of a person other than a local social services authority being named as guardian, the agreement of that person to act as guardian is recorded in the form set out in Part 2 of that Form.

(5) A hospital patient who is detained in a registered establishment –

(a) may be transferred from that registered establishment to another registered establishment where both are under the same management, and paragraph (2) shall not apply, and

(b) where such a patient is maintained under a contract with a Strategic Health Authority, Local Health Board, Primary Care Trust, National Health Service trust, National Health Service foundation trust, a Special Health Authority or the Welsh Ministers, any authority for transfer required under paragraph (2)(a) or, as the case may be, (4)(a), and the record (where relevant) required under paragraph

(4)(d), may be made or given by an officer of that authority, board or trust authorised by that authority, board or trust in that behalf, or by those Ministers, instead of by the managers.

(6) The functions of the managers referred to in this regulation may be performed by an officer authorised by them in that behalf.

## Transfer from guardianship to guardianship or hospital

8. (1) A guardianship patient may be transferred into the guardianship of another local social services authority or person where –

    (a) an authority for transfer is given by the guardian in the form set out in Part 1 of Form G7;

    (b) that transfer has been agreed by the receiving local social services authority, which will be the responsible local social services authority if the proposed transfer takes effect;

    (c) that local social services authority has specified the date on which the transfer shall take place;

    (d) the guardian has recorded the agreement of the receiving local social services authority mentioned in paragraph (b) and the date for transfer mentioned in paragraph (c) in Part 1 of that Form;

    (e) a person other than a local social services authority is named in the authority for transfer as proposed guardian, the statement of willingness of that person to act as guardian is recorded in the form set out in Part 2 of that Form.

   (2) An authority for transfer to hospital of a guardianship patient may be given by the responsible local social services authority in the form set out in Part 1 of Form G8 where –

    (a) an application for admission for treatment has been made by an approved mental health professional in the form set out in Form A6;

    (b) that application is founded on medical recommendations given by two registered medical practitioners in accordance with section 12 in the form set out –

       (i) in the case of joint recommendations, in Form A7;

       (ii) in any other case, in Form A8;

    (c) the responsible local social services authority is satisfied that arrangements have been made for the admission of the patient to that hospital within the period of 14 days beginning with the date on which the patient was last examined by a registered medical practitioner for the purposes of paragraph (b).

   (3) Where paragraph (2)(a) applies, for the purposes of the application referred to in that paragraph, sections 11(4) (consultation with nearest relative) and 13 (duty of approved mental health professional) shall apply as if the proposed transfer were an application for admission for treatment.

   (4) On the transfer of a guardianship patient referred to in paragraph (2), a record of admission shall be made by the managers of the hospital to which the patient is transferred in the form set out in Part 2 of Form G8 and shall be attached to the application referred to in paragraph (2)(a).

   (5) Where the conditions of paragraph (2) are satisfied, the transfer of the patient must be effected within 14 days of the date on which the patient was last examined, failing which the patient will remain subject to guardianship.

(6) The functions of the managers referred to in this regulation may be performed by an officer authorised by them in that behalf.

## Transfer of community patients recalled to hospital

9. (1) The managers of a hospital in which a community patient is detained, having been recalled to hospital, may authorise the transfer of that patient to another hospital.

(2) Where the hospital to which the patient has been recalled and the hospital to which the patient is being transferred are not under the same management, a transfer may only take place if the requirements of paragraphs (3) to (5) are satisfied.

(3) Those requirements are that the managers of the hospital to which the patient was recalled –

(a) authorise the transfer of the patient in the form set out in Part 1 of Form CTO6, and

(b) are satisfied that arrangements have been made for the admission of the patient to the hospital to which the patient is being transferred.

(4) The managers of the hospital from which the patient is being transferred shall furnish the managers of the hospital to which the patient is being transferred with a copy of Form CTO4 (record of patient's detention in hospital after recall) before, or at the time of, the patient's transfer.

(5) On the transfer of the patient, the managers of the hospital to which the patient is transferred shall record the patient's admission in the form set out in Part 2 of Form CTO6.

(6) Where –

(a) a patient has been recalled to a registered establishment, and

(b) that patient is maintained under a contract with a Strategic Health Authority, Local Health Board, Primary Care Trust, National Health Service trust, National Health Service foundation trust, a Special Health Authority or the Welsh Ministers, any authority for transfer required under paragraph (3)(a) may be given by an officer of that authority, board or trust authorised by that authority, board or trust in that behalf, or by those Ministers, instead of the managers.

(7) The functions of the managers referred to in this regulation may be performed by an officer authorised by them in that behalf.

## Transfers from England to Wales and from Wales to England

10. (1) Where a patient who is liable to be detained or is subject to guardianship under the Act is transferred from a hospital or guardianship in England to a hospital or guardianship in Wales, that transfer shall be subject to the conditions in these Regulations.

(2) Where a patient who is liable to be detained or is subject to guardianship under the Act is transferred from a hospital or guardianship in Wales to a hospital or guardianship in England, that transfer and the duty to record the admission of a patient so transferred shall be subject to such conditions as may be prescribed in Regulations made by the Welsh Ministers to similar effect for Wales.

(3) Where paragraph (2) applies and any Regulations made by the Welsh Ministers to similar effect for Wales provide for authority to convey a patient in Wales, those Regulations shall provide authority to convey the patient whilst in England.

## Conveyance to hospital on transfer from hospital or guardianship

11. (1) Where the conditions of regulation 7(2) or 8(2) are satisfied, the authority for transfer given in accordance with those regulations shall be sufficient authority for the following persons to take the patient and convey the patient to the hospital to which the patient is being transferred within the periods specified –

    (a) in a case to which regulation 7(2) applies –

        (i) an officer of the managers of either hospital, or

        (ii) any person authorised by the managers of the hospital to which the patient is being transferred, within the period of 28 days beginning with the date of the authority for transfer;

    (b) in a case to which regulation 8(2) applies –

        (i) an officer of, or

        (ii) any person authorised by, the responsible local social services authority, within the period of 14 days beginning with the date on which the patient was last examined by a medical practitioner for the purposes of regulation 8(2)(b).

  (2) Paragraph (1) shall apply to a patient who –

    (a) is liable to be detained under the Act and is removed to another hospital in circumstances to which section 19(3) applies, as if the authority given by the managers for that transfer were an authority for transfer given in accordance with regulation 7(2);

    (b) is liable to be detained in a hospital at which high security psychiatric services are provided and who, pursuant to a direction given by the Secretary of State under section 123(1) or (2) (transfers to and from special hospitals), is removed or transferred to another hospital, as if that direction were an authority for transfer given in accordance with regulation 7(2).

  (3) In a case to which regulation 7(5)(a) applies, an officer of or any other person authorised by the managers of the registered establishment may take and convey the patient to the registered establishment to which the patient is being transferred.

## Conveyance from hospital to hospital following recall of community patients

12. (1) Where the conditions of regulation 9(1) or (3) are satisfied, the authority for transfer given in accordance with that regulation shall be sufficient authority for the following persons to take the patient and convey him to the hospital to which he is being transferred –

    (a) an officer of the managers of either hospital, or

    (b) any person authorised by the managers of the hospital to which the patient is being transferred, within the period of 72 hours beginning with the time of the patient's detention pursuant to the patient's recall under section 17E (power to recall to hospital).

## Renewal of authority for detention or guardianship and extension of community treatment period

13. (1) Any report for the purposes of section 20(3) (medical recommendation for renewal of authority to detain) shall be in the form set out in Parts 1 and 3 of Form H5.

  (2) The statement for the purposes of section 20(5A) (agreement with medical recommendation for renewal of authority to detain) shall be in the form set out in Part 2 of Form H5.

(3)  The receipt of Form H5 shall be recorded by the managers of the hospital in which the patient is liable to be detained in the form set out in Part 4 of that Form.

(4)  Any report for the purposes of section 20(8) (medical recommendation for renewal of guardianship) shall be in the form set out in Part 1 of Form G9.

(5)  The responsible social services authority shall record receipt of Form G9 in the form set out in Part 2 of that Form.

(6)  For the purposes of section 20A (community treatment period) –

(a)  a report for the purposes of subsection (4) of that section (responsible clinician's report extending the community treatment period) shall be in the form set out in Parts 1 and 3 of Form CTO7;

(b)  a statement for the purposes of subsection (8) of that section (approved mental health professional's statement that it is appropriate to extend the order) shall be in the form set out in Part 2 of Form CTO7.

(7)  The managers of the responsible hospital shall record the receipt of Form CTO7 in the form set out in Part 4 of that Form.

## Detention, guardianship or community treatment after absence without leave for more than 28 days

14.  (1)  In relation to a patient who is liable to be detained –

(a)  any report for the purposes of section 21B(2) (authority for detention or guardianship of patients who are taken into custody or return after more than 28 days) shall be in the form set out in Part 1 of Form H6, and

(b)  the receipt of that report shall be recorded by the managers of the hospital in which the patient is liable to be detained in the form set out in Part 2 of that Form.

(2)  In relation to a patient who is subject to guardianship –

(a)  any report for the purposes of section 21B(2) shall be in the form set out in Part 1 of Form G10, and

(b)  the receipt of that report shall be recorded by the responsible local social services authority in the form set out in Part 2 of that Form.

(3)  In relation to a community patient –

(a)  any report for the purposes of section 21B(2) shall be in the form set out in Part 1 of Form CTO8, and

(b)  the receipt of that report shall be recorded by the managers of the responsible hospital in the form set out in Part 2 of that Form.

## Removal to England

15.  (1)  This regulation shall apply to a patient who is removed from Scotland, Northern Ireland, any of the Channel Islands or the Isle of Man to England ("a removed patient") under –

(a)  section 82, 84 or 85 (as the case may be), or

(b)  regulations made under section 290 of the Mental Health (Care and Treatment) (Scotland) Act 2003 (removal and return of patients within United Kingdom).

(2) Where a removed patient is liable to be detained in a hospital, the managers of the hospital shall record the date on which the patient is admitted to the hospital in the form set out in Form M1.

(3) The managers of the hospital shall take such steps as are reasonably practicable to inform the person (if any) appearing to them to be the patient's nearest relative as soon as practicable of the patient's admission to hospital.

(4) Where a removed patient is received into guardianship –

(a) the guardian shall record the date on which the patient arrives at the place at which the patient is to reside on the patient's reception into guardianship under the Act in the form set out in Form M1;

(b) the guardian shall take such steps as are reasonably practicable to inform the person (if any) appearing to them to be the patient's nearest relative as soon as practicable that the patient has been received into guardianship under the Act;

(c) a private guardian shall notify the responsible local social services authority of the –

(i) date mentioned in sub-paragraph (a), and

(ii) particulars mentioned in regulation 22(1)(b) and (e).

## Removal to England of patients subject to compulsion in the community

16. (1) This regulation shall apply to a patient who is removed from Scotland, any of the Channel Islands or the Isle of Man to England under –

(a) section 289(1) of the Mental Health (Care and Treatment) (Scotland) Act 2003 (crossborder transfer: patients subject to requirement other than detention) in the case of Scotland; or

(b) section 85ZA (responsibility for community patients transferred from any of the Channel Islands or the Isle of Man) in the case of any of the Channel Islands or the Isle of Man.

(2) The managers of the responsible hospital shall record the date on which the patient arrived at the place where the patient is to reside in the form set out in Form M1.

(3) The managers of the hospital shall take such steps as are reasonably practicable to inform the person (if any) appearing to them to be the patient's nearest relative as soon as practicable that the patient is a community patient.

(4) The conditions specified by the responsible clinician under section 80C(5) (removal of patients subject to compulsion in the community from Scotland) or section 85ZA(4), shall be recorded by that responsible clinician in Part 1 of Form CTO9.

(5) The approved mental health professional's agreement to the conditions referred to in paragraph (4) shall be recorded by that approved mental health professional in Part 2 of Form CTO9.

## Assignment of responsibility for community patients

17. (1) This regulation applies to a community patient whether or not the patient has been recalled to hospital in accordance with section 17E (power to recall to hospital).

(2) Responsibility for a patient referred to in paragraph (1) may be assigned by the managers of the responsible hospital to any other hospital whether or not that other hospital is under the same management as the responsible hospital.

(3) Responsibility for a patient shall not be assigned to a hospital which is not under the same management as the responsible hospital unless –

  (a) an authority for the assignment is given by the managers of the assigning responsible hospital in the form set out in Part 1 of Form CTO10;

  (b) that transfer has been agreed by the managers of the hospital which will be the responsible hospital if the proposed transfer takes effect;

  (c) the managers of the hospital referred to in (b) have specified the date on which the transfer shall take place;

  (d) the managers of the assigning responsible hospital record –

    (i) the agreement of the managers of the new responsible hospital to the assignment, and

    (ii) the date on which the assignment is to take place, in the form set out in that Form.

(4) The managers of the receiving hospital must notify the patient in writing of –

  (a) the assignment, either before it takes place or as soon as reasonably practicable thereafter; and

  (b) their name and address (irrespective of whether or not there are any changes in the managers).

(5) Where responsibility for a patient is assigned from a responsible registered establishment to another hospital which is not under the same management and the patient is maintained under a contract with a Strategic Health Authority, Local Health Board, Primary Care Trust, National Health Service trust, National Health Service foundation trust, a Special Health Authority or the Welsh Ministers, any authority for transfer required under paragraph (3)(a), and the record required under paragraph (3)(b), may be given by an officer of that authority, board or trust authorised by it in that behalf, or by those Ministers, instead of by the managers.

(6) Any hospital to which a patient has been assigned may, in accordance with the provisions of this regulation, assign the patient to another hospital.

(7) The functions of the managers referred to in this regulation may be performed by an officer authorised by them in that behalf.

## Discharge of patients

18. (1) For the purposes of section 23 (discharge of patients) a responsible clinician's order for the discharge of –

  (a) a patient liable to be detained under the Act, or a community patient, shall be sent to the managers of the hospital in which the patient is liable to be detained or the responsible hospital (as applicable) as soon as practicable after it is made;

  (b) a guardianship patient, shall be sent to the guardian as soon as practicable after it is made.

## Delegation of hospital managers' functions under the Act

19. (1) The functions of the managers of a hospital in respect of the following –

  (a) notifying local social services authorities under section 14 (social reports) of patients detained on the basis of applications by their nearest relatives;

(b)  authorising persons under section 17(3) (leave of absence from hospital) to keep in custody patients who are on leave of absence who are subject to a condition that they remain in custody;

(c)  authorising persons under sections 18(1) and (2A) (return and readmission of patients absent without leave) to take and return detained and community patients respectively who are absent without leave, may be performed by any person authorised by them in that behalf.

## Delegation of managers' functions under the Domestic Violence, Crime and Victims Act 2004

20.  (1)  The functions of the managers of a hospital under sections 35 to 44B of the Domestic Violence, Crime and Victims Act 2004 (provision of information to victims of patients under the Act etc.) may be performed by any person authorised by them in that behalf.

## Delegation by local social services authorities

21.  (1)  Except as provided by paragraph (2), a local social services authority may delegate its functions under Parts 2 and 3 of the Act and these Regulations in the same way and to the same persons as its functions referred to in the Local Government Act 1972 may be delegated in accordance with section 101 of that Act.

(2)  The function of the local social services authority under section 23 (discharge of patients) may not be delegated otherwise than in accordance with that section.

## PART 3: FUNCTIONS OF GUARDIANS AND NEAREST RELATIVES

## Duties of private guardians

22.  (1)  It shall be the duty of a private guardian –

(a)  to appoint a registered medical practitioner to act as the nominated medical attendant of the patient;

(b)  to notify the responsible local social services authority of the name and address of the nominated medical attendant;

(c)  in exercising the powers and duties of a private guardian conferred or imposed by the Act and these Regulations, to comply with such directions as that authority may give;

(d)  to furnish that authority with all such reports or other information with regard to the patient as the authority may from time to time require;

(e)  to notify that authority –

(i)  on the reception of the patient into guardianship, of the private guardian's address and the address of the patient,

(ii)  except in a case to which paragraph (f) applies, of any permanent change of either address, before or not later than seven days after the change takes place;

(f)  on any permanent change of the private guardian's address, where the new address is in the area of a different local social services authority, to notify that authority –

(i)  of that address and that of the patient,

(ii) of the particulars mentioned in paragraph (b), and to notify the authority which was formerly responsible of the permanent change in the private guardian's address;

(g) in the event of the death of the patient, or the termination of the guardianship by discharge, transfer or otherwise, to notify the responsible local social services authority as soon as reasonably practicable.

(2) Any notice, reports or other information under this regulation may be given or furnished in any other way (in addition to the methods of serving documents provided for by regulation 3(1)) to which the relevant local social services authority agrees, including orally or by electronic communication.

## Visits to patients subject to guardianship

23. (1) The responsible local social services authority shall arrange for every patient received into guardianship under the Act to be visited at such intervals as the authority may decide, but –

(a) in any case at intervals of not more than three months, and

(b) at least one such visit in any year shall be made by an approved clinician or a practitioner approved by the Secretary of State for the purposes of section 12 (general provisions as to medical recommendations).

## Performance of functions of nearest relative

24. (1) Subject to the conditions of paragraph (7), any person other than –

(a) the patient;

(b) a person mentioned in section 26(5) (persons deemed not to be the nearest relative), or

(c) a person in respect of whom the court has made an order on the grounds set out in section 29(3)(b) to (e) (which sets out the grounds on which an application to the court for the appointment of a person to exercise the functions of a nearest relative may be made) for so long as an order under that section is in effect, may be authorised in accordance with paragraph (2) to act on behalf of the nearest relative in respect of the matters mentioned in paragraph (3).

(2) Subject to paragraph (8), the authorisation mentioned in paragraph (1) must be given in writing by the nearest relative.

(3) The matters referred to in paragraph (1) are the performance in respect of the patient of the functions conferred upon the nearest relative under –

(a) Part 2 of the Act (as modified by Schedule 1 to the Act as the case may be), and

(b) section 66 (applications to tribunals).

(4) An authorisation given under paragraph (1) shall take effect upon its receipt by the person authorised.

(5) Subject to the conditions of paragraph (7), the nearest relative of a patient may give notice in writing revoking that authorisation.

(6) Any revocation of such authorisation shall take effect upon the receipt of the notice by the person authorised.

(7) The conditions mentioned in paragraphs (1) and (5) are that the nearest relative shall immediately notify –

(a) the patient;

(b) in the case of a patient liable to be detained in a hospital, the managers of that hospital;

(c) in the case of a patient subject to guardianship, the responsible local social services authority and the private guardian, if any;

(d) in the case of a community patient, the managers of the responsible hospital, of the authorisation or, as the case may be, its revocation.

(8) An authorisation or notification referred to in this regulation may be transmitted by means of electronic communication if the recipient agrees.

## Discharge by nearest relative

25. (1) Any report given by the responsible clinician for the purposes of section 25 (restrictions on discharge by nearest relative) –

(a) shall be in the form set out in Part 1 of Form M2, and

(b) the receipt of that report by –

(i) the managers of the hospital in which the patient is liable to be detained, or

(ii) the managers of the responsible hospital in the case of a community patient, shall be in the form set out in Part 2 of that Form.

(2) In addition to the methods of serving documents provided for by regulation 3(1), reports under this regulation may be furnished by –

(a) transmission by facsimile, or

(b) the transmission in electronic form of a reproduction of the report, if the managers of the hospital agree.

## PART 4: PROVISION OF INFORMATION

26. (1) Unless the patient requests otherwise, where –

(a) a patient is to be or has been transferred from hospital to hospital pursuant to section 19 or section 123 (regulations as to transfer of patients and transfer to and from special hospitals respectively), the managers of the hospital to which the patient is to be or has been transferred shall take such steps as are reasonably practicable to cause the person (if any) appearing to them to be the patient's nearest relative to be informed of that transfer before it takes place or as soon as practicable thereafter;

(b) a patient's detention is renewed pursuant to a report furnished under section 20 (duration of authority), the managers of the responsible hospital shall take such steps as are reasonably practicable to cause the person (if any) appearing to them to be the patient's nearest relative to be informed of that renewal as soon as practicable following their decision not to discharge the patient;

(c) by virtue of section 21B(7) (patients who are taken into custody or return after more than 28 days) a patient's detention is renewed pursuant to a report furnished under section 21B(2), the managers of the responsible hospital in which the patient is liable to be detained shall take such steps as are reasonably practicable to cause the person (if any) appearing to them to be the patient's nearest relative to be informed of that renewal as soon as practicable following their decision not to discharge the patient;

(d) by virtue of section 21B(5) and (6) (patients who are taken into custody or return after more than 28 days), a patient's detention is renewed retrospectively pursuant to a report furnished under section 21B(2), the managers of the hospital in which the patient is liable to be detained shall take such steps as are reasonably practicable to cause the patient and the person (if any) appearing to them to be the patient's nearest relative to be informed of that renewal as soon as practicable following their receipt of that report;

(e) a patient's period of community treatment is extended pursuant to a report furnished under section 20A (community treatment period), the managers of the responsible hospital shall take such steps as are reasonably practicable to cause the person (if any) appearing to them to be the patient's nearest relative to be informed of that extension as soon as practicable following their decision not to discharge the patient;

(f) by virtue of section 21B(7A) (patients who are taken into custody or return after more than 28 days) a patient's period of community treatment is extended pursuant to a report furnished under section 21B(2), the managers of the responsible hospital shall take such steps as are reasonably practicable to cause the person (if any) appearing to them to be the patient's nearest relative to be informed of that extension as soon as practicable following their decision not to discharge the patient;

(g) by virtue of section 21B(6A) and (6B) (patients who are taken into custody or return after more than 28 days) a patient's period of community treatment is extended retrospectively pursuant to a report furnished under section 21B(2), the managers of the responsible hospital shall take such steps as are reasonably practicable to cause the patient and the person (if any) appearing to them to be the patient's nearest relative to be informed of that extension as soon as practicable following their receipt of that report;

(h) a patient is to be or has been assigned to another hospital which assumes responsibility for that patient as a community patient, the managers of the hospital to which the patient is to be or has been assigned shall take such steps as are reasonably practicable to cause the person (if any) appearing to them to be the patient's nearest relative to be informed of that assignment before or as soon as practicable following it taking place;

(i) a patient is to be or has been transferred from hospital to guardianship pursuant to section 19 (regulations as to transfer of patients), the responsible local social services authority shall take such steps as are reasonably practicable to cause the person appearing to it to be the patient's nearest relative to be informed of that transfer before it takes place or as soon as practicable thereafter;

(j) a patient is to be or has been transferred from the guardianship of one person to the guardianship of another person pursuant to section 19 (regulations as to transfer of patients), the new responsible local social services authority shall take such steps as are reasonably practicable to cause the person (if any) appearing to it to be the patient's nearest relative to be informed of that transfer before it takes place or as soon as practicable thereafter;

(k) a patient's guardianship becomes vested in the local social services authority or the functions of a guardian are, during the guardian's incapacity, transferred to the authority or a person approved by it under section 10 (transfer of guardianship in case of death, incapacity, etc. of guardian), the responsible local social services authority shall take such steps as are reasonably practicable to cause the person (if any) appearing to it to be the patient's nearest relative to be informed of that vesting, or as the case may be, transfer before it takes place or as soon as practicable thereafter;

(l) patient's guardianship is renewed pursuant to a report furnished under section 20 (duration of authority), the responsible local social services authority shall take such steps as are reasonably practicable to cause the person (if any) appearing to it to be the patient's nearest relative to be informed of that renewal as soon as practicable following the decision of the responsible local social services authority to discharge the patient;

(m) by virtue of section 21B(7) (patients who are taken into custody or return after more than 28 days) a patient's guardianship is renewed pursuant to a report furnished under section 21B(7), the responsible local social services authority shall take such steps as are reasonably practicable to cause the person (if any) appearing to it to be the patient's nearest relative to be informed of that renewal as soon as practicable following the decision of the responsible local social services authority not to discharge the patient;

(n) by virtue of section 21B(5) and (6) (patients who are taken into custody or return after more than 28 days) a patient's guardianship is renewed retrospectively pursuant to a report furnished under section 21B(2), the responsible local social services authority shall take such steps as are reasonably practicable to cause the patient and person (if any) appearing to it to be the patient's nearest relative to be informed of that renewal as soon as practicable following the receipt by the responsible local social services authority of that report.

(2) Where paragraph (1)(m) or (n) applies, the responsible local social services authority shall, as soon as practicable inform the private guardian (if any) of its receipt of a report furnished under section 21B (patients who are taken into custody or return after more than 28 days).

(3) Upon a patient becoming subject to guardianship under the Act, the responsible local social services authority shall take such steps as are reasonably practicable to cause to be informed both the patient and the person (if any) appearing to the authority to be the patient's nearest relative of the rights referred to in paragraph (4).

(4) Those rights are –

(a) the patient's rights under section 66 (applications to tribunals),

(b) the nearest relative's right, as the case may be, to –

(i) discharge the patient under section 23 (discharge of patients), or

(ii) make an application under section 69 (application to tribunals concerning patients subject to hospital and guardianship orders where the patient is, or is treated as being, subject to guardianship under section 37).

(5) Where information referred to in paragraph (1)(d), (g) or (n), or in paragraph (3) is to be given to the patient, it shall be given both orally and in writing.

(6) Where information referred to in paragraph (1) is to be given to the person appearing to be the patient's nearest relative, it shall be given in writing.

(7) Where information referred to in paragraph (2) is to be given to the private guardian, it shall be given in writing.

(8) Information that is to be given in writing under paragraphs (6) and (7) may be transmitted by means of electronic communication if the recipient agrees.

(9) The functions of the managers referred to in this regulation may be performed by an officer authorised by them in that behalf.

## PART 5: CONSENT TO TREATMENT

### Consent to treatment

27. (1) For the purposes of section 57 (treatment requiring consent and a second opinion) –

    (a) the form of treatment to which that section shall apply, in addition to the treatment mentioned in subsection (1)(a) of that section (any surgical operation for destroying brain tissue or for destroying the functioning of brain tissue), shall be the surgical implantation of hormones for the purpose of reducing male sexual drive, and

    (b) the certificates required for the purposes of subsection (2)(a) and (b) of that section shall be in the form set out in Form T1.

    (2) For the purposes of section 58 (treatment requiring consent or a second opinion) the certificates required for the purposes of subsection (3)(a) and (b) of that section shall be in the form set out in Forms T2 and T3 respectively.

    (3) For the purposes of section 58A (electro-convulsive therapy, etc.) –

    (a) the form of treatment to which that section shall apply, in addition to the administration of electro-convulsive therapy mentioned in subsection (1)(a) of that section, shall be the administration of medicine as part of that therapy; and

    (b) the certificates required for the purposes of subsections (3), (4) and (5) of that section shall be in the form set out in Forms T4, T5 and T6 respectively.

    (4) Section 58A does not apply to treatment by way of the administration of medicine as part of electro-convulsive therapy where that treatment falls within section 62(1)(a) or (b) (treatment immediately necessary to save the patient's life or to prevent a serious deterioration in the patient's condition).

## PART 6: TREATMENT OF COMMUNITY PATIENTS NOT RECALLED TO HOSPITAL

28. (1) For the purposes of Part 4A of the Act (treatment of community patients not recalled to hospital), the certificates required for the purposes of sections 64B(2)(b) and 64E(2)(b) (which set out when treatment under Part 4A of the Act may be given to adult and child community patients respectively) shall be in the form set out in Form CTO11.

    (2) Treatment of a patient to whom section 64B(3)(b) or section 64E(3)(b) applies (adult and child patients for whom treatment is immediately necessary), may include treatment by way of administration of medicine as part of electro-convulsive therapy but only where that treatment falls within section 64C(5)(a) or (b) (treatment immediately necessary to save the patient's life or to prevent a serious deterioration in the patient's condition).

    (3) Treatment of a patient to whom section 64G (emergency treatment for patients lacking capacity or competence) applies may include treatment by way of the administration of medicine as part of electro-convulsive therapy but only where that treatment falls within section 64G(5)(a) or (b) (treatment immediately necessary to save the patient's life or to prevent a serious deterioration in the patient's condition).

## PART 7: CORRESPONDENCE OF PATIENTS

### Inspection and opening of postal packets

29. (1) Where under section 134(4) (inspection and opening of postal packets addressed to or by patients in hospital) any postal packet is inspected and opened, but neither the packet nor anything contained in it is withheld under section 134(1) or (2) the person appointed who inspected and opened it, shall record in writing –

    (a) that the packet had been so inspected and opened,

    (b) that nothing in the packet has been withheld, and

    (c) the name of the person appointed and the name of the hospital, and shall, before resealing the packet, place the record in that packet.

  (2) Where under section 134(1) or (2) any postal packet or anything contained in it is withheld by the person appointed –

    (a) that person shall record in a register kept for the purpose –

      (i) that the packet or anything contained in it has been withheld,

      (ii) the date on which it was so withheld,

      (iii) the grounds on which it was so withheld,

      (iv) a description of the contents of the packet withheld or of any item withheld, and

      (v) the name of the person appointed; and

    (b) if anything contained in the packet is withheld, the person appointed shall record in writing –

      (i) that the packet has been inspected and opened,

      (ii) that an item or items contained in the packet have been withheld,

      (iii) a description of any such item,

      (iv) the name of the person appointed and the name of the hospital, and

      (v) in any case to which section 134(1)(b) or (2) applies, the further particulars required for the purposes of section 134(6), and shall, before resealing the packet, place the record in that packet.

  (3) In a case to which section 134(1)(b) or (2) applies –

    (a) the notice required for the purposes of section 134(6) shall include –

      (i) a statement of the grounds on which the packet in question or anything contained in it was withheld, and

      (ii) the name of the person appointed who so decided to withhold that packet or anything contained in it and the name of the hospital; and

    (b) where anything contained in a packet is withheld the record required by paragraph (2)(b) shall, if the provisions of section 134(6) are otherwise satisfied, be sufficient notice to the person to whom the packet is addressed for the purposes of section 134(6).

  (4) For the purposes of this regulation "the person appointed" means a person appointed under section 134(7) to perform the functions of the managers of the hospital under that section.

## Review of decisions to withhold postal packets

30. (1) Every application for review by the Commission under section 121(7) (review of any decision to withhold a postal packet, or anything contained in it, under section 134) shall be –

    (a) made in such manner as the Commission may accept as sufficient in the circumstances of any particular case or class of case and may be made otherwise than in writing, and

    (b) made, delivered or sent to an office of the Commission.

    (2) Any person making such an application shall furnish to the Commission the notice of the withholding of the postal packet or anything contained in it, given under section 134(6), or a copy of that notice.

    (3) For the purpose of determining any such application the Commission may direct the production of such documents, information and evidence as it may reasonably require.

## Patient advocacy and liaison services and independent mental capacity advocate services

31. (1) In section 134 (correspondence of patients), for the purposes of subsection (3)(ea) "patient advocacy and liaison service" means a service affording assistance in the form of advice and liaison for patients, their families and carers provided by –

    (a) an NHS trust,

    (b) an NHS foundation trust, or

    (c) a Primary Care Trust.

    (2) For the purposes of section 134(3A)(b)(iii), the prescribed arrangements are arrangements in respect of independent mental capacity advocates made under section 35 to 41 of the Mental Capacity Act 2005 (independent advocacy service).

## PART 8: REVOCATIONS

## Revocations

32. (1) The Regulations specified in column 1 of Schedule 2 are hereby revoked to the extent mentioned in column 3 of that Schedule.

Signed by authority of the Secretary of State for Health.

*Ivan Lewis*

Parliamentary Under-Secretary of State

Department of Health

28th April 2008

379

# SCHEDULE 1 Regulations 4–9, 13–17, 25, 27 and 28

## FORMS FOR USE IN CONNECTION WITH COMPULSORY ADMISSION TO HOSPITAL, GUARDIANSHIP AND TREATMENT

**Form A1** *Regulation 4(1)(a)(i)*

**Mental Health Act 1983 section 2 – application by nearest relative for admission for assessment**

To the managers of [name and address of hospital]

I [PRINT your full name and address] apply for the admission of [PRINT full name and address of patient] for assessment in accordance with Part 2 of the Mental Health Act 1983.

*Complete (a) or (b) as applicable and delete the other.*

(a)   To the best of my knowledge and belief I am the patient's nearest relative within the meaning of the Act.

I am the patient's [state your relationship with the patient].

(b)   I have been authorised to exercise the functions under the Act of the patient's nearest relative by a county court/the patient's nearest relative *<delete the phrase which does not apply>*, and a copy of the authority is attached to this application.

I last saw the patient on [date], which was within the period of 14 days ending on the day this application is completed.

This application is founded on two medical recommendations in the prescribed form.

If neither of the medical practitioners had previous acquaintance with the patient before making their recommendations, please explain why you could not get a recommendation from a medical practitioner who did have previous acquaintance with the patient –

...........................................................................................................................................

...........................................................................................................................................

...........................................................................................................................................

[If you need to continue on a separate sheet please indicate here [ ] and attach that sheet to this form]

Signed.............................................

Date.............................................

**Form A2** *Regulation 4(1)(a)(ii)*

## Mental Health Act 1983 section 2 – application by an approved mental health professional for admission for assessment

To the managers of [name and address of hospital]

I [PRINT your full name and address] apply for the admission of [PRINT full name and address of patient] for assessment in accordance with Part 2 of the Mental Health Act 1983.

I am acting on behalf of [PRINT name of local social services authority] and am approved to act as an approved mental health professional for the purposes of the Act by <*delete as appropriate*> that authority

[name of local social services authority that approved you, if different]

*Complete the following if you know who the nearest relative is.*

*Complete (a) or (b) as applicable and delete the other.*

(a)  To the best of my knowledge and belief [PRINT full name and address] is the patient's nearest relative within the meaning of the Act.

(b)  I understand that [PRINT full name and address] has been authorised by a county court/the patient's nearest relative* to exercise the functions under the Act of the patient's nearest relative.

<*Delete the phrase which does not apply*>

I have/have not yet* informed that person that this application is to be made and of the nearest relative's power to order the discharge of the patient. <*Delete the phrase which does not apply*>

*Complete the following if you do not know who the nearest relative is.*

*Delete (a) or (b).*

(a)  I have been unable to ascertain who is the patient's nearest relative within the meaning of the Act.

(b)  To the best of my knowledge and belief this patient has no nearest relative within the meaning of the Act.

*The remainder of the form must be completed in all cases.*

I last saw the patient on [date], which was within the period of 14 days ending on the day this application is completed.

I have interviewed the patient and I am satisfied that detention in a hospital is in all the circumstances of the case the most appropriate way of providing the care and medical treatment of which the patient stands in need.

This application is founded on two medical recommendations in the prescribed form.

If neither of the medical practitioners had previous acquaintance with the patient before making their recommendations, please explain why you could not get a recommendation from a medical practitioner who did have previous acquaintance with the patient –

.................................................................................................................................

.................................................................................................................................

.................................................................................................................................

[If you need to continue on a separate sheet please indicate here [ ] and attach that sheet to this form]

Signed............................................

Date............................................

**Form A3** *Regulation 4(1)(b)(i)*

## Mental Health Act 1983 section 2 – joint medical recommendation for admission for assessment

We, registered medical practitioners, recommend that [PRINT full name and address of patient] be admitted to a hospital for assessment in accordance with Part 2 of the Mental Health Act 1983.

I [PRINT full name and address of first practitioner] last examined this patient on [date].

*    I had previous acquaintance with the patient before I conducted that examination.

*    I am approved under section 12 of the Act as having special experience in the diagnosis or treatment of mental disorder.

<*Delete if not applicable>

I [PRINT full name and address of second practitioner] last examined this patient on [date].

*    I had previous acquaintance with the patient before I conducted that examination.

*    I am approved under section 12 of the Act as having special experience in the diagnosis or treatment of mental disorder.

<*Delete if not applicable>

In our opinion,

(a)  this patient is suffering from mental disorder of a nature or degree which warrants the detention of the patient in hospital for assessment (or for assessment followed by medical treatment) for at least a limited period,

AND

(b)  ought to be so detained

    (i)   in the interests of the patient's own health

    (ii)  in the interests of the patient's own safety

    (iii) with a view to the protection of other persons.

<Delete the indents not applicable>

Our reasons for these opinions are:

[Your reasons should cover both (a) and (b) above. As part of them: describe the patient's symptoms and behaviour and explain how those symptoms and behaviour lead you to your opinion; explain why the patient ought to be admitted to hospital and why informal admission is not appropriate.]

.....................................................................................................................................

.....................................................................................................................................

.....................................................................................................................................

[If you need to continue on a separate sheet please indicate here [ ] and attach that sheet to this form]

Signed............................................

Date............................................

Signed............................................

Date............................................

NOTE: AT LEAST ONE OF THE PRACTITIONERS SIGNING THIS FORM MUST BE APPROVED UNDER SECTION 12 OF THE ACT.

## Form A4   *Regulation 4(1)(b)(ii)*

### Mental Health Act 1983 section 2 – medical recommendation for admission for assessment

I [PRINT full name and address of medical practitioner], a registered medical practitioner,

recommend that [PRINT full name and address of patient] be admitted to a hospital for assessment in accordance with Part 2 of the Mental Health Act 1983. I last examined this patient on [date].

*    I had previous acquaintance with the patient before I conducted that examination.

*    I am approved under section 12 of the Act as having special experience in the diagnosis or treatment of mental disorder.

<*Delete if not applicable>

In my opinion,

(a)   this patient is suffering from mental disorder of a nature or degree which warrants the detention of the patient in hospital for assessment (or for assessment followed by medical treatment) for at least a limited period,

AND

(b)   ought to be so detained

    (i)  in the interests of the patient's own health

    (ii)  in the interests of the patient's own safety

    (iii)  with a view to the protection of other persons.

<Delete the indents not applicable>

My reasons for these opinions are:

[Your reasons should cover both (a) and (b) above. As part of them: describe the patient's symptoms and behaviour and explain how those symptoms and behaviour lead you to your opinion; explain why the patient ought to be admitted to hospital and why informal admission is not appropriate.]

..........................................................................................................................

..........................................................................................................................

..........................................................................................................................

[If you need to continue on a separate sheet please indicate here [ ] and attach that sheet to this form]

Signed............................................

Date............................................

**Form A5** *Regulation 4(1)(c)(i)*

## Mental Health Act 1983 section 3 – application by nearest relative for admission for treatment

To the managers of [name and address of hospital]

I [PRINT your full name and address] apply for the admission of [PRINT full name and address of patient] for treatment in accordance with Part 2 of the Mental Health Act 1983.

*Complete either (a) or (b) as applicable and delete the other.*

(a)   To the best of my knowledge and belief I am the patient's nearest relative within the meaning of the Act.

I am the patient's [state your relationship with the patient].

(b)   I have been authorised to exercise the functions under the Act of the patient's nearest relative by a county court/the patient's nearest relative *<delete the phrase which does not apply>*, and a copy of the authority is attached to this application.

I last saw the patient on [date], which was within the period of 14 days ending on the day this application is completed.

This application is founded on two medical recommendations in the prescribed form.

If neither of the medical practitioners had previous acquaintance with the patient before making the recommendations, please explain why you could not get a recommendation from a medical practitioner who did have previous acquaintance with the patient –

........................................................................................................................................

........................................................................................................................................

........................................................................................................................................

[If you need to continue on a separate sheet please indicate here [ ] and attach that sheet to this form]

Signed............................................

Date............................................

**Form A6**  *Regulation 4(1)(c)(ii)*

## Mental Health Act 1983 section 3 – application by an approved mental health professional for admission for treatment

To the managers of [name and address of hospital]

I [PRINT your full name and address] apply for the admission of [PRINT full name and address of patient] for treatment in accordance with Part 2 of the Mental Health Act 1983.

I am acting on behalf of [name of local social services authority] and am approved to act as an approved mental health professional for the purposes of the Act by *<delete as appropriate>* that authority

[name of local social services authority that approved you, if different]

*Complete the following where consultation with the nearest relative has taken place. Complete (a) or (b) and delete the other.*

(a)   I have consulted [PRINT full name and address] who to the best of my knowledge and belief is the patient's nearest relative within the meaning of the Act.

(b)   I have consulted [PRINT full name and address] who I understand has been authorised by a county court/the patient's nearest relative* to exercise the functions under the Act of the patient's nearest relative.

*<\*Delete the phrase which does not apply>*

That person has not notified me or the local social services authority on whose behalf I am acting that he or she objects to this application being made.

*Complete the following where the nearest relative has not been consulted. Delete whichever two of (a), (b) and (c) do not apply.*

(a)   I have been unable to ascertain who is this patient's nearest relative within the meaning of the Act.

(b)   To the best of my knowledge and belief this patient has no nearest relative within the meaning of the Act.

(c)   I understand that [PRINT full name and address] is

  (i)   this patient's nearest relative within the meaning of the Act,

  (ii)   authorised to exercise the functions of this patient's nearest relative under the Act, *<delete either (i) or (ii)>* but in my opinion it is not reasonably practicable/would involve unreasonable delay *<delete as appropriate>* to consult that person before making this application, because –

...............................................................................................................................................

...............................................................................................................................................

...............................................................................................................................................

[If you need to continue on a separate sheet please indicate here [ ] and attach that sheet to this form]

*The remainder of this form must be completed in all cases.*

I saw the patient on [date], which was within the period of 14 days ending on the day this application is completed.

I have interviewed the patient and I am satisfied that detention in a hospital is in all the circumstances of the case the most appropriate way of providing the care and medical treatment of which the patient stands in need.

This application is founded on two medical recommendations in the prescribed form.

If neither of the medical practitioners had previous acquaintance with the patient before making their recommendations, please explain why you could not get a recommendation from a medical practitioner who did have previous acquaintance with the patient –

.............................................................................................................................

.............................................................................................................................

.............................................................................................................................

[If you need to continue on a separate sheet please indicate here [ ] and attach that sheet to this form]

Signed............................................

Date............................................

## Form A7  *Regulation 4(1)(d)(i)*

### Mental Health Act 1983 section 3 – joint medical recommendation for admission for treatment

We, registered medical practitioners, recommend that [PRINT full name and address of patient] be admitted to a hospital for treatment in accordance with Part 2 of the Mental Health Act 1983.

I [PRINT full name and address of first practitioner] last examined this patient on [date].

*    I had previous acquaintance with the patient before I conducted that examination.

*    I am approved under section 12 of the Act as having special experience in the diagnosis or treatment of mental disorder.

*<\*Delete if not applicable>*

I [PRINT name and address of second practitioner]

*    I had previous acquaintance with the patient before I conducted that examination.

*    I am approved under section 12 of the Act as having special experience in the diagnosis or treatment of mental disorder.

*<\*Delete if not applicable>*

In our opinion,

(a)   this patient is suffering from mental disorder of a nature or degree which makes it appropriate for the patient to receive medical treatment in a hospital,

AND

(b)   it is necessary

    (i)   for the patient's own health

    (ii)   for the patient's own safety

    (iii)   for the protection of other persons

*<delete the indents not applicable>*

that this patient should receive treatment in hospital,

AND

(c)   such treatment cannot be provided unless the patient is detained under section 3 of the Act,

because – [Your reasons should cover (a), (b) and (c) above. As part of them: describe the patient's symptoms and behaviour and explain how those symptoms and behaviour lead you to your opinion; say whether other methods of treatment or care (e.g. out-patient treatment or social services) are available and, if so, why they are not appropriate; indicate why informal admission is not appropriate.]

..............................................................................................................................

..............................................................................................................................

..............................................................................................................................

[If you need to continue on a separate sheet please indicate here [ ] and attach that sheet to this form]

..............................................................................................................................

We are also of the opinion that, taking into account the nature and degree of the mental disorder from which the patient is suffering and all the other circumstances of the case, appropriate medical treatment is available to the patient at the following hospital (or one of the following hospitals): –

[Enter name of hospital(s). If appropriate treatment is available only in a particular part of the hospital, say which part.]

..............................................................................................................................

..............................................................................................................................

..............................................................................................................................

[If you need to continue on a separate sheet please indicate here [ ] and attach that sheet to this form]

Signed..............................................

Date..............................................

Signed..............................................

Date..............................................

NOTE: AT LEAST ONE OF THE PRACTITIONERS SIGNING THIS FORM MUST BE APPROVED UNDER SECTION 12 OF THE ACT.

**Form A8** *Regulation 4(1)(d)(ii)*

## Mental Health Act 1983 section 3 – medical recommendation for admission for treatment

I [PRINT full name and address of practitioner], a registered medical practitioner, recommend that [PRINT full name and address of patient] be admitted to a hospital for treatment in accordance with Part 2 of the Mental Health Act 1983.

I last examined this patient on [date].

*    I had previous acquaintance with the patient before I conducted that examination.

*    I am approved under section 12 of the Act as having special experience in the diagnosis or treatment of mental disorder.

<*Delete if not applicable>

In my opinion,

(a)   this patient is suffering from mental disorder of a nature or degree which makes it appropriate for the patient to receive medical treatment in a hospital,

AND

(b)   it is necessary

     (i)   for the patient's own health

     (ii)   for the patient's own safety

     (iii)   for the protection of other persons

<delete the indents not applicable>

that this patient should receive treatment in hospital, AND

(c)   such treatment cannot be provided unless the patient is detained under section 3 of the Act,

because – [Your reasons should cover (a), (b) and (c) above. As part of them: describe the patient's symptoms and behaviour and explain how those symptoms and behaviour lead you to your opinion; say whether other methods of treatment or care (e.g. out-patient treatment or social services) are available and, if so, why they are not appropriate; indicate why informal admission is not appropriate.]

......................................................................................................................................

......................................................................................................................................

......................................................................................................................................

[If you need to continue on a separate sheet please indicate here [ ] and attach that sheet to this form]

I am also of the opinion that, taking into account the nature and degree of the mental disorder from which the patient is suffering and all the other circumstances of the case, appropriate medical treatment is available to the patient at the following hospital (or one of the following hospitals): –

.........................................................................................................................................

.........................................................................................................................................

[Enter name of hospital(s). If appropriate treatment is available only in a particular part of the hospital, say which part.]

Signed............................................

Date............................................

**Form A9** *Regulation 4(1)(e)(i)*

**Mental Health Act 1983 section 4 – emergency application by nearest relative for admission for assessment**

THIS FORM IS TO BE USED ONLY FOR AN EMERGENCY APPLICATION

To the managers of [name and address of hospital]

I [PRINT your full name and address] apply for the admission of [PRINT full name and address of patient] for assessment in accordance with Part 2 of the Mental Health Act 1983.

*Complete (a) or (b) as applicable and delete the other.*

(a)   To the best of my knowledge and belief I am the patient's nearest relative within the meaning of the Act.

I am the patient's [state your relationship with the patient].

(b)   I have been authorised to exercise the functions under the Act of the patient's nearest relative by a county court/the patient's nearest relative <*delete the phrase which does not apply*>, and a copy of the authority is attached to this application.

I last saw the patient on [date], which was within the last 24 hours.

In my opinion it is of urgent necessity for the patient to be admitted and detained under section 2 of the Act and compliance with the provisions of Part 2 of the Act relating to applications under that section would involve undesirable delay.

This application is founded on a medical recommendation in the prescribed form.

If the medical practitioner did not have previous acquaintance with the patient before making the recommendation, please explain why you could not get a recommendation from a medical practitioner who did have previous acquaintance with the patient –

...............................................................................................................................................................

...............................................................................................................................................................

...............................................................................................................................................................

[If you need to continue on a separate sheet please indicate here [ ] and attach that sheet to this form]

Signed.............................................

Date.............................................

Time.............................................

## Form A10   Regulation 4(1)(e)(ii)

**Mental Health Act 1983 section 4 – emergency application by an approved mental health professional for admission for assessment**

THIS FORM IS TO BE USED ONLY FOR AN EMERGENCY APPLICATION

To the managers of [name and address of hospital]

I [PRINT your full name and address] apply for the admission of [PRINT full name and address of patient] for assessment in accordance with Part 2 of the Mental Health Act 1983.

I am acting on behalf of [name of local social services authority] and am approved to act as an approved mental health professional for the purposes of the Act by <*delete as appropriate*> that authority

[name of local social services authority that approved you, if different].

I last saw the patient on [date] at [time], which was within the last 24 hours.

I have interviewed the patient and I am satisfied that detention in a hospital is in all the circumstances of the case the most appropriate way of providing the care and medical treatment of which the patient stands in need.

In my opinion it is of urgent necessity for the patient to be admitted and detained under section 2 of the Act and compliance with the provisions of Part 2 of the Act relating to applications under that section would involve undesirable delay.

This application is founded on a medical recommendation in the prescribed form.

If the medical practitioner did not have previous acquaintance with the patient before making the recommendation, please explain why you could not get a recommendation from a medical practitioner who did have previous acquaintance with the patient –

.................................................................................................................................................

.................................................................................................................................................

.................................................................................................................................................

[If you need to continue on a separate sheet please indicate here [ ] and attach that sheet to this form]

Signed.............................................

Date.............................................

Time.............................................

**Form A11** *Regulation 4(1)(f)*

## Mental Health Act 1983 section 4 – medical recommendation for emergency admission for assessment

THIS FORM IS TO BE USED ONLY FOR AN EMERGENCY APPLICATION

I [PRINT name and address of medical practitioner], a registered medical practitioner, recommend that [PRINT full name and address of patient] be admitted to a hospital for assessment in accordance with Part 2 of the Mental Health Act 1983.

I last examined this patient on [date] at [time].

* I had previous acquaintance with the patient before I conducted that examination.

* I am approved under section 12 of the Act as having special experience in the diagnosis or treatment of mental disorder.

<*Delete if not applicable>

I am of the opinion,

(a) this patient is suffering from mental disorder of a nature or degree which warrants the detention of the patient in hospital for assessment (or for assessment followed by medical treatment) for at least a limited period,

AND

(b) this patient ought to be so detained

    (i) in the interests of the patient's own health

    (ii) in the interests of the patient's own safety

    (iii) with a view to the protection of other persons

<delete the indents not applicable>

AND

(c) it is of urgent necessity for the patient to be admitted and detained under section 2 of the Act.

My reasons for these opinions are: [Your reasons should cover (a), (b) and (c) above. As part of them: describe the patient's symptoms and behaviour and explain how those symptoms and behaviour lead you to your opinion; and explain why the patient ought to be admitted to hospital urgently and why informal admission is not appropriate.]

..............................................................................................................................................

..............................................................................................................................................

..............................................................................................................................................

[If you need to continue on a separate sheet please indicate here [ ] and attach that sheet to this form]

Compliance with the provisions of Part 2 of the Act relating to applications under section 2 would involve undesirable delay, because – [Say approximately how long you think it would take to obtain a second medical recommendation and what risk such a delay would pose to the patient or to other people.]

.......................................................................................................................................................

.......................................................................................................................................................

[If you need to continue on a separate sheet please indicate here [ ] and attach that sheet to this form]

Signed...........................................

Date............................................

Time............................................

**Form H1** *Regulation 4(1)(g)*

**Mental Health Act 1983 section 5(2) – report on hospital in-patient**

PART 1

*(To be completed by a medical practitioner or an approved clinician qualified to do so under section 5(2) of the Act)*

To the managers of [name and address of hospital]

I am [PRINT full name]

and I am *<delete (a) or (b) as appropriate>*

(a) the registered medical practitioner/the approved clinician (who is not a registered medical practitioner)*<delete the phrase which does not apply>*

(b) a registered medical practitioner/an approved clinician (who is not a registered medical practitioner)* who is the nominee of the registered medical practitioner or approved clinician (who is not a registered medical practitioner) *<\*delete the phrase which does not apply>*

in charge of the treatment of [PRINT full name of patient], who is an in-patient in this hospital and

not at present liable to be detained under the Mental Health Act 1983.

It appears to me that an application ought to be made under Part 2 of the Act for this patient's admission to hospital for the following reasons –

...............................................................................................................................

...............................................................................................................................

...............................................................................................................................

[The full reasons why informal treatment is no longer appropriate must be given. If you need to continue on a separate sheet please indicate here [ ] and attach that sheet to this form.]

I am furnishing this report by: *<delete the phrase which does not apply>*

consigning it to the hospital managers' internal mail system today at [time]

delivering it (or having it delivered) by hand to a person authorised by the hospital managers to receive it.

Signed.............................................

Date.............................................

PART 2

*(To be completed on behalf of the hospital managers)*

This report was *<delete the phrase which does not apply>*

furnished to the hospital managers through their internal mail system delivered to me in person as someone authorised by the hospital managers to receive this report at [time] on [date]

Signed...........................................

on behalf of the hospital managers

PRINT NAME...........................................

Date...........................................

**Form H2** *Regulation 4(1)(h)*

**Mental Health Act 1983 section 5(4) – record of hospital in-patient**

To the managers of [name and address of hospital]

[PRINT full name of the patient]

It appears to me that –

(a)  this patient, who is receiving treatment for mental disorder as an in-patient of this hospital, is suffering from mental disorder to such a degree that it is necessary for the patient's health or safety or for the protection of others for this patient to be immediately restrained from leaving the hospital;

AND

(b)  it is not practicable to secure the immediate attendance of a registered medical practitioner or an approved clinician (who is not a registered practitioner) for the purpose of furnishing a report under section 5(2) of the Mental Health Act 1983.

I am [PRINT full name], a nurse registered –

*<delete whichever do not apply>*

(a)  in Sub-Part 1 of the register, whose entry includes an entry to indicate the nurse's field of practice is mental health nursing;

(b)  in Sub-Part 2 of the register, whose entry includes an entry to indicate the nurse's field of practice is mental health nursing;

(c)  in Sub-Part 1 of the register, whose entry includes an entry to indicate the nurse's field of practice is learning disabilities nursing;

(d)  in Sub-Part 2 of the register, whose entry includes an entry to indicate the nurse's field of practice is mental health nursing.

Signed............................................

Date............................................

Time............................................

399

**Form H3**   *Regulation 4(4) and (5)*

**Mental Health Act 1983 sections 2, 3 and 4 – record of detention in hospital**

*(To be attached to the application for admission)*

PART 1

[Name and address of hospital]

[PRINT full name of patient]

*Complete (a) if the patient is not already an in-patient in the hospital.*

*Complete (b) if the patient is already an in-patient.*

*Delete the one which does not apply.*

(a)   The above named patient was admitted to this hospital on [date of admission to hospital] at [time] in pursuance of an application for admission under section [state section] of the Mental Health Act 1983.

(b)   An application for the admission of the above named patient (who had already been admitted to this hospital) under section [state section] of the Mental Health Act 1983 was received by me on behalf of the hospital managers on [date] at [time] and the patient was accordingly treated as admitted for the purposes of the Act from that time.

Signed...........................................

on behalf of the hospital managers

PRINT NAME...........................................

Date...........................................

PART 2

*(To be completed only if the patient was admitted in pursuance of an emergency application under section 4 of the Act)*

On [date] at [time] I received, on behalf of the hospital managers, the second medical recommendation in support of the application for the admission of the above named patient.

Signed...........................................

on behalf of the hospital managers

PRINT NAME...........................................

Date...........................................

NOTE: IF THE PATIENT IS BEING DETAINED AS A RESULT OF A TRANSFER FROM GUARDIANSHIP, THE PATIENT'S ADMISSION SHOULD BE RECORDED IN PART 2 OF THE FORM G8 WHICH AUTHORISED THE TRANSFER.

**Form H4**   *Regulation 7(2)(a) and 7(3)*

**Mental Health Act 1983 section 19 – authority for transfer
from one hospital to another under different managers**

PART 1

*(To be completed on behalf of the managers of the hospital where the patient is detained)*

Authority is given for the transfer of [PRINT full name of patient] from [name and address of hospital in which the patient is liable to be detained] to [name and address of hospital to which patient is to be transferred] in accordance with the Mental Health (Hospital, Guardianship and Treatment) (England) Regulations 2008 within 28 days beginning with the date of this authority.

Signed............................................

on behalf of the hospital managers

PRINT NAME............................................

Date............................................

**PART 2**

RECORD OF ADMISSION

*(This is not part of the authority for transfer but is to be completed at the hospital to which the patient is transferred)*

This patient was transferred to [name of hospital] in pursuance of this authority for transfer and admitted to that hospital on [date of admission to receiving hospital] at [time].

Signed............................................

on behalf of the hospital managers

PRINT NAME............................................

Date............................................

**Form H5** *Regulation 13(1), (2) and (3)*

**Mental Health Act 1983 section 20 – renewal of authority for detention**

PART 1

*(To be completed by the responsible clinician)*

To the managers of [name and address of hospital in which the patient is liable to be detained] I examined [PRINT full name of patient] on [date of examination].

The patient is liable to be detained for a period ending on [date authority for detention is due to expire].

I have consulted [PRINT full name and profession of person consulted] who has been professionally concerned with the patient's treatment.

In my opinion,

(a)   this patient is suffering from mental disorder of a nature or degree which makes it appropriate for the patient to receive medical treatment in a hospital,

AND

(b)   it is necessary

 (i)   for the patient's own health

 (ii)   for the patient's own safety

 (iii)   for the protection of other persons

*<delete the indents not applicable>*

that this patient should receive treatment in hospital, because – [Your reasons should cover both (a) and (b) above. As part of them: describe the patient's symptoms and behaviour and explain how those symptoms and behaviour lead you to your opinion; say whether other methods of treatment or care (e.g. out-patient treatment or social services) are available and, if so, why they are not appropriate.]

.............................................................................................................................

.............................................................................................................................

.............................................................................................................................

[If you need to continue on a separate sheet please indicate here [ ] and attach that sheet to this form]

Such treatment cannot be provided unless the patient continues to be detained under the Act, for the following reasons – [Reasons should indicate why informal admission is not appropriate.]

.............................................................................................................................

.............................................................................................................................

.............................................................................................................................

[If you need to continue on a separate sheet please indicate here [ ] and attach that sheet to this form]

I am also of the opinion that, taking into account the nature and degree of the mental disorder from which the patient is suffering and all the other circumstances of the case, appropriate medical treatment is available to the patient.

Signed.............................................

PRINT NAME.............................................

Profession.............................................

Date.............................................

PART 2

*(To be completed by a professional who has been professionally concerned with the patient's medical treatment and who is of a different profession from the responsible clinician)*

I agree with the responsible clinician that: this patient is suffering from mental disorder of a nature or degree which makes it appropriate for the patient to receive medical treatment in a hospital; it is necessary for the patient's own health or safety or for the protection of other persons that the patient should receive treatment and it cannot be provided unless the patient continues to be detained under the Act; and that, taking into account the nature and degree of the mental disorder from which the patient is suffering and all other circumstances of the case, appropriate medical treatment is available to the patient.

Signed.............................................

PRINT NAME.............................................

Profession.............................................

Date.............................................

PART 3

*(To be completed by the responsible clinician)*

I am furnishing this report by: *<delete the phrase which does not apply>*

today consigning it to the hospital managers' internal mail system.

sending or delivering it without using the hospital managers' internal mail system.

Signed.............................................

PRINT NAME.............................................

Date.............................................

PART 4

*(To be completed on behalf of the hospital managers)*

This report was *<delete the phrase which does not apply>*

furnished to the hospital managers through their internal mail system.

received by me on behalf of the hospital managers on [date].

*Signed.............................................*

*on behalf of the hospital managers*

*PRINT NAME.............................................*

*Date.............................................*

**Form H6**  *Regulation 14(1)(a) and (b)*

**Mental Health Act 1983 section 21B – authority for detention after absence without leave for more than 28 days**

PART 1

*(To be completed by the responsible clinician)*

To the managers of [name and address of hospital in which the patient is liable to be detained]

I examined [PRINT full name of patient] on [date of examination] who:

(a)  was absent without leave from hospital or the place where the patient ought to have been beginning on [date absence without leave began];

(b)  was/is* liable to be detained for a period ending on [date authority for detention would have expired, apart from any extension under section 21, or date on which it will expire]; <*delete the phrase which does not apply> and

(c)  returned to the hospital or place on [date].

I have consulted [PRINT full name of approved mental health professional] who is an approved mental health professional.

I have also consulted [PRINT full name and profession of person consulted] who has been professionally concerned with the patient's treatment.

In my opinion,

(a)  this patient is suffering from mental disorder of a nature or degree which makes it appropriate for the patient to receive medical treatment in a hospital,

AND

(b)  it is necessary

(i)  for the patient's own health

(ii)  for the patient's own safety

(iii)  for the protection of other persons

*<delete the indents not applicable>*

that this patient should receive treatment in hospital,

because – [Your reasons should cover both (a) and (b) above. As part of them: describe the patient's symptoms and behaviour and explain how those symptoms and behaviour lead you to your opinion; say whether other methods of treatment or care (e.g. out-patient treatment or social services) are available and, if so, why they are not appropriate.]

.............................................................................................................................................................

.............................................................................................................................................................

.............................................................................................................................................................

[If you need to continue on a separate sheet please indicate here [ ] and attach that sheet to this form]

405

Such treatment cannot be provided unless the patient continues to be detained under the Act, for the following reasons – [Reasons should indicate why informal admission is not appropriate.]

..............................................................................................................................................

..............................................................................................................................................

..............................................................................................................................................

[If you need to continue on a separate sheet please indicate here [ ] and attach that sheet to this form]

I am also of the opinion that, taking into account the nature and degree of the mental disorder from which the patient is suffering and all other circumstances of the case, appropriate medical treatment is available to the patient.

The authority for the detention of the patient is/is not* due to expire within a period of two months beginning with the date on which this report is to be furnished to the hospital managers.

<*Delete the phrase which does not apply>

*Complete the following only if the authority for detention is due to expire within that period of two months.*

This report shall/shall not* have effect as a report duly furnished under section 20(3) for the renewal of the authority for the detention of the patient. <*Delete the phrase which does not apply>

*Complete the following in all cases.*

I am furnishing this report by: <delete the phrase which does not apply>

today consigning it to the hospital managers' internal mail system.

sending or delivering it without using the hospital managers' internal mail system.

Signed..............................................

PRINT NAME..............................................

Date..............................................

PART 2

*(To be completed on behalf of the hospital managers)*

This report was <delete the phrase which does not apply>

furnished to the hospital managers through their internal mail system

received by me on behalf of the hospital managers on [date]

Signed..............................................

on behalf of the hospital managers

PRINT NAME..............................................

Date..............................................

**Form G1** *Regulation 5(1)(a)(i) and (1)(b)*

**Mental Health Act 1983 section 7 – guardianship application by nearest relative**

PART 1

*(To be completed by the nearest relative)*

To the [name of local social services authority]

I [PRINT your full name and address] apply for the reception of [PRINT full name and address of patient] into the guardianship of [PRINT full name and address of proposed guardian] in accordance with Part 2 of the Mental Health Act 1983.

*Complete (a) or (b) as applicable and delete the other.*

(a)   To the best of my knowledge and belief I am the patient's nearest relative within the meaning of the Act.

I am the patient's [state your relationship with the patient].

(b)   I have been authorised to exercise the functions under the Act of the patient's nearest relative by a county court/the patient's nearest relative *<delete the phrase which does not apply>*, and a copy of the authority is attached to this application.

*       The patient's date of birth is [date]

OR

*       I believe the patient is aged 16 years or over.

*<\*Delete the phrase which does not apply.>*

I last saw the patient on [date], which was within the period of 14 days ending on the day this application is completed.

This application is founded on two medical recommendations in the prescribed form.

If neither of the medical practitioners had previous acquaintance with the patient before making their recommendations, please explain why you could not get a recommendation from a medical practitioner who did have previous acquaintance with the patient –

..............................................................................................................................................

..............................................................................................................................................

..............................................................................................................................................

[If you need to continue on a separate sheet please indicate here [ ] and attach that sheet to this form]

Signed............................................

Date............................................

PART 2*

<*Complete only if proposed guardian is not a local social services authority>

*(To be completed by the proposed guardian)*

My full name and address is as entered in Part 1 of this form and I am willing to act as the guardian of the above named patient in accordance with Part 2 of the Mental Health Act 1983.

Signed............................................

Date............................................

**Form G2** *Regulation 5(1)(a)(ii) and 5(1)(b)*

**Mental Health Act 1983 section 7 – guardianship application
by an approved mental health professional**

PART 1

*(To be completed by the approved mental health professional)*

To the [name of local social services authority]

I [PRINT your full name and address] apply for the reception of [PRINT full name and address of patient] into the guardianship of

[PRINT full name and address of proposed guardian] in accordance with Part 2 of the Mental Health Act 1983.

I am acting on behalf of [name of local social services authority] and am approved to act as an approved mental health professional for the purposes of the Act by *<delete as appropriate>* that authority

[name of local social services authority that approved you, if different.]

*Complete the following where consultation with the nearest relative has taken place.*

*Complete (a) or (b) as applicable and delete the other.*

(a) I have consulted [PRINT full name and address] who to the best of my knowledge and belief is the patient's nearest relative within the meaning of the Act;

(b) I have consulted [PRINT full name and address] who I understand has been authorised by a county court/the patient's nearest relative to exercise the functions under the Act of the patient's nearest relative. *<Delete the phrase which does not apply>*

That person has not notified me or the local social services authority on whose behalf I am acting that he or she objects to this application being made.

*Complete the following where the nearest relative has not been consulted. Delete whichever two of (a), (b) and (c) do not apply.*

(a) I have been unable to ascertain who is this patient's nearest relative within the meaning of the Act,

OR

(b) to the best of my knowledge and belief this patient has no nearest relative within the meaning of the Act,

OR

(c) [PRINT full name and address] is

(i) this patient's nearest relative within the meaning of the Act,

(ii) authorised to exercise the functions of this patient's nearest relative under the Act,

*<delete either (i) or (ii)>*

but in my opinion it is not reasonably practicable/would involve unreasonable delay

*<delete as appropriate>* to consult that person before making this application, because –

................................................................................................................................................

................................................................................................................................................

................................................................................................................................................

[If you need to continue on a separate sheet please indicate here [ ] and attach that sheet to this form]

*The remainder of Part 1 of this form must be completed in all cases.*

I last saw the patient on [date], which was within the period of 14 days ending on the day this application is completed.

\*     The patient's date of birth is [date]

OR

\*     I believe the patient is aged 16 years or over.

*<\*Delete the phrase which does not apply.>*

This application is founded on two medical recommendations in the prescribed form. If neither of the medical practitioners had previous acquaintance with the patient before making their recommendations, please explain why you could not get a recommendation from a medical practitioner who did have previous acquaintance with the patient –

................................................................................................................................................

................................................................................................................................................

................................................................................................................................................

[If you need to continue on a separate sheet please indicate here [ ] and attach that sheet to this form]

*Signed*..............................................

*Date*..............................................

PART 2\*

*<\*Complete only if proposed guardian is not a local social services authority>*

*(To be completed by the proposed guardian)*

My full name and address is as entered in Part 1 of this form and I am willing to act as the guardian of the above named patient in accordance with Part 2 of the Mental Health Act 1983.

Signed..............................................

Date..............................................

**Form G3** *Regulation 5(1)(c)(i)*

## Mental Health Act 1983 section 7 – joint medical recommendation for reception into guardianship

We, registered medical practitioners, recommend that [PRINT full name and address of patient] be received into guardianship in accordance with Part 2 of the Mental Health Act 1983.

I [PRINT full name and address of first practitioner] last examined this patient on [date], and

*<*delete if not applicable>*

* I had previous acquaintance with the patient before I conducted that examination.

* I am approved under section 12 of the Act as having special experience in the diagnosis or treatment of mental disorder.

I [PRINT full name and address of second practitioner] last examined this patient on [date], and

*<*delete if not applicable>*

* I had previous acquaintance with the patient before I conducted that examination.

* I am approved under section 12 of the Act as having special experience in the diagnosis or treatment of mental disorder.

In our opinion,

(a) this patient is suffering from mental disorder of a nature or degree which warrants the patient's reception into guardianship under the Act,

AND

(b) it is necessary

    (i) in the interests of the welfare of the patient

    (ii) for the protection of other persons

*<delete (i) or (ii) unless both apply>*

that the patient should be so received.

Our reasons for these opinions are:

[Your reasons should cover both (a) and (b) above. As part of them: describe the patient's symptoms and behaviour and explain how those symptoms and behaviour lead you to your opinion; and explain why the patient cannot appropriately be cared for without powers of guardianship.]

.................................................................................................................................................

.................................................................................................................................................

.................................................................................................................................................

[If you need to continue on a separate sheet please indicate here [ ] and attach that sheet to this form]

Signed.............................................

Date..............................................

Signed.............................................

Date..............................................

NOTE: AT LEAST ONE OF THE PRACTITIONERS SIGNING THIS FORM MUST BE APPROVED UNDER SECTION 12 OF THE ACT.

**Form G4** *Regulation 5(1)(c)(ii)*

**Mental Health Act 1983 section 7 – medical recommendation for reception into guardianship**

I [PRINT full name and address of practitioner], a registered medical practitioner recommend

that [PRINT full name and address of patient] be received into guardianship in accordance with Part 2 of the Mental Health Act 1983.

I last examined this patient on [date].

* I had previous acquaintance with the patient before I conducted that examination.

* I am approved under section 12 of the Act as having special experience in the diagnosis or treatment of mental disorder. <*Delete if not applicable>

In my opinion,

(a) this patient is suffering from mental disorder of a nature or degree which warrants the patient's reception into guardianship under the Act,

AND

(b) it is necessary

　(i) in the interests of the welfare of the patient

　(ii) for the protection of other persons

<delete (i) or (ii) unless both apply>

that the patient should be so received.

My reasons for these opinions are:

[Your reasons should cover both (a) and (b) above. As part of them: describe the patient's symptoms and behaviour and explain how those symptoms and behaviour lead you to your opinion; and explain why the patient cannot appropriately be cared for without powers of guardianship.]

..............................................................................................................................

..............................................................................................................................

..............................................................................................................................

[If you need to continue on a separate sheet please indicate here [ ] and attach that sheet to this form]

Signed.............................................

Date.............................................

**Form G5** *Regulation 5(2)*

**Mental Health Act 1983 section 7 – record of acceptance of guardianship application**

*(To be attached to the guardianship application)*

[PRINT full name and address of patient]

This application was accepted by/on behalf* of the local social services authority on [date].

*<\*Delete the phrase that does not apply>*

Signed..........................................

on behalf of the responsible local social services authority

PRINT NAME..........................................

Date..........................................

**Form G6**  *Regulation 7(4)(a),(d) and (e)*

**Mental Health Act 1983 section 19 – authority for transfer from hospital to guardianship**

PART 1

*(To be completed on behalf of the managers of the hospital where the patient is detained)*

Authority is given for the transfer of [PRINT full name of patient] who is at present liable to be detained in [name and address of hospital] to the guardianship of [PRINT full name and address of proposed guardian] in accordance with the Mental Health (Hospital, Guardianship and Treatment) (England) Regulations 2008.

This transfer was agreed by the [name of local social services authority] on [date of confirmation]. The transfer is to take place on [date].

Signed.............................................

on behalf of the responsible local social services authority

PRINT NAME.............................................

Date.............................................

PART 2*

<*Complete only if proposed guardian is not a local social services authority>

*(To be completed by the proposed private guardian)*

My full name and address is as entered in Part 1 of this form and I am willing to act as the guardian of the above named patient in accordance with Part 2 of the Mental Health Act 1983.

Signed.............................................

Date.............................................

IF THE GUARDIAN IS TO BE A PRIVATE GUARDIAN, THE TRANSFER MAY NOT TAKE PLACE UNTIL BOTH PARTS OF THIS FORM ARE COMPLETED

**Form G7** *Regulation 8(1)(a), (d)and (e)*

## Mental Health Act 1983 section 19 – authority for transfer of a patient from the guardianship of one guardian to another

PART 1

*(To be completed by the present guardian)*

Authority is given for the transfer of [PRINT full name and address of patient] from the guardianship of [PRINT full name and address of the present guardian] to the guardianship of

[PRINT full name and address of the proposed guardian] in accordance with the Mental Health (Hospital, Guardianship and Treatment) (England) Regulations 2008.

This transfer was agreed by the [name of local social services authority] on [date of confirmation]. The transfer is to take place on [date].

Signed............................................

the guardian/on behalf of the local social services

*<Delete whichever does not apply>*

PRINT NAME............................................

Date............................................

PART 2*

<*Complete only if proposed guardian is not a local social services authority>

*(To be completed by the proposed private guardian)*

My full name and address is as entered in Part 1 of this form and I am willing to act as the guardian of the above named patient in accordance with Part 2 of the Mental Health Act 1983.

Signed............................................

Date............................................

IF THE NEW GUARDIAN IS TO BE A PRIVATE GUARDIAN, THE TRANSFER MAY NOT TAKE PLACE UNTIL BOTH PARTS OF THIS FORM ARE COMPLETED.

**Form G8**  *Regulation 8(2) and (4)*

**Mental Health Act 1983 section 19 – authority for transfer from guardianship to hospital**

PART 1

*(To be completed on behalf of the local social services authority)*

Authority is given for the transfer of [PRINT full name and address of patient] who is at present under the guardianship of [name and address of guardian] to [name and address of hospital] in accordance with the Mental Health (Hospital, Guardianship and Treatment) (England) Regulations 2008.

Signed............................................

on behalf of the local social services authority

PRINT NAME............................................

Date............................................

PART 2

RECORD OF ADMISSION

*(This is not part of the authority for transfer but is to be completed at the hospital to which the patient is transferred)*

This patient was admitted to the above named hospital in pursuance of this authority for transfer on [date of admission to receiving hospital] at [time].

Signed............................................

on behalf of the managers of the receiving hospital

PRINT NAME............................................

Date............................................

**Form G9** *Regulation 13(4) and (5)*

**Mental Health Act 1983 section 20 – renewal of authority for guardianship**

PART 1

*(To be completed by the responsible clinician or nominated medical attendant)*

To [name of guardian]

[name of responsible local social services authority if it is not the guardian]

I examined [PRINT full name and address of patient] on [date].

The patient is subject to guardianship for a period ending on [date authority for guardianship is due to expire].

In my opinion,

(a)  this patient is suffering from mental disorder of a nature or degree which warrants the patient's reception into guardianship under the Act,

AND

(b)  it is necessary

   (i)  in the interests of the welfare of the patient

   (ii)  for the protection of other persons

*<delete (i) or (ii) unless both apply>*

that the patient should remain under guardianship under the Act.

My reasons for these opinions are:

[Your reasons should cover both (a) and (b) above. As part of them: describe the patient's symptoms and behaviour and explain how those symptoms and behaviour lead you to your opinion; and explain why the patient cannot appropriately be cared for without powers of guardianship.]

......................................................................................................................

......................................................................................................................

......................................................................................................................

[If you need to continue on a separate sheet please indicate here [ ] and attach that sheet to this form]

Signed............................................

*Responsible clinician

*Nominated medical attendant

<* Delete whichever does not apply>

PRINT NAME.............................................

Date.............................................

PART 2

(To be completed on behalf of the responsible local social services authority)

This report was received by me on behalf of the local social services authority on [date].

Signed.............................................

on behalf of the local social services authority

PRINT NAME.............................................

Date.............................................

**Form G10** *Regulation 14(2)(a) and (b)*

**Mental Health Act 1983 section 21B – authority for guardianship after absence without leave for more than 28 days**

PART 1

*(To be completed by the responsible clinician or nominated medical attendant)*

To [name of guardian]

[name of responsible local social services authority if it is not the guardian]

I examined [PRINT full name and address of patient] on [date of examination] who:

(a)  was absent without leave from the place where the patient is required to reside beginning on [date absence without leave began];

(b)  was/is* subject to guardianship for a period ending on [date authority for guardianship would have expired, apart from any extension under section 21, or date on which it will expire]; <*delete phrase which does not apply> and

(c)  returned to that place on [date].

In my opinion,

(a)  this patient is suffering from mental disorder of a nature or degree which warrants the patient's reception into guardianship under the Act,

AND

(b)  it is necessary

    (i)  in the interests of the welfare of the patient

    (ii)  for the protection of other persons

<delete (i) or (ii) unless both apply>

that the patient should remain under guardianship under the Act.

My reasons for these opinions are:

[Your reasons should cover both (a) and (b) above. As part of them: describe the patient's symptoms and behaviour and explain how those symptoms and behaviour lead you to your opinion; and explain why the patient cannot appropriately be cared for without powers of guardianship.]

..................................................................................................................................

..................................................................................................................................

..................................................................................................................................

[If you need to continue on a separate sheet please indicate here [ ] and attach that sheet to this form]

The authority for the guardianship of the patient is/is not* due to expire within a period of two months beginning with the date on which this report is to be furnished. *<*Delete the phrase which does not apply>*

*Complete the following only if the authority for guardianship is due to expire within that period of two months.*

This report shall/shall not* have effect as a report duly furnished under section 20(6) for the renewal of the authority for the guardianship of the patient. *<*Delete the phrase which does not apply>*

Signed.............................................

*Responsible clinician

*Nominated medical attendant

*<* Delete whichever does not apply>*

PRINT NAME.............................................

Date.............................................

PART 2

*(To be completed on behalf of the responsible local social services authority)*

This report was received by me on behalf of the local social services authority on [date].

Signed.............................................

on behalf of the local social services authority

PRINT NAME.............................................

Date.............................................

**Form M1   Regulation 15(2), (4)(a) and 16(2)**

**Mental Health Act 1983 Part 6 – date of reception of a patient in England**

[PRINT full name of patient]

*   was admitted to [name and address of hospital] at [time] on [date]

*   was received into the guardianship of [name and address of guardian] on [date]

*   became a community patient as if discharged from [name and address of responsible hospital], on [date].

*<\*Complete as appropriate and delete the others>*

Signed.............................................

on behalf of the hospital managers/on behalf of the local social services authority/

the private guardian

*<Delete whichever do not apply>*

PRINT NAME.............................................

Date.............................................

**Form M2** *Regulation 25(1)(a) and (b)*

**Mental Health Act 1983 section 25 – report barring discharge by nearest relative**

PART 1

*To be completed by the responsible clinician)*

To the managers of [name and address of hospital]

[Name of nearest relative] gave notice at [time] on [date] of an intention to discharge [PRINT full name of patient].

I am of the opinion that the patient, if discharged, would be likely to act in a manner dangerous to other persons or to himself or herself.

The reasons for my opinion are –

.............................................................................................................................................

.............................................................................................................................................

.............................................................................................................................................

[If you need to continue on a separate sheet please indicate here [ ] and attach that sheet to this form]

I am furnishing this report by: <*delete the phrase which does not apply*>

consigning it to the hospital managers' internal mail system today at [time].

sending or delivering it without using the hospital managers' internal mail system.

Signed...........................................

Responsible clinician

PRINT NAME...........................................

Date...........................................

Time...........................................

PART 2

*(To be completed on behalf of the hospital managers)*

This report was: <*delete the phrase which does not apply*>

furnished to the hospital managers through their internal mail system.

received by me on behalf of the hospital managers at [time] on [date].

Signed...........................................

on behalf of the hospital managers

PRINT NAME...........................................

Date...........................................

**Form T1** *Regulation 27(1)(b)*

## Mental Health Act 1983 section 57 – certificate of consent to treatment and second opinion

*(Both parts of this certificate must be completed)*

PART 1

I [PRINT full name and address], a registered medical practitioner appointed for the purposes of Part 4 of the Act (a SOAD), and we [PRINT full name, address and profession], being two persons appointed for the purposes of section 57(2)(a) of the Act, certify that [PRINT full name and address of patient]

(a)   is capable of understanding the nature, purpose and likely effects of: [Give description of treatment or plan of treatment. Indicate clearly if the certificate is only to apply to any or all of the treatment for a specific period.]

..................................................................................................................................................

..................................................................................................................................................

..................................................................................................................................................

[If you need to continue on a separate sheet please indicate here [ ] and attach that sheet to this form]

AND

(b)   has consented to that treatment.

Signed...........................................

Date...........................................

Signed...........................................

Date...........................................

Signed...........................................

Date...........................................

PART 2

*(To be completed by SOAD only)*

I, the above named registered medical practitioner appointed for the purposes of Part 4 of the Act have consulted [PRINT full name of nurse] a nurse and [PRINT full name and profession] who have been professionally concerned with the medical treatment of the patient named above and certify that it is appropriate for the treatment to be given.

My reasons are as below/I will provide a statement of my reasons separately. *<Delete as appropriate>* [When giving reasons please indicate if, in your opinion, disclosure of the reasons to the patient would be likely to cause serious harm to the physical or mental health of the patient or to that of any other person.]

...............................................................................................................................

...............................................................................................................................

...............................................................................................................................

[If you need to continue on a separate sheet please indicate here [ ] and attach that sheet to this form]

Signed..........................................

Date..........................................

**Form T2** *Regulation 27(2)*

**Mental Health Act 1983 section 58(3)(a) – certificate of consent to treatment**

I [PRINT full name and address], the approved clinician in charge of the treatment described below/a registered medical practitioner appointed for the purposes of Part 4 of the Act (a SOAD) <*delete the phrase which does not apply*> certify that [PRINT full name and address of patient]

(a) is capable of understanding the nature, purpose and likely effects of: [Give description of treatment or plan of treatment. Indicate clearly if the certificate is only to apply to any or all of the treatment for a specific period.]

....................................................................................................................................

....................................................................................................................................

....................................................................................................................................

[If you need to continue on a separate sheet please indicate here [ ] and attach that sheet to this form]

AND

(b) has consented to that treatment.

Signed.............................................

Date.............................................

**Form T3**  *Regulation 27(2)*

**Mental Health Act 1983 section 58(3)(b) – certificate of second opinion**

I [PRINT full name and address], a registered medical practitioner appointed for the purposes of Part 4 of the Act (a SOAD), have consulted [PRINT full name of nurse], a nurse and [PRINT full name and profession] who have been professionally concerned with the medical treatment of

[PRINT full name and address of patient].

I certify that the patient – *<delete the phrase which does not apply>*

(a)   is not capable of understanding the nature, purpose and likely effects of

(b)   has not consented to

the following treatment: [Give description of treatment or plan of treatment. Indicate clearly if the certificate is only to apply to any or all of the treatment for a specific period.]

...........................................................................................................................................

...........................................................................................................................................

...........................................................................................................................................

[If you need to continue on a separate sheet please indicate here [ ] and attach that sheet to this form]

but that it is appropriate for the treatment to be given.

My reasons are as below/I will provide a statement of my reasons separately. *<Delete as appropriate>* [When giving reasons please indicate if, in your opinion, disclosure of the reasons to the patient would be likely to cause serious harm to the physical or mental health of the patient, or to that of any other person.]

...........................................................................................................................................

...........................................................................................................................................

...........................................................................................................................................

[If you need to continue on a separate sheet please indicate here [ ] and attach that sheet to this form]

Signed............................................

Date............................................

427

**Form T4** *Regulation 27(3)(b)*

**Mental Health Act 1983 section 58A(3) – certificate of consent to treatment (patients at least 18 years old)**

THIS FORM IS NOT TO BE USED FOR PATIENTS UNDER 18 YEARS OF AGE

I [PRINT full name and address], the approved clinician in charge of the treatment described below/a registered medical practitioner appointed for the purposes of Part 4 of the Act (a SOAD) <*delete as appropriate*> certify that [PRINT full name and address of patient] who has attained the age of 18 years,

(a) is capable of understanding the nature, purpose and likely effects of: [Give description of treatment or plan of treatment. Indicate clearly if the certificate is only to apply to any or all of the treatment for a specific period.]

.........................................................................................................................................

.........................................................................................................................................

.........................................................................................................................................

[If you need to continue on a separate sheet please indicate here [ ] and attach that sheet to this form]

AND

(b) has consented to that treatment.

Signed............................................

Date............................................

**Form T5** *Regulation 27(3)(b)*

## Mental Health Act 1983 section 58A(4) – certificate of consent to treatment and second opinion (patients under 18)

THIS FORM IS ONLY TO BE USED FOR PATIENTS UNDER 18 YEARS OF AGE

I [PRINT full name and address], a registered medical practitioner appointed for the purposes of Part 4 of the Act (a SOAD) certify that [PRINT full name and address of patient] who has not yet attained the age of 18 years,

(a) is capable of understanding the nature, purpose and likely effects of: [Give description of treatment or plan of treatment. Indicate clearly if the certificate is only to apply to any or all of the treatment for a specific period.]

................................................................................................................................................

................................................................................................................................................

................................................................................................................................................

[If you need to continue on a separate sheet please indicate here [ ] and attach that sheet to this form]

AND

(b) has consented to that treatment.

In my opinion it is appropriate for that treatment to be given.

My reasons are as below/I will provide a statement of my reasons separately. *<Delete as appropriate>* [When giving reasons please indicate if, in your opinion, disclosure of the reasons to the patient would be likely to cause serious harm to the physical or mental health of the patient, or to that of any other person.]

................................................................................................................................................

................................................................................................................................................

................................................................................................................................................

[If you need to continue on a separate sheet please indicate here [ ] and attach that sheet to this form]

Signed............................................

Date............................................

**Form T6** *Regulation 27(3)(b)*

**Mental Health Act 1983 section 58A(5) – certificate of second opinion (patients who are not capable of understanding the nature, purpose and likely effects of the treatment)**

I [PRINT full name and address], a registered medical practitioner appointed for the purposes of Part 4 of the Act (a SOAD), have consulted [PRINT full name of nurse] a nurse and [PRINT full name and profession] who have been professionally concerned with the medical treatment of [PRINT full name and address of patient].

I certify that the patient is not capable of understanding the nature, purpose and likely effects of: [Give description of treatment or plan of treatment. Indicate clearly if the certificate is only to apply to any or all of the treatment for a specific period.]

..................................................................................................................................

..................................................................................................................................

..................................................................................................................................

[If you need to continue on a separate sheet please indicate here [ ] and attach that sheet to this form]

but that it is appropriate for the treatment to be given.

My reasons are as below/I will provide a statement of my reasons separately. *<Delete as appropriate>* [When giving reasons please indicate if, in your opinion, disclosure of the reasons to the patient would be likely to cause serious harm to the physical or mental health of the patient or to that of any other person.]

..................................................................................................................................

..................................................................................................................................

..................................................................................................................................

[If you need to continue on a separate sheet please indicate here [ ] and attach that sheet to this form]

I further certify that giving the treatment described above to the patient would not conflict with –

(i) any decision of an attorney appointed under a Lasting Power of Attorney or deputy (appointed by the Court of Protection) of the patient as provided for by the Mental Capacity Act 2005

(ii) any decision of the Court of Protection, or

(iii) any Advance Decision to refuse treatment that is valid and applicable under the Mental Capacity Act 2005.

Signed.............................................

Date.............................................

**Form CTO1**  *Regulation 6(1)(a), (b) and 6(2)(a)*

**Mental Health Act 1983 section 17A – community treatment order**

*(Parts 1 and 3 of this form are to be completed by the responsible clinician and Part 2 by an approved mental health professional)*

PART 1

I [PRINT full name and address of the responsible clinician] am the responsible clinician for

[PRINT full name and address of patient].

In my opinion,

(a)  this patient is suffering from mental disorder of a nature or degree which makes it appropriate for the patient to receive medical treatment,

(b)  it is necessary for

(i)  the patient's health

(ii)  the patient's safety

(iii)  the protection of other persons

*<delete any phrase which is not applicable>*

that the patient should receive such treatment;

(c)  such treatment can be provided without the patient continuing to be detained in a hospital provided the patient is liable to being recalled to hospital for medical treatment;

(d)  it is necessary that the responsible clinician should be able to exercise the power under section 17E(1) to recall the patient to hospital;

(e)  taking into account the nature and degree of the mental disorder from which the patient is suffering and all other circumstances of the case, appropriate medical treatment is available to the patient.

My opinion is founded on the following grounds –

..................................................................................................................................................

..................................................................................................................................................

..................................................................................................................................................

[If you need to continue on a separate sheet please indicate here [ ] and attach that sheet to this form]

I confirm that in determining whether the criterion at (d) above is met, I have considered what risk there would be of deterioration of the patient's condition if the patient were not detained in hospital, with regard to the patient's history of mental disorder and any other relevant factors.

*Conditions to which the patient is to be subject by virtue of this community treatment order*

The patient is to make himself or herself available for examination under section 20A, as requested.

If it is proposed to give a certificate under Part 4A of the Act in the patient's case, the patient is to make himself or herself available for examination to enable the certificate to be given, as requested.

The patient is also to be subject to the following conditions (if any) under section 17B(2) of the Act:

.................................................................................................................................................

.................................................................................................................................................

.................................................................................................................................................

[If you need to continue on a separate sheet please indicate here [ ] and attach that sheet to this form]

I confirm that I consider the above conditions to be made under section 17B(2) of the Act are necessary or appropriate for one or more of the following purposes:

\*      to ensure that the patient receives medical treatment

\*      to prevent risk of harm to the patient's health or safety

\*      to protect other persons.

Signed.............................................

Date.............................................

PART 2

I [PRINT full name and address] am acting on behalf of [name of local social services authority]and am approved to act as an approved mental health professional for the purposes of the Act by

<delete as appropriate>

that authority

[name of local social services authority that approved you, if different].

I agree that:

(i)  the above patient meets the criteria for a community treatment order to be made

(ii)  it is appropriate to make a community treatment order, and

(iii)  the conditions made above under section 17B(2) are necessary or appropriate for one or more of the purposes specified.

Signed.............................................

Approved mental health professional

Date.............................................

PART 3

I exercise my power under section 17A of the Mental Health Act 1983 to make a community treatment order in respect of the patient named in Part 1 of this Form.

This community treatment order is to be effective from [date] at [time].

Date............................................

Responsible clinician

Date............................................

THIS COMMUNITY TREATMENT ORDER IS NOT VALID UNLESS ALL THREE PARTS ARE COMPLETED AND SIGNED.

IT MUST BE FURNISHED AS SOON AS PRACTICABLE TO THE MANAGERS OF THE HOSPITAL IN WHICH THE PATIENT WAS LIABLE TO BE DETAINED BEFORE THE ORDER WAS MADE.

**Form CTO2** *Regulation 6(2)(b)*

**Mental Health Act 1983 section 17B – variation of conditions of a community treatment order**

I [PRINT full name and address of the responsible clinician] am the responsible clinician for [PRINT full name and address of the community patient].

I am varying the conditions attaching to the community treatment order for the above named patient.

The conditions made under section 17B(2), as varied, are: [List the conditions as varied in full (including any which are not being varied) or state that there are no longer to be any such conditions.]

.................................................................................................................................

.................................................................................................................................

.................................................................................................................................

[If you need to continue on a separate sheet please indicate here [ ] and attach that sheet to this form]

The variation is to take effect from [date].

I confirm that I consider the above conditions to be necessary or appropriate for one or more of the following purposes:

* to ensure that the patient receives medical treatment

* to prevent risk of harm to the patient's health or safety

* to protect other persons.

Signed..........................................

Responsible clinician

Date..........................................

THIS FORM MUST BE FURNISHED AS SOON AS PRACTICABLE TO THE MANAGERS OF THE RESPONSIBLE HOSPITAL.

**Form CTO3**  *Regulation 6(3)(a)*

**Mental Health Act 1983 section 17E – community treatment order: notice of recall to hospital**

*(To be completed by the responsible clinician)*

I notify you, [PRINT name of community patient], that you are recalled to [PRINT full name and address of the hospital] under section 17E of the Mental Health Act 1983.

*Complete either (a) or (b) below and delete the one which does not apply.*

(a)  In my opinion,

   (i)  you require treatment in hospital for mental disorder, AND

   (ii)  there would be a risk of harm to your health or safety or to other persons if you were not recalled to hospital for that purpose.

This opinion is founded on the following grounds –

...................................................................................................................................................

...................................................................................................................................................

...................................................................................................................................................

[If you need to continue on a separate sheet please indicate here [ ] and attach that sheet to this form]

(b)  You have failed to comply with the condition imposed under section 17B of the Mental Health Act 1983 that you make yourself available for examination for the purpose of:

*<delete as appropriate>*

 (i)  consideration of extension of the community treatment period under section 20A

(ii)  enabling a Part 4A certificate to be given.

Signed............................................

Responsible clinician

PRINT NAME............................................

Date............................................

Time............................................

A COPY OF THIS NOTICE IS TO BE FORWARDED TO THE MANAGERS OF THE HOSPITAL TO WHICH THE PATIENT IS RECALLED AS SOON AS POSSIBLE AFTER IT IS SERVED ON THE PATIENT. IF THAT HOSPITAL IS NOT THE RESPONSIBLE HOSPITAL, YOU SHOULD INFORM THE HOSPITAL MANAGERS THE NAME AND ADDRESS OF THE RESPONSIBLE HOSPITAL.

*This notice is sufficient authority for the managers of the named hospital to detain the patient there in accordance with the provisions of section 17E of the Mental Health Act 1983.*

**Form CTO4**   *Regulation 6(3)(d)*

**Mental Health Act 1983 section 17E – community treatment order: record of patient's detention in hospital after recall**

[PRINT full name and address of patient] ("the patient") is currently a community patient.

In pursuance of a notice recalling the patient to hospital under section 17E of the Act, the patient was detained in [full name and address of hospital] on [enter date and time at which the patient's detention in the hospital as a result of the recall notice began].

Signed............................................

on behalf of the hospital managers

PRINT NAME............................................

Date............................................

Time............................................

**Form CTO5** *Regulation 6(8)(a) and (b)*

**Mental Health Act 1983 section 17F(4) – revocation of community treatment order**

*(Parts 1 and 3 of this form are to be completed by the responsible clinician and Part 2 by an approved mental health professional)*

*PART 1*

I [PRINT full name and address of the responsible clinician] am the responsible clinician for

[PRINT full name and address of community patient] who is detained in [name and address of hospital] having been recalled to hospital under section 17E(1) of the Act.

In my opinion,

(a)   this patient is suffering from mental disorder of a nature or degree which makes it appropriate for the patient to receive medical treatment in a hospital,

AND

(b)   it is necessary for

 (i)  the patient's own health

 (ii)  the patient's own safety

 (iii)  the protection of other persons

*<delete the indents not applicable>*

that this patient should receive treatment in hospital,

AND

(c)   such treatment cannot be provided unless the patient is detained for medical treatment under the Act,

because – [Your reasons should cover (a), (b) and (c) above. As part of them: describe the patient's symptoms and behaviour and explain how those symptoms and behaviour lead you to your opinion; say whether other methods of treatment or care (e.g. out-patient treatment or social services) are available and, if so, why they are not appropriate; indicate why informal admission is not appropriate.]

...........................................................................................................................................

...........................................................................................................................................

...........................................................................................................................................

[If you need to continue on a separate sheet please indicate here [ ] and attach that sheet to this form]

I am also of the opinion that taking into account the nature and degree of the mental disorder from which the patient is suffering and all other circumstances of the case, appropriate medical treatment is available to the patient at the hospital named above.

Signed..............................................

Responsible clinician

Date..............................................

PART 2

I [PRINT full name and address] am acting on behalf of [name of local social services authority] and am approved to act as an approved mental health professional for the purposes of the Act by

*<delete as appropriate>*

that authority

[name of local social services authority that approved you, if different].

I agree that:

(i)   the patient meets the criteria for detention in hospital set out above and

(ii)   it is appropriate to revoke the community treatment order.

Signed..............................................

Approved mental health professional

Date..............................................

PART 3

I exercise my power under section 17F(4) to revoke the community treatment order in respect of the patient named in Part 1 who has been detained in hospital since [time] on [date], having been recalled under section 17E(1).

Signed..............................................

Responsible clinician

Date..............................................

THIS REVOCATION ORDER IS NOT VALID UNLESS ALL THREE PARTS ARE COMPLETED AND SIGNED. IT MUST BE SENT AS SOON AS PRACTICABLE TO THE MANAGERS OF THE HOSPITAL IN WHICH THE PATIENT IS DETAINED.

**Form CTO6** *Regulation 9(3)(a) and (5)*

## Mental Health Act 1983 section 17F(2) – authority for transfer of recalled community patient to a hospital under different managers

*(To be completed on behalf of the managers of the hospital in which the patient is detained by virtue of recall)*

PART 1

This form authorises the transfer of [PRINT full name of patient] from [name and address of hospital in which the patient is detained] to [name and address of hospital to which patient is to be transferred] in accordance with the Mental Health (Hospital, Guardianship and Treatment) (England) Regulations 2008.

I attach a copy of Form CTO4 recording the patient's detention in hospital after recall.

\* 	The hospital in which the patient is currently detained is the patient's responsible hospital.

\* 	The hospital to which the patient is to be transferred is the patient's responsible hospital.

\* 	The patient's responsible hospital is [name and address of responsible hospital].

<*Delete the phrases which do not apply>

Signed..........................................

on behalf of managers of the first named hospital

PRINT NAME..........................................

Date..........................................

PART 2

RECORD OF ADMISSION

*(This is not part of the authority for transfer but is to be completed at the hospital to which the patient is transferred)*

This patient was admitted to [name of hospital] in pursuance of this authority for transfer on [date of admission to receiving hospital] at [time].

Signed..........................................

on behalf of managers of the receiving hospital

PRINT NAME..........................................

Date..........................................

**Form CTO7** *Regulation 13(6)(a) and (b), and 13(7)*

**Mental Health Act 1983 section 20A – community treatment order: report extending the community treatment period**

*Parts 1 and 3 of this form are to be completed by the responsible clinician and Part 2 by an approved mental health professional. Part 4 is to be completed by or on behalf of the managers of the responsible hospital.*

PART 1

To the managers of [name and address of the responsible hospital]

I am [PRINT full name and address of the responsible clinician] the responsible clinician for

[PRINT full name and address of patient].

The patient is currently subject to a community treatment order made on [enter date].

I examined the patient on [date].

In my opinion,

(a) this patient is suffering from mental disorder of a nature or degree which makes it appropriate for the patient to receive medical treatment;

(b) it is necessary for

    (i) the patient's health

    (ii) the patient's safety

    (iii) the protection of other persons

*<delete any indent which is not applicable>*

that the patient should receive such treatment;

(c) such treatment can be provided without the patient continuing to be detained in a hospital provided the patient is liable to being recalled to hospital for medical treatment;

(d) it is necessary that the responsible clinician should continue to be able to exercise the power under section 17E(1) to recall the patient to hospital;

(e) taking into account the nature and degree of the mental disorder from which the patient is suffering and all other circumstances of the case, appropriate medical treatment is available to the patient.

My opinion is founded on the following grounds –

..............................................................................................................................................

..............................................................................................................................................

[If you need to continue on a separate sheet please indicate here [ ] and attach that sheet to this form]

I confirm that in determining whether the criterion at (d) above is met, I have considered what risk there would be of deterioration of the patient's condition if the patient were to continue not to be detained in hospital, with regard to the patient's history of mental disorder and any other relevant factors.

Signed............................................

Responsible clinician

Date............................................

PART 2

I [PRINT full name and address] am acting on behalf of [name of local social services authority] and am approved to act as an approved mental health professional for the purposes of the Act by

*<delete as appropriate>*

that authority

[name of local social services authority that approved you, if different].

I agree that:

(i)   the patient meets the criteria for the extension of the community treatment period and

(ii)  it is appropriate to extend the community treatment period.

Signed............................................

Approved mental health professional

Date............................................

PART 3

Before furnishing this report, I consulted [PRINT full name and profession of person consulted] who has been professionally concerned with the patient's treatment.

I am furnishing this report by: *<delete the phrase which does not apply>*

today consigning it to the hospital managers' internal mail system.

sending or delivering it without using the hospital managers' internal mail system.

Signed............................................

Responsible clinician

Date............................................

THIS REPORT IS NOT VALID UNLESS PARTS 1, 2 & 3 ARE COMPLETED AND SIGNED

PART 4

This report was <*delete the phrase which does not apply*>

furnished to the hospital managers through their internal mail system.

received by me on behalf of the hospital managers on [date].

Signed..........................................

on behalf of the managers of the responsible hospital

PRINT NAME..........................................

Date..........................................

**Form CTO8** *Regulation 14(3)(a) and (b)*

**Mental Health Act 1983 section 21B – authority for extension of community treatment period after absence without leave for more than 28 days**

PART 1

*(To be completed by the responsible clinician)*

To the managers of [enter name and address of responsible hospital]

I am [PRINT full name and address of the responsible clinician] the responsible clinician for [PRINT full name and address of patient].

I examined the patient on [date of examination] who:

(a)  was recalled to hospital on [date] under section 17E of the Mental Health Act 1983;

(b)  was absent without leave from hospital beginning on [date absence without leave began];

(c)  was/is *<delete as appropriate>* subject to a community treatment order for a period ending on [date community treatment order would have expired, apart from any extension under section 21, or date on which it will expire]; and

(d)  returned to the hospital on [date].

I have consulted [PRINT full name of approved mental health professional] who is an approved mental health professional.

I have also consulted [PRINT full name and profession of person consulted] who has been professionally concerned with the patient's treatment.

In my opinion,

(a)  this patient is suffering from mental disorder of a nature or degree which makes it appropriate for the patient to receive medical treatment;

(b)  it is necessary for

(i)  the patient's health

(ii)  the patient's safety

(iii)  the protection of other persons

*<delete any indent which is not applicable>*

that the patient should receive such treatment;

(c)  such treatment can be provided without the patient continuing to be detained in a hospital provided the patient is liable to being recalled to hospital for medical treatment;

(d)  it is necessary that the responsible clinician should continue to be able to exercise the power under section 17E(1) to recall the patient to hospital;

(e)  taking into account the nature and degree of the mental disorder from which the patient is suffering and all other circumstances of the case, appropriate medical treatment is available to the patient.

I confirm that in determining whether the criterion at (d) above is met, I have considered what risk there would be of deterioration of the patient's condition if the patient were to continue not to be detained in hospital, with regard to the patient's history of mental disorder and any other relevant factors.

My opinion is founded on the following grounds –

..............................................................................................................................................................

..............................................................................................................................................................

[If you need to continue on a separate sheet please indicate here [ ] and attach that sheet to this form]

The community treatment order is/is not* due to expire within a period of two months beginning with the date on which this report is to be furnished to the managers of the responsible hospital.

<*Delete the phrase which does not apply>

*Complete the following only if the authority for detention is due to expire within that period of two months.*

This report shall/shall not* have effect as a report duly furnished under section 20A(4) for the extension of the community treatment period for this patient. <*Delete the phrase which does not apply>

*Complete the following in all cases.*

I am furnishing this report by: <delete the phrase which does not apply>

today consigning it to the hospital managers' internal mail system.

sending or delivering it without using the hospital managers' internal mail system.

Signed..........................................

Date..........................................

PART 2

*(To be completed on behalf of the managers of the responsible hospital)*

This report was <delete the phrase which does not apply>

furnished to the hospital managers through their internal mail system.

received by me on behalf of the hospital managers on [date].

Signed..........................................

on behalf of the hospital managers

PRINT NAME..........................................

Date..........................................

**Form CTO9** *Regulation 16(4) and (5)*

**Mental Health Act 1983 Part 6 – community patients transferred to England**

PART 1

*(To be completed by the responsible clinician)*

I [PRINT full name and address of the responsible clinician] am the responsible clinician for

[PRINT full name and address of patient] who is treated as if subject to a community treatment order having been transferred to England.

The patient is to be subject to the following conditions by virtue of that community treatment order: The patient is to make himself or herself available for examination under section 20A, as requested.

If it is proposed to give a certificate under Part 4A of the Act in the patient's case, the patient is to make himself or herself available for examination to enable the certificate to be given, as requested.

The patient is also to be subject to the following conditions (if any) under section 17B(2) of the Act:

...................................................................................................................................

...................................................................................................................................

[If you need to continue on a separate sheet please indicate here [ ] and attach that sheet to this form]

I confirm that I consider the above conditions to be made under section 17B(2) of the Act are necessary or appropriate for one or more of the following purposes:

* to ensure that the patient receives medical treatment

* to prevent risk of harm to the patient's health or safety

* to protect other persons.

Signed............................................

Responsible clinician

Date............................................

PART 2

*(To be completed by the approved mental health professional)*

I [PRINT full name and address] am acting on behalf of [name of local social services authority]

and am approved to act as an approved mental health professional for the purposes of the Act by

*<delete as appropriate>*

that authority

[name of local social services authority that approved you, if different].

I agree that the conditions made above under section 17B(2) are necessary or appropriate for one or more of the purposes specified.

Signed...........................................

Approved mental health professional

Date...........................................

THE PATIENT IS NOT SUBJECT TO THE CONDITIONS SET OUT IN THIS FORM UNLESS BOTH PARTS OF THE FORM ARE COMPLETED.

**Form CTO10** *Regulation 17(3)(a) and (d)(i) and (ii)*

**Mental Health Act 1983 section 19A – authority for assignment of responsibility for community patient to hospital under different managers**

*(To be completed on behalf of the responsible hospital)*

This form gives authority for the assignment of responsibility for [PRINT full name and address of patient] from [name and address of responsible hospital] to [name and address of hospital to which responsibility is to be assigned] in accordance with the Mental Health (Hospital, Guardianship and Treatment) (England) Regulations 2008.

This assignment was agreed by the managers of the hospital to which the responsibility is to be assigned on [date of confirmation].

The assignment is to take place on [date].

Signed..............................................

on behalf of managers of first named hospital

PRINT NAME..............................................

Date..............................................

**Form CTO11   Regulation 28(1)**

**Mental Health Act 1983 section 64C(4) – certificate of appropriateness of treatment to be given to community patient**

(Part 4A certificate)

*(To be completed on behalf of the responsible hospital)*

I [PRINT full name and address] am a registered medical practitioner appointed for the purposes of Part 4 of the Act (a SOAD).

I have consulted [PRINT full name and profession] and [full name and profession] who have been professionally concerned with the medical treatment of [PRINT full name and address of patient] who is subject to a community treatment order.

I certify that it is appropriate for the following treatment to be given to this patient while the patient is not recalled to hospital, subject to any conditions specified below. The treatment is:

[Give description of treatment or plan of treatment.]

..............................................................................................................................

..............................................................................................................................

I specify the following conditions (if any) to apply: [Conditions may include time-limits on the approval of any or all of the treatment.]

..............................................................................................................................

..............................................................................................................................

I certify that it is appropriate for the following treatment (if any) to be given to this patient following any recall to hospital under section 17E of the Act, subject to any conditions specified below. The treatment is: [Give description of treatment or plan of treatment].

..............................................................................................................................

..............................................................................................................................

I specify the following conditions (if any) to apply to the treatment which may be given to the patient following any recall to hospital under section 17E: [Conditions may include time-limits on the approval of any or all of the treatment.]

..............................................................................................................................

..............................................................................................................................

My reasons are as below/I will provide a statement of my reasons separately. *<Delete as appropriate>* [When giving reasons please indicate if, in your opinion, disclosure of the reasons to the patient would be likely to cause serious harm to the physical or mental health of the patient, or to that of any other person.]

..............................................................................................................................

..............................................................................................................................

[If you need to continue on a separate sheet for any of the above please indicate here [ ] and attach that sheet to this form]

Signed................................................

Date................................................

# 3B – MENTAL HEALTH (WALES)

## Statutory Instrument No. 2439 (W 212) 2008

The Mental Health (Hospital, Guardianship, Community Treatment and Consent to Treatment) (Wales) Regulations 2008

| | |
|---|---|
| *Made* | *15 September 2008* |
| *Laid before the National Assembly for Wales* | *17 September 2008* |
| *Coming into force* | *3 November 2008* |

39. Forms of treatment under Part 4A of the Act

40. Certificates for administration of treatment


## PART 9

## CORRESPONDENCE OF PATIENTS

41. Inspection and opening of postal packets

42. Independent Advocacy Services


## PART 10
## REVOCATIONS

43. Revocations


## SCHEDULES

Schedule 1 Forms

Schedule 2 Revocations

The Welsh Ministers in exercise of the powers conferred by sections 9, 17F(2), 19(1) and (4), 19A, 32(1), (2) and (3), 57(1)(b), 58A(1)(b), 64(2), 64H(2) and 134(3A)(a) and (8) of the Mental Health Act 1983(F1F), after consultation with such bodies as appear to them to be concerned in accordance with section 57(4) and 58A(8), hereby make the following regulations –


## PART 1 – GENERAL

### Title, application and commencement

1. The title of these Regulations is the Mental Health (Hospital, Guardianship, Community Treatment and Consent to Treatment) (Wales) Regulations 2008, they apply in relation to Wales and come into force on 3 November 2008.

### Interpretation

2.–(1) In these Regulations, unless the context otherwise requires –

"the Act" ("*y Ddeddf*") means the Mental Health Act 1983;

"bank holiday" ("*g_yl banc")* means a bank holiday under the Banking and Financial Dealings Act 1971(F1F);

"business day" ("*diwrnod busnes*") means any day except Saturday, Sunday or a bank holiday;

"document" ("*dogfen*") means any application, recommendation, record, report, order, notice or other document;

"electronic communication" ("*cyfathrebiad electronig*") has the same meaning as in section 15(1) of the Electronic Communications Act 2000(F2F);

"private guardian" ("*gwarcheidwad preifat*"), in relation to a patient, means a person, other than a local social services authority, who acts as a guardian under the Act;

"served" ("*cyflwyno*"), in relation to a document, includes addressed, delivered, given, forwarded, furnished or sent;

"special hospital" (*"ysbyty arbennig"*) means a hospital at which high security psychiatric services are provided

"tribunal" (*"tribiwnlys"*) means the Mental Health Tribunal for Wales or the First-tier Tribunal established under the Tribunals, Courts and Enforcement Act 2007(F3F) as the case may be.

(2) Except in so far as the context otherwise requires, any reference in these Regulations to –

    (a) a numbered section is to the section of the Act bearing that number;

    (b) a numbered regulation or Schedule is to the regulation in or Schedule to these regulations bearing that number;

    (c) any reference in a regulation to a numbered paragraph is a reference to the paragraph of that regulation bearing that number;

    (d) an alphanumeric form is a reference to the form in Schedule 1 bearing that designation.

## Documents

3.–(1) Except in a case to which paragraphs (2), (3) (4) or (5) apply, any document required or authorised to be served upon any <u>authority</u>, body or person by or under Part 2 of the Act (compulsory admission to hospital, guardianship and supervised community treatment) or these Regulations may be served –

    (a) by delivering it to the authority, body or person upon whom it is to be served; or

    (b) by delivering it to any person authorised by that authority, body or person to receive it; or

    (c) by sending it by pre-paid post addressed to –

        (i) the authority or body at their registered or principal office, or

        (ii) to the person upon whom it is to be served at the person's usual or last known residence; or

    (d) by delivering it using an internal mail system operated by the authority, body or person.

(2) Any application for the admission of a patient to a hospital under Part 2 of the Act must be served by delivering the application to an officer of the managers of the hospital, to which it is proposed that the patient will be admitted, authorised by them to receive it.

(3) Where a patient is liable to be detained in a hospital under Part 2 of the Act –

    (a) any order by the nearest relative of the patient under section 23 for the patient's discharge, and

    (b) the notice of such order under section 25(1), must be served by –

        (i) delivering the order or notice at that hospital to an officer of the managers authorised by them to receive it, or

        (ii) sending it by pre-paid post to those managers at that hospital, or

        (iii) delivering it using an internal mail system operated by the managers upon whom it is to be served, if those managers agree.

(4) Where a patient is a community patient –

    (a) any order by the nearest relative of the patient under section 23(1A) for the patient's discharge, and

    (b) the notice of such order given under section 25(1A), must be served by –

        (i) delivery of the order or notice at the patient's responsible hospital to an officer of the managers authorised by them to receive it, or

        (ii) by sending it by prepaid post to those managers at that hospital, or

        (iii) delivering it using an internal mail system operated by the managers upon whom it is to be served, if those managers agree.

(5) Any report made under section 5(2) (detention of patient already in hospital for 72 hours) must be served by –

    (a) delivery of the report to an officer of the managers of the hospital authorised by them to receive it, or

    (b) delivering it using an internal mail system operated by the managers upon whom it is to be served, if those managers agree.

(6) Where a document referred to in this regulation is sent by prepaid –

    (a) first class post, service is deemed to have taken place on the second business day following the day of posting;

    (b) second class post, service is deemed to have taken place on the fourth business day following posting, unless the contrary is shown.

(7) Where a document under this regulation is delivered using an internal mail system, service is considered to have taken place immediately it is delivered into the internal mail system.

(8) Subject to sections 6(3) and 8(3) (proof of applications), any document required or authorised by or under Part 2 of the Act or these Regulations and purporting to be signed by a person required or authorised by or under that Part or these Regulations to do so may be received in evidence and be deemed to be such a document without further proof, unless the contrary is shown.

(9) Any document required to be addressed to the managers of a hospital in accordance with the Act or these Regulations will be deemed to be properly addressed to such managers if addressed to the administrator of that hospital.

(10) Where under Part 2 of the Act or these Regulations the managers of a hospital are required to make any record or report, that function may be performed by an officer authorised by those managers in that behalf.

(11) Where under these Regulations the decision to accept service by a particular method requires the agreement of the managers of a hospital, that agreement may be given by an officer authorised by those managers in that behalf.

## PART 2 – PROCEDURES AND RECORDS RELATING TO HOSPITAL ADMISSIONS

Procedure for and record of hospital admissions

4.–(1) For the purposes of admission to hospital under Part 2 of the Act –

    (a) any application for admission for assessment under section 2 must be in the form set out –

       (i)   where made by the nearest relative, in Form HO 1;

       (ii)  where made by an approved mental health professional, in Form HO 2;

(b)  any medical recommendations for the purposes of section 2 must be in the form set out –

       (i)   in the case of joint recommendations, in Form HO 3;

       (ii)  in any other case, in Form HO 4;

(c)  any application for admission for treatment under section 3 must be in the form set out –

       (i)   where made by the nearest relative, in Form HO 5;

       (ii)  where made by an approved mental health professional, in Form HO 6;

(d)  any medical recommendations for the purposes of section 3 must be in the form set out –

       (i)   in the case of joint recommendations, in Form HO 7;

       (ii)  in any other case, in Form HO 8;

(e)  any emergency application under section 4 must be in the form set out –

       (i)   where made by the nearest relative, in Form HO 9;

       (ii)  where made by an approved mental health professional, in Form HO 10;

(f)  any medical recommendation for the purposes of section 4 must be in the form set out in Form HO 11;

(g)  any report made under subsection (2) of section 5 (detention of patient already in hospital for 72 hours) by –

       (i)   the registered medical practitioner or approved clinician in charge of the treatment of the patient, or

       (ii)  any such person nominated by the registered medical practitioner or approved clinician to act for them must be in the form set out in Part 1 of Form HO 12 and the hospital managers must record receipt of that report in Part 2 of that Form;

(h)  any record made under subsection (4) of section 5 (power to detain an in-patient for a maximum of 6 hours) by a nurse of the class for the time being prescribed for the purposes of that subsection(F1F) must be in the form set out in Form HO 13.

(2)  For the purposes of rectifying applications or recommendations under section 15, the managers of the hospital to which a patient has been admitted in pursuance of an application for assessment or for treatment may authorise in writing an officer on their behalf –

(a)  to consent under subsection (1) of that section to the amendment of the application or any medical recommendation given for the purposes of the application;

(b)  to consider the sufficiency of a medical recommendation and, if the recommendation is considered insufficient, to give written notice as required by subsection (2) of that section.

(3)  Where a patient has been admitted to a hospital pursuant to an application under section 2, 3 or 4, a record of the same must be made by the managers of that hospital in

the form set out in Form HO 14 and be attached to the application or, as the case may be, recommendation.

(4) For the purposes of any medical recommendation under sections 2, 3 and 4 (admission for assessment, admission for treatment and admission for assessment in cases of emergency respectively) in the case of –

(a) a single recommendation made in respect of a patient whom a doctor has examined in England, the medical recommendation must be in the form required by Regulations made by the Secretary of State to similar effect for England;

(b) joint recommendations made in respect of a patient whom both doctors have examined in England, the medical recommendation must be in the form required by Regulations made by the Secretary of State to similar effect for England;

(c) joint recommendations made in respect of a patient whom one doctor has examined in Wales and one doctor has examined in England, the medical recommendation must either be in the form required by these Regulations or in the form required by Regulations made by the Secretary of State to similar effect for England.

## Renewal of authority to detain

5.–(1) For the purposes of renewing authority to detain a patient admitted to hospital in pursuance of an application for treatment –

(a) any report made by a responsible clinician for the purposes of section 20(3) (medical recommendation for renewal of authority to detain) must be in the form set out in Parts 1 and 3 of Form HO 15;

(b) the statement made by a person who has been professionally concerned with the patient's medical treatment for the purposes of section 20(5A) (agreement with medical recommendation) must be in the form set out in Part 2 of Form HO 15;

(c) the renewal of authority for detention under section 20(8) must be recorded by the managers of the hospital in which the patient is liable to be detained in the form set out in Part 4 of Form HO 15.

## Detention after absence without leave for more than 28 days

6. In relation to a patient who is liable to be detained after being taken into custody or returning after absence without leave for more than 28 days –

(a) any report made under section 21B(2) (authority for detention for patients who are taken into custody or return after more than 28 days) must be in the form set out in Part 1 of Form HO 16;

(b) the receipt of that report must be recorded by the managers of the hospital in which the patient is liable to be detained in the form set out in Part 2 of Form HO 16.

## Discharge of patients liable to be detained by responsible clinicians or hospital managers

7. Any order made by the responsible clinician or hospital managers under section 23(2)(a) (discharge of patients) for the discharge of a patient who is liable to be detained under the Act must be in the form set out in Form HO 17 and in the event of the order being made by the patient's responsible clinician must be served on the managers of the hospital in which the patient is liable to be detained.

### Provision of information – patients liable to be detained

8.  Unless the patient requests otherwise, where –

(a)  a patient's detention is renewed pursuant to a report furnished under section 20 (duration of authority), the managers of the responsible hospital must take such steps as are reasonably practicable to cause the person (if any) appearing to them to be the patient's nearest relative to be informed of that renewal as soon as practicable following their decision not to discharge the patient;

(b)  by virtue of section 21B(7) (patients who are taken into custody or return after more than 28 days) a patient's detention is renewed pursuant to a report furnished under section 21B(2), the managers of the responsible hospital in which the patient is liable to be detained must take such steps as are reasonably practicable to cause the person (if any) appearing to them to be the patient's nearest relative to be informed of that renewal as soon as practicable following their decision not to discharge the patient;

(c)  by virtue of section 21B(5) and (6) (patients who are taken into custody or return after more than 28 days), a patient's detention is renewed retrospectively pursuant to a report furnished under section 21B(2), the managers of the hospital in which the patient is liable to be detained must take such steps as are reasonably practicable to cause the person (if any) appearing to them to be the patient's nearest relative to be informed of that renewal as soon as practicable following their receipt of that report.

### PART 3 – PROCEDURES AND RECORDS RELATING TO GUARDIANSHIP

Procedure for and acceptance of guardianship applications

9.–(1)  For the purposes of applying for guardianship under section 7 –

(a)  an application for guardianship must be in the form set out –

(i)  where made by the nearest relative, in Part 1 of Form GU 1;

(ii)  where made by an approved mental health professional, in Part 1 of Form GU 2;

(b)  where a person named as guardian will be a private guardian, the statement by that person that he or she is willing to act must be in the form set out in Part 2 of Form GU 1 or, as the case may be, Part 2 of Form GU 2;

(c)  any medical recommendation must be in the form set out –

(i)  in the case of a joint recommendation, in Form GU 3;

(ii)  in any other case, in Form GU 4.

(2)  For the purposes of any medical recommendation under section 7 in the case of –

(a)  a single recommendation made in respect of a patient whom a doctor has examined in England, the medical recommendation must be in the form required by Regulations made by the Secretary of State to similar effect for England;

(b)  joint recommendations made in respect of a patient whom both doctors have examined in England, the medical recommendation must be in the form required by Regulations made by the Secretary of State to similar effect for England;

(c)  joint recommendations made in respect of a patient whom one doctor has examined in Wales and one doctor has examined in England, the medical recommendation must either be in the form required by these Regulations or in the form required by Regulations made by the Secretary of State to similar effect for England.

(3) Where an application made under section 7 is accepted by the responsible local social services authority it must record its acceptance of the application in the form set out in Form *GU 5*, which must be attached to the application.

## Visits to patients subject to guardianship

10. The responsible local social services authority must arrange for every patient received into guardianship under the Act to be visited at such intervals as the authority may decide, but –

    (a) in any case at intervals of not more than three months, and

    (b) at least one such visit in any year must be made by an approved clinician or a practitioner approved by the Welsh Ministers for the purposes of section 12 (general provisions as to medical recommendations).

## Duties of private guardians

11.–(1) It is the duty of a private guardian –

    (a) to appoint a registered medical practitioner to act as the nominated medical attendant of the patient;

    (b) to notify the responsible local social services authority of the name and address of the nominated medical attendant;

    (c) in exercising the powers and duties conferred or imposed upon the private guardian by the Act and these Regulations, to comply with such directions as the responsible local social services authority may give;

    (d) to furnish that authority with all such reports or other information with regard to the patient as the responsible local social services authority may from time to time require;

    (e) to notify the responsible local social services authority –

        (i) on the reception of the patient into guardianship, of his or her address and the address of the patient,

        (ii) except in a case to which paragraph (f) applies, of any permanent change of either address, before or not later than seven days after the change takes place;

    (f) where on any permanent change of his or her address, the new address is in the area of a different local social services authority, to notify both that authority and the authority which was formerly responsible of –

        (i) his or her address and that of the patient,

        (ii) the particulars mentioned in paragraph (b); and

    (g) in the event of the death of the patient, or the termination of the guardianship by discharge, transfer or otherwise, to notify the responsible local social services authority of the same as soon as reasonably practicable.

(2) Any notice, reports or other information under this regulation may be given or furnished in any other way (in addition to the methods of serving documents provided for by regulation 3(1)) to which the relevant local social services authority agrees, including orally or by electronic communication.

### Renewal of guardianship

12.  For the purposes of renewing guardianship –

(a)  any report made under section 20(6) (report renewing guardianship) must be in the form set out in Part 1 of Form GU 6;

(b)  any renewal of authority for guardianship under section 20(8) must be recorded by the responsible local social services authority in the form set out in Part 2 of Form GU 6.

### Guardianship after absence without leave for more than 28 days

13.  In relation to the return of a patient subject to guardianship who is taken into custody or returns after absence without leave after more than 28 days –

(a)  any report made under section 21B(2) (authorisation for guardianship of patients who are taken into custody or return after more than 28 days) must be in the form set out in Part 1 of Form GU 7;

(b)  the receipt of that report must be recorded by the responsible local social services authority in the form set out in Part 2 of Form GU 7.

### Discharge of patients subject to guardianship by responsible clinicians or responsible local social services authorities

14.  Any order made by the responsible clinician or responsible local social services authority of the patient under section 23(2)(b) for discharge of a patient subject to guardianship under the Act must be in the form set out in Form GU 8 and in the event of the order being made by the patient's responsible clinician must be served on the responsible local social services authority.

### Provision of information – patients subject to guardianship

15.–(1)  Upon a patient becoming subject to guardianship under the Act, the responsible local social services authority must take such steps as are practicable to cause to be informed both the patient and the person (if any) appearing to the authority to be the patient's nearest relative of the rights referred to in paragraph (2).

(2)  The rights are –

(a)  the patient's right to apply to a Tribunal under section 66;

(b)  the nearest relative's right, as the case may be, to –

(i)  discharge the patient under section 23, or

(ii)  apply to a Tribunal under section 69 (where the patient is, or is treated as being, subject to guardianship under section 37).

(3)  Where information referred to in paragraph (1) –

(a)  is to be given to the patient, it must be given both orally and in writing;

(b)  is to be given to the nearest relative it must be given in writing.

(4)  Unless the patient requests otherwise, where –

(a)  a patient's guardianship is renewed pursuant to a report furnished under section 20, the responsible local social services authority must take such steps as are reasonably practicable to cause the person (if any) appearing to it to be the patient's nearest relative to be informed of that renewal as soon as practicable following the decision of the responsible local social services authority not to discharge the patient;

(b) by virtue of section 21B(7) a patient's guardianship is renewed pursuant to a report furnished under section 21B(2), the responsible local social services authority must take such steps as are reasonably practicable to cause the person (if any) appearing to it to be the patient's nearest relative to be informed of that renewal as soon as practicable following the decision of the responsible local social services authority not to discharge the patient;

(c) by virtue of section 21B(5) and (6) a patient's guardianship is renewed retrospectively pursuant to a report furnished under section 21B(2), the responsible local social services authority must take such steps as are reasonably practicable to cause the person (if any) appearing to it to be the patient's nearest relative to be informed of that renewal as soon as practicable following the receipt by the responsible local social services authority of that report.

(5) Where paragraph (4)(b) or (c) applies, the responsible local social services authority must, as soon as practicable inform the private guardian (if any) of its receipt of a report furnished under section 21B.

## PART 4 – PROCEDURES AND RECORDS RELATING TO COMMUNITY TREATMENT

### Procedures for and record of community treatment orders

16.–(1) For the purposes of making community treatment orders under section 17A and attaching conditions to the same under section 17B –

(a) any order made by the responsible clinician under section 17A(1) must be in the form set out in Parts 1 and 3 of Form CP 1;

(b) the conditions specified in the order under section 17B(3) and any other conditions under section 17B(2) must be in the applicable form set out in Part 1 of Form CP 1;

(c) any statement of an approved mental health professional made under section 17A(4) or, as the case may be, section 17B(2) must be in the applicable form set out in Part 2 of Form CP 1;

(d) any community treatment order must be furnished to the managers of the responsible hospital as soon as reasonably practicable.

(2) Any variation to conditions specified in a community treatment order under section 17B(4) must be recorded in the form set out in Form CP 2 and the order so varying the conditions must be furnished to the managers of the responsible hospital as soon as reasonably practicable.

### Extension of community treatment periods

17. For the purposes of extending community treatment periods under section 20A –

(a) any report by a responsible clinician made under section 20A(4) must be in the form set out in Parts 1 and 3 of Form CP 3;

(b) any statement of an approved mental health professional made under section 20A(8) must be in the form set out in Part 2 of Form CP 3;

(c) any extension of a community treatment period under section 20A(3) must be recorded by the managers of the responsible hospital in the form set out in Part 4 of Form CP 3.

### Community treatment after absence without leave for more than 28 days

18. In relation to the return of a community patient who is taken into custody or returns after absence without leave after more than 28 days –

    (a) any report made under section 21B(2) must be in the form set out in Part 1 of Form CP 4;

    (b) the receipt of that report must be recorded by the managers of the responsible hospital in the form set out in Part 2 of Form CP 4.

### Recall and release of community patients

19.–(1) For the purpose of recalling a patient to hospital under section 17E(1) –

    (a) a responsible clinician's notice under section 17E(5) must be in the form set out in Form CP 5;

    (b) the responsible clinician must furnish a copy of the notice to the managers of the responsible hospital as soon as reasonably practicable;

    (c) where the patient is recalled to a hospital which is not the responsible hospital, the responsible clinician must –

        (i) furnish the managers of that hospital with a copy of the notice, and

        (ii) notify those managers of the name and address of the responsible hospital; and

    (d) the managers of the hospital to which the patient is recalled must record the time and date of the patient's detention pursuant to that notice in the form set out in Part 1 of Form CP 6.

(2) In relation to the release of a community patient recalled to hospital under section 17F(5), the responsible clinician must notify the managers of the responsible hospital of any such release and those managers must record the time and date of the patient's release in the form set out in Part 2 of Form CP 6.

(3) Where the patient's responsible hospital is in England, the patient's recall must be effected in accordance with Regulations made by the Secretary of State to similar effect for England.

(4) A responsible clinician's notice recalling a patient to hospital for the purposes of section 17E (power to recall a community patient to hospital) in Form CP 5 must be served by –

    (a) delivering it by hand to the patient,

    (b) delivering it by hand to the patient's usual or last known address, or

    (c) sending it by pre-paid first class post addressed to the patient at the patient's usual or last known address.

(5) Notice of recall in Form CP 5 is considered served –

    (a) in the case of paragraph 4(a), immediately on delivery of the notice to the patient;

    (b) in the case of paragraph 4(b), on the day (which does not have to be a business day) after it is delivered;

    (c) in the case of paragraph 4(c), on the second business day after it was posted.

## Revocation of community treatment orders

20. For the purpose of revoking a community treatment order under section 17F(4) (powers in respect of recalled patients) –

    (a) a responsible clinician's order revoking a community treatment order must be in the form set out in Parts 1 and 3 of Form CP 7;

    (b) any statement of an approved mental health professional made under section 17F(4)(b) must be in the form set out in Part 2 of Form CP 7;

    (c) the responsible clinician must furnish the managers of the hospital to which the patient has been recalled with the revocation order;

    (d) where the patient has been recalled to a hospital which is not the responsible hospital, the responsible clinician must (as soon as reasonably practicable) furnish the managers of the hospital which was the patient's responsible hospital prior to the revocation of the patient's community treatment order, with a copy of that revocation order;

    (e) the managers of the hospital in which the patient is detained upon revocation of the community treatment order must record receipt of the copy of the revocation order and the time and date of the revocation in the form set out in Part 4 of Form CP 7.

## Discharge of community patients by responsible clinicians or hospital managers

21. Any order made by the responsible clinician or hospital managers under section 23(2)(c) for the discharge of a community patient must be in the form set out in Form CP 8 and in the event of the order being made by the patient's responsible clinician must be served on the managers of the responsible hospital.

## Provision of information – community patients

22.–(1) As soon as practicable following the recall of a patient under section 17E, the managers of the responsible hospital must take such steps as are reasonably practicable to –

    (a) cause the patient to be informed, both orally and in writing, of the provisions of the Act under which the patient is for the time being detained and the effect of those provisions, and

    (b) ensure that the patient understands the effect, so far as is relevant to the patient's case, of sections 56 to 64 (consent to treatment).

    (2) Unless the patient requests otherwise, where –

    (a) a patient's period of community treatment is extended pursuant to a report furnished under section 20A (community treatment period), the managers of the responsible hospital must take such steps as are reasonably practicable to cause the person (if any) appearing to them to be the patient's nearest relative to be informed of that extension as soon as practicable following their decision not to discharge the patient;

    (b) by virtue of section 21B(7A) (patients who are taken into custody or return after more than 28 days) a patient's period of community treatment is extended pursuant to a report furnished under section 21B(2), the managers of the responsible hospital must take such steps as are reasonably practicable to cause the person (if any) appearing to them to be the patient's nearest relative to be informed of that extension as soon as practicable following their decision not to discharge the patient;

(c) by virtue of section 21B(6A) and (6B) (patients who are taken into custody or return after more than 28 days) a patient's period of community treatment is extended retrospectively pursuant to a report furnished under section 21B(2), the managers of the responsible hospital must take such steps as are reasonably practicable to cause the person (if any) appearing to them to be the patient's nearest relative to be informed of that extension as soon as practicable following their receipt of that report.

## PART 5 – TRANSFER AND CONVEYANCE

### Transfer from hospital to hospital or guardianship

23.–(1) This regulation applies in respect of any patient to whom section 19(1)(a) as modified by Schedule 1 to the Act applies ("hospital patient"), who is not a patient transferred under –

(a) section 19(3) (transfer between hospitals under the same managers), or

(b) section 123(1) and (2) (transfers between and from special hospitals).

(2) A hospital patient may be transferred to another hospital where –

(a) an authority for transfer in the form set out in Part 1 of Form TC 1 is given by the managers of the hospital in which the patient is liable to be detained; and

(b) those managers are satisfied that arrangements have been made for the admission of the patient to the hospital to which it is proposed that he or she is to be transferred.

(3) On the transfer of that patient, the managers of the hospital to which he or she is transferred must record the patient's admission in the form set out in Part 2 of Form TC 1.

(4) A hospital patient may be transferred into the guardianship of a local social services authority, or of any person approved by a local social services authority, where –

(a) an authority for transfer in the form set out in Part 1 of Form TC 2 is given by the managers of the hospital in which the patient is liable to be detained;

(b) the transfer has been agreed by the local social services authority, which will be the responsible one if the proposed transfer takes effect;

(c) that local social services authority has specified the date on which the transfer will take place; and

(d) where the person named in the authority for transfer as guardian will be a private guardian, the agreement of that person has been obtained and recorded in the form set out in Part 2 of Form TC 2.

(5) On the transfer of that patient, the responsible local social services authority must record the patient's transfer in the form set out in Part 3 of Form TC 2.

(6) Where a hospital patient is detained in a registered establishment –

(a) he or she may be transferred from that establishment to another registered establishment where both establishments are under the management of the same managers, and paragraph (2) will not apply;

(b) if he or she is maintained under a contract with a National Health Service Trust, Local Health Board, Strategic Health Authority, Primary Care Trust, NHS Foundation Trust, Special Health Authority or the Welsh Ministers, any authority for transfer required under paragraph (2)(a) or, as the case may be, (4)(a) may be given by a duly authorised officer of that trust, board or authority instead of by the managers, or, as the case may be, by the Welsh Ministers instead of the managers.

(7) In this regulation the functions of the managers may be performed by an officer authorised by them in that behalf.

(8) Where the conditions of paragraphs (2) or (4), as the case may be, are satisfied, the transfer of the patient must be effected within 28 days of the date of the authority as provided under sub- paragraph (a) of paragraphs (2) or (4), failing which the authority for the transfer will cease.

## Transfer from guardianship to guardianship or hospital

24.–(1) This regulation applies in respect of any patient who is for the time being subject to guardianship under the Act ("guardianship patient").

(2) A guardianship patient may be transferred into the guardianship of another local social services authority or another person where –

(a) an authority for transfer is given by the guardian in the form set out in Part 1 of Form TC 3;

(b) the transfer has been agreed by the local social services authority, which will be the responsible one if the proposed transfer takes effect;

(c) that local social services authority has specified the date on which the transfer will take place; and

(d) where the person named in the authority for transfer as proposed guardian will be a private guardian, the agreement of that person has been obtained and recorded in the form set out in Part 2 of Form TC 3.

(3) On the transfer of that patient, the responsible local social services authority must record the patient's transfer of guardianship in the form set out in Part 3 of Form TC 3.

(4) An authority for transfer to hospital of a guardianship patient may be given by the responsible local social services authority in the form set out in Part 1 of Form TC 4 where –

(a) an application for admission for treatment has been made by an approved mental health professional in the form set out in Form HO 6 and, for the purposes of that application, sections 11(4) (consultation with nearest relative) and 13 (duty of approved mental health professional) will apply as if the proposed transfer were an application for admission for treatment;

(b) an application for admission for treatment has been made by the nearest relative in the form set out in Form HO 5;

(c) the application is founded on medical recommendations given by two registered medical practitioners in accordance with section 12 and regulation 4(1)(d);

(d) the responsible local social services authority is satisfied that arrangements have been made for the admission of the patient to that hospital.

(5) On the transfer of that patient to hospital, a record of admission must be made by the managers of the hospital to which the patient is transferred in the form set out in Part 2 of Form TC 4.

(6) The functions of the managers referred to in this regulation may be performed by an officer authorised by them in that behalf.

(7) Where the conditions of paragraph (2) are satisfied, the transfer of the patient must be effected within 28 days of the date of the authority as provided under sub-paragraph (a) of paragraph (2), failing which the patient will remain in the guardian-ship of the initial guardian.

(8) Where the conditions of paragraph (4) are satisfied, the transfer of the patient must be effected within 14 days of the date on which the patient was last examined, failing which the patient will remain subject to guardianship.

## Assignment of responsibility for community patients

25.–(1) This regulation applies in respect of any patient who is for the time being a community patient.

(2) Responsibility for a community patient may be assigned to another hospital under different management from the responsible hospital ("other hospital") where –

    (a) an authority for assignment in the form set out in Part 1 of Form TC 5 is given by the managers of the assigning responsible hospital prior to assignment;

    (b) those managers are satisfied that arrangements have been made for the assignment of responsibility of the patient to the other hospital within a period of 28 days beginning with the date of the authority for assignment;

    (c) on assignment, the managers of the other hospital must record the assignment in the form set out in Part 2 of Form TC 5.

(3) Where the conditions of paragraph (2) are satisfied, the assignment of responsibility must be effected within 28 days of the date of the authority as provided under sub-paragraph (a) of that paragraph, failing which responsibility for the community treatment order will remain with the hospital so responsible prior to assignment.

(4) Responsibility for a community patient to whom this regulation applies may be assigned to another hospital managed by the same hospital managers, in which event the provisions of paragraphs (2) and (3) and regulation 32 (b) will not apply.

(5) Where responsibility for a patient is assigned from a responsible hospital which is a registered establishment to another hospital under different management from the assigning hospital and the patient is maintained under a contract with a National Health Service Trust, Local Health Board, Strategic Health Authority, Primary Care Trust, NHS Foundation Trust, Special Health Authority or the Welsh Ministers any authority for assignment required under paragraph (2)(a) may be given by an duly authorised officer of that trust, board or authority, or by the Welsh Ministers, instead of the managers.

(6) The functions of the managers referred to in this regulation may be performed by an officer authorised by them in that behalf.

## Transfer of recalled patients to hospital

26.–(1) This regulation applies in respect of any patient who is for the time being recalled from a community treatment order under section 17E.

(2) Where the hospital to which the patient has been recalled and the hospital to which the patient is being transferred are not under the same management, a transfer may only take place if the requirements in paragraphs (3) to (5) are satisfied.

(3) Subject to paragraph (5), a patient referred to in paragraph (1) may be transferred to another hospital where –

    (a) an authority for transfer in the form set out in Part 1 of Form TC 6 is given by the managers of the hospital in which the patient is detained prior to transfer, and

    (b) those managers are satisfied that arrangements have been made for the admission of the patient to the hospital to which it is proposed that he or she is to be transferred.

(4) On the transfer of that patient, the managers of the hospital to which he or she is transferred must record the patient's admission in the form set out in Part 2 of Form TC 6.

(5) The managers of the hospital from which the patient is being transferred must furnish the managers of the hospital to which the patient is being transferred with a copy of Form CP 6 (record of patient's detention in hospital after recall) before, or at the time of, the patient's transfer.

(6) Where –

    (a) a patient has been recalled to a hospital which is a registered establishment; and

    (b) that patient is maintained under a contract with a National Health Service Trust, Local Health Board, Strategic Health Authority, Primary Care Trust, NHS Foundation Trust, Special Health Authority or the Welsh Ministers, any authority for transfer required under paragraph (3) may be given by an duly authorised officer of that trust, board or authority, or by the Welsh Ministers, instead of the managers.

(7) In this regulation the functions of the managers may be performed by an officer authorised by them in that behalf.

## Conveyance to hospital on transfer

27.–(1) Where the conditions of regulation 23(2), 24(4) or 26(2), as the case may be, are satisfied, the authority for transfer given in accordance with those regulations will be sufficient authority for the following persons to take the patient and convey him or her to the hospital to which the patient is being transferred within the periods specified –

    (a) in a case to which regulation 23(2) applies, an officer of the managers of either hospital, or any person authorised by those managers, within the period of 28 days beginning with the date of the authority for transfer;

    (b) in a case to which regulation 24(4) applies, an officer of, or any person authorised by, a local social services authority, within the period of 14 days beginning with the date on which the patient was last examined by a medical practitioner for the purposes of regulation 24(4)(c).

    (c) in a case to which regulation 26 applies, an officer of, or any other person authorised by the managers of the hospital to which the patient is being transferred, within the period of 72 hours beginning with the time of the patient's detention pursuant to the patient's recall under section 17E.

(2) Paragraph (1) also applies to a patient who –

    (a) is liable to be detained under the Act and is removed to another hospital in circumstances to which section 19(3) applies, as if the authority given by the managers for that transfer were an authority for transfer given in accordance with regulation 23(2);

(b) is liable to be detained in a special hospital and who, pursuant to a direction given by the Welsh Ministers under section 123(1) or (2), is removed to another special hospital or transferred to another hospital, as if that direction were an authority for transfer given in accordance with regulation 23(2).

(3) In a case to which regulation 23(6)(a) applies, an officer of or any other person authorised by the managers of the registered establishment may take and convey the patient to the registered establishment to which he or she is being transferred.

### Transfers from Wales to England and from England to Wales

28.–(1) Where a patient who is liable to be detained or is subject to guardianship under the Act is transferred from a hospital or guardianship in Wales to a hospital or guardianship in England, that transfer will be subject to such conditions as may be prescribed in these Regulations.

(2) Where a patient who is liable to be detained or is subject to guardianship under the Act is transferred from a hospital or guardianship in England to a hospital or guardianship in Wales, that transfer and the duty to record the admission of a patient so transferred will be subject to such conditions as may be prescribed in Regulations made by the Secretary of State to similar effect for England.

(3) Where paragraph (2) applies and any Regulations made by the Secretary of State to similar effect for England provide for authority to convey a patient in England, those Regulations will provide authority to convey the patient whilst in Wales.

### Removal of patients

29.–(1) Paragraphs (2) and (3) apply to a patient who is removed from Scotland, Northern Ireland, any of the Channel Islands or the Isle of Man to Wales under –

(a) section 82, 84 or 85 (as the case may be), or

(b) Regulations made under section 290 of the Mental Health (Care and Treatment) (Scotland) Act 2003(1) (removal and return of patients within United Kingdom).

(2) Where a patient to whom this paragraph applies is liable to be detained in a hospital, the managers of the hospital must –

(a) record in the form set out in Form TC 7 the date on which the patient is admitted to the hospital, and

(b) take such steps as are reasonably practicable to inform the person (if any) appearing to be the patient's nearest relative or performing such functions as correspond to those performed by nearest relatives of the patient's admission.

(3) Where a patient to whom this paragraph applies is received into guardianship the guardian must –

(a) record in the form set out in Form TC 7 the date on which the patient arrives at the place at which the patient is to reside on his or her reception into guardianship under the Act;

(b) take such steps as are reasonably practicable to inform the person (if any) appearing to be the patient's nearest relative or performing such functions as correspond to those performed by nearest relatives that the patient has been received into guardianship under the Act; and

(c)  a private guardian must notify the responsible local social services authority of the date mentioned in sub-paragraph (a) and of the particulars mentioned in regulation 11(1)(b) and (e).

(4)  Paragraph (5) applies to a patient who is removed from Scotland, any of the Channel Islands or the Isle of Man to Wales under –

(a)  section 289 of the Mental Health (Care and Treatment) (Scotland) Act 2003; or

(b)  section 85ZA (responsibility for community patients transferred from any of the Channel Islands or the Isle of Man)(F2F) in the case of any of the Channel Islands or the Isle of Man.

(5)  Where a patient to whom this paragraph applies is to receive treatment in the community –

(a)  the conditions specified by the responsible clinician under section 80C(5) or 85ZA(4) for the purposes of section 17B(1) must be in the form set out in Part 1 of Form TC 8;

(b)  the agreement of the approved mental health professional required under section 80C(6) must be in the form set out in Part 2 of Form TC 8;

(c)  the managers of the responsible hospital in respect of which the patient is treated as having been admitted by virtue of section 80C(2) must record in the form set out in Part 3 of Form TC 8 the date on which the patient arrived at the place he or she is to reside in Wales (and in consequence of which the patient is treated as if a community treatment order had been made discharging him or her from hospital).

## Provision of information – transfer

30.  In the event of the proposed or actual transfer of –

(a)  a hospital patient under regulation 23(2) to a hospital with different hospital managers from that from which the patient was transferred, the managers of the hospital to which the patient is to be or is transferred must notify the patient and, save where a patient requests otherwise, must take such steps as are reasonably practicable to notify the person (if any) appearing to be the patient's nearest relative, in writing, of the transfer and name and address of the hospital and the details of those hospital managers;

(b)  a hospital patient into guardianship under regulation 23(4) the responsible local social services authority must, save where the patient requests otherwise, take such steps as are reasonably practicable to notify the person (if any) appearing to be the patient's nearest relative of the date of the patient's transfer or, where it has not done so, record its reasons for not doing so;

(c)  a guardianship patient into the guardianship of another authority or person under regulation 24(2) the responsible local social services authority must, save where the patient requests otherwise, take such steps as are reasonably practicable to notify the person (if any) appearing to be the patient's nearest relative of the date of the patient's transfer or, where it has not done so, record its reasons for not doing so;

(d)  a guardianship patient to hospital under regulation 24(4), the hospital managers of the hospital to which the patient is to be or has been transferred must notify to the patient and, save where the patient requests otherwise, take such steps as are reasonably practicable to notify the person (if any) appearing to be the patient's nearest relative, in writing, of the name and address of the hospital and the details of the hospital managers.

## Provision of information – transfer in case of death, incapacity etc. of guardian

31.  Unless the patient requests otherwise, where a patient's guardianship becomes vested in the local social services authority or the functions of a guardian are, during the guardian's incapacity, transferred to the authority or a person approved by it under section 10 (transfer of guardianship in case of death, incapacity, etc. of guardian), the responsible local social services authority must take such steps as are reasonably practicable to cause the person (if any) appearing to be the patient's nearest relative to be informed of that vesting, or as the case may be, transfer before it takes place or as soon as practicable thereafter.

## Provision of information – assignment of responsibility for community patients

32.  In the event of the proposed or actual assignment of responsibility for a community patient, the hospital managers of the hospital to which responsibility has been assigned must –

   (a)  notify the patient, in writing, of the name and address of the responsible hospital and the details of the hospital managers (irrespective of whether or not there are any changes in the hospital managers); and

   (b)  unless the patient requests otherwise, where the assignment is made to a hospital under different management from the assigning hospital under regulation 25(2), take such steps as are reasonably practicable to notify the person (if any) appearing to be the patient's nearest relative, the name and address of responsible hospital and the details of the hospital managers of that hospital.

### PART 6 – FUNCTIONS OF NEAREST RELATIVES

## Performance of functions of nearest relative

33.–(1)  Subject to paragraph (8) and the conditions in paragraph (7), the nearest relative of a patient may authorise in writing any person other than –

   (a)  the patient; or

   (b )a person mentioned in section 26(5) (persons deemed not to be the nearest relative), to act on his or her behalf in respect of the matters mentioned in paragraph (2).

   (2)  Those matters are the performance in respect of the patient of the functions conferred upon the nearest relative under –

   (a)  Part 2 of the Act (as modified by Schedule 1 to the Act as the case may be); and

   (b)  section 66 (applications to tribunals).

   (3)  Such an authority confers upon the person authorised all the rights of the nearest relative that are reasonably necessary for and incidental to the performance of the functions referred to in paragraph (2) or are reasonably necessary to carry those functions into full effect.

   (4)  Any such authority takes effect upon receipt of the authority by the person authorised.

   (5)  Subject to the conditions in sub-paragraph (7)(b), the nearest relative of a patient may revoke such authority.

   (6)  Any revocation of such authority takes effect upon the receipt of the notice by the person authorised.

(7) The conditions mentioned in paragraphs (1) and (5) are, as relevant, that –

    (a) the person to be authorised has given his or her consent; and

    (b) on making or revoking such authority, the nearest relative must give notice in writing of that fact to –

        (i) the person authorised;

        (ii) the patient;

        (iii) in the case of a patient liable to be detained in a hospital, the managers of that hospital;

        (iv) in the case of a patient subject to guardianship, the responsible local social services authority and the private guardian, if any;

        (v) in the case of a community patient, the managers of the responsible hospital.

(8) A nearest relative of a patient may not authorise any person under paragraph (1) to perform functions on his or her behalf in the event of any person having made an application to the court for displacement of that nearest relative under section 29 on the grounds listed in sub-paragraphs (b) to (e) of subsection (3) of that section.

(9) An authorisation or notification referred to in this regulation may be transmitted by means of electronic communication if the recipient agrees.

## Restriction on discharge by nearest relative

34.–(1) Any report given by the responsible clinician for the purposes of section 25 (restrictions on discharge by nearest relative) –

    (a) must be in the form set out in Part 1 of Form NR 1; and

    (b) the receipt of that report by –

        (i) the managers of the hospital in which the patient is liable to be detained

        (ii) the managers of the responsible hospital in the case of a community patient must be in the form set out in Part 2 of Form NR 1.

(2) In addition to the methods of serving documents provided for by regulation 3(1), reports under this regulation may be furnished by –

    (a) transmission by facsimile, or

    (b) the transmission in electronic form of a reproduction of the report, if the managers of the hospital agree.

## PART 7 – DELEGATION

## Delegation of hospital managers' functions under the Act

35. The functions of the managers of a hospital in respect of the following –

    (a) notifying local social services authorities under section 14 (social reports) of patients detained on the basis of applications by their nearest relatives;

    (b) authorising persons under section 17(3) (leave of absence from hospital) to keep in custody patients who are on leave of absence who are subject to a condition that they remain in custody;

(c) authorising person under sections 18(1) and (2A) (return and readmission of patients absent without leave) to take and return detained and community patients respectively who are absent without leave, may be performed by any person authorised by them in that behalf.

## Delegation of hospital managers' functions under the Domestic Violence, Crime and Victims Act 2004

36. The functions of the managers of a hospital under sections 35 to 44B of the Domestic Violence, Crime and Victims Act 2004 (provision of information to victims of patients under the Act etc.)(F1F) may be performed by any person authorised by them in that behalf.

## Delegation by local social services authorities

37.–(1) Except as provided by paragraph (2), a local social services authority may delegate its functions under Parts 2 and 3 of the Act and these Regulations in the same way and to the same persons as its functions referred to in the Local Government Act 1972(F2F) may be delegated in accordance with section 101 of that Act.

(2) The function of the local social services authority under section 23 (discharge of patients) may not be delegated otherwise than in accordance with that section.

## PART 8 – CONSENT TO TREATMENT

## Forms of treatment under Part 4 of the Act

38.–(1) For the purposes of section 57 (treatment requiring consent and a second opinion) the form of treatment to which that section applies, in addition to the treatment mentioned in subsection (1)(a) of that section (any surgical operation for destroying brain tissue or for destroying the functioning of brain tissue), is the surgical implantation of hormones for the purpose of reducing male sexual drive.

(2) For the purposes of section 58A (electro-convulsive therapy, etc.) the form of treatment to which that section applies, in addition to the administration of electro-convulsive therapy mentioned in subsection (1)(a) of that section, is the administration of medicines as part of that therapy.

(3) Section 58A does not apply to treatment by way of the administration of medicines as part of electro-convulsive therapy where that treatment falls within section 62(1)(a) or (b) of the Act (treatment immediately necessary to save the patient's life or to prevent a serious deterioration in his or her condition).

## Forms of treatment under Part 4A of the Act

39. For the purposes of Part 4A of the Act (treatment of community patients not recalled to hospital) –

(a) treatment of a patient to whom section 64B(3)(b) or section 64E(3)(b) (which set out when treatment under Part 4A of the Act may be given to adult and child community patients respectively) applies may include treatment by way of the administration of medicines as part of electro-convulsive therapy but only where that treatment falls within section 64C(5)(a) or (b);

(b) treatment of a patient to whom section 64G (emergency treatment for community patients lacking capacity or competence) applies may include treatment by way of medicines used in connection with electro-convulsive therapy but only where that treatment falls within section 64C(5)(a) or (b).

## Certificates for administration of treatment

40.–(1) The certificate required under sections 57(2)(a) and (b) (treatment requiring consent and a second opinion) must be in the form set out in Form CO 1.

(2) The certificates required under sections 58(3)(a) and (b) (treatment requiring consent or a second opinion) must be in the form set out in Forms CO 2 and CO 3 respectively.

(3) The certificates required under sections 58A(3)(c), (4)(c) and (5) (electro-convulsive therapy, etc.) must be in the form set out in Forms CO 4, CO 5 and CO 6 respectively.

(4) The certificate required under sections 64B(2)(b) or 64E(2)(b) (treatment of community patients) must be in the form set out in Form CO 7.

## PART 9 – CORRESPONDENCE OF PATIENTS

## Inspection and opening of postal packets

41.–(1) Where under section 134(4) (inspection and opening of postal packets addressed to or by patients in hospital) any postal packet is inspected and opened, but neither the packet nor anything contained in it is withheld under section 134(1), the person appointed must record in writing –

(a) that the packet had been so inspected and opened;

(b) that nothing in the packet has been withheld; and

(c) his or her name and the name of the hospital, and must, before resealing the packet, place the record in that packet and keep a copy of that record.

(2) Where under section 134(1) any postal packet or anything contained in it is withheld by the person appointed –

(a) he or she must record in a register kept for the purpose –

(i) that the packet or anything contained in it has been withheld,

(ii) the date on which it was so withheld,

(iii) the grounds on which it was so withheld,

(iv) a description of the contents of the packet withheld or of any item withheld, and

(v) his or her name and the name of the hospital; and

(b) if anything contained in the packet is withheld, he or she must record in writing –

(i) that the packet has been inspected and opened,

(ii) that an item or items contained in the packet have been withheld,

(iii) a description of any such item, and

(iv) his or her name and the name of the hospital, and must, before resealing the packet, place the record in that packet.

(3)  For the purposes of this regulation "the person appointed" means a person appointed under section 134(7) to perform the functions of the managers of the hospital under that section.

## Independent advocacy services

42.  For the purposes of section 134(3A)(b)(iii), the prescribed arrangements are arrangements in respect of independent mental capacity advocates made under sections 35 to 41 of the Mental Capacity Act 2005(F1F) (independent advocacy service).

## PART 10 – REVOCATIONS
## Revocations

43.  The Regulations specified in Schedule 2 are revoked in relation to Wales.

Edwina Hart

Minister for Health and Social Services, one of the Welsh Ministers

15 September 2008

## SCHEDULE 2

Regulation 43

## REVOCATIONS

The Mental Health (Hospital, Guardianship and Consent to Treatment) Regulations 1983 (SI 1983/893)

The Mental Health (Hospital, Guardianship and Consent to Treatment) (Amendment) Regulations 1993 (SI 1993/2156)

The Mental Health (Hospital, Guardianship and Consent to Treatment) (Amendment) Regulations 1996 (SI 1996/540)

The Mental Health (Hospital, Guardianship and Consent to Treatment) (Amendment) Regulations 1997 (SI 1997/801)

The Mental Health (Hospital, Guardianship and Consent to Treatment) (Amendment) Regulations 1998 (SI 1998/2624)

# *Appendix 4*

# The Mental Health (Care and Treatment) (Scotland) Act 2003 (Consequential Provisions) Order 2005 (SI 2005/2078)

## Citation, commencement, interpretation and extent

1.–(1)  This Order may be cited as the Mental Health (Care and Treatment) (Scotland) Act 2003 (Consequential Provisions) Order 2005 and, subject to paragraph (2), shall come into force on 5 October 2005.

(2)  The entry in Schedule 3 to this Order in respect of the Mental Health (Scotland) Act 1984 shall come into force immediately after the coming into force of the entry in Schedule 5 to the 2003 Act in respect of the Mental Health (Scotland) Act 1984.

(3)  In this Order, unless the context otherwise requires –

"the 1995 Act" means the Criminal Procedure (Scotland) Act 1995;

"the 2003 Act" means the Mental Health (Care and Treatment) (Scotland) Act 2003;

"hospital", except as provided in articles 2(7) and 4(8), has the meaning given in section 329(1) of the 2003 Act;

"hospital direction" means a direction made under section 59A of the 1995 Act;

"patient" has the meaning given in section 329(1) of the 2003 Act;

"restriction order" means an order made under section 59 of the 1995 Act; and

"transfer for treatment direction" has the meaning given by section 136 of the 2003 Act.

(4)  A reference in this Order to "a patient whose detention in hospital was authorised by virtue of the 2003 Act or the 1995 Act" shall be read as including references to a patient in respect of whom a certificate under one of the provisions listed in section 290(7)(a) of the 2003 Act is in operation.

(5)  ...

(6)  Articles 4, 5, 6, 7 and 9 extend to Northern Ireland only.

(7)   Articles 8, 10, 11 and 12(2) extend to England and Wales and Northern Ireland only.

(8)   Articles 12(1), 13 and 14 extend to Scotland only.

(9)   Subject to paragraph (10), the modifications in Schedules 1 and 2 and the repeals in Schedule 3 have the same extent as the provisions being modified or repealed.

(10)  Those modifications and repeals do not extend to Scotland other than the modifications in paragraphs 1(4)(b), 5 and 6 of Schedule 1 and paragraph 20 of Schedule 2 and the repeal in Schedule 3 of the Mental Health (Scotland) Act 1984.

# Removal to England and Wales of hospital patients from Scotland

Repealed by Mental Health Act 2007

# Transfer of patients to England and Wales from Scotland: conditional discharge

Repealed by Mental Health Act 2007

# Patients absent from hospitals or other places in Scotland

8.–(1)  Subject to the provisions of this article, any person who may be taken into custody in Scotland under –

(a)   sections 301 to 303 of the 2003 Act; or

(b)   regulations made under section 289, 290, 309, 309A or 310 of that Act, may be taken into custody in, and returned to Scotland from, any other part of the United Kingdom.

(2)   For the purposes of the enactments referred to in paragraph (1), in their application by virtue of this article to England and Wales or Northern Ireland –

(a)   "constable" includes a constable in England or Wales or a constable of the Police Service of Northern Ireland, as the case may be; and

(b)   "mental health officer" includes

(i)    in England and Wales, any approved mental health professional within the meaning of the Mental Health Act 1983; and

(ii)   in Northern Ireland, any approved social worker within the meaning of the Mental Health (Northern Ireland) Order 1986.

# Assisting patients to absent themselves without leave etc.

10.–(1)  Any person who in England and Wales or Northern Ireland does anything in relation to a person whose detention in hospital is authorised by the 2003 Act which, if done in Scotland, would make him guilty of an offence under section 316 of the 2003 Act shall be guilty of an offence.

(2) Where a person is charged with an offence under paragraph (1) as it applies to section 316(1)(b) of the 2003 Act, it shall be a defence for such person to prove that the doing of that with which the person is charged –

(a) did not obstruct the discharge by any person of a function conferred or imposed on that person by virtue of the 2003 Act or this Order; and

(b) was intended to protect the interests of the patient.

(3) Any person guilty of an offence under this article shall be liable –

(a) on summary conviction, to imprisonment for a term not exceeding 3 months or to a fine not exceeding level 5 on the standard scale;

(b) on conviction on indictment, to imprisonment for a term not exceeding two years or to a fine, or both.

# Provisions as to custody, removal and detention

11.–(1) Any person required or authorised by or by virtue of the 2003 Act or by virtue of this Order to be moved to any place or to be kept in custody or detained in a place of safety shall, while being so moved, kept or detained, as the case may be, be deemed to be in legal custody.

(2) A constable or any other person required or authorised by or by virtue of that Act or by virtue of this Order to take any person into custody, or to move or detain any person shall, for the purposes of taking him into custody or moving or detaining him, have all the powers, authorities, protection and privileges which a constable has –

(a) in the case of a constable, within the area for which he acts as constable; and

(b) in the case of any other person, in the area where he has taken any person into custody or is moving or detaining him.

# Protection for acts done under this Order

12.–(1) No person shall be liable, whether on ground of want of jurisdiction or on any other ground, to any civil or criminal proceedings to which he would have been liable apart from this paragraph in respect of any act purporting to be done in pursuance of this Order, unless the act was done in bad faith or without reasonable care.

(2) Section 139 of the Mental Health Act 1983 (which relates to protection for acts done in pursuance of that Act) shall apply in respect of any act purporting to be done in pursuance of articles 4 to 11 of this Order.

# *Appendix 5*

# The Human Rights
# Act 1998

Some key sections of the Human Rights Act are followed by Articles of the European Convention of Human Rights that are enshrined in English law and relevant to mental health law.

**Section 1** identifies which of the Convention rights are covered by the Human Rights Act. These are:

(a)  Articles 2 to 12 and 14 of the Convention,

(b)  Articles 1 to 3 of the First Protocol, and

(c)  Articles 1 and 2 of the Sixth Protocol

as read with Articles 16 to 18 of the Convention.

**Section 2** requires courts or tribunals determining questions which have arisen in connection with a Convention right to take into account the decisions of Strasbourg (the European Court and Commission of Human Rights and the Committee of Ministers) so far as is relevant.

**Section 3** requires legislation to be interpreted as far as possible in a way which is compatible with the Convention rights.

**Section 4** gives the higher courts a power to make a "declaration of incompatibility" where they find that primary legislation is incompatible with a Convention right. This does not strike down the existing legislation but relies on the Government making a remedial order or introducing new law.

**Section 6** makes it unlawful for a public authority to act in a way which is incompatible with a Convention right unless it is required to do so by primary legislation. A public authority would include a court or tribunal or any person certain of whose functions are of a public nature.

**Section 7** states that victims may rely on the Convention rights in legal proceedings in UK courts and tribunals or the may institute separate proceedings. Separate proceedings must usually be brought within one year of the date on which the act complained of took place.

**Section 10** allows the relevant Minister to amend infringing legislation by order following a declaration of incompatibility or a finding of the European Court of Human Rights if he is satisfied that there is a compelling reason to do so.

**Section 11** states that the Act does not restrict any existing rights that an individual might have under UK law or his right to bring proceedings under existing law.

**Section 13** obliges courts to have particular regard to the importance of the right to freedom of thought, conscience and religion.

**Section 19** requires that when legislation is introduced into either House for a second reading, the Minister responsible must make a written statement that he considers the Bill is

*477*

compatible with the Convention rights or that he is unable to make such a statement but wishes Parliament to proceed with the Bill anyway.

# The text of the European Convention of Human Rights

(This includes those articles which are enshrined in English law as a result of the Human Rights Act).

### ARTICLE 2: RIGHT TO LIFE

1. Everyone's right to life shall be protected by law. No one shall be deprived of his life intentionally save in the execution of a sentence of a court following his conviction of a crime for which this penalty is provided by law.

2. Deprivation of life shall not be regarded as inflicted in contravention of this Article when it results from the use of force which is no more than absolutely necessary:

   (a) in defence of any person from unlawful violence;

   (b) in order to effect a lawful arrest or to prevent the escape of a person lawfully detained;

   (c) in action lawfully taken for the purpose of quelling a riot or insurrection.

### ARTICLE 3: PROHIBITION OF TORTURE

No one shall be subjected to torture or to inhuman or degrading treatment or punishment.

### ARTICLE 4: PROHIBITION OF SLAVERY AND FORCED LABOUR

1. No one shall be held in slavery or servitude.

2. No one shall be required to perform forced or compulsory labour.

3. For the purpose of this Article the term "forced or compulsory labour" shall not include:

   (a) any work required to be done in the ordinary course of detention imposed according to the provisions of Article 5 of this Convention or during conditional release from such detention;

   (b) any service of a military character or, in case of conscientious objectors in countries where they are recognised, service exacted instead of compulsory military service;

   (c) any service exacted in case of an emergency or calamity threatening the life or wellbeing of the community;

   (d) any work or service which forms part of normal civic obligations.

### ARTICLE 5: RIGHT TO LIBERTY AND SECURITY

1. Everyone has the right to liberty and security of person. No one shall be deprived of his liberty save in the following cases and in accordance with a procedure prescribed by law:

   (a) the lawful detention of a person after conviction by a competent court;

   (b) the lawful arrest or detention of a person for non-compliance with the lawful order of a court or in order to secure the fulfilment of any obligation prescribed by law;

(c)   the lawful arrest or detention of a person effected for the purpose of bringing him before the competent legal authority on reasonable suspicion of having committed an offence or when it is reasonably considered necessary to prevent his committing an offence or fleeing after having done so;

(d)   the detention of a minor by lawful order for the purpose of educational supervision or his lawful detention for the purpose of bringing him before the competent legal authority;

(e)   the lawful detention of persons for the prevention of the spreading of infectious diseases, of persons of unsound mind, alcoholics or drug addicts or vagrants;

(f)   the lawful arrest or detention of a person to prevent his effecting an unauthorised entry into the country or of a person against whom action is being taken with a view to deportation or extradition.

2.   Everyone who is arrested shall be informed promptly, in a language which he understands, of the reasons for his arrest and of any charge against him.

3.   Everyone arrested or detained in accordance with the provisions of paragraph 1(c) of this Article shall be brought promptly before a judge or other officer authorised by law to exercise judicial power and shall be entitled to trial within a reasonable time or to release pending trial. Release may be conditioned by guarantees to appear for trial.

4.   Everyone who is deprived of his liberty by arrest or detention shall be entitled to take proceedings by which the lawfulness of his detention shall be decided speedily by a court and his release ordered if the detention is not lawful.

5.   Everyone who has been the victim of arrest or detention in contravention of the provisions of this Article shall have an enforceable right to compensation.

## ARTICLE 6: RIGHT TO A FAIR TRIAL

1.   In the determination of his civil rights and obligations or of any criminal charge against him, everyone is entitled to a fair and public hearing within a reasonable time by an independent and impartial tribunal established by law. Judgement shall be pronounced publicly but the press and public may be excluded from all or part of the trial in the interest of morals, public order or national security in a democratic society, where the interest of juveniles or the protection of the private life of the parties so require, or to the extent strictly necessary in the opinion of the court in special circumstances where publicity would prejudice the interests of justice.

2.   Everyone charged with a criminal offence shall be presumed innocent until proved guilty according to law.

3.   Everyone charged with a criminal offence has the following minimum rights:

(a)   to be informed promptly, in a language which he understands and in detail, of the nature and cause of the accusation against him;

(b)   to have adequate time and facilities for the preparation of his defence;

(c)   to defend himself in person or through legal assistance of his own choosing or, if he has not sufficient means to pay for legal assistance, to be given it free when the interests of justice so require;

(d) to examine or have examined witnesses against him and to obtain the attendance and examination of witnesses on his behalf under the same conditions as witnesses against him;

(e) to have the free assistance of an interpreter if he cannot understand or speak the language used in court.

## ARTICLE 7: NO PUNISHMENT WITHOUT LAW

1. No one shall be held guilty of any criminal offence on account of any act or omission which did not constitute a criminal offence under national or international law at the time when it was committed. Nor shall a heavier penalty be imposed than the one that was applicable at the time the criminal offence was committed.

2. This Article shall not prejudice the trial and punishment of any person for any act or omission which, at the time when it was committed, was criminal according to the general principles of law recognised by civilised nations.

## ARTICLE 8: RIGHT TO RESPECT FOR PRIVATE AND FAMILY LIFE

1. Everyone has the right to respect for his private and family life, his home and his correspondence.

2. There shall be no interference by a public authority with the exercise of this right except such as is in accordance with the law and is necessary in a democratic society in the interests of national security, public safety or the economic wellbeing of the country, for the prevention of disorder or crime, for the protection of health or morals, or for the protection of the rights and freedoms of others.

## ARTICLE 9: FREEDOM OF THOUGHT, CONSCIENCE AND RELIGION

1. Everyone has the right to freedom of thought, conscience and religion; this right includes freedom to change his religion or belief and freedom, either alone or in community with others and in public or private, to manifest his religion or belief, in worship, teaching, practice and observance.

2. Freedom to manifest one's religion or beliefs shall be subject only to such limitations as are prescribed by law and are necessary in a democratic society in the interests of public safety, for the protection of public order, health or morals, or for the protection of the rights and freedoms of others.

## ARTICLE 10: FREEDOM OF EXPRESSION

1. Everyone has the right to freedom of expression. This right shall include freedom to hold opinions and to receive and impart information and ideas without interference by public authority and regardless of frontiers. This Article shall not prevent States from requiring the licensing of broadcasting, television or cinema enterprises.

2. The exercise of these freedoms, since it carries with it duties and responsibilities, may be subject to such formalities, conditions, restrictions or penalties as are prescribed by law and are necessary in a democratic society, in the interests of national security, territorial integrity or public safety, for the prevention of disorder or crime, for the protection of health or morals, for the protection of the reputation or rights of others, for preventing the disclosure of information received in confidence, or for maintaining the authority and impartiality of the judiciary.

### ARTICLE 11: FREEDOM OF ASSEMBLY AND ASSOCIATION

1.  Everyone has the right to freedom of peaceful assembly and to freedom of association with others, including the right to form and to join trade unions for the protection of his interests.

2.  No restrictions shall be placed on the exercise of these rights other than such as are prescribed by law and are necessary in a democratic society in the interests of national security or public safety, for the prevention of disorder or crime, for the protection of health or morals or for the protection of the rights and freedoms of others. This Article shall not prevent the imposition of lawful restrictions on the exercise of these rights by members of the armed forces, of the police or of the administration of the State.

### ARTICLE 12: RIGHT TO MARRY

Men and women of marriageable age have the right to marry and to found a family, according to the national laws governing the exercise of this right.

### ARTICLE 14: PROHIBITION OF DISCRIMINATION

The enjoyment of the rights and freedoms set forth in this Convention shall be secured without discrimination on any ground such as sex, race, colour, language, religion, political or other opinion, national or social origin, association with a national minority, property, birth or other status.

### ARTICLE 16: RESTRICTIONS ON POLITICAL ACTIVITY OF ALIENS

Nothing in Articles 10, 11 and 14 shall be regarded as preventing the High Contracting Parties from imposing restrictions on the political activity of aliens.

### ARTICLE 17: PROHIBITION OF ABUSE OF RIGHTS

Nothing in this Convention may be interpreted as implying for any State, group or person any right to engage in any activity or perform any act aimed at the destruction of any of the rights and freedoms set forth herein or at their limitation to a greater extent than is provided for in the Convention.

### ARTICLE 18: LIMITATION ON USE OF RESTRICTIONS ON RIGHTS

The restrictions permitted under this Convention to the said rights and freedoms shall not be applied for any purpose other than those for which they have been prescribed.

# Part 2. The First Protocol

### ARTICLE 1. PROTECTION OF PROPERTY

Every natural or legal person is entitled to the peaceful enjoyment of his possessions. No one shall be deprived of his possessions except in the public interest and subject to the conditions provided for by law and by the general principles of international law.

The preceding provisions shall not, however, in any way impair the right of a State to enforce such laws as it deems necessary to control the use of property in accordance with the general interest or to secure the payment of taxes or other contributions or penalties.

### ARTICLE 2. RIGHT TO EDUCATION

No person shall be denied the right to education. In the exercise of any functions which it assumes in relation to education and to teaching, the State shall respect the right of parents to ensure such education and teaching in conformity with their own religious and philosophical convictions.

### ARTICLE 3. RIGHT TO FREE ELECTIONS

The High Contracting Parties undertake to hold free elections at reasonable intervals by secret ballot, under conditions which will ensure the free expression of the opinion of the people in the choice of the legislature.

# Part 3. The Sixth Protocol

### ARTICLE 1. ABOLITION OF THE DEATH PENALTY

The death penalty shall be abolished. No one shall be condemned to such penalty or executed.

### ARTICLE 2. DEATH PENALTY IN TIME OF WAR

A State may make provision in its law for the death penalty in respect of acts committed in time of war or of imminent threat of war; such penalty shall be applied only in the instances laid down in the law and in accordance with its provisions. The State shall communicate to the Secretary General of the Council of Europe the relevant provisions of that law.

# Appendix 6
## Case law

### A PCT v LDV et al. (2013) EWHC 272 (Fam)

ISSUE

What information did a patient need to be able to understand about coming into hospital for treatment for mental disorder for them to be capable of being admitted informally?

DECISION

The "salient details" (see *CC v KK and STCC* (2012) EWHC 2136 (COP)) this patient needed to be able to understand included that:

* she is in hospital to receive care and treatment for a mental disorder;

* the care and treatment will include varying levels of supervision (including supervision in the community), use of physical restraint and the prescription and administration of medication to control her mood;

* staff at the hospital will be entitled to carry out property and personal searches;

* she must seek permission of the nursing staff to leave the hospital, and, until the staff at the hospital decide otherwise, will only be allowed to leave under supervision;

* if she left the hospital without permission and without supervision, the staff would take steps to find and return her, including contacting the police.

IMPLICATIONS

While not creating a precedent, the court set a high threshold for understanding which many elderly people, or those with dementia or learning disability, will be unlikely to reach. Thus, given that since *Cheshire West* (2014) such patients are likely to be deprived of their liberty when admitted, they are likely to have to be made subject to an authorisation under the MHA or DoLS and will not be able to be admitted informally as they will be unable to consent to such conditions (which would negate deprivation of liberty under Article 5). This is reflected in the new Codes of Practice (E Para. 13.53; W Para. 13.39).

The Courts seem increasingly prepared to give guidance as to relevant and irrelevant factors in making a wide range of decisions. See, e.g., *Derbyshire CC v AC et al.* (2014) EWCOP 38; *LBX v K, L, M* (2013) EWHC 3230 (Fam); and *Re A* (2019) EWCOP 2.

### Aerts v Belgium (2000) 29 EHRR 50

ISSUE

Where must a person detained on grounds of mental disorder be held?

## DECISION

Although the Convention does not carry an entitlement to specific treatment for mental disorder, persons detained on this ground must be held in a therapeutic environment. The psychiatric wing of a prison did not qualify as such.

## IMPLICATIONS

Although the conditions in which a person was held might fail to reach the level of severity required to amount to inhuman or degrading treatment under Article 3, there could be a breach of Article 5(1) if he was not held in a "hospital, clinic or other appropriate institution authorised for that purpose".

# *AH v W London MHT* (2011) UKUT 74 (AAC)

### ISSUE

In what circumstances should Tribunal proceedings be held in public?

### DECISION

Open justice is a right, which does not require justification on a case by case basis. On the contrary it is the exceptions which need to be justified. A "threshold test" must be applied, comprising four questions:

Is it consistent with the subjective and informed wishes of the applicant?

Will it have an adverse effect on the applicant's mental health in the short or long term? Are there any other special factors for or against a public hearing?

Can practical arrangements be made for an open hearing without disproportionate burden on the authority?

A public hearing was directed despite the practical problems and expense involved.

### IMPLICATIONS

Despite the decision in this case, compared to old Rule 21, new Rule 38 in fact appears to reflect a shift from the wishes of the patient to more general interests of justice in determining if a hearing should be in public. It is likely that the costs would have to be considerably greater than the £150,000 annual anticipated sum for Broadmoor Hospital for its 170 Tribunals before this would influence a court against ordering a public hearing.

# *AJ v A LA* (2015) EWCOP 5

### ISSUE

How can the DoLS regime be made compatible with Article 5(4)?

### DECISION

To be compatible with Article 5(4) there must be a means of speedy and effective challenge to deprivation of liberty. There may need to be special procedural safeguards in place to ensure this right is enjoyed by people with mental disabilities unable to exercise it themselves. To make the DoLS scheme compatible with Article 5(4) the judge construed the provisions as collectively ensuring that a person objecting to DoLS has that authorisation challenged in the Court of

Protection. The LA must ensure that the RPR appointment is appropriate and that s/he or the IMCA bring such a challenge, failing which the LA itself must bring the matter to Court. The IMCA's role is not to bring a challenge if s/he judges this to be in the person's best interests but whenever the person objects.

It is only in exceptional cases that an authorisation need not be sought before deprivation of liberty begins.

## IMPLICATIONS

This case, together with *LBH v Neary* (2011) EWCH 1377 (qv), *Re RD et al.* (2016) EWCOP 49 (qv) and *MH v UK* (Application No. 11577/06) (2014) 58 EHRR 35, illustrates that the courts are increasingly alert to the need to ensure that persons lacking capacity and detained under either the DoLS or the MHA regime have the right to an effective challenge, which must be a reality and not merely theoretical. At least under the MHA if a patient does not challenge his detention, in the end someone will refer the matter to a Tribunal. No equivalent right exists under DoLS, which relies on heroic efforts by the judiciary to attempt to construe the scheme so as to plug the human rights gap.

# *AM v SLAM and Secretary of State for Health* (2013) UKUT 0365 (AAC)

## ISSUE

To what extent should decision-makers consider the availability of both DoLS and the MHA as routes for the admission to hospital of a person for treatment of mental disorder? How should the choice be made where it exists?

## DECISION

A Tribunal deciding discharge of a patient on s2 must consider if MHA is warranted on the basis that MCA/DoLS might be less restrictive. This applies equally to all MHA/MCA decision-makers. DoLS is an alternative to MHA for authorising dol for a range of purposes including assessment of mental disorder in hospital, so assessors must consider if it is available and whether the MHA alternative is necessary/warranted.

Refining his decision in *GJ v The Foundation Trust* (2009) EWHC 2972 (Fam) (qv), the judge asserted that MHA does **not** have general primacy. If on consideration (e.g. Does the patient lack capacity to decide on admission? Is he objecting? Will he be compliant? Is he likely to be deprived of his liberty?) DoLS and MHA both remain possible options, decision-makers should balance the impacts of the respective regimes upon the person to decide which best achieves the objective of s2/3-type assessment/treatment in the least restrictive way.

## IMPLICATIONS

The Tribunal Practice Direction in England requires reports to include the consideration of the availability and appropriateness of DoLS as an alternative to the Mental Health Act. The Code for England stresses at Para. 13.60 that the decision should not be based on a general preference for one regime rather than the other because of greater familiarity, or on a view that one regime is generally more restrictive than another, or provides greater safeguards: "a decision should always be made depending on the unique circumstances of each case". See also *Northants Trust v ML* (2014) EWCOP 2: "It is clear that the magnetic north when contemplating dol of those … within Case E (i.e. admission to hospital for treatment for mental disorder) is … the MHA."

# B v Barking Havering etc. NHS Trust (1999) 1 FLR 106

## ISSUE

Was it lawful to renew a patient's detention under s20 while he was largely continuing on s17 leave?

## DECISION

Provided that the patient's treatment as a whole involved treatment as an inpatient in a hospital, the fact that the patient was on s17 leave at the time of renewal did not invalidate it.

The court did not specify how much time in hospital as an in-patient was required.

## IMPLICATIONS

This case marks the beginning of the use of "long leash" s17 leave.

In *R (DR) v Mersey Care NHS Trust* ((2002) EWHC 1810 (Admin)) the judge took matters further, stating that there was no requirement for any of the treatment to be delivered as an in-patient. What mattered was treatment at a hospital not in a hospital. That treatment must, however, be an essential part of the patient's overall care plan, i.e. the requirement to attend a hospital ensures compliance by the patient with the overall care plan.

This principle has been applied in the context of an application to a Tribunal – see *R (CS) v Mental Health Review Tribunal* ((2004) EWHC 2958 (Admin)) in which a decision of the Tribunal not to discharge a patient was upheld in circumstances in which in the closing stages of treatment in hospital the RMO's (now RC's) grasp on the patient was "gossamer thin", being engaged in a delicate balancing act by which she was, with as light a touch as she could, encouraging progress to discharge. The patient during this time had very limited contact with the hospital, but it remained an essential ingredient of the care plan.

The manner in which the courts have successively extended the reach of s17 leave means that the distinction between leave and the use of a CTO is far from clear, not to say artificial (see discussion in Chapter 3).

The lawfulness of using s17 leave long term was recently upheld in *SL v Ludlow Street Healthcare* (2015) UKUT 398 (AAC), which makes the guidance in the Code of Practice for England at Para. 31.5 that it should not normally be granted for more than a month inexplicable. Further it is advocated by the Mental Health Casework Section of the Prison and Probation service as a solution to the problem posed by the decision in *SoS Justice v MM* (2018) UKSC 60 (qv) that a Mental Health Tribunal has no power to attach conditions amounting to a deprivation of liberty to a conditional discharge order.

# CC v KK and STCC (2012) EWHC 2136 (COP)

## ISSUE

How to approach assessments of capacity?

## DECISION

Professionals must avoid conflating a capacity assessment with a best interests analysis by attaching excessive weight to their own views of how physical safety may be best protected and insufficient weight to the person's own views of how their emotional needs may best be met.

Different individuals may give different weight to different factors, e.g. as to the importance of avoiding or accepting varying degrees of risk.

It is imperative to have regard to MCA s1(3), i.e. whether all practical steps have been taken to help the person make the decision. This involves presenting them with detailed options so that their capacity to weigh up those options can be fairly assessed.

The person need only comprehend and weigh the salient details relevant to the decision and not all the peripheral detail. (See *A PCT v LDV et al.* (2013) EWHC 272 (Fam).)

### IMPLICATIONS

The case reinforces increasing moves by the courts to emphasise the need to respect the wishes of the person and not to conclude that they are making an incapacitated as opposed to an unwise decision just because the professionals take a different view. In terms of the s3 MCA test for the inability to make a decision, the substitution of "the salient details" for the "information relevant to the decision" perhaps does not take us much further. However the same judge in *A PCT v LDV et al.* (2013) EWHC 272 (Fam) (qv) was drawn to be more specific in the context of a decision to be admitted to hospital for the purpose of treatment of mental disorder, and other judges have since increasingly been prepared to give specific guidance as to the "salient details" in a variety of contexts (see, e.g., *Derbyshire CC v AC et al.* (2014) EWCOP 38; *LBX v K, L, M* (2013) EWHC 3230 (Fam); and *Re A* (2019) EWCOP 2).

See also *Re CD* (2015) EWCOP 74: the wishes and feelings of P should be confined to the best interests analysis and not undermine a capacity assessment (P wanted the operation but lacked capacity to consent to it).

# *D (A Child) Deprivation of Liberty* (2015) EWHC 922 (Fam)

### ISSUE

May a parent deprive a child under the age of 16 of their liberty or authorise another to do so? If so, would this fall within the scope of parental responsibility (PR)? (See *D (A Child)* (2019) UKSC 42 for the legal situation when this child reached 16 but lacked capacity to consent to confinement.)

### DECISION

Case involved a 15-year-old with ADHD, Asperger's and Tourette's admitted to a six-bed psychiatric unit with school room attached and not allowed to leave without staff or a family member. Court held that the *Cheshire West* (2014) "acid test" applied irrespective of the child's disabilities and that objectively there was deprivation of liberty. *RK v BCC et al.* (2011) EWCA Civ 1305, in which the court held that a parent could not authorise the deprivation of liberty of their child was wrongly decided and arguably inconsistent with *Cheshire West* (2014).

What fell within the scope of PR might differ according to the disabilities and needs of the child. For an autistic child with erratic, challenging and potentially harmful behaviours the scope of PR might include more than for a child without disabilities.

### IMPLICATIONS

The case survived the Supreme Court decision in *D (A Child)* (2019) UKSC 42 and remains good law. It is therefore possible for professionals in some circumstances to rely on parental consent to admit a child to hospital for treatment of mental disorder without the need to use the compulsory powers of the Mental Health Act. The introduction of such a comparator in this way is arguably inconsistent with *Cheshire West* (2014) as being discriminatory. The same judge said in *A LA v D* (2015) EWHC 3125 (Fam) that his conclusions did not apply if child was in care. See also *A LA v D, E, C* (2016) EWHC 3473 (Fam) where it was held that a Gillick competent under-16-year-old could consent to deprivation of liberty and so negate it.

# D (A Child) (2019) UKSC 42

### ISSUE

If a 16- or 17-year-old lacks capacity to consent to circumstances of confinement amounting to deprivation of liberty within the meaning of Article 5, can consent by someone with parental responsibility ("PR") negate what would otherwise be a breach of Article 5?

### DECISION (Majority 3–2)

In the case of a young person of D's age the restrictions imposed went beyond what was normal and met the "acid test" for deprivation of liberty (dol). The fact that the arrangements might be in his best interests or imposed from benign motives was not relevant. The fact that D suffered from mental disabilities made no difference as the comparator was that of a young person without such disabilities and D was entitled to the same protections under Article 5.

A parent cannot give substituted consent to such confinement and thereby negate the dol. This falls outside the scope of PR for a 16- or 17-year-old.

Even where the state was not directly involved in the confinement, if it knew or should have known of the circumstances of a private confinement this would be attributable to the state and so caught by Article 5.

### IMPLICATIONS

Although Lady Hale said that her conclusions would "logically" apply to a child under 16 whose liberty was restricted beyond what was normal for his age she did not, and nor did Lady Black, express a concluded view. Lord Carnwarth confirmed that the decision in *D (A Child) (Deprivation of Liberty)* (2015) EWHC 922 (Fam) (qv) (which concerned the same child at a younger age), and thus what fell within PR for such a child, remained good law.

This case is limited to the issue of PR in the context of confinement. Other areas of PR, such as in relation to consent to medical treatment of those under 18, are not directly affected. Also, what arrangements meet the "acid test" of dol will continue to require careful analysis post Cheshire West.

One consequence of the judgement is that more young people will require a formal authorisation for their confinement whether under s25 Children Act 1989, the Mental Health Act or from the court. From October 2020 the Liberty Protection Safeguards (the successor scheme to DoLS) will be available for 16- and 17-year-olds.

Lady Black considered (obiter) the meaning of secure accommodation within s25 Children Act and reached a tentative conclusion that this turned on the nature of the accommodation itself rather than on the nature of the regime operating within it.

NOTE: Once a capacitated child reaches 16, PR cannot authorise dol in a hospital for treatment of mental disorder (s131 (2)–(5) Mental Health Act 1983).

# DL-H v Devon Partnership NHS Trust v Secretary of State (2010) UKUT 102 (AAC)

## ISSUE

What constitutes "mental disorder"? What is the meaning and scope of the "availability of appropriate medical treatment" test?

## DECISION

Neither DSM-IV nor ICD-10 nor the Code defines "mental disorder". Note the warnings re ICD-10 (diagnostic criteria *for research*), and DSM-IV (… the clinical diagnosis of a DSM-IV mental disorder not sufficient to establish the existence for legal purposes of a "mental disorder" …). "[This] leaves open … how a patient's mental state is to be classified for the purposes of the MHA" and produces the danger that a patient for whom no appropriate treatment is available may be contained for public safety rather than detained for treatment.

Danger is avoided by asking: What treatment could be provided? What benefit might it have for the patient? Is the benefit related to the patient's mental disorder? Is the patient truly resistant to engagement?

MHA definition of medical treatment is broad enough to include attempts by nursing staff to encourage the patient to engage.

## IMPLICATIONS

Whether for *legal purposes of the MHA* a person's signs and symptoms constitute a mental disorder does not depend on its presence in or absence from one of the manuals. Confirms that "mental disorder" is to be broadly construed (see *MD v Nottingham Healthcare NHS Trust (2010) UKUT 59 (AAC)*).

# Dorset Healthcare NHS Foundation Trust v MHRT (2009) UKUT 4 (AAC)

## ISSUE

What approach should be taken by Tribunals in relation to Rule 14 regarding disclosure?

## DECISION

The starting point should be that full disclosure should be given.

The parties (particularly when represented) should attempt to reach agreement on issues of disclosure without making an application to the Tribunal.

## IMPLICATIONS

Detailed guidance was given as to the steps each party should take where disclosure is an issue. When the Tribunal does have to resolve a dispute about disclosure this will be dealt with as a preliminary issue, either on the day of the hearing or exceptionally at a separate hearing. The parties may agree to (or the Tribunal may order) disclosure to the patient's solicitor on an undertaking not to disclose to anyone else without the Tribunal's consent.

# F (Mental Health Act: Guardianship), Re (2001) 1 FLR 192

## ISSUE

What meaning should be given to the words "seriously irresponsible conduct" in s1?

## DECISION

A restrictive interpretation should be adopted such that in this case the wish of a learning disabled person to return home to possible abuse was not considered to amount to "seriously irresponsible conduct".

## IMPLICATIONS

In *Newham LBC v S* (adult: court's jurisdiction) ((2003) EWHC 1909 (Fam)), the court held similarly that a tendency to rush into the road without looking did not constitute "seriously irresponsible conduct". However the case law is not consistent. The court reached the opposite conclusion on similar facts in *GC v Managers of Kingswood Centre et al.* (CO/7784/2008).

The definition of learning disability in amended s1 of the Act (see discussion in Chapter 4) is qualified by similar wording in relation to use of the longer-term compulsory powers including guardianship.

As a result of the court's interpretation of this phrase its inclusion in the amended Act means that guardianship will continue not to be available for many learning disabled individuals unless they are suffering from other forms of mental disorder in addition. Use will have to be made of the MCA, which contains fewer protections.

# Gillick v West Norfolk and Wisbech AHA (1986) AC 112

## ISSUE

Can a child under the age of 16 give a valid consent to medical treatment?

## DECISION

A child under the age of 16 can consent to medical treatment if he has sufficient maturity and intelligence to understand the nature and effects of the proposed treatment.

## IMPLICATIONS

Unlike for a 16/17-year-old there is no presumption of capacity for an under-16-year-old.

In *Re W (a minor)* ((1992) 4 All ER 627) the Court of Appeal drew a distinction between a child consenting to and a child refusing treatment. "No minor of whatever age has power by refusing consent to treatment to override a consent to treatment by someone who has parental responsibility … and … by the court." This decision does not just apply to those under the age of 16. However in the light of more recent case law (e.g. *Storck v Germany* (2005) below) and concerns that to rely on parental consent to override a child's competent refusal in such circumstances might in the future be held to amount to a breach of the child's Convention rights, the Code of Practice advises against such reliance (see discussion in Chapter 18); instead the MHA should be considered if appropriate and if the criteria are met, or alternatively an application made to the court.

Even if a child's competent refusal may in theory be overridden, the child's wishes should carry very great weight. There is no requirement on the part of a doctor to rely on parental consent, merely the legal right to do so in appropriate circumstances.

# GJ v The Foundation Trust et al. (2009) EWHC 2972 (Fam)

### ISSUE

How is the "eligibility" assessment under DoLS to be understood and applied? Where is the dividing line to be drawn between use of DoLS and detention under the MHA?

### DECISION

The eligibility assessment is required to determine three things:

Are the MHA criteria met? Assessor must assume medical recommendations have been given and that no alternative is available under MCA (MCA Schedule 1A Para. 12). The MHA has primacy.

Is GJ to be accommodated in hospital for the purpose of medical treatment for mental disorder (or is the real reason for hospital admission treatment of a physical condition)? Apply the "but for" test – i.e. but for need for treatment of the physical condition, would detention in hospital be sought?

Does GJ object to what is proposed to be authorised by DoLS (bearing in mind past and present behaviour, beliefs, wishes and feelings)? Low threshold set for objection.

### IMPLICATIONS

Professional discretion is curtailed:

> It is not lawful for [decision-makers under both the MHA and MCA] to proceed on the basis that they can pick and choose between the two statutory regimes as they think fit having regard to general considerations (e.g. the preservation or promotion of a therapeutic relationship with P) that they consider render one regime preferable to the other in the circumstances of the case.

Possibility of a new "gap": person may object sufficiently to be ineligible for DoLS but not sufficiently to justify use of MHA compulsory powers. Judge implies MHA should be used in these circumstances under the "primacy" principle.

Treatment of mental disorder in *hospital* under compulsion will in most cases be under MHA not DoLS where there is a deprivation of liberty.

See also *AM v SLAM and Secretary of State for Health* (2013) UKUT 0365 (AAC), where the same judge stated that his comments in GJ that the MHA had primacy were not of general application.

# HL v UK (2004) 40 EHRR 761

### ISSUE

Did the detention under the common law doctrine of necessity of a patient who lacked capacity to consent to admission to psychiatric hospital, but who did not resist being taken there, constitute a breach of Article 5 of the Convention?

## DECISION

Patient was deprived of his liberty.

Patient could have been detained under the MHA.

Patient's detention at common law was not in accordance with a procedure prescribed by law (lack of procedural safeguards, rules and formal admission procedures) and was thus arbitrary and in breach of Article 5(1).

The lack of an effective means of challenge to his detention (e.g. no possible Tribunal application) was in breach of patient's rights under Article 5(4).

## IMPLICATIONS

Article 5 does not prohibit restriction of movement.

Distinction between deprivation of liberty and restriction of movement is one of degree and intensity not nature or substance.

No single factor is determinative of deprivation of liberty. All circumstances of patient's care had to be considered in reaching a conclusion.

An important factor was that the healthcare professionals assumed "complete and effective control" of the patient's movements.

The Deprivation of Liberty Safeguards procedure is designed to permit lawful deprivation of liberty without use of MHA or Court of Protection order.

# *JE v DE and Surrey CC* (2006) EWHC 3459 (Fam)

### ISSUE

What constitutes deprivation of liberty as opposed to restriction of movement?

### DECISION

Distinction made between restrictions of person's movements within an institution and his not being free to leave it and live where he chooses.

Not being free to leave institution and live with his wife at home constituted a deprivation of person's liberty.

### IMPLICATIONS

Hard to reconcile this case with *HL v UK* (2004) and other case law, which had identified that no single factor was determinative of a deprivation of liberty.

Does this case elevate not being free to leave and live where he chooses above all other factors when deciding whether a person was deprived of his liberty? Is it no longer a question of degree and intensity?

What weight should be attached to the apparent wishes of a person lacking capacity to make the relevant decision in determining whether he is deprived of his liberty? See *LBH v GP* ((2009) FD08P01058), which suggests that even though the person lacked capacity to consent to where he was to reside, his views had to be given considerable weight.

Does this decision mean that guardianship under the Mental Health Act might constitute a deprivation of liberty?

This case now needs to be read in the light of *Cheshire West* (2014) in relation to "freedom to leave", where it was quoted by the Supreme Court but it is unclear whether this was with approval or not.

# *JT v UK* (2000) 30 EHRR CD 77

## ISSUE

Did the lack of a legal right under the MHA to apply for the removal of his NR breach a patient's rights to privacy under Article 8 of the Convention?

## DECISION

The Government conceded that the lack of such a right amounted to a breach of the patient's Article 8 rights and undertook to bring in legislative change.

## IMPLICATIONS

In *R (M) v Secretary of State for Health* ((2003) EWHC 1094 (Admin)) the court made a declaration of incompatibility (see Chapter 17) in similar circumstances.

The limited amendments to s29 MHA to add patients to the list of those able to apply to court for appointment of a different NR, and add the new ground for removal of the NR as being unsuitable to act as such, may be insufficient to prevent continued breach of the patient's rights under Article 8.

The implications of the case of *R (E) v Bristol City Council* (2005) (see below and Chapter 17) survive the amendments to s29.

# *LBH v Neary* (2011) EWHC 1377

## ISSUE

What approach should local authorities take towards use of DoLS in the face of disputes with a person's family? When should reference be made to the Court of Protection?

## DECISION

LA's powers strictly limited in the face of dispute with family carers (see also *A LA v A* (2010) EWHC 978). Role is to support, not impose its own will. It must demonstrate its own arrangements are better than the family's.

Faced with dispute with a person's family, LA should not impose its will by use of DoLS but refer to the Court of Protection.

There was breach of Article 8 as there had been no effective balanced assessment of the alternatives. The supervisory body must scrutinise assessments with care: perfunctory best interests assessments will be unlawful and DoLS authorisation will not render it lawful (see also *A CC v MB* (2010) EWHC 2508).

MCA Schedule A1 states authorisation must be given if assessments are positive but this only applies if the supervisory body is satisfied assessment is thorough and adequate.

There was a breach of Article 5(4) because no IMCA was appointed; there was no effective review of DoLS authorisation and no speedy review by a *court*. There is a positive obligation of the supervisory body to enable and ensure review by referring to court.

The need to make the DoLS compliant with Article 5(4) was developed further in *AJ v A LA* (2015) EWCOP 5 and *Re RD et al.* (2016) EWCOP 49 (qv).

### IMPLICATIONS

The case is an example of the court attempting to make the DoLS safeguards a reality, rather than a mere procedure. See also *A CC v MB* ((2010) EWHC 2508). *Neary* involved a dispute between the LA and the family, but the judge did not specifically limit his conclusions to such cases and it is an open question whether (and if so when) in all cases of DoLS authorisations (even where no such dispute exists) a reference to the Court of Protection must be made to ensure the person has his Article 5(4) right to a speedy review of detention by a court protected. The problem arises because, unlike under the MHA, there is no provision for automatic referral to a Tribunal (which is a court for MHA purposes).

There is a need to beware of potential for serious conflicts of interests where the DoLS assessor, decision-maker and managing authority are the same.

# *MD v Nottingham Healthcare NHS Trust* (2010) UKUT 59 (AAC)

### ISSUE

What is the meaning and scope of the "availability of appropriate medical treatment" test?

### DECISION

Merely benefitting from the ward "milieu" meant that appropriate medical treatment was available. Detention without possibility of reduction of risk did not merely amount to containment. Treatment must be appropriate but not need to reduce risk. The argument that a theoretical capacity to engage with psychological therapy did not equate to a practical ability to benefit from treatment was "untenable".

### IMPLICATIONS

This case reinforces the view that the threshold for meeting the test is low and that "medical treatment" is to be very broadly construed. As a consequence it is easier to justify use and renewal of (inter alia) the s3 compulsory powers than when the previous "treatability" test had to be met. See also the case of *DL-H v Devon Partnership NHS Trust v Secretary of State* ((2010) UKUT 102 (AAC)).

# *MH v UK* (Application No. 11577/06) (2014) 58 EHRR 35

### ISSUE

What does Article 5(4) require in relation to a person lacking capacity to challenge their own detention?

### DECISION

Article 5(4) requires special safeguards for persons lacking capacity to place them as near as possible in same position as someone with capacity.

## IMPLICATIONS

Echoing *LBH v Neary* (2011) EWCH 1377, *AJ v A LA* (2015) EWCOP 5 and *Re RD et al.* (2016) EWCOP 49 (qv), the courts increasingly expect authorities to go the extra mile to **ensure** (rather than just make available) safeguards for vulnerable people. Note the introduction via MHA2007 of s68(2) longstop duty of managers to refer patient to Tribunal six months after s2 admission. The Code of Practice (E 37.46; W 37.41) requires managers to refer to the Secretary of State where, inter alia, P lacks capacity to request a reference.

# *Montgomery v Lanarkshire Health Board* (2015) UKSC 11

### ISSUE

What is the test for whether a doctor has given sufficient information to a patient prior to treatment for consent to be valid?

### DECISION

The House of Lords in *Sidaway* (1985) AC 871 had decided that both (a) what information is given to the patient and (b) whether this is sufficient were to be subjectively determined by the doctor with the protection of a *Bolam* defence. In *Montgomery v Lanarkshire Health Board* (2015), the Supreme Court held that *Sidaway* was wrong. As far as (a) was concerned it remained for the doctor to determine the risks, etc. of a procedure, but as to (b) what material risks were to be discussed with the patient was to be determined by the reasonable man test, not by reference to a *Bolam* competent body.

### IMPLICATIONS

The doctor could, as a limited therapeutic exception, withhold information from the patient if he reasonably considered that disclosure would be seriously detrimental, but this was not to be abused.

The application of this judgement to those with impaired capacity is not entirely clear. All practicable steps will need to be taken to give the patient a broad general understanding of the "salient points".

# *MS v UK* (24527/08) (2012) ECHR 804

### ISSUE

Did the conditions in which the patient was kept in a police cell under s136 amount to inhuman and degrading treatment in breach of Article 3?

### DECISION

The patient's mental state was rapidly deteriorating in his cell: shouting, smearing himself with faeces and food, drinking from the toilet. The psychiatrists said he met MHA admission criteria, but there was no space at clinic and the admission was not seen as urgent, as he might be charged with criminal offences. The patient remained in the cell for more than the maximum 72 hours permitted under s136. (Now reduced to 24 hours with a possible 12-hour extension.) The ECHR accepted the psychiatrists' judgement, but said he was highly vulnerable and "in dire need of treatment". The situation "diminished excessively his fundamental human dignity". This amounted to degrading treatment and violated his Article 3 rights.

## IMPLICATIONS

The case suggests that the high threshold for what constitutes a breach of Article 3 may be reducing (see also *Keenan v UK* ((27229/95) (2001) 33 EHRR38). There might also have been a breach of Article 5 in that the maximum period under s136 was exceeded, but no claim was made in this respect.

# Nottinghamshire Healthcare NHS Trust v RC (2014) EWHC 1317 (COP)

## ISSUE

Was it lawful to withhold treatment with blood products of a detained Jehovah's Witness patient with capacity to refuse and who had made an advance decision to refuse treatment, even though the power to treat existed under s63 of the Mental Health Act and his life would be at risk without treatment?

## DECISION

Treatment given in such circumstances unquestionably fell within s63. However this was a *power* not an *obligation* to treat. The judge stated "it would be an abuse of power in such circumstances even to think about imposing a blood transfusion". This was so, even though the patient's decision might lead to his death.

## IMPLICATIONS

The need to demonstrate that treatment is in the patient's best interests even when detained under the Mental Health Act and subject to compulsory treatment provisions is a clear reinforcement of numerous decisions placing the patient's wishes at the heart of the decision-making process; this applies whether the patient has capacity or not (see, e.g., *Wye Valley NHS Trust v Mr B* (2015) EWCOP 60), is detained or informal, and whether the decision is wise or unwise. See also *X v Finland* (2012) separately summarised and the Code of Practice for England at E Paras 24.6 and 24.41.

The judge stated that where a responsible clinician was faced with such a decision, an application to court should be made.

# P v Cheshire West and Chester Council and P & Q v Surrey County Council (2014) UKSC 19 ("Cheshire West")

## ISSUE

What constituted deprivation of liberty within the meaning of Article 5 for P in a staffed bungalow, MEG in a small residential home and MIG in her foster mother's home, all suffering from varying levels of disability and restrictions?

## DECISION

The "acid test" of the objective element of a deprivation of liberty was whether a person was under continuous supervision and control **and** not free to leave. The tacit compliance of a person did not constitute valid consent to the restrictions so as to negate a deprivation of liberty.

The beneficial purpose or relative normality of the restrictions were irrelevant. Under this test the majority of the Supreme Court held that P, MEG and MIG were all deprived of their liberty, so that authorisations were required.

## IMPLICATIONS

The full implications of the judgement are in the process of being worked out. What does the "acid test" mean? At what point does supervision become "continuous"? When does support for everyday activities become control?

Does "free to leave" mean free to go to the shops and return, or free to live somewhere else with whomsoever one chooses? It is clear that the question does not turn on whether the person is actively seeking to leave or passively remaining, but on whether if (however unlikely that may be) they attempted to leave they would be prevented.

In what circumstances is the deprivation of liberty to be regarded as imputable to the State? Does the "acid test" apply without modification in a general hospital (see *NHS Trust-v-FG* (2015) I WLR 1984), in an ICU (see *Ferreira-v-Coroner for Inner S. London* (2017) EWCA Civ 31), in a hospice, to respite placements? How does the test apply to children and young people? (*D (A Child) Deprivation of Liberty* (2015) EWHC 922 (Fam) and *D (A Child)* (2019) UKSC 42 qv).

Huge numbers of people with learning disability or dementia may now be regarded as deprived of their liberty as the result of the lowering of the threshold, which has major practical implications for local and health authorities and care home managers amongst others in obtaining the necessary authorisation to make the detention lawful. Applying the test to the domestic or supported living context (where DoLS are not available) means a large increase in court applications. Conditions attaching to a guardianship order, a CTO or conditional discharge, which previously might have been regarded merely as restrictions of movement, might now meet the acid test for deprivation of liberty and so require separate authorisation which may not always be possible (*Welsh Ministers v PJ* (2018) UKSC 66, and *SoS for Justice v MM* (2018) UKSC 60 qv).

# *PC and NC v City of York Council* (2013) EWCA Civ 478

## ISSUE

How to approach the assessment of capacity under the Mental Capacity Act. Whether capacity is decision specific.

## DECISION

Capacity is decision or matter specific not "act" or "person" specific. MCA Code of Practice Guidance on the assessment process states that stage 1 is the "diagnostic" test (s2) and stage 2 is the "functional" test (s3) but in this case the Court of Appeal suggests the reverse, i.e. that assessors should first identify the decision to be made, then determine whether on balance of probabilities the person is unable to make it (s3) before turning to s2 and deciding whether the inability to make the decision is because of an impairment, etc. Unless the inability to make a decision is *because of* an impairment, etc. it will not fall to be dealt with under the MCA and the matter may need to be referred to the High Court (not Court of Protection) for how to proceed and protect the person concerned under its inherent jurisdiction.

## IMPLICATIONS

Does "because of" mean "to the exclusion of all possible reasons"? What if there is a combination of reasons, e.g. an impairment and undue influence? The inability to make the causal link will perhaps most frequently be encountered where the person may be under the "undue influence" of another and so unable to make their own decision. See also *LB Redbridge v G* (2014) EWHC 485 (COP). The advice to reverse the order of assessment was followed in *Kings College Trust v C & E* (2015) EWCOP 85.

# R (AN) v MHRT (Northern Region) (2005) EWCA Civ 1605

### ISSUE

What is the standard of proof required at a Tribunal hearing?

### DECISION

The requirement is that the Tribunal is satisfied on the balance of probabilities, not on any higher criminal standard.

Section 72(1)(b)(i) and (ii) criteria are cumulative and the Tribunal must discharge if the detaining authority fails to satisfy as to either.

### IMPLICATIONS

The Court of Appeal held that "the standard of proof will have a much more important part to play in the determination of disputed issues of fact than it will generally have in matters of judgement as to appropriateness and necessity".

Tribunals should be alert to the dangers of hearsay evidence and look to the medical records for contemporaneous evidence of assertions relied on.

The burden of proof before the Tribunal lies at all times on those arguing for the continued detention of the patient – see *R (H) v MHRT for NE London* ((2001) 3 WLR 512).

# R (C) v A LA et al. (2011) EWHC 1539 (Admin)

### ISSUE

What is application of the MHA and MCA Codes of Practice to circumstances not directly within their remit?

### DECISION

DoLS Code of Practice relevant even where DoLS not possible (because not detention in hospital or care home).

MHA Code of Practice should be deemed to apply even if the patient is not detained under MHA, where prima facie his condition falls within the MHA definition of mental disorder, and possibly even where it does not. This would apply to seclusion. Section 118(1)(b) MHA is broad enough to cover patients not formally detained under the Act.

### IMPLICATIONS

This case involved an 18-year-old. The court stated that LA should have referred to the Court of Protection when P was 16 (as DoLS not applicable) – i.e. before any deprivation of liberty occurred.

# R (E) v Bristol City Council (2005) EWHC 74 Admin

## ISSUE

What is the meaning of the words "practicable" and "reasonably practicable" in s11(3) and (4) in relation to the requirement of the ASW (AMHP) to inform or consult with the patient's NR?

## DECISION

Guidance in the (then) Code of Practice that the words meant that the duty to inform or consult with the NR arose if he was "available" was wrong.

The words could be construed as more akin to "appropriate", so that if it was detrimental to the patient's well-being and in breach of his right to respect for privacy under Article 8, there was no need to inform or consult.

## IMPLICATIONS

The case can be seen as an example of the requirement of a court under the Human Rights Act to construe a statutory provision if at all possible in a way that does not breach a person's Convention rights.

Because of the limited nature of the amendments to s29, which allow a patient in defined circumstances to apply to court for the displacement of his NR (but do not give him the right to choose who it should be) this case will continue to be relevant to the consideration by the AMHP of his obligations to consult or inform the patient's existing NR. This is particularly so given that the opportunity for applying to court will often occur for a patient when at his most vulnerable and least able to pursue it.

In *TW v Enfield Borough Council* (2014) EWCA Civ 362, the court put a gloss on this decision, stating that the AMHP had to balance the patient's right not to be detained other than in accordance with a procedure prescribed by law (Article 5) and their right to a private and family life under Article 8(1).

# R (IH) v Secretary of State for the Home Department (2003) UKHL 59

## ISSUE

What if conditions attached to a deferred discharge by MHRT cannot be met?

## DECISION

The obligation is not absolute but is to use best endeavours to meet conditions, so the Tribunal's inability to enforce conditions is not in breach of Article 5. MHRTs must adopt a flexible approach and adjourn/revisit decisions. The new Tribunal approach set by Court of Appeal approved by House of Lords.

## IMPLICATIONS

Does ruling extend beyond deferred conditional discharge patients under s73? Is a community RC a public authority?

Professional autonomy of psychiatrists preserved.

How long the patient is lawfully detained as a result depends on whether he is still suffering from mental disorder.

# R v MHRT for South Thames Region, ex parte Smith (1999) COD 148

### ISSUE

What do the words "nature or degree" mean in relation to the criteria for use of the compulsory powers?

### DECISION

"Nature" refers to the particular mental disorder from which the patient suffers. "Degree" refers to its current manifestation.

The symptoms or manifestations of a patient's disorder may be largely in abeyance, and yet continued detention in hospital is warranted where the underlying nature of the disorder is serious enough that if he ceases to take medication his history shows he is likely to relapse.

See also *CM v Derbyshire Healthcare NHS Foundation Trust et al.* ((2011) UKUT 129 (AAC)), which confirmed earlier case law that a relapsing mental disorder may justify detention on the basis of its nature but only if the risk is of relapse in the near future.

### IMPLICATIONS

Taken together with the cases on long leash s17 leave dealt with under *B v Barking* (1999) above, the consequences are that patients may remain liable to be detained for longer and this raises issues in relation to possible breach of Article 5. This may progressively lead to use of CTOs, whose safeguards for patients make them arguably less arbitrary than s17 leave, although concerns have been expressed that patients may be being kept on CTOs for longer than necessary rather than being discharged (which is reflected in guidance in the Code of Practice at E Paras 29.75, 29.39 and 32.13) and, since *Cheshire West* (2014), that the conditions may sometimes constitute an unlawful breach of Article 5.

# R (Munjaz) v Mersey Care NHS Trust (2005) UKHL 58

### ISSUE

What is the legal status and effect of the Code of Practice? Is seclusion lawful?

### DECISION

The Code does not have statutory force.

The Code is guidance which should be considered with great care and is more than advice which a person under an obligation to have regard to it is free to follow or not.

The Code should only be departed from for cogent reasons. Seclusion is not per se unlawful even at common law.

Seclusion (according to the Court of Appeal) can constitute medical treatment for mental disorder under s63.

In a patient subject to the compulsory powers of the MHA, it is not seclusion which constitutes a deprivation of liberty but the fact that he has been sectioned.

## IMPLICATIONS

The question is less whether a patient is being managed in accordance with Code of Practice guidance, and more whether his treatment breaches his rights under the Convention.

Appropriate local policies and procedures in relation to seclusion can prevent a breach of the patient's rights under Articles 3 and 8, even if they allow for a departure from the Code's guidance.

The judgement is of general application, not just to the issue of seclusion.

Legal requirements cannot be left to the Code of Practice.

This case reached the ECHR under the name *Munjaz v UK* (2012) MHLR 351. The Court affirmed the decision of the House of Lords but stated that the seclusion of a patient might in some circumstances amount to a breach of their residual right to liberty under Article 5.

# R (von Brandenburg) v E London and City Mental Health NHS Trust (2003) UKHL 58

## ISSUE

In what circumstances may a patient just discharged by a Tribunal be re-sectioned without breach of Article 5(4)?

## DECISION

A patient may not be re-sectioned following Tribunal discharge unless the ASW (now AMHP) bona fide believes he has information not known to the Tribunal which would have placed a significantly different complexion on the matter.

## IMPLICATIONS

The House of Lords stressed the different roles of the ASW who made the decision whether to admit, and the doctors who provided the recommendations upon which the ASW had a discretion whether to act.

The decision did not imply that the ASW must have new information, merely that it was information not previously known to the Tribunal. It was not a "change of circumstances" test.

The need for ASWs to act quickly following the Tribunal decision emphasises the importance of Tribunals giving early and reasoned decisions.

If the Tribunal has apparently erred in law, an alternative course to re-sectioning is to apply for a stay and then challenge the Tribunal decision (*R (H) v Ashworth Hospital Authority* (2002) EWCA Civ 923).

See also *R (IH) v Secretary of State for the Home Department* ((2003) UKHL 59), in which the House of Lords stated that the obligation on a health authority was to use best endeavours to implement conditions that a Tribunal was minded to attach to the deferred discharge of a restricted patient. This case is discussed in Chapter 12.

# Re RD et al. (2016) EWCOP 49

## ISSUE

When and in what circumstances should a DoLS authorisation be appealed to the Court of Protection (COP)?

## DECISION

The judge revisited his decision in *AJ v A LA* (2015) EWCOP 5 (qv) and set out substantive guidance in particular at Para. 86. It is largely for the relevant person's representative (RPR) not the IMCA to decide and act upon this issue. IMCA's role under S 38(7)–(9) is to assist. There is a low threshold for capacity to appeal. Does P understand that COP can decide he should not be subject to DoLS? If the person has capacity his wishes must be followed. If he lacks capacity a wish to appeal may possibly be indirectly inferred from his behaviour. If so it is not the role of RPR to decide if this would be in P's best interests. RPR must decide if he should appeal even if not responding to P's wishes. In this case the best interests principle **does** apply.

## IMPLICATIONS

(See *AJ v A LA* (2015) EWCOP 5 and LBH v Neary (2011) EWCH 1377.) RPR may consider alternatives of Part 8 Review, or working collaboratively to make alternative (e.g. less restrictive) arrangements, but **not** so as to frustrate Court application if P would wish it.

# Reed (Trainer) v Bronglais Hospital et al. (2001) EWHC Admin 792

## ISSUE

What constitutes "previous acquaintance" of the patient in s12 in relation to the medical recommendation?

## DECISION

What was required was that the doctor should not be coming to the patient "cold".

The extent of previous acquaintance required is relatively low. The reference in the then Code of Practice to "personal" knowledge did not import any greater requirement.

## IMPLICATIONS

If it is not practicable to ensure that either of the doctors providing recommendations has previous acquaintance of the patient, then the second doctor should preferably also be s12 approved.

The Code of Practice for the amended Act now states: "preferably this should be a doctor who has personally treated the patient. But it is sufficient for the doctor to have had some previous knowledge of the patient's case."

See also *TTM v Hackney BC et al.* ((2011) EWCA Civ 4), in which it was stated that even if this requirement could have been met but was not, this would not have invalidated the section.

# Reid v Secretary of State for Scotland (1999) AC 512

## ISSUE

What does "medical treatment" constitute as defined in s145?

## DECISION

Medical treatment is broad enough to include "treatment the purpose of which may extend from cure to containment".

Medical treatment includes treatment "which is designed to alleviate or to prevent a deterioration of the mental disorder ... or of the symptoms of the mental disorder".

## IMPLICATIONS

This case seems to foreshadow the provisions of s145(4), introduced by the MHA2007 – see the discussion in Chapter 4 – although the use of the word "manifestations" in s145(4) might broaden the definition's effect still further in practice.

Similar comments were made as to the meaning of "medical treatment" in *R (Munjaz) v Mersey Care NHS Trust* (2005) above.

See also *MD v Nottingham Healthcare NHS Trust* ((2010) UKUT 59 (AAC)) and *DL-H v Devon Partnership NHS Trust v Secretary of State* ((2010) UKUT 102 (AAC)).

# RM v St Andrew's Healthcare (2010) UKUT 119 (AAC)

## ISSUE

In what circumstances may information (in this case that he was being covertly medicated) be withheld from a patient in Tribunal proceedings?

## DECISION

The situation is now governed by Rule 14. There is discretion to prohibit disclosure of reports in Tribunal proceedings if disclosure would be likely to cause serious harm to the patient or another and if proportionate with regard to interests of justice. The patient does not have absolute or unqualified right to see every document, but in this case the Upper Tribunal concluded that if the information was withheld the patient would not be able effectively to challenge his detention because he did not know that he was being covertly medicated.

Disclosure was therefore ordered in the interests of justice, even though such disclosure would be likely to cause serious harm to the patient's health.

## IMPLICATIONS

The requirement under Article 6 for a fair trial was considered to be of greater importance than the avoidance of likely serious harm to the patient. It is interesting to speculate whether the same decision would have been reached if the prospect was of serious harm to someone other than the patient.

# Savage v SE Essex Partnership NHS Foundation Trust (2008) UKHL 74

## ISSUE

What is the nature and extent of the obligation owed to a detained patient under Article 2?

## DECISION

A health authority's obligation to such a patient to prevent his committing suicide was akin to that laid down in *Osman v United Kingdom* ((1999) 1 FLR 193) in relation to a public authority: a positive obligation to employ competent staff and adopt systems of work which would protect the patient's life and an obligation to take all reasonable steps to prevent his suicide where they knew or ought to have known that such a risk existed.

## IMPLICATIONS

In *Rabone v Pennine Care NHS Trust* (2012) UKSC 2, the court held that the same duty may be owed even to an informal patient, depending on the presence of relevant factors such as the assumption of responsibility for the individual's welfare by the state, the victim's vulnerability and the nature of the risk.

# Sec of State for Justice v MM (2018) UKSC 60

### ISSUE

Can a Mental Health Tribunal attach to a conditional discharge order conditions which amount to a deprivation of P's liberty within the meaning of Article 5 ECHR?

### DECISION

There is no express power in the MHA for a Tribunal to impose conditions amounting to dol, and this cannot be implied. Moreover such a power would be contrary to the whole scheme of the MHA which provides for only two forms of detention (in a place of safety for up to 36 hours or a hospital). P cannot consent to such conditions (thereby in theory negating the deprivation of liberty) because he might be compliant with the conditions merely to get out of hospital and might subsequently withdraw his "coerced" consent.

### IMPLICATIONS

The SC acknowledged that this decision placed the capacitated P at a disadvantage compared to the incapacitated P who might possibly be made subject to a Court of Protection order or even a DoLS authorisation of his deprivation of liberty and so discharged from hospital. If the conditions could not be reduced so that they amounted to a mere restriction of movement the capacitated P might have to remain in hospital detention.

The alternative suggested by the MoJ of use of long term S17 leave to permit management of the capacitated P in the community is of dubious legality, not least because case law has established the need for such management to require an element of hospital treatment if it is to be lawful. In Herts CC v AB (2018) EWHC 3103 (Fam) the court used its inherent jurisdiction to authorise dol of such a P, but this approach is specifically rejected in the guidance though without any obvious legal basis and was not considered or endorsed by the Supreme Court.

Thus it seems that only amending legislation giving Tribunals the missing power can resolve the current impasse satisfactorily.

# Storck v Germany (2005) 43 EHRR 96

### ISSUE

What is the nature of the State's positive obligation under Article 1 to secure Convention rights for those within its jurisdiction?

## DECISION

The State had an obligation to ensure proper supervision and review of the deprivation of a person's liberty even if confined in a private institution. It could not delegate its responsibilities.

The State's obligation extended to decisions to treat a patient against his will.

The involvement of the State through the police in bringing a patient back to a private institution meant that it was implicated in the patient's detention and resultant breach of Articles 5 and 8 of the Convention.

The State was under an obligation to consider the need for special safeguards for the vulnerable mentally ill.

## IMPLICATIONS

Detention of a competent refusing child on the basis of parental authority might no longer be lawful.

# *TTM v Hackney BC et al.* (2011) EWCA Civ 4

## ISSUE

What is the effect of an honest but mistaken belief that the nearest relative had no objection to s3 application? Who is responsible for the legal consequence of such a mistake? What if neither doctor had "previous acquaintance" with the patient?

## DECISION

The detention was unlawful *ab initio* not merely from when a court so declared.

The fact that the hospital trust did not act unlawfully within s6(3) in admitting and detaining the patient did not retrospectively render the detention itself lawful.

Section 139 could not be interpreted so as to render lawful what was unlawful. Article 5(1) had been breached so the patient was entitled to compensation.

The local authority was liable to pay the claim, not the hospital trust (as detaining authority).

There was no breach of MHA s6(3) by the hospital trust in admitting the patient without either doctor having previous acquaintance. "Practicable" was to be broadly construed. Even if it had been practicable this would not have invalidated the application.

## IMPLICATIONS

Managers' duties to check and scrutinise applications are limited: the first stage is to check that the documents appear to amount to an application that has been duly made; the second stage is to scrutinise for defects which fundamentally invalidate the application.

Managers were entitled to rely on the AMHP's confirmation that there had been no objection by the nearest relative; when P's solicitors asserted post-admission that the nearest relative had objected, managers acted sufficiently in checking with the AMHP who again assured them that this was not the case.

Managers also acted correctly in treating solicitors' allegation as nearest relative exercising his right to discharge P and so a barring order was correctly made.

# *Welsh Ministers v PJ* (2018) UKSC 66

### ISSUE

Can a responsible clinician for a detained patient attach conditions to a community treatment order (CTO) which objectively amount to a deprivation of liberty (dol) within the meaning of Article 5?

### DECISION

There was no express power in the MHA (which could not be implied) to permit imposition of conditions amounting to dol. The fact that medication cannot be forced on a CTO patient supports the view that Parliament did not intend such a power to be implied. The fact that the conditions are not directly enforceable does not mean they cannot amount to dol: the focus is on the concrete position of the patient. The MHT has no power to revoke or vary the conditions, merely to discharge the CTO. The patient must challenge alleged consequential unlawful dol by judicial review or habeas corpus.

### IMPLICATIONS

The SC was silent as to the place of a concurrent DoLS for the incapacitated P or the effect of a capacitated P's consent to conditions amounting to dol but following the decision in *Sec of State for Justice v MM* (2018) UKSC 60 (qv) it is unlikely the patient could negate dol by such consent. If the dol was imposed not by the CTO conditions but by the care plan, consent might be possible and a DoLS authorisation might be possible where the patient lacked capacity. It is unclear whether the High Court would consider using its inherent jurisdiction to resolve the issue as in *Herts CC v AB* (2018) EWHC 3103 (Fam).

# *Wilkinson v UK* (Application 14659/02, Admissibility Decision Feb 06)

### ISSUE

Does s58 treatment forced on a capacitated patient breach his Convention rights?

### DECISION

Safeguards built into the MHA (such as SOAD), and the remedy of judicial review prevented the high threshold for breach of Article 3 (prohibition against inhuman and degrading treatment) being reached.

There was a breach of Article 8(1) (right to private and family life) but this was justified by Article 8(2) (for the protection of the patient's health).

### IMPLICATIONS

Would treatment with ECT have led to the same result? (ECT in face of capacitated refusal now only permitted under limited s62 exceptions.)

For treatment under s58 against the wishes of a capacitated patient to be lawful it must be convincingly shown to be a therapeutic necessity – see *Herczegfalvy v Austria* ((1992) 15 EHRR 437), and *R (N) v Dr M et al.* ((2003) 1 WLR 3284), in which the relevant factors were identified.

Note also the case of *Keenan v UK* ((2001) 33 EHRR 38), which indicates that the failure to provide appropriate psychiatric input to a patient known to be seriously mentally disordered might constitute a breach of the prohibition under Article 3 against inhuman and degrading treatment.

If that failure leads to the patient's death there might also be a breach of his right to life under Article 2.

See also *X v Finland* (34806/04) (2012) MHLR 318 ECHR and *Nottinghamshire Healthcare NHS Trust v RC* (2014) EWHC 1317 (COP), which are separately summarised in this Appendix, for further discussion of the limits to the use of the compulsory powers to treat detained patients.

# *Winterwerp v Netherlands* (1979) 2 EHRR 387

## ISSUE

What constitutes a lawful deprivation of liberty under Article 5(1)(e) of the Convention in relation to a person of unsound mind?

## DECISION

There must be objective medical expertise establishing a true mental disorder, save in an emergency.

The mental disorder must be of a kind or degree which justifies detention.

To justify continued detention there must be a persistence of the mental disorder.

## IMPLICATIONS

True mental disorder is to be distinguished from behaviour which merely deviates from society's norms. This may have implications for use of the compulsory powers to detain, e.g. a paedophile.

Will approved clinicians who are not doctors have the necessary "medical expertise" upon which lawfully to base the use of the compulsory powers in the MHA, in particular the renewal of a patient's detention under s20?

# *X v Finland* (34806/04) (2012) MHLR 318 ECHR

## ISSUE

Did compulsory treatment of a capacitated refusing detained patient constitute an unlawful breach of Articles 3 and 8?

## DECISION

ECtHR held there was a breach of Article 8 because Finnish law permitted the forced administration of medication by doctors despite refusal by patient, without immediate judicial scrutiny of its lawfulness and proportionality and without the court being able to order its discontinuance.

## IMPLICATIONS

It could be argued that MHA s63 creates a similar power. However, the combined effect of the procedural requirements of the MHA, the power of Tribunals to discharge and in particular the cases of *Wilkinson v UK* (2006) MHLR 142; *R (JB) v Dr Haddock* (2006) EWCA Civ 961; *R (N) v Dr M* (2002) EWCA Civ 1789; *R (PS) v Dr G and Dr W* (2003) EWHC 2335 (Admin); and *R (B) v Dr SS* (2006) EWCA Civ 28 may mean that sufficient safeguards have been built into the scheme for compulsory treatment for UK law to be compliant with Article 8. Convincingly demonstrating the therapeutic need to proceed is akin to importing a best interests test into MHA. See also *Nottinghamshire Healthcare NHS Trust v RC* (2014) EWHC 1317 (COP), which is separately summarised. The Code of Practice for England guidance reflects this case law at E Paras 24.6 and 24.41.

# *Appendix 7*

## Conversion chart for forms used in Wales and England

This chart shows the equivalent statutory forms in England for the forms prescribed in Wales. Not all of the forms in England share the same title as those in Wales, and there are some differences in content of the forms. Welsh forms are in the left-hand column, with English equivalents on the right. To fill in some gaps in the sequence of the right-hand column the English forms are inserted but in italics. Generally these forms then appear again when their place in the Welsh sequence arrives. Abbreviations:

AMHP = approved mental health professional. AWOL = absent without leave. CTO = community treatment order. LSSA = local social services authority. NR = nearest relative. RC = responsible clinician. S = Section.

| Wales | Title of Form | England |
|---|---|---|
| HO1 | S2 – application by NR for admission for assessment | A1 |
| HO2 | S2 – application by an AMHP for admission for assessment | A2 |
| HO3 | S2 – joint medical recommendation for admission for assessment | A3 |
| HO4 | S2 – medical recommendation for admission for assessment | A4 |
| HO5 | S3 – application by NR for admission for treatment | A5 |
| HO6 | S3 – application by an AMHP for admission for treatment | A6 |
| HO7 | S3 – joint medical recommendation for admission for treatment | A7 |
| HO8 | S3 – medical recommendation for admission for treatment | A8 |
| HO9 | S4 – emergency application by NR for admission for assessment | A9 |
| HO10 | S4 – emergency application by AMHP for admission for assessment | A10 |
| HO11 | S4 – medical recommendation for emergency admission for assessment | A11 |
| HO12 | S5(2) – report on hospital in-patient | H1 |
| HO13 | S5(4) – record of hospital in-patient | H2 |
| HO14 | S2, 3 and 4 – record of detention in hospital | H3 |
| *TC1* | *authority for transfer from one hospital to another under different managers* | *(H4)* |
| HO15 | S20 – renewal of authority for detention | H5 |
| HO16 | S21B – authority for detention after AWOL for more than 28 days | H6 |

| | | |
|---|---|---|
| HO17 | S23 – discharge by the responsible clinician or the hospital managers | No form |
| GU1 | S7 – guardianship application by NR | G1 |
| GU2 | S7 – guardianship application by an AMHP | G2 |
| GU3 | S7 – joint medical recommendation for reception into guardianship | G3 |
| GU4 | S7 – medical recommendation for reception into guardianship | G4 |
| GU5 | S7 – record of acceptance of guardianship application | G5 |
| *TC2* | *S19 – authority for transfer from hospital to guardianship* | *G6* |
| *TC3* | *S19 – authority for transfer of a patient from the guardianship of one guardian to another* | *G7* |
| *TC4* | *S19 – authority for transfer from guardianship to hospital.* | *G8* |
| GU6 | S20 – renewal of authority for guardianship | G9 |
| GU7 | S21B – authority for guardianship after AWOL more than 28 days | G10 |
| GU8 | S23 – discharge by the RC or the responsible LSSA | No form |
| CP1 | S17A – CTO | CTO1 |
| CP2 | S17B – variation of conditions on a CTO | CTO2 |
| CP3 | S20A – report extending the community treatment period | CTO7 |
| CP4 | S21B – authority for community treatment after AWOL for more than 28 days | CTO8 |
| CP5 | S17E – notice of recall to hospital | CTO3 |
| CP6 | S17E – record of patients detention in hospital after recall | CTO4 |
| CP7 | S17F – revocation of CTO | CTO5 |
| *TC6* | *S17F(2) – authority for transfer of recalled community patient to a hospital under different managers* | *CTO6* |
| *TC8* | *Part 6 – transfer of patient subject to compulsion in the community* | *CTO9* |
| *TC5* | *S19A – authority for assignment of responsibility for a community patient from one hospital to another under different managers* | *CTO10* |
| CP8 | S23 – discharge by the RC or the hospital managers | No form |
| TC1 | S19 – authority for transfer from one hospital to another under different managers | H4 |
| TC2 | S19 – authority for transfer from hospital to guardianship | G6 |
| TC3 | S19 – authority for transfer of a patient from the guardianship of one guardian to another | G7 |
| TC4 | S19 – authority for transfer from guardianship to hospital. | G8 |
| TC5 | S19A – authority for assignment of responsibility for a community patient from one hospital to another under different managers | CTO10 |
| TC6 | S17F(2) – authority for transfer of recalled community patient to a hospital under different managers | CTO6 |
| TC7 | Part 6 – date of reception of a patient to hospital or into guardianship in Wales | M1 |

| TC8 | Part 6 – transfer of patient subject to compulsion in the community | CTO9 |
|---|---|---|
| NR1 | S25 – report barring discharge by NR | M2 |
| CO1 | S57 – certificate of consent to treatment and second opinion | T1 |
| CO2 | S58(3)(a) – certificate of consent to treatment | T2 |
| CO3 | S58(3)(b) – certificate of second opinion | T3 |
| CO4 | S58A(3)(c) – certificate of consent to treatment (patients at least 18 years of age) | T4 |
| CO5 | S58A(4)(c) – certificate of consent to treatment and second opinion (patients under 18 years of age) | T5 |
| CO6 | S58A(5) – certificate of second opinion (patients not capable of understanding nature, purpose and likely effects of the treatment) | T6 |
| CO7 | Part 4A – certificate of appropriateness of treatment to be given to a community patient (Part 4A Certificate) | CTO11 |

# Appendix 8

# Transfer of patients between jurisdictions

This guidance is taken from the Reference Guide (Chapters 34–38) which was written for use in England but is also used in practice in Wales. Form numbers given are for England. See Appendix 7 for the equivalent Welsh forms. Before reprinting the key chapters, here are some useful addresses from the Reference Guide:

### England

For advice on proposals to transfer a patient from England to another jurisdiction please contact: Department of Health, Richmond House, 79 Whitehall, London SW1A 2NS Telephone: 020 7210 5359 or 020 7210 5775.

### Scotland

Directorate for Population Health Improvement Mental Health, St Andrews House, Regents Road, Edinburgh, EH1 3DG Telephone: 0131 244 5668 Email: andy.lawson2@scotland.gsi.gov.uk.

For cases concerned with criminal proceedings email: restrictedpatients@scotland.gsi.gov.uk.

### Northern Ireland

Mental Health Unit, Department of Health, Social Services and Public Safety, D1.4 Castle Buildings, Stormont Estate, Belfast BT4 3SQ Telephone: 028 9052 2562 Fax: 028 9052 2500.

Email: mentalhealthunit@dhsspsni.gov.uk.

### States of Jersey

Community Mental Health Service, 20 La Chasse, St Helier, Jersey, Channel Islands, JE24UE Telephone: 01534 445841 Fax: 01534 445140.

Email: health@gov.je.

### Bailiwick of Guernsey

Corporate Headquarters, Rue Mignot, St Andrews, Guernsey, Channel Islands, GY6 8TW Telephone: 10481 725241 Fax: 01481 235341.

Email: healthandwellbeing@gov.gg.

### Isle of Man

Department of Health and Social Care, Mental Health Service, Cronk Coar, Noble's Hospital, Braddan, Isle of Man, IM4 4RF Telephone: 01624 656015 Fax: 01624 642805.

Email: mentalhealthcustomerservices.dh@gov.im.

# Chapter 34 – Transfer of patients from outside England and Wales

## INTRODUCTION

34.1 This chapter describes the provisions of the Act, which deal with the transfer of patients from Scotland, Northern Ireland, the Isle of Man or any of the Channel Islands. These provisions are mainly to be found in Part 6 of the Act. Details to do with transfers between England and Wales are included in chapter 10.

## RELEVANT SECTIONS OF THE ACT

34.2 The sections of the Act dealing with the transfer of patients (or responsibility for patients) to England (and Wales) from corresponding or similar provision elsewhere are set out in Figure 89.

| From | Scotland | Northern Ireland | Isle of Man/Channel Islands |
|------|----------|------------------|------------------------------|
| Detention in hospital | Section 80B | Section 82 | Section 85 |
| Community treatment | Section 80C | n/a | Section 85ZA |
| Conditional discharge | Section 80D | Section 82A | Section 85A |
| Guardianship | n/a | Section 82 | Section 85 |

*Figure 89   Sections of the Act dealing with cross-border transfers to England*

## GENERAL RULES APPLICABLE TO TRANSFERS FROM ALL JURISDICTIONS

34.3 Although some of the precise details differ, the following basic rules apply in all cases.

### Transfer to detention in hospital

34.4 When the equivalent of a Part 2 patient is transferred to detention under the Act, they are treated on their admission to hospital in England or Wales as if they had been admitted on that date as a result of a corresponding application for admission under Part 2 of the Act. In other words, they are treated as if they were a newly detained patient.

34.5 If patients were subject to the equivalent of a hospital order, hospital direction or transfer direction before being transferred, then instead of being treated as detained on the basis of an application, they are treated as if subject to the corresponding order or direction under Part 3 of the Act given on the date of their admission.

34.6 This means that these patients are also, for the most part, treated as if they had been newly detained under Part 3 of the Act. There are some differences, described below. In particular, patients treated as becoming subject to an unrestricted hospital order on their transfer may apply to the Tribunal in the six months following their transfer, even though such patients would normally not be able to apply unless or until their detention had been renewed after six months...

34.7 If they were restricted patients or the equivalent before they were transferred, they are treated on admission to hospital as if they are also subject to a restriction order, limitation direction, or restriction direction as applicable.

34.8 If they were subject to the equivalent of hospital and limitation directions or a transfer direction under s47, the associated sentence of imprisonment or equivalent is treated as if it had been imposed by a court in England or Wales. If there is more than one associated sentence, they are all treated in that way. Similarly, the restriction order or direction will cease on the date that the first restriction order or direction would have ceased.

## Transfer to a CTO

34.9 When a patient is transferred from the equivalent of a community treatment order (CTO), they are treated as if they had been detained and then immediately discharged onto a CTO on the day they arrived at the place they are to live in England or Wales. Specifically, they are treated as if, on that day:

- an application for their admission under Part 2, or an order or direction for their detention under Part 3 (as applicable), had been made, equivalent to the authority to which they were subject before being transferred;

- they had been admitted to the hospital whose managers have agreed to be the responsible hospital; and

34.10 their responsible clinician had then immediately made a CTO. The hospital from which they are treated as having been discharged onto a CTO becomes their responsible hospital.

## Transfer to guardianship

34.11 When patients from Jersey or the Isle of Man are transferred from guardianship, they are treated as if a guardianship application under Part 2 was accepted, or a guardianship order under Part 3 was made as applicable on the day they arrived at the place they are to live in England or Wales.

## Transfer of responsibility for conditionally discharged patients

34.12 Responsibility for conditionally discharged patients can only be transferred if the Secretary of State for Justice agrees to take over that responsibility.

34.13 Where the Secretary of State agrees to the transfer of responsibility, patients are treated as if they:

- are subject to a hospital order and restriction order, or hospital and limitation directions, or a transfer direction and restriction direction (depending on which corresponds to their position before transfer); and

- had been conditionally discharged on the day responsibility is transferred.

## Restricted patients (detained or conditionally discharged)

34.14 None of the above affects the date on which a restriction order, limitation direction or restriction direction is due to expire, if the equivalent to which a patient was previously subject outside England or Wales was due to expire on a fixed date.

### ARRANGEMENTS FOR TRANSFERS

34.15 It is up to the authorities in the jurisdiction from which the patient is being transferred to decide whether to authorise the transfer in accordance with the local legislation.

34.16 The authorities will almost certainly require evidence that arrangements have been made for the patient to be received in England before they will agree to the transfer. In practice, they will generally ask the Department of Health (or the Ministry of Justice for restricted patients) to confirm this with the relevant English hospital or local authority.

34.17 The Secretary of State for Justice will not, in practice, agree to the transfer of a restricted patient to England unless satisfied that the proposed arrangements will enable the patient's safe management in England.

## RECORD OF TRANSFER – MANAGERS' AND GUARDIANS' DUTIES
## (REGULATION 15)

34.18 Hospital managers in England are required to record the admission of patients transferred to detention in their hospital from outside England or Wales using Form M1. The managers must then take whatever steps are reasonably practical to inform the person they think is the patient's nearest relative of the patient's admission unless the patient has asked that such information not be given or does not have a nearest relative. Restricted patients, by definition, will not have a nearest relative.

34.19 The managers of the responsible hospital must similarly record the arrival of patients transferred to a CTO using Form M1. In this case, arrival means the day on which the patient arrives at the place they are to live in England or Wales. The managers must then take whatever steps are reasonably practical to inform the person they think is the patient's nearest relative that the patient is now a CTO patient unless the patient has asked that such information not be given or does not have a nearest relative.

34.20 In both cases, the record on Form M1 may be made by an officer authorised by the managers to do so.

34.21 Guardians (whether local authorities or private guardians) must record the arrival of patients transferred to their guardianship using Form M1. Again, arrival means the day on which the patient arrives at the place they are to live in England or Wales. The guardian must then take whatever steps are reasonably practical to inform the person they think is the patient's nearest relative that the patient is now subject to guardianship in England unless the patient has asked that such information not be given or does not have a nearest relative.

34.22 A private guardian must also inform the responsible local authority of their own address, the patient's address and the name and address of the patient's nominated medical attendant...

34.23 These duties are in addition to the normal duties that hospital managers and local authorities have to give information to patients who are newly detained, or who become CTO patients or guardianship patients and their nearest relatives.

## PATIENTS TRANSFERRED TO A CTO – RESPONSIBLE CLINICIAN'S DUTY TO SET CONDITIONS
## (SECTIONS 80C AND 85ZA AND REGULATION 16)

34.24 As soon as practicable after patients are treated as having become CTO patients the responsible clinician must specify the conditions which are to be included in their CTO under section 17B of the Act.... Those conditions must first be agreed by an approved mental health professional (AMHP). The conditions which are specified are deemed to be included in the patient's CTO.

34.25 The responsible clinician must specify those conditions using Form CT09 and the AMHP must confirm agreement using the same form.

## TRANSFERS FROM SCOTLAND – FURTHER DETAILS
## (SECTIONS 80B, 80C AND 80D)

34.26 Transfers to England and Wales can only take place with the approval of Scottish Ministers in accordance with regulations made under the following provisions of the Mental Health (Care and Treatment) (Scotland) Act 2003:

Section 289    Patients who are not subject to a measure authorising detention in hospital, i.e. the equivalent of CTO patients

Section 290    Patients who are liable to be detained (including those who are on the equivalent of leave of absence) and conditionally discharged patients

34.27 An application for a transfer should be made to the Scottish Government.

34.28 In practice, the Scottish Government will generally ask the Department of Health (or the Ministry of Justice for restricted patients) to confirm that arrangements have been made. The Secretary of State for Justice will not, in practice, agree to the transfer of a restricted patient to England unless satisfied that the proposed arrangements will enable the patient's safe management in England.

34.29 Although the Act does not specify which of its provisions are to be considered equivalent to those in Scotland, they are likely to be as set out in Figure 88.

| Scotland | England and Wales |
| --- | --- |
| Emergency detention certificate under s36 of the Mental Health (Care and Treatment) (Scotland) Act 2003 | Emergency application (s4) |
| Short term detention certificate under s44 of the Mental Health (Care and Treatment) (Scotland) Act 2003 | Application for admission for assessment (s2) |
| Compulsory treatment order under s64 of the Mental Health (Care and Treatment) (Scotland) Act 2003 authorising detention in hospital | Application for admission for treatment (s3) |
| Compulsory treatment order under s64 of the Mental Health (Care and Treatment) (Scotland) Act 2003 not authorising detention in hospital | CTO following detention under an application for admission for treatment (s3 and s17A) |
| Compulsion order under s57A of the Criminal Procedure (Scotland) Act 1995 authorising detention in hospital, without a restriction order | Hospital order (s37) |
| Compulsion order under s57A of the Criminal Procedure (Scotland) Act 1995 authorising detention in hospital, with a restriction order under s59 of that Act | Hospital order (s37) with restriction order (s41) |
| Compulsion order under s57A of the Criminal Procedure (Scotland) Act 1995 not authorising detention in hospital | CTO following detention under an unrestricted hospital order (s37 and s17A as applied by Part 1 of Schedule 1) |

*(Continued)*

*Figure 88   (Continued)*

| Scotland | England and Wales |
| --- | --- |
| Hospital direction under s59A of the Criminal Procedure (Scotland) Act 1995 | Hospital and limitation directions (s45A) |
| Transfer for treatment direction under s136 of the Mental Health (Care and Treatment) (Scotland) Act 2003 | Restricted transfer direction for sentenced prisoner (s47 and s49) |

*Figure 88   Transfers from Scotland: likely corresponding provisions*

34.30   At the time of publication, Scottish regulations do not permit the transfer of patients subject to treatment orders, assessment orders, interim compulsion orders, temporary compulsion orders or remands for inquiries into their mental condition. Between them, these are roughly equivalent to remands under s35 or s36 of the Act, interim hospital orders under s38 and transfer directions for unsentenced prisoners under s48.

## TRANSFERS FROM NORTHERN IRELAND – FURTHER DETAILS
## (SECTIONS 82 AND 82A)

34.31   Transfers from Northern Ireland must be approved by the Department of Health, Social Services and Public Safety (DHSSPS) for Northern Ireland under section 82 of the Act, unless the patient is restricted. At the time of publication, transfers of restricted detained patients, and transfers of conditionally discharged patients under section 82A, must be approved by the Department of Justice in Northern Ireland.

34.32   Before authorising a transfer, the DHSSPS or the Department of Justice in Northern Ireland as applicable must deem or judge it to be in the patient's interests after all appropriate investigations and assessments have been completed. The level of investigation and assessment required would depend on the gravity of the decision involved. More serious decisions, including decisions to transfer a patient against his ascertainable wishes and those of his family, would require the highest level of informed scrutiny.

34.33   In practice, the Northern Ireland authorities will generally ask the Department of Health (or the Ministry of Justice for restricted patients) to confirm that arrangements have been made for the patient to be admitted to hospital or received into guardianship in England or Wales. The Secretary of State for Justice will not, in practice, agree to the transfer of a restricted patient to England unless satisfied that the proposed arrangements will enable the patient's safe management in England.

34.34   Section 82 specifies the provisions to which certain patients are to be treated as subject if transferred to England or Wales, as set out in Figure 89.

34.35   Although the Act does not specify which of its provisions are to be considered equivalent to those in Northern Ireland in other cases, they are likely to be as set out in Figure 90.

| Liable to be detained in Northern Ireland immediately before the transfer on the basis of | To be treated as liable to be detained in England and Wales on the basis of |
| --- | --- |
| a report under Article 12(1) or 13 of the Mental Health (Northern Ireland) Order 1986 | an application for admission for treatment (section 3) |
| an application for assessment under Article 4 of that Order | an application for admission for assessment (section 2) |

*Figure 89    Transfers from Northern Ireland: corresponding provisions as set out in section 82*

| Northern Ireland (Mental Health (Northern Ireland) Order 1986) | England and Wales |
| --- | --- |
| Liable to be detained under Article 44, without restrictions on discharge | Hospital order (s37) |
| Liable to be detained under Article 44, with restrictions under Article 47 | Hospital order (s37) and restriction order (s41) |
| Liable to be detained under Article 53, without restrictions on discharge | Transfer direction for sentenced prisoner (s47) |
| Liable to be detained under Article 53, with restrictions under Article 57 | Transfer direction for sentenced prisoner (s47) with restriction direction (s49) |
| Liable to be detained under Article 54, without restrictions on discharge | Transfer direction for unsentenced prisoner (s48) |
| Liable to be detained under Article 54, with restrictions under Article 57 | Transfer direction for unsentenced prisoner (s48) with restriction direction (s49) |
| Subject to guardianship on the basis of an application under Article 18 | Guardianship application (s7) |
| Subject to guardianship order under Article 44 | Guardianship order (s37) |

*Figure 90    Transfers from Northern Ireland: likely corresponding provisions in other cases*

## TRANSFERS FROM THE ISLE OF MAN OR THE CHANNEL ISLANDS – FURTHER DETAILS (SECTIONS 85, 85ZA AND 85A)

34.36    Transfers from the Isle of Man or any of the Channel Islands require the approval of the relevant island authorities, in accordance with local legislation.

34.37    In practice, the island authorities will generally ask the Department of Health (or the Ministry of Justice for restricted patients) to confirm that arrangements have been made for the transfer. The Secretary of State for Justice will not, in practice, agree to the transfer of a restricted patient to England unless satisfied that the proposed arrangements will enable the patient's safe management in England.

34.38 Patients transferred from the Isle of Man or the Channel Islands are treated on their arrival in England or Wales as if subject to the application, order or direction which corresponds to the provisions to which they were subject in the island in question. Advice should be sought from the island authorities or from the Department of Health or the Ministry of Justice as applicable if there is doubt about what the relevant corresponding provision is. Patients subject to the equivalent of remand to hospital under sections 35 or 36, or an interim hospital order under section 38, cannot be transferred.

34.39 For patients transferred from the Isle of Man who become subject to the equivalent of hospital directions or restriction directions in England, detention under sections 53 and 54 of the Mental Health Act 1998 is treated where relevant as if it were a sentence of imprisonment which has been given by a court in England or Wales.

### OFFENDERS FOUND INSANE IN THE ISLE OF MAN OR THE CHANNEL ISLANDS (SECTION 84)

34.40 Under section 84, the Secretary of State for Justice may direct that an offender be removed to a hospital in England or Wales if the offender:

- has been found insane by a court in the Isle of Man or any of the Channel Islands, or to have been insane at the time of the alleged offence; and

- has been ordered to be detained during Her Majesty's pleasure.

34.41 When admitted to the hospital in England or Wales, the patient is treated as if subject to a hospital order and restriction order. The Secretary of State may subsequently direct that the patient be returned to the island, to be dealt with as if never transferred in the first place.

# Chapter 35 – Transfer of patients to Scotland

### INTRODUCTION

35.1 This chapter describes the provisions of the Act under which patients may be transferred from detention, community [treatment] order (CTO) or conditional discharge in England to the equivalent in Scotland. The provisions in question are mainly to be found in Part 6 of the Act.

### PURPOSE OF TRANSFERS UNDER THE ACT

35.2 A transfer under the Act is only necessary where the patient concerned needs to remain subject to detention, conditional discharge or the equivalent of a CTO on arrival in Scotland.

### TRANSFER OF DETAINED PATIENTS TO SCOTLAND (SECTIONS 80 AND 92)

35.3 The Secretary of State may issue a warrant ("a transfer warrant") authorising the transfer of the detained patients from England to Scotland if they are detained under one of the provisions set out in Figure 91.

| Patients liable to be detained on the basis of | Relevant section |
|---|---|
| an application for admission for assessment | 2 or 4 |
| an application for admission for treatment | 3 |
| a hospital order (with or without a restriction order) | 37 (or 51) |

| | |
|---|---|
| a hospital direction (with or without a limitation direction) | 45A |
| a transfer direction (with or without a restriction direction) | 47 or 48 |

and

patients treated as detained on the basis of one of the above (e.g. as a result of transfer from guardianship or from outside England or Wales).

*Figure 91    Detained patients who may be transferred to Scotland*

35.4    A warrant cannot be issued for the transfer of patients remanded to hospital under section 35 or 36, subject to an interim hospital order under section 38, or detained in a hospital as a place of safety under section 135 or 136. In practice, it is unlikely that a warrant would be issued for the transfer of patients detained in hospital under the "holding powers" in section 5.

35.5    A warrant may only be issued if the Secretary of State is satisfied that it is in the patient's interests to be removed to Scotland and that arrangements have been made for the patient to be admitted to hospital in Scotland or (if the patient is not, in fact, to be admitted immediately to hospital) for the possibility of the patient's detention in hospital to be authorised under the relevant Scottish legislation.

### REQUESTING A TRANSFER WARRANT FOR SCOTLAND FOR A DETAINED PATIENT

35.6    In practice, a request for a transfer warrant should be made by, or on behalf of, the managers of the hospital in which the patient is detained in England.

35.7    The request should explain why the hospital thinks the transfer would be in the patient's interests (not the interests of the hospital) and the arrangements that have been agreed for the patient to be received in Scotland.

35.8    For patients other than restricted patients, a pro-forma to be used for such requests is available from the Department of Health.

35.9    Requests for the transfer of restricted patients should be made to the Ministry of Justice. The Act only provides for the transfer of patients between hospitals in different jurisdictions but not the transfer between a prison in one jurisdiction and a hospital in another. If such a transfer is being contemplated, it will need to be undertaken in two stages. Either the patient will be transferred from prison to hospital and from there to a hospital in the other jurisdiction or from prison to another prison and then prison to hospital. Although this might appear complicated, it can be agreed in principle with the patient only having to move once.

35.10    For patients detained under section 2 of the Act, the Scottish authorities require there to be at least 10 days and preferably 14 days remaining on the section 2 when the transfer takes place. This means that the pro-forma for such a transfer should be completed as soon as it is known that the patient is to be transferred to Scotland and the hospital in England has been advised that there is a bed available for the patient at the receiving hospital in Scotland. The completed pro-forma should be faxed or emailed to the Department of Health by day 11 (day 14 at the very latest) and the hospital in England would need to transfer the patient by day 18 (preferably by day 14). A warrant issued for a patient detained under section 2 would not be valid beyond day 18 of the patient's detention.

35.11 Transfer to Scotland requires the approval of Scottish Ministers in accordance with Scottish legislation. The Department of Health (or the Ministry of Justice) will seek this directly from the Scottish Government. If necessary, they may need to ask the hospital in England for any further information which the Scottish Ministers require.

## CONVEYANCE OF DETAINED PATIENTS TO SCOTLAND (SECTIONS 80 AND 137)

35.12 If the Secretary of State issues a warrant, it will include any necessary directions allowing the patient to be conveyed to the relevant hospital (or other place) in Scotland by specified people (normally anyone authorised by the hospital managers) within a fixed period. This is normally 14 days, unless the patient's current period of detention is due to expire sooner or, in a section 2 case, day 18 will be reached in less than 14 days.

35.13 The Scottish Ministers may also give directions about the patient's conveyance once in Scotland under Scottish regulations (or authorise the patient's intended responsible medical officer in Scotland to do so).

35.14 While being conveyed to Scotland in accordance with the transfer warrant, the patient is considered to be in legal custody under the Act.

## EFFECT OF TRANSFER OF A DETAINED PATIENT (SECTION 91)

35.15 When the transfer is completed, the application, order or direction on the basis of which the patient was detained in England ceases to have effect and cannot be revived.

35.16 The transfer is completed when the patient is admitted to the relevant hospital in Scotland. If the patient is not in fact to be detained (e.g. because the patient is to be given the equivalent of leave of absence under Scottish legislation without first being admitted to the new hospital), the transfer is completed when the possibility of detention is authorised under the relevant Scottish legislation.

35.17 The patient will then be subject to the relevant legislation in Scotland – which differs in many respects from that in England.

35.18 For the patient to return to England, a further transfer would be necessary, in accordance with Scottish legislation, which will require the agreement of the Scottish Ministers.

## TRANSFER OF RESPONSIBILITY FOR CONDITIONALLY DISCHARGED PATIENTS TO SCOTLAND (SECTIONS 80A AND 92)

35.19 If the Secretary of State for Justice thinks it would be in the patient's interests, the Secretary of State may agree with the relevant Scottish Minister that the latter will take over responsibility for a conditionally discharged patient who is subject to a restriction order. If responsibility is transferred to the Scottish Minister in this way, the patient will become subject to the arrangements for conditional discharge under the relevant legislation in Scotland.

## TRANSFER OF RESPONSIBILITY FOR PATIENTS ON A CTO TO SCOTLAND (SECTIONS 80ZA AND 91)

35.20 The Secretary of State for Health may authorise the transfer of responsibility for a patient on a CTO to Scotland.

35.21 Such a transfer of responsibility may only be authorised if the Secretary of State thinks that it is in the patient's interests and that arrangements have been made for the patient to be made subject to provisions under Scottish legislation which correspond or are similar to CTOs. At the time of publication, the relevant legislation is the Mental Health (England and Wales cross-border transfer: patients subject to requirements other than detention) (Scotland) Regulations 2008 (SSI 2008/356).

35.22 In practice, this means a CTO under the Mental Health (Care and Treatment) (Scotland) Act 2003 (or a compulsion order under the Criminal Procedure (Scotland) Act 1995), which does not authorise the patient's detention in hospital.

35.23 The Secretary of State may not authorise a transfer of responsibility for patients on a CTO while they are recalled to hospital (which includes any period during which they are absent without leave from the hospital while recalled).

35.24 If the Secretary of State authorises a transfer of responsibility, responsibility for the patient passes to the appropriate body in Scotland from whatever time is specified in the authority. When responsibility passes to Scotland, the patient's CTO ceases to have effect and the patient ceases to be a patient on a CTO. In other words, the patient is no longer liable to recall to or detention in hospital in England or Wales. The patient will then be subject to the relevant legislation in Scotland.

35.25 In practice, a request for the transfer of patient on a CTO should be made to the Department of Health by, or on behalf of, the managers of the patient's responsible hospital using the same pro-forma as for detained patients. A transfer of responsibility for a patient on a CTO does not give anyone any power to convey the patient to Scotland against the patient's will.

## TRANSFER OF GUARDIANSHIP PATIENTS TO SCOTLAND

35.26 It is not possible to transfer guardianship patients to guardianship (or any other form of compulsory measure) in Scotland.

# Chapter 27 – Transfer of patients to Northern Ireland

## INTRODUCTION

35.3 This chapter describes the provisions of the Act under which patients may be transferred from detention, a CTO, guardianship or conditional discharge in England to the equivalent in Northern Ireland. The provisions in question are mainly to be found in Part 6 of the Act.

## PURPOSE OF TRANSFERS UNDER THE ACT

35.4 A transfer under the Act is only necessary where the patient concerned needs to remain subject to detention, guardianship, conditional discharge or the equivalent of a CTO on arrival in Northern Ireland.

## TRANSFER OF DETAINED PATIENTS TO NORTHERN IRELAND (SECTIONS 81 AND 92)

35.5 The Secretary of State may issue a warrant ("a transfer warrant") authorising the transfer of detained patients from England to Northern Ireland if they are detained under one of the provisions set out in Figure 91.

35.6 A warrant cannot be issued for the transfer of patients remanded to hospital under section 35 or 36, or subject to an interim hospital order under section 38, or detained in a hospital as a place of safety under section 135 or 136. And in practice, it is very unlikely that a warrant would be issued for the transfer of patients detained in hospital under the "holding powers" in section 5.

35.7    A transfer warrant may only be issued if the Secretary of State is satisfied that it is in the patient's interests to be removed to Northern Ireland and that arrangements have been made for the patient to be admitted to hospital in Northern Ireland.

## REQUESTING A TRANSFER WARRANT FOR NORTHERN IRELAND FOR A DETAINED PATIENT

35.8    In practice, a request for a transfer warrant should be made by, or on behalf of, the managers of the hospital in which the patient is detained in England.

35.9    The request should explain why the hospital thinks the transfer would be in the patient's interests (not the interests of the hospital) and the arrangements that have been agreed for the patient to be received in Northern Ireland.

35.10   For patients other than restricted patients, a pro-forma to be used for such requests is available from the Department of Health.

35.11   Requests for the transfer of restricted patients should be made to the Ministry of Justice. The Act only provides for the transfer of patients between hospitals in different jurisdictions but not the transfer between a prison in one jurisdiction and a hospital in another. If such a transfer is being contemplated, it will need to be undertaken in two stages. Either the patient will be transferred from prison to hospital and from there to a hospital in the other jurisdiction, or from prison to another prison and then prison to hospital. Although this might appear complicated, it can be agreed in principle with the patient only having to move once.

## CONVEYANCE OF DETAINED PATIENTS TO NORTHERN IRELAND (SECTIONS 81 AND 137)

35.12   If the Secretary of State issues a warrant, it will include any necessary directions allowing the patient to be conveyed to the relevant hospital in Northern Ireland by specified people (normally anyone authorised by the hospital managers) within a fixed period (normally 14 days, unless the patient's current period of detention is due to expire sooner).

35.13   While being conveyed in accordance with the warrant, the patient is considered to be in legal custody, whether in England or Northern Ireland.

## EFFECT OF TRANSFER OF A DETAINED PATIENT (SECTION 91)

35.14   When the transfer is completed, the application, order or direction on the basis of which the patient was detained in England ceases to have effect and cannot be revived. For the patient to return to England, a further transfer would be necessary, in accordance with section 82 of the Act (see Chapter 34).

35.15   The transfer is completed when the patient is admitted to the relevant hospital in Northern Ireland. From that point, the patient is treated as if subject to the corresponding provision of legislation in force in Northern Ireland. In particular:

35.16   Patients subject to a hospital direction, or transfer direction under section 47 given while they were serving a prison sentence (as defined in section 47(5)) imposed by a court in England or Wales, are treated, on their transfer, as if the associated prison sentence(s) had been imposed by a court in Northern Ireland.

35.17   If they were subject to a restriction direction or a limitation direction due to end on a fixed date (e.g. because they are serving a prison sentence of fixed duration, rather than a life sentence), the equivalent restriction direction will still expire on that date. The same applies to patients who were subject to a restriction order of limited duration before their transfer.

| If the patient, immediately before being transferred to Northern Ireland, was liable to be detained on the basis of | The patient is treated, on admission to hospital in Northern Ireland, as if |
|---|---|
| an application for admission for assessment (section 2) | admitted to the hospital on the basis of an application for assessment under Article 4 of the Mental Health (Northern Ireland) Order 1986 made on the date of admission to that hospital. |
| an application for admission for treatment (section 3) | detained for treatment under Part 2 of the Mental Health (Northern Ireland) Order 1986 by virtue of a report under Article 12(1) of that Order made on the date of admission. |

*Figure 92   Transfer of a detained patient to Northern Ireland*

### TRANSFER OF RESPONSIBILITY FOR CONDITIONALLY DISCHARGED PATIENTS TO NORTHERN IRELAND (SECTIONS 81A AND 92)

35.18   If the Secretary of State for Justice thinks it would be in the patient's interests, the Secretary of State may agree with the Secretary of State for Northern Ireland that the latter will take over responsibility for a conditionally discharged patient.

35.19   If a transfer of responsibility is agreed, patients are treated as if they were subject to a hospital order and restriction order, or transfer direction and restriction direction (as applicable), under the corresponding legislation in Northern Ireland, and as if they had been conditionally discharged on the day of the transfer.

35.20   The transfer does not affect the day on which the patient's restriction order or direction expires, if it was due to expire on a fixed date.

### TRANSFER OF PATIENTS ON A CTO TO NORTHERN IRELAND (SECTION 81ZA)

35.21   At the time of publication, there is no equivalent of a CTO under Northern Ireland legislation, so responsibility for patients on a CTO may not be transferred to a hospital in Northern Ireland.

35.22   However, if it is in their interests, patients on a CTO may instead be transferred to detention in Northern Ireland under a transfer warrant as described earlier in this chapter, as if (in effect) they had never become a patient on a CTO.

35.23   In practice, a request for the transfer of a patient on a CTO should be made to the Department of Health by, or on behalf of, the managers of the patient's responsible hospital.

### TRANSFER OF GUARDIANSHIP PATIENTS TO NORTHERN IRELAND (SECTION 81)

35.24   The Secretary of State may also issue a transfer warrant authorising the transfer of a guardianship patient to guardianship in Northern Ireland. This may only be done if the Secretary of State thinks that it is in the patient's interests to be removed to Northern Ireland and that arrangements have been made for the patient to be received into guardianship in Northern Ireland.

35.25   In practice, a request for a transfer warrant should be made by, or on behalf of, the patient's responsible local authority in England to the Department of Health using the same pro-forma as for detained patients. The request should explain why the transfer would be in the patient's interests, the arrangements that have been agreed for the patient to be received into guardianship in Northern Ireland, and whether, and if so why, the patient needs to be kept in custody while being taken there.

35.26   If the Secretary of State for Health issues a warrant, it will (if appropriate) include directions allowing the patient to be conveyed to the place where they are to live in Northern Ireland, so that the patient is treated as being in legal custody on the journey.

35.27   The transfer is complete once the patient has arrived at that place. From then on, a patient who was previously subject to guardianship on the basis of a guardianship application under the Act is treated as if subject to guardianship on the basis of a corresponding application accepted under the legislation in Northern Ireland on the day the transfer was completed. Similarly, a patient previously subject to a guardianship order under the Act is treated as if given an equivalent order or direction under Northern Ireland legislation on that day.

# Chapter 28 – Transfer of patients to the Isle of Man or the Channel Islands

## INTRODUCTION

37.1   This chapter describes the provisions of the Act under which patients may be transferred from detention, a CTO guardianship or conditional discharge in England to the equivalent in the Isle of Man or any of the Channel Islands. The provisions in question are mainly to be found in Part 6 of the Act.

## PURPOSE OF TRANSFERS UNDER THE ACT

37.2   A transfer under the Act is only necessary where the patient concerned needs to remain subject to detention, or the equivalent of a CTO, guardianship or conditional discharge, on arrival in the island in question if equivalent arrangements are available there.

## TRANSFER OF DETAINED PATIENTS TO THE ISLE OF MAN OR THE CHANNEL ISLANDS (SECTIONS 83 AND 92)

37.3   The Secretary of State may issue a warrant ("a transfer warrant") authorising the transfer of a detained patient from England to the Isle of Man or any of the Channel Islands if they are detained under one of the provisions set out in Figure 93.

| Patients liable to be detained on the basis of | Relevant section |
| --- | --- |
| an application for admission for assessment | 2 or 4 |
| an application for admission for treatment | 3 |
| a hospital order (with or without a restriction order (s41)) | 37 (or 51) |

| | |
|---|---|
| a hospital direction (with or without a limitation direction) | 45A |
| a transfer direction (with or without a restriction direction (s49)) | 47 or 48 |

and

patients treated as detained on the basis of one of the above (e.g. as a result of transfer to or from guardianship or from outside England or Wales).

*Figure 93   Detained patients who may be transferred to the Isle of Man or Channel Islands*

37.4    A warrant cannot be issued for the transfer of a patient remanded to hospital under section 35 or 36, subject to an interim hospital order under section 38, or detained in hospital as a place of safety under section 135 or 136. And in practice, it is very unlikely that a warrant would be issued for the transfer of a patient detained in hospital under the "holding powers" in section 5.

37.5    A transfer warrant may only be issued if the Secretary of State is satisfied that it is in the patient's interests to be removed to the island in question and that arrangements have been made for the patient to be admitted to hospital there.

### REQUESTING A TRANSFER WARRANT FOR THE ISLE OF MAN OR THE CHANNEL ISLANDS FOR A DETAINED PATIENT

37.6    In practice, a request for a transfer warrant should be made by, or on behalf of, the managers of the hospital in which the patient is detained in England.

37.7    The request should explain why the hospital thinks the transfer would be in the patient's interests (not the interests of the hospital), and the arrangements that have been agreed for the patient to be received in the island in question.

37.8    For patients other than restricted patients, a pro-forma to be used for such requests is available from the Department of Health.

37.9    Requests for the transfer of restricted patients should be made to the Ministry of Justice. The Act only provides for the transfer of patients between hospitals in different jurisdictions but not the transfer between a prison in one jurisdiction and a hospital in another. If such a transfer is being contemplated, it will need to be undertaken in two stages. Either the patient will be transferred from prison to hospital and from there to a hospital in the other jurisdiction or from prison to another prison and then prison to hospital. Although this might appear complicated, it can be agreed in principle with the patient only having to move once.

37.10   Transfers may require the approval of the relevant island authorities in accordance with the local legislation. The Department of Health (or the Ministry of Justice) will seek this as necessary. They may need to ask the hospital in England for any further information which island authorities require.

### CONVEYANCE TO THE ISLE OF MAN OR THE CHANNEL ISLANDS OF DETAINED PATIENTS (SECTIONS 83 AND 137)

37.11   If the Secretary of State issues a warrant, it will include any necessary directions allowing the patient to be conveyed to the relevant hospital (or other place) in the island by specified people (normally anyone authorised by the hospital managers) within a fixed period (normally 14 days, unless the patient's current period of detention is due to expire sooner).

37.12 While being conveyed in accordance with the warrant, the patient is considered to be in legal custody while in England or Wales. Once the patient reaches the territory of the relevant island, local legislation governs whether they may be kept in custody and whether, by whom and during what period, they may be retaken if they abscond. The receiving hospital or the island authorities may be able to advise on this as necessary.

## EFFECT OF TRANSFER OF A DETAINED PATIENT (SECTION 91)

37.13 When the transfer is completed, the application, order or direction on the basis of which the patient was detained in England ceases to have effect and cannot be revived. For the patient to return to England a further transfer would be necessary, in accordance with section 85 of the Act (see Chapter 34).

37.14 The transfer is completed when the patient is admitted to the relevant hospital in the island in question. The patient will then be subject to the relevant local legislation – which may be significantly different from that in England.

## TRANSFER OF RESPONSIBILITY FOR CONDITIONALLY DISCHARGED PATIENTS TO THE ISLE OF MAN OR THE CHANNEL ISLANDS (SECTIONS 83A AND 92)

37.15 If the Secretary of State for Justice thinks that it would be in the patient's interests, the Secretary of State may agree with the relevant authorities in the Isle of Man or any of the Channel Islands that those authorities will take over responsibility for a conditionally discharged patient. If responsibility is transferred in this way, the patient becomes subject to arrangements corresponding to conditional discharge under the relevant local legislation.

## TRANSFER OF RESPONSIBILITY FOR SCT PATIENTS TO THE ISLE OF MAN OR THE CHANNEL ISLANDS (SECTION 83ZA)

37.16 If the local legislation in force in the Isle or Man or any of the Channel Islands includes provisions corresponding to or similar to a CTO, the Secretary of State for Health may authorise the transfer of responsibility for a patient on a CTO to that island.

37.17 Such a transfer of authority may only be authorised if the Secretary of State thinks that it is in the patient's interests and that arrangements have been made for the patient to be made subject to the relevant local provisions.

37.18 The Secretary of State may not authorise a transfer of responsibility for patients on a CTO while they are recalled to hospital which includes any period during which they are absent without leave while recalled.

37.19 If the Secretary of State authorises a transfer of responsibility, responsibility for the patient passes to the appropriate authority or person in the island from whatever date is specified in the authority, and at that point the patient's CTO ceases to have effect and the patient ceases to be a patient on a CTO. In other words, the patient is no longer liable to recall to or detention in hospital in England or Wales. Instead they become subject to the local legislation, which may be different in significant respects.

37.20 A transfer of responsibility for a patient on a CTO does not give anyone any power to convey the patient to the island against the patient's will. The island authorities should be able to advise on what, if any, powers would be available if the patient did not arrive as expected.

37.21 If there is no equivalent of a CTO in the island in question, patients on a CTO may instead be transferred to detention in the island under a transfer warrant as described earlier in this chapter, as if (in effect) they had never become a patient on a CTO.

37.22 In practice, a request for the transfer of a patient on a CTO should be made to the Department of Health by, or on behalf of, the managers of the patient's responsible hospital. At the time of publication the Isle of Man legislation contains provision for 'Aftercare under supervision' (section 28 *et seq*). The Jersey Mental Health Act 1969 contains no provision equivalent to the CTO. The Mental Health Law 2010 of the Bailiwick of Guernsey does contain provision for CTOs (section 26 *et seq*).

## TRANSFER OF GUARDIANSHIP PATIENTS TO THE ISLE OF MAN OR THE
## CHANNEL ISLANDS (SECTION 83)

37.23 The Secretary of State may also issue a transfer warrant authorising the transfer of a guardianship patient to guardianship in the Isle of Man or any of the Channel Islands. This may only be done if the Secretary of State thinks that it is in the patient's interests to be removed to the island and that arrangements have been made for the patient to be received into guardianship there.

37.24 In practice, a request for a transfer warrant should be made by, or on behalf of, the patient's responsible local social services authority in England to the Department of Health. The request should explain why the transfer would be in the patient's interests, the arrangements that have been agreed for the patient to be received into guardianship in the island in question, and whether, and if so why, the patient needs to be kept in custody while being taken there. The transfer may also have to be agreed with the relevant island authorities in accordance with local legislation.

37.25 If the Secretary of State for Health issues a warrant, it will (if appropriate) include directions allowing the patient to be conveyed to the relevant island. Those directions have the same effect as directions in a transfer warrant for a detained patient (see paragraph 37.12).

37.26 The transfer is complete once the patient has been placed under guardianship in the island. From that point, the patient is no longer subject to guardianship or a guardianship order in England or Wales, but is subject to the relevant local legislation instead, which may be different.

# Chapter 29 – Removal of foreign patients

## INTRODUCTION

38.1 This chapter describes the provisions in Part 6 of the Act under which certain detained patients may be repatriated (or otherwise moved) to a jurisdiction outside the UK, the Isle of Man and the Channel Islands.

## PURPOSE OF THESE PROVISIONS

38.2 A removal warrant under the Act is only necessary where patients are not willing to travel or need to be kept in custody on the journey. A warrant is not necessary if patients are willing to travel and it is safe for them to do so without being in legal custody.

## SECRETARY OF STATE'S POWER TO AUTHORISE REMOVAL OF PATIENT (SECTION 86)

38.3   The Secretary of State may authorise a person's removal to a place in a jurisdiction outside the UK, the Isle of Man or the Channel Islands if that person is:

- neither a British citizen nor a Commonwealth citizen with the right of abode in the UK;

- receiving in-patient treatment in hospital for mental disorder in England or Wales; and

- detained pursuant to an application for admission for treatment, a hospital order, a hospital direction or a transfer direction.

38.4   This may only be done if the Secretary of State thinks that removal is in the interests of the patient and that proper arrangements have been made for:

- the patient's removal to the other place; and

- care or treatment for the patient there.

   and the proposed removal has been agreed by the First-tier Tribunal (or the Upper Tribunal on appeal) or the Mental Health Review tribunal for Wales, or the Mental Health Review Tribunal for Northern Ireland (the Tribunal).

38.5   In practice, this provision is not likely to be used often, not least because of the difficulty of being sure that patients who need to remain detained can and will be detained under the legislation of the country to which it is proposed they be removed.

## PROPOSALS FOR REMOVAL

38.6   Proposals for the removal of a patient detained on the basis of an application for admission under Part 2 should be made to the Department of Health. If the patient is detained under Part 3, the Ministry for Justice should be contacted instead.

38.7   The Ministry of Justice guidance document "Foreign national restricted patients: Guidance on repatriation" (25 March 2009) states that "use of s. 86 is not appropriate where the patient is likely to be discharged within 6 months" (p4).

38.8   Before deciding whether to seek the agreement of the Tribunal, the Department of Health or the Ministry of Justice will need to have details of the reasons for the proposed transfer and the arrangements that have or could be made for the patient's transport (in the UK and abroad) and for the patient's subsequent care and treatment. In practice, the Departments will expect the managers of the hospital in which the patient is detained to provide this information and (if the case is referred to the Tribunal) to provide any further information which the Tribunal requires.

## EFFECT OF SECRETARY OF STATE'S WARRANT

38.9   If the Secretary of State obtains the Tribunal's approval and decides to authorise the patient's transfer, the Secretary of State will issue a warrant which will include any appropriate directions to allow the patient to be conveyed, while remaining in legal custody, out of the UK. This includes being kept in custody while en route to another country, e.g. on a plane or ship. But the Secretary of State cannot authorise the patient being kept in custody or detained once the patient has arrived in another country – so any escort arrangements for the rest of the journey would have to be made under the law of that country, if that is allowed.

## EFFECT OF REMOVAL FROM ENGLAND (SECTION 91)

38.10    In most cases, when patients are removed from England and Wales under these arrangements, the authority for their detention ceases to have effect when they are received into hospital (or another institution) in the country to which they have been removed. But where the patient is subject to a restricted hospital order, it will remain in force so that it will apply again should the patient return to England or Wales, unless the restriction order is for a fixed period, in which case both it and the hospital order will expire at the end of that period.

## ALTERNATIVE MEANS OF REPATRIATION

38.11    It may also be possible to arrange repatriation of certain patients detained in hospital under Part 3 of the Act under the Repatriation of Prisoners Act 1984. Advice should be sought from the Ministry of Justice.

# *Appendix 9*
## Approved clinician competences

There are some differences in the way these are worded in the two countries, so both versions are reproduced here. Doctors, nurses, occupational therapists, psychologists and social workers may seek to become approved clinicians. The regulations and competences for AMHPs for both England and Wales are reproduced in a sister volume (Brown, 2016). The AC instructions for England changed in 2016.

## SCHEDULE 2

RELEVANT COMPETENCIES

**Relevant competencies for approved clinicians**

1. The relevant competencies are those set out in paragraphs 2 to 9.

**The role of the approved clinician and responsible clinician**

2. A comprehensive understanding of the role, legal responsibilities and key functions of an approved clinician and the responsible clinician.

**Legal and policy framework**

3.1. Applied knowledge of –

   (a) mental health legislation, related codes of practice and national and local policy and guidance;

   (b) other relevant legislation, codes of practice and national and local policy guidance, in particular, relevant parts of the Human Rights Act 1998, the Mental Capacity Act 2005, the Children Act 1989 and the Children Act 2004; and

   (c) relevant guidance issued by the National Institute for Health and Clinical Excellence.

3.2. In the above paragraph "relevant" means relevant to the decisions likely to be taken by an approved clinician or responsible clinician.

**Assessment**

4.1. Ability to –

   (a) identify the presence of mental disorder;

   (b) identify the severity of the mental disorder; and

   (c) determine whether the mental disorder is of a kind or degree warranting compulsory detention.

4.2. Ability to assess all levels of clinical risk, including risks to the safety of the patient and others within an evidence based framework for risk assessment and management.

4.3. Ability to undertake mental health assessments incorporating biological, psychological, cultural and social perspectives.

**Treatment**

5.1. Understanding of –

(a) mental health-related treatments, which include physical, psychological and social interventions;

(b) different evidence-based treatment approaches and their applicability to different patients; and

(c) the range of appropriate treatments and treatment settings which can be provided in the least restrictive environment and will deliver the necessary health and social outcomes.

5.2. High level of skill in determining whether a patient has capacity to consent to treatment.

5.3. Ability to formulate, review appropriately and lead on treatment in relation to which the clinician is appropriately qualified in the context of a multidisciplinary team.

5.4. Ability to communicate clearly the aims of the treatment to patients, carers and the team.

**Care planning**

6. Ability to manage and develop care plans which combine health (including measures relating to physical and psychological health and medication), social services (including housing and employment) and other resources, preferably within the context of the Care Programme Approach.

**Leadership and multidisciplinary team working**

7.1. Ability to effectively lead a multidisciplinary team.

7.2. Ability to assimilate the (potentially diverse) views and opinions of other professionals, patients and carers, whilst maintaining an independent view.

7.3. Ability to manage and take responsibility for making decisions in complex cases without the need to refer to supervision in each individual case.

7.4. Understanding and recognition of the limits of the person's own skills and an ability to seek professional views from others to inform a decision, for example, through peer review and appraisal.

**Equality and cultural diversity**

8.1. Up-to-date knowledge and understanding of relevant equality issues.

8.2. Ability to identify, challenge, and where possible and appropriate redress discrimination and inequality in relation to approved clinician practice.

8.3. Understanding of the need to sensitively and actively promote equality and diversity.

8.4. Understanding of how cultural factors and personal values can affect practitioners' judgements and decisions concerning the application of mental health legislation and policy.

## Communication

**9.1.** Ability to communicate effectively with professionals, patients, carers and others, particularly in relation to decisions taken and the underlying reasons for these.

**9.2.** Ability to keep appropriate records and an awareness of the legal requirements in relation to record keeping, including the processing of all personal data or sensitive personal data in accordance with the Data Protection Act 1998.

**9.3.** Understanding of, and ability to manage, the competing requirements of confidentiality and effective information sharing, to the benefit of the patient and other stakeholders.

**9.4.** Ability to compile and complete statutory documentation and to provide written reports as required of an approved clinician.

**9.5.** Ability to present evidence to courts and tribunals.

# NATIONAL HEALTH SERVICE (WALES) ACT 2006

Mental Health Act 1983 Approved Clinician (Wales) Directions 2008

### SCHEDULE 2

Relevant competencies

### 1. The role of the approved clinician

**1.1.** A comprehensive understanding of the role, legal responsibilities and key functions of the approved clinician and the responsible clinician.

### 2. Values-based practice

**2.1.** The ability to identify what constitutes least restrictive health and social care for those dealt with or who may be dealt with under the Act.

**2.2.** Understanding and respect of individuals' qualities, abilities and diverse backgrounds.

**2.3.** Sensitivity to individuals' needs in terms of respect to the patient and the patient's choice, dignity and privacy whilst exercising the role of approved clinician or responsible clinician.

**2.4.** The ability to promote the rights, dignity and self determination of patients consistent with their own needs and wishes, to enable them to contribute to the decisions made affecting their quality of life and liberty.

### 3. Assessment

**3.1.** Able to identify the presence or absence of mental disorder and the severity of the disorder, including whether it is of a kind or degree warranting the use of detention under the Act.

**3.2.** Able to undertake a mental health assessment incorporating biological, psychological, cultural and social perspectives.

**3.3.** Able to assess all levels of clinical risk, and the safety of the patient and others within an evidence-based framework for risk assessment and management.

3.4. Demonstrate a high level of skill in determining whether a patient has capacity to consent to treatment.

## 4. Care planning

4.1. Possesses the skills and knowledge necessary to undertake safe, effective and efficient care planning, being able to:

    (a) involve patients and (where appropriate) their families and carers in care planning;

    (b) assess patients' needs;

    (c) formulate individual care plans to meet identified needs;

    (d) ensure that care plans are implemented as agreed;

    (e) review and evaluate care plans (and revise as necessary).

## 5. Treatment

5.1. Has the skills and knowledge necessary to harness the specialist treatment expertise of the multidisciplinary team, for the benefit of the patient. Specifically, must be able to understand the roles and specialist competences of the various members of a multidisciplinary team, in relation to specific treatments and therapies.

5.2. Broad understanding of all mental health related treatments, i.e. physical, psychological and social interventions.

## 6. Leadership and multidisciplinary team working

6.1. Possesses the skills and knowledge necessary to:

    (a) lead effectively a multidisciplinary team in the delivery of coordinated programmes of care, in order to meet the needs of patients for whom he or she is responsible;

    (b) take into account the views and opinions of patients and (where appropriate) their families and carers when developing programmes of care involving the team;

    (c) consider objectively the professional opinions of other colleagues within the team when formulating programmes of care, so as to ensure that care and treatment decisions are multidisciplinary and based on sound evidence.

6.2. An advanced level of skills in making and taking responsibility for complex judgements and decisions, without referring to supervision in each individual case.

## 7. Equality and cultural diversity

7.1. Demonstrates an up to date knowledge of race equality legislation and other equality issues, including disability, sexual orientation and gender.

7.2. Has a broad grasp of issues of social exclusion.

7.3. Understands the need to promote equality and diversity.

7.4. Aware of how cultural factors and personal values can affect practitioners' judgements and decisions in the application of mental health legislation.

7.5. Ability to identify, challenge, and where possible redress discrimination and inequality in all its forms in relation to approved clinician practice.

## 8. Mental health legislation and policy

8.1.   Up to date working knowledge of:

(a)   the Act;

(b)   relevant NICE Guidelines:

(c)   relevant parts of other related legislation (including the Mental Capacity Act 2005, the Human Rights Act 1998 and the Children Acts);

(d)   all other relevant codes, national policies and protocols related to mental health;

(e)   case law relevant to the practice of approved clinicians and responsible clinicians.

## 9. Communication

9.1.   Able to communicate effectively with professions, service users, carers and others, particularly in relation to decisions taken and the underlying reasons for these.

9.2.   Consideration of the needs of individuals for whom Welsh is their language of choice.

9.3.   Able to demonstrate appropriate record keeping and an awareness of the legal requirements with respect to record keeping.

9.4.   Ability to compile and complete statutory documentation and to provide written reports as required of an approved clinician.

9.5.   Ability with regard to effective report writing.

9.6.   Ability to competently present evidence both verbal and written, to courts and tribunals.

# Appendix 10

# The Mental Health Regulations

## 10A – THE MENTAL HEALTH (CONFLICTS OF INTEREST) (ENGLAND) REGULATIONS 2008

### Statutory Instrument No. 1205 2008

The Secretary of State, in exercise of the powers conferred by section 12A of the Mental Health Act 1983, makes the following Regulations:

### Citation, commencement and application

1.  (1)  These Regulations may be cited as the Mental Health (Conflicts of Interest) (England) Regulations 2008 and shall come into force on 3 November 2008.

    (2)  These Regulations apply in relation to England only.

### Interpretation

2.  In these Regulations –

    "the Act" means the Mental Health Act 1983;

    "AMHP" means an approved mental health professional;

    "application" means an application mentioned in section 11(1) of the Act;

    "assessor" means –

    (a)  an AMHP, or

    (b)  a registered medical practitioner.

### General

3.  Regulations 4 to 7 set out the circumstances in which there would be a potential conflict of interest within the meaning of section 12A(1) of the Act such that an AMHP shall not make an application or a registered medical practitioner shall not give a medical recommendation.

### Potential conflict for financial reasons

4.  (1)  An assessor shall have a potential conflict of interest for financial reasons if the assessor has a financial interest in the outcome of a decision whether or not to make an application or give a medical recommendation.

(2) Where an application for the admission of the patient to a hospital which is a registered establishment is being considered, a registered medical practitioner who is on the staff of that hospital shall have a potential conflict of interest for financial reasons where the other medical recommendation is given by a registered medical practitioner who is also on the staff of that hospital.

## Potential conflict of interest for business reasons

5. (1) When considering making an application or considering giving a medical recommendation in respect of a patient, an assessor shall have a potential conflict of interest for business reasons if both the assessor and the patient or another assessor are closely involved in the same business venture, including being a partner, director, other office-holder or major shareholder of that venture.

(2) Where the patient's nearest relative is making an application, a registered medical practitioner who is considering giving a medical recommendation in respect of that patient shall have a potential conflict of interest for business reasons if that registered medical practitioner and the nearest relative are both closely involved in the same business venture, including being a partner, director, other office-holder or major shareholder of that venture.

## Potential conflict of interest for professional reasons

6. (1) When considering making an application or considering giving a medical recommendation in respect of a patient, an assessor shall have a potential conflict of interest for professional reasons if the assessor –

   (a) directs the work of, or employs, the patient or one of the other assessors making that consideration;

   (b) except where paragraph (3) applies, is a member of a team organised to work together for clinical purposes on a routine basis and –

      (i) the patient is a member of the same team, or

      (ii) the other two assessors are members of the same team.

(2) Where the patient's nearest relative is making an application, a registered medical practitioner who is considering giving a medical recommendation in respect of that patient shall have a potential conflict of interest for professional reasons if that registered medical practitioner –

   (a) directs the work of, or employs, the nearest relative, or

   (b) works under the direction of, or is employed by, the patient's nearest relative.

(3) Paragraph (1)(b) shall not prevent a registered medical practitioner giving a medical recommendation or an AMHP making an application if, in their opinion, it is of urgent necessity for an application to be made and a delay would involve serious risk to the health or safety of the patient or others.

## Potential conflict of interest on the basis of a personal relationship

7. (1) An assessor who is considering making an application or considering giving a medical recommendation in respect of a patient, shall have a potential conflict of interest on the basis of a personal relationship if that assessor is –

   (a) related to a relevant person in the first degree;

   (b) related to a relevant person in the second degree;

    (c)   related to a relevant person as a half-sister or half-brother;

    (d)   the spouse, ex-spouse, civil partner or ex-civil partner of a relevant person; or

    (e)   living with a relevant person as if they were a spouse or a civil partner.

(2)   For the purposes of this regulation –

    (a)   "relevant person" means another assessor, the patient, or, if the nearest relative is making the application, the nearest relative;

    (b)   "related in the first degree" means as a parent, sister, brother, son or daughter and includes step relationships;

    (c)   "related in the second degree" means as an uncle, aunt, grandparent, grandchild, first cousin, nephew, niece, parent-in-law, grandparent-in-law, grandchild-in-law, sister-in-law, brother-in-law, son-in-law or daughter-in-law and includes step relationships;

    (d)   references to step relationships and in-laws in sub-paragraphs (b) and (c) are to be read in accordance with section 246 of the Civil Partnership Act 2004.

# 10B – THE MENTAL HEALTH (CONFLICTS OF INTEREST) (WALES) REGULATIONS 2008

## Statutory Instrument No. 2440 (W 213) 2008

The Welsh Ministers, in exercise of the powers conferred upon them by section 12A of the Mental Health Act 1983, hereby make the following Regulations:

### Title, commencement and extent

1.  (1) The title of these Regulations is the Mental Health (Conflict of Interest) (Wales) Regulations 2008 and they come into force on 3 November 2008.

    (2) These Regulations apply in relation to Wales.

### Interpretation

2.   In these Regulations –

"the Act" ("*y Ddeddf*") means the Mental Health Act 1983;

"AMHP" ("*GPIMC*") means an approved mental health professional;

"application" ("*cais*") means an application mentioned in section 11(1) of the Act;

"assessor" ("*asesydd*") means –

(a) an AMHP considering making an application, or

(b) a registered medical practitioner considering giving a medical recommendation;

"medical recommendation" ("*argymhelliad meddygol*") means a medical recommendation as mentioned in section 12(1) of the Act for the purposes of an application;

references to "nearest relative" ("*perthynas agosaf*") include any person for the time being appointed to carry out the functions of the nearest relative by virtue of an order made under section 29 of the Act, regulation 33 of the Mental Health (Hospital, Guardianship, Community Treatment and Consent to Treatment) (Wales) Regulations 2008 or regulation 24 of the Mental Health (Hospital, Guardianship and Treatment) (England) Regulations 2008.

### Potential conflict of interest for professional reasons

3.  (1) When considering a patient, an assessor will have a potential conflict of interest if he or she –

    (a) works under the direction of, or is employed by, one of the other assessors considering the patient;

    (b) is a member of a team organised to work together for clinical purposes on a routine basis of which the other two assessors are also members.

    (2) Where the patient's nearest relative is making an application, an assessor will have a potential conflict of interest if he or she –

    (a) works under the direction of, or is employed by, that patient's nearest relative;

    (b) employs the patient's nearest relative or the nearest relative works under his or her direction;

    (c) is a member of a team organised to work together for clinical purposes on a routine basis of which the nearest relative is also a member.

(3) When considering a patient, an assessor will have a potential conflict of interest if he or she –

    (a) works under the direction of, or is employed by, the patient;

    (b) employs the patient or the patient works under his or her direction;

    (c) is a member of a team organised to work together for clinical purposes on a routine basis of which the patient is also a member.

## Potential conflict for financial reasons

**4.**  (1) Subject to paragraph (4), an assessor will have a potential conflict of interest if he or she stands to make financial gain dependent upon whether or not he or she decides to make an application or give a medical recommendation.

    (2) Where the application is for the admission of the patient to a hospital which is not a registered establishment, one (but not more than one) of the medical recommendations may be given by a registered medical practitioner who is on the staff of that hospital or who receives or has an interest in the receipt of any payments made on account of the maintenance of the patient.

    (3) Where the application is for the admission of the patient to a hospital which is a registered establishment, neither of the medical recommendations may be given by a registered medical practitioner who is on the staff of that hospital or who receives or has an interest in the receipt of any payments made on account of the maintenance of the patient.

    (4) For the purposes of this regulation the term "financial gain" does not include any fee paid to a practitioner in respect of the examination of a patient pursuant to section 12 of the Act or the provision of any recommendation as a result of such examination.

## Potential conflict of interest for business reasons

**5.**  (1) When considering a patient, an assessor will have a potential conflict of interest if he or she is closely involved in the same business venture as another assessor, the patient or the patient's nearest relative including being a partner, director, other office-holder or major shareholder of that venture.

    (2) Where the patient's nearest relative is making an application, an assessor will have a potential conflict of interest if he or she is closely involved in the same business venture as the nearest relative including being a partner, director, other office-holder or major shareholder of that venture.

## Potential conflict of interest on the basis of a personal relationship

**6.**  (1) An assessor will have a potential conflict of interest in considering a patient, if he or she is –

    (a) related to a relevant person in the first degree;

    (b) related to a relevant person in the second degree;

    (c) related to a relevant person as a half-sister or half-brother;

    (d) the spouse, ex-spouse, civil partner or ex-civil partner of a relevant person;

    (e) living with a relevant person as if he or she were a spouse or a civil partner.

(2)  For the purposes of this regulation –

   (a)  "relevant person" means another assessor, the patient, or if the patient's nearest relative is making the application, the nearest relative;

   (b)  "related in the first degree" means as a parent, sister, brother, daughter or son; and includes step relationships;

   (c)  "related in the second degree" means as an uncle, aunt, grandparent, grandchild, first cousin, niece, nephew, parent-in-law, grandparent-in-law, grandchild-in-law, sister-in-law, brother-in-law, daughter-in-law or son-in-law and includes step relationships;

   (d)  references to step relationships and in-laws in paragraphs (b) and (c) above are to be read in accordance with section 246 of the Civil Partnership Act 2004(1).

## Emergency provision

7.  These Regulations do not prevent an AMHP making an application or a registered medical practitioner giving a medical recommendation if there would otherwise be delay involving serious risk to the health or safety of the patient or others.

# *Appendix 11*

# Mental Health Act 1983 (Places of Safety) Regulations 2017

## Statutory Instrument No. 1036 2017

Citation, commencement and application

1.  (1)  These Regulations may be cited as the Mental Health Act 1983 (Places of Safety) Regulations 2017 and come into force on 11th December 2017.

    (2)  In these Regulations –

        "the Act" means the Mental Health Act 1983;

        "custody officer" means a person who is appointed as, or who is performing the functions of, a custody officer within the meaning given in section 36 of the Police and Criminal Evidence Act 1984;

        "healthcare professional" means a person who is a member of a profession mentioned in section 60(2) of the Health Act 1999.

Circumstances in which a police station may be used as a place of safety

2.  (1)  An adult ("A") may only be removed to, kept at, or taken to, a place of safety that is a police station in the exercise of a power to which section 136A of the Act applies where –

        (a)  the decision-maker is satisfied that –

            (i)  the behaviour of A poses an imminent risk of serious injury or death to A, or to another person,

            (ii)  because of that risk, no place of safety other than a police station in the relevant police area can reasonably be expected to detain A, and

            (iii)  the requirement in sub-paragraph (b) of regulation 4(1) will be met, and

        (b)  where the decision-maker is not an officer of the rank of inspector or above, an officer of that rank or above authorises that A may be removed to, kept at, or taken to a place of safety that is a police station.

    (2)  Before determining that the circumstances in paragraphs (i) to (iii) of paragraph (1)(a) exist, a decision-maker who is a constable must, if it is reasonably practicable to do so, consult –

> (a) a registered medical practitioner,
>
> (b) a registered nurse,
>
> (c) an approved mental health professional, or
>
> (d) a person of a description specified in regulation 8(1).

(3) In this regulation –

"decision-maker" means –

> (a) in relation to the exercise of a power under section 135(1) or 136(1) of the Act, the constable exercising that power,
>
> (b) in relation to the exercise of a power under section 135(3A) or 136(3) of the Act, the constable or approved mental health professional who –
>
> > (i) exercises that power, or
> >
> > (ii) authorises a person to exercise that power,

"relevant police area" means the police area in which A is located when a power to which section 136A of the Act applies begins to be exercised in relation to A.

### Requirements when a police station is used as a place of safety

3. Regulations 4 to 7 apply when an adult is detained at a police station under section 135 or section 136 of the Act.

4. (1) A custody officer at the police station must ensure that –

> (a) the welfare of the detained adult ("D") is checked by a healthcare professional at least once every thirty minutes, and any appropriate action is taken for the treatment and care of D, and
>
> (b) so far as is reasonably practicable, a healthcare professional is present and available to D throughout the period in which D is detained at the police station.

(2) Subject to regulation 7, in any case where either or both of the requirements in paragraph (1)(a) and (b) is not met, the custody officer must arrange for D to be taken to another place of safety.

5. (1) A custody officer at the police station must, subject to paragraph (2) and regulations 6 and 7 –

> (a) review the behaviour of D at least once an hour and determine whether the circumstances in regulation 2(1)(a)(i) and (ii) exist, and
>
> (b) where those circumstances are determined not to exist, arrange for D to be taken to a place of safety other than a police station.

(2) Before making a determination under paragraph (1)(a), the custody officer must, where reasonably practicable, consult the healthcare professional that carried out the most recent check by virtue of regulation 4(1)(a).

6. The frequency of the reviews referred to in regulation 5(1)(a) may be reduced, to no less than once every three hours, where –

> (a) D is sleeping, and

(b) a healthcare professional who has checked D's welfare by virtue of regulation 4(1)(a) has not, in the most recent check, identified any risk that would require D to be woken more frequently.

7. The requirements to take D to a place of safety in regulation 4(2) and regulation 5(1)(b) do not apply where –

(a) arrangements have been made which would enable an assessment of D for the purpose of section 135 or (as the case may be) section 136 of the Act to be commenced sooner at the police station than at another place of safety, and

(b) to postpone the assessment would be likely to cause distress to D.

## Persons to be consulted

1. The following persons are specified for the purposes of section 136(1C)(d) of the Act –

(a) an occupational therapist,

(b) a paramedic.

2. For the purposes of paragraph (1) –

(a) an occupational therapist is a person registered in the register established and maintained by the Health and Care Professions Council under article 5 of the Health and Social Work Professions Order 2001, in the part relating to occupational therapists, and

(b) a paramedic is a person registered in that register, in the part relating to paramedics.

# References

Bartlett, P. and Sandland, R. (2014) *Mental Health Law: Policy and Practice*, 4th edition, Oxford.

Bowen, P. (2007) *Blackstone's Guide to the Mental Health Act 2007*, Oxford.

Bradley, K. (2009) *The Bradley Report*, Department of Health.

Brown, R. (2019) *The Approved Mental Health Professional's Guide to Mental Health Law*, 5th edition, Sage.

Brown, R., Adshead, G. and Pollard, A. (2009) *The Approved Mental Health Professional's Guide to Psychiatry and Medication*, 2nd edition, Learning Matters.

Brown, R., Barber, P. and Martin, D. (2015) *The Mental Capacity Act 2005: A Guide For Practice*, 3rd edition, Sage.

Burns, T., Rugkåsa, J., Molodynski, A., Dawson, J., Yeeles, K., Vazquez-Montes, M., Voysey, M., Sinclair, J. and Priebe, S. (2013) "Community treatment orders for patients with psychosis (OCTET): A randomised controlled trial", *The Lancet*, 381, pp. 1627–1633.

Care Quality Commission (2018) *Monitoring the Use of the Mental Health Act in 2017/18*, CQC.

Churchill, R. et al. (2007) *International Experiences of Using Community Treatment Orders*, Institute of Psychiatry.

Council of Europe (1950) *The European Convention on Human Rights*.

Department for Constitutional Affairs (2007) *Mental Capacity Act 2005: Code of Practice*, HMSO.

Department of Health (2000) *Reforming the Mental Health Act*, Cm 50161, HMSO.

Department of Health (2004) "Advice on the Decision of the European Court of Human Rights in the Case of *HL v UK* (the '*Bournewood*' Case)" [gateway reference 4269].

Department of Health (2007) "Adult Protection, Care Reviews and Independent Mental Capacity Advocates (IMCA): Guidance on Interpreting the Regulations Extending the IMCA Role" [gateway reference 7557].

Department of Health (2007) "Explanatory Notes to Mental Health Act 2007", The Stationery Office.

Department of Health (2008) *Reference Guide to the Mental Health Act 1983*, The Stationery Office.

Department of Health (2009) "IMHAs: Supplementary Guidance on Access to Patient Records", Department of Health.

Department of Health (2011) **www.dh.gov.uk/en/socialcare/deliveringsocialcare/mentalcapacity**

Department of Health (2015) *Mental Health Act 1983, Code of Practice*, TSO.

Department of Health (2015) *Reference Guide to the Mental Health Act 1983*, TSO.

Department of Health and Home Office (2017) *Guidance for the Implementation of Changes to Police Powers and Places of Safety Provisions in the Mental Health Act 1983*. Department of Health.

Department of Health and Social Care (2018) *Modernising the Mental Health Act*, Gov.UK.

Eldergill, A. (1998) *Mental Health Review Tribunals*, Sweet and Maxwell.

Fennell, P. (2011) *Mental Health Law and Practice*, Jordans.

Gostin, L. (1975) *A Human Condition*, Vol. 1, MIND.

Gostin, L. (1977) *A Human Condition*, Vol. 2, MIND.

Gostin, L. and Fennell, P. (1992) *Mental Health: Tribunal Procedure*, Longman.

Hale, B. (2017) *Mental Health Law*, 6th edition, Sweet and Maxwell.

Harbour, A. (2008) *Children with Mental Disorder and the Law*, Jessica Kingsley.

Hewitt, D. (2007) *The Nearest Relative Handbook*, Jessica Kingsley.

Hoggett, B. (1996) *Mental Health Law*, Sweet and Maxwell.

Jones, R. (ed.) (2001) *Mental Health Act Manual*, 7th edition, Sweet and Maxwell.

Jones, R. (2008) "Deprivations of Liberty: Mental Health Act or Mental Capacity Act?" *Journal of Mental Health Law*, pp. 170–173, Northumbria Law Press.

Jones, R. (ed.) (2011) *Mental Health Act Manual*, 14th edition, Sweet and Maxwell.

Law Commission (1991) "Mentally Incapacitated Adults and Decision-Making: An Overview", Consultation Paper No. 119, HMSO.

Law Commission (1995) *Mental Incapacity*, Law Com No. 231.

Law Society (1989) *Decision-Making and Mental Incapacity: A Discussion Document*, Memorandum by the Law Society's Mental Health Sub-Committee.

Law Society (2015) *Identifying a Deprivation of Liberty: A Practical Guide*, The Law Society.

Lord Chancellor's Department (1997) *Who Decides? Making Decisions on Behalf of Mentally Incapacitated Adults.* Cmnd 3803.

Lord Chancellor's Department (1999) *Making Decisions.* Cmnd 4465.

Martin, E. and Law, J. (eds) (2009) *Oxford Dictionary of Law*, Oxford University Press.

Mental Health Act Commission (2008) *"Rights, Risk, Recovery": The Twelfth Biennial Report 2005–2007*, TSO.

Montgomery, J. (2002) *Health Care Law*, Oxford University Press.

Puri, B., Brown, R., McKee, H. and Treasaden, I. (2005) *Mental Health Law*, Hodder Arnold.

The Oxford Community Treatment Order Evaluation Trial (OCTET) 2008 reported in Burns, T., Rugkåsa, J., Molondynski, A., Dawson, J., Yeeles, K., Vazquez-Montes, M., Voysey, M., Sinclair, J. and Priebe, S. (2013) "Community Treatment Orders for Patients with Psychosis (OCTET): A Randomised Controlled Trial", *The Lancet*, Vol. 381.

Welsh Government (2016) *Mental Health Act 1983, Code of Practice for Wales*, OGL.

Yeates, V. (2005) "Death of the Nearest Relative? Carers' and Families' Rights to Challenge Compulsion Under Current and Proposed Mental Health Legislation", *Journal of Mental Health Law*, pp. 123–137.

# Inquiries

Department of Health (2005) *The Kerr/Haslam Inquiry* (Cmnd 6440), TSO.

# Statutes

1948 National Assistance Act

1969 Family Law Reform Act

1976 and 2000 Race Relations Acts

1977 National Health Service Act

1983 Mental Health Act

1984 Police and Criminal Evidence Act

1985 Enduring Powers of Attorney Act

1989 Children Act

1990 National Health Service and Community Care Act

1998 Human Rights Act

1999 Health Act

2000 Care Standards Act

2004 Domestic Violence, Crime and Victims Act

2005 Mental Capacity Act

2007 Mental Health Act

2007 Tribunals, Courts and Enforcement Act

2014 Care Act

2017 Policing and Crime Act

# Regulations and Statutory Instruments

The Court of Protection Rules (SI 2007, No 1744)

The Court of Protection Fees Order (SI 2007, No 1745)

Lasting Powers of Attorney, Enduring Powers of Attorney and Public Guardian Regulations (SI 2007, No 1253)

The Mental Capacity Act 2005 (Independent Mental Capacity Advocates) (General) Regulations (SI 2006, No 1832)

The Mental Capacity Act 2005 (Independent Mental Capacity Advocates) (Expansion of Role) Regulations (SI 2006, No 2883)

The Mental Capacity Act 2005 Loss of Capacity during Research Project (England) Regulations (SI 2007, No 679)

The Mental Capacity Act 2005 (Transitional and Consequential Provisions) Order 2007 (SI 2007 No 1898)

The Mental Capacity Act 2005 (Transfer of Proceedings) Order (SI 2007, No 1899)

The Mental Health Act 1983 (Places of Safety) Regulations 2017 (2017 No. 1036)

The Public Guardian (Fees etc.) Regulations (SI 2007, No 2051)

# Case law

*A CC v MB* (2010) EWHC 2508

*A LA v A* (2010) EWHC 978

*A LA v D* (2015) EWHC 3125 (Fam)

*A PCT v LDV et al.* (2013) EWHC 272 (Fam)

*Aerts v Belgium* (2000) 29 EHRR 50

*AH v W London MHT* (2011) UKUT 74 (AAC)

*AJ v A LA* (2015) EWCOP 5 (qv)

*AM v SLAM and Secretary of State for Health* (2013) UKUT 0365 (ACC)

*B v Barking Havering etc. NHS Trust* (1999) 1 FLR 106

*BB v Cygnet Healthcare and Another* (2008) EWHC 1259 Admin

*Bibby v Chief Constable of Essex Police* (Court of Appeal 2000) EWCA Civ 113

*Birmingham CC v D and W* (2016) EWCOP 8

*CC v KK and STCC* (2012) EWHC 2136 (COP)

*Cheshire and Chester v P* (2011) EWCA Civ 1257; (2011) EWHC 1330 (Fam)

*Cheshire West* (2014) UKSC 14

*CM v Derbyshire Healthcare NHS Foundation Trust et al.* (2011) UKUT 129 (AAC)

*D (A Child)* (2017) EWCA Civ 1695

*Derbyshire CC v AC et al.* (2014) EWCOP 38

*DL-H v Devon Partnership NHS Trust v Secretary of State* (2010) UKUT 102 (AAC)

*Dorset Healthcare NHS Foundation Trust v MHRT* (2009) UKUT 4 (AAC)

*F (Mental Health Act: Guardianship), Re* (2001) 1 FLR 192

*G v E v A Local Authority v F* (2010) EWCA (Civ 822)

*GC v Managers of the Kingswood Centre et al.* (CO/7784/2008)

*Gillick v West Norfolk and Wisbech AHA* (1986) AC 112

*GJ v The Foundation Trust et al.* (2009) EWHC 2972 (Fam)

*Hereford County Council v AB* (2018) EWHC 3103 (Fam)

*Herczegfalvy v Austria* ((1992) 15 EHRR 437)

*Hillingdon v Neary* (2011) EWHC 1377 (COP)

*HL v UK* (2004) 40 EHRR 761 (the *Bournewood* case)

*ITW v Z* (2009) EWHC 2525 (Fam)

*JE v DE and Surrey CC* (2006) EWHC 3459 (Fam) (Deprivation of liberty)

*JT v UK* (2000) 30 EHRR CD 77

*Keenan v UK* (27229/95) (2001) 33 EHRR 38

*Kings College Trust v C and E* (2015) EWCOP 85

*KL v Somerset Partnership NHS Foundation Trust* (2011) UKUT 233 (AAC)

*LB Redbridge v G* (2014) EWHC 485 (COP)

*LBH v GP* (2009) FD08P01058

*LBH v Neary* (2011) EWHC 1377

*LBX v K, L, M* (2013) EWHC 3230 (Fam)

*Local Authority X v MM (by the Official Solicitor) and KM* (2007) EWHC 2003 (Fam), (2009) 1 FLR 443

*McNaghten's case* [1843–60] All ER Rep 229, HL

*MD v Nottingham Healthcare NHS Trust* (2010) UKUT 59 (AAC)

*MH v UK* (Application No. 11577/06) (2014) 58 EHRR 35

*MM v WL* (2015) UKUT 644

*Montgomery v Lanarkshire Health Board* (2015) UKSC 11

*MS v UK* (24527/08) (2012) ECHR 804

*Newham LBC v S* (adult: court's jurisdiction) (2003) EWHC 1909 (Fam)

*NM v Kent CC* (2015) UKUT 125 (AAC)

*Northants Trust v ML* (2014) EWCOP 2

*Nottinghamshire Healthcare NHS Trust v RC* (2014) EWCOP 1317

*Osman v United Kingdom* (1999) 1 FLR 193

*P v Cheshire West and Chester Council and P & Q v Surrey County Council* (2014) UKSC 19 ("Cheshire West")

*P and Q (aka Mig and Meg) v Surrey CC et al.* (2011) EWCA Civ 190

*PC and NC v City of York Council* (2013) EWCA Civ 478

*PJ v A Local Health Board* (2015) UKUT 480 (AAC)

*R (on the application of S) v Plymouth City Council* (2002) EWCA Civ 388

*R (AN) v MHRT (Northern Region)* (2005) EWCA Civ 1605

*R (B) v Dr SS* (2006) EWCA Civ 28

*R (C) v A LA et al.* (2011) EWHC 1539 (Admin)

*R (CS) v Mental Health Review Tribunal* (2004) EWHC 2958 (Admin)

*R (DR) v Mersey Care NHS Trust* (2002) EWHC 1810 (Admin)

*R (E) v Bristol City Council* (2005) EWHC 74 (Admin)

*R (H) v Ashworth Hospital Authority* (2002) EWCA Civ 923

*R (H) v MHRT for NE London* (2001) 3 WLR 512

*R (IH) v Secretary of State for the Home Department* (2003) UKHL 59

*R (JB) v Dr Haddock* (2006) EWCA Civ 961

*R (M) v Sec of State for Health* (2003) EWHC 1094

*R (MH) v Secretary of State for Health* (2005) UKHL 60 (Admin)

*R v MHRT for South Thames Region, ex parte Smith* (1999) COD 148

*R v MHRT for West Midlands and North West ex parte H* (2000)

*R (Munjaz) v Mersey Care NHS Trust* (2005) UKHL 58

*R (N) v Dr M* (2002) EWCA Civ 1789

*R (N) v Dr M et al.* (2003) 1 WLR 3284

*R (PS) v Dr G and Dr W* (2003) EWHC 2335 (Admin)

*R (RD) v MHRT* (2007) EWHC 781 (Admin)

*R (S) v Mental Health Review Tribunal* (2002) EWHC Admin 2522

*R (von Brandenburg) v E London and City Mental Health NHS Trust* (2003) UKHL 58

*Rabone v Pennine Care NHS Trust* (2010) EWCA Civ 698

*Rabone v Pennine Care NHS Trust* (2012) UKSC 2

*Re A (Capacity: Social Media and Internet Use: Best Interests)* (2019) EWCOP 2

*Re B (Capacity: Social Media: Care and Contact)* (2019) EWCOP 3

*Re CD* (2015) EWCOP 74

*Re (D) (Mental patient: Habeas corpus)* (Court of Appeal, 2000)

*Re (F) (Mental Health Act: Guardianship), Re* (2001) 1 FLR 192

*Re KB (Adult) (Mental patient: medical treatment)* (1994) Family Division

*Re W (a minor)* (1992) 4 All ER 627

*Reed (Trainer) v Bronglais Hospital et al.* (2001) EWHC Admin 792

*Reid v Secretary of State for Scotland* (1999) AC 512

*RK v BCC et al.* (2011) EWCA Civ 1305

*RM v St Andrew's Healthcare* (2010) UKUT 119 (AAC)

*Savage v SE Essex Partnership NHS Foundation Trust* (2008) UKHL 74

*Secretary of State for the Home Department v JJ and others* (2007) (FC) (Respondents) UKHL 45

*Secretary of State for Justice v MM* (2018) UKSC 60

*Sessay v South London and Maudsley NHS Foundation Trust & The Commissioner of Police for the Metropolis* (2011) EWHC 2617

*Sidaway* (1985) AC 871

*SL v Ludlow Street Healthcare* (2015) UKUT 398 (AAC)

*South Stafford and Shropshire Healthcare NHSFT v St George's Hospital* (2016) EWHC 1196 (Admin)

*SSJ v KC* (2015) UKUT 0376

*Storck v Germany* (2005) 43 EHRR 96

*Trust A v X and A Local Authority* (2015) EWHC 922 (Fam)

*TTM v Hackney BC et al.* (2011) EWCA Civ 4

*TW v Enfield Borough Council* (2014) EWCA Civ 362

*W City Council v Mrs L* (2015) EWCOP 20

*Welsh Ministers (Respondent) v PJ (Appellant)* (2018) UKSC 66

*WH v Partnerships in Care* (2015) UKUT 695 (AAC)

*Wilkinson v UK* (Application 14659/02, Admissibility Decision Feb 06)

*Wilkinson v UK* (2006) MHLR 142

*Winterwerp v Netherlands* (1979) 2 EHRR 387

*Wye Valley NHS Trust v Mr B* (2015) EWCOP 60

*X v Finland* (34806/04) (2012) MHLR 318 ECHR

*ZH v Commissioner of the Police for the Metropolis* (2013) EWCA Civ 69

# Some useful websites

Mental Health Law information **www.mentalhealthlaw.co.uk**

Public Guardianship Office via **www.direct.gov.uk**

Ministry of Justice **www.justice.gov.uk**

Department of Health **www.dh.gov.uk**

Care Quality Commission **www.cqc.org.uk**

Healthcare Inspectorate Wales **www.hiw.org.uk**

Welsh Government **www.wales.gov.uk**

Social Work England **www.socialworkengland.org.uk**

# Index

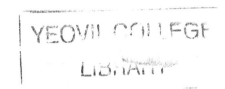